COMMENTARIES ON EZEKIEL

BY

Matthew Henry

COMMENTARIES ON EZEKIEL

Published by Scriptura Press

New York City, NY

First published circa 1714

Copyright © Scriptura Press, 2015

All rights reserved

ABOUT SCRIPTURA PRESS

<u>Scriptura Press</u> is a Christian company that makes Christian works available and affordable to all. We are a non-denominational publishing group that shares the teachings of the Scripture, whether in the form of sermons or histories of the Church.

Ezekiel

An Exposition, with Practical Observations, of The Book of the Prophet Ezekiel

When we entered upon the writings of the prophets, which speak of the things that should be hereafter, we seemed to have the same call that St. John had (Rev 4:1), Come up hither; but, when we enter upon the prophecy of this book, it is as if the voice said, Come up higher; as we go forward in time (for Ezekiel prophesied in the captivity, as Jeremiah prophesied just before it), so we soar upward in discoveries yet more sublime of the divine glory. These waters of the sanctuary still grow deeper; so far are they from being fordable that in some places they are scarcely fathomable; yet, deep as they are, out of them flow streams which make glad the city of our God, the holy place of the tabernacles of the Most High. As to this prophecy now before us, we may enquire, I. Concerning the penman of it-it was Ezekiel; his name signifies, The strength of God, or one girt or strengthened of God. He girded up the loins of his mind to the service, and God put strength into him. Whom God calls to any service he will himself enable for it; if he give commission, he will give power to execute it. Ezekiel's name was answered when God said (and no doubt did as he said), I have made thy face strong against their faces. The learned Selden, in his book De Diis Syris, says that it was the opinion of some of the ancients that the prophet Ezekiel was the same with that Nazaratus Assyrius whom Pythagoras (as himself relates) had for his tutor for some time, and whose lectures he attended. It is agreed that they lived much about the same time; and we have reason to think that many of the Greek philosophers were acquainted with the sacred writings and borrowed some of the best of their notions from them. If we may give credit to the tradition of the Jews, he was put to death by the captives in Babylon, for his faithfulness and boldness in reproving them; it is stated that they dragged him upon the stones till his brains were dashed out. An Arabic historian says that he was put to death and was buried in the sepulchre of Shem the son of Noah. So Hottinger relates, Thesaur. Philol. lib. 2 cap. 1. II. Concerning the date of it-the place whence it is dated and the time when. The scene is laid in Babylon, when it was a house of bondage to the Israel of God; there the prophecies of this book were preached, there they were written, when the prophet himself, and the people to whom he prophesied, were captives there. Ezekiel and Daniel are the only writing prophets of the Old Testament who lived and prophesied any where but in the land of Israel, except we add Jonah, who was sent to Nineveh to prophesy. Ezekiel prophesied in the beginning of the captivity, Daniel in the latter end of it. It was an indication of God's good-will to them, and his gracious designs concerning them in their affliction, that he raised up prophets among them, both to convince them when, in the beginning of their troubles, they were secure and unhumbled, which was Ezekiel's business, and to comfort them when, in the latter end of their troubles, they were dejected and discouraged. If the Lord had been pleased to kill them, he would not have used such apt and proper means to cure them. III. Concerning the matter and scope of it. 1. There is much in it that is very mysterious, dark, and hard to be understood, especially in the beginning and the latter end of it, which therefore the Jewish rabbin forbade the reading of to their young men, till they came to be thirty years of age, lest by the difficulties they met with there they should be prejudiced against the scriptures; but if we read these difficult parts of scripture with humility and reverence, and search them diligently, though we may not be able to untie all the knots we meet with, any more than we can solve all the phenomena in the book of nature, yet we may from them, as from the book of nature, gather a great deal for the confirming of our faith and the encouraging of our hope in the God we worship. 2. Though the visions here be intricate, such as an elephant may swim in, yet the sermons are mostly plain, such as a lamb may wade in; and the chief design of them is to show God's people their transgressions, that in their captivity they might be repenting and not repining. It should seem the prophet was constantly attended (for we read of their sitting before him as God's people sat to hear his words, Eze 33:31), and that he was occasionally consulted, for we read of the elders of Israel who came to enquire of the Lord by him, Eze 14:1, Eze 14:3. And as it was of great use to the oppressed captives themselves to have a prophet with them, so it was a testimony to their holy religion against their oppressors who ridiculed it and them. 3. Though the reproofs and the threatenings here are very sharp and bold, yet towards the close of the book very comfortable assurances are given of great mercy God had in store for them; and there, at length, we shall meet with something that has reference to gospel times, and which was to have its accomplishment in the kingdom of the Messiah, of whom indeed this prophet speaks less than almost any of the prophets. But by opening the terrors of the Lord he prepares Christ's way. By the law is the knowledge of sin, and so it becomes our school-master to bring us to Christ. The visions which were the prophet's credentials we have ch. 1-3, the reproofs and threatenings ch. 4-24 betwixt which and the comforts which we have in the latter part of the book we have messages sent to the nations that bordered upon the land of Israel, whose destruction is foretold (ch. 25-35), to make way for the restoration of God's Israel and the re-establishment of their city and temple, which are foretold ch. 36 to the end. Those who would apply the comforts to themselves must apply the convictions to themselves.

Ezekiel Chapter 1

In this chapter we have, I. The common circumstances of the prophecy now to be delivered, the time when it was delivered (Eze 1:1), the place where (Eze 1:2), and the person by whom (Eze 1:3). II. The uncommon introduction to it by a vision of the glory of God, 1. In his attendance and retinue in the upper world, where his throne is surrounded with angels, here called "living creatures," (Eze 1:4-14). 2. In his providences concerning the lower world, represented by the wheels and their motions (Eze 1:15-25). 3. In the face of Jesus Christ sitting upon the throne (Eze 1:26-28). And the more we are acquainted, and the more intimately we converse, with the glory of God in these three branches of it, the more commanding influence will divine revelation have upon us and the more ready shall we be to submit to it, which is the thing aimed at in prefacing the prophecies of this book with these visions. When such a God of glory speaks, it concerns us to hear with attention and reverence; it is at our peril if we do not.

Ezekiel 1:1

The circumstances of the vision which Ezekiel saw, and in which he received his commission and instructions, are here very particularly set down, that the narrative may appear to be authentic and not romantic. It may be of use to keep an account when and where God has been pleased to manifest himself to our souls in a peculiar manner, that the return of the day, and our return to the place of the altar (Gen 13:4), may revive the pleasing grateful remembrance of God's favour to us. "Remember, O my soul! and never forget what communications of divine love thou didst receive at such a time, at such a place; tell others what God did for thee."

I. The time when Ezekiel had this vision is here recorded. It was in the thirtieth year, v. 1. Some make it the thirtieth year of the prophet's age; being a priest, he was at that age to enter upon the full execution of the priestly office, but being debarred from that by the iniquity and calamity of the times, now that they had neither temple nor altar, God at that age called him to the dignity of a prophet. Others make it to be the thirtieth year from the beginning of the reign of Nabopolassar, the father of Nebuchadnezzar, from which the Chaldeans began a new computation of time, as they had done from Nabonassar 123 years before. Nabopolassar reigned nineteen years, and this was the eleventh of his son, which makes the thirty. And it was proper enough for Ezekiel, when he was in Babylon, to use the computation they there used, as we in foreign countries date by the new style; and he afterwards uses the melancholy computation of his own country, observing (Eze 1:2) that it was the fifth year of Jehoiachin's captivity. But the Chaldee paraphrase fixes upon another era, and says that this was the thirtieth year after Hilkiah the priest found the book of the law in the house of the sanctuary, at midnight, after the setting of the moon, in the days of Josiah the king. And it is true that this was just thirty years from that time; and that was an event so remarkable (as it put the Jewish state upon a new trial) that it was proper enough to date form it; and perhaps therefore the prophet speaks indefinitely of thirty years, as having an eye both to that event and to the Chaldean computation, which were coincident. It was in the fourth month, answering to our June, and in the fifth day of the month, that Ezekiel had this vision, Eze 1:2. It is probably that it was on the sabbath day, because we read (Eze 3:16) that at the end of seven days, which we may well suppose to be the next sabbath, the word of the Lord came to him again. Thus John was in the Spirit on the Lord's day, when he saw the visions of the Almighty, Rev 1:10. God would hereby put an honour upon his sabbaths, when the enemies mocked at them, Lam 1:7. And he would thus encourage his people to keep up their attendance on the ministry of his prophets every sabbath day, by the extraordinary manifestations of himself on some sabbath days.

II. The melancholy circumstances he was in when God honoured him, and thereby favoured his people, with this vision. he was in the land of the Chaldeans, among the captives, by the river of Chebar, and it was in the fifth year of king Jehoiachin's captivity. Observe,

1. The people of God were now, some of them, captives in the land of the Chaldeans. The body of the Jewish nation yet remained in their own land, but these were the first-fruits of the captivity, and they were some of the best; for in Jeremiah's vision these were the good figs, whom God had sent into the land of the Chaldeans for their good (Jer 24:5); and, that it might be for their good, God raised up a prophet among them, to teach them out of the law, then when he chastened them, Psa 94:12. Note, It is a great mercy to have the word of God brought to us, and a great duty to attend to it diligently, when we are in affliction. The word of instruction and the rod of correction may be of great service to us, in concert and concurrence with each other, the word to explain the rod and the rod to enforce the word: both together give wisdom. It is happy for a man, when he is sick and in pain, to have a messenger with him, an interpreter, one among a thousand, if he have but his ear open to discipline, Job 36:10. One of the quarrels God had with the Jews, when he sent them into captivity, we for mocking his messengers and misusing his prophets; and yet, when they were suffering for this sin, he favoured them with this forfeited mercy. It were ill with us if God did not sometimes graciously thrust upon us those means of grace and salvation which we have foolishly thrust from us. In their captivity they were destitute of ordinary helps for their souls, and therefore God raised them up these extraordinary ones; for God's children, if they be hindered in their education one way, shall have it made up another way. But observe, It was in the fifth year of the captivity that Ezekiel was raised up amongst them, and not before. So long God left them without any prophet, till they began to lament after the Lord and to complain that they saw not their signs and there was none to tell them how long (Psa 74:9), and then they would know how to value a prophet, and God's discoveries of himself to them by him would be the more acceptable and comfortable. The Jews that remained in their own land had Jeremiah with them, those that had gone into captivity had Ezekiel with them; for wherever the children of God are scattered abroad he will find out tutors for them.

2. The prophet was himself among the captives, those of them that were posted by the river

Chebar; for it was by the rivers of Babylon that they sat down, and on the willow-trees by the river's side that they hanged their harps, Psa 137:1,Psa 137:2. The planters in America keep along by the sides of the rivers, and perhaps those captives were employed by their masters in improving some parts of the country by the rivers' sides that were uncultivated, the natives being generally employed in war; or they employed them in manufactures, and therefore chose to fix them by the sides of rivers, that the good they made might the more easily be conveyed by water-carriage. Interpreters agree not what river this of Chebar was, but among the captives by that river Ezekiel was, and himself a captive. Observe here, (1.) The best men, and those that are dearest to God, often share, not only in the common calamities of this life, but in the public and national judgments that are inflicted for sin; those feel the smart who contributed nothing to the guilt, by which it appears that the difference between good and bad arises not from the events that befal them, but from the temper and disposition of their spirits under them. And since not only righteous men, but prophets, share with the worst in present punishments, we may infer thence, with the greatest assurance, that there are rewards reserved for them in the future state. (2.) Words of conviction, counsel, and comfort, come best to those who are in affliction from their fellow sufferers. The captives will be best instructed by one who is a captive among them and experimentally knows their sorrows. (3.) The spirit of prophecy was not confined to the land of Israel, but some of the brightest of divine revelations were revealed in the land of the Chaldeans, which was a happy presage of the carrying of the church, with that divine revelation upon which it is built, into the Gentile world; and, as now, so afterwards, when the gospel kingdom was to be set up, the dispersion of the Jews contributed to the spreading of the knowledge of God. (4.) Wherever we are we may keep up our communion with God. Undique ad coelos tantundem est viae-From the remotest corners of the earth we may find a way open heavenward. (5.) When God's ministers are bound the word of the Lord is not bound, Ti2 2:9. When St. Paul was a prisoner the gospel had a free course. When St. John was banished into the Isle of Patmos Christ visited him there. Nay, God's suffering servants have generally been treated as favourites, and their consolations have much more abounded when affliction has abounded, Co2 1:5.

III. The discovery which God was pleased to make of himself to the prophet when he was in these circumstances, to be by him communicated to his people. He here tells us what he saw, what he heard, and what he felt. 1. He saw visions of God, Eze 1:1. No man can see God and live; but many have seen visions of God, such displays of the divine glory as have both instructed and affected them; and commonly, when God first revealed himself to any prophet, he did it by an extraordinary vision, as to Isaiah (Isa 6:1-13), to Jeremiah (ch. 1), to Abraham (Act 7:2), to settle a correspondence and a satisfactory way of intercourse, so that there needed not afterwards a vision upon ever revelation. Ezekiel was employed in turning the hearts of the people to the Lord their God, and therefore he must himself see the visions of God. Note, It concerns those to be well acquainted with God themselves, and much affected with what they know of him, whose business it is to bring others to the knowledge and love of him. That he might see the visions of God the heavens were opened; the darkness and distance which hindered

vii

his visions were conquered, and he was let into the light of the glories of the upper world, as near and clear as if heaven had been opened to him. 2. He heard the voice of God (Eze 1:3): The word of the Lord came expressly to him, and what he saw was designed to prepare him for what he was to hear. The expression is emphatic. Essendo fuit verbum Dei-The word of the Lord was as really it was to him. There was no mistake in it; it came to him in the fulness of its light and power, in the evidence and demonstration of the Spirit; it came close to him, nay, it came into him, took possession of him and dwelt in him richly. It came expressly, or accurately, to him; he did himself clearly understand what he said and was abundantly satisfied f the truth of it. The essential Word (so we may take it), the Word who is, who is what he is, came to Ezekiel, to send him on his errand. 3. He felt the power of God opening his eyes to see the visions, opening his ear to hear the voice, and opening his heart to receive both: The hand of the Lord was there upon him. Note, The hand of the Lord goes along with the word f the Lord, and so it becomes effectual; those only understand and believe the report to whom the arm of the Lord is revealed. The hand of God was upon him, as upon Moses, to cover him, that he should not be overcome by the dazzling light and lustre of the visions he saw,Exo 33:22. It was upon him (as upon St. John, Rev 1:17), to revive and support him, that he might bear up, and not faint, under these discoveries, that he might neither be lifted up nor cast down with the abundance of the revelations. God's grace is sufficient for him, and, in token of that, his hand is upon him.

Ezekiel 1:4

The visions of God which Ezekiel here saw were very glorious, and had more particulars than those which other prophets saw. It is the scope and intention of these vision, 1. To possess the prophet's mind with very great, and high, and honourable thoughts of that God by whom he was commissioned and for whom he was employed. It is the likeness of the glory of the Lord that he sees (Eze 1:28), and hence he may infer that it is his honour to serve him, for he is one whom angels serve. He may serve him with safety, for he has power sufficient to bear him out in his work. It is at his peril to draw back from his service, for he has power to pursue him, as he did Jonah. So great a God as this must be served with reverence and godly fear; and with assurance may Ezekiel foretel what this God will do, for he is able to make his words good. 2. To strike a terror upon the sinners who remained in Zion, and those who had already come to Babylon, who were secure, and bade defiance to the threatenings of Jerusalem's ruin, as we have found in Jeremiah's prophecy, and shall find in this, many did. "Let those who said, We shall have peace though we go on, know that our God is a consuming fire, whom they cannot stand before." That this vision had a reference to the destruction of Jerusalem seems plain from Jer 43:3, where he says that it was the vision which he saw when he came to destroy the city, that is, to prophesy the destruction of it. 3. To speak comfort to those that feared God, and trembled at his word, and humbled themselves under his mighty hand. "Let them know that, though they are captives in Babylon, yet they have God nigh unto them; though they have not the place of the sanctuary to be their glorious high throne, they have the God of the sanctuary." Dr. Lightfoot observes, "Now that the church is to be planted for a long time in another country, the Lord shows a glory in the midst of them, as he had done at their first constituting into a church in the wilderness; and out of a cloud and fire, as he had done there, he showed himself; and from between living creatures, as from between the cherubim, he gives his oracles." This put an honour upon them, by which they might value themselves when the Chaldeans insulted over them, and this might encourage their hopes of deliverance in due time.

Now, to answer these ends, we have in these verses the first part of the vision, which represents God as attended and served by an innumerable company of angels, who are all his messengers, his ministers, doing his commandments and hearkening to the voice of his word. This denotes his grandeur, as it magnifies an earthly prince to have a splendid retinue and numerous armies at his command, which engages his allies to trust him and his enemies to fear him.

I. The introduction to this vision of the angels is very magnificent and awakening, Eze 1:4. The prophet, observing the heavens to open, looked, looked up (as it was time), to see what discoveries God would make to him. Note, When the heavens are opened it concerns us to have our eyes open. To clear the way, behold, a whirlwind came out of the north, which would drive away the interposing mists of this lower region. Fair weather comes out of the north, and thence the wind comes that drives away rain. God can by a whirlwind clear the sky and air, and produce that serenity of mind which is necessary to our communion with Heaven. Yet this whirlwind was attended with a great cloud. When we think that the clouds which arise from this earth are dispelled and we can see beyond them, yet still there is a cloud which heavenly things are wrapped in, a cloud from above, so that we cannot order our speech concerning them by reason of darkness. Christ here descended, as he ascended, in a cloud. Some by this whirlwind and cloud understand the Chaldean army coming out of the north against the land of Judah, bearing down all before them as a tempest; and so it agrees with that which was signified by one of the first of Jeremiah's visions (Jer 1:14, Out of the north an evil shall break forth); but I take it here as an introduction rather than to the vision than to the sermons. This whirlwind came to Ezekiel (as that to Elijah, Kgl 19:11), to prepare the way of the Lord, and to demand attention. He that has eyes, that has ears, let him see, let him hear.

II. The vision itself. A great cloud was the vehicle of this vision, in which it was conveyed to the prophet; for God's pavilion in which he rests, his chariot in which he rides, is darkness and thick clouds, Psa 18:11; Psa 104:3. Thus he holds back the face of his throne, lest its dazzling light and lustre should overpower us, by spreading a cloud upon it. Now,

1. The cloud is accompanied with a fire, as upon Mount Sinai, where God resided in a thick cloud; but the sight of his glory was like a devouring fire (Exo 24:16, Exo 24:17), and his first appearance to Moses was in a flame of fire in the bush; for our God is a consuming fire. This was a fire enfolding itself, a globe, or orb, or wheel of fire. God being his own cause, his own rule, and his own end, if he be as a fire, he is as a fire enfolding itself, or (as some read it) kindled by itself. The fire of God's glory shines forth, but it quickly enfolds itself; for he lets us

ix

know but part of his ways; the fire of God's wrath breaks forth, but it also quickly enfolds itself, for the divine patience suffers not all his wrath to be stirred up. If it were not a fire thus enfolding itself, O Lord! who shall stand?

2. The fire is surrounded with a glory: A brightness was about it, in which it enfolded itself, yet it made some discovery of itself. Though we cannot see into the fire, cannot by searching find out God to perfection, yet we see the brightness that is round about it, the reflection of this fire from the thick cloud. Moses might see God's back parts, but not his face. We have some light concerning the nature of God, from the brightness which encompasses it, though we have not an insight into it, by reason of the cloud spread upon it. Nothing is more easy than to determine that God is, nothing more difficult than to describe what he is. When God displays his wrath as fire, yet there is a brightness about it; for his holiness and justice appear very illustrious in the punishment of sin and sinners: even about the devouring fire there is a brightness, which glorified saints will for ever admire.

3. Out of this fire there shines the colour of amber. We are not told who or what it was that had this colour of amber, and therefore I take it to be the whole frame of the following vision, which came into Ezekiel's view out of the midst of the fire and brightness; and the first thing he took notice of before he viewed the particulars was that it was of the colour of amber, or the eye of amber; that is, it looked as amber does to the eye, of a bright flaming fiery colour, the colour of a burning coal; so some think it should be read. The living creatures which he saw coming out of the midst of the fire were seraphim-burners; for he maketh his angels spirits, his ministers a flaming fire.

4. That which comes out of the fire, of a fiery amber colour, when it comes to be distinctly viewed, is the likeness of four living creatures; not the living creatures themselves (angels are spirits, and cannot be seen), but the likeness of them, such a hieroglyphic, or representation, as God saw fit to make use of for the leading of the prophet, and us with him, into some acquaintance with the world of angels (a matter purely of divine revelation), so far as is requisite to possess us with an awful sense of the greatness of that God who has angels for his attendants, and the goodness of that God who has appointed them to be attendants on his people. The likeness of these living creatures came out of the midst of the fire; for angels derive their being and power from God; they are in themselves, and to us, what he is pleased to make them; their glory is a ray of his. The prophet himself explains this vision (Eze 10:20): I knew that the living creatures were the cherubim, which is one of the names by which the angels are known in scripture. To Daniel was made known their number, ten thousand times ten thousand, Dan 7:10. But, though they are many, yet they are one, and that is made known to Ezekiel here; they are one in nature and operation, as an army, consisting of thousands, is yet called a body of men. We have here an account of,

(1.) Their nature. They are living creatures; they are the creatures of God, the work of his hands; their being is derived; they have not life in and of themselves, but receive it from him who is the fountain of life. As much as the living creatures of this lower world excel the vegetables that are the ornaments of earth, so much do the angels, the living creatures of the upper world, excel the sun, moon, and stars, the ornaments of the heavens. The sun (say some) is a flame of fire enfolding itself, but it is not a living creature, as angels, those flames of fire, are. Angels are living creatures, living beings, emphatically so. Men on earth are dying creatures, dying daily (in the midst of life we are in death), but angels in heaven are living creatures; they live indeed, live to good purpose; and, when saints come to be equal unto the angels, they shall not die any more, Luk 20:36.

(2.) Their number. They are four; so they appear here, though they are innumerable; not as if these were four particular angels set up above the rest, as some have fondly imagined, Michael and Gabriel, Raphael and Uriel, but for the sake of the four faces they put on, and to intimate their being sent forth towards the four winds of heaven, Mat 24:31. Zechariah saw them as four chariots going forth east, west, north, and south, Zac 6:1. God has messengers to send every way; for his kingdom is universal, and reaches to all parts of the world.

(3.) Their qualifications, by which they are fitted for the service of their Maker and Master. These are set forth figuratively and by similitude, as is proper in visions, which are parables to the eye. Their description here is such, and so expressed, that I think it is not possible by it to form an exact idea of them in our fancies, or with the pencil, for that would be a temptation to worship them; but the several instances of their fitness for the work they are employed in are intended in the several parts of this description. Note, It is the greatest honour of God's creatures to be in a capacity of answering the end of their creation; and the more ready we are to every good work the nearer we approach to the dignity of angels. These living creatures are described here, [1.] By their general appearance: They had the likeness of a man; they appeared, for the main, in a human shape, First, To signify that these living creatures are reasonable creatures, intelligent beings, who have the spirit of a man which is the candle of the Lord. Secondly, To put an honour upon the nature of man, who is made lower, yet but a little lower, than the angels, in the very next rank of beings below them. When the invisible intelligences of the upper world would make themselves visible, it is in the likeness of man. Thirdly, To intimate that their delights are with the sons of men, as their Master's are (Pro 8:31), that they do service to men, and men may have spiritual communion with them by faith, hope, and holy love. Fourthly, The angels of God appear in the likeness of man because in the fulness of time the Son of God was not only to appear in that likeness, but to assume that nature; they therefore show this love to it. [2.] By their faces: Every one had four faces, looking four several ways. In St. John's vision, which has a near affinity with this, each of the four living creatures has one of these faces here mentioned (Rev 4:7); here each of them has all four, to intimate that they have all the same qualifications for service; though, perhaps, among the angels of heaven, as among the angels of the churches, some excel in one gift and others in another, but all for the common service. Let us contemplate their faces till we be in some measure changed into the same image, that we may do the will of God as the angels do it in heaven. They all four had the face of a man (for in that likeness they appeared, Eze 1:5), but, besides that, they had the face of a lion, an ox, and an eagle, each masterly in its kind, the lion among wild beasts, the ox among tame ones, and the eagle among fowls, Eze 1:10. Does God make use of them for the executing of judgments upon his enemies? They are fierce and strong as the lion and the eagle in tearing their prey. Does he make use of them for the good of his people? They are as oxen strong for labour and inclined to serve. And in both they have the understanding of a man. The scattered perfections of the living creatures on earth meet in the angels of heaven. They have the likeness of man; but, because there are some things in which man is excelled even by the inferior creatures, they are therefore compared to some of them. They have the understanding of a man, and such as far exceeds it; they also resemble man in tenderness and humanity. But, First, A lion excels man in strength and boldness, and is much more formidable; therefore the angels, who in this resemble them, put on the face of a lion. Secondly, An ox excels man in diligence, and patience, and painstaking, and an unwearied discharge of the work he has to do; therefore the angels, who are constantly employed in the service of God and the church, put on the face of an ox. Thirdly, An eagle excels man in quickness and piercingness of sight, and in soaring high; and therefore the angels, who seek things above, and see far into divine mysteries, put on the face of a flying eagle. [3.] By their wings: Every one had four wings, Eze 1:6. In the vision Isaiah had of them they appeared with six, now with four; for they appeared above the throne, and had occasion for two to cover their faces with. The angels are fitted with wings to fly swiftly on God's errands; whatever business God sends them upon they lose no time. Faith and hope are the soul's wings, upon which it soars upward; pious and devout affections are its wings on which it is carried forward with vigour and alacrity. The prophet observes here, concerning their wings, First, That they were joined one to another, Eze 1:9 and again Eze 1:11. They did not make use of their wings for fighting, as some birds do; there is no contest among the angels. God makes peace, perfect peace, in his high places. But their wings were joined, in token of their perfect unity and unanimity and the universal agreement there is among them. Secondly, That they were stretched upward, extended, and ready for use, not folded up, or flagging. Let an angel receive the least intimation of the divine will, and he has nothing to seek, but is upon the wings immediately; while our poor dull souls are like the ostrich, that with much difficulty lifts up herself on high. Thirdly, That two of their wings were made use of in covering their bodies, the spiritual bodies they assumed. The clothes that cover us are our hindrance in work; angels need no other covering than their own wings, which are their furtherance. They cover their bodies from us, so forbidding us needless enquiries concerning them. Ask not after them, for they are wonderful, Jdg 13:18. They cover them before God, so directing us, when we approach to God, to see to it that we be so clothed with Christ's righteousness that the shame of our nakedness may not appear. [4.] By their feet, including their legs and thighs: They were straight feet (Eze 1:7); they stood straight, and firm, and steady; no burden of service could make their legs to bend under them. The spouse makes this part of the description of her beloved, that his legs were as pillars of marble set upon sockets of fine gold (Sol 5:15); such are the angels' legs. The sole of their feet was like that of a calf's foot, which divides the hoof and is therefore clean: as it were the sole of a round foot (as the Chaldee words it); they were ready for motion any way. Their feet were winged (so the Septuagint); they went so swiftly that it was as if they flew. And their very feet sparkled like the colour of burnished brass; not only the faces, but the very feet, of those are beautiful whom God sends on his errands (Isa 52:7); every step the angels take is glorious. In the vision John had of Christ it is said, His feet were like unto fine brass, as if they burned in a furnace, Rev 1:15. [5.] By their hands (Eze 1:8): They had the hands of a man under their wings on their four sides, an arm and a hand under every wing. They had not only wings for motion, but hands for action. Many are quick who are not active; they hurry about a great deal, but do nothing to purpose, bring nothing to pass; they have wings, but no hands: whereas God's servants, the angels, not only go when he sends them and come when he calls them, but do what he bids them. They are the hands of a man, which are wonderfully made and fitted for service, which are guided by reason and understanding; for what angles do they do intelligently and with judgment. They have calves' feet; this denotes the swiftness of their motion (the cedars of Lebanon are said to skip like a calf, Psa 29:6); but they have a man's hand, which denotes the niceness and exactness of their performances, as the heavens are said to be the work of God's fingers. Their hands were under their wings, which concealed them, as they did the rest of their bodies. Note, The agency of angels is a secret thing and their work is carried on in an invisible way. In working for God, though we must not, with the sluggard, hide our hand in our bosom, yet we must, with the humble, not let our left hand know what our right hand doeth. We may observe that where these wings were their hands were under their wings; wherever their wings carried them they carried hands along with them, to be still doing something suitable something that the duty of the place requires.

(4.) Their motions. The living creatures are moving. Angels are active beings; it is not their happiness to sit still and do nothing, but to be always well employed; and we must reckon ourselves then best when we are doing good, doing it as the angels do it, or whom it is here observed, [1.] That whatever service they went about they went every one straight forward (Eze 1:9, Eze 1:12), which intimates, First, That they sincerely aimed at the glory of God, and had a single eye to that, in all they did. Their going straight forward supposes that they looked straight forward, and never had any sinister intentions in what they did. And, if thus our eye be single, our whole body will be full of light. The singleness of the eye is the sincerity of the heart. Secondly, That they were intent upon the service they were employed in, and did it with a close application of mind. They went forward with their work; for what their hand found to do they did with all their might and did not loiter in it. Thirdly, That they were unanimous in it: They went straight forward, every one about his own work; they did not thwart or jostle one another, did not stand in one another's light, in one another's way. Fourthly, That they perfectly understood their business, and were thoroughly apprised of it, so that they needed not to stand still, to pause of hesitate, but pursue their work with readiness, as those that knew what they had to do and how to do it. Fifthly, They were steady and constant in their work. They did not fluctuate, did not tire, did not vary, but were of a piece with themselves. They moved in a direct line, and so went the nearest way to work in all they did and lost no time. When we go straight we go forward; when we serve God with one heart we rid ground, we rid work. [2.] They turned not when they went, Eze 1:9,Eze 1:12. First, They made no blunders or mistakes, which would give them occasion to turn back to rectify them; their work needed no correction, and therefore needed not to be gone over again. Secondly, They minded no diversions; as they turned not back, so they turned not aside, to trifle with any thing that was foreign to their business. [3.] They went whither the Spirit was to go (Eze 1:12), either, First, Whither their own spirit was disposed to go; thither they went, having no bodies, as we have, to clog or hinder them. It is our infelicity and daily burden that, when the spirit if willing, yet the flesh is weak and cannot keep pace with it, so that the good which we would do we do it not; but angels and glorified saints labour under no such impotency; whatever they incline or intend to do they do it, and never come short of it. Or, rather, Secondly, Whithersoever the Spirit of God would have them go, thither they went. Though they had so much wisdom of their own, yet in all their motions and actions they subjected themselves to the guidance and government of the divine will. Whithersoever the divine Providence was to go they went, to serve its purposes and to execute its orders. The Spirit of God (says Mr. Greenhill) is the great agent that sets angels to work, and it is their honour that they are led, they are easily led, by the Spirit. See how tractable and obsequious these noble creatures are. Whithersoever the Spirit is to go they go immediately, with all possible alacrity. Note, Those that walk after the Spirit do the will of God as the angels do it. [4.] They ran and returned like a flash of lightning, Eze 1:14. This intimates, First, That they made haste; they were quick in their motions, as quick as lightning. Whatever business they went about they despatched it immediately, in a moment, in the twinkling of an eye. Happy they that have no bodies to retard their motion in holy exercises. And happy shall we be when we come to have spiritual bodies for spiritual work. Satan falls like lightning into his own ruin, Luk 10:18. Angels fly like lightning in their Master's work. The angel Gabriel flew swiftly. Secondly, That they made haste back: They ran and returned; ran to do their work and execute their orders, and then returned to give an account of what they had done and receive new instructions, that they might be always doing. They ran into the lower world, to do what was to be done there; but, when they had done it, they returned like flash of lightning to the upper world again, to the beatific vision of their God, which they could not with any patience be longer from than their service did require. Thus we should be in the affairs of this world as out of our element. Though we run into them, we must not repose in them, but our souls must quickly return like lightning to God their rest and centre.

5. We have an account of the light by which the prophet saw these living creatures, or the looking-glass in which he saw them, Eze 1:13. (1.) He saw them by their own light, for their appearance was like burning coals of fire; they are seraphim-burners, denoting the ardour of their love to God, their fervent zeal in his service, their splendour and brightness, and their terror against God's enemies. When God employs them to fight his battles they are as coals of fire (Psa 18:12) to devour the adversaries, as lightnings shot out to discomfit them. (2.) He saw them by the light of some lamps, which went up and down among them, the shining whereof was very bright. Satan's works are works of darkness; he is the ruler of the darkness of this world. But the

angels of light are in the light, and, though they conceal their working, they show their work, for it will bear the light. But we see them and their works only by candle-light, but the dim light of lamps that go up and down among them; when the day breaks, and the shadows flee away, we shall see them clearly. Some make the appearance of these burning coals, and of the lightning that issues out of the fire, to signify the wrath of God, and his judgments, that were now to be executed upon Judah and Jerusalem for their sins, in which angels were to be employed; and accordingly we find afterwards coals of fire scattered upon the city to consume it, which were fetched from between the cherubim, Eze 10:2. But by the appearance of the lamps then we may understand the light of comfort which shone forth to the people of God in the darkness of this present trouble. If the ministry of the angels is as a consuming fire to God's enemies, it is as a rejoicing light to his own children. To the one this fire is bright, it is very reviving and refreshing; to the other, out of the fire comes fresh lightning to destroy them. Note, Good angels are our friends, or enemies, according as God is.

Ezekiel 1:15

The prophet is very exact in making and recording his observations concerning this vision. And here we have,

I. The notice he took of the wheels, Eze 1:15-21. The glory of God appears not only in the splendour of his retinue in the upper world, but in the steadiness of his government here in this lower world. Having seen how God does according to his will in the armies of heaven, let us now see how he does according to it among the inhabitants of the earth; for there, on the earth, the prophet saw the wheels, Eze 1:15. As he beheld the living creatures, and was contemplating the glory of that vision and receiving instruction from it, this other vision presented itself to his view. Note, Those who make a good use of the discoveries God has favoured them with may expect further discoveries; for to him that hath shall be given. We are sometimes tempted to think there is nothing glorious but what is in the upper world, whereas, could we with an eye of faith discern the beauty of Providence and the wisdom, power, and goodness, which shine in the administration of that kingdom, we should see, and say, Verily he is a God that judgeth in the earth and acts like himself. There are many things in this vision which give us some light concerning the divine Providence. 1. The dispensations of Providence are compared to wheels, either the wheels of a chariot, in which the conqueror rides in triumph, or rather the wheels of a clock or watch, which all contribute to the regular motion of the machine. We read of the course or wheel of nature (Jam 3:6), which is here set before us as under the direction of the God of nature. Wheels, though they move not of themselves, as the living creatures do, are yet made movable and are almost continually kept in action. Providence, represented by these wheels, produces changes; sometimes one spoke of the wheel is uppermost and sometimes another; but the motion of the wheel on its own axletree, like that of the orbs above, is very regular and steady. The motion of the wheels is circular; by the revolutions of Providence things are brought to the same posture and pass which they were in formerly; for the thing that is is that which has been, and there is no new thing under the sun, Ecc 1:9,Ecc 1:10. 2. The wheel is said to be by the living creatures, who attended it to direct its motion; for the angels are employed as the ministers of God's providence, and have a greater hand in directing the motions of second causes to serve the divine purpose than we think they have. Such a close connexion is there between the living creatures and the wheels that they moved and rested together. Were angels busily employed? Men were busily employed as instruments in their hand, whether of mercy or judgment, though they themselves were not aware of it. Or, Are men active to compass their designs? Angels at the same time are acting to control and overrule them. This is much insisted on here (Eze 1:19): When the living creatures went, to bring about any business, the wheels went by them; when God has work to do by the ministry of angels second causes are all found, or made, ready to concur in it; and (Eze 1:21) when those stood these stood; when the angels had done their work the second causes had done theirs. If the living creatures were lifted up from the earth, were elevated to any service above the common course of nature and out of the ordinary road (as suppose in the working of miracles, the dividing of the water, the standing still of the sun), the wheels, contrary to their own natural tendency, which is towards the earth, move in concert with them, and are lifted up over against them; this is thrice mentioned, Eze 1:19-21. Note, All inferior creatures are, and move, and act, as the Creator, by the ministration of angels, directs and influences them. Visible effects are managed and governed by invisible causes. The reason given of this is because the spirit of the living creatures was in the wheels; the same wisdom, power, and holiness of God, the same will and counsel of his, that guides and governs the angels and all their performances, does, by them, order and dispose of all the motions of the creatures in this lower world and the events and issues of them. God is the soul of the world, and animates the whole, both that above and that beneath, so that they move in perfect harmony, as the upper and lower parts of the natural body do, so that whithersoever the Spirit is to go (whatever God wills and purposes to be done and brought to pass) thither their spirit is to go; that is, the angels, knowingly and designedly, set themselves to bring it about. And their spirit is in the wheels, which are therefore lifted up over against them; that is, both the powers of nature and the wills of men are all made to serve the intention, which they infallibly and irresistibly effect, though perhaps they mean not so, neither doth their heart think so, Isa 10:7; Mic 4:11, Mic 4:12. Thus, though the will of God's precept be not done on earth as it is done in heaven, yet the will of his purpose and counsel is, and shall be. 3. The wheel is said to have four faces, looking four several ways (Eze 1:15), denoting that the providence of God exerts itself in all parts of the world, east, west, north, and south, and extends itself to the remotest corners of it. Look which way you will upon the wheel of Providence, and it has a face towards you, a beautiful one, which you may admire the features and complexion of; it looks upon you as ready to speak to you, if you be but ready to hear the voice of it; like a well-drawn picture, it has an eye upon all that have an eye upon it. The wheel had so four faces that it had in it four wheels, which went upon their four sides, Eze 1:17. At first Ezekiel saw it as one wheel (Eze 1:15), one sphere; but afterwards he saw it was four, but they four had one likeness (Eze 1:16); not only they were like one another, but they were as if they had been one. This intimates, (1.) That one event of providence is like whence it is easy to infer that whatever God by his prophets either promises or threatens to do he is able to effect it. Angels are his servants; men are his tools. But now that a divine revelation is to be given to a prophet, and by him to the church, we must look higher than the living creatures or the wheels, and must expect that from the eternal Word, of whom we have an account in these verses. Ezekiel, hearing a voice from the firmament, looked up, as John did, to see the voice that spoke with him, and he saw one like unto the Son of man, Rev 1:12, Rev 1:13. The second person sometimes tried the fashion of a man occasionally before he clothed himself with it for good and all; and the Spirit of prophecy is called the Spirit of Christ (Pe1 1:11) and the testimony of Jesus, Rev 19:10. 1. This glory of Christ that the prophet saw was above the firmament that was over the heads of the living creatures, Eze 1:26. Note, The heads of angels themselves are under the feet of the Lord Jesus; for the firmament that is over their heads is under his feet. Angels, principalities, and powers are made subject to him, Pe1 3:22. This dignity and dominion of the Redeemer before his incarnation magnify his condescension in his incarnation, when he was made a little lower than the angels, Heb 2:9. 2. The first thing he observed was a throne; for divine revelation comes backed and supported with a royal authority. We must have an eye of faith to God and Christ as upon a throne. The first thing that John discovered in his visions was a throne set in heaven (Rev 4:2), which commands reverence and subjection. It is a throne of glory, a throne of grace, a throne of triumph, a throne of government, a throne of judgment. The Lord has prepared his throne in the heavens, has prepared it for his Son, whom he has set King on his holy hill of Zion. 3. On the throne he saw the appearance of a man. This is good new to the children of men, that the throne above the firmament is filled with one that is not ashamed to appear, even there, in the likeness of man. Daniel, in vision, saw the kingdom and dominion given to one like the Son of man, who therefore has authority given him to execute judgment because he is the Son of man (Joh 5:27), so appearing in these visions. 4. He saw him as a prince and judge upon this throne. Though he appeared in fashion as a man, yet he appeared in more than human glory, Eze 1:27. (1.) Is God a shining light? So is he: when the prophet saw him he saw as the colour of amber, that is, a brightness round about; for God dwells in light, and covers himself with light as with a garment. How low did the Redeemer stoop for us when, to bring about our salvation, he suffered his glory to be eclipsed by the veil of his humanity! (2.) Is God a consuming fire? So is he: from his loins, both upward and downward, there was the appearance of fire. The fire above the loins was round about within the amber; it was inward and involved. That below the loins was more outward and open, and yet that also had brightness round about. Some make the former to signify Christ's divine nature, the glory and virtue of which are hidden within the colour of amber; it is what no man has seen nor can see. The latter they suppose to be his human nature, the glory of which there were those who saw; the glory as of the only begotten of the Father, full of grace and truth, Joh 1:14. He had rays coming out of his hand, and yet there was the hiding of his power, Hab 3:4. The fire in which the Son of man appeared here might be intended to signify the judgments that were ready to be executed upon Judah and Jerusalem, coming form that fiery indignation of the Almighty which devours the adversaries. Nothing is more dreadful to the most daring sinners than the wrath of him that sits upon the throne, and of the Lamb, Rev 6:16. The day is coming when the Lord Jesus shall be revealed in flaming fire, Th2 1:7, Th2 1:8. It concerns us therefore to kiss the Son lest he be angry. 5. The throne is surrounded with a rainbow, Eze 1:28. It is so in St. John's vision, Rev 4:3. The brightness about it was of divers colours, as the bow that is in the cloud in the day of rain, which, as it is a display of majesty, and looks very great, so it is a pledge of mercy, and looks very kind; for it is a confirmation of that gracious promise God has made that he will not drown the world again, and he has said, I will look upon the bow and remember the covenant, Gen 9:16. This intimates that he who sits upon the throne is the Mediator of the covenant, that his dominion is for our protection, not our destruction, that he interposes between us and the judgments our sins have deserved, and that all the promises of God are in him yea and amen. Now that the fire of God's wrath was breaking out against Jerusalem bounds should be set to it, and he would not make an utter destruction of it, for he would look upon the bow and remember the covenant, as he promised in such a case, Lev 26:42.

Lastly, We have the conclusion of this vision. Observe, 1. What notion the prophet himself had of it: This was the appearance of the likeness of the glory of the Lord. Here, as all along, he is careful to guard against all gross corporeal thoughts of God, which might derogate from the transcendent purity of his nature. he does not say, This was the Lord (for he is invisible), but, This was the glory of the Lord, in which he was pleased to manifest himself a glorious being; yet it is not the glory of the Lord, but the likeness of that glory, some faint resemblance of it; nor is it any adequate likeness of that glory, but only the appearance of that likeness, a shadow of it, and not the very image of the thing,Heb 10:1. 2. What impressions it made upon him: When I saw it, I fell upon my face. (1.) He was overpowered by it; the dazzling lustre of it conquered him and threw him upon his face; for who is able to stand before this holy Lord God? Or, rather, (2.) He prostrated himself in a humble sense of his own unworthiness of the honour now done him, and of the infinite distance which he now, more than ever, perceived to be between him and God; he fell upon his face in token of that holy awe and reverence of God with which his mind was possessed and filled. Note, The more God is pleased to make known of himself to us the more low we should be before him. He fell upon his face to adore the majesty of God, to implore his mercy and to deprecate the wrath he saw ready to break out against the children of his people. 3. What instructions he had from it. All he saw was only to prepare him for that which he was to hear; for faith comes by hearing. He therefore heard a voice of one that spoke; for we are taught by words, not merely by hieroglyphics. When he fell on his face, ready to received the word, then he heard the voice of one that spoke; for God delights to teach the humble.

Ezekiel Chapter 2

Ezekiel

What our Lord Jesus said to St. Paul (Act 26:16) may fitly be applied to the prophet Ezekiel, to whom the same Jesus is here speaking, "Rise and stand upon thy feet, for I have appeared unto thee for this purpose, to make thee a minister." We have here Ezekiel's ordination to his office, which the vision was designed to fit him for, not to entertain his curiosity with uncommon speculations, but to put him into business. Now here, I. He is commissioned to go as a prophet to the house of Israel, now captives in Babylon, and to deliver God's messages to them from time to time (Eze 2:1-5). II. He is cautioned not to be afraid of them (Eze 2:6). III. He is instructed what to say to them, and has words put into his mouth, signified by the vision of a roll, which he was ordered to eat (Eze 2:7-10), and which, in the next chapter, we find he did eat.

Ezekiel 2:1

The title here given to Ezekiel, as often afterwards, is very observable. God, when he speaks to him, calls him, Son of man (Eze 2:1, Eze 2:3), Son of Adam, Son of the earth. Daniel is once called so (Dan 8:17) and but once; the compellation is used to no other of the prophets but to Ezekiel all along. We may take it, 1. As a humble diminishing title. Lest Ezekiel should be lifted up with the abundance of the revelations, he is put in mind of this, that sill he is a son of man, a mean, weak, mortal creature. Among other things made known to him, it was necessary he should be made to know this, that he was a son of man, and therefore that it was wonderful condescension in God that he was pleased thus to manifest himself to him. Now he is among the living creatures, the angels; yet he must remember that he is himself a man, a dying creature. What is man, or the son of man, that he should be thus visited, thus dignified? Though God had here a splendid retinue of holy angels about his throne, who were ready to go on his errands, yet he passes them all by, and pitches on Ezekiel, a son of man, to be his messenger to the house of Israel; for we have this treasure in earthen vessels, and God's messages sent us by men like ourselves, whose terror shall not make us afraid nor their hand be heavy upon us. Ezekiel was a priest, but the priesthood was brought low and the honour of it laid in the dust. It therefore became him, and all of his order, to humble themselves, and to lie low, as sons of men, common men. he was now to be employed as a prophet, God's ambassador, and a ruler over the kingdoms (Jer 1:10), a post of great honour, but he must remember that he is a son of man, and, whatever good he did, it was not by any might of his own, for he was a son of man, but in the strength of divine grace, which must therefore have all the glory. Or, 2. We may take it as an honourable dignifying title; for it is one of the titles of the Messiah in the Old Testament (Dan 7:13, I saw one like the Son of man come with the clouds of heaven), whence Christ borrows the title he often calls himself by, The Son of man. The prophets were types of him, as they had near access

xxi

to God and great authority among men; and therefore as David the king is called the Lord's anointed, or Christ, so Ezekiel the prophet is called son of man.

I. Ezekiel is here set up, and made to stand, that he might receive his commission, Eze 2:1, Eze 2:2. He is set up,

1. By a divine command: Son of man, stand upon thy feet. His lying prostrate was a posture of greater reverence, but his standing up would be a posture of greater readiness and fitness for business. Our adorings of God must not hinder, but rather quicken and excite, our actings for God. He fell on his face in a holy fear and awe of God, but he was quickly raised up again; for those that humble themselves shall be exalted. God delights no in the dejections of his servants, but the same that brings them low will raise them up; the same that is a Spirit of bondage will be a Spirit of adoption. Stand, and I will speak to thee. Note, We may expect that God will speak to us when we stand ready to do what he commands us.

2. By a divine power going along with that command, Eze 2:2. God bade him stand up; but, because he had not strength of his own to recover his feet nor courage to face the vision, the Spirit entered into him and set him upon his feet. Note, God is graciously pleased to work that in us which he requires of us and raises those whom he bids rise. We must stir up ourselves, and then God will put strength into us; we must work out our salvation, and then God will work in us. He observed that the Spirit entered into him when Christ spoke to him; for Christ conveys his Spirit by his word as the ordinary means and makes the word effectual by the Spirit. The Spirit set the prophet upon his feet, to raise him up from his dejections, for he is the Comforter. Thus, in a similar case, Daniel was strengthened by a divine touch (Dan 10:18) and John was raised by the right hand of Christ laid upon him, Rev 1:17. The Spirit set him upon his feet, made him willing and forward to do as he was bidden, and then he heard him that spoke to him. He heard the voice before (Eze 1:28), but now he heard it more distinctly and clearly, heard it and submitted to it. The Spirit sets us upon our feet by inclining our will to our duty, and thereby disposes the understanding to receive the knowledge of it.

II. Ezekiel is here sent, and made to go, with a message to the children of Israel (Eze 2:3): I send thee to the children of Israel. God had for many ages been sending to them his servants the prophets, rising up betimes and sending them, but to little purpose; they were now sent into captivity for abusing God's messengers, and yet even there God sends this prophet among them, to try if their ears were open to discipline, now that they were holden in the cords of affliction. As the supports of life, so the means of grace, are continued to us after they have been a thousand times forfeited. Now observe,

1. The rebellion of the people to whom this ambassador is sent; he is sent to reduce them to their allegiance, to bring back the children of Israel to the Lord their God. let the prophet know that there is occasion for his going on this errand, for they are a rebellious nation (Eze 2:3), a

was Ezekiel's business, and to comfort them when, in the latter end of their troubles, they were dejected and discouraged. If the Lord had been pleased to kill them, he would not have used such apt and proper means to cure them. III. Concerning the matter and scope of it. 1. There is much in it that is very mysterious, dark, and hard to be understood, especially in the beginning and the latter end of it, which therefore the Jewish rabbin forbade the reading of to their young men, till they came to be thirty years of age, lest by the difficulties they met with there they should be prejudiced against the scriptures; but if we read these difficult parts of scripture with humility and reverence, and search them diligently, though we may not be able to untie all the knots we meet with, any more than we can solve all the phenomena in the book of nature, yet we may from them, as from the book of nature, gather a great deal for the confirming of our faith and the encouraging of our hope in the God we worship. 2. Though the visions here be intricate, such as an elephant may swim in, yet the sermons are mostly plain, such as a lamb may wade in; and the chief design of them is to show God's people their transgressions, that in their captivity they might be repenting and not repining. It should seem the prophet was constantly attended (for we read of their sitting before him as God's people sat to hear his words, Eze 33:31), and that he was occasionally consulted, for we read of the elders of Israel who came to enquire of the Lord by him, Eze 14:1, Eze 14:3. And as it was of great use to the oppressed captives themselves to have a prophet with them, so it was a testimony to their holy religion against their oppressors who ridiculed it and them. 3. Though the reproofs and the threatenings here are very sharp and bold, yet towards the close of the book very comfortable assurances are given of great mercy God had in store for them; and there, at length, we shall meet with something that has reference to gospel times, and which was to have its accomplishment in the kingdom of the Messiah, of whom indeed this prophet speaks less than almost any of the prophets. But by opening the terrors of the Lord he prepares Christ's way. By the law is the knowledge of sin, and so it becomes our school-master to bring us to Christ. The visions which were the prophet's credentials we have ch. 1-3, the reproofs and threatenings ch. 4-24 betwixt which and the comforts which we have in the latter part of the book we have messages sent to the nations that bordered upon the land of Israel, whose destruction is foretold (ch. 25-35), to make way for the restoration of God's Israel and the re-establishment of their city and temple, which are foretold ch. 36 to the end. Those who would apply the comforts to themselves must apply the convictions to themselves.

ABOUT SCRIPTURA PRESS

Scriptura Press is a Christian company that makes Christian works available and affordable to all. We are a non-denominational publishing group that shares the teachings of the Scripture, whether in the form of sermons or histories of the Church.

Ezekiel

An Exposition, with Practical Observations, of The Book of the Prophet Ezekiel

When we entered upon the writings of the prophets, which speak of the things that should be hereafter, we seemed to have the same call that St. John had (Rev 4:1), Come up hither; but, when we enter upon the prophecy of this book, it is as if the voice said, Come up higher; as we go forward in time (for Ezekiel prophesied in the captivity, as Jeremiah prophesied just before it), so we soar upward in discoveries yet more sublime of the divine glory. These waters of the sanctuary still grow deeper; so far are they from being fordable that in some places they are scarcely fathomable; yet, deep as they are, out of them flow streams which make glad the city of our God, the holy place of the tabernacles of the Most High. As to this prophecy now before us, we may enquire, I. Concerning the penman of it-it was Ezekiel; his name signifies, The strength of God, or one girt or strengthened of God. He girded up the loins of his mind to the service, and God put strength into him. Whom God calls to any service he will himself enable for it; if he give commission, he will give power to execute it. Ezekiel's name was answered when God said (and no doubt did as he said), I have made thy face strong against their faces. The learned Selden, in his book De Diis Syris, says that it was the opinion of some of the ancients that the prophet Ezekiel was the same with that Nazaratus Assyrius whom Pythagoras (as himself relates) had for his tutor for some time, and whose lectures he attended. It is agreed that they lived much about the same time; and we have reason to think that many of the Greek philosophers were acquainted with the sacred writings and borrowed some of the best of their notions from them. If we may give credit to the tradition of the Jews, he was put to death by the captives in Babylon, for his faithfulness and boldness in reproving them; it is stated that they dragged him upon the stones till his brains were dashed out. An Arabic historian says that he was put to death and was buried in the sepulchre of Shem the son of Noah. So Hottinger relates, Thesaur. Philol. lib. 2 cap. 1. II. Concerning the date of it-the place whence it is dated and the time when. The scene is laid in Babylon, when it was a house of bondage to the Israel of God; there the prophecies of this book were preached, there they were written, when the prophet himself, and the people to whom he prophesied, were captives there. Ezekiel and Daniel are the only writing prophets of the Old Testament who lived and prophesied any where but in the land of Israel, except we add Jonah, who was sent to Nineveh to prophesy. Ezekiel prophesied in the beginning of the captivity, Daniel in the latter end of it. It was an indication of God's good-will to them, and his gracious designs concerning them in their affliction, that he raised up prophets among them, both to convince them when, in the beginning of their troubles, they were secure and unhumbled, which rebellious house, Eze 2:5. They are called children of Israel; they retain the name of their pious ancestors, but they have wretchedly degenerated, they have become Goim-nations, the word commonly used for the Gentiles. The children of Israel have become as the children of the Ethiopian (Amo 9:7), for they are rebellious; and rebels at home are much more provoking to a prince than enemies abroad. Their idolatries and false worships were the sins which, more than any thing, denominated them a rebellious nation; for thereby they set up another prince in opposition to their rightful Sovereign, and did homage and paid tribute to the usurper, which is the highest degree of rebellion that can be. (1.) They had been all along a rebellious generation and had persisted in their rebellion: They and their fathers have transgressed against me. Note, Those are not always in the right that have antiquity and the fathers on their side; for there are errors and corruptions of long standing: and it is so far from being an excuse for walking in a bad way that our fathers walked in it that it is really an aggravation, for it is justifying the sin of those that have gone before us. They have continued in their rebellion even unto this very day; notwithstanding the various means and methods that have been made use of to reclaim them, to this day, when they are under divine rebukes for their rebellion, they continue rebellious; many among them, like Ahaz, even in their distress, trespass yet more; they are not the better for all the changes that have befallen them, but still remain unchanged. (2.) They were now hardened in their rebellion. They are impudent children, brazen-faced, and cannot blush; they are still-hearted, self-willed, and cannot bend, cannot stoop, neither ashamed nor afraid to sin; they will not be wrought upon by the sense either of honour or duty. We are willing to hope this was not the character of all, but of many, and those perhaps the leading men. Observe, [1.] God knew this concerning them, how inflexible, how incorrigible, they were. Note, God is perfectly acquainted with every man's true character, whatever his pretensions and professions may be. [2.] He told the prophet this, that he might know the better how to deal with them and what handle to take them by. He must rebuke such men as those sharply, cuttingly, must deal plainly with them, though they call it dealing roughly. God tells him this, that it might be no surprise or stumbling-block to him if he found that his preaching should not make that impression upon them, which he had reason to think it would.

2. The dominion of the prince by whom this ambassador is sent. (1.) He has authority to command him whom he sends: "I do send thee unto them, and therefore thou shalt say thus and thus unto them," Eze 2:4. Note, it is the prerogative of Christ to send prophets and ministers and to enjoin them their work. St. Paul thanked Christ Jesus who put him into the ministry (Ti1 1:12); for, as he was sent of the Father, ministers are sent by him; and as he received the Spirit without measure he gives the Spirit by measure, saying, Receive you the Holy Ghost. They are impudent and rebellious, and yet I send thee unto them. Note, Christ gives the means of grace to many who he knows will not make a good use of those means, puts many a price into the hand of fools to get wisdom, who not only have no heart to it, but have their hearts turned against it. Thus he will magnify his own grace, justify his own judgment, leave them inexcusable, and make their condemnation more intolerable. (2.) He has authority by him to command those to whom he sends him: Thou shalt say unto them, Thus saith the Lord God. All he said to them must be

spoken in God's name, enforced by his authority, and delivered as from him. Christ delivered his doctrines as a Son-Verily, verily, I say unto you; the prophets as servants-Thus saith the Lord God, our Master and yours. Note, The writings of the prophets are the word of God, and so are to be regarded by every one of us. (3.) He has authority to call those to an account to whom he sends his ambassadors. Whether they will hear or whether they will forbear, whether they will attend to the word or turn their backs upon it, they shall know that there has been a prophet among them, shall know by experience. [1.] If they hear and obey, they will know by comfortable experience that the word which did them good was brought to them by one that had a commission from God and a divine power going along with him in the execution of it. Thus those who were converted by St. Paul's preaching are said to be the seals of his apostleship, Col 9:2. When men's hearts are made to burn under the word, and their wills to bow to it, then they know and bear the witness in themselves that it is not the word of men, but of God. [2.] If they forbear, if they turn a deaf ear to the word (as it is to be feared they will, for they are a rebellious house), yet they shall be made to know that he whom they slighted was indeed a prophet, by the reproaches of their own consciences and the just judgments of God upon them for refusing him; they shall know it to their cost, know it to their confusion, know it by sad experience, what a pernicious dangerous thing it is to despise God's messengers. They shall know by the accomplishment of the threatenings that the prophet who denounced them was sent of God; thus the word will take hold of men, Zac 1:6. Note, First, Those to whom the word of God is sent are upon their trial whether they will hear or whether they will forbear, and accordingly will their doom be. Secondly, Whether we be edified by the word or no, it is certain that God will be glorified and his word magnified and made honourable. Whether it be a savour of life unto life or of death unto death, either way it will appear to be of divine original.

Ezekiel 2:6

The prophet, having received his commission, here receives a charge with it. It is a post of honour to which he is advanced, but withal it is a post of service and work, and it is here required of him,

I. That he be bold. He must act in the discharge of this trust with an undaunted courage and resolution, and not be either driven off from his work or made to drive on heavily, by the difficulties and oppositions that he would be likely to meet with in it: Son of man, be not afraid of them, Eze 2:6. Note, Those that will do any thing to purpose in the service of God must not be afraid of the face of man; for the fear of men will bring a snare, which will be very entangling to us in the work of God. 1. God tells the prophet what was the character of those to whom he sent him, as before, Eze 2:3, Eze 2:4. They are briers and thorns, scratching, and tearing, and vexing a man, which way soever he turns. They are continually teazing God's prophets and entangling them in their talk (Mat 22:15); they are pricking briers and grieving thorns. The best of them is as a brier, and the most upright sharper than a thorn-hedge, Mic 7:4. Thorns and briers are the fruit of sin and the curse, and of equal date with the enmity between the seed of the woman and the seed of the serpent. Note, Wicked men, especially the persecutors of God's prophets and people, are as briers and thorns, which are hurtful to the ground, choke the good seed, hinder God's husbandry, are vexatious to his husbandmen; but they are nigh unto cursing and their end is to be burned. Yet God makes use of them sometimes for the correction and instruction of his people, as Gideon taught the men of Succoth with thorns and briers, Jdg 8:16. Yet this is not the worst of their character: they are scorpions, venomous and malignant. The sting of a scorpion is a thousand times more hurtful than the scratch of a brier. persecutors are a generation of vipers, are of the serpent's seed, and the poison of asps is under their tongue; and they are more subtle than any beast of the field. And, which makes the prophet's case the more grievous, he dwells among these scorpions; they are continually about him, so that he cannot be safe nor quiet in his own house; these bad men are his bad neighbours, who thereby have many opportunities, and will let slip none, to do him a mischief. God takes notice of this to the prophet, as Christ to the angel of one of the churches, Rev 2:13. I know thy works, and where thou dwellest, even where Satan's seat is. Ezekiel had been, in vision, conversing with angels, but when he comes down from this mount he finds he dwells with scorpions. 2. He tells him what would be their conduct towards him, that they would do what they could to frighten him with their looks and their words; they would hector him and threaten him, would look scornfully and spitefully at him, and do their utmost to face him down and put him our of countenance, that they might drive him off from being a prophet, or at least from telling them of their faults and threatening them with the judgments of God; or, if they could not prevail in this, that they might vex and perplex him, and disturb the repose of his mind. They were now themselves in subjection, divested of all power, so that they had no other way of persecuting the prophet than with their looks and their words; and so they did persecute him. Behold, thou hast spoken and done evil things as thou couldest, Jer 3:5. If they had had more power, they would have done more mischief. They were now in captivity, smarting for their rebellion, and particularly their misusing God's prophets; and yet they are as bad as ever. Though thou brag a fool in a mortar, yet will not his foolishness depart from him; no providences will of themselves humble and reform men, unless the grace of God work with them. But, how malicious soever they were, Ezekiel must not be afraid of them nor dismayed, he must not be deterred from his work, or any part of it, nor be disheartened or dispirited in it by all their menaces, but go on in it with resolution and cheerfulness, assuring himself of safety under the divine protection.

II. It is required that he be faithful, Eze 2:7. 1. he must be faithful to Christ who sent him: Thou shalt speak my words unto them. Note, As it is the honour of prophets that they are entrusted to speak God's words, so it is their duty to cleave closely to them and to speak nothing but what is agreeable to the words of God. Ministers must always speak according to that rule. 2. He must be faithful to the souls of those to whom he was sent: Whether they will hear of whether they will forbear, he must deliver his message to them as he received it. He must bring them to comply with the word, and not study to accommodate the word to their humours. "It is true they are most rebellious, they are rebellion itself; but, however, speak my words to them, whether they are pleasing or unpleasing." Note, The untractableness and unprofitableness of people under the word are no good reason why ministers should leave off preaching to them; nor must we decline an opportunity by which good may be done, though we have a great deal of reason to think no good will be done.

III. It is required that he be observant of his instructions.

1. Here is a general intimation what the instructions were that were given him, in the contents of the book which was spread before him, Eze 2:10. (1.) His instructions were large; for the roll was written within and without, on the inside and on the outside of the roll. It was as a sheet of paper written on all the four sides. One side contained their sins; the other side contained the judgments of God coming upon them for those sins. Note, God has a great deal to say to his people when they have degenerated and become rebellious. (2.) His instructions were melancholy. He was sent on a sad errand; the matter contained in the book was, lamentations, and mourning, and woe. The idea of his message is taken from the impression it would make upon the minds of those that carefully attended to it; it would set them a weeping and crying out, Woe! and, Alas! Both the discoveries of sin and the denunciations of wrath would be matter of lamentation. What could be more lamentable, more mournful, more woeful, than to see a holy happy people sunk into such a state of sin and misery as it appears by the prophecy of this book the Jews were at this time? Ezekiel echoes to Jeremiah's lamentations. Note, Though God is rich in mercy, yet impenitent sinners will find there are even among his words lamentations and woe.

2. Here is an express charge given to the prophet to observe his instructions, both in receiving his message and delivering it. he is now to receive it and is here commanded, (1.) To attend diligently to it: son of man, hear what I say unto thee, Eze 2:8. Note, Those that speak from God to others must be sure to hear from God themselves and be obedient to his voice: "Be not thou rebellious; do not refuse to go on this errand, or to deliver it; do not fly off, as Jonah did, for fear of disobliging thy countrymen. They are a rebellious house, among whom thou livest; but be not thou like them, do not comply with them in any thing that is evil." If ministers, who are reprovers by office, connive at sin and indulge sinners, either show them not their wickedness or show them not the fatal consequences of it, for fear of displeasing them and getting their ill-will, they hereby make themselves partakers of their guilt and are rebellious like them. If people will not do their duty in reforming, yet let ministers do theirs in reproving, and they will have the comfort of it in the reflection, whatever the success be, as that prophet had, Isa 50:5. The Lord God has opened my ear, and I was not rebellious. Even the best of men, when their lot is cast in bad times and places, have need to be cautioned against the worst of crimes. (2.) To digest it in his own mind by an experience of the favour and power of it: "Do not only hear what I say unto thee, but open thy mouth, and eat that which I give thee. Prepare to eat it and eat it willingly and with an appetite." All God's children are content to be at their heavenly father's finding, and to eat whatever he gives them. That which God's hand reached out to Ezekiel was a roll of a book, or the volume of a book, a book or scroll of paper or parchment fully written and rolled up. Divine revelation comes to us from the hand of Christ; he gave it to the prophets, Rev 1:1. When we

look at the roll of thy book we must have an eye to the hand by which it is sent to us. He that brought it to the prophet spread it before him, that he might now swallow it with an implicit faith, but might fully understand the contents of it, and then receive it and make it his own. Be not rebellious, says Christ, but eat what I give thee. If we receive not what Christ in his ordinances and providences allots for us, if we submit not to his word and rod, and reconcile not ourselves to both, we shall be accounted rebellious.

Ezekiel Chapter 3

Ezekiel

In this chapter we have the further preparation of the prophet for the work to which God called him. I. His eating the roll that was presented to him in the close of the foregoing chapter (Eze 3:1-3). II. Further instructions and encouragements given him to the same purport with those in the foregoing chapter (Eze 3:4-11). III. The mighty impulse he was under, with which he was carried to those that were to be his hearers (Eze 3:12-15). IV. A further explication of his office and business as a prophet, under the similitude of a watchman (Eze 3:16-21). V. The restraining and restoring of the prophet's liberty of speech, as God pleased (Eze 3:22-27).

Ezekiel 3:1

These verses are fitly joined by some translators to the foregoing chapter, as being of a piece with it and a continuation of the same vision. The prophets received the word from God that they might deliver it to the people of God, furnished themselves that they might furnish them with the knowledge of the mind and will of God. Now here the prophet is taught,

I. How he must receive divine revelation himself, Eze 3:1. Christ (whom he saw upon the throne, Eze 1:26) said to him, "Son of man, eat this roll, admit this revelation into thy understanding, take it, take the meaning of it, understand it aright, admit it into thy heart, apply it, and be affected with it; imprint it in thy mind, ruminate and chew the cud upon it; take it as it is entire, and make no difficulty of it, nay, take a pleasure in it as thou dost in thy meat, and let thy soul be nourished and strengthened by it; let it be meat and drink to thee, and as thy necessary food; be full of it, as thou art of the meat thou hast eaten." Thus ministers should in their studies and meditations take in that word of God which they are to preach to others. Thy words were found, and I did eat them, Jer 15:16. They must be both well acquainted and much affected with the things of God, that they may speak of them both clearly and warmly, with a great deal of divine light and heat. Now observe, 1. How this command is inculcated upon the prophet. In the foregoing chapter, Eat what I give thee; and here (Eze 3:1), "Eat that thou findest, that which is presented to thee by the hand of Christ." Note, Whatever we find to be the word of God, whatever is brought to us by him who is the Word of God, we must receive it without disputing. What we find set before us in the scripture, that we must eat. And again (Eze 3:3), "Cause thy belly to eat, and fill thy bowels with this roll; do not eat it and bring it up again, as that which is nauseous, but eat it and retain it, as that which is nourishing and grateful to the stomach. Feast upon this vision till thou be full of matter, as Elihu was, Job 32:18. Let the word have a place in thee, the innermost place." We must take pains with our own hearts, that we may cause them duly to receive and entertain the word of God, that every faculty may do its office, in order to the due digesting of the word of God, that it may be turned in succum et sanguinem-into blood and spirits. We must empty ourselves of worldly things, that we may fill our bowels with this roll. 2. How this command is explained (Eze 3:10): "All my words that I shall speak unto thee, to be spoken unto the people, thou must receive in thy heart, as well as hear with thy ears, receive them in the love of them." Let these sayings sink down into your ears, Luk 9:44. Christ demands the prophet's attention not only to what he now says, but to all that he shall at any time hereafter speak: Receive it all in thy heart; meditate on these things and give thyself wholly to them, Ti1 4:15. 3. How this command was obeyed in vision. He opened his mouth and Christ caused him to eat the roll, Eze 3:2. If we be truly willing to receive the word into our hearts, Christ will by his Spirit bring it into them and cause it to dwell in us richly. If he that opens the roll, and by his Spirit, as a Spirit of revelation, spreads it before us, did not also open our understanding, and by his Spirit, as a Spirit of wisdom, give us the knowledge of it and cause us to eat it, we should be for ever strangers to it. The prophet had reason to fear that the roll would be an unpleasant morsel and a sorry dish to make a meal of, but it proved to be in his mouth as honey for sweetness. Note, if we readily obey even the most difficult commands, we shall find that comfort in the reflection which will make us abundant amends for all the hardships we meet with in the way of our duty. Though the roll was filled with lamentations, and mourning, and woe, yet it was to the prophet as honey for sweetness. Note, Gracious souls can receive those truths of God with great delight which speak most terror to wicked people. We find St. John let into some part of the revelation by such a sign as this, Rev 10:9, Rev 10:10. He took the book out of the angel's hand, and ate it up, and it was, as this, in his mouth sweet as honey; but it was bitter in the belly; and we shall find that this was so too, for (Eze 3:14) the prophet went in bitterness.

II. How he must deliver that divine revelation to others which he himself had received (Eze 3:1): Eat this roll, and then go, speak to the house of Israel. He must not undertake to preach the things of God to others till he did himself fully understand them; let him not go without his errand, nor take it by the halves. But when he does himself fully understand them he must be both busy and bold to preach them for the good of others. We must not conceal the words of the Holy One (Job 6:10), for that is burying a talent which was given us to trade with. He must go and speak to the house of Israel; for it is their privilege to have God's statutes and judgments made known to them; as the giving of the law (the lively oracles), so prophecy (the living oracles) pertains to them. He is not sent to the Chaldeans to reprove them for their sins, but to the house of Israel to reprove them for theirs; for the father corrects his own child if he do amiss, not the child of a stranger.

1. The instructions given him in speaking to them are much the same with those in the foregoing chapter.

(1.) He must speak to them all that, and that only, which God spoke to him. he had said before (Eze 2:7): Thou shalt speak my words to them; here he says (Eze 3:4), Thou shalt speak with my words unto them, or in my words. He must not only say that which for substance is the same that God had said to him, but as near as may be in the same language and expressions. Blessed Paul, though a man of a very happy invention, yet speaks of the things of God in the words which the Holy Ghost teaches, Col 2:13. Scripture truths look best in scripture language, their native dress; and how can we better speak God's mind than with his words?

(2.) He must remember that they are the house of Israel whom he is sent to speak to, God's house and his own; and therefore such as he ought to have a particular concern for and to deal faithfully and tenderly with. They were such as he had an intimate acquaintance with, being not only their countryman, but their companion in tribulation; they and he were fellow-sufferers, and had lately been fellow-travellers, in very melancholy circumstances, from Judea to Babylon, and had often mingled their tears, which could not but knit their affections to each other. It was well for the people that they had a prophet who knew experimentally how to sympathize with them, and could not but be touched with the feeling of their infirmities. It was well for the prophet that he had to do with those of his own nation, not with a people of strange speech and a hard language, deep of lip, so that thou canst not fathom their meaning, and heavy of tongue, whom it is intolerable and impossible to converse with. Every strange language seems to us to be deep and heavy. "Thou art not sent to many such people, whom thou couldst neither speak to nor hear from, neither understand nor be understood among but by an interpreter." The apostles indeed were sent to many people of a strange speech, but they could not have done any good among them if they had not had the gift of tongues; but Ezekiel was sent only to one people, those but a few, and his own, whom having acquaintance with he might hope to find acceptance with.

(3.) He must remember what God had already told him of the bad character of those to whom he was sent, that, if he met with discouragement and disappointment in them, he might not be offended. They are impudent and hard-hearted (Eze 3:7), no convictions of sin would make them blush, no denunciations of wrath would make them tremble. Two things aggravated their obstinacy:-[1.] That they were more obstinate than their neighbours would have been if the prophet had been sent to them. had God sent him to any other people, though of a strange speech, surely they would have hearkened to him; they would at least have given him a patient hearing and shown him that respect which he could not obtain of his own countrymen. The Ninevites were wrought upon by Jonah's preaching when the house of Israel, that was compassed about with so great a cloud of prophets, was unhumbled and unreformed. But what shall we say to these things? The means of grace are given to those that will not improve them and withheld from those that would have improved them. We must resolve this into the divine sovereignty, and say, Lord, thy judgments are a great deep. [2.] That they were obstinate against God himself: "They will not hearken unto thee, and no marvel, for they will not hearken unto me;" they will not regard the word of the prophet, for they will not regard the rod of God, by which the Lord's voice cries in the city. If they believe not God speaking to them by a minister, neither would they believe though he should speak to them by a voice from heaven; nay, therefore they reject what the prophet says, because it comes from God, whom the carnal mind is enmity to. They are prejudiced against the law of God, and for that reason turn a deaf ear to his prophets, whose business it is to enforce his law.

(4.) He must resolve to put on courage, and Christ promises to steel him with it, Eze 3:8, Eze 3:9. He is sent to such as are impudent and hard-hearted, who will receive no impressions nor be wrought upon either by fair means or foul, who will take a pride in affronting God's messenger and confronting the message. It will be a hard task to know how to deal with them; but, [1.] God will enable him to put a good face on it: "I have made thy face strong against their faces, endued thee with all the firmness and boldness that the case calls for." Perhaps Ezekiel was naturally bashful and timorous, but, if God did not find him fit, yet by his grace he made him fit, to encounter the greatest difficulties. Note, The more impudent wicked people are in their opposition to religion the more openly and resolutely should God's people appear in the practice and defence of it. let the innocent stir up himself against the hypocrite, Job 17:8. When vice is daring let not virtue be sneaking. And, when God has work to do, he will animate men for it and give them strength according to the day. If there be occasion, God can and will by his grace make the foreheads of faithful ministers as an adamant, so that the most threatening powers shall not dash them out of countenance. The Lord God will help men, therefore have I set my face like a flint, Isa 50:7. [2.] He is therefore commanded to have a good heart on it, and to go on in his work with a holy security, not valuing either the censures or the threats of his enemies: "Fear not, neither be dismayed at their looks; let not the menaces of their impotent malice cast either a damp upon thee or a stumbling-block before thee." Bold sinners must have bold reprovers; evil beasts must be rebuked cuttingly (Tit 1:12, Tit 1:13), must be saved with fear, Jde 1:23. Those that keep closely to the service of God may be sure of the favour of God, and then they need not be dismayed at the proud looks of men. Let not the angry countenance that drives away a back-biting tongue give any check to a reproving tongue.

(5.) He must continue instant with them in his preaching, whatever the success was, Eze 3:11. he must go to those of the captivity, who, being in affliction, it was to be hoped would receive instruction; he must look upon them as the children of his people, to whom he was nearly allied, and for whom he therefore ought to have a very tender concern, as Paul for his kinsmen, Rom 9:3. And he must tell them not only what the Lord said, but that the Lord said it; let him speak in God's name, and back what he said with his authority: Thus saith the Lord God; tell them so, whether they will hear or whether they will forbear. Not that it may be indifferent to us what success our ministry has, but, whatever it be, we must go on with our work and leave the issue to God. We must not say "Here are some so good that we do not need to speak to them," or, "Here are others so bad that it is to no purpose to speak to them;" but, however it be, deliver thy message faithfully, tell them, The Lord God saith so and so, let them reject it at their peril.

2. Full instructions being thus given to the prophet, pursuant to his commission, we are here told,

(1.) With what satisfaction this mission of his was applauded by the holy angels, who were very well pleased to see one of a nature inferior to their own thus honourable employed and entrusted. He heard a voice of a great rushing (Eze 3:12), as if the angels thronged and crowded to see the inauguration of a prophet; for to them is known by the church (that is, by reflection from the church) the manifold wisdom of God, Eph 3:10. They seemed to strive who should get nearest to this great sight. he heard the noise of their wings that touched, or (as the word is) kissed one another, denoting the mutual affections and assistances of the angels. He heard also the noise of the wheels of Providence moving over-against the angels and in concert with them. All this was to engage his attention and to convince him that the God who sent him, having such a glorious train of attendants, no doubt had power sufficient to bear him out in his work. But all this noise ended in the voice of praise. He heard them saying, Blessed be the glory of the Lord from his place. [1.] From heaven, his place above, whence his glory was now in vision descending, or whither perhaps it was now returning. Let the innumerable company of angels above join with those employed in this vision in saying, Blessed be the glory of the Lord. Praise you the Lord from the heavens. Praise him, all his angels, Psa 148:1, Psa 148:2. [2.] From the temple, his place on earth, whence his glory was now departing. They lament the departure of the glory, but adore the righteousness of God in it: however it be, yet God is blessed and glorious, and ever will be so. The prophet Isaiah heard God thus praised when he received his commission (Isa 6:3); and a comfort it is to all the faithful servants of God, when they see how much God is dishonoured in this lower world, to think how much he is admired and glorified in the upper world. The glory of the Lord has many slights from our place, but many praises from his place.

(2.) With what reluctance of his own spirit, and yet with what a mighty efficacy of the Spirit of God, the prophet was himself brought to the execution of his office. The grace given to him was not in vain; for, [1.] The Spirit led him with a strong hand. God bade him go, but he stirred not till the Spirit took him up. The Spirit of the living creatures that was in the wheels now was in the prophet too, and took him up, first to hear more distinctly the acclamations of the angels (Eze 3:12), but afterwards (Eze 3:14) lifted him up, and took him away to his work, which he was backward to, being very loth either to bring trouble upon himself or foretel it to his people. he would gladly have been excused, but must own, as another prophet does (Jer 20:7), Thou was stronger than I, and hast prevailed. Ezekiel would willingly have kept all he heard and saw to himself, that it might go no further, but the hand of the Lord was strong upon him and overpowered him; he was carried on contrary to his own inclinations by the prophetical impulse, so that he could not but speak the things which he had heard and seen, as the apostles, Act 4:20. Note, Those whom God calls to the ministry, as he furnishes their heads for it, so he bows their hearts to it. [2.] He followed with a sad heart: The Spirit took me away, says he, and then I went, but it was in bitterness, in the heat of my spirit. He had perhaps seen what a hard task Jeremiah had at Jerusalem when he appeared as a prophet, what pains he took, what opposition he met with, how he was abused by hand and tongue, and what ill treatment he met with, and all to no purpose. "And" (thinks Ezekiel) "must I be set up for a mark like him?" The life of a captive was bad enough; but what would the life of a prophet in captivity be? Therefore he went in this fret and under this discomposure. Note, There may in some cases be a great reluctance of corruption even where there is a manifest predominance of grace. "I went, not disobedient to the heavenly vision, or shrinking from the work, as Jonah, but I went in bitterness, not at all pleased with it." When he received the divine revelation himself, it was to him sweet as honey (Eze 3:3); he could with abundance of pleasure have spent all his days in meditating upon it; but when he is to preach it to others, who, he foresees, will be hardened and exasperated by it, and have their condemnation aggravated, then he goes in bitterness. Note, It is a great grief to faithful ministers, and makes them go on in their work with a heavy heart, when they find people untractable and hating to be reformed. he went in the heat of his spirit, because of the discouragements he foresaw he should meet with; but the hand of the Lord was strong upon him, not only to compel him to his work, but to fit him for it, to carry him through it, and animate him against the difficulties he would meet with (so we may understand it); and, when he found it so, he was better reconciled to his business and applied himself to it: Then he came to those of the captivity (Eze 3:15), to some place where there were many of them together, and sat where they sat, working, or reading, or talking, and continued among them seven days to hear what they said and observe what they did; and all that time he was waiting for the word of the Lord to come to him. Note, Those that would speak suitably and profitably to people about their souls must acquaint themselves with them and with their case, must do as Ezekiel did here, must sit where they sit, and speak familiarly to them of the things of God, and put themselves into their condition, yea, though they sit by the rivers of Babylon. But observe, He was there astonished, overwhelmed with grief for the sins and miseries of his people and overpowered by the pomp of the vision he had seen. he was there desolate (so some read it); God showed him no visions, men made him no visit. Thus was he left to digest his grief, and come to a better temper, before the word of the Lord should come to him. Note, Those whom god designs to exalt and enlarge he first humbles and straitens for a time.

Ezekiel 3:16

These further instructions God gave to the prophet at the end of seven days, that is, on the seventh day after the vision he had; and it is very probably that both that and this were on the sabbath day, which the house of Israel, even in their captivity, observed as well as they could in those circumstances. We do not find that their conquerors and oppressors tied them to any constant service, as their Egyptian task-masters had formerly done, but that they might observe the sabbath-rest for a sign to distinguish between them and their neighbours; but for the sabbath-work they had not the convenience of temple or synagogue, only it should seem they had a place by the river side where prayer was wont to be made (as Act 16:13); there they met on the sabbath day; there their enemies upbraided them with the songs of Zion (Psa 137:1, Psa 137:3); there Ezekiel met them, and the word of the Lord then and there came to him. He that had been musing and meditating on the things of God all the week was fit to speak to the people in God's name on the sabbath day, and disposed to hear God speak to him. This sabbath day Ezekiel was not so honoured with visions of the glory of God as he had been the sabbath before; but he is plainly, and by a very common similitude, told his duty, which he is to communicate to the people. Note, Raptures and transports of joy are not the daily bread of God's children, however they may upon special occasions be feasted with them. We must not deny but that we have truly communion with God (Jo1 1:3) though we have it not always so sensibly as at some times. And, though the mysteries of the kingdom of heaven may sometimes be looked into, yet ordinarily it is plain preaching that is most for edification. God here tells the prophet what his office was, and what the duty of that office; and this (we may suppose) he was to tell the people, that they might attend to what he said and improve it accordingly. Note, It is good for people to know and consider what a charge their ministers have of them and what an account they must shortly give of that charge. Observe,

I. What the office is to which the prophet is called: Son of man, I have made thee a watchman to the house of Israel, Eze 3:17. The vision he saw astonished him: he knew not what to make of that, and therefore God used this plain comparison, which served better to lead him to the understanding of his work and so to reconcile him to it. he sat among the captives, and said little, but God comes to him, and tells him that will not do; he is a watchman, and has something to say to them; he is appointed to be as a watchman in the city, to guard against fire, robbers, and disturbers of the peace, as a watchman over the flock, to guard against thieves and beasts of prey, but especially as a watchman in the camp, in an invaded country or a besieged town, that is to watch the motions of the enemy, and to sound an alarm upon the approach, nay, upon the first appearance, of danger. This supposes the house of Israel to be in a military state, and exposed to enemies, who are subtle and restless in their attempts upon it; yea, and each of the particular members of that house to be in danger and concerned to stand upon their guard. Note, Ministers are watchmen on the church's walls (Isa 62:6), watchmen that go about the city, Sol 3:3. It is a toilsome office. Watchmen must keep awake, be they ever so sleepy, and keep abroad, be it ever so cold; they must stand all weathers upon the watch-tower, Isa 21:8; Gen 31:40. It is a dangerous office. Sometimes they cannot keep their post, but are in peril of death from the enemy, who gain their point if they kill the sentinel; and yet they dare not quit their post upon pain of death from their general. Such a dilemma are the church's watchmen in; men will curse them if they be faithful, and God will curse them if they be false. But it is a needful office; the house of Israel cannot be safe without watchmen, and yet, except the Lord keep it, the watchman waketh but in vain, Psa 127:1, Psa 127:2.

II. What is the duty of this office. The work of a watchman is to take notice and to give notice.

1. The prophet, as a watchman, must take notice of what God said concerning this people, not only concerning the body of the people, to which the prophecies of Jeremiah and other prophets had most commonly reference, but concerning particular persons, according as their character was. He must not, as other watchmen, look round to spy danger and gain intelligence, but he must look up to God, and further he need not look: Hear the word at my mouth, Eze 3:17. Note, Those that are to preach must first hear; for how can those teach others who have not first

learned themselves?

2. He must give notice of what he heard. As a watchman must have eyes in his head, so he must have a tongue in his head; if he be dumb, it is as bad as if he were blind, Isa 56:10. Thou shalt give them warning from me, sound an alarm in the holy mountain; not in his own name, or as from himself, but in God's name, and from him. Ministers are God's mouth to the children of men. The scriptures are written for our admonition. By them is thy servant warned, Psa 19:11. But, because that which is delivered viv voce-by the living voice, commonly makes the deepest impression, God is pleased, by men like ourselves, who are equally concerned, to enforce upon us the warnings of the written word. Now the prophet, in his preaching, must distinguish between the wicked and the righteous, the precious and the vile, and in his applications must suit his alarms to each, giving every one his portion; and, if he did this, he should have the comfort of it, whatever the success was, but, if not, he was accountable.

(1.) Some of those he had to do with were wicked, and he must warn them not to go on in their wickedness, but to turn from it, Eze 3:18, Eze 3:19. We may observe here, [1.] That the God of heaven has said, and does say, to every wicked man, that if he go on still in his trespasses he shall surely die. His iniquity shall undoubtedly be his ruin; it tends to ruin and will end in ruin. Dying thou shalt die, thou shalt die so great a death, shalt die eternally, be ever dying, but never dead. The wicked man shall die in his iniquity, shall fie under the guilt of it, die under the dominion of it. [2.] That if a wicked man turn from his wickedness, and from his wicked way, he shall live, and the ruin he is threatened with shall be prevented; and, that he may do so, he is warned of the danger he is in. The wicked man shall die if he go on, but shall live if he repent. Observe, he is to turn from his wickedness and from his wicked way. It is not enough for a man to turn from his wicked way by an outward reformation, which may be the effect of his sins leaving him rather than of his leaving his sins, but he must turn from his wickedness, from the love of it and the inclination to it, by an inward regeneration; if he do not so much as turn from his wicked way, there is little hope that he will turn from his wickedness. [3.] That it is the duty of ministers both to warn sinners of the danger of sin and to assure them of the benefit of repentance, to set before them how miserable they are if they go on in sin, and how happy they may be if they will but repent and reform. Note, The ministry of the word is concerning matters of life and death, for those are the things it sets before us, the blessing and the curse, that we may escape the curse and inherit the blessing. [4.] That, though ministers do not warn wicked people as they ought of their misery and danger, yet that shall not be admitted as an excuse for those that go on still in their trespasses; for, though the watchman did not give them warning, yet they shall die in their iniquity, for they had sufficient warning given them by the providence of God and their own consciences; and, if they would have taken it, they might have saved their lives. [5.] That if ministers be not faithful to their trust, if they do not warn sinners of the fatal consequences of sin, but suffer them to go on unreproved, the blood of those that perish through their carelessness will be required at their hand. It shall be charged upon them in the day of account that it was owing to their unfaithfulness that such and such precious souls perished in sin; for who knows but if they had had fair warning given them they might have fled in time from the wrath to come? And, if it contract so heinous a guilt as it does to be accessory to the murder of a dying body, what is it to be accessory to the ruin of an immortal soul? [6.] That if ministers do their duty in giving warning to sinners, though the warning be not taken, yet they may have this satisfaction, that they are clear from their blood, and have delivered their own souls, though they cannot prevail to deliver theirs. Those that are faithful shall have their reward, though they be not successful.

(2.) Some of those he had to deal with were righteous, at least he had reason to think, in a judgment of charity, that they were so; and he must warn them not to apostatize and turn away from their righteousness, Eze 3:20, Eze 3:21. We may observe here, [1.] That the best men in the world have need to be warned against apostasy, and to be told of the danger they are in of it and the danger they are in by it. God's servants must be warned (Psa 19:11) that they do not neglect his work and quit his service. One good means to keep us from falling is to keep up a holy fear of falling, Heb 4:1. Let us therefore fear; and (Rom 11:20) even those that stand by faith must not be high-minded, but fear, and must therefore be warned. [2.] There is a righteousness which a man may turn from, a seeming righteousness, and, if men turn from this, it thereby appears that it was never sincere, how passable, nay, how plausible soever it was; for, if they had been of us, they would no doubt have continued with us, Jo1 2:19. There are many that begin in the spirit, but end in the flesh, that set their faces heavenward, but look back; that had a first love, but have lost it, and turned from the holy commandment. [3.] When men turn from their righteousness they soon learn to commit iniquity. When they grow careless and remiss in the duties of God's worship, neglect them, or a re negligent in them, they become an easy prey to the tempter. Omissions make way for commissions. [4.] When men turn from their righteousness, and commit iniquity, it is just with God to lay stumbling-blocks before them, that they may grow worse and worse, till they are ripened for destruction. When Pharaoh hardened his heart God hardened it. When sinners turn their back upon God, desert his service, and so cast a reproach upon it, he does, in a way of righteous judgment, not only withdraw his restraining grace and give them up to their own hearts' lusts, but order them by his providence into such circumstances as occasion their sin and hasten their ruin. There are those to whom Christ himself is a stone of stumbling and a rock of offence, Pe1 2:8. [5.] The righteousness which men relinquish shall never be remembered to their honour or comfort; it will stand them in no stead in this world or the other. Apostates lose all that they have wrought; their services and sufferings are all in vain, and shall never be brought to an account, because not continued in. It is a rule in the law, Factum non dicitur, quod non perseverat-We are said to do only that which we do perseveringly, Gal 3:3, Gal 3:4. [6.] If ministers do no give fair warning, as they ought, of the weakness of the best, their aptness to stumble and fall, the particular temptations they are in and the fatal consequences of apostasy, the ruin of those that do apostatize will be laid at their door, and they shall answer for it. Not but that there are those who are warned against it, and yet turn from their righteousness; but that case is not put here, as was concerning the wicked man, but, on the contrary, that a righteous man, being warned, takes the warning and does not sin (Eze 3:21); for, if you give instruction to a wise man, he will be yet wiser. We must not only not flatter the wicked, but not flatter even the righteous as if they were perfectly safe any where on this side heaven. [7.] If ministers give warning, and people take it, it is well for both. Nothing is more beautiful than a wise reprover upon an obedient ear; the one shall live because he is warned and the other has delivered his soul. What can a good minister desire more than to save himself and those that hear him? Ti1 4:16.

Ezekiel 3:22

After all this large and magnificent discovery which God had made of himself to the prophet, and the full instructions he had given him how to deal with those to whom he sent him with an ample commission, we should have expected presently to see him preaching the word of God to a great congregation of Israel; but here we find it quite otherwise. his work here, at first, seems not at all proportionable to the pomp of his call.

I. We have him here retired for further learning. By his unwillingness to go it should seem as if he were not so thoroughly convinced as he might have been of the ability of him that sent him to bear him out; and therefore, to encourage him against the difficulties he foresaw, God will favour him with another vision of his glory, which (if any thing) would put life into him and animate him for his work. In order for this, God calls him out to the plain (Eze 3:22) and there he will have some talk with him. See and admire the condescension of God in conversing thus familiarly with a man, a son of man, a poor captive, nay, with a sinful man, who, when God sent him went in bitterness of spirit, and was at this time out of humour with his work. And let us own ourselves for ever indebted to the mediation of Christ for this blessed intercourse and communion between God and man, between heaven and earth. See here the benefit of solitude, and how much it befriends contemplation. It is very comfortable to be alone with God, withdrawn from the word for converse with him, to hear from him, to speak to him; and a good man will say that he is never less along than when thus alone. Ezekiel went forth into the plain more willingly than he went among those of the captivity (Eze 3:15); for those that know what it is to have communion with God cannot but prefer that before any converse with this world, especially such as is commonly met with. He went out into the plain, and there he saw the same vision that he had seen by the river of Chebar; for God is not tied to places. Note, Those who follow God shall meet with his consolations, wherever they go. God called him out to talk with him, but did more than that: he showed him his glory, Eze 3:23. We are not now to expect such visions, but we must own that we have a favour done us no way inferior if we so by faith behold the glory of the Lord as to be changed into the same image, by the Spirit of the Lord; and this honour have all his saints. Praise you the Lord, Co2 3:18.

II. We have him here restrained from further teaching for the present. When he saw he fell on his face, being struck with an awe of God's majesty and a dread of his displeasure; but the Spirit entered into him to raise him up, and then he recovered himself and got upon his feet and heard what the Spirit whispered to him, which is very surprising. One would have expected now that God would send him directly to the chief place of concourse, would give him favour in the eyes of his brethren, and make him and his message acceptable to them, that he would have a wider door of opportunity opened to him and that God would give him a door of utterance to open his mouth boldly; but what is here said to him is the reverse of all this.

1. Instead of sending him to a public assembly, he orders him to confine himself to his own lodgings: Go, shut thyself within thy house, Eze 3:24. He was not willing to appear in public, and, when he did, the people did not regard him, nor show him the respect he deserved, and as a just rebuke both to him and them, to him for his shyness of them and to them for their coldness towards him, God forbids him to appear in public. Note, Our choice is often made our punishment; and it is a righteous thing with God to remove teachers into corners when they, or their people, or both, grow indifferent to solemn assemblies. Ezekiel must shut up himself, some think, to give a sign of the besieging of Jerusalem, in which the people should be closely shut up as he was in his house, and which he speaks of in the next chapter. He must shut himself within his house, that he might receive further discoveries of the mind of God and might abundantly furnish himself with something to say to the people when he went abroad. We find that the elders of Judah visited him and sat before him sometimes in his house (Eze 8:1), to be witnesses of his ecstasies; but it was not till Eze 11:25that he spoke to those of the captivity all the things that the Lord had shown him. Note, Those that are called to preach must find time to study, and a great deal of time too, must often shut themselves up in their houses, that they may give attendance to reading and meditation, and so their profiting may appear to all.

2. Instead of securing him an interest in the esteem and affections of those to whom he sent him he tells him that they shall put bands upon him and bind him (Eze 3:25), either (1.) As a criminal. They shall bind him in order to the further punishing of him as a disturber of the peace; though they were themselves sent into bondage in Babylon for persecuting the prophets, yet there they continue to persecute them. Or, rather, (2.) As a distracted man. They would go about to bind him as one beside himself; for to that they imputed his violent motions in his raptures. The captains asked Jehu, Wherefore came this mad fellow unto thee? Festus said to Paul, Thou art beside thyself; and so the Jews said of our Lord Jesus, Mar 3:21. Perhaps this was the reason why he must keep within doors, because otherwise they would bind him, under pretence of his being mad, and therefore he must not go out among them. Justly are prophets forbidden to go to those that will abuse them.

3. Instead of opening his lips that his mouth might show forth God's praise, God silence him, made his tongue cleave to the roof of his mouth, so that he was dumb for a considerable time, Eze 3:26. The pious captives in Babylon used this imprecation upon themselves, that, if they should forget Jerusalem, there tongue might cleave to the roof of their mouth, Psa 137:6. Ezekiel remembers Jerusalem more than any of them, and yet his tongue cleaves to the roof of his mouth, and he that can speak best is forbidden to speak at all; and the reason given is because they are a

rebellious house to whom he is sent, and they are not worthy to have him for a reprover. He shall not give them instructions and admonitions, for they are lost and thrown away upon them. he is before commanded to speak boldly to them because they are most rebellious (Eze 2:7); but, since that proves to no purpose, he is now for that reason enjoined silence and shall not speak at all to them. Note, Those whose hearts are hardened against conviction are justly deprived of the mans of conviction. Why should not the reprovers be dumb, if, after long trials, it be found that the reproved resolve to be deaf? If Ephraim be joined to idols, let him alone. Thou shalt be dumb, and not be a reprover, implying that unless he were dumb he would be reproving; if he could speak at all, he would witness against the wickedness of the wicked. But when God speaks with him, and designs to speak by him, he will open his mouth, Eze 3:27. Note, Though God's prophets may be silenced awhile, there will come a time when God will give them the opening of the mouth again. And, when God speaks to his ministers, he not only opens their ears to hear what he says, but opens their mouth to return an answer. Moses, who had a veil on his face when he went down to the people, took it off when he went up again to God, Exo 34:34.

4. Instead of giving him assurance of success when he should at any time speak to the people, he here leaves the matter very doubtful, and Ezekiel must not perplex and disquiet himself about it, but let it be as it will. He that hears, let him hear, and he is welcome to the comfort of it; let him hear, and his soul shall live; but he that forbears, let him forbear at his peril, and take what comes. If thou scornest, thou alone shalt bear it; neither God nor his prophet shall be any losers by it; but the prophet shall be rewarded for his faithfulness in reproving the sinner, and God will have the glory of his justice in condemning him for not taking the reproof.

Ezekiel Chapter 4

Ezekiel

Ezekiel was now among the captives in Babylon, but they there had Jerusalem still upon their hearts; the pious captives looked towards it with an eye of faith (as Dan 6:10), the presumptuous ones looked towards it with an eye of pride, and flattered themselves with a conceit that they should shortly return thither again; those that remained corresponded with the captives, and, it is likely, bouyed them up with hopes that all would be well yet, as long as Jerusalem was standing in its strength, and perhaps upbraided those with their folly who had surrendered at first; therefore, to take down this presumption, God gives the prophet, in this chapter, a very clear and affecting foresight of the besieging of Jerusalem by the Chaldean army and the calamities which would attend that siege. Two things are here represented to him in vision:-I. The fortifications that should be raised against the city; this is signified by the prophet's laying siege to the portraiture of Jerusalem (Eze 4:1-3) and laying first on one side and then on the other side before it (Eze 4:4-8). II. The famine that should rage within the city; this is signified by his eating very coarse fare, and confining himself to a little of it, so long as this typical representation lasted (Eze 4:9-17).

Ezekiel 4:1

The prophet is here ordered to represent to himself and others by signs which would be proper and powerful to strike the fancy and to affect the mind, the siege of Jerusalem; and this amounted to a prediction.

I. He was ordered to engrave a draught of Jerusalem upon a tile, Eze 4:1. It was Jerusalem's honour that while she kept her integrity God had graven her upon the palms of his hands (Isa 49:16), and the names of the tribes were engraven in precious stones on the breast-plate of the high priest; but, now that the faithful city has become a harlot, a worthless brittle tile or brick is thought good enough to portray it upon. This the prophet must lay before him, that the eye may affect the heart.

II. He was ordered to build little forts against this portraiture of the city, resembling the batteries raised by the besiegers, Eze 4:2. Between the city that was besieged and himself that was the besieger he was to set up an iron pan, as an iron wall, Eze 4:3. This represented the inflexible resolution of both sides; the Chaldeans resolved, whatever it cost them, that they would make themselves masters of the city and would never quit it till they had conquered it; on the other side, the Jews resolved never to capitulate, but to hold out to the last extremity.

III. He was ordered to lie upon his side before it, as it were to surround it, representing the Chaldean army lying before it to block it up, to keep the meat from going in and the mouths from going out. He was to lie on his left side 390 days (Eze 4:5), about thirteen months; the siege of Jerusalem is computed to last eighteen months (Jer 52:4-6), but if we deduct from that five months' interval, when the besiegers withdrew upon the approach of Pharaoh's army (Jer 37:5-8), the number of the days of the close siege will be 390. Yet that also had another signification. The 390 days, according to the prophetic dialect, signified 390 years; and, when the prophet lies so many days on his side, he bears the guilt of that iniquity which the house of Israel, the ten tribes, had borne 390 years, reckoning from their first apostasy under Jeroboam to the destruction of Jerusalem, which completed the ruin of those small remains of them that had incorporated with Judah. He is then to lie forty days upon his right side, and so long to bear the iniquity of the house of Judah, the kingdom of the two tribes, because the measure-filling sins of that people were those which they were guilty of during the last forty years before their captivity, since the thirteenth year of Josiah, when Jeremiah began to prophesy (Jer 1:1, Jer 1:2), or, as some reckon it, since the eighteenth, when the book of the law was found and the people renewed their covenant with God. When they persisted in their impieties and idolatries, notwithstanding they had such a prophet and such a prince, and were brought into the bond of such a covenant, what could be expected but ruin without remedy? Judah, that had such helps and advantages for reformation, fills the measure of its iniquity in less time than Israel does. Now we are not to think that the prophet lay constantly night and day upon his side, but every day, for so many days together, at a certain time of the day, when he received visits, and company came in, he was found lying 390 days on his left side and forty days on his right side before his portraiture of Jerusalem, which all that saw might easily understand to mean the close besieging of that city, and people would be flocking in daily, some for curiosity and some for conscience, at the hour appointed, to see it and to take their different remarks upon it. His being found constantly on the same side, as if bands were laid upon him (as indeed they were by the divine command), so that he could not turn himself from one side to another till he had ended the days of the siege, did plainly represent the close and constant continuance of the besiegers about the city during that number of days, till they had gained their point.

IV. He was ordered to prosecute the siege with vigour (Eze 4:7): Thou shalt set thy face towards the siege of Jerusalem, as wholly intent upon it and resolved to carry it; so the Chaldeans would be, and neither bribed nor forced to withdraw from it. Nebuchadnezzar's indignation at Zedekiah's treachery in breaking his league with him made him very furious in pushing on this siege, that he might chastise the insolence of that faithless prince and people; and his army promised themselves a rich booty of that pompous city; so that both set their faces against it, for they were very resolute. Nor were they less active and industrious, exerting themselves to the utmost in all the operations of the siege, which the prophet was to represent by the uncovering of his arm, or, as some read it, the stretching out of his arm, as it were to deal blows about without mercy. When God is about to do some great work he is said to make bare his arm, Isa 52:10. In short, The Chaldeans will go about their business, and go on in it, as men in earnest, who resolve to go through with it. Now, 1. This is intended to be a sign to the house of Israel (Eze 4:3), both to those in Babylon, who were eye-witnesses of what the prophet did, and to those also who remained in their own land, who would hear the report of it. The prophet was dumb and could not speak (Eze 3:26); but as his silence had a voice, and upbraided the people with their deafness, so even then God left not himself without witness, but ordered him to make signs, as dumb men are accustomed to do, and as Zacharias did when he was dumb, and by them to make known his mind (that is, the mind of God) to the people. And thus likewise the people were upbraided with their stupidity and dulness, that they were not capable of being taught as men of sense are, by words, but must be taught as children are, by pictures, or as deaf men are, by signs. Or, perhaps, they are hereby upbraided with their malice against the prophet. Had he spoken in words at length what was signified by these figures, they would have entangled him in his talk, would have indicted him for treasonable expressions, for they knew how to make a man an offender for a word (Isa 29:21), to avoid which he is ordered to make use of signs. Or the prophet made use of signs for the same reason that Christ made use of parables, that hearing they might hear and not understand, and seeing they might see and not perceive, Mat 13:14, Mat 13:15. They would not understand what was plain, and therefore shall be taught by that which is difficult; and herein the Lord was righteous. 2. Thus the prophet prophesies against Jerusalem (Eze 4:7); and there were those who not only understood it so, but were the more affected with it by its being so represented, for images to the eye commonly make deeper impressions upon the mind than words can, and for this reason sacraments are instituted to represent divine things, that we might see and believe, might see and be affected with those things; and we may expect this benefit by them, and a blessing to go along with them, while (as the prophet here) we make use only of such signs as God himself has expressly appointed, which, we must conclude, are the fittest. Note, The power of imagination, if it be rightly used, and kept under the direction and correction of reason and faith, may be of good use to kindle and excite pious and devout affections, as it was here to Ezekiel and his attendants. "Methinks I see so and so, myself dying, time expiring, the world on fire, the dead rising, the great tribunal set, and the like, may have an exceedingly good influence upon us: for fancy is like fire, a good servant, but a bad master." 3. This whole transaction has that in it which the prophet might, with a good colour of reason, have hesitated at and excepted against, and yet, in obedience to God's command, and in execution of his office, he did it according to order. (1.) It seemed childish and ludicrous, and beneath his gravity, and there were those that would ridicule him for it; but he knew the divine appointment put honour enough upon that which otherwise seemed mean to save his reputation in the doing of it. (2.) It was toilsome and tiresome to do as he did; but our ease as well as our credit must be sacrificed to our duty, and we must never call God's service in any instance of it a hard service. (3.) It could not but be very much against the grain with him to appear thus against Jerusalem, the city of God, the holy city, to act as an enemy against a place to which he was so good a friend; but he is a prophet, and must follow his instructions, not his affections, and must plainly preach the ruin of a sinful place, though its welfare is what he passionately desires and earnestly prays for. 4. All this that the prophet sets before the children of his people concerning the destruction of Jerusalem is designed to bring them to repentance, by showing them sin, the provoking cause of this destruction, sin the ruin of that once flourishing city, than which surely nothing could be more effectual to make them hate sin and turn from it; while he thus in lively colours describes the calamity with a great deal of pain and uneasiness to himself, he is bearing the iniquity of Israel and Judah. "Look here" (says he) "and see what work sin makes, what an evil and bitter thing it is to depart form God; this comes of sin, your sins and the sin of your fathers; let that therefore be the daily matter of your sorrow and shame now in your captivity, that you may make your peace with God and he may return in mercy to you." But observe, It is a day of punishment for a year of sin: I have appointed thee each day for a year. The siege is a calamity of 390 days, in which God reckons for the iniquity of 390 years; justly therefore d they acknowledge that God had punished them less than their iniquity deserved, Ezr 9:13. But let impenitent sinners know that, though now God is long-suffering towards them, in the other world there is an everlasting punishment. When God laid bands upon the prophet, it was to show them how they were bound with the cords of their own transgression (Lam 1:14), and therefore they were now holden in the cords of affliction. But we may well think of the prophet's case with compassion, when God laid upon him the bands of duty, as he does on all his ministers (Col 9:16, Necessity is laid upon me, and woe unto me if I preach not the gospel); and yet men laid upon him bonds of restraint (Eze 3:25); but under both it is satisfaction enough that they are serving the interests of God's kingdom among men.

Ezekiel 4:9

The best exposition of this part of Ezekiel's prediction of Jerusalem's desolation is Jeremiah's lamentation of it, Lam 4:3, Lam 4:4, etc., and Lam 4:10, where he pathetically describes the terrible famine that was in Jerusalem during the siege and the sad effects of it.

I. The prophet here, to affect the people with the foresight of it, must confine himself for 390 days to coarse fare and short commons, and that ill-dressed, for they should want both food and fuel.

1. His meat, for the quality of it, was to be of the worst bread, made of but little wheat and barley, and the rest of beans, and lentiles, and millet, and fitches, such as we feed horses or fatted hogs with, and this mixed, as mill corn, or as that in the beggar's bag, that has a dish full of one sort of corn at one house and of another at another house; of such corn as this must the prophet's bread be made while he underwent the fatigue of lying on his side, and needed something better to support him, Eze 4:9. Note, It is our wisdom not to be too fond of dainties and pleasant bread, because we know not what hard meat we may be tied to, nay, and may be glad of, before we die. The meanest sort of food is better than we deserve, and therefore must not be despised nor wasted, nor must those that use it be looked upon with disdain, because we know not what may be our own lot.

2. For the quantity of it, it was to be of the least that a man could be kept alive with, to signify that the besieged should be reduced to short allowance and should hold out till all the bread in the city was spent, Jer 37:21. The prophet must eat but twenty shekels' weight of bread a day (Eze 4:10), that was about ten ounces; and he must drink but the sixth part of a hin of water, that was half a pint, about eight ounces, Eze 4:11. The stint of the Lessian diet is fourteen ounces of meat and sixteen of drink. The prophet in Babylon had bread enough and to spare, and was by the river side, where there was plenty of water; and yet, that he might confirm his own prediction and be a sign to the children of Israel, God obliges him to live thus sparingly, and he submits to it. Note, God's servants must learn to endure hardness, and to deny themselves the use of lawful delights, when they may thereby serve the glory of God, evidence the sincerity of their faith, and express their sympathy with their brethren in affliction. The body must be kept under and brought into subjection. Nature is content with a little, grace with less, but lust with nothing. It is good to stint ourselves of choice, that we may the better bear it if ever we should come to be stinted by necessity. And in times of public distress and calamity it ill becomes us to make much of ourselves, as those that drank wine in bowls and were not grieved for the affliction of Joseph, Amo 6:4-6.

3. For the dressing of it, he must bake it with a man's dung (Eze 4:12); that must be dried, and serve for fuel to heat his oven with. The thought of it would almost turn one's stomach; yet the coarse bread, thus baked, he must eat as barley-cakes, as freely as if it were the same bread he had been used to. This nauseous piece of cookery he must exercise publicly in their sight, that they might be the more affected with the calamity approaching, which was signified by it, that in the extremity of the famine they should not only have nothing that was dainty, but nothing that was cleanly, about them; they must take up with what they could get. To the hungry soul every bitter thing is sweet. This circumstance of the sign, the baking of his bread with man's dung, the prophet with submission humbly desired might be dispensed with (Eze 4:14); it seemed to have in it something of a ceremonial pollution, for there was a law that man's dung should be covered with earth, that God might see no unclean thing in their camp, Deu 23:13, Deu 23:14. And must he go and gather a thing so offensive, and use it in the dressing of his meat in the sight of the people? "Ah! Lord God," says he, "behold, my soul has not been polluted, and I am afraid lest by this it be polluted." Note, The pollution of the soul by sin is what good people dread more than any thing; and yet sometimes tender consciences fear it without cause, and perplex themselves with scruples about lawful things, as the prophet here, who had not yet learned that it is not that which goes into the mouth that defiles the man, Mat 15:11. But observe he does not plead, "Lord, from my youth I have been brought up delicately and have never been used to any thing but what was clean and nice" (and there were those who were so brought up, who in the siege of Jerusalem did embrace dunghills, Lam 4:5), but that he had been brought up conscientiously, and had never eaten any thing that was forbidden by the law, that died of itself or was torn in pieces; and therefore, "Lord, do not put this upon me now." Thus Peter pleaded (Act 10:14), Lord, I have never eaten any thing that is common or unclean. Note, it will be comfortable to us, when we are reduced to hardships, if our hearts can witness for us that we have always been careful to abstain

from sin, even from little sins, and the appearances of evil. Whatever God commands us, we may be sure, is good; but, if we be put upon any thing that we apprehend to be evil, we should argue against it, from this consideration, that hitherto we have preserved our purity-and shall we lose it now? Now, because Ezekiel with a manifest tenderness of conscience made this scruple, God dispensed with him in this matter. Note, Those who have power in their hands should not be rigorous in pressing their commands upon those that are dissatisfied concerning them, yea, though their dissatisfactions be groundless or arising from education and long usage, but should recede from them rather than grieve or offend the weak, or put a stumbling-block before them, in conformity to the example of God's condescension to Ezekiel, though we are sure his authority is incontestable and all his commands are wise and good. God allowed Ezekiel to use cow's dung instead of man's dung, Eze 4:15. This is a tacit reflection upon man, as intimating that he being polluted with sin his filthiness is more nauseous and odious than that of any other creature. How much more abominable and filthy is man! Job 15:16.

II. Now this sign is particularly explained here; it signified,

1. That those who remained in Jerusalem should be brought to extreme misery for want of necessary food. All supplies being cut off by the besiegers, the city would soon find the want of the country, for the king himself is served of the field; and thus the staff of bread would be broken in Jerusalem, Eze 4:16. God would not only take away from the bread its power to nourish, so that they should eat and not be satisfied (Lev 26:26), but would take away the bread itself (Isa 3:1), so that what little remained should be eaten by weight, so much a day, so much a head, that they might have an equal share and might make it last as long as possible. But to what purpose, when they could not make it last always, and the besieged must be tired out before the besiegers? They should eat and drink with care, to make it go as far as might be, and with astonishment, when they saw it almost spent and knew not which way to look for a recruit. They should be astonished one with another; whereas it is ordinarily some alleviation of a calamity to have others share with us in it (Solamen miseris socios habuisse doloris), and some ease to the spirit to complain of the burden, it should be an aggravation of the misery that it was universal, and their complaining to one another should but make them all the more uneasy and increase the astonishment. And the event shall be as bad as their fears; they cannot make it worse than it is, for they shall consume away for their iniquity; multitudes of them shall die of famine, a lingering death, worse than that by the sword (Lam 4:9); they shall dies so as to feel themselves die. And it is sin that brings all this misery upon them: They shall consume away in their iniquity (so it may be read); they shall continue hardened and impenitent, and shall die in their sins, which is more miserable than to die on a dunghill. Now, (1.) Let us see here what woeful work sin makes with a people, and acknowledge the righteousness of God herein. Time was when Jerusalem was filled with the finest of the wheat (Psa 147:14); but now it would be glad of the coarsest, and cannot have it. Fulness of bread, as it was one of Jerusalem's mercies, so it had become one of her sins, Eze 16:49. The plenty was abused to luxury and excess, which were therefore thus justly punished with famine. It is a righteous thing with God to deprive us of those enjoyments which

we have made the food and fuel of our lusts. (2.) Let us see what reason we have to bless God for plenty, not only for the fruits of the earth, but for the freedom of commerce, that the husbandman can have money for his bread and the tradesman bread for his money, that there is abundance not only in the field, but in the market, that those who live in cities and great towns, though they sow not, neither do they reap, are yet fed from day to day with food convenient.

2. It signified that those who were carried into captivity should be forced to eat their defiled bread among the Gentiles (Eze 4:13), to eat meat made up by Gentile hands otherwise than according to the law of the Jewish church, which they were always taught to call defiled, and which they would have as great an aversion to as a man would have to bread prepared with dung, that is (as perhaps it may be understood) kneaded and moulded with dung. Daniel and his fellows confined themselves to pulse and water, rather than they would eat the portion of the king's meat assigned them, because they apprehended it would defile them, Dan 1:8. Or they should be forced to eat putrid meat, such as their oppressors would allow them in their slavery, and such as formerly they would have scorned to touch. Because they served not God with cheerfulness in the abundance of all things, God will make them serve their enemies in the want of all things.

Ezekiel Chapter 5

In this chapter we have a further, and no less terrible, denunciation of the judgments of God, which were coming with all speed and force upon the Jewish nation, which would utterly ruin it; for when God judges he will overcome. This destruction of Judah and Jerusalem is here, I. Represented by a sign, the cutting, and burning, and scattering of hair (Eze 5:1-4). II. That sign is expounded, and applied to Jerusalem. 1. Sin is charged upon Jerusalem as the cause of this desolation-contempt of God's law (Eze 5:5-7) and profanation of his sanctuary (Eze 5:11). 2 Wrath is threatened, great wrath (Eze 5:8-10), a variety of miseries (Eze 5:12, Eze 5:16, Eze 5:17), such as should be their reproach and ruin (Eze 5:13-15).

Ezekiel 5:1

We have here the sign by which the utter destruction of Jerusalem is set forth; and here, as before, the prophet is himself the sign, that the people might see how much he affected himself with, and interested himself in, the case of Jerusalem, and how it lay to his heart, even when he foretold the desolations of it. he was so much concerned about it as to take what was done to it as done to himself, so far was he from desiring the woeful day.

I. He must shave off the hair of his head and beard (Eze 5:1), which signified God's utter rejecting and abandoning that people, as a useless worthless generation, such as could well be spared, nay, such as it would be his honour to part with; his judgments, and all the instruments he made use of in cutting them off, were this sharp knife and this razor, that were proper to be made use of, and would do execution. Jerusalem had been the head, but, having degenerated, had become as the hair, which, when it grows thick and long, is but a burden which a man wishes to get clear of, as God of the sinners in Zion. Ah! I will ease me of my adversaries, Isa 1:24. Ezekiel must not cut off that hair only which was superfluous, but cut it all off, denoting the full end that God would make of Jerusalem. The hair that would not be trimmed and kept neat and clean by the admonitions of the prophets must be all shaved off by utter destruction. Those will be ruined that will not be reformed.

II. He must weigh the hair and divide it into three parts. This intimates the very exact directing of God's judgments according to equity (by him men and their actions are weighed in the unerring balance of truth and righteousness) and the proportion which divine justice observes in punishing some by one judgment and others by another; one way or other, they shall all be met with. Some make the shaving of the hair to denote the loss of their liberty and of their honour: it was looked upon as a mark of ignominy, as in the disgrace Hanun put on David's ambassadors. It denotes also the loss of their joy, for they shaved their heads upon occasion of great mourning; I may add the loss of their Nazariteship, for the shaving of the head was a period to that vow (Num 6:18), and Jerusalem was now no longer looked upon as a holy city.

III. He must dispose of the hair so that it might all be destroyed or dispersed, Eze 5:2. 1. One third part must be burnt in the midst of the city, denoting the multitudes that should perish by famine and pestilence, and perhaps many in the conflagration of the city, when the days of the siege were fulfilled. Or the laying of that glorious city in ashes might well be looked upon as a third part of the destruction threatened. 2. Another third part was to be cut in pieces with a knife, representing the many who, during the siege, were slain by the sword, in their sallies out upon the besiegers, and especially when the city was taken by storm, the Chaldeans being then most furious and the Jews most feeble. 3. Another third part was to be scattered in the wind, denoting the carrying away of some into the land of the conqueror and the flight of others into the neighbouring countries for shelter; so that they were hurried, some one way and some another, like loose hairs in the wind. But, lest they should think that this dispersion would be their escape, God adds, I will draw out a sword after them, so that wherever they go evil shall pursue them. Note, God has variety of judgments wherewith to accomplish the destruction of a sinful people and to make an end when he begins.

IV. He must preserve a small quantity of the third sort that were to be scattered in the wind, and bind them in his skirts, as one would bind that which he is very mindful and careful of, Eze 5:3. This signified perhaps that little handful of people which were left under the government of Gedaliah, who, it was hoped, would keep possession of the land when the body of the people was carried into captivity. Thus God would have done well for them if they would have done well for themselves. But these few that were reserved must be taken and cast into the fire, Eze 5:4. When Gedaliah and his friends were slain the people that put themselves under his protection were scattered, some gone into Egypt, others carried off by the Chaldeans, and in short the land totally cleared of them; then this was fulfilled, for out of those combustions a fire came forth into all the house of Israel, who, as fuel upon the fire, kindled and consumed one another. Note, It is ill with a people when those are taken away in wrath that seemed to be marked for monuments of mercy; for then there is no remnant or escaping, none shut up or left.

Ezekiel 5:5

We have here the explanation of the foregoing similitude: This is Jerusalem. Thus it is usual in scripture language to give the name of the thing signified to the sign; as when Christ said, This is my body. The prophet's head, which was to be shaved, signified Jerusalem, which by the judgments of God was now to be stripped of all its ornaments, to be emptied of all its inhabitants, and to be set naked and bare, to be shaved with a razor that is hired, Isa 7:20. The head of one that was a priest, a prophet, a holy person, was fittest to represent Jerusalem the holy city. Now the contents of these verses are much the same with what we have often met with, and still shall, in the writings of the prophets. Here we have,

I. The privileges Jerusalem was honoured with (Eze 5:5): I have set it in the midst of the nations and countries that are round about her, and those famous nations and very considerable. Jerusalem was not situated in a remote obscure corner of the world, far from neighbours, but in the midst of kingdoms that were populous, polite, and civilized, famed for learning, arts, and sciences, and which then made the greatest figure in the world. But there seems to be more in it than this. 1. Jerusalem was dignified and preferred above the neighbouring nations and their cities. it was set in the midst of them as excelling them all. This holy mountain was exalted above all the hills, Isa 2:2. Why leap you, you high hills? This is the hill which God desires to dwell in, Psa 68:16. Jerusalem was a city upon a hill, conspicuous and illustrious, and which all the neighbouring nations had an eye upon, some for good-will, some for ill-will. 2. Jerusalem was designed to have a good influence upon the nations and countries round about, was set in the midst of them as a candle upon a candlestick, to spread the light of divine revelation, which she was blessed with, to all the dark corners of the neighbouring nations, that from them it might diffuse itself further, even to the ends of the earth. Jerusalem was set in the midst of the nations, to be as the heart in the body, to invigorate this dead world with a divine life as well as to enlighten this dark world with a divine light, to be an example of every thing that was good. The nations that observed what excellent statutes and judgments they had concluded them to be a wise and understanding people (Deu 4:6), fit to be consulted as an oracle, as they were in Solomon's time, Kg1 4:34. And, had they preserved this reputation and made a right use of it, what a blessing would Jerusalem have been to all the nations about! But, failing to be so, the accomplishment of this intention was reserved for its latter days, when out of Zion went forth the gospel law and the word of the Lord Jesus from Jerusalem, and there repentance and remission began to be preached, and thence the preachers of them went forth into all nations. And, when that was done, Jerusalem was levelled with the ground. Note, When places and persons are made great, it is with design that they may do good and that those about them may be the better for them, that their light may shine before men.

II. The provocations Jerusalem was guilty of. A very high charge is here drawn up against that city, and proved beyond contradiction sufficient to justify God in seizing its privileges and putting it under military execution. 1. She has not walked in God's statutes, nor kept his judgments (Eze 5:7); nay, the inhabitants of Jerusalem had refused his judgments and his statutes (Eze 5:6); they did not do their duty, nay, they would not, they said that they would not. Those statutes and judgments which their neighbours admired they despised, which they should have set before their face they cast behind their back. Note, A contempt of the word and law of God opens a door to all manner of iniquity. God's statutes are the terms on which he deals with men; those that refuse his terms cannot expect his favours. 2. She had changed God's judgments into wickedness (Eze 5:6), a very high expression of profaneness, that the people had not only broken God's laws, but had so perverted and abused them that they had made them the excuse and colour of their wickedness. They introduced the abominable customs and usages of the heathen, instead of God's institutions; this was changing the truth of God into a lie (Rom 1:25) and the glory of God into shame, Psa 4:2. Note, Those that have been well educated, if they live ill, put the highest affront imaginable upon God, as if he were the patron of sin and his judgments were turned into wickedness. 3. She had been worse than the neighbouring nations, to whom she should have set a good example: She has changed my judgments, by idolatries and false worship, more than the nations (Eze 5:6), and she has multiplied (that is, multiplied idols and altars, gods and temples, multiplied those things the unity of which was their praise) more than the nations that were round about. Israel's God is one, and his name one, his altar one; but they, not content with this one God, multiplied their gods to such a degree that according to the number of their cities so were their gods, and their altars were as heaps in the furrows of the field; so that they exceeded all their neighbours in having gods many and lords many. They corrupted revealed religion more than the Gentiles had corrupted natural religion. Note, If those who have made a profession of religion, and have had a pious education, apostatize from it, they are commonly more profane and vicious than those who never made any profession; they have seven other spirits more wicked. 4. She had not done according to the judgments of the nations, Eze 5:7. Israel had not acted towards their God, as the nations had acted towards their gods, though they were false gods; they had not been so observant of him nor so constant to him. Has a nation changed its gods, or slighted them, so as they have? Jer 2:11. or it may refer to their morals; instead of reforming their neighbors, they came short of them; and many who were of the uncircumcision kept the righteousness of the law better than those who were of the circumcision, Rom 2:26, Rom 2:27. Those who had the light of scripture did not according to the judgments of many who had only the light of nature. Note, There are those who are called Christians who will in the great day be condemned by the better tempers and better lives of sober heathens. 5. The particular crime charged upon Jerusalem is profaning the holy things, which she had been both entrusted and honoured with (Eze 5:11): Thou hast defiled my sanctuary with all thy detestable things, with thy idols and idolatries. The images of their pretended deities, and the groves erected in honour of them, were brought into the temple; and the ceremonies used by idolaters were brought into the worship of God. Thus every thing that is sacred was polluted. Note, Idols are detestable things any where, but more especially so in the sanctuary.

III. The punishments that Jerusalem should fall under for these provocations: Shall not God visit for these things? No doubt he shall. The matter of the sentence here passed upon Jerusalem is very dreadful, and the manner of expression makes it yet more so; the judgments are various, and the threatenings of them varied, reiterated, inculcated, that one may well say, Who is able to stand in God's sight when once he is angry?

1. God will take this work of punishing Jerusalem into his own hands; and who knows the power of his anger and what a fearful thing it is to fall into his hands? Observe what a strong emphasis is laid upon it (Eze 5:8): I, even I, am against thee. God had been for Jerusalem, to defend and save it; but miserable is its case when he has turned to be its enemy and fights against it. If God be against us, the whole creation is at war with us, and nothing can be for us so as to

stand us in any stead: "You think it is only the Chaldean army that is against you, but they are God's hand, or rather the staff in his hand; it is I, even I, that am against thee, not only to speak against thee by prophets, but to act against thee by providence. I will execute judgments in thee (Eze 5:10), in the midst of thee (Eze 5:8), not only in the suburbs, but in the heart of the city, not only in the borders, but in the bowels of the country." Note, Those who will not observe the judgments of God's mouth shall not escape the judgments of his hand; and God's judgments, when they come with commission, will penetrate into the midst of a people, will enter into the soul, into the bowels like water and like oil into the bones. I will execute judgments. Note, God himself undertakes to execute his own judgments, according to the true and full intent of them; whatever are the instruments, he is the principal agent.

2. These punishments shall come from his displeasure. As to the body of the people, it shall not be a correction in love, but he will execute judgments in anger, and in fury, and in furious rebukes (Eze 5:15), strange expressions to come from a God who has said, Fury is not in me, and who has declared himself gracious, and merciful, and slow to anger. But they are designed to show the malignity of sin, and the offence it gives to the just and holy God. That must needs be a very evil thing which provokes him to such resentments, and against his own people too, that had been so high in his favour, and expressed with so much satisfaction (Eze 5:13): "My anger, which has long been withheld, shall now be accomplished, and I will cause my fury to rest upon them; it shall not only light upon them, but lie upon them, and fill them as vessels of wrath fitted by their own wickedness to destruction; and, justice being hereby glorified, I will be comforted, I will be entirely satisfied in what I have done." As, when God is dishonoured by the sins of men, he is said to be grieved (Psa 95:10), so when he is honoured by their destruction he is said to be comforted. The struggle between mercy and judgment is over, and in this case judgment triumphs, triumphs indeed; for mercy that has been so long abused is now silent and gives up the cause, has not a word more to say on the behalf of such an ungrateful incorrigible people: My eye shall not spare, neither will I have any pity, Eze 5:11. Divine compassion defers the punishment, or mitigates it, or supports under it, or shortens it; but here is judgment without mercy, wrath without any mixture or allay of pity. These expressions are thus sharpened and heightened perhaps with design to look further, to the vengeance of eternal fire, which some of the destructions we read of in the Old Testament were typical of, and particularly that of Jerusalem; for surely it is nowhere on this side hell that this word has its full accomplishment, My eye shall not spare, but I will cause my fury to rest. Note, Those who live and die impenitent will perish for ever unpitied; there is a day coming when the Lord will not spare.

3. Punishments shall be public and open: I will execute these judgments in the sight of the nations (Eze 5:8); the judgments themselves shall be so remarkable that all the nations far and near shall take notice of them; they shall be all the talk of that part of the world, and the more for the conspicuousness of the place and people on which they are inflicted. Note, Public sins, as they call for public reproofs (those that sin rebuke before all), so, if those prevail not, they call for public judgments. He strikes them as wicked men in the open sight of others (Job 34:26), that

he may maintain and vindicate the honour of his government, for (as Grotius descants upon it here) why should he suffer it to be said, See what wicked lives those lead who profess to be the worshippers of the only true God! And, as the publicity of the judgments will redound to the honour of God, so it will serve, (1.) To aggravate the punishment, and to make it lie the more heavily. Jerusalem, being made waste, becomes a reproach among the nations in the sight of all that pass by, Eze 5:14. The more conspicuous and the more peculiar any have been in the day of their prosperity the greater disgrace attends their fall; and that was Jerusalem's case. The more Jerusalem had been a praise in the earth the more it is now a reproach and a taunt, Eze 5:15. This she was warned of as much as any thing when her glory commenced (Kg1 9:8), and this was lamented as much as any thing when it was laid in the dust, Lam 2:15. (2.) To teach the nations to fear before the God of Israel, when they see what a jealous God he is, and how severely he punishes sin even in those that are nearest to him: It shall be an instruction to the nations, Eze 5:15. Jerusalem should have taught her neighbours the fear of God by her piety and virtue, but, she not doing that, God will teach it to them by her ruin; for they have reason to say, If this be done in the green tree, what shall be done in the dry? If judgment begin at the house of God, where will it end? If those be thus punished who only had some idolaters among them, what will become of us who are all idolaters? Note, The destruction of some is designed for the instruction of others. Malefactors are publicly punished in terrorem-that others may take warning.

4. These punishments, in the kind of them, shall be very severe and grievous. (1.) They shall be such as have no precedent or parallel. Their sins being more provoking than those of others, the judgments executed upon them should be uncommon (Eze 5:9): "I will do in thee that which I have not done in thee before, though thou hast long since deserved it; nay, that which I have not done in any other city." This punishment of Jerusalem is said to be greater than that of Sodom (Lam 4:6), which was more grievous than all that went before it; nay, it is such as "I will not do any more the like, all the circumstances taken in, to any other city, till the like come to be done again to this city, in the final overthrow by the Romans." This is a rhetorical expression of the most grievous judgments, like that character of Hezekiah, that there was none like him, before or after him. (2.) They shall be such as will force them to break the strongest bonds of natural affection to one another, which will be a just punishment of them for their wilfully breaking the bonds of their duty to God (Eze 5:10): The fathers shall eat the sons, and the sons shall eat the fathers, through the extremity of the famine, or shall be compelled to do it by their barbarous conquerors. (3.) There shall be a complication of judgments, any one of them terrible enough, and desolating; but what then would they be when they came all together and in perfection? Some shall be taken away by the plague (Eze 5:12); the pestilence shall pass through thee (Eze 5:17), sweeping all before it, as the destroying angel; others shall be consumed with famine, shall gradually waste away as men in a consumption (Eze 5:12); this is again insisted on (Eze 5:16): I will send upon them the evil arrows of famine; hunger shall make them pine, and shall pierce them to the heart, as if arrows, evil arrows, poisoned darts, were shot into them. God has many arrows, evil arrows, in his quiver; when some are discharged, he has still more in reserve. I will increase the famine upon you. A famine in a bereaved country may decrease as fruits spring

forth; but a famine in a besieged city will increase of course; yet god speaks of it as his act: "I will increase it, and will break your staff of bread, will take away the necessary supports of life, will disappoint you of all that which you depend upon, so that there is no remedy, but you must fall to the ground." Life is frail, is weak, is burdened, so that, if it have not daily bread for its staff to lean upon, it cannot but sink, and is soon gone if that staff be broken. Others shall fall by the sword round about Jerusalem, when they sally out upon the besiegers; it is a sword which God will bring, Eze 5:17. The sword of the Lord, that used to be drawn for Jerusalem's defence, is now drawn for its destruction. Others are devoured by evil beasts, which will make a prey of those that fly for shelter to the deserts and mountains. They shall meet their ruin where they expected refuge, for there is no escaping the judgments of God, Eze 5:17. And, lastly, those who escape shall be scattered into all parts of the world, into all the winds (so it is expressed, Eze 5:10, Eze 5:12), intimating that they should not only be dispersed, but hurried, and tossed, and driven to and fro, as chaff before the wind. Nay, and Cain's curse (to be fugitives and vagabonds) is not the worst of it neither; their restless life shall be cut off by a bloody death: "I will draw out a sword after them, which shall follow them wherever they go." Evil pursues sinners; and the curse shall come upon them and overtake them.

5. These punishments will prove their ruin by degrees. They shall be diminished (Eze 5:11); their strength and glory shall grow less and less. They shall be bereaved (Eze 5:17), emptied of all that which was their joy and confidence. God sends these judgments on purpose to destroy them, Eze 5:16. The arrows are not sent (as those which Jonathan shot) for their direction, but for their destruction; for god will accomplish his fury upon them (Eze 5:13); the day of God's patience is over, and the ruin is remediless. Though this prophecy was to have its accomplishment now quickly, in the destruction of Jerusalem by the Chaldeans, yet the executioners not being named here, but the criminal only (this is Jerusalem), we may well suppose that it looks further, to the final destruction of that great city by the Romans when God made a full end of the Jewish nation, and caused his fury to rest upon them.

6. All this is ratified by the divine authority and veracity: I the Lord have spoken it, Eze 5:15 and again Eze 5:17. The sentence is passed by him that is Judge of heaven and earth, whose judgment is according to truth, and the judgments of whose hand are according to the judgments of his mouth. he has spoken it who can do it, for with him nothing is impossible. He has spoken it who will do it, for he is not a man that he should lie. He has spoken it whom we are bound to hear and heed, whose ipse dixit-word commands the most serious attention and submissive assent: And they shall know that I the Lord have spoken it, Eze 5:13. There were those who thought it was only the prophet that spoke it in his delirium; but God will make them know, by the accomplishment of it, that he has spoken it in his zeal. Note, Sooner or later, God's word will prove itself.

Ezekiel Chapter 6

In this chapter we have, I. A threatening of the destruction of Israel for their idolatry, and the destruction of their idols with them (Eze 6:1-7). II. A promise of the gracious return of a remnant of them to God, by true repentance and reformation (Eze 6:8-10). III. Directions given to the prophet and others, the Lord's servants, to lament both the iniquities and the calamities of Israel (Eze 6:11-14).

Ezekiel 6:1

Here, I. The prophecy is directed to the mountains of Israel (Eze 6:1, Eze 6:2); the prophet must set his face towards them. If he could see so far off as the land of Israel, the mountains of that land would be first and furthest seen; towards them therefore he must look, and look boldly and stedfastly, as the judge looks at the prisoner, and directs his speech to him, when he passes sentence upon him. Though the mountains of Israel be ever so high and ever so strong, he must set his face against them, as having judgments to denounce that should shake their foundation. The mountains of Israel had been holy mountains, but now that they had polluted them with their high places God set his face against them and therefore the prophet must. Israel is here put, not, as sometimes, for the ten tribes, but for the whole land. The mountains are called upon to hear the word of the Lord, to shame the inhabitants that would not hear. The prophets might as soon gain attention from the mountains as from that rebellious and gainsaying people, to whom they all day long stretched out their hands in vain. Hear, O mountains! the Lord's controversy (Mic 6:1, Mic 6:2), for God's cause will have a hearing, whether we hear it or no. But from the mountains the word of the Lord echoes to the hills, to the rivers, and to the valleys; for to them also the Lord God speaks, intimating that the whole land is concerned in what is now to be delivered and shall be witnesses against this people that they had fair warning given them of the judgments coming, but they would not take it; nay, they contradicted the message and persecuted the messengers, so that God's prophets might more safely and comfortably speak to the hills and mountains than to them.

II. That which is threatened in this prophecy is the utter destruction of the idols and the idolaters, and both by the sword of war. God himself is commander-in-chief of this expedition against the mountains of Israel. It is he that says, Behold, I, even I, will bring a sword upon you (Eze 6:3); the sword of the Chaldeans is at God's command, goes where he sends it, comes where he brings it, and lights as he directs it. In the desolations of that war,

1. The idols and all their appurtenances should be destroyed. The high places, which were on

the tops of mountains (Eze 6:3), shall be levelled and made desolate (Eze 6:6); they shall not be beautified, shall not be frequented as they had been. The altars, on which they offered sacrifice and burnt incense to strange gods, shall be broken to pieces and laid waste; the images and idols shall be defaced, shall be broken and cease, and be cut down, and all the fine costly works about them shall be abolished, Eze 6:4, Eze 6:6. Observe here, (1.) That war makes woeful desolations, which those persons, places, and things that were esteemed most sacred cannot escape; for the sword devours one as well as another. (2.) That God sometimes ruins idolatries even by the hands of idolaters, for such the Chaldeans themselves were; but, as if the deity were a local thing, the greatest admirers of the gods of their own country were the greatest despisers of the gods of other countries. (3.) It is just with God to make that a desolation which we make an idol of; for he is a jealous God and will not bear a rival. (4.) If men do not, as they ought, destroy idolatry, God will, first or last, find out a way to do it. When Josiah had destroyed the high places, altars, and images, with the sword of justice, they set them up again; but God will now destroy them with the sword of war, and let us see who dares re-establish them.

2. The worshippers of idols and all their adherents should be destroyed likewise. As all their high places shall be laid waste, so shall all their dwelling-places too, even all their cities, Eze 6:6. Those that profane God's dwelling-place as they had done can expect no other than that he should abandon theirs, Eze 5:11. If any man defile the temple of God, him will God destroy, Col 3:17. It is here threatened that their slain shall fall in the midst of them (Eze 6:7); there shall be abundance slain, even in those places which were thought most safe; but it is added as a remarkable circumstance that they shall fall before their idols (Eze 6:4), that their dead carcases should be laid, and their bones scattered, about their altars, Eze 6:5. (1.) Thus their idols should be polluted, and those places profaned by the dead bodies which they had had in veneration. If they will not defile the covering of their graven images, God will, Isa 30:22. The throwing of the carcases among them, as upon the dunghill, intimates that they were but dunghill-deities. (2.) Thus it was intimated that they were but dead things, unfit to be rivals with the living God; for the carcases of dead men, that, like them, have eyes and see not, ears and hear not, were the fittest company for them. (3.) Thus the idols were upbraided with their inability to help their worshippers, and idolaters were upbraided with the folly of trusting in them; for, it should seem, they fell by the sword of the enemy when they were actually before their idols imploring their aid and putting themselves under their protection. Sennacherib was slain by his sons when he was worshipping in the house of his god. (4.) The sin might be read in this circumstance of the punishment; the slain men are cast before the idols, to show that therefore they are slain, because they worshipped those idols; see Jer 8:1, Jer 8:2. let the survivors observe it, and take warning not to worship images; let them see it, and know that God is the Lord, that the Lord he is God and he alone.

Ezekiel 6:8

Judgment had hitherto triumphed, but in these verses mercy rejoices against judgment. A sad end is made of this provoking people, but not a full end. The ruin seems to be universal, and yet will I leave a remnant, a little remnant, distinguished from the body of the people, a few of many, such as are left when the rest perish; and it is God that leaves them. This intimates that they deserved to be cut off with the rest, and would have been cut off if God had not left them. See Isa 1:9. And it is God who by his grace works that in them which he has an eye to in sparing them. Now,

I. It is a preserved remnant, saved from the ruin which the body of the nation is involved in (Eze 6:8): That you may have some who shall escape the sword. God said (Eze 5:12) that he would draw a sword after those who were scattered, that destruction should pursue them in their dispersion; but here is mercy remembered in the midst of that wrath, and a promise that some of the Jews of the dispersion, as they were afterwards called, should escape the sword. None of those who were to fall by the sword about Jerusalem shall escape; for they trust to Jerusalem's walls for security, and shall be made ashamed of that vain confidence. but some of them shall escape the sword among the nations, where, being deprived of all other stays, they stay themselves upon God only. They are said to have those who shall escape; for they shall be the seed of another generation, out of which Jerusalem shall flourish again.

II. It is a penitent remnant (Eze 6:9): Those who escape of you shall remember me. Note, To those whom god designs for life he will give repentance unto life. They are reprieved, and escape the sword, that they may have time to return to God. Note, God's patience both leaves room for repentance and is an encouragement to sinners to repent. Where God designs grace to repent he allows space to repent; yet many who have the space want the grace, many who escape the sword do not forsake the sin, as it is promised that these shall do. This remnant, here marked for salvation, is a type of the remnant reserved out of the body of mankind to be monuments of mercy, who are made safe in the same way that these were, by being brought to repentance. Now observe here,

1. The occasion of their repentance, and that is a mixture of judgment and mercy-judgment, that they were carried captives, but mercy, that they escaped the sword in the land of their captivity. They were driven out of their own land, but not out of the land of the living, not chased out of the world, as other were and they deserved to be. Note, The consideration of the just rebukes of Providence we are under, and yet of the mercy mixed with them, should engage us to repent, that we may answer God's end in both. And true repentance shall be accepted of God, though we are brought to it by our troubles; nay, sanctified afflictions often prove means of conversion, as to Manasseh.

2. The root and principle of their repentance: They shall remember me among the nations. Those who forgot God in the land of their peace and prosperity, who waxed fat and kicked, were brought to remember him in the land of their captivity. The prodigal son never bethought himself of his father's house till he was ready to perish for hunger in the far country. Their remembering

God was the first step they took in returning to him. Note, Then there begins to be some hopes of sinners when they have sinned against, and to enquire, Where is God my Maker? Sin takes rise in forgetting God, Jer 3:21. Repentance takes rise from the remembrance of him and of our obligations to him. God says, They shall remember me, that is, "I will give them grace to do so;" for otherwise they would for ever forget him. That grace shall find them out wherever they are, and by bringing God to their mind shall bring them to their right mind. The prodigal, when he remembered his father, remembered how he has sinned against Heaven and before him; so do these penitents. (1.) They remember the base affront they had put upon God by their idolatries, and this is that which an ingenuous repentance fastens upon and most sadly laments. They had departed from God to idols, and given that honour to pretended deities, the creatures of men's fancies and the work of men's hands, which they should have given to the God of Israel. They departed from God, from his word, which they should have made their rule, from his work, which they should have made their business. Their hearts departed from him. The heart, which he requires and insists upon, and without which bodily exercise profits nothing, the heart, which should be set upon him, and carried out towards him, when that departs from him, is as the treacherous elopement of a wife from her husband or the rebellious revolt of a subject from his sovereign. Their eyes also go after their idols; they doted on them, and had great expectations from them. Their hearts followed their eyes in the choice of their gods (they must have gods that they could see), and then their eyes followed their hearts in the adoration of them. Now the malignity of this sin is that it is spiritual whoredom; it is a whorish heart that departs from God; and they are eyes that go a whoring after their idols. Note, Idolatry is spiritual whoredom; it is the breach of a marriage-covenant with God; it is the setting of the affections upon that which is a rival with him, and the indulgence of a base lust, which deceives and defiles the soul, and is a great wrong to God in his honour, (2.) They remember what a grief this was to him and how he resented it. They shall remember that I am broken with their whorish heart and their eyes that are full of this spiritual adultery, not only angry at it, but grieved, as a husband is at the lewdness of a wife whom he dearly loved, grieved to such a degree that he is broken with it; it breaks his heart to think that he should be so disingenuously dealt with; he is broken as an aged father is with the undutiful behaviour of a rebellious and disobedient son, which sinks his spirits and makes him to stoop. Forty years long was I grieved with this generation, Psa 95:10. God's measures were broken (so some); a stop was put to the current of his favours towards them, and he was even compelled to punish them. This they shall remember in the day of their repentance, and it shall affect and humble them more than any thing, not so much that their peace was broken, and their country broken, as that God was broken by their sin. Thus they shall look on him whom they have pierced and shall mourn, Zac 12:10. Note, Nothing grieves a true penitent so much as to think that his sin has been a grief to God and to the Spirit of his grace.

3. The product and evidence of their repentance: They shall loathe themselves for the evils which they have committed in all their abominations. Thus God will give them grace to qualify them for pardon and deliverance. Though he had been broken by their whorish heart, yet he would not quite cast them off. See Isa 57:17, Isa 57:18; Hos 2:13, Hos 2:14. His goodness takes

occasion from their badness to appear the more illustrious. note, (1.) True penitents see sin to be an abominable thing, that abominable thing which the Lord hates and which makes sinners, and even their services, odious to him, Jer 44:4; Isa 1:11. It defiles the sinner's own conscience, and makes him, unless he be past feeling, an abomination to himself. An idol is particularly called an abomination, Isa 44:19. Those gratifications which the hearts of sinners were set upon as delectable things the hearts of penitents are turned against as detestable things. (2.) There are many evils committed in these abominations, many included in them, attendant on them, and flowing from them, many transgressions in one sin, Lev 16:21. In their idolatries they were sometimes guilty of whoredom (as in the worship of Peor), sometimes of murder (as in the worship of Moloch); these were evils committed in their abominations. Or it denotes the great malignity there is in sin; it is an abomination that has abundance of evil in it. (3.) Those that truly loathe sin cannot but loathe themselves because of sin; self-loathing is evermore the companion of true repentance. Penitents quarrel with themselves, and can never be reconciled to themselves till they have some ground to hope that God is reconciled to them; nay, then they shall lie down in their shame, when he is pacified towards them, Eze 16:63.

4. The glory that will redound to God by their repentance (Eze 6:10): "They shall know that I am the Lord; they shall be convinced of it by experience, and shall be ready to own it, and that I have not said in vain that I would do this evil unto them, finding that what I have said is made good, and made to work for good, and to answer a good intention, and that it was not without just provocation that they were thus threatened and thus punished." Note, (1.) One way or other God will make sinners to know and own that he is the lord, either by their repentance or by their ruin. (2.) All true penitents are brought to acknowledge both the equity and the efficacy of the word of God, particularly the threatenings of the word, and to justify God in them and in the accomplishment of them.

Ezekiel 6:11

The same threatenings which we had before in the foregoing chapter, and in the former part of this, are here repeated, with a direction to the prophet to lament them, that those he prophesied to might be the more affected with the foresight of them.

I. He must by his gestures in preaching express the dep sense he had both of the iniquities and of the calamities of the house of Israel (Eze 6:11): Smite with thy hand and stamp with thy foot. Thus he must make it to appear that he was in earnest in what he said to them, that he firmly believed it and laid it to heart. Thus he must signify the just displeasure he had conceived at their sins, and the just dread he was under of the judgments coming upon them. Some would reject this use of these gestures, and call them antic and ridiculous; but God bids him use them because they might help to enforce the word upon some and give it the setting on; and those that know the worth of souls will be content to be laughed at by the wits, so they may but edify the weak. Two things the prophet must thus lament:-1. National sins. Alas! for all the evil abominations of the house of Israel. Note, The sins of sinners are the sorrows of God's faithful servants, especially the evil abominations of the house of Israel, whose sins are more abominable and have more evil in them than the sins of others. Alas! What will be in the end hereof? 2. National judgments. To punish them for these abominations they shall fall by the sword, by the famine, and by the pestilence. Note, It is our duty to be affected not only with our own sins and sufferings, but with the sins and sufferings of others; and to look with compassion upon the miseries that wicked people bring upon themselves; as Christ beheld Jerusalem and wept over it.

II. He must inculcate what he had said before concerning the destruction that was coming upon them. 1. They shall be run down and ruined by a variety of judgments which shall find them out and follow them wherever they are (Eze 6:12): He that is far off, and thinks himself out of danger, because out of the reach of the Chaldeans' arrows, shall find himself not out of the reach of God's arrows, which fly day and night (Psa 91:5): He shall die of the pestilence. He that is near a place of strength, which he hopes will be to him a place of safety, shall fall by the sword, before he can retreat. He that is so cautious as not to venture out, but remains in the city, shall there die by the famine, the saddest death of all. Thus will God accomplish his fury, that is, do all that against them which he had purposed to do. 2. They shall read their sin in their punishment; for their slain men shall be among their idols, round about their altars, as was threatened before, Eze 6:5-7. There, where they had prostrated themselves in honour of their idols, God will lay them dead, to their own reproach and the reproach of their idols. They lived among them and shall die among them. They had offered sweet odours to their idols, but there shall their dead carcases send forth an offensive smell, as it were to atone for that misplaced incense. 3. The country shall be all laid waste, as, before, the cities (Eze 6:6): I will make the land desolate. That fruitful, pleasant, populous country, that has been as the garden of the Lord, the glory of all lands, shall be desolate, more desolate than the wilderness towards Diblath, Eze 6:14. It is called Diblathaim (Num 33:46;Jer 48:22), that great and terrible wilderness which is described, Deu 8:15, wherein were fiery serpents and scorpions. The land of Canaan is at this day one of the most barren desolate countries in the world. City and country are thus depopulated, that the altars may be laid waste and made desolate, Eze 6:6. Rather than their idolatrous altars shall be left standing, both town and country shall be laid in ruins. Sin is a desolating thing; therefore stand in awe and sin not.

Ezekiel Chapter 7

In this chapter the approaching ruin of the land of Israel is most particularly foretold in affecting expressions often repeated, that if possible they might be awakened by repentance to prevent it. The prophet must tell them, I. That it will be a final ruin, a complete utter destruction, which would make an end of them, a miserable end (Eze 7:1-6). II. That it is an approaching ruin, just at the door (Eze 7:7-10). III. That it is an unavoidable ruin, because they had by sin brought it upon themselves (Eze 7:10-15). IV. That their strength and wealth should be no fence against it (Eze 7:16-19). V. That the temple, which they trusted in, should itself be ruined (Eze 7:20-22). VI. That it should be a universal ruin, the sin that brought it having been universal (Eze 7:23-27).

Ezekiel 7:1

We have here fair warning given of the destruction of the land of Israel, which was now hastening on apace. God, by the prophet, not only sends notice of it, but will have it inculcated in the same expressions, to show that the thing is certain, that it is near, that the prophet is himself affected with it and desires they should be so too, but finds them deaf, and stupid, and unaffected. When the town is on fire men do no seek for fine words and quaint expressions in which to give an account of it, but cry about the streets, with a loud and lamentable voice, "Fire! fire!" So the prophet here proclaims, An end! an end! it has come, it has come; behold, it has come. He that hath ears to hear let him hear.

I. An end has come, the end has come (Eze 7:2), and again (Eze 7:3, Eze 7:6), Now has the end come upon thee-the end which all their wickedness had a tendency to, and which God had often told them it would come to at last, when by his prophets he had asked them, What will you do in the end hereof?-the end which all the foregoing judgments had been working towards, as means to bring it about (their ruin shall now be completed)-or the end, that is, the period of their state, the final destruction of their nation, as the deluge was the end of all flesh, Gen 6:13. They had flattered themselves with hopes that they should shortly see an end of their troubles. "Yea," says God, "An end has come, but a miserable one, not the expected end" (which is promised to the pious remnant among them, Jer 29:11); "it is the end, that end which you have been so often warned of, that last end which Moses wished you to consider (Deu 32:29), and which, because Jerusalem remembered not, therefore she came down wonderfully," Lam 1:9. This end was long in coming, but now it has come. Though the ruin of sinners comes slowly, it comes surely. "It has come; it watches for thee, ready to receive thee." This perhaps looks further, to the last destruction of that nation by the Romans, which that by the Chaldeans was an earnest of; and still further to the final destruction of the world of the ungodly. The end of all things is at hand; and Jerusalem's last end was a type of the end of the world, Mat 24:3. Oh that we could all see that end of time and days very near, and the end of our own time and days much nearer, that we may secure a happy lot at the end of the days! Dan 12:13. This end comes upon the four corners of the land. The ruin, as it shall be final, so it shall be total; no part of the land shall escape; no, not that which lies most remote. Such will the destruction of the world be; all these things shall be dissolved. Such will the destruction of sinners be; none can avoid it. Oh that the wickedness of the wicked might come to an end, before it bring them to an end!

II. An evil, an only evil, behold, has come, Eze 7:5. Sin is an evil, an only evil, an evil that has no good in it; it is the worst of evils. But this is spoken of the evil of trouble; it is an evil, one evil, and that one shall suffice to affect and complete the ruin of the nation; there needs no more to do its business; this one shall make an utter end, affliction needs not rise up a second time, Nah 1:9. It is an evil without precedent or parallel, an evil that stands alone; you cannot produce such another instance. It is to the impenitent an evil, an only evil; it hardens their hearts and irritates their corruptions, whereas there were those to whom it was sanctified by the grace of God and made a means of much good; they were sent into Babylon for their good, Jer 24:5. The wicked have the dregs of that cup to drink which to the righteous is full of mixtures of mercy, Psa 75:8. The same affliction is to us either a half evil or an only evil according as we conduct ourselves under it and make use of it. But when an end, the end, has come upon the wicked world, then an evil, an only evil, comes upon it, and not till then. The sorest of temporal judgments have their allays, but the torments of the damned are an evil, an only evil.

III. The time has come, the set time, for the inflicting of this only evil and the making of this full end; for to all God's purposes there is a time, a proper time, and that prefixed, in which the purpose shall have its accomplishment; particularly the time of reckoning with wicked people, and rendering to them according to their desserts, is fixed, the day of the revelation of the righteous judgment of god; and he sees, whether we see it or no, that his day is coming. This they are here told of again and again (Eze 7:10): Behold, the day that has lingered so long has come at last, behold, it has come. The time has come, the day draws near, the day of trouble is near, Eze 7:7, Eze 7:12. Though threatened judgments may be long deferred, yet they shall not be dropped; the time for executing them will come. Though God's patience may put them off, nothing but man's sincere repentance and reformation will put them by. The morning has come unto thee (Eze 7:7), and again (Eze 7:10), The morning has gone forth; the day of trouble dawns, the day of destruction is already begun. The morning discovers that which was hidden; they thought their secret sins would never come to light, but now they will be brought to light. They used to try and execute malefactors in the morning, and such a morning of judgment and execution is now coming upon them, a day of trouble to sinners, the year of their visitation. See how stupid these people were, that, though the day of their destruction was already begun, yet they were not aware of it, but must be thus told of it again and again. The day of trouble, real trouble, is near, and not the sounding again of the mountains, that is, not a mere echo or report of troubles, as they were willing to think it was, nothing but a groundless surmise; as if the men that came against them were but the shadow of the mountains (as Zebul suggested to Gaal, Jdg 9:36) and the intelligence they received were but an empty sound, reverberated from the mountains. No; the trouble is not a fancy, and so you will soon find.

IV. All this comes from God's wrath, not allayed, as sometimes it has been, with mixtures of mercy. This is the fountain from which all these calamities flow; and this is the wormwood and the gall in the affliction and the misery, which make it bitter indeed (Eze 7:3): I will send my anger upon thee. Observe, God is Lord of his anger; it does not break out but when he pleases, nor fasten upon any but as he directs it and gives it commission. The expression rises higher (Eze 7:8): Now will I shortly pour out my fury upon thee in full vials, and accomplish my anger, all the purposes and all the products of it, upon thee. This wrath does not single out here and there one to be made examples, but it is upon all the multitude thereof (Eze 7:12, Eze 7:14); the whole body of the nation has become a vessel of wrath, fitted for destruction. God does sometimes in wrath remember mercy, but now he says, My eye shall not spare thee, neither will I have pity,Eze 7:4 and again Eze 7:9. Those shall have judgment without mercy who made light of mercy when it was offered them.

V. All this is the just punishment of their sins, and it is what they have by their own folly brought upon themselves. This is much insisted on here, that they might be brought to justify God in all he had brought upon them. God never sends his anger but in wisdom and justice; and therefore it follows, "I will judge thee according to thy ways, Eze 7:3. I will examine what thy ways have been, compare them with the law, and then deal with thee according to the merit of them, and recompense them to thee," Eze 7:4. Note, In the heaviest judgments God inflicts upon sinners he does but recompense their own ways upon them; they are beaten with their own rod. And, when God comes to reckon with a sinful people, he will bring every provocation to account: "will recompense upon thee all thy abominations (Eze 7:3); and now thy iniquity shall be found to be hateful (Psa 36:2) and thy abominations shall be in the midst of thee" (Eze 7:4); that is, the secret wickedness shall now be brought to light, and that shall appear to have been in the midst of thee which before was not suspected; and thy sin shall now become an abomination to thyself. So the abomination of iniquity will be when it comes to be an abomination of desolation, Mat 24:15. Or, Thy abominations (that is, the punishments of them) shall be in the midst of thee; they shall reach to thy heart. See Jer 4:18. Or therefore God will not spare, nor have pity, because, even when he is recompensing their ways upon them, yet in their distress they trespass yet more; their abominations are still in the midst of them, indulged and harboured in their hearts. It is repeated again (Eze 7:8,Eze 7:9), I will judge thee, I will recompense thee. Two sins are particularly specified as provoking God to bring these judgments upon them-pride and oppression. 1. God will humble them by his judgments, for they have magnified themselves. The rod of affliction has blossomed, but it was pride that budded,Eze 7:10. What buds in sin will blossom in some judgment or other. The pride of Judah and Jerusalem appeared among all orders and degrees of men, as buds upon the tree in spring. 2. Their enemies shall deal hardly with them, for they have dealt hardly with one another (Eze 7:11): Violence has risen up into a rod of wickedness; that is, their injuriousness to one another is protected and patronised by the power of the magistrate. The rod of government had become a rod of wickedness, to such a degree of impudence was violence risen up. I saw the place of judgment, that wickedness was there, Ecc 3:16; Isa 5:7. Whatever are the fruits of God's judgments, it is certain that our sin is the root of them.

VI. There is no escape from these judgments nor fence against them, for they shall be universal and shall bear down all before them, without remedy. 1. Death in its various shapes shall ride triumphantly, both in town and in country, both within the city and without it, Eze 7:15. Men shall be safe nowhere; for he that is in the field shall die by the sword (every field shall be to them a field of battle) and he that is in the city, though it be a holy city, yet it shall not be his protection, but famine and pestilence shall devour him. Sin had abounded both in city and country, Iliacos intra muros peccator et extra-Trojans and Greeks offend alike; and therefore among both desolations are made. 2. None of those that are marked for death shall escape: There shall none of them remain. None of those proud oppressors that did violence to their poor neighbours with the rod of wickedness, none of them shall be left, but they shall be all swept away by the desolation that is coming (Eze 7:11): None of their multitude, that is, of the rabble, whom they set on to do mischief, and to countenance them in doing it, to cry, "Crucify, crucify," when they were resolved on the destruction of any, none of them shall remain, nor any of theirs; their families shall all be destroyed, and neither root nor branch left them. This multitude, this mob, divine vengeance will in a particular manner fasten upon; for wrath is upon all the multitude thereof (Eze 7:12, Eze 7:14) and the vision was touching the whole multitude thereof (Eze 7:13), the bulk of the common people. The judgments coming shall carry them away by wholesale, and they shall neither secure themselves nor their masters whose creatures and tools they were. God's judgments, when they come with commission, cannot be overpowered by multitudes. Though hand join in hand, yet shall not the wicked go unpunished. 3. Those that fall shall not be lamented (Eze 7:11): There shall be no wailing for them, for there shall be none left to bewail them, but such as are hastening apace after them. And the times shall be so bad that men shall rather congratulate than lament the death of their friends, as reckoning those happy that are taken away from seeing these desolations and sharing in them, Jer 16:4, Jer 16:5. 4. They shall not be able to make any resistance. The decree has gone forth, and the vision concerning them shall not return, Eze 7:13. God will not reveal it, and they cannot defeat it; and therefore it shall not return re infecta-without having accomplished any thing, but shall accomplish that for which he sends it. God's word will take place, and then, (1.) Particular persons cannot make their part good against God: No man shall strengthen himself in the iniquity of his life; it will be to no purpose for sinners to set God and his judgments at defiance as they used to do. None ever hardened his heart against God and prospered. Those that strengthen themselves in their wickedness will be found not only to weaken, but to ruin, themselves, Psa 52:7. (2.) The multitude cannot resist the torrent of these judgments, nor make head against them (Eze 7:14): They have blown the trumpet, to call their soldiers together, and to animate and encourage those whom they have got together, and thus they think to make all ready; but all in vain; none enlist themselves, or those that do have not courage to face the enemy. Note, If God be against us, none can be for us to do us any service. 5. They shall have no hope of the return of their prosperity, with which to support themselves in their adversity; they shall have given up all for gone; and therefore, "Let not the buyer rejoice that he is increasing his estate and has become a purchaser; nor let the seller mourn that he is lessening his estate and has become a bankrupt," Eze 7:12. See the vanity of the things of this world, and how worthless they are-that in a time of trouble, when we have most need of them, we may perhaps make least account of them. Those that have sold are the more easy, having the less to lose, and those that have bought have but increased their own cares and fears. Because the fashion of this world passes away, let those that buy be as though they possessed not, because they know not how soon they may be dispossessed,Col 7:29-31. It is added (Eze 7:13), "The seller shall not return, at the year of jubilee, to that which is sold, according to the law, though he should escape the sword and pestilence, and live till that year comes; for no inheritances shall be enjoyed here till the seventy years be accomplished, and then men shall return to their possessions, shall claim and have their own again." In the belief of this, Jeremiah, about this time, bought his uncle's field, yet, according to the charge, the buyer did not rejoice, but complain, Jer 32:25. 6. God will be glorified in all: "You shall know that I am the Lord (Eze 7:4), that I am the Lord that smiteth,Eze 7:9. You look at second causes, and think it is Nebuchadnezzar that smites you, but you shall be made to know he is but the staff: it is the hand of the Lord that smiteth you, and who knows the weight of his hand?" Those who would not know it was the Lord that did them goo shall be made to know it is the Lord that smiteth them; for, one way or other, he will be owned.

Ezekiel 7:16

We have attended the fate of those that are cut off, and are now to attend the flight of those that have an opportunity of escaping the danger; some of them shall escape (Eze 7:16), but what the better? As good die once as, in a miserable life, die a thousand deaths, and escape only like Cain to be fugitives and vagabonds, and afraid of being slain by every one they meet; so shall these be.

I. They shall have no comfort or satisfaction in their own minds, but be in continual anguish and terror; for, wherever they go, they carry about with them guilty consciences, which make them a burden to themselves. 1. They shall be always solitary and under prevailing melancholy; they shall not be in the cities, or places of concourse, but all alone upon the mountains, not caring for society, but shy of it, as being ashamed of the low circumstances to which they are reduced. 2. They shall be always sorrowful. Those have reason to be so that are under the tokens of God's displeasure; and God can make those so that have been most jovial and have set sorrow at defiance. Those that once thought themselves as the lions of the mountains, so daring were they, now become as the doves of the valleys, so timid are they, and so dispirited, ready to flee when none pursues and to tremble at the shaking of a leaf. They are all of them mourning (not with a godly sorrow, but with the sorrow of the world, which works death), every one for his iniquity, that is, for those calamities which they now see their iniquity has brought upon them, not only the iniquity of the land, but their own: they shall then be brought to acknowledge what they have each of them contributed to the national guilt. Note, Sooner or later sin will have sorrow of one kind or other; and those that will not repent of their iniquity may justly be left to pine away in it; those that will not mourn for it as it is an offence to God shall be made to mourn for it as it is a shame and ruin to themselves, to mourn at the last, when the flesh and the body are consumed, and to say, How have I hated instruction! Pro 5:11, Pro 5:12. 3. They shall be deprived of all their strength of body and mind (Eze 7:17): All hands shall be feeble, so that they shall not be able to fight, or defend themselves, and all knees shall be weak as water, so that they shall neither be able to flee nor to stand their ground; they shall feel a universal colliquation: their knees shall flow as water, so that they must fall of course. Note, It is folly for the strong man to glory in his strength, for God can soon weaken it. 4. They shall be deprived of all their hopes and shall abandon themselves to despair (Eze 7:18); they shall have nothing to hold up their spirits with; their aspects shall show what are their prospects, all dreadful, for they shall gird themselves with sackcloth, as having no expectation ever to wear better clothing. Horror shall cover them, and shame, and baldness, all the expressions of a desperate sorrow, Isa 17:11. Note, Those that will not be kept from sin by fear and shame shall by fear and shame be punished for it; such is the confusion that sin will end in.

II. They shall have no benefit from their wealth and riches, but shall be perfectly sick of them, Eze 7:19. Those that were reduced to this distress were such as had had abundance of silver and gold, money, and plate, and jewels, and other valuable goods, from which they promised themselves a great deal of advantage in times of public trouble. They thought their wealth would be their strong city, that with it they could bribe enemies and buy friends, that it would be the ransom of their lives, that they could never want bread as long as they had money, and that money would answer all things; but see how it proved. 1. Their wealth had been a great temptation to them in the day of their prosperity; they set their affections upon it, and put their confidence in it. By their eager pursuit of it they were drawn into sin, and by their plentiful enjoyment of it they were hardened in sin; and thus it was the stumbling-block of their iniquity; it occasioned their falling into sin and obstructed their return to God. Note, There are many whose wealth is their snare and ruin. The gaining of the world is the losing of their souls; it makes them proud, secure, covetous, oppressive, voluptuous; and that which, it well used, might have been the servant of their piety, being abused, becomes the stumbling-block of their iniquity. 2. It was no relief to them now in the day of their adversity; for, (1.) Their gold and silver could not protect them from the judgments of God. They shall not be able to deliver them in the day of the wrath of the Lord; they shall not serve to atone his justice, or turn away his wrath, nor to screen them from the judgments he is bringing upon them. Note, Riches profit not in the day of wrath, Pro 11:4. They neither set them so high that god's judgments cannot reach them nor make them so strong that they cannot conquer them. There is a day of wrath coming, when it will appear that men's wealth is utterly unable to deliver them or do them any service. What the better was the rich man for his full barns when his soul was required of him, or that other rich man for his purple, and scarlet, and sumptuous fare, when in hell he could not procure a drop of water to cool his tongue? Money is no defence against the arrests of death, nor any alleviation to the miseries of the damned. (2.) Their gold and silver could not give them any content under their calamities. [1.] They could not fill their bowels; when there was no bread left in the city, none to be had for love or money, their silver and gold could not satisfy their hunger, nor serve to make one meal's meat for them. Note, We could better be without mines of gold than fields of corn; the products of the earth, which may easily be gathered from the surface of it, are much greater blessings to mankind than its treasures, which are with so much difficulty and hazard dug out of its bowels. If God give us daily bread, we have reason to be thankful, and no reason to complain, though silver and gold we have none. [2.] Much less could they satisfy their souls, or yield them any inward comfort. Note, The wealth of this world has not that in it which will answer the desires of the soul, or be any satisfaction to it in a day of distress. He that loves silver shall not be satisfied with silver, much less he that loses it. (3.) Their gold and silver shall be thrown into the streets, either by the hands of the enemy, who shall have more spoil than they care for or can carry away (silver shall be nothing accounted of; they shall cast that in the streets; but the gold, which is more valuable, shall be removed and brought to Babylon); or they themselves shall throw away their silver and gold, because it would be an incumbrance to them and retard their flight, or because it would expose them and be a temptation to the enemy to cut their throats for their money, or in indignation at it, because, after all the care and pains they had taken to scrape it together and hoard it up, they found that it would stand them in no stead, but do them a mischief rather. Note, The world passes away, and the lusts thereof, Jol 2:17. The time may come when worldly men will be as weary of their wealth as now they are wedded to it, when those will fare best that have least.

III. God's temple shall stand them in no stead, Eze 7:20-22. This they had prided themselves in, and promised themselves security from (Jer 7:4; Mic 3:11); but this confidence of theirs shall fail them. Observe, 1. The great honour God had done to that people in setting up his sanctuary among them (Eze 7:20): As for the beauty of his ornament, that holy and beautiful house, where they and their fathers praised God (Isa 64:11), which was therefore beautiful because holy (it was called the beauty of holiness, and holiness is the beauty of its ornament; it was also adorned with gold and gifts)-as for this, he set it in majesty; every thing was contrived to make it magnificent, that it might help to make the people of Israel the more illustrious among their neighbours. He built his sanctuary like high palaces, Psa 78:69. It was a glorious high throne from the beginning, Jer 17:12. But, 2. Here is the great dishonour they had done to God in profaning his sanctuary; they made the images of their counterfeit deities, which they set up in rivalship with God, and which are here called their abominations and their detestable things (for so they were to God, and so they should have been to them), and these they set up in God's temple, than which a greater affront could not be put upon him. And therefore, 3. It is here threatened that they shall be deprived of the temple, and it shall be no succour to them: Therefore have I set it far from them, that is, sent them far from it, so that it is out of the reach of their services and they are out of the reach of its influences. Note, God's ordinances, and the privileges of a profession of religion, will justly be taken away from those that despise and profane them. Nay, they shall not only be kept at a distance from the temple, but the temple itself shall be involved in the common desolation (Eze 7:21); the Chaldeans, who are strangers, and therefore have no veneration for it, who are the wicked of the earth, and therefore have an antipathy to it, shall have it for a prey and for a spoil; all the ornaments and treasures of it shall fall into their hands, who will make no difference between that and other plunder. This was a grief to the saints in Zion, who complained of nothing so much as of that which the enemy did wickedly in the sanctuary (Psa 74:3); but it was the punishment of the sinners in Zion, who, by profaning the temple with strange gods, provoked God to suffer it to be profaned by strange nations, and to turn his face from those that did it as if he had not seen them and their crimes and from those that deprecated it as not regarding them and their prayers. Let the soldiers do as they will; let them enter into the secret place, into the holy of holies, as robbers; let them strip it, let them pollute it; its defence has departed, and then farewell all its glory. Note, Those are unworthy to be honoured with the form of godliness who will not be governed by the power of godliness.

Ezekiel 7:23

Here is, I. The prisoner arraigned: Make a chain, in which to drag the criminal to the bar, and set him before the tribunal of divine justice; let him stand in fetters (as a notorious malefactor), stand pinioned to receive his doom. Note, Those that break the bands of God's law asunder, and cast away those cords from them, will find themselves bound and held by the chains of his judgments, which they cannot break nor cast from them. The chain signified the siege of Jerusalem, or the slavery of those that were carried into captivity, or that they were all bound over to the righteous judgment of God, reserved in chains.

II. The indictment drawn up against the prisoner: The land is full of bloody crimes, full of the judgments of blood (so the word is), that is, of the guilt of blood which they had shed under colour of justice and by forms of law, with the solemnity of a judgment. The innocent blood which Manasseh shed, probably thus shed, by the judgment of the blood, was the measure-filling sin of Jerusalem, Kg2 24:4. Or, It is full of such crimes as by the law were to be punished with death, the judgment of blood. Idolatry, blasphemy, witchcraft, Sodomy, and the like, were bloody crimes, for which particular sinners were to die; and therefore, when they had become national, there was no remedy but the nation must be cut off. Note, Bloody crimes will be punished with bloody judgments. The city, the city of David, the holy city, that should have been the pattern of righteousness, the protector of it, and the punisher of wrong, is now full of violence; the rulers of that city, having greater power and reputation, are greater oppressors than any others. This was sadly to be lamented. How has the faithful city become a harlot!

III. Judgment given upon this indictment. God will reckon with them not only for the profaning of his sanctuary, but for the perverting of justice between man and man; for, as holiness becomes his house, so the righteous Lord loves righteousness and is the avenger of unrighteousness. Now the judgment given is, 1. That since they had walked in the way of the heathen, and done worse than they, God would bring the worst of the heathen upon them to destroy them and lay them waste, the most barbarous and outrageous, that have the least compassion to mankind and the greatest antipathy to the Jews. Note, Of the heathen some are worse than others, and God sometimes picks out the worst to be a scourge to his own people, because he intends them for the fire when the work is done. 2. That since they had filled their houses with goods unjustly gotten, and used their pomp and power for the crushing and oppressing of the weak, God would give their houses to be possessed and all the furniture of them to be enjoyed by strangers, and make the pomp of the strong to cease, so that their great men should not dazzle the eyes of the weak-sighted with their pomp, nor with their might at any time prevail against right, as they had done. 3. That, since they had defiled the holy places with their idolatries, God would defile them with his judgments, since they had set up the images of other gods in the temple, God would remove thence the tokens of the presence of their own God. When the holy places are deserted by their God they will soon be defiled by their enemies. 4. Since they had followed one sin with another, God would pursue them with one judgment upon another: "Destruction comes, utter destruction (Eze 7:25); for there shall come mischief upon mischief to ruin you, and rumour upon rumour to frighten you, like the waves in a storm, one upon the neck of another." Note, Sinners that are marked for ruin shall be prosecuted to it; for God will overcome when he judges. 5. Since they had disappointed God's expectations from them, he would disappoint their expectations from him; for, (1.) They shall not have the deliverance out of their troubles that they expect. They shall seek peace; they shall desire it and pray for it; they shall aim at and expect it: but there shall be none; their attempts both to court their enemies and to conquer them shall be in vain, and their troubles shall grow worse and worse. (2.) They shall not have the direction in the trouble that they expect (Eze 7:26): They shall seek a vision of the prophet, shall desire, for their support under their troubles, to be assured of a happy issue out of them. They did not desire a vision to reprove them for sin, nor to warn them of danger, but to promise them deliverance. Such messages they longed to hear. But the law shall perish from the priest; he shall have no words either of counsel or comfort to say to them. They would not hear what God had to say to them by ways of conviction, and therefore he has nothing to say to them by way of encouragement. Counsel shall perish from the ancients; the elders of the people, that should advise them what to do in this difficult juncture, shall be infatuated and at their wits' end. It is bad with a people when those that should be their counsellors know not how to consider within themselves, consult with one another, or counsel them. 6. Since they had animated and encouraged one another to sin, God would dispirit and dishearten them all, so that they should not be able to make head against the judgments of God that were breaking in upon them. All orders and degrees of men shall lie down by consent under the load (Eze 7:27): The king, that should inspire life into them, and the prince, that should lead them onto attack the enemy, shall mourn and be clothed with desolation; their heads and hearts shall fail, their politics and their courage; and then no wonder if the hands of the people of the land, that should fight for them, be troubled. None of the men of might shall find their hands. What can men contrive or do for themselves when God has departed from them and appears against them? All must needs be in tears, all in trouble, when God comes to judge them according to their deserts, and so make then know, to their cost, that he is the Lord, the God to whom vengeance belongs.

Ezekiel Chapter 8

Ezekiel

God, having given the prophet a clear foresight of the people's miseries that were hastening on, here gives him a clear insight into the people's wickedness, by which God was provoked to bring these miseries upon them, that he might justify God in all his judgments, might the more particularly reprove the sins of the people, and with the more satisfaction foretel their ruin. Here God, in vision, brings him to Jerusalem, to show him the sins that were committed there, though God had begun to contend with them (Eze 8:1-4), and there he sees, I. The image of jealousy set up at the gate of the altar (Eze 8:5, Eze 8:6). II. The elders of Israel worshipping all manner of images in a secret chamber (Eze 8:7-12). III. The women weeping for Tammuz (Eze 8:13, Eze 8:14). IV. The men worshipping the sun (Eze 8:15, Eze 8:16). And then appeals to him whether such a provoking people should have any pity shown them (Eze 8:17, Eze 8:18).

Ezekiel 8:1

Ezekiel was now in Babylon; but the messages of wrath he had delivered in the foregoing chapters related to Jerusalem, for in the peace or trouble thereof the captives looked upon themselves to have peace or trouble, and therefore here he has a vision of what was done at Jerusalem, and this vision is continued to the close of the 11th chapter.

I. Here is the date of this vision. The first vision he had was in the fifth year of the captivity, in the fourth month and the fifth day of the month, Eze 1:1, Eze 1:2. This was just fourteen months after. Perhaps it was after he had lain 390 days on his left side, to bear the iniquity of Israel, and before he began the forty days on his right side, to bear the iniquity of Judah; for now he was sitting in the house, not lying. Note, God keeps a particular account of the messages he sends to us, because he will shortly call us to account about them.

II. The opportunity is taken notice of, as well as the time. 1. The prophet was himself sitting in his house, in a sedate composed frame, deep perhaps in contemplation. Note, The more we retreat from the world, and retire into our own hearts, the better frame we are in for communion with God: those that sit down to consider what they have learned shall be taught more. Or, he sat in his house, ready to preach to the company that resorted to him, but waiting for instructions what to say. God will communicate more knowledge to those who are communicative of what they do know. 2. The elders of Judah, that were now in captivity with him, sat before him. It is probable that it was on the sabbath day, and that it was usual for them to attend on the prophet every sabbath day, both to hear the word from him and to join with him and prayer and praise: and how could they spend the sabbath better, now that they had neither temple nor synagogue, neither priest nor altar? It was a great mercy that they had opportunity to spend it so well, as the good people in Elisha's time, Kg2 4:23. But some think it was on some extraordinary occasion that they attended him, to enquire of the Lord, and sat down at his feet to hear his word. Observe here, (1.) When the law had perished from the priests at Jerusalem, whose lips should keep knowledge (Eze 7:26), those in Babylon had a prophet to consult. God is not tied to places or persons. (2.) Now that the elders of Judah were in captivity they paid more respect to God's prophets, and his word in their mouth, than they did when they lived in peace in their own land. When God brings men into the cords of affliction, then he opens their ears to discipline, Job 36:8, Job 36:10;Psa 141:6. Those that despised vision in the valley of vision prized it now that the word of the Lord precious and there was no open vision. (3.) When our teachers are driven into corners, and are forced to preach in private houses, we must diligently attend them there. A minister's house should be a church for all his neighbours. Paul preached in his own hired house at Rome, and God owned him there, and no man forbad him.

III. The divine influence and impression that the prophet was now under: The hand of the Lord fell there upon me. God's hand took hold of him, and arrested him, as it were, to employ him in this vision, but at the same time supported him to bear it.

IV. The vision that the prophet saw, Eze 8:2. He beheld a likeness, of a man we may suppose, for that was the likeness he saw before, but it was all brightness above the girdle and all fire below, fire and flame. This agrees with the description we had before of the apparition he saw, Eze 1:27. It is probably that it was the same person, the man Christ Jesus. It is probable that the elders that sat with him (as the men that journeyed with Paul) saw a light and were afraid, and this happy sight they gained by attending the prophet in a private meeting, but they had no distinct view of him that spoke to him, Act 22:9.

V. The prophet's remove, in vision, to Jerusalem. The apparition he saw put forth the form of a hand, which took him by a lock of his head, and the Spirit was that hand which was put forth, for the Spirit of God is called the finger of God. Or, The spirit within him lifted him up, so that he was borne up and carried on by an internal principle, not an external violence. A faithful ready servant of God will be drawn by a hair, by the least intimation of the divine will, to his duty; for he has that within him which inclines him to a compliance with it, Psa 27:8. He was miraculously lifted up between heaven and earth, as if he were to fly away upon eagles' wings. This, it is probable (so Grotius thinks), the elders that sat with him saw; they were witnesses of the hand taking him by the lock of hair, and lifting him up, and then perhaps laying him down again in a trance of ecstasy, while he had the following visions, whether in the body or out of the body, we may suppose, he could not tell, any more than Paul in a like case, much less can we. Note, Those are best prepared for communion with God and the communications of divine light that by divine grace are raised up above the earth and the things of it, to be out of their attractive force. But, being lifted up towards heaven, he was carried in vision to Jerusalem, and to God's sanctuary there; for those that would go to heaven must take that in their way. The Spirit represented to his mind the city and temple as plainly as if he had been there in person. O that by faith we could thus enter into the Jerusalem, the holy city, above, and see the things that are invisible!

VI. The discoveries that were made to him there.

1. There he saw the glory of God (Eze 8:4): Behold, the glory of the god of Israel was there, the same appearance of the living creatures, and the wheels, and the throne, that he had seen, ch. 1. Note, God's servants, wherever they are and whithersoever they go, ought to carry about with them a believing regard to the glory of God and to set that always before them; and those that have seen God's power and glory in the sanctuary should desire to see them again, so as they have seen them, Psa 63:2. Ezekiel has this repeated vision of the glory of God both to give credit to and to put honour upon the following discoveries. But it seems to have a further intention here; it was to aggravate this sin of Israel, in changing their own God, the God of Israel (who is a God of so much glory as here he appears to be), for dunghill gods, scandalous gods, false gods, and indeed no gods. Note, The more glorious we see God to be the more odious we shall see sin to be, especially idolatry, which turns his truth into a lie, his glory into shame. It was also to aggravate their approaching misery, when this glory of the Lord should remove from them (Eze 11:23) and leave the house and city desolate.

2. There he saw the reproach of Israel-and that was the image of jealousy, set northward, at the gate of the altar, Eze 8:3, Eze 8:5. What image this was is uncertain, probably an image of Baal, or of the grove, which Manasseh made and set in the temple (Kg2 21:7, Ch2 33:3), which Josiah removed, but his successors, it seems, replace there, as probably they did the chariots of the sun which he found at the entering in of the house of the Lord (Kg2 23:11), and this is here said to be in the entry. But the prophet, instead of telling us what image it was, which might gratify our curiosity, tells us that it was the image of jealousy, to convince our consciences that, whatever image it was, it was in the highest degree offensive to God and provoked him to jealousy. he resented it as a husband would resent the whoredoms of his wife, and would certainly revenge it; for God is jealous, and the Lord revenges, Nah 1:2.

(1.) The very setting up of this image in the house of the Lord was enough to provoke him to jealousy; for it is in the matters of his worship that we are particularly told, I the Lord thy God am a jealous God. Those that placed this image at the door of the inner gate, where the people assembled, called the gate of the altar (Eze 8:5), thereby plainly intended, [1.] To affront God, to provoke him to his face, by advancing an idol to be a rival with him for the adoration of his people, in contempt of his law and in defiance of his justice. [2.] To debauch the people, and pick them up as they were entering into the courts of the Lord's house to bring their offerings to him, and to tempt them to offer them to this image; like the adulteress Solomon describes, that sits at the door of her house, to call passengers who go right on their ways, Whoso is simple, let him turn in hither, Pro 9:14-16. With good reason therefore is this called the image of jealousy.

(2.) We may well imagine what a surprise and what a grief it was to Ezekiel to see this image in the house of God, when he was in hopes that the judgments they were under had, by this time, wrought some reformation among them; but there is more wickedness in the world, in the church, than good men think there is. And now, [1.] God appeals to him whether this was not bad enough, and a sufficient ground for God to go upon in casting off this people and abandoning them to ruin. Could he, or any one else, expect any other than that God should go far from his sanctuary, when there were such abominations committed there, in that very place; nay, was he not perfectly driven thence? They did these things designedly, and on purpose that he should leave his sanctuary, and so shall their doom be; they have hereby, in effect, like the Gadarenes, desired him to depart out of their coasts, and therefore he will depart; he will no more dignify and protect his sanctuary, as he has done, but will give it up to reproach and ruin. But, [2.] Though this is bad enough, and serves abundantly to justify God in all that he brings upon them, yet the matter will appear to be much worse: But turn thyself yet again, and thou wilt be amazed to see greater abominations than these. Where there is one abomination it will be found that there are many more. Sins do not go alone.

Ezekiel 8:7

We have here a further discovery of the abominations that were committed at Jerusalem, and within the confines of the temple, too. Now observe,

I. How this discovery is made. God, in vision, brought Ezekiel to the door of the court, the outer court, along the sides of which the priests' lodgings were. God could have introduced him at first into the chambers of imagery, but he brings him to them by degrees, partly to employ his own industry in searching out these mysteries of iniquity, and partly to make him sensible with what care and caution those idolaters concealed their idolatries. Before the priests' apartments they had run up a wall, to make them the more private, that they might not lie open to the observation of those who passed by-a shrews sign that they did something which they had reason to be ashamed of. He that doth evil hates the light. They were not willing that those who saw them in God's house should see them in their own, lest they should see them contradict themselves and undo in private what they did in public. But, behold, a hole in the wall, (Eze 8:7), a spy-hole, by which you might see that which would give cause to suspect them. When hypocrites screen themselves behind the wall of an external profession, and with it think to conceal their wickedness from the eye of the world and carry on their designs the more successfully, it is hard for them to manage it with so much art by that there is some hole or other left in the wall, something that betrays them, to those who look diligently, not to be what they pretend to be. The ass's ears in the fable appeared from under the lion's skin. This hole in the wall Ezekiel made wider, and behold a door, v. 8. This door he goes in by into the treasury, or some of the apartments of the priests, and sees the wicked abominations that they do there, v. 9. Note, Those that would discover the mystery of iniquity in others, or in themselves, must accomplish a diligent search; for Satan has his wiles, and depths, and devices, which we should not be ignorant of, and the heart is deceitful above all things; in the examining of it therefore we are concerned to be very strict.

II. What the discovery is. It is a very melancholy one. 1. He sees a chamber set round with idolatrous pictures (Eze 8:10): All the idols of the house of Israel, which they had borrowed from the neighbouring nations, were portrayed upon the wall round about, even the vilest of them, the forms of creeping things, which they worshipped, and beasts, even abominable ones, which are poisonous and venomous; at least they were abominable when they were worshipped. This was a sort of panthenon, a collection of all the idols together which they paid their devotions to. Though the second commandment, in the letter of it, forbids only graven images, yet painted ones are as bad and as dangerous. 2. He sees this chamber filled with idolatrous worshippers (Eze 8:11): There were seventy men of the elders of Israel offering incense to these painted idols. here was a great number of idolaters strengthening one another's hands in this wickedness; though it was in a private chamber, and the meeting industriously concealed, yet here were seventy men engaged in it. I doubt these elders were many more than those in Babylon that sat before the prophet in his house, Eze 8:1. They were seventy men, the number of the great Sanhedrim, or chief council of the nation, and, we have reason to fear, the same men; for they were the ancients of the house of Israel, not only in age, but in office, who were bound, by the duty of their place, to restrain and punish idolatry and to destroy and abolish all superstitious images wherever they found them; yet these were those that did themselves worship them in private, so undermining that religion which in public they professed to own and promote only because by it they held their preferments. They had every man his censer in his hand; so fond were they of the idolatrous service that they would all be their own priests, and very prodigal they were of their perfumes in honour of these images, for a thick cloud of incense went up, that filled the room. O that the zeal of these idolaters might shame the worshippers of the true God out of their indifference to his service! The prophet took particular notice of one whom he knew, who stood in the midst of these idolaters, as chief among them, being perhaps president of the great council at this time or most forward in this wickedness. No wonder the people were corrupt when the elders were so. The sins of leaders are leading sins.

III. What the remark is that made upon it (Eze 8:12): "Son of man, hast thou seen this? Couldst thou have imagined that there was such wickedness committed?" It is here observed concerning it, 1. That it was done in the dark; for sinful works are works of darkness. They concealed it, lest they should lose their places, or at least their credit. There is a great deal of secret wickedness in the world, which the day will declare, the day of the revelation of the righteous judgment of God. 2. That this one idolatrous chapel was but a specimen of many the like. Here they met together, to worship their images in concert, but, it should seem, they had every man the chamber of his imagery besides, a room in his own house for this purpose, in which every man gratified his own fancy with such pictures as he liked best. Idolaters had their household gods, and their family worship of them in private, which is a shame to those who call themselves Christians and yet have no church in their house, no worship of God in their family. Had they chambers of imagery, and shall not we have chambers of devotion? 3. That atheism was at the bottom of their idolatry. They worship images in the dark, the images of the gods of other nations, and they say, "Jehovah, the God of Israel, whom we should serve, seeth us not. Jehovah hath forsaken the earth, and we may worship what God we will; he regards us not." (1.) They think themselves out of God's sight: They say, The Lord seeth us not. They imagined, because the matter was carried on so closely that men could not discover it, nor did any of their neighbours suspect them to be idolaters, that therefore it was hidden from the eye of God; as if there were any darkness, or shadow of death, where the workers of iniquity may hide themselves. Note, A practical disbelief of God's omniscience is at the bottom of our treacherous departures from him; but the church argues justly, as to this very sin of idolatry (Psa 44:20, Psa 44:21), If we have forgotten the name of our God, and stretched forth our hand to a strange god, will not God search this out? No doubt he will. (2.) They think themselves out of God's care: "The Lord has forsaken the earth, and looks not after the affairs of it; and then we may as well worship any other god as him." Or, "He has forsaken our land, and left it to be a prey to its enemies; and therefore it is time for us to look out for some other god, to whom to commit the protection of it. Our one God cannot, or will not, deliver us; and therefore let us have many." This was a blasphemous reflection upon God, as if he had forsaken them first, else they would not have forsaken him. Note, Those are ripe indeed for ruin who have arrived at such a pitch of impudence as to lay the blame of their sins upon God himself.

Ezekiel 8:13

Here we have,

I. More and greater abominations discovered to the prophet. He thought that what he had seen was bad enough and yet (Eze 8:13): Turn thyself again, and thou shalt see yet greater abominations, and greater still, Eze 8:15, as before,Eze 8:6. There are those who live in retirement who do no think what wickedness there is in this world; and the more we converse with it, and the further we go abroad into it, the more corrupt we see it. When we have seen that which is bad we may have our wonder at it made to cease by the discovery of that which, upon some account or other, is a great deal worse. We shall find it so in examining our own hearts and searching into them; there is a world of iniquity in them, a great abundance and variety of abominations, and, when we have found out much amiss, still we shall find more; for the heart is desperately wicked, who can know it perfectly? Now the abominations here discovered were, 1. Women weeping for Tammuz, Eze 8:14. An abominable thing indeed, that any should choose rather to serve an idol in tears than to serve the true God with joyfulness and gladness of heart! Yet such absurdities as these are those guilty of who follow after lying vanities and forsake their own mercies. Some think it was for Adonis, an idol among the Greeks, other for Osiris, an idol of the Egyptians, that they shed these tears. The image, they say, was made to weep, and then the worshippers wept with it. They bewailed the death of this Tammuz, and anon rejoiced in its returning to life again. These mourning women sat at the door of the gate of the Lord's house, and there shed their idolatrous tears, as it were in defiance of God and the sacred rites of his worship, and some think, with their idolatry, prostrating themselves also to corporeal whoredom; for these two commonly went together, and those that dishonoured the divine nature by the one were justly given up to vile affections and a reprobate sense to dishonour the human nature, which nowhere ever sunk so far below itself as in these idolatrous rites. 2. Men worshipping the sun, Eze 8:16. And this was so much the greater an abomination that it was practised in the inner court of the Lord's house at the door of the temple of the lord, between the porch and the altar. There, where the most sacred rites of their holy religion used to be performed, was this abominable wickedness committed. Justly might God in jealousy say to those who thus affronted him at his own door, as the king to Haman, Will he force the queen also before me in the house? Here were about twenty-five men giving that honour to the sun which is due to God only. Some think they were the king and his princes; it should rather seem that they were priests, for this was the court of the priests, and the proper place to find them in. Those that were entrusted with the true religion, had it committed to their care and were charged with the custody of it, they were the men that betrayed it. (1.) They turned their backs towards the temple of the Lord, resolvedly forgetting it and designedly slighting it and putting contempt upon it. Note, When men turn their backs upon God's institutions, and despise them, it is no marvel if they wander endlessly after their own inventions. Impiety is the beginning of idolatry and all iniquity. (2.) They turned their faces towards the east, and worshipped the sun, the rising sun. This was an ancient instance of idolatry; it is mentioned in Job's time (Job 31:26), and had been generally practised among the nations, some worshipping the sun under one name, others under another. These priests, finding it had antiquity and general consent and usage on its side (the two pleas which the papists use at this day in defence of their superstitious rites, and particularly this of worshipping towards the east), practised it in the court of the temple, thinking it an omission that it was not inserted in their ritual. See the folly of idolaters in worshipping that as a god, and calling it Baal-a lord, which God made to be a servant to the universe (for such the sun is, and so his name Shemesh signified, Deu 4:19), and in adoring the borrowed light and despising the Father of lights.

II. The inference drawn from these discoveries (Eze 8:17): "Hast thou seen this, O son of man! and couldst thou have thought ever to see such things done in the temple of the Lord?" Now, 1. he appeals to the prophet himself concerning the heinousness of the crime. Can he think it is a light thing to the house of Judah, who know and profess better things, and are dignified with so many privileges above other nations? Is it an excusable thing in those that have God's oracles and ordinances that they commit the abominations which they commit here? Do not those deserve to suffer that thus sin? Should not such abominations as these make desolate? Dan 9:27. 2. He aggravates it from the fraud and oppression that were to be found in all parts of the nations: They have filled the land with violence. It is not strange if those that wrong God thus make no conscience of wronging one another, and with all that is sacred trample likewise upon all that is just. And their wickedness in their conversations made even the worship they paid to their own God an abomination (Isa 1:11, etc.): "They fill the land with violence, and then they return to the temple to provoke me to anger there; for even their sacrifices, instead of making an atonement, do but add to their guilt. They return to provoke me (they repeat the provocation, do it, and do it again), and, lo, they put the branch to their nose"-a proverbial expression denoting perhaps their scoffing at God and having him in derision; they snuffed at his service, as men do when they put a branch to their nose. Or it was some custom used by idolaters in honour of the idols they served. We read of garlands used in their idolatrous worships (Act 14:13), out of which every zealot took a branch which they smelled to as a nosegay. Dr. Lightfoot (Hor. Heb. in John 15.6) gives another sense of this place: They put the branch to their wrath, or to his wrath, as the Masorites read it; that is, they are still bringing more fuel (such as the withered branches of the vine) to the fire of divine wrath, which they have already kindled, as if that wrath did not burn hot enough already. Or putting the branch to the nose may signify the giving of a very great affront and provocation either to God or man; they are an abusive generation of men. 3. he passes sentence upon them that they shall be utterly cut off: Therefore, because they are thus furiously bent upon sin, I will also deal in fury with them, Eze 8:18. They filled the land with their violence, and God will fill it with the violence of their enemies; and he will not lend a favourable ear to the suggestions either, (1.) Of his own pity: My eye shall not spare, neither will I have pity; repentance shall be hidden from his eyes; or, (2.) Of their prayers: Though they cry in my ears with a loud voice, yet will I not hear them; for still their sins cry more loudly for vengeance than their prayers cry for mercy. God will now be as deaf to their prayers as their own idols were, on whom they cried aloud, but in vain, Kg1 18:26. Time was when God was ready to hear even before they cried and to answer while they were yet speaking; but now they shall seek me early and not find me, Pro 1:28. It is not the loud voice, but the upright heart, that God will regard.

Ezekiel Chapter 9

The prophet had, in vision, seen the wickedness that was committed at Jerusalem, in the foregoing chapter, and we may be sure that it was not represented to him worse than really it was; now here follows, of course, a representation of their ruin approaching; for when sin goes before judgments come next. Here is, I. Preparation made of instruments that were to be employed in the destruction of the city (Eze 9:1, Eze 9:2). II. The removal of the Shechinah from the cherubim to the threshold of the temple (Eze 9:3). III. Orders given to one of the persons employed, who is distinguished from the rest, for the marking of a remnant to be preserved from the common destruction (Eze 9:3, Eze 9:4). IV. The warrant signed for the execution of those that were not marked, and the execution begun accordingly (Eze 9:5-7). V. The prophet's intercession for the mitigation of the sentence, and a denial of any mitigation, the decree having now gone forth (Eze 9:8-10). VI. The report made by him that was to mark the pious remnant of what he had done in that matter (Eze 9:11). And this shows a usual method of Providence in the government of the world.

Ezekiel 9:1

In these verses we have,

I. The summons given to Jerusalem's destroyers to come forth and give their attendance. He that appeared to the prophet (Eze 8:2), that had brought him to Jerusalem and had shown the wickedness that was done there, he cried, Cause those that have charge over the city to draw near (Eze 9:1), or, as it might better be read, and nearer the original, Those that have charge over the city are drawing near. He had said (Eze 8:18), I will deal in fury; now, says he to the prophet, thou shalt see who are to be employed as the instruments of my wrath. Appropinquaverunt visitationes civitatis-The visitations (or visitors) of the city are at hand. They would not know the day of their visitations in mercy, and now they are to be visited in wrath. Observe, 1. how the notice of this is given to the prophet: He cried it in my ears with a loud voice, which intimates the vehemency of him that spoke; when men are highly provoked, and threaten in anger, they speak aloud. Those that regard not the counsels God gives them in a still small voice shall be made to hear the threatenings, to hear and tremble. It denotes also the prophet's unwillingness to be told this: he was deaf on that ear, but there is no remedy, their sin will not admit an excuse and therefore their judgment will not admit a delay: "He cried it in my ears with a loud voice; he made me hear it, and I heard it with a sad heart." 2. What this notice is. There are those that have charge over the city to destroy it, not the Chaldean armies, they are to be indeed employed in this work, but they are not the visitors, they are only the servants, or tools rather. God's angels have received a charge now to lay that city waste, which they had long had a charge to protect and watch over. They are at hand, as destroying angels, as ministers of wrath, for every man has his destroying weapon in his hand, as the angel that kept the way of the tree of life with a flaming sword. Note, Those that have by sin made God their enemy have made the good angels their enemies too. These visitors are called and caused to draw near. Note, God has ministers of wrath always within call, always at command, invisible powers, by whom he accomplishes is purposes. The prophet is made to see this in vision, that he might with the greater assurance in his preaching denounce these judgments. God told it him with a loud voice, taught it him with a strong hand (Isa 8:11), that it might make the deeper impression upon him and that he might thus proclaim it in the people's ears.

II. Their appearance, upon this summons, is recorded. Immediately six men came (Eze 9:2), one for each of the principal gates of Jerusalem. Two destroying angels were sent against Sodom, but six against Jerusalem; for Jerusalem's doom in the judgment will be thrice as heavy as that of Sodom. There is an angel watching at every gate to destroy, to bring in judgments from every quarter, and to take heed that none escape. One angel served to destroy the first-born of Egypt, and the camp of the Assyrians, but here are six. In the Revelation we find seven that were to pour out the vials of God's wrath, Rev 16:1. They came with every one a slaughter-weapon in his hand, prepared for the work to which they were called. The nations of which the king of Babylon's army was composed, which some reckon to be six, and the commanders of his army (of whom six are named as principal, Jer 39:3), may be called the slaughter-weapons in the hands of the angels. The angels are thoroughly furnished for every service. 1. Observe whence they came-from the way of the higher gate, which lies towards the north (Eze 9:2), either because the Chaldeans came from the north (Jer 1:14, Out of the north an evil shall break forth) or because the image of jealousy was set up at the door of the inner gate that looks towards the north, Eze 8:3, Eze 8:5. At that gate of the temple the destroying angels entered, to show what it was that opened the door to them. Note, That way that sin lies judgments may be expected to come. 2. Observe where they placed themselves: They went in and stood beside the brazen altar, on which sacrifices were wont to be offered and atonement made. When they acted as destroyers they acted as sacrificers, not from any personal revenge or ill-will, but with a pure and sincere regard to the glory of God; for to his justice all they slew were offered up as victims. They stood by the altar, as it were to protect and vindicate that, and plead its righteous cause, and avenge the horrid profanation of it. At the altar they were to receive their commission to destroy, to intimate that the iniquity of Jerusalem, like that of Eli's house, was not to be purged by sacrifice.

III. The notice taken of one among the destroying angels distinguished in his habit from the rest, from whom some favour might be expected; it should seem he was not one of the six, but among them, to see that mercy was mixed with judgment, Eze 9:2. This man was clothed with linen, as the priests were, and he had a writer's inkhorn hanging at his side, as anciently attorneys and lawyers' clerks had, which he was to make use of, as the other six were to make use of their destroying weapons. Here the honours of the pen exceeded those of the sword, but he was the

Lord of angels that made use of the writer's inkhorn; for it is generally agreed, among the best interpreters, that this man represented Christ as Mediator saving those that are his from the flaming sword of divine justice. He is our high priest, clothed with holiness, for that was signified by the fine linen, Rev 19:8. As prophet he wears the writer's inkhorn. The book of life is the Lamb's book. The great things of the law and gospel which God has written to us are of his writing; for it is the Spirit of Christ, in the writers of the scripture, that testifies to us, and the Bible is the revelation of Jesus Christ. Note, It is a matter of great comfort to all good Christians that, in the midst of the destroyers and the destructions that are abroad, there is a Mediator, a great high priest, who has an interest in heaven, and whom saints on earth have an interest in.

IV. The removal of the appearance of the divine glory from over the cherubim. Some think this was that usual display of the divine glory which was between the cherubim over the mercy seat, in the most holy place, that took leave of them now, and never returned; for it is supposed that it was not in the second temple. Others think it was that display of the divine glory which the prophet now saw over the cherubim in vision; and this is more probable, because this is called the glory of the God of Israel (Rev 8:4), and this is it which he had now his eye upon; this was gone to the threshold of the house, as it were to call to the servants that attended without the door, to send them on their errand and give them their instructions. And the removal of this, as well as the former, might be significant of God's departure from them, and leaving them their house desolate; and when God goes all good goes, but he goes from none till they first drive him from them. He went at first no further than the threshold, that he might show how loth he was to depart, and might give them both time and encouragement to invite his return to them and his stay with them. Note, God's departures from a people are gradual, but gracious souls are soon award of the first step he takes towards a remove. Ezekiel immediately observed that the glory of the god of Israel had gone up from the cherub: and what is a vision of angels if God be gone?

V. The charge given to the man clothed in linen to secure the pious remnant from the general desolation. We do not read that this Saviour was summoned and sent for, as the destroyers were; for he is always ready, appearing in the presence of God for us; and to him, as the most proper person, the care of those that are marked for salvation is committed, Eze 9:4. Now observe, 1. The distinguishing character of this remnant that is to be saved. They are such as sigh and cry, sigh in themselves, as men in pain and distress, cry to God in prayer, as men in earnest, because of all the abominations that are committed in Jerusalem. It was not only the idolatries they were guilty of, but all their other enormities, that were abominations to God. These pious few had witnessed against those abominations and had done what they could in their places to suppress them; but, finding all their attempts for the reformation of manners fruitless, they sat down, and sighted, and cried, wept in secret, and complained to God, because of the dishonour done to his name by their wickedness and the ruin it was bringing upon their church and nation. Note, It is not enough that we do not delight in the sins of others, and that we have not fellowship with them, but we must mourn for them, and lay them to heart; we must grieve for that which we cannot help, as those that hate sin for its own sake, and have a tender concern for the souls of others, as David (Psa 119:136), and Lot, who vexed his righteous soul with the wicked conversation of his neighbours. The abominations committed in Jerusalem are to be in a special manner lamented, because they are in a particular manner offensive to God. 2. The distinguishing care taken of them. Orders are given to find those all out that are of such a pious public spirit: "Go through the midst of the city in quest of them, and though they are ever so much dispersed, and ever so closely hid from the fury of their persecutors, yet see that you discover them, and set a mark upon their foreheads," (1.) To signify that God owns them for his, and he will confess them another day. A work of grace in the soul is to God a mark upon the forehead, which he will acknowledge as his mark, and by which he knows those that are his. (2.) To give to them who are thus marked an assurance of God's favour, that they may know it themselves; and the comfort of knowing it will be the most powerful support and cordial in calamitous times. Why should we perplex ourselves about this temporal life if we know by the mark that we have eternal life? (3.) To be a direction to the destroyers whom to pass by, as the blood upon the door-posts was an indication that that was an Israelite's house, and the first-born there must not be slain. Note, Those who keep themselves pure in times of common iniquity God will keep safe in times of common calamity. Those that distinguish themselves shall be distinguished; those that cry for other men's sins shall not need to cry for their own afflictions, for they shall be either delivered from them or comforted under them. God will set a mark upon his mourners, will book their sighs and bottle their tears. The sealing of the servants of God in their foreheads mentioned in Rev 7:3 was the same token of the care God has of his own people with this related here; only this was to secure them from being destroyed, that from being seduced, which is equivalent.

Ezekiel 9:5

In these verses we have,

I. A command given to the destroyers to do execution according to their commission. They stood by the brazen altar, waiting for orders; and orders are here given them to cut off and destroy all that were either guilty of, or accessory to, the abominations of Jerusalem, and that did not sigh and cry for them. Note, When God has gathered his wheat into his garner nothing remains but to burn up the chaff, Mat 3:12.

1. They are ordered to destroy all, (1.) Without exception. They must go through the city, and smite; they must slay utterly, slay to destruction, give them their death's wound. They must make no distinction of age or sex, but cut off old and young; neither the beauty of the virgins, nor the innocency of the babes, shall secure them. This was fulfilled in the death of multitudes by famine and pestilence, especially by the sword of the Chaldeans, as far as the military execution went. Sometimes even such bloody work as this has been God's work. But what an evil thing is sin, then, which provokes the God of infinite mercy to such severity! (2.) Without compassion: "Let not your eye spare, neither have you pity (Eze 9:5); you must not save any whom God has

doomed to destruction, as Saul did Agag and the Amalekites, for that is doing the work of God deceitfully, Jer 48:10. None need to be more merciful than God is; and he had said (Eze 8:18), My eye shall not spare, neither will I have pity." Note, Those that live in sin, and hate to be reformed, will perish in sin, and deserve not to be pitied; for they might easily have prevented the ruin, and would not.

2. They are warned not to do the least hurt to those that were marked for salvation: "Come not near any man upon whom is the mark; do not so much as threaten or frighten any of them; it is promised them that there shall no evil come nigh them, and therefore you must keep at a distance from them." The king of Babylon gave particular orders that Jeremiah should be protected. Baruch and Ebed-melech were secured, and, it is likely, others of Jeremiah's friends, for his sake. God had promised that it should go well with his remnant and they should be well treated (Jer 15:11); and we have reason to think that none of the mourning praying remnant fell by the sword of the Chaldeans, but that God found out some way or other to secure them all, as, in the last destruction of Jerusalem by the Romans, the Christians were all secured in a city called Pella, and none of them perished with the unbelieving Jews. Note, None of those shall be lost whom God has marked for life and salvation; for the foundation of God stands sure.

3. They are directed to begin at the sanctuary (Eze 9:6), that sanctuary which, in the chapter before, he had seen the horrid profanation of; they must begin there because there the wickedness began which provoked God to send these judgments. The debaucheries of the priests were the poisoning of the springs, to which all the corruption of the streams was owing. The wickedness of the sanctuary was of all wickedness the most offensive to God, and therefore there the slaughter must begin: "Begin there, to try if the people will take warning by the judgments of God upon their priests, and will repent and reform; begin there, that all the world may see and know that the Lord, whose name is Jealous, is a jealous God, and hates sin most in those that are nearest to him." Note, When judgements are abroad they commonly begin at the house of God, Pe1 4:17. You only have I known, and therefore I will punish you, Amo 3:2. God's temple is a sanctuary, a refuge and protection for penitent sinners, but not for any that go on still in their trespasses; neither the sacredness of the place nor the eminency of their place in it will be their security. It should seem the destroyers made some difficulty of putting men to death in the temple, but God bids them not to hesitate at that, but (Eze 9:7), Defile the house, and fill the courts with slain. They will not be taken from the altar (as was appointed by the law, Exo 21:14), but think to secure themselves by keeping hold of the horns of it, like Joab, and therefore, like him, let them die there, Kg1 2:30, Kg1 2:31. There the blood of one of God's prophets had been shed (Mat 23:35) and therefore let their blood be shed. Note, If the servants of God's house defile it with their idolatries, God will justly suffer the enemies of it to defile it with their violences, Psa 79:1. But these acts of necessary justice were really, whatever they were ceremonially, rather a purification than a pollution of the sanctuary; it was putting away evil from among them. 4. They are appointed to go forth into the city, Eze 9:6, Eze 9:7. Note, Wherever sin has gone before judgement will follow after; and, though judgement begins at the house of God, yet it shall not

end there. The holy city shall be no more a protection to the wicked people then the holy house was to the wicked priests.

II. Here is execution done accordingly. They observed their orders, and, 1. They began at the elders, the ancient men that were before the house, and slew them first, either those seventy ancients who worshipped idols in their chambers (Eze 8:12) or those twenty-five who worshipped the sun between the porch and the altar, who might more properly be said to be before the house. Note, Ringleaders in sin may expect to be first met with by the judgements of God; and the sins of those who are in the most eminent and public stations call for the most exemplary punishments. 2. They proceeded to the common people: They went forth and slew in the city; for, when the decree has gone forth, there shall be no delay; if God begin, he will make an end.

III. Here is the prophet's intercession for a mitigation of the judgement, and a reprieve for some (Eze 9:8): While they were slaying them, and I was left, I fell upon my face. Observe here, 1. How sensible the prophet was of God's mercy to him, in that he was spared when so many round about him were cut off. Thousands fell on his right hand, and on his left, and yet the destruction did not come nigh him; only with his eyes did he behold the just reward of the wicked,Psa 91:7, Psa 91:8. He speaks as one that narrowly escaped the destruction, attributing it to God's goodness, not his own deserts. Note, The best saints must acknowledge themselves indebted to sparing mercy that they are not consumed. And when desolating judgements are abroad, and multitudes fall by them, it ought to be accounted a great favor if we have our lives given us for a prey; for we might justly have perished with those that perished. 2. Observe how he improved this mercy; he looked upon it that therefore he was left that he might stand in the gap to turn away the wrath of God. Note, We must look upon it that for this reason we are spared, that we may do good in our places, may do good by our prayers. Ezekiel did not triumph in the slaughter he made, but his flesh trembled for the fear of God, (as David's, Psa 119:120); he fell on his face, and cried, not in fear for himself (he was one of those that were marked), but in compassion to his fellow-creatures. Those that sigh and cry for the sins of sinners cannot but sigh and cry for their miseries too; yet the day is coming when all this concern will be entirely swallowed up in a full satisfaction in this, that God is glorified; and those that now fall on their faces, and cry, Ah! Lord God, will lift up their heads, and sing, Hallelujah, Rev 19:1, Rev 19:3. The prophet humbly expostulates with God: "Wilt thou destroy all the residue of Israel, and shall there be none left but the few that are marked? Shall the Israel of God be destroyed, utterly destroyed? When there are but a few left shall those be cut off, who might have been the seed of another generation? And will the God of Israel be himself their destroyer? Wilt thou now destroy Israel, who wast wont to protect and deliver Israel? Wilt thou so pour out thy fury upon Jerusalem as by the total destruction of the city to ruin the whole country too? Surely thou wilt not!" Note, Though we acknowledge that God is righteous, yet we have leave to plead with him concerning his judgements, Jer 12:1.

IV. Here is God's denial of the prophet's request for a mitigation of the judgement and his justification of himself in that denial, Eze 9:9, Eze 9:10. 1. Nothing could be said in extenuation of this sin. God was willing to show mercy as the prophet could desire; he always is so. But here the case will not admit of it; it is such that mercy cannot be granted without wrong to justice; and it is not fit that one attribute of God should be glorified at the expense of another. Is it any pleasure to the Almighty that he should destroy, especially that he should destroy Israel? By no means. But the truth is their crimes are so flagrant that the reprieve of the sinners would be a connivance at the sin: "The iniquity of the house of Judah and Israel is exceedingly great; there is no suffering them to go on at this rate. The land is filled with the innocent blood, and, when the city courts are appealed to for the defence of injured innocency, the remedy is as bad as the disease, for the city is full of perverseness, or wrestling of judgement; and that which they support themselves with in this iniquity is the same atheistical profane principle with which they flattered themselves in their idolatry, Eze 8:12. The Lord has forsaken the earth, and left it to us to do what we will in it; he will not intermeddle in the affairs of it; and, whatever wrong we do, he sees not; he either knows it not, or will not take cognizance of it." Now how can those expect benefit by the mercy of God who thus bid defiance to his justice? No; nothing can be offered by an advocate in excuse of the crimes while the criminal puts in such a plea as this in his own vindication; and therefore. 2. Nothing can be done to mitigate the sentence (Eze 9:10): "Whatever thou thinkest of it, as for me, my eye shall not spare, neither will I have pity; I have borne with them as long as it was fit that such impudent sinners should be borne with; and therefore now I will recompense their way on their head." Note, Sinners sink and perish under the weight of their own sins; it is their own way, which they deliberately chose rather than the way of God, and which they obstinately persisted in, in contempt of the word of God, that is recompensed on them. Great iniquities justify God in great severities; nay, he is ready to justify himself, as he does here to the prophet, for he will be clear when he judges.

V. Here is a return made of the writ of protection which was issued out for the securing of those that mourned in Zion (Eze 9:11): The man clothed with linen reported the matter, gave an account of what he had done in pursuance of his commission; he had found out all that mourned in secret for the sins of the land, and cried out against them by a public testimony, and had marked them all in the forehead. Lord, I have done as thou hast commanded me. We do not find that those who were commissioned to destroy reported what destruction they had made, but he who was appointed to protect reported his matter; for it would be more pleasing both to God and to the prophet to hear of those that were saved than of those that perished. Or this report was made now because the thing was finished, whereas the destroying work would be a work of time, and when it was brought to an end then the report should be made. See how faithful Christ is to the trust reposed in him. Is he commanded to secure eternal life to the chosen remnant? He has done as was commanded him. Of all that thou hast given me I have lost none.

Ezekiel Chapter 10

The prophet had observed to us (Eze 8:4) that when he was in vision at Jerusalem he saw the same appearance of the glory of God there that he had seen by the river Chebar; now, in this chapter, he gives us some account of the appearance there, as far as was requisite for the clearing up of two further indications of the approaching destruction of Jerusalem, which God here gave the prophet:-I. The scattering of the coals of fire upon the city, which were taken from between the cherubim (Eze 10:1-7). II. The removal of the glory of God from the temple, and its being upon the wing to be gone (Eze 10:8-22). When God goes out from a people all judgments break in upon them.

Ezekiel 10:1

To inspire us with a holy awe and dread of God, and to fill us with his fear, we may observe, in this part of the vision which the prophet had,

I. The glorious appearance of his majesty. Something of the invisible world is here in the visible, some faint representations of its brightness and beauty, some shadows, but such as are no more to be compared with the truth and substance than a picture with the life; yet here is enough to oblige us all to the utmost reverence in our thoughts of God and approaches to him, if we will but admit the impressions this discovery of him will make. 1. He is here in the firmament above the head of the cherubim, Eze 10:1. He manifests his glory in the upper world, where purity and brightness are both in perfection; and the vast expanse of the firmament aims to speak the God that dwells there infinite. It is the firmament of his power and of his prospect too; for thence he beholds all the children of men. The divine nature infinitely transcends the angelic nature, and God is above the head of the cherubim, in respect not only of his dignity above them, but of his dominion over them. Cherubim have great power, and wisdom, and influence, but they are all subject to God and Christ. 2. He is here upon the throne, or that which had the appearance of the likeness of a throne (for God's glory and government infinitely transcend all the brightest ideas our minds can either form or receive concerning them); and it was as it were a sapphire-stone, pure and sparkling; such a throne has God prepared in the heavens, far exceeding the thrones of any earthly potentates. 3. He is here attended with a glorious train of holy angels. When God came into his temple the cherubim stood on the right side of the house (Eze 10:3), as the prince's life-guard, attending the gate of his palace. Christ has angels at command. The orders given to all the angels of God are, to worship him. Some observe that they stood on the right side of the house, that is, the south side, because on the north side the image of jealousy was, and other instances of idolatry, from which they would place themselves at as great a distance as might be.

4. The appearance of his glory is veiled with a cloud, and yet out of that cloud darts forth a dazzling lustre; in the house and inner court there was a cloud and darkness, which filled them, and yet either the outer court, or the same court after some time, was full of the brightness of the Lord's glory, Eze 10:3, Eze 10:4. There was a darting forth of light and brightness; but if any over curious eye pried into it, it would find itself lost in a cloud. His righteousness is conspicuous as the great mountains, and the brightness of it fills the court; but his judgements are a great deep, which we cannot fathom, a cloud which we cannot see through. The brightness discovers enough to awe and direct our consciences, but the cloud forbids us to expect the gratifying of our curiosity; for we cannot order our speech by reasons of darkness. Thus (Hab 3:4) he had rays coming out of his hand, and yet there was the hiding of his power. Nothing is more clear than that God is, nothing more dark than what he is. God covers himself with light, and yet, as to us, makes darkness his pavilion. God took possession of the tabernacle and the temple in a cloud, which was always the symbol of his presence. In the temple above there will be no cloud, but we shall see face to face. 5. The cherubim, made a dreadful sound with their wings, Eze 10:5. The vibration of them, as of the strings of musical instruments, made a curious melody; bees, and other winged insects, make a noise with their wings. Probably this intimated their preparing to remove, by stretching forth and lifting up their wings, which made this noise as it were to give warning of it. This noise is said to be as the voice of the almighty God when he speaks, as the thunder, which is called the voice of the Lord (Psa 29:3), or as the voice of the Lord when he spoke to Israel on Mount Sinai; and therefore he then gave the law with abundance of terror, to signify with what terror he would reckon for the violation of it, which he was now about to do. This noise of their wings was heard even to the outer court, the court of the people; for the Lord's voice, in his judgements, cries in the city, which those may hear that do not, as Ezekiel, see the visions of them.

II. The terrible directions of his wrath. This vision has a further tendency than merely to set forth the divine grandeur; further orders are to be given for the destruction of Jerusalem. The greatest devastations are made by fire and sword. For a general slaughter of the inhabitants of Jerusalem orders were given in the foregoing chapter; now here we have a command to lay the city in ashes, by scattering coals of fire upon it, which in the vision were fetched from between the cherubim.

1. For the issuing out of orders to do this the glory of the Lord was lifted up from the cherub (as in the chapter before for the giving of orders there, Eze 10:3) and stood upon the threshold of the house, in imitation of the courts of judgement, which they kept in the gates of their cities. The people would not hear the oracles which God had delivered to them from his holy temple, and therefore they shall thence be made to hear their doom.

2. The man clothed in linen who had marked those that were to be preserved is to be employed in this service; for the same Jesus that is the protector and Saviour of those that believe, having all judgement committed to him, that of condemnation as well as that of absolution, will come in

a flaming fire to take vengeance on those that obey not his gospel. He that sits on the throne calls to the man clothed in linen to go in between the wheels, and fill his hand with coals of fire from between the cherubim, and scatter them over the city. This intimates, (1.) That the burning of the city and temple by the Chaldeans was a consumption determined, and that therein they executed God's counsel, did what he designed before should be done. (2.) That the fire of divine wrath, which kindles judgement upon a people, is just and holy, for it is fire fetched from between the cherubim. The fire on God's altar, where atonement was made, had been slighted, to avenge which fire is here fetched from heaven, like that by which Nadab and Abihu were killed for offering strange fire. If a city, or town, or house, be burnt, whether by design or accident, if we trace it in its original, we shall find that the coals which kindled the fire came from between the wheels; for there is not any evil of that kind in the city, but the Lord has done it. (3.) That Jesus Christ acts by commission from the Father, for from him he receives authority to execute judgement, because he is the Son of man. Christ came to send fire on the earth (Luk 12:49) and in the great day will speak this world into ashes. By fire from his hand, the earth, and all the works that are therein, will be burnt up.

3. This man clothed with linen readily attended to this service; though, being clothed with linen, he was very unfit to go among the burning coals, yet, being called, he said, Lo, I come; this commandment he had received of his Father, and he complied with it; the prophet saw him go in, Eze 10:2. He went in, and stood beside the wheels, expecting to be furnished there with the coals he was to scatter; for what Christ was to give he first received, whether for mercy or judgement. He was directed to take fire, but he staid till he had it given him, to show how slow he is to execute judgement, and how long-suffering to us-ward.

4. One of the cherubim reached him a handful of fire from the midst of the living creatures. The prophet, when he first saw this vision, observed that there were burning coals of fire, and lamps, that went up and down among the living creatures (Eze 1:13); thence this fire was taken, Eze 10:7. The spirit of burning, the refiner's fire, by which Christ purifies his church, is of a divine original. It is by a celestial fire, fire from between the cherubim, that wonders are wrought. The cherubim put it into his hand; for the angels are ready to be employed by the Lord Jesus and to serve all his purposes.

5. When he had taken the fire he went out, no doubt to scatter it up and down upon the city, as he was directed. And who can abide the day of his coming? Who can stand before him when he goes out in his anger?

Ezekiel 10:8

We have here a further account of the vision of God's glory which Ezekiel saw, here intended to introduce that direful omen of the departure of that glory from them, which would open the door for ruin to break in.

I. Ezekiel sees the glory of God shining in the sanctuary, as he had seen it by the river of Chebar, and gives an account of it, that those who had by their wickedness provoked God to depart from them might know what they had lost and might lament after the Lord, groaning out their Ichabod, Where is the glory? Ezekiel here sees the operations of divine Providence in the government of the lower world, and the affairs of it, represented by the four wheels; and the perfections of the holy angels, the inhabitants of the upper world, and their ministrations, represented by the four living creatures, every one of which had four faces. The agency of the angels in directing the affairs of this world is represented by the close communication that was between the living creatures and the wheels, the wheels being guided by them in all their motions, as the chariot is by him that drives it. But the same Spirit being both in the living creatures and in the wheels denoted the infinite wisdom which serves its own purposes by the ministration of angels and all the occurrences of this lower world. So that this vision gives out faith a view of that throne which the Lord has prepared in the heavens, and that kingdom of which rules over all, Psa 103:19. The prophet observes that this was the same vision with that he saw by the river of Chebar (Eze 10:15, Eze 10:22), and yet in one thing there seems to be a material difference, that that which was there was the face of an ox, and was on the left side (Eze 1:10), is here the face of a cherub, and is the first face (Eze 10:14), whence some have concluded that the peculiar face of a cherub was that of an ox, which the Israelites had an eye to when they made the golden calf. I rather think that in this latter vision the first face was the proper appearance or figure of a cherub, which Ezekiel knew very well, being a priest, by what he had seen in the temple of the Lord (Kg1 6:29), but which we now have no certainty of at all; and by this Ezekiel knew assuredly, whereas before he only conjectured it, that they were all cherubim, though putting on different faces, Eze 10:20. And this first appearing in the proper figure of a cherub, and yet it being proper to retain the number of four, that of the ox is left out and dropped, because the face of the cherub had been most abused by the worship of an ox. As sometimes when God appeared to deliver his people, so now when he appeared to depart from them, he rode on a cherub, and did fly. Now observe here, 1. That this world is subject to turns, and changes, and various revolutions. The course of affairs in it is represented by wheels (Eze 10:9); sometimes one spoke is uppermost and sometimes another; they are still ebbing and flowing like the sea, waxing and waning like the moon, Sa1 2:4, etc. Nay, their appearance is as if there were a wheel in the midst of a wheel (Eze 10:10), which intimates the mutual references of providence to each other, their dependences on each other, and the joint tendency of all to one common end, while their motions as to us are intricate, and perplexed, and seemingly contrary. 2. That there is an admirable harmony and uniformity in the various occurrences of providence (Eze 10:13): As for the wheels, though they moved several ways, yet it was cried to them, O wheel! they were all as one, being guided by one Spirit to one end; for God works all according to the counsel of his own will, which is one, for his own glory, which is one. And this makes the disposal of Providence truly admirable, and to be looked upon with wonder. As the works of his creation, considered separately, were good, but all together very good, so the wheels of Providence, considered by themselves, are wonderful, but put them together and they are very wonderful. O wheel! 3. That the motions of Providence are steady and regular, and whatever the Lord pleases that he does and is never put upon new counsels. The wheels turned not as they went (Eze 10:11), and the living creatures went every one straight forward, Eze 10:22. Whatever difficulties lay in their way, they were sure to get over them, and were never obliged to stand still, turn aside, or go back. So perfectly known to God are all his works that he never put upon to new counsels. 4. That God make more use of the ministration of angels in the government of this lower world than we are aware of: The four wheels were by the cherubim, one wheel by one cherub and another wheel by another cherub, Eze 10:9. What has been imagined by some concerning the spheres above, that every orb has its intelligence to guide it, is here intimated concerning the wheels below, that every wheel has its cherub to guide it. We think it a satisfaction to us if under the wise God there are wise men employed in managing the affairs of the kingdoms and churches; whether there be so or no, it appears by this that there are wise angels employed, a cherub to every wheel. 5. That all the motions of Providence and all the ministrations of angels are under the government of the great God. They are all full of eyes, those eyes of the Lord which run to and fro through the earth and which the angels have always an eye to, Eze 10:12. The living creatures and the wheels concur in their motions and rests (Eze 10:17); for the Spirit of life, as it may be read, or the Spirit of the living creatures, is in the wheels. The Spirit of God directs all the creatures, both upper and lower, so as to make them serve the divine purpose. Events are not determined by the wheel of fortune, which is blind, but by the wheels of Providence, which are full of eyes.

II. Ezekiel sees the glory of God removing out of the sanctuary, the place where God's honour had long dwelt, and this sight is as sad as the other was grateful. It was pleasant to see that God had not forsaken the earth (as the idolaters suggested, Eze 9:9), but sad to see that he was forsaking his sanctuary. The glory of the Lord stood over the threshold, having thence given the necessary orders for the destruction of the city, and it stood over the cherubim, not those in the most holy place, but those that Ezekiel now saw in vision, Eze 10:18. It ascended that stately chariot, as the judge, when he comes off the bench, goes into his coach and is gone. And immediately the cherubim lifted up their wings (Eze 10:19), as they were directed, and they mounted up from the earth, as birds upon the wing; and, when they went out, the wheels of this chariot were not drawn, but went by instinct, beside them, by which it appeared that the Spirit of the living creatures was in the wheels. Thus, when God is leaving a people in displeasure, angels above, and all events here below, shall concur to further his departure. But observe here, In the courts of the temple where the people of Israel had dishonoured their God, had cast off his yoke and withdrawn the shoulder from it, blessed angels appear very ready to serve him, to draw in his chariot, and to mount upwards with it. God has shown the prophet how the will of God was disobeyed by men on earth (ch. 8); here he shows him how readily it is obeyed by angels and inferior creatures; and it is a comfort to us, when we grieve for the wickedness of the wicked, to think how his angels do his commandments, hearkening to the voice of his word, Psa 103:20. Let us now, 1. Take a view of this chariot in which the glory of the God of Israel rides triumphantly. He that is the God of Israel is the God of heaven and earth, and has the command of all the powers of both. Let the faithful Israelites comfort themselves with this, that he who is their God is above the cherubim; their Redeemer is so (Pe1 3:22) and has the sole and sovereign disposal of all events; the living creatures and the wheels agree to serve him, so that he is head over all things to the church. The rabbin call this vision that Ezekiel had Mercabah-the vision of the chariot; and thence they call the more abstruse part of divinity, which treats concerning God and spirits, Opus currs-The work of the chariot, as they do the other part, that is more plain and familiar, Opus bereshith-The work of the creation.-2. Let us attend the motions of this chariot: The cherubim, and the glory of God above them, stood at the door of the east gate of the Lord's house, Eze 10:19. But observe with how many stops and pauses God departs, as loth to go, as if to see if there be any that will intercede with him to return. None of the priests in the inner court, between the temple and the altar, would court his stay; therefore he leaves their court, and stands at the east gate, which led into the court of the people, to see if any of them would yet at length stand in the gap. Note, God removes by degrees from a provoking people; and, when he is ready to depart in displeasure, would return to them in mercy if they were but a repenting praying people.

Ezekiel Chapter 11

This chapter concludes the vision which Ezekiel saw, and this part of it furnished him with two messages:-I. A message of wrath against those who continued still at Jerusalem, and were there in the height of presumption, thinking they should never fall (Eze 11:1-13). II. A message of comfort to those who were carried captives into Babylon and were there in the depth of despondency, thinking they should never rise. And, as the former are assured that God has judgments in store for them notwithstanding their present security, so the later are assured that God has mercy in store for them notwithstanding their present distress (Eze 11:14-21). And so the glory of God removes further (Eze 11:22, Eze 11:23). The vision disappears (Eze 11:24), and Ezekiel faithfully gives his hearers an account of it (Eze 11:25).

Ezekiel 11:1

We have here,

I. The great security of the prince's of Jerusalem, notwithstanding the judgements of God that were upon them, The prophet was brought, in vision, to the gate of the temple where these princes sat in council upon the present arduous affairs of the city: The Spirit lifted me up, and brought me to the east gate of the Lord's house, and behold twenty-five men were there. See how obsequious the prophet was to the Spirit's orders and how observant of all the discoveries that were made to him. It should seem, these twenty-five men were not the same with those twenty-five whom we saw at the door of the temple, worshipping towards the east (Eze 8:16); those seen to have been priests or Levites, for they were between the porch and the altar, but these were princes sitting in the gate of the Lord's house, to try causes (Jer 26:10), and they are here charged, not with corruptions in worship, but with mal-administration in the government; two of them are named, because they were the most active leading men, and perhaps because the prophet knew them, though he had been some years absent-Pelatiah and Jaazaniah, not that mentioned Eze 8:11, for he was the son of Shaphan, this is the son of Azur. Some tell us that Jerusalem was divided into twenty-four wards, and that these were the governors or aldermen of those wards, with their mayor or president. Now observe, 1. The general character which God gives of these men to the prophet (Eze 11:2): "These are the men that devise mischief; under pretence of concerting measures for the public safety they harden people in their sins, and take off their fear of God's judgements which they are threatened with by the prophets; they gave wicked counsel in this city, counselling them to restrain and silence the prophets, to rebel against the king of Babylon, and to resolve upon holding the city out to the last extremity." Note, It is bad with a people when the things that belong to their peace are hidden from the eyes of those who are entrusted with their counsels. And, when mischief is done, God knows at whose door to lay it, and, in the day of discovery and recompence, will be sure to lay it at the right door, and will say, These are the men that devised it, though they are great men, and pass for wise men, and must not now be contradicted or controlled. 2. The particular charge exhibited against them in proof of this character. They are indicted for words spoken at their council-board, which he that stands in the congregation of the mighty would take cognizance of (Eze 11:3); they said to this effect, "It is not near; the destruction of our city, that has been so often threatened by the prophets, is not near, not so near as they talk of." They are conscious to themselves of such an enmity to reformation that they cannot but conclude it will come at last; but they have such an opinion of God's patience (though they have long abused it) that they are willing to hope it will not come this great while. Note, Where Satan cannot persuade men to look upon the judgement to come as a thing doubtful and uncertain, yet he gains his point by persuading them to look upon it as a thing at a distance, so that it loses its force: if it be sure, yet it is not near; whereas, in truth, the Judge stands before the door. Now, if the destruction is not near, they conclude, Let us build houses; let us count upon a continuance, for this city is the caldron and we are the flesh. This seems to be a proverbial expression, signifying no more than this, "We are as safe in this city as flesh in a boiling pot; the walls of the city shall be to us as walls of brass, and shall receive no more damage from the besiegers about it than the cauldron does from the fire under it. Those that think to force us out of our city into captivity shall find it to be as much at their peril as it would be to take the flesh out of a boiling pot with their hands." This appears to be the meaning of it, by the answer God gives to it (Eze 11:9): "I will bring you out of the midst of the city, where you think yourselves safe, and then it will appear (Eze 11:11) that this is not your caldron, neither are you the flesh." Perhaps it has a particular reference to the flesh of the peace-offerings, which it was so great an offence for the priests themselves to take out of the caldron while it was in seething (as we find Sa1 2:13, Sa1 2:14), and then it intimates that they were the more secure because Jerusalem was the holy city, and they thought themselves a holy people in it, not to be meddled with. Some think this was a banter upon Jeremiah, who in one of his first visions saw Jerusalem represented by a seething pot, Jer 1:13. "Now," say they, in a way of jest and ridicule, "if it be a seething pot, we are as the flesh in it, and who dares meddle with us?" Thus they continued mocking the messengers of the Lord, even while they suffered for so doing; but be you not mockers, lest your bands be made strong. Those hearts are indeed which are made more secure by those words of God which were designed for warning to them.

II. The method taken to awaken them out of their security. One would think that the providences of God which related to them were enough to startle them; but, to help them to understand and improve those, the word of God is sent to them to give them warning (Eze 11:4): Therefore prophesy against them, and try to undeceive them; prophesy, O son of man! upon these dead and dry bones. Note, The greatest kindness ministers can do to secure sinners is to preach against them, and to show them their misery and danger, though they are ever so unwilling to see them. We then act most for them when we appear most against them. But the prophet, being at a loss what to say to men that were hardened in sin, and that bade defiance to the judgments of God, the Spirit of the Lord fell upon him, to make him full of power and courage, and said unto him, Speak. Note, When sinners are flattering themselves into their own ruin it is time to speak, and to tell them that they shall have no peace if they go on. Ministers are sometimes so bashful and timorous, and so much at a loss, that they must be put on to speak, and to speak boldly. But he that commands the prophet to speak gives him instructions what to say; and he must address himself to them as the house of Israel (Eze 11:5), for not the princes only, but all the people, were concerned to know the truth of their cause, to know the worst of it. They are the house of Israel, and therefore the God of Israel is concerned, in kindness to them, to give them warning; and they are concerned in duty to him to take the warning. And what is it that the must say to them in God's name? 1. Let them know that the God of heaven takes notice of the vain confidences with which they support themselves (Eze 11:5): "I know the things which come into your minds every one of them, what secret reasons you have for these resolutions, and what you aim at in putting so good a face upon a matter you know to be bad." Note, God perfectly knows not only the things that come out of our mouths, but the things that come into our minds, not only all we say, but all we think; even those thoughts that are most suddenly darted into our minds, and that as suddenly slip out of them again, so that we ourselves are scarcely aware of them, yet God knows them. He knows us better than we know ourselves; he understands our thoughts afar off. The consideration of this should oblige us to keep our hearts with all diligence, that no vain thoughts come into them or lodge within them. 2. Let them know that those who advised the people to stand it out should be accounted before God the murderers of all who had fallen, or should yet fall, in Jerusalem, by the sword of the Chaldeans; and those slain were the only ones that should remain in the city, as the flesh in the caldron. "You have multiplied your slain in the city, not only those whom you have by the sword of justice unjustly put to death under colour of law, but those whom you have by your wilfulness and pride unwisely exposed to the sword of war, though you were told by the prophets that you should certainly go by the worst. Thus you, with your stubborn humour, have filled the streets of Jerusalem with the slain,"Eze 11:6. Note, Those who are either unrighteous or imprudent in beginning or carrying on a war bring upon themselves a great deal of the guilt of blood; and those who are slain in the battles or sieges which they, by such a reasonable peace as the war aimed at, might have prevented, will be called their slain. Now these slain are the only flesh that shall be left in this caldron, Eze 11:7. There shall none remain to keep possession of the city but those that are buried in it. There shall be no inhabitants of Jerusalem but the inhabitants of the graves there, no freemen of the city but the free among the dead. 3. Let them know that, how impregnable soever they thought their city to be, they should be forced out of it, either driven to flight or dragged into captivity: I will bring you forth out of the midst of it, whether you will or no, Eze 11:7, Eze 11:9. They had provoked God to forsake the city, and thought they should do well enough by their own policy and strength when he was gone; but God will make them know that there is no peace to those that have left their God. If they have by their sins driven God from his house, he will soon by his judgments drive them from theirs; and it will be found that those are least safe that are most secure: "This city shall not be your caldron, neither shall you be the flesh; you shall not soak away in it as you promise yourselves, and die in your nest; you think yourself safe in the midst thereof, but you shall not be long there." 4. Let them know that when God has got them out of the midst of Jerusalem he will pursue them with his judgments wherever he finds them, the judgments which they thought to shelter themselves from by keeping close in Jerusalem. They feared the sword if they should go out to the Chaldeans, and therefore would abide in their caldron, but, says God, I will bring a sword upon you (Eze 11:8) and you shall fall by the sword, Eze 11:10. Note, The fear of the wicked shall come upon him. And there is no fence against the judgments of God when they come with commission, no, not in walls of brass. They were afraid of trusting to the mercy of strangers. "But," says God, "I will deliver you into the hands of strangers, whose resentments you shall feel, since you were not willing to lie at their mercy." See Jer 38:17, Jer 38:18. They thought to escape the judgments of God, but God says that he will execute judgments upon them; and whereas they resolved, if they must be judged, that it should be in Jerusalem, God tells them (Eze 11:10 and again Eze 11:11) that he will judge them in the borders of Israel, which was fulfilled when Nebuchadnezzar slew all the nobles of Judah at Riblah in the land of Hamath, on the utmost border of the land of Canaan. Note, Those who have taken ever so deep root in the place where they live cannot be sure that in that place they shall die. 5. Let them know that all this is the due punishment of their sin, and the revelation of the righteous judgment of God against them: You shall know that I am the Lord, Eze 11:10 and again Eze 11:12. Those shall be made to know by the sword of the Lord who would not be taught by his word what a hatred he has to sin, and what a fearful thing it is for impenitent sinners to fall into his hands. I will execute judgments, and then you shall know that I am the Lord, for the Lord is known by the judgments which he executes upon those that have not walked in his statutes. Hereby it is known that he made the law, because he punishes the breach of it. I will execute judgments among you (says God) because you have not executed my judgments, Eze 11:12. Note, The executing of the judgments of God's mouth by us, in a uniform steady course of obedience to his law, is the only way to prevent the executing of the judgments of his hand upon us in our ruin and confusion. One way or other. God's judgments will be executed; the law will take place either in its precept or in its penalty. If we do not give honour to God by executing his judgments as he has commanded, he will get him honour upon us by executing his judgments as he has threatened; and thus we shall know that he is the Lord, the sovereign Lord of all, that will not be mocked. And observe, When they cast off God's statutes, and walked not in them, they did after the manners of the heathen that were round about them, and introduced into their worship all their impure, ridiculous, and barbarous usages. When men leave the settled rule of divine institutions, they wander endlessly. Justly therefore was this made the reason why they should keep God's ordinances, that they might not commit the abominable customs of the heathen,Lev 18:30.

III. This awakening word is here immediately followed by an awakening providence, Eze 11:13. Here we may observe, 1. With what power Ezekiel prophesied, or, rather, what a divine power went along with it: It came to pass, when I prophesied, that Pelatiah the son of Benaiah died; he was mentioned (Eze 11:1) as a principal man among the twenty-five princes that made all the mischief in Jerusalem. It should seem, this was done in vision now, as the slaying of the ancient men (Eze 9:6) upon occasion of which Ezekiel prayed (Eze 11:8) as he did here; but it was an assurance that when this prophecy should be published it should be done in fact. The death of Pelatiah was an earnest of the complete accomplishment of this prophecy. Note, God is pleased often-times to single out some sinners, and to make them monuments of his justice, for warning to others of what is coming; and some that thought themselves very safe and snatched away suddenly, and drop down dead in an instant, as Ananias and Sapphira at Peter's feet when he prophesied. 2. With what pity Ezekiel prayed. Thought the sudden death of Pelatiah was a confirmation of Ezekiel's prophecy, and really an honour to him, yet he was in deep concern about it, and laid it to heart as if he had been his relation or friend: He fell on his face and cried with a loud voice, as one in earnest, "Ah! Lord God, wilt thou make a full end of the remnant of Israel? Many are swept away by the judgments we have been under; and shall the remnant which have escaped the sword die thus by the immediate hand of heaven? Then thou wilt indeed make a full end." Perhaps it was Ezekiel's infirmity to bewail the death of this wicked prince thus, as it was Samuel's to mourn so long for Saul; but thus he showed how far he was from desiring the woeful day he foretold. David lamented the sickness of those that hated and persecuted him. And we ought to be much affected with the sudden death of others, yea, though they are wicked.

Ezekiel 11:14

Prophecy was designed to exalt every valley as well as to bring low every mountain and hill (Isa 40:4), and prophets were to speak not only conviction to the presumptuous and secure, but comfort to the despised and desponding that trembled at God's word. The prophet Ezekiel, having in the former part of this chapter received instructions for the awakening of those that were at ease in Zion, is in these verses furnished with comfortable words for those that mourned in Babylon and by the rivers there sat weeping when they remembered Zion. Observe,

I. How the pious captives were trampled upon and insulted over by those who continued in Jerusalem, Eze 11:15. God tells the prophet what the inhabitants of Jerusalem said of him and the rest of them that were already carried away to Babylon. God had owned them as good figs, and declared it was for their good that he had sent them into Babylon; but the inhabitants of Jerusalem abandoned them, supposing those that were really the best saints to be the greatest sinners of all men that dwelt in Jerusalem. Observe, 1. How they are described: They are thy brethren (says God to the prophet), whom thou hast a concern and affection for; they are the men of thy kindred (the men of thy redemption, so the word is), thy next of kin, to whom the right of redeeming the alienated possession belongs, but who are so far from being able to do it that they have themselves gone into captivity. They are the whole house of Israel; God so accounts of them because they only have retained their integrity, and are bettered by their captivity. They were not only of the same family and nation with Ezekiel, but of the same spirit; they were his hearers, and he had communion with them in holy ordinances; and perhaps upon that account they are called his brethren and the men of his kindred. 2. How they were disowned by the inhabitants of Jerusalem; they said of them, Get you far from the Lord. Those that were at ease and proud themselves scorned their brethren that were humbled and under humbling providences. (1.) They cut them off from being members of their church. Because they had separated themselves from their rulers and in compliance with the will of God had surrendered themselves to the king of Babylon, they excommunicated them, and said, "Get you far from the Lord; we will have nothing to do with you." Those that were superstitious were very willing to shake off those that were conscientious, and were severe in their censures of them and sentences against them, as if they were forsaken and forgotten of the Lord and were cut off from the communion of the faithful. (2.) They cut them off from being members of the commonwealth too, as if they had no longer any part or lot in the matter: "Unto us is this land given in possession, and you have forfeited your estates by surrendering to the king of Babylon, and we have thereby become entitled to them." God takes notice of, and is much displeased with, the contempt which those that are in prosperity put upon their brethren that are in affliction.

II. The gracious promises which God made to them in consideration of the insolent conduct of their brethren towards them. Those that hated them and cast them out said, Let the Lord be glorified; but he shall appear to their joy, Isa 66:5. God owns that his hand had gone out against them, which had given occasion to their brethren to triumph over them (Eze 11:16): "It is true I have cast them far off among the heathen and scattered them among the countries; they look as if they were an abandoned people, and so mingled with the nations that they will be lost among them; but I have mercy in store for them." Note, God takes occasion from the contempts which are put upon his people to speak comfort to them, as David hoped God would reward him good for Shimei's cursing. His time to support his people's hopes is when their enemies are endeavouring to drive them to despair. Now God promises,

1. That he will make up to them the want of the temple and the privileges of it (Eze 11:16): I will be to them as a little sanctuary, in the countries where they shall come. Those at Jerusalem have the temple, but without God; those in Babylon have God, though without the temple. (1.) God will be a sanctuary to them; that is, a place of refuge; to him they shall flee, and in him they shall be safe, as he was that took hold on the horns of the altar. Or, rather, they shall have such communion with God in the land of their captivity as it was thought could be had nowhere but in the temple. They shall there see God's power and his glory, as they used to see them in the sanctuary; they shall have the tokens of God's presence with them, and his grace in their hearts shall sanctify their prayers and praises, as well as ever the altar sanctified the gift, so that they shall please the Lord better than an ox or bullock. (2.) He will be a little sanctuary, not seen or observed by their enemies, who looked with an evil and an envious eye upon that house at Jerusalem which was high and great, Kg1 9:8. They were but few and mean, and a little sanctuary was fittest for them. God regards the low estate of his people, and suits his favours to their circumstances. Observe the condescensions of divine grace. The great God will be to his people a little sanctuary. Note, Those that are deprived of the benefit of public ordinances, if it be not their own fault, may have the want of them abundantly made up in the immediate

communications of divine grace and comforts.

2. That God would in due time put an end to their afflictions, bring them out of the land of their captivity, and settle them again, them or their children, in their own land (Eze 11:17): "I will gather even you that are thus dispersed, thus despised, and given over for lost by your own countrymen; I will gather you from the people, distinguish you from those with whom you are mingled, deliver you from those by whom you are held captives, and assemble you in a body out of the countries where you have been scattered; you shall not come back one by one, but all together, which will make your return more honourable, safe, and comfortable; and then I will give you the land of Israel, which now your brethren look upon you as for ever shut out from." Note, It is well for us that men's severe censures cannot cut us off from God's gracious promises. There are many that will be found to have a place in the holy land whom uncharitable men, by their monopolies of it to themselves, had secluded from it. I will give you the land of Israel, give it to you again by a new grant, and they shall come thither. If there be any thing in the change of the person from you to them, it may signify the posterity of those to whom the promise is made. "You shall have the title as the patriarchs had, and those that come after shall have the possession."

3. That God by his grace would part between them and their sins, Eze 11:18. Their captivity shall effectually cure them of their idolatry: When they come thither to their own land again they shall take away all the detestable things thereof. Their idols, that had been their delectable things, should now be looked upon with detestation, not only the idols of Babylon, where they were captives, but the idols of Canaan, where they were natives; they should not only not worship them as they had done, but they should not suffer any monuments of them to remain: They shall take all the abominations thereof thence. Note, Then it is in mercy that we return to a prosperous estate, when we return not to the sins and follies of that state. What have I to do any more with idols?

4. That God would powerfully dispose them to their duty; they shall not only cease to do evil, but they shall learn to do well, because there shall be not only an end of their troubles, but a return to their peace.

(1.) God will plant good principles in them; he will make the tree good, Eze 11:19. This is a gospel promise, and is made good to all those whom God designs for the heavenly Canaan; for God prepares all for heaven whom he has prepared heaven for. It is promised, [1.] That God will give them one heart, a heart entire for the true God and not divided as it had been among many gods, a heart firmly fixed and resolved for God and not wavering, steady and uniform, and not inconstant with itself. One heart is a sincere and upright heart, its intentions of a piece with its professions. [2.] That he will put a new spirit within them, a temper of mind agreeable to the new circumstances into which God in his providence would bring them. All that are sanctified have a new spirit, quite different from what it was; they act from new principles, walk by new rules, and aim at new ends. A new name, or a new face, will not serve without a new spirit. If any man be in Christ, he is a new creature. [3.] That he will take away the stony heart out of their flesh, out of their corrupt nature. Their hearts shall no longer be, as they have been, dead and dry, and hard and heavy, as a stone, no longer incapable of bearing good fruit, so that the good seed is lost upon it, as it was on the stony ground. [4.] That he will give them a heart of flesh, not dead or proud flesh, but living flesh; he will make their hearts sensible of spiritual pains and spiritual pleasures, will make them tender, and apt to receive impressions. This is God's work, it is his gift, his gift by promise; and a wonderful and happy change it is that is wrought by it, from death to life. This is promised to those whom God would bring back to their own land; for then such a change of the condition is for the better indeed when it is accompanied with such a change of the heart; and such a change must be wrought in all those that shall be brought to the better country, that is, the heavenly.

(2.) Their practices shall be consonant to those principles: I will give them a new spirit, not that they may be able to discourse well of religion and to dispute for it, but that they may walk in my statues in their whole conversation and keep my ordinances in all acts of religious worship, Eze 11:20. These two must go together; and those to whom God has given a new heart and a new spirit will make conscience of both; and then they shall be my people and I will be their God. The ancient covenant, which seemed to be broken and forgotten, shall be renewed. By their idolatry, it should seem, they had cast God off; by their captivity, it should seem, God had cast them off. But when they were cured of their idolatry, and delivered out of their captivity, God and his Israel own one another again. God, by his good work in them, will make them his people; and then, by the tokens of his good-will towards them, he will show that he is their God.

III. Here is a threatening of wrath against those who hated to be reformed. As, when judgments are threatened, the righteous are distinguished so as not to share in the evil of those judgments, so, when favours are promised, the wicked are distinguished so as not to share in the comfort of those favours; they have no part nor lot in the matter, Eze 11:21. But, as for those that have no grace, what have they to do with peace? Observe, 1. Their description. Their heart walks after the heart of their detestable things; they have as great a minds to worship devils as devils have to be worshipped. Or, in opposition to the new heart which God gives his people, which is a heart after his own heart, they have a heart after the heart of their idols; in their temper and practice they conformed to the characters and accounts given them of their idols, and the ideas they had of them, and of them they learned lewdness and cruelty. Here lies the root of all their wickedness, the corruption of the heart; as the root of their reformation is laid in the renovation of the heart. The heart has its walks, and according as those are the man is. 2. Their doom. It carries both justice and terror in it: I will recompense their way upon their own heads; I will deal with them as they deserve. There needs no more than this to speak God righteous, that he does but render to men according to their deserts: and yet such are the deserts of sin that there needs no more than this to speak the sinner miserable.

Here is, 1. The departure of God's presence from the city and temple. When the message was committed to the prophet, and he was fully apprized of it, fully instructed how to separate between the precious and the vile, then the cherubim lifted up their wings and the wheels beside them (Eze 11:22) as before, Eze 10:19. Angels, when they have done their errands in this lower world, are upon the wing to be gone, for they lose no time. We left the glory of the Lord last at the east gate of the temple (Eze 10:19), which is here said to be in the midst of the city. Now here we are told that, finding and wondering that there was none to intercede, none to uphold, none to invite its return, it removed next to the mountain which is on the east side of the city (Eze 11:23); that was the mount of Olives. On this mountain they had set up their idols, to confront God in his temple, when he dwelt there (Kg1 11:7), and thence it was called the mount of corruption (Kg2 23:13); therefore there God does as it were set up his standard, his tribunal, as it were to confront those who thought to keep possession of the temple for themselves now that God had left it. From that mountain there was a full prospect of the city; thither God removed, to make good what he had said (Deu 32:20), I will hide my face from them, I will see what their end shall be. It was from this mountain that Christ beheld the city and wept over it, in the foresight of its last destruction by the Romans. The glory of the Lord removed thither, to be as it were yet within call, and ready to return if now at length, in this their day, they would have understood the things that belonged to their peace. Loth to depart bids oft farewell. God, by going away thus slowly, thus gradually, intimated that he left them with reluctance, and would not have gone if they had not perfectly forced him from them. He did now, in effect, say, How shall I give thee up, Ephraim? How shall I deliver thee, Israel? But, though he bear long, he will not bear always, but will at length forsake those, and cast them off for ever, who have forsaken him and cast him off. 2. The departure of this vision from the prophet. At length it went up from him (Eze 11:24); he saw it mount upwards, till it went out of sight, which would be a confirmation to his faith that it was a heavenly vision, that it descended from above, for thitherward it returned. Note, The visions which the saints have of the glory of God will not be constant will they come to heaven. They have glimpses of that glory, which they soon lose again, visions which go up from them, tastes of divine pleasures, but not a continual feast. It was from the mount of Olives that the vision went up, typifying the ascension of Christ to heaven from that very mountain, when those that had seen him manifested in the flesh saw him no more. It was foretold (Zac 14:4) that his feet should stand upon the mount of Olives, stand last there. 3. The prophet's return to those of the captivity. The same spirit that had carried him in a trance or ecstasy to Jerusalem brought him back to Chaldea; for there the bounds of his habitation are at present appointed, and that is the place of his service. The Spirit came to him, not to deliver him out of captivity, but (which was equivalent) to support and comfort him in his captivity. 4. The account which he gave to his hearers of all he had seen and heard, Eze 11:25. He received that he might give, and he was faithful to him that appointed him; he delivered his message very honestly: he spoke all that, and that only, which God had shown him. He told them of the great wickedness he had seen at Jerusalem, and the ruin that was hastening towards that city, that they might not repent of their surrendering themselves to the king of Babylon as Jeremiah advised them, and blame themselves for it, nor envy those that staid behind, and laughed at them for going when they did, nor wish themselves there again, but be content in their captivity. Who would covet to be in a city so full of sin and so near to ruin? It is better to be in Babylon under the favour of God than in Jerusalem under his wrath and curse. But, though this was delivered immediately to those of the captivity, yet we may suppose that they sent the contents of it to those at Jerusalem, with whom they kept up a correspondence; and well would it have been for Jerusalem if she had taken the warning hereby given.

Ezekiel Chapter 12

Though the vision of God's glory had gone up from the prophet, yet his word comes to him still, and is by him sent to the people, and to the same purport with that which was discovered to him in the vision, namely, to set forth the terrible judgments that were coming upon Jerusalem, by which the city and temple should be entirely laid waste. In this chapter, I. The prophet, by removing his stuff, and quitting his lodgings, must be a sign to set forth Zedekiah's flight out of Jerusalem in the utmost confusion when the Chaldeans took the city (v. 1-16). II. The prophet, by eating his meat with trembling, must be a sign to set forth the famine in the city during the siege, and the consternation that the inhabitants should be in (Eze 12:17-20). III. A message is sent from God to the people, to assure them that all these predictions should have their accomplishment very shortly, and not be deferred, as they flattered themselves they would be (Eze 12:21-28).

Ezekiel 12:1

Perhaps Ezekiel reflected with so much pleasure upon the vision he had had of the glory of God that often, since it went up from him, he was wishing it might come down to him again, and, having seen it once and a second time, he was willing to hope he might be a third time so favoured; but we do not find that he ever saw it any more, and yet the word of the Lord comes to him; for God did in divers manners speak to the fathers (Heb 1:1) and they often heard the words of God when they did not see the visions of the Almighty. Faith comes by hearing that word of prophecy which is more sure than vision. We may keep up our communion with God without raptures and ecstasies. In these verses the prophet is directed,

I. By what signs and actions to express the approaching captivity of Zedekiah king of Judah; that was the thing to be foretold, and it is foretold to those that are already in captivity, because as long as Zedekiah was upon the throne they flattered themselves with hopes that he would make his part good with the king of Babylon, whose yoke he was now projecting to shake off, from which, it is probable, these poor captives promised themselves great things; and it may be, when he was forming that design, he privately sent encouragement to them to hope that he would rescue them shortly, or procure their liberty by exchange of prisoners. While they were fed with these vain hopes they could not set themselves either to submit to their affliction or to get good by their affliction. It was therefore necessary, but very difficult, to convince them that Zedekiah, instead of being their deliverer, should very shortly be their fellow-suffered. Now, one would think it might have been sufficient if the prophet had only told them this in God's name, as he does afterwards (Eze 12:10); but, to prepare them for the prophecy of it, he must first give them a sign of it, must speak it to their eyes first and then to their ears: and here we have, 1. The reason why he must take this method (Eze 12:2): It is because they are a stupid, dull, unthinking people, that will not heed or will soon forget what they only hear of, or at least will not be at all affected with it; it will make no impression at all upon them: Thou dwellest in the midst of a rebellious house, whom it is next to impossible to work any good upon. They have eyes and ears, they have intellectual powers and faculties, but they see not, they hear not. They were idolaters, whose character it was that they were like the idols they worshipped, which have eyes and see not, ears and hear not, Psa 115:5, Psa 115:6, Psa 115:8. Note, Those are to be reckoned rebellious that shut their eyes against the divine light and stop their ears to the divine law. The ignorance of those that are wilfully ignorant, that have faculties and means and will not use them, is so far from being their excuse that it adds rebellion to their sin. None so blind, so deaf, as those that will not see, that will not hear. They see not, they hear not; for they are a rebellious house. The cause is all from themselves: the darkness of the understanding is owing to the stubbornness of the will. Now this is the reason why he must speak to them by signs, as deaf people are taught, that they might be either instructed or ashamed. Note, Ministers must accommodate themselves not only to the weakness, but to the wilfulness of those they deal with, and deal with them accordingly: if they dwell among those that are rebellious they must speak to them the more plainly and pressingly, and take that course that is most likely to work upon them, that they may be left inexcusable. 2. The method he just take to awaken and affect them; he must furnish himself with all necessaries for removing (Eze 12:3), provide for a journey clothes and money; he must remove from one place to another, as one unsettled and forced to shift; this he must do by day, in the sight of the people; he must bring out all his household goods, to be packed up and sent away (Eze 12:4); and, because all the doors and gates were either locked up that they could not pass through them or so guarded by the enemy that they durst not, he must therefore dig through the wall, and convey his goods away clandestinely through that breach in the wall, Eze 12:5. He must carry his goods away himself upon his own shoulders, for want of a servant to attend him; he must do this in the twilight, that he might not be discovered; and, when he has made what shift he can to secure some of the best of his effects, he must himself steal away at evening in their sight, with fear and trembling, and must go as those that go forth into captivity (Eze 12:4); that is, he must cover his face (Eze 12:6) as being ashamed to be seen and afraid to be known, or in token of very great sorrow and concern; he must go away as a poor broken tradesman, who, when he is forced to shut up shop, hides his head, or quits his country. Thus Ezekiel must be himself a sign to them; and when perhaps he seemed somewhat backward to put himself to all this trouble, and to expose himself to be bantered and ridiculed for it, to reconcile him to it God says (Eze 12:3) "It may be they will consider, and will by it be taken off from their vain confidence, though they be a rebellious house." Note, We must not despair even of the worst, but that yet they may be brought to bethink themselves and repent; and therefore we must continue the use of proper means for their conviction and conversion, because, while there is life, there is hope. And ministers must be willing to go through the most difficult and inconvenient offices (for such was this of Ezekiel's removing), though there be but the it may be of success. If but one soul be awakened to consider, our care and pains will be well bestowed. 3. Ezekiel's ready and punctual obedience to the orders God gave him (Eze 12:7): I did so as I was commanded. Hereby he teaches us all, and ministers especially, (1.) To obey with cheerfulness every command of God, even the most difficult. Christ himself learned obedience, and so we must all. (2.) To do all we can for the good of the souls of others, to put ourselves to any trouble or pains for the conviction of those that are unconvinced. We do all things (that is, we are willing to do any thing), dearly beloved, for your edifying. (3.) To be ourselves affected with those things wherewith we desire to affect others. When Ezekiel would give his hearers a melancholy prospect he does himself put on a melancholy aspect. (4.) To sit loose to this world, and prepare to leave it, to carry out our stuff for removing, because we have here no continuing city. Arise, depart, this it not your rest, for it is polluted. Thou dwellest in a rebellious house, therefore prepare for removing; for who would not be willing to leave such a house, such a wicked world as this is?

II. He is directed by what words to explain those signs and actions, as Agabus, when he bound his own hands and feet, told whose binding was thereby signified. But observe, It was not till morning that God gave him an exposition of the sign, till the next morning, to keep up in him a continual dependence upon God for instruction. As what God does, so what he directs us to do, perhaps we know not now, but shall know hereafter.

1. It was supposed that the people would ask the meaning of this sing, or at least they should (Eze 12:9): "Hath not the house of Israel said unto thee, What doest thou? Yes, I know they have. Though they are a rebellious house, yet they are inquisitive concerning the mind of God," as those (Isa 58:2) who sought God daily. Therefore the prophet must do such a strange uncouth thing, that they might enquire what it meant; and then, it may be hoped, people will take notice of what is told them, and profit by it, when it comes to them in answer to their enquiries. But some understand it as an intimation that they had not made any such enquiries: "Hath not this rebellious house so much as asked thee, What doest thou? No; they take no notice of it; but tell them the meaning of it, though they do not ask." Note, When God sends to us by his ministers he observes what entertainment we give to the messages he sends us; he hearkens and hears what we say to them, and what enquiries we make upon them, and is much displeased if we pass them by without taking any notice of them. When we have heard the word we should apply to our ministers for further instruction; and then we shall know if we thus follow on to know.

2. The prophet is to tell them the meaning of it. In general (Eze 12:10), This burden concerns the prince in Jerusalem; they knew who that was, and gloried in it now that they were in captivity that they had a prince of their own in Jerusalem, and that the house of Israel was yet entire there, and therefore doubted not but in time to do well enough. "But tell them," says God, "that in what thou hast done they may read the doom of their friends at Jerusalem. Say, I am your sign," Eze 12:11. As the conversation of ministers should teach the people what they should do, so the providences of God concerning them are sometimes intended to tell them what they must expect.

The unsettled state and removals of ministers give warning to people what they must expect in this world, no continuance, but constant changes. When times of trouble are coming on Christ tells his disciples, They shall first lay their hands on you, Luk 21:12. (1.) The people shall be led away into captivity (Eze 12:11): As I have done, so shall it be done unto them; they shall be forced away from their own houses, no more to return to them, neither shall their place know them any more. We cannot say concerning our dwelling-place that it is our resting-place; for how far we may be tossed from it before we die we cannot foresee. (2.) The prince shall in vain attempt to make his escape; for he also shall go into captivity. Jeremiah had told Zedekiah the same to his face (Jer 34:3): Thou shalt not escape, but shalt surely be taken. Ezekiel here foretels it to those who made him their confidence and promised themselves relief from him. [1.] That he shall himself carry away his own goods: He shall bear upon his shoulder some of his most valuable effects. Note, The judgments of God can turn a prince into a porter. He that was wont to have the regalia carried before him, and to march through the city at noon-day, shall now himself carry his goods on his back and steal away out of the city in the twilight. See what a change sin makes with men! All the avenues to the palace being carefully watched by the enemy, they shall dig through the wall to carry out thereby. Men shall be their own house-breakers, and steal away their own goods; so it is when the sword of war has cancelled all right and property. [2.] That he shall attempt to escape in a disguise, with a mask or a visor on, which shall cover his face, so that he shall be able only to look before him, and shall not see the ground with his eyes. He who, when he was in pomp, affected to be seen, now that he is in his flight is afraid to be seen; let none therefore either be proud of being looked at or over-much pleased with looking about them, when they see a king with his face covered, that he cannot see the ground. [3.] That he shall be made a prisoner and carried captive into Babylon (Eze 12:13): My net will I spread upon him and he shall be taken in my snare. It seemed to be the Chaldeans' net and their snare, but God owns them for his. Those that think to escape the sword of the Lord will find themselves taken in his net. Jeremiah had said that king Zedekiah should see the king of Babylon and that he should go to Babylon; Ezekiel says, He shall be brought to Babylon, yet he shall not see it, though he shall die there. Those that were disposed to cavil would perhaps object that these two prophets contradicted one another; for one said, He shall see the king of Babylon, the other said, He shall not see Babylon; and yet both proved true: he did see the king of Babylon at Riblah, where he passed sentence upon him for his rebellion, but there he had his eyes put out, so that he did not see Babylon when he was brought thither. These captives expected to see their prince come to Babylon as a conqueror, to bring them out of their trouble; but he shall come thither a prisoner, and his disgrace will be a great addition to their troubles. Little joy could they have in seeing him when he could not see them. [4.] That all his guards should be dispersed and utterly disabled for doing him any service (Eze 12:14): I will scatter all that are about him to help him, so that he shall be left helpless; I will scatter them among the nations and disperse them in the countries (Eze 12:15), to be monuments of divine justice wherever they go. But are there not hopes that they may rally again? (he that flies one time may fight another time); no: I will draw out the sword after them, which shall cut them off wherever if finds them; for the sword that God draws out will be sure to do the execution designed. Yet of Zedekiah's scattered troops some shall escape (Eze 12:16): I will leave a few men of them. Though they shall all be scattered, yet they shall not all be cut off; some shall have their lives given them for a prey. And the end for which they are thus remarkably spared is very observable: That they may declare all their abominations among the heathen whither they come; the troubles they are brought into will bring them to themselves and to their right mind, and then they will acknowledge the justice of God in all that is brought upon them and will make an ingenuous confession of their sins, which provoked God thus to contend with them; and, as by this it shall appear that they were spared in mercy, so hereby they will make a suitable grateful return to God for his favours to them in sparing them. Note, When God has remarkably delivered us from the deaths wherewith we were surrounded we must look upon it that for this end, among others, we were spared, that we might glorify God and edify others by making a penitent acknowledgment of our sins. Those that by their afflictions are brought to this are then made to know that God is the Lord and may help to bring others to the knowledge of him. See how God brings good out of evil. The dispersion of sinners, who had done God much dishonour and disservice in their own country, proves the dispersion of penitents, who shall do him much honour and service in others countries. The Levites are by a curse divided in Jacob and scattered in Israel, yet it is turned into a blessing, for thereby they have the fairest opportunity to teach Jacob God's laws.

Ezekiel 12:17

Here again the prophet is made a sign to them of the desolations that were coming on Judah and Jerusalem. 1. He must himself eat and drink in care and fear, especially when he was in company, Eze 12:17, Eze 12:18. Though he was under no apprehension of danger to himself, but lived in safety and plenty, yet he must eat his bread with quaking (the bread of sorrows, Psa 127:2) and drink his water with trembling and with carefulness, that he might express the calamitous condition of those that should be in Jerusalem during the siege; not that he must dissemble and pretend to be in fear and care when really he was not; but having to foretel this judgment, to show that he firmly believed it himself, and yet was far from desiring it, in the prospect of it he was himself affected with grief and fear. Note, When ministers speak of the ruin coming upon impenitent sinners they must endeavour to speak feelingly, as those that know the terrors of the Lord; and they must be content to endure hardness, so that they may but do good. 2. He must tell them that the inhabitants of Jerusalem should in like manner eat and drink with care and fear, Eze 12:19, Eze 12:20. Both those that have their home in Jerusalem and those of the land of Israel that come to shelter themselves there, shall eat their bread with carefulness and drink their water with astonishment, either because they are afraid it will not hold out, but they shall want shortly, or because they are continually expecting the alarms of the enemy, their life hanging in doubt before them (Deu 28:66), so that what they have they shall have no enjoyment of nor will it do them any good. Note, Care and fear, if they prevail, are enough to embitter all our comforts and are themselves very sore judgments. They shall be reduced to these straits that thus by degrees, and by the hand of those that thus straiten them, both city and country may be laid in ruins; for it is no less than an utter destruction of both that is aimed at in these judgments-that her land may be desolate from all the fulness thereof, may be stripped of all its ornaments and robbed of all its fruits, and then of course the cities that are inhabited shall be laid waste, for they are served by the field. This universal desolation was coming upon them, and then no wonder that they eat their bread with care and fear. Now we are here told, (1.) How bad the cause of this judgment was; it is because of the violence of all those that dwell therein, their injustice and oppression, and the mischief they did one another, for which God would reckon with them, as well as for the affronts put upon him in his worship. Note, The decay of virtue in a nation brings on a decay of every thing else; and when neighbours devour one another it is just with God to bring enemies upon them to devour them all. (2.) How good the effect of this judgment should be: You shall know that I am the Lord; and if, by these judgments, they learn to know him aright, that will make up the loss of all they are deprived of by these desolations. Those are happy afflictions, how grievous soever to flesh and blood, that help to introduce us into and improve us in an acquaintance with God.

Ezekiel 12:21

Various methods had been used to awaken this secure and careless people to an expectation of the judgments coming, that they might be stirred up, by repentance and reformation, to prevent them. The prophecies of their ruin were confirmed by visions, and illustrated by signs, and all with such evidence and power that one would think they must needs be wrought upon; but here we are told how they evaded the conviction, and guarded against it, namely, by telling themselves, and one another, that though these judgments threatened should come at last yet they would not come of a long time. This suggestion, with which they bolstered themselves up in their security, is here answered, and shown to be vain and groundless, in two separate messages which God sent to them by the prophet at different times, both to the same purport; such care, such pains, must the prophet take to undeceive them, Eze 12:21, Eze 12:26. Observe,

I. How they flattered themselves with hopes that the judgments should be delayed. One saying they had, which had become proverbial in the land of Israel, Eze 12:22. They said, "The days are prolonged; the judgments have not come when they were expected to come, but seem to be still put off de die in diem-from day to day, and therefore we may conclude that every vision fails, because it should seem that some do, that because the destruction has not come yet it will never come; we will never trust a prophet again, for we have been more frightened than hurt." And another saying they had which, if it would not conquer their convictions, yet would cool their affections and abate their concern, and that was, "The vision is for a great while to come; it refers to events at a vast distance, and he prophesies of things which, though they may be true, are yet very far off, so that we need not trouble our heads about them (Eze 12:27); we may die in honour and peace before these troubles come." And, if indeed the troubles had been thus adjourned, they might have made themselves easy, as Hezekiah did. Is it not well if peace and truth shall be in my days? But it was a great mistake, and they did but deceive themselves into their own ruin;

and God is here much displeased at it; for, 1. It was a wretched abuse of the patience of God, who, because for a time he kept silence, was thought to be altogether such a one as themselves, Psa 50:21. That forbearance of God which should have led them to repentance hardened them in sin. They were willing to think their works were not evil because sentence against them was not executed speedily; and therefore concluded the vision itself failed, because the days were prolonged. 2. It received countenance form the false prophets that were among them, as should seem from the notice God takes (Eze 12:24) of the vain visions, and flattering divinations, even within the house of Israel, to whom were committed the oracles of God. No marvel if those that deceived themselves by worshipping pretended deities deceived themselves also by crediting pretended prophecies, to which strong delusions God justly gave them up for their idolatries. 3. These sayings had become proverbial; they were industriously spread among the people, so that they had got into very one's mouth, and not only so, but were generally assented to, as proverbs usually are, not only the proverbs of the ancients, but those of the moderns too. Note, It is a token of universal degeneracy in a nation when corrupt and wicked sayings have grown proverbial; and it is an artifice of Satan by them to confirm men in their prejudices against the word and ways of God, and a great offence to the God of heaven. It will not serve for an excuse, in saying ill, to plead that it is a common saying.

II. How they are assured that they do but deceive themselves, for the judgments shall be hastened, these profane proverbs shall be confronted: Tell them, therefore, The days are at hand (Eze 12:23), and again, There shall none of my words be prolonged any more, Eze 12:28. Their putting the evil day far from them does but provoke God to bring it the sooner upon them; and it will be so much the sorer, so much the heavier, so much the more a surprise and terror to them when it does come. He must tell them,

1. That God will certainly silence the lying proverbs, and the lying prophecies, with which they buoyed up their vain hopes, and will make them ashamed of both: (1.) I will make this proverb to cease; for when they find the days of vengeance have come, and not one iota or tittle of the prediction falls to the ground, they will be ashamed to use it as a proverb in Israel, The days are prolonged, and the vision fails. Note, Those that will not have their eyes opened and their mistakes rectified, by the word of God, shall be undeceived by his judgments: for every mouth that speaks perverse things shall be stopped. (2.) There shall be no more any vain vision, Eze 12:24. The false prophets, who told the people they should have peace and should soon see an end of their troubles, shall be disproved by the event, and then shall be ashamed of their pretensions, and shall hide their heads and impose silence upon themselves. Note, As truth was older than error, so it will survive it; it got the start, and it will get the race. The true prophets' visions and predictions stand, and are in full force, power, and virtue; they give law, and receive credit, when the vain visions, and the flattering divinations, are lost and forgotten, and shall be no more in the house of Israel; for great is the truth, and will prevail.

2. That God will certainly, and very shortly, accomplish every word that he has spoken. With

what majesty does he say it (Eze 12:25): I am the Lord! I am Jehovah! That glorious name of his speaks him a God giving being to his word by the performance of it, and therefore to the patriarchs, who lived by faith in a promise not yet performed, he was not known by his name Jehovah, Exo 6:3. But, as he is Jehovah in making good his promise, so he is in making good his threatenings. Let them know then that God, with whom they have to do, is the great Jehovah, and therefore, (1.) He will speak, whether they will hear or whether they will forbear: I am the Lord, I will speak. God will have his saying, whoever gainsays it. God's oracles are called lively ones, for they still speak when the pagan oracles are long ago struck dumb. There has been, and shall be, a succession of God's ministers to the end of the world, by whom he will speak; and, though contempt may be put upon them, that shall not put a period to their ministration: In your days, O rebellious house! will I say the word. Even in the worst ages of the church God left not himself without witness, but raised up men that spoke for him, that spoke from him. I will say the word, the word that shall stand. (2.) The word that he speaks shall come to pass; it shall infallibly be accomplished according to the true intent and meaning of it, and according to the full extent and compass of it: I will say the word and will perform it (Eze 12:25), for his mind is never changed, nor his arm shortened, nor is Infinite Wisdom ever nonplussed. With men saying and doing are two things, but they are not so with God; with him it is dictum, factum-said, and done. In the works of providence, as in those of creation, he speaks and it is done; for he said, Let there be light, and there was light-Let there be a firmament, and there was a firmament, Num 23:19; Sal 15:29. Whereas they had said, Every vision fails (Eze 12:22), God says, "No, there shall be the effect of every vision (Eze 12:23); it shall not return void, but every sign shall be answered by the thing signified." Those that see the visions of the Almighty do not see vain visions; God confirms the word of his servants by performing it. (3.) It shall be accomplished very shortly: "The days are at hand when you shall see the effect of every vision, Eze 12:23. It is said, it is sworn, that delay shall be no longer (Rev 10:6); the year of God's patience has now just expired, and he will no longer defer the execution of the sentence. It shall be no more prolonged (Eze 12:25); he has borne with you a great while, but he will not bear always. In your days, O rebellious house! shall the word that is said be performed, and you shall see the threatened judgments and share in them. Behold, the Judge stands at the door. The righteous are taken away from the evil to come, but this rebellious house shall not be so quietly taken away; no, they shall live to be hurried away, to be chased out of the world." This is repeated (Eze 12:28): "There shall none of my words be prolonged any more, but judgment shall now hasten on apace; and the longer the bow has been in the drawing the deeper shall the arrow pierce." When we tell sinners of death and judgment, heaven and hell, and think by them to persuade them to a holy life, though we do not find them downright infidels (they will own that they do believe there is a state of rewards and punishments in the other world), yet they put by the force of those great truths, and void the impressions of them, by looking upon the things of the other world as very remote; they tell us, "The vision you see is for many days to come, and you prophesy of the times that are very far off; it will be time enough to think of them when they come nearer," whereas really there is but a step between us and death, between us and an awful eternity; yet a little while and the vision shall speak and not lie, and therefore it concerns us to redeem time, and get ready with all speed for a future state; for, though it is future, it is very near, and while impenitent sinners slumber their damnation slumbers not.

Ezekiel Chapter 13

Mention had been made, in the chapter before, of the vain visions and flattering divinations with which the people of Israel suffered themselves to be imposed upon (v. 24); now this whole chapter is levelled against them. God's faithful prophets are nowhere so sharp upon any sort of sinners as upon the false prophets, not because they were the most spiteful enemies to them, but because the put the highest affront upon God and did the greatest mischief to his people. The prophet here shows the sin and punishment, I. Of the false prophets (v. 1-16). II. Of the false prophetesses (Eze 13:17-23). Both agreed to sooth men up in their sins, and, under pretence of comforting God's people, to flatter them with hopes that they should yet have peace; but the prophets shall be proved liars, their prophecies mere shams, and the expectations of the people illusions; for God will let them know that "the deceived and the deceiver are his," are both accountable to him, Job 12:16.

Ezekiel 13:1

The false prophets, who are here prophesied against, were some of them at Jerusalem (Jer 23:14): I have seen in the prophets at Jerusalem a horrible thing; some of them among the captives in Babylon, for to them Jeremiah writes (Jer 29:8), Let not your diviners, that be in the midst of you, deceive you. And as God's prophets, though at a distance from each other in place or time, yet preached the same truths, which was an evidence that they were guided by one and the same good Spirit, so the false prophets prophesied the same lies, being actuated by one and the same spirit of error. There were little hopes of bringing them to repentance, they were so hardened in their sin; yet Ezekiel must prophesy against them, in hopes that the people might be cautioned not to hearken to them; and thus a testimony will be left upon record against them, and they will thereby be left inexcusable.

Ezekiel had express orders to prophesy against the prophets of Israel; so they called themselves, as if none but they had been worthy of the name of Israel's prophets, who were indeed Israel's deceivers. But it is observable that Israel was never imposed upon by pretenders to prophecy till after they had rejected and abused the true prophets; as, afterwards, they were never deluded by counterfeit messiahs till after they had refused the true Messiah and rejected him. These false prophets must be required to hear the word of the Lord. They took upon them to speak what concerned others as from God; let them now hear what concerned themselves as from him. And two things the prophet is directed to do:-

I. To discover their sin to them, and to convince them of that if possible, or thereby to prevent their proceeding any further, by making manifest their folly unto all men, Ti2 3:9. They are here called foolish prophets (Eze 13:3), men that did not at all understand the business they pretended to; to make fools of the people they made fools of themselves, and put the greatest cheat upon their own souls. Let us see what is here laid to their charge. 1. They pretend to have a commission from God, whereas he never sent them. They thrust themselves into the prophetic office, without warrant from him who is the Lord God of the holy prophets, which was a foolish thing; for how could they expect that God should own them in a work to which he never called them? They are prophets out of their own hearts (so the margin reads it, Eze 13:2), prophets of their own making, Eze 13:6. They say, The Lord saith; they pretend to be his messengers, but the Lord has not sent them, has not given them any orders. They counterfeit the broad seal of heaven, than which they cannot do a greater indignity to mankind, for hereby they put a reproach upon divine revelation, lessen its credit, and weaken its credibility. When these pretenders are found to be deceivers atheists and infidels will thence infer, They are all so. The Lord has not sent them; for though crafty enough in other things like the foxes, and very wise for the world, yet they are foolish prophets and have no experimental acquaintance with the things of God. Note, Foolish prophets are not of God's sending, for whom he sends he either finds fit or makes fit. Where he gives warrant he gives wisdom. 2. They pretend to have instructions from God, whereas he never made himself and his mind known to them: They followed their own spirit (Eze 13:3); they delivered that as a message from God which was the product either of their subtle invention, to serve a turn for themselves, or of their own crazed and heated imagination, to give vent to a fancy. For they have seen nothing, they have not really had any heavenly vision; they pretend that what they say the Lord saith it, but God disowns it: "I have not spoken it, I never said it, never meant any such thing." What they delivered was not what they had seen or heard, as that is which the ministers of Christ deliver (Jo1 1:1), but either what they had dreamed or what they thought would please those they coveted to make an interest in; this is called their seeing vanity and lying divination (Eze 13:6); they pretended to have seen that which they did not see, and produced that as a divine truth which they knew to be false. To the same purport (Eze 13:7): You have see a vain vision and spoken a lying divination, which had no divine original and would have no effect, but would certainly be disproved by the event; the words are changed (Eze 13:8): You have spoken vanity and seen lies; what they saw and what they said was all alike, a mere sham; they saw nothing, they said nothing, to the purpose, nothing that could be relied on or that deserved regard. Again (Eze 13:9), They see vanity and divine lies; they pretended to have had visions, as the true prophets had, whereas really they had none, but either it was the creature of their own fancy (they thought they had a vision, as men in a delirium do, that was seeing vanity) or it was a fiction of their own politics, and they knew they had none, and then they saw lies, and divined lies. See Jer 23:16, etc. Note, Since the devil is universally know to be the father of lies, those put the highest affront imaginable upon God who tell lies, and then father them upon him. But those that had put God's character upon Satan, in worshipping devils, arrived at length at such a pitch of impiety as to put Satan's character upon God. 3. They took no care to prevent the judgments of God that were breaking in upon the kingdom. They are like the foxes in the deserts, running to and fro, and seeming to be in a great hurry, but it was to get away and shift for their own safety, not to do any good: The hireling flees, and leaves the sheep. They are like foxes that are greedy of prey for themselves, crafty and cruel to feed themselves. But (Eze 13:5), "You have not gone up into the gaps, nor made up the hedge of the house of Israel. A breach is made in their fences, at which judgments are ready to pour in upon them, and then, if ever, is the time to do them service; but you have done nothing to help them." They should have made intercession for them, to turn away the wrath of God; but they were not praying prophets, had no interest in heaven nor intercourse with heaven (as prophets used to have, Gen 20:7) and so could do them no service that way. They should have made it their business by preaching and advice to bring people to repentance and reformation, and so have made up the hedge, and put a stop to the judgments of God; but this was none of their care: they contrived how to pleased people, not how to profit them. They saw a deluge of profaneness and impiety breaking in upon the land, waging war with virtue and holiness, and threatening to crush them and bear them down, and then they should have come in to the help of the Lord, to the help of the Lord against the mighty, by witnessing against the wickedness of the time and place they lived in; but they thought that would be as dangerous a piece of service as standing in a breach to make it good against the besiegers, and therefore they declined it, did nothing to stem the tide, stood not in the battle against vice and immorality, but basely deserted the cause of religion and reformation, in the day of the Lord, when it was proclaimed, Who is on the Lord's side? Who will rise up for me against the evil-doers? Psa 94:16. Those were unworthy the name of prophets that could think so favourably of sin, and had so little zeal for God and the public welfare. 4. They flattered people into a vain hope that the judgments God had threatened would never come, whereby they hardened those in sin whom they should have endeavoured to turn from sin (Eze 13:6): They have made others to hope that all should be well, and they should have peace, though they went on still in their trespasses, and that the event would confirm the word. They were still ready to say, "We will warrant you that these troubles will be at an end quickly, and we shall be in prosperity again." as if their warrants would confirm false prophecies, in defiance of God himself.

II. He is directed to denounce the judgments of God against them for these sins, from which their pretending to the character of prophets would not exempt them. 1. In general, here is a woe against them (Eze 13:3), and what that woe is we are told (Eze 13:8). Behold, I am against you, saith the Lord God. Note, Those are in a woeful condition that have God against them. Woe, and a thousand woes, to those that have made him their enemy. 2. In particular, they are sentenced to be excluded from all the privileges of the commonwealth of Israel, for they are adjudged to have forfeited them all (Eze 13:9): God's hand shall be upon them, to seize them and bring them to his bar, to shut them out from his presence, and they will find it a fearful thing to fall into his hands. They pretend to be prophets, particular favourites of heaven, and authorized to preside in the congregation of his church on earth; but, by pretending to the honours they were not entitled to, they lost those that otherwise they might have enjoyed, Mat 5:19. Their doom is, (1.) To be expelled from the communion of saints, and not to be looked upon as belonging to it: They shall not be in the secret of my people; their folly shall be so clearly manifested that they shall never be consulted, nor their advice asked; they shall not be present at any debates about public affairs. Or, rather, they shall not be in the assembly of God's people for religious worship, for they shall be ashamed to show their heads there, when they are proved by the events to be false prophets, and, like Cain, shall go out from the presence of the Lord. The people that are deceived by them shall abandon them, and resolve to have no more to do with them. Those that usurped Moses's chair shall not be allowed so much as a door-keeper's place. In the great day they shall not stand in the congregation of the righteous (Psa 1:5), when God gathers his saints together to him (Psa 50:5, Psa 50:16), to be for ever with him. (2.) To be expunged out of the book of the living. They shall die in their captivity, and shall die childless, shall leave no posterity to take their denomination from them, and so their names shall not be found among those who either themselves or their posterity returned out of Babylon, of whom a particular account was kept in a public register, which was called the writing of the house of Israel, such as we have Ezra 2. They shall not be found among the living in Jerusalem, Isa 4:3. Or they shall not be found written among those whom God has from eternity chosen to be vessels of his mercy to eternity. We read of those who prophesied in Christ's name, and yet he will tell them that he never knew them (Mat 7:22, Mat 7:23), because they were not among those that were given to him. The Chaldee paraphrase reads it, They shall not be written in the writing of eternal life, which is written for the righteous of the house of Israel. See Psa 69:28. (3.) To be for ever excluded from the land of Israel. God has sworn in his wrath concerning them that they shall never enter with the returning captives into the land of Canaan, which a second time remains a rest for them. Note, Those who oppose the design of God's threatenings, and will not be awed and influenced by them, forfeit the benefit of his promises, and cannot expect to be comforted and encouraged by them.

Ezekiel 13:10

We have here more plain dealing with the false prophets, and some further articles of their doom. We have seen the people made ashamed of the false prophets (though sometimes they had been fond of them) and casting them away, as they shall do their false gods, with indignation; now here we find them as much ashamed of their false prophecies, which they had sometimes depended upon with much assurance. Observe,

I. How the people are deceived by the false prophets. Those flatterers seduce them, saying, Peace, and there was no peace, Eze 13:10. They pretended to have seen visions of peace, Eze 13:16. But that could not be, for there was no peace, saith the Lord God. There was no prosperity designed for them, and therefore there could be no ground for their security; yet they told them that God was at peace with them, and had mercy in reserve for them, and that the war they were engaged in with the Chaldeans should soon end in an honourable peace, and their land should enjoy a happy repose and tranquillity. They told the idolaters and other sinners that there was neither harm nor danger in the way they were in. Thus they seduced God's people; they put a cheat upon them, led them into mistakes, and drew them aside out of that way of repentance and reformation which the other prophets were endeavouring to bring them into. Note, Those are the most dangerous seducers who suggest to sinners that which tends to lessen their dread of sin and their fear of God. Now this is compared to the building of a slight rotten wall, or, according to our Saviour's similitude, which is to the same purport with this (Mat 7:26), the building of a house upon the sand, which seems to be a shelter and protection for a while, but will fall when a storm comes. One false prophet built the wall, set up the notion that God was not at all displeased with Jerusalem, but that the city should be confirmed in its flourishing state, and be victorious over the powers that now threatened it. This notion was very pleasing, and he that started it made himself very acceptable by it and was caressed by every body, which invited others to say the same. They made the matter look yet more plausible and promising; they daubed the wall, which the first had built, but it was with untempered mortar, sorry stuff, that will not bind nor hold the bricks together; they had no ground for what they said, nor had it any consistency with itself, but was like ropes of sand. They did not strengthen the wall, were in no care to make it firm, to see that they went upon sure grounds; they only daubed it to hide the cracks and make it look well to the eye. And the wall thus built, when it comes to any stress, much more to any distress, will bulge and totter, and come down by degrees. Note, Doctrines that are groundless, though ever so grateful, that are not built upon a scripture foundation nor fastened with a scripture cement, though ever so plausible, ever so pleasing, are not of any worth, nor will stand men in any stead; and those hopes of peace and happiness which are not warranted by the word of God will but cheat men, like a wall that is well daubed indeed, but ill-built.

II. How they will be soon undeceived by the judgment of God, which, we are sure, is according to truth. 1. God will in anger bring a terrible storm that shall beat fiercely and furiously upon the wall. The descent which the Chaldean army shall make upon Judah, and the siege which they shall lay to Jerusalem, will be as an overflowing shower, or inundation (such as Solomon calls a sweeping rain that leaves no food, Pro 28:3), will bear down all before it, as the deluge did in Noah's time: You, O great hailstones! shall fall, the artillery of heaven, every hailstone like a cannon-ball, battering this wall, and with these a stormy wind, which is sometimes so strong as to rend the rocks (Kg1 19:11), much more an ill-built wall, Eze 13:11. But that which makes this rain, and hail, and wind, most terrible is that they arise from the wrath of God, and are enforced by that; it is that which sends them; it is that which gives them the setting on (Eze 13:13); it is a stormy wind in my fury, and an overflowing shower in my anger, and great hailstones in my fury. The fury of Nebuchadnezzar and his princes, who highly resented Zedekiah's treachery, made the invasion very formidable, but that was nothing in comparison with God's displeasure. The staff in their hand is my indignation, Isa 10:5. Note, An angry God has winds and storms at command wherewith to alarm secure sinners; and his wrath makes them frightful and forcible indeed; for who can stand before him when he is angry? 2. This storm shall overturn the wall: it shall fall, and the wind shall rend it (Eze 13:11), the hailstones shall consume it (Eze 13:13); I will break it down (Eze 13:14) and bring it to the ground, so that the foundation thereof shall be discovered; it will appear how false, how rotten it was, to the prophetical reproach of the builders. When the Chaldean army has made Judah and Jerusalem desolate then this credit of the prophets, and the hopes of the people, will both sink together; the former will be found false in flattering the people and the latter foolish in suffering themselves to be imposed upon by them, and so exposed to so much the greater confusion, when the judgment shall surprise them in their security. Note, Whatever men think to shelter themselves with against the judgments of God, while they continue unreformed, will prove but a refuge of lies and will not profit them in the day of wrath. See Isa 28:17. Men's anger cannot shake that which God has built (for the blast of the terrible ones is but as a storm against the wall, which makes a great noise, but never stirs the wall; see Isa 25:4), but God's anger will overthrow that which men have built in opposition to him. They and all their attempts, they and all the securities wherein they intrench themselves, shall be as a bowing wall and as a tottering fence (Psa 62:3, Psa 62:10); and when their vain predictions are disproved, and their vain expectations disappointed, then it will be discovered that there was no ground for either, Hab 3:13. The day will declare what every man's work is, and the fire will try it, Col 3:13. 3. The builders of the wall, and those that daubed it, will themselves be buried in the ruins of it: It shall fall, and you shall be consumed in the midst thereof, Eze 13:14. And thus the threatenings of God's wrath, and all the just intentions of it, shall be accomplished to the uttermost, both upon the wall and upon those that have daubed it, Eze 13:15. The same judgments that will prove the false prophets to be false will punish them for their falsehood; and they themselves shall be involved in the calamity which they made the people believe there was no danger of, and become monuments of that justice which they bade defiance to. Thus, if the blind lead the blind, both the blind leaders and the blind followers will fall together into the ditch. Note, Those that deceive others will in the end prove to have deceived themselves; and no doom will be more fearful than that of unfaithful ministers, that flattered sinners in their sins. 4. Both the deceivers and the deceived, when they thus perish together, will justly be ridiculed and triumphed over (Eze 13:12): When the wall has fallen shall it not be said unto you, by those that gave credit to the true prophets, and feared the word of the Lord, "Now where is the daubing wherewith you have daubed the wall? What has become of all the fine soft words and fair promises wherewith you flattered your wicked neighbours, and all the assurances you gave them that the troubles of the nation should soon be at an end?" The righteous shall laugh at them, the righteous God shall, righteous men shall, saying, Lo, this is the man that made not God his strength, Psa 52:6,Psa 52:7. I also will laugh at your calamity, Pro 1:26. They will say unto you (Eze 13:15), "The wall is no more, neither he that daubed it; your hopes have vanished, and those that supported them, even the prophets of Israel," Eze 13:16. Note, Those that usurp the honours that do not belong to them will shortly be filled with the shame that does.

Ezekiel 13:17

As God has promised that when he pours out his Spirit upon his people both their sons and their daughters shall prophesy, so the devil, when he acts as a spirit of lies and falsehood, is so in the mouth not only of false prophets, but of false prophetesses too, and those are the deceivers whom the prophet is here directed to prophesy against; for they are not such despicable enemies to God's truths as deserve not to be taken notice of, nor yet will either the weakness of their sex excuse their sin or the tenderness and respect that are owing to it exempt them from the reproaches and threatenings of the word of God. No: Son of man, set they face against the daughters of thy people, Eze 13:17. God takes no pleasure in owning them for his people. They are thy people, as Exo 32:7. The women pretend to a spirit of prophecy, and are in the same song with the men, as Ahab's prophets were: Go on, and prosper. They prophesy out of their own heart too; they say what comes uppermost and what they know nothing of. Therefore prophesy against them from God's own mouth. The prophet must set his face against them, and try if they can look him in the face and stand to what they say. Note, When sinners grow very impudent it is time for reprovers to be very bold. Now observe,

I. How the sin of these false prophetesses is described, and what are the particulars of it. 1. They told deliberate lies to those who consulted them, and came to them to be advised, and to be told their fortune: "You do mischief by your lying to my people that hear your lies (Eze 13:19); they come to be told the truth, but you tell them lies; and, because you humour them in their sins, they are willing to hear you." Note, It is ill with those people who can better hear pleasing lies than unpleasing truths; and it is a temptation to those who lie in wait to deceive to tell lies when they find people willing to hear them and to excuse themselves with this, Si populus vult decipi, decipiatur-If the people will be deceived, let them. 2. They profaned the name of God by pretending to have received those lies from him (Eze 13:19): "You pollute my name among my people, and make use of that for the patronising of your lies and the gaining of credit to them." Note, Those greatly pollute God's holy name that make use of it to give countenance to falsehood and wickedness. Yet this they did for handfuls of barley and pieces of bread. They did it for gain; they cared not what dishonour they did to God's name by their lying, so they could but make a hand of it for themselves. There is nothing so sacred which men of mercenary spirits, in whom the love of this world reigns, will not profane and prostitute, if they can but get money by the bargain. But they did it for poor gain; if they could get no more for it, rather than break they would sell you a false prophecy that should please you to a nicety for the beggar's dole, a piece of bread or a handful of barley; and yet that was more than it was worth. Had they asked it as an alms, for God's sake, surely they might have had it, and God would have been honoured; but, taking it as a fee for a false prophecy, God's name if polluted, and the smallness of the reward heightens the offence. For a piece of bread that man will transgress, Pro 28:21. Had their poverty been their temptation to steal, and so to take the name of the Lord in vain, it would not have been nearly so bad as when it tempted them to prophesy lies in his name and so to profane it. 3. They kept people in awe, and terrified them with their pretensions: "You hunt the souls of my people (Eze 13:18), hunt them to make them flee (Eze 13:20), hunt them into gardens (so the margin reads it); you use all the arts you have to court or compel them into those places where you deliver your pretended predictions, or you have got such an influence upon them that you make them do just as you would have them do, and tyrannise over them." It was indeed the people's fault that they did regard them, but it was their fault by lies and falsehoods to command that regard; they pretended to save the souls alive that came to them,Eze 13:18. If they would but be hearers of them, and contributors to them, they might be sure of salvation; thus they beguiled unstable souls that had a concern about salvation as their end but did not rightly understand the way, and therefore hearkened to those who were most confident in promising it to them. "But will you pretend to save souls, or secure salvation to your party?" Those are justly suspected that make such pretensions. 4. They discouraged those that were honest and good, and encouraged those that were wicked and profane: You slay the souls that should not die, and save those alive that should not live, Eze 13:19. This is explained (Eze 13:22): You have made the heart of the righteous sad, whom I have not made sad; because they would not, they durst not, countenance your pretensions, you thundered out the judgments of God against them, to their great grief and trouble; you put them under invidious characters, to make them either despicable or odious to the people, and pretended to do it in God's name, which made them go many a time with a sad heart; whereas it was the will of God that they should be comforted, and by having respect put upon them should have encouragement given them. But on the other side, and which is still worse, you have strengthened the hands of the wicked and emboldened them to go on in their wicked ways and not to return from them, which was the thing the true prophets with earnestness called them to. "You have promised sinners life in their sinful ways, have told them that they shall have peace though they go on, by which their hands have been strengthened and their hearts hardened." Some think this refers to the severe censures they passed upon those who had already gone into captivity (who were humbled under their affliction, by which their hearts were made sad), and the commendations they gave to those who rebelled against the king of Babylon, who were hardened in their impieties, by which their hands were strengthened; or by their polluting the name of God they saddened the hearts of good people who have a value and veneration for the word of God, and confirmed atheists and infidels in their contempt of divine revelation and furnished them with arguments against it. Note, Those have a great deal to answer for who grieve the spirits, and weaken the hands, of good people, and who gratify the lusts of sinners, and animate them in their opposition to God and religion. Nor can any thing strengthen the hands of sinners more than to tell them that they may be saved in their sins without repentance, or that there may be repentance though they do not return from their wicked ways. 5. They mimicked the true prophets, by giving signs for the illustrating of their false predictions (as Hananiah did, Jer 28:10), and they were signs agreeable to their sex; they sewed little pillows to the people's arm-holes, to signify that they might be easy and repose themselves, and needed not be disquieted with the apprehensions of trouble approaching. And they made kerchiefs upon the head of every stature, of persons of every age, young and old, distinguishable by their stature, Eze 13:18. These kerchiefs were badges of liberty or triumph, intimating that they should not only be delivered from the Chaldeans, but be victorious over them. Some think these were some superstitious rites which they used with those to whom they delivered their divinations, preparing them for the reception of them by putting enchanted pillows under their arms and handkerchiefs on their heads, to raise their fancies and their expectations of something great. Or perhaps the expressions are figurative: they did all they could to make people secure, which is signified by laying them easy, and to make people proud, which is signified by dressing them fine with handkerchiefs, perhaps laid or embroidered on their heads.

II. How the wrath of God against them is expressed. Here is a woe to them (Eze 13:18), and God declares himself against the methods they took to delude and deceive, Eze 13:20. But what course will God take with them? 1. They shall be confounded in their attempts, and shall proceed no further; for (Eze 13:23) you shall see no more vanity nor divine revelations; not that they shall themselves lay down their pretensions in a way of repentance, but when the event gives them the lie they shall be silent for shame; or their fancies and imaginations shall not be disposed to receive impressions which assist them in their divinations as they have been; or they themselves shall be cut off. 2. God's people shall be delivered out of their hands. When they see themselves deluded by them into a false peace and a fool's paradise, and that though they would not leave their sin their sin has left them, and they see no more vanity nor divine divinations, they shall turn their back upon them, shall slight their predictions. The righteous shall be no more saddened by them, no, nor the wicked strengthened: The pillows shall be torn from their arms, and the kerchiefs from their heads; the fallacies shall be discovered, their frauds detected, and the people of God shall no more be in their hand, to be hunted as they had been. Note, It is a great mercy to be delivered from a servile regard to, and fear of, those who, under colour of a divine authority, impose upon and tyrannise over the consciences of men, and say to their souls, Bow down, that we may go over. But it is a sore grief to those who delight in such usurpations to have their power broken and the prey delivered; such was the reformation to the church of Rome. And, when God does this, he makes it to appear that he is the Lord, that it is his prerogative to give law to souls.

Ezekiel Chapter 14

Ezekiel

Hearing the word, and prayer, are two great ordinances of God, in which we are to give honour to him and may hope to find favour and acceptance with him; and yet in this chapter, to our great surprise, we find some waiting upon God in the one and some in the other and yet not meeting with success as they expected. I. The elders of Israel come to hear the word, and enquire of the prophet, but, because they are not duly qualified, they meet with a rebuke instead of acceptance (Eze 14:1-5) and are called upon to repent of their sins and reform their lives, else it is at their peril to enquire of God (Eze 14:6-11). II. Noah, Daniel, and Job, are supposed to pray for this people, and yet, because the decree has gone forth, and the destruction of them is determined by a variety of judgments, their prayers shall not be answered (Eze 14:12-21). And yet it is promised, in the close, that a remnant shall escape (Eze 14:22, Eze 14:23).

Ezekiel 14:1

Here is, I. The address which some of the elders of Israel made to the prophet, as an oracle, to enquire of the Lord by him. They came, and sat before him, Eze 14:1. It is probable that they were not of those who were now his fellow-captives, and constantly attended his ministry (such as those we read of Eze 8:1), but some occasional hearers, some of the grandees of Jerusalem who had come upon business to Babylon, perhaps public business, on an embassy from the king, and in their way called on the prophet, having heard much of him and being desirous to know if he had any message from God, which might be some guide to them in their negotiation. By the severe answer given them one would suspect they had a design to ensnare the prophet, or to try if they could catch hold of any thing that might look like a contradiction to Jeremiah's prophecies, and so they might have occasion to reproach them both. However, they feigned themselves just men, complimented the prophet, and sat before him gravely enough, as God's people used to sit. Note, It is no new thing for bad men to be found employed in the external performances of religion.

II. The account which God gave the prophet privately concerning them. They were strangers to him; he only knew that they were elders of Israel; that was the character they wore, and as such he received them with respect, and, it is likely, was glad to see them so well disposed. But God gives him their real character (Eze 14:3); they were idolaters, and did only consult Ezekiel as they would any oracle of a pretended deity, to gratify their curiosity, and therefore he appeals to the prophet himself whether they deserved to have any countenance or encouragement given them: "Should I be enquired of at all by them? Should I accept their enquiries as an honour to myself, or answer them for satisfaction to them? No; they have no reason to expect it;" for, 1.

They have set up their idols in their heart; they not only have idols, but they are in love with them, they dote upon them, are wedded to them, and have laid them so near their hearts, and have given them so great a room in their affections, that there is no parting with them. The idols they have set up in their houses, though they are now at a distance from the chambers of their imagery, yet they have them in their hearts, and they are ever and anon worshipping them in their fancies and imaginations. They have made their idols to ascend upon their hearts (so the word is); they have subjected their hearts to their idols, they are upon the throne there. Or when they came to enquire of the prophet they pretended to put away their idols, but it was in pretence only; they still had a secret reserve for them. They kept them up in their hearts; and, if they left them for a while, it was cum animo revertendi-with an intention to return to them, not a final farewell. Or it may be understood of spiritual idolatry; those whose affections are placed upon the wealth of the world and the pleasures of sense, whose god is their money, whose god is their belly, they set up their idols in their heart. Many who have no idols in their sanctuary have idols in their hearts, which is no less a usurpation of God's throne and a profanation of his name. Little children, keep yourselves from those idols. 2. They put the stumbling-block of their iniquity before their face. Their silver and gold were called the stumbling-block of their iniquity (Eze 7:19), their idols of silver and gold, by the beauty of which they were allured to idolatry, and so it was the block at which they stumbled, and fell into that sin; or their iniquity is their stumbling-block, which throws them down, so that they fall into ruin. Note, Sinners are their own tempters (every man is tempted when he is drawn aside of his own lust), and so they are their own destroyers. If thou scornest, thou alone shalt bear it; and thus they put the stumbling-block of their iniquity before their own faces, and stumble upon it though they see it before their eyes. It intimates that they are resolved to go on in sin, whatever comes of it. I have loved strangers, and after them I will go; that is the language of their hearts. And should God be enquired of by such wretches? Do they not hereby rather put an affront upon him than do him any honour, as those did who bowed the knee to Christ in mockery? Can those expect an answer of peace from God who thus continue their acts of hostility against him? "Ezekiel, what thinkest thou of it?"

III. The answer which God, in just displeasure, orders Ezekiel to give them, Eze 14:4. Let them know that it is not out of any disrespect to their persons that God refuses to give them an answer, but it is laid down as a rule for every man of the house of Israel, whoever he be, that if he continue in love and league with his idols, and come to enquire of God, God will resent it as an indignity done to him, and will answer him according to his real iniquity, not according to his pretended piety. He comes to the prophet, who, he expects, will be civil to him, but God will give him his answer, by punishing him for his impudence: I the Lord, who speak and it is done, I will answer him that cometh, according to the multitude of his idols. Observe, Those who set up idols in their hearts, and set their hearts upon their idols, commonly have a multitude of them. Humble worshippers God answers according to the multitude of his mercies, but bold intruders he answers according to the multitude of their idols, that is, 1. According to the desire of their idols; he will give them up to their own hearts' lust, and leave them to themselves to be as bad as they have a mind to be, till they have filled up the measure of their iniquity. Men's corruptions are idols in their hearts, and they are of their own setting up; their temptations are the stumbling-block of their iniquity, and they are of their own putting, and God will answer them accordingly; let them take their course. 2. According to the desert of their idols; they shall have such an answer as it is just that such idolaters should have. God will punish them as he usually punishes idolaters, that is, when they stand in need of his help he will send them to the gods whom they have chosen, Jdg 10:13, Jdg 10:14. Note, The judgment of God will dwell with men according to what they are really (that is, according to what their hearts are), not according to what they are in show and profession. And what will be the end of this? What will this threatened answer amount to? He tells them (Eze 14:5): That I may take the house of Israel in their own heart, may lay them open to the world, that they may be ashamed; nay, lay them open to the curse, that they may be ruined. Note, The sin and shame, and pain and ruin, of sinners, are all from themselves, and their own hearts are the snares in which they are taken; they seduce them, they betray them; their own consciences witness against them, condemn them, and are a terror to them. If God take them, if he discover them, if he convict them, if he bind them over to his judgment, it is all by their own hearts. O Israel! thou hast destroyed thyself. The house of Israel is ruined by its own hands, because they are all estranged from me through their idols. Note, (1.) The ruin of sinners is owing to their estrangement from God. (2.) It is through some idol or other that the hearts of men are estranged from God; some creature has gained that place and dominion in the heart that God should have.

IV. The extent of this answer which God had given them-to all the house of Israel, Eze 14:7, Eze 14:8. The same thing is repeated, which intimates God's just displeasure against hypocrites, who mock him with the shows and forms of devotion, while their hearts are estranged from him and at war with him. Observe, 1. To whom this declaration belongs. It concerns not only every one of the house of Israel (as before, Eze 14:4), but the stranger that sojourns in Israel; let him not think it will be an excuse for him in his idolatries that he is but a stranger and a sojourner in Israel, and does but worship the gods that his father served and that he himself was bred up in the service of; no, let him not expect any benefit from Israel's oracles or prophets unless he thoroughly renounce his idolatry. Note, Even proselytes shall not be countenanced if they be not sincere: a dissembled conversion is no conversion. 2. The description here given of hypocrites: They separate themselves from God by their fellowship with idols; they cut themselves off from their relation to God and their interest in him; they break off their acquaintance and intercourse with him, and set themselves at a distance from him. Note, Those that join themselves to idols separate themselves from God; nor shall any be for ever separated from the vision and fruition of God, but such as now separate themselves from his service and wilfully withdraw their allegiance from him. But there are those who thus separate themselves from God, and yet come to the prophets with a seeming respect and deference to their office, to enquire of them concerning God, in order to satisfy a vain curiosity, to stop the mouth of a clamorous conscience, or to get or save a reputation among men, but without any desire to be acquainted with God or any design to be ruled by him. 3. The doom of those who thus trifle with God and think to impose upon him: "I the Lord will answer him by myself; let me alone to deal with him; I will give him an answer that shall fill him with confusion, that shall make him repent of his daring impiety." He shall have his answer, not by the words of the prophet, but by the judgments of God. And I will set my face against that man, which denotes great displeasure against him and a fixed resolution to ruin him. God can outface the most impenitent sinner. The hypocrite thought to save his credit, nay, and to gain applause, but, on the contrary, God will make him a sign and a proverb, will inflict such judgments upon him as shall make him remarkable and contemptible in the eyes of all about him; his misery shall be made use of to express the greatest misery, as when the worst of sinners are said to have their portion appointed them with hypocrites, Mat 24:51. God will make him an example; his judgments upon him shall be for warning to others to take heed of mocking God: for thus shall it be done to the man that separates himself from God, and yet pretends to enquire concerning him. The hypocrite thought to pass for one of God's people, and to crowd into heaven among them; but God will cut him off from the midst of his people, will discover him, and pluck him out from the thickest of them; and by this, says God, you shall know that I am the Lord. By the discovery of hypocrites it appears that God is omniscient: ministers know not how people stand affected when they come to hear the word, but God does. And by the punishment of hypocrites it appears that he is a jealous God, and one that cannot and will not be imposed upon.

V. The doom of those pretenders to prophecy who give countenance to these pretenders to piety, Eze 14:9, Eze 14:10. These hypocritical enquirers, though Ezekiel will not give them a comfortable answer, yet hope to meet with some other prophets that will; and if they do, as perhaps they may, let them know that God permits those lying prophets to deceive them in part of punishment: "If the prophet that flatters them be deceived, and gives them hopes which there is no ground for, I the Lord have deceived that prophet, have suffered the temptation to be laid before him, and suffered him to yield to it, and overruled it for the hardening of those in their wicked courses who were resolved to go on in them." We are sure that God is not the author of sin, but we are sure that he is the Lord of all and the Judge of sinners, and that he often makes use of one wicked man to destroy another, and so of one wicked man to deceive another. Both are sins in him who does them, and so they are not from God; both are punishments to him to whom they are done, and so they are from God. We have a full instance of this in the story of Ahab's prophets, who were deceived by a lying spirit, which God put into their mouths (Kg1 22:23), and another in those whom God gives up to strong delusions, to believe a lie, because they received not the love of the truth, Th2 2:10, Th2 2:11. But read the fearful doom of the lying prophet: I will stretch out my hand upon him and will destroy him. When God has served his own righteous purposes by him he shall be reckoned with for his unrighteous purposes. As, when God had made use of the Chaldeans for the wasting of a sinful people, he justly punished them for their rage, so when he had made use of false prophets, and afterwards of false Christs, for the deceiving of a sinful people, he justly punished them for their falsehood. But herein we must acknowledge (as Calvin upon this place reminds us) that God's judgments are a great deep, that we are incompetent judges of them, and that, though we cannot account for the equity of God's proceedings to the satisfying and silencing of every caviller, yet there is a day coming when he will be justified before all the world, and particularly in this instance, when the punishment of the prophet that flattereth the hypocrite in his evil way shall be as the punishment of the hypocrite that seeketh to him and bespeaks smooth things only, Isa 30:10. The ditch shall be the same to the blind leader and the blind followers.

VI. The good counsel that is given them for the preventing of this fearful doom (Eze 14:6): "Therefore repent, and turn yourselves from your idols. Let this separate between you and them, that they separate between you and God; because they set God's face against you, do you turn away your faces from them," which denotes, not only forsaking them, but forsaking them with loathing and detestation: "Turn from them as from abominations that you are sick of; and then you will be welcome to enquire of the Lord. Come now, and let us reason together."

VII. The good issue of all this as to the house of Israel; therefore the pretending prophets, and the pretending saints, shall perish together by the judgments of God, that, some being made examples, the body of the people may be reformed, that the house of Israel may go no more astray from me, Eze 14:11. Note, The punishments of some are designed for the prevention of sin, that others may hear, and fear, and take warning. When we see what becomes of those that go astray from God we should thereby be engaged to keep close to him. And, if the house of Israel go not astray, they will not be polluted any more. Note, Sin is a polluting thing; it renders the sinner odious in the eyes of the pure and holy God, and in his own eyes too whenever conscience is awakened; and therefore they shall no more be polluted, that they may be my people and I may be their God. Note, Those whom God takes into covenant with himself must first be cleansed from the pollutions of sin; and those who are so cleansed shall not only be saved from ruin, but be entitled to all the privileges of God's people.

Ezekiel 14:12

The scope of these verses is to show,

I. That national sins bring national judgments. When virtue is ruined and laid waste every thing else will soon be ruined and laid waste too (Eze 14:13): When the land sins against me, when vice and wickedness become epidemical, when the land sins by trespassing grievously, when the sinners have become very numerous and their sins very heinous, when gross impieties and immoralities universally prevail, then will I stretch forth my hand upon it, for the punishment of it. The divine power shall be vigorously and openly exerted; the judgments shall be extended and stretched forth to all the corners of the land, to all the concerns and interests of the nation. Grievous sins bring grievous plagues.

II. That God has a variety of sore judgments wherewith to punish sinful nations, and he has them all at command and inflicts which he pleases. He did indeed give David his choice what judgment he would be punished with for his sin in numbering the people; for any of them would serve to answer the end, which was to lessen the numbers he was proud of; but David, in effect, referred it to God again: "Let us fall into the hands of the Lord; let him choose with what rod we shall be beaten." But he uses a variety of judgments that it may appear he has a universal dominion, and that in all our concerns we may see our dependence on him. Four sore judgments are here specified:-1. Famine, Eze 14:13. The denying and withholding of common mercies is itself judgment enough, there needs no more to make a people miserable. God needs not bring the staff of oppression, it is but breaking the staff of bread and the work is soon done; he cuts off man and beast by cutting off the provisions which nature makes for both in the annual products of the earth. God breaks the staff of bread when, though we have bread, yet we are not nourished and strengthened by it. Hag 1:6, You eat, but you have not enough. 2. Hurtful beasts, noisome and noxious, either as poisonous or as ravenous. God can make these to pass through the land (Eze 14:15), to increase in all parts of it, and to bereave it, not only of the tame cattle, preying upon their flocks and herds, but of their people, devouring men, women, and children, so that no man may pass through because of the beasts; none dare travel even in the high roads for fear of being pulled in pieces by lions, or other beasts of prey, as the children of Beth-el by two bears. Note, When men revolt from their allegiance to God, and rebel against him, it is just with God that the inferior creatures should rise up in arms against men, Lev 26:22. 3. War. God often chastises sinful nations by bringing a sword upon them, the sword of a foreign enemy, and he gives it its commission and orders what execution it shall do (Eze 14:17): he says, Sword, go through the land. It is bad enough if the sword do but enter into the borders of a land, but much worse when it goes through the bowels of a land. By it God cuts off man and beast, horse and foot. What execution the sword does God does by it; for it is his sword, and it acts as he directs. 4. Pestilence (Eze 14:19), a dreadful disease, which has sometimes depopulated cities; by it God pours out his fury in blood (that is, in death); the pestilence kills as effectually as if the blood were shed by the sword, for it is poisoned by the disease, the sickness we call it. See how miserable the case of mankind is that lies thus exposed to deaths in various shapes. See how dangerous the case of sinners is against whom God has so many ways of fighting, so that, though they escape one judgment, God has another waiting for them.

III. That when God's professing people revolt from him, and rebel against him, they may justly expect a complication of judgments to fall upon them. God has various ways of contending with a sinful nation; but if Jerusalem, the holy city, become a harlot, God will send upon her all his four sore judgments (Eze 14:21); for the nearer any are to God in name and profession the more severely will he reckon with them if they reproach that worthy name by which they are called and give the lie to that profession. They shall be punished seven times more.

IV. That there may be, and commonly are, some few very good men, even in those places that by sin are ripened for ruin. It is no foreign supposition that, even in a land that has trespassed grievously, there may be three such men as Noah, Daniel, and Job. Daniel was now living, and at this time had scarcely arrived at the prime of his eminency, but he was already famous (at least this word of God concerning him would without fail make him so); yet he was carried away into captivity with the first of all, Dan 1:6. Some of the better sort of people in Jerusalem might perhaps think that, if Daniel (of whose fame in the king of Babylon's court they had heard much) had but continued in Jerusalem, it would have been spared for his sake, as the magicians in Babylon were. "No," says God, "though you had him, who was as eminently good in bad times and places as Noah in the old world and Job in the land of Uz, yet a reprieve should not be obtained." In the places that are most corrupt, and in the ages that are most degenerate, there is a remnant which God reserves to himself, and which still hold fast their integrity and stand fair for the honour of delivering the land, as the innocent are said to do, Job 22:30.

V. That God often spares very wicked places for the sake of a few godly people in them. This is implied here as the expectation of Jerusalem's friends in the day of its distress: "Surely God will stay his controversy with us; for are there not some among us that are emptying the measure of national guilt by their prayers, as others are filling it by their sins? And, rather than God will destroy the righteous with the wicked, he will preserve the wicked with the righteous. If Sodom might have been spared for the sake of ten good men, surely Jerusalem may."

VI. That such men as Noah, Daniel, and Job, will prevail, if any can, to turn away the wrath of God from a sinful people. Noah was a perfect man, and kept his integrity when all flesh had corrupted their way; and, for his sake, his family, though one of them was wicked (Ham), was saved in the ark. Job was a great example of piety, and mighty in prayer for his children, for his friends; and God turned his captivity when he prayed. Those were very ancient examples, before Moses, that great intercessor; and therefore God mentions them, to intimate that he had some very peculiar favourites long before the Jewish nation was formed or founded, and would have such when it was ruined, for which reason, it should seem, those names were made use of, rather than Moses, Aaron, or Samuel; and yet, lest any should think that God was partial in his respects to the ancient days, here is a modern instance, a living one, placed between those two that were the glories of antiquity, and he now a captive, and that is Daniel, to teach us not to lessen the useful good men of our own day by over-magnifying the ancients. Let the children of the captivity know that Daniel, their neighbour, and companion in tribulation, being a man of great humility, piety, and zeal for God, and instant and constant in prayer, had as good an interest in heaven as Noah or Job had. Why may not God raise up as great and good men now as he did formerly, and do as much for them?

VII. That when the sin of a people has come to its height, and the decree has gone forth for their ruin, the piety and prayers of the best men shall not prevail to finish the controversy. This is here asserted again and again, that, though these three men were in Jerusalem at this time, yet they should deliver neither son nor daughter; not so much as the little ones should be spared for their sakes, as the little ones of Israel were upon the prayer of Moses, Num 14:31. No; the land shall be desolate, and God would not hear their prayers for it, though Moses and Samuel stood before him, Jer 15:1. Note, Abused patience will turn at last into inexorable wrath; and it should seem as if God would be more inexorable in Jerusalem's case than in another (Eze 14:6), because, besides the divine patience, they had enjoyed greater privileges than any other people, which were the aggravations of their sin.

VIII. That, though pious praying men may not prevail to deliver others, yet they shall deliver their own souls by their righteousness, so that, though they may suffer in the common calamity, yet to them the property of it is altered; it is not to them what it is to the wicked; it is unstrung, and does them no hurt; it is sanctified, and does them good. Sometimes their souls (their lives) are remarkably delivered, and given them for a prey; at least their souls (their spiritual interests) are secured. If their bodies be not delivered, yet their souls are. Riches indeed profit not in the day of wrath, but righteousness delivers from death, from so great a death, so many deaths as are here threatened. This should encourage us to keep our integrity in times of common apostasy, that, if we do so, we shall be hidden in the day of the Lord's anger.

IX. That, even when God makes the greatest desolations by his judgments, he reserves some to be the monuments of his mercy, Eze 14:22, Eze 14:23. In Jerusalem itself, though marked for utter ruin, yet there shall be left a remnant, who shall not be cut off by any of those sore judgments before mentioned, but shall be carried into captivity, both sons and daughters, who shall be the seed of a new generation. The young ones, who had not grown up to such an obstinacy in sin as their fathers had who were therefore cut off as incurable, these shall be brought forth out of the ruins of Jerusalem by the victorious enemy, and behold they shall come forth to you that are in captivity, they shall make a virtue of a necessity, and shall come the more willingly to Babylon because so many of their friends have gone thither before them and are there ready to receive them; and, when they come, you shall see their ways and their doing; you shall hear them make a free and ingenuous confession of the sins they had formerly been guilty of, and a humble profession of repentance for them, with promises of reformation; and you shall see instances of their reformation, shall see what good their affliction has done them, and how prudently and patiently they conduct themselves under it. Their narrow escape shall have a good effect upon them; it shall change their temper and conversation, and make them new men. And this will redound, 1. To the satisfaction of their brethren: They shall comfort you when you see their ways. Note, It is a very comfortable sight to see people, when they are under the rod, repenting and humbling themselves, justifying God and accepting the punishment of their iniquity. When we sorrow (as we ought to do) for the afflictions of others, it is a great comfort to us in our sorrow to see them improving their afflictions and making a good use of them. When those captives told their friends how bad they had been, and how righteous God was in bringing these judgments upon them, it made them very easy, and helped to reconcile them to the calamities of Jerusalem, to the justice of God in punishing his own people so, and to the goodness of God, which now appeared to have had kind intentions in all; and thus "You shall be comforted concerning all the evil that I have brought upon Jerusalem, and, when you better understand the thing, shall not have such direful apprehensions concerning it as you have had." Note, It is a debt we owe to our brethren, if we have got good by our afflictions, to comfort them by letting them know it. 2. It will redound to the honour of God: "You shall know that I have not done without cause, not without a just provocation, and yet not without a gracious design, all that I have done in it." Note, When afflictions have done their work, and have accomplished that for which they were sent, then will appear the wisdom and goodness of God in sending them, and God will be not only justified, but glorified in them.

Ezekiel Chapter 15

Ezekiel has again and again, in God's name, foretold the utter ruin of Jerusalem; but, it should seem, he finds it hard to reconcile himself to it, and to acquiesce in the will of God in this severe dispensation; and therefore God takes various methods to satisfy him not only that it shall be so, but that there is no remedy: it must be so; it is fit that it should be so. Here, in this short chapter, he shows him (probably with design that he should tell the people) that it was as requisite Jerusalem should be destroyed as that the dead and withered branches of a vine should be cut off and thrown into the fire. I. The similitude is very elegant (Eze 15:1-5), but, II. The explanation of the similitude is very dreadful (Eze 15:6-8).

Ezekiel 15:1

The prophet, we may suppose, was thinking what a glorious city Jerusalem was, above any city in the world; it was the crown and joy of the whole earth; and therefore what a pity it was that it should be destroyed; it was a noble structure, the city of God, and the city of Israel's solemnities. But, if these were the thoughts of his heart, God here returns an answer to them by comparing Jerusalem to a vine. 1. It is true, if a vine be fruitful, it is a most valuable tree, none more so; it was one of those that were courted to have dominion over the trees, and the fruit of it is such as cheers God and man (Jdg 9:12, Jdg 9:13); it makes glad the heart, Psa 104:15. So Jerusalem was planted a choice and noble vine, wholly a right seed (Jer 2:21); and, if it had brought forth fruit suitable to its character as a holy city, it would have been the glory both of God and Israel. It was a vine which God's right hand had planted, a branch out of a dry ground, which, though its original was mean and despicable, God had made strong for himself (Psa 80:15), to be to him for a name and for a praise. 2. But, if it be not fruitful, it is good for nothing, it is as worthless and useless a production of the earth as even thorns and briers are: What is the vine-tree, if you take the tree by itself, without consideration of the fruit? What is it more than any tree, that it should have so much care taken of it and so much cost laid out upon it? What is a branch of the vine, though it spread more than a branch which is among the trees of the forest, where it grows neglected and exposed? Or, as some read it, What is the vine more than any tree if the branch of it be as the trees of the forest; that is, if it bear no fruit, as forest-trees seldom do, being designed for timber-trees, not fruit-trees? Now there are some fruit-trees which, if they do not bear, are nevertheless of good use, as the wood of them may be made to turn to a good account; but the vine is not of this sort: if that do not answer its end as a fruit-tree, it is worth nothing as a timber-tree. Observe,

I. How this similitude is expressed here. The wild vine, that is among the trees of the forest, or the empty vine (which Israel is compared to, Hos 10:1), that bears no more fruit than a forest-tree, is good for nothing; it is as useless as a brier, and more so, for that will add some sharpness to the thorny hedge, which the vine-branch will not do. He shows, 1. That it is fit for no use. The wood of it is not taken to do any work; one cannot so much as make a pin of it to hand a vessel upon, Eze 15:3. See how variously the gifts of nature are dispensed for the service of man. Among the plants, the roots of some, the seeds or fruits of others, the leaves of others, and of some the stalks, are most serviceable to us; so, among trees, some are strong and not fruitful, as the oaks and cedars; others are weak but very fruitful, as the vine, which is unsightly, low, and depending, yet of great use. Rachel is comely but barren, Leah homely but fruitful. 2. That therefore it is made use of for fuel; it will serve to heat the oven with. Because it is not meet for any work, it is cast into the fire, Eze 15:4. When it is good for nothing else it is useful this way, and answers a very needful intention, for fuel is a thing we must have, and to burn any thing for fuel which is good for other work is bad husbandry. To what purpose is this waste? The unfruitful vine is disposed of in the same way with the briers and thorns, which are rejected, and whose end is to be burnt, Heb 6:8. And what care is taken of it then? If a piece of solid timber be kindled, somebody perhaps may snatch it as a brand out of the burning, and say, "It is a pity to burn it, for it may be put to some better use;" but if the branch of a vine be on fire, and, as usual, both the ends of it and the middle be kindled together, nobody goes about to save it. When it was whole it was meet for no work, much less when the fire has devoured it (Eze 15:5); even the ashes of it are not worth saving.

II. How this similitude is applied to Jerusalem. 1. That holy city had become unprofitable and good for nothing. It had been as the vine-tree among the trees of the vineyard, abounding in the fruits of righteousness to the glory of God. When religion flourished there, and the pure worship of God was kept up, many a joyful vintage was then gathered in from it; and, while it continued so, God made a hedge about it; it was his pleasant plant (Isa 5:7); he watered it every moment and kept it night and day (Isa 27:3); but it had now become the degenerate plant of a strange vine, of a wild vine (such as we read of Kg2 4:39), a vine-tree among the trees of the wild grapes (Isa 5:4), which are not only of no use, but are nauseous and noxious (Deu 32:32), their grapes are grapes of gall, and their clusters are bitter. It is explained (Eze 15:8): "They have trespassed a trespass, that is, they have treacherously prevaricated with God and perfidiously apostatized from him;" for so the word signifies. Note, Professors of religion, if they do not live up to their profession, but contradict it, if they degenerate and depart from it, are the most unprofitable creatures in the world, like the salt that has lost its savour and is thenceforth good for nothing, Mar 9:50. Other nations were famed for valour or politics, some for war, others for trade, and retained their credit; but the Jewish nation, being famous as a holy people, when they lost their holiness, and became wicked, were thenceforth good for nothing; with that they lost all their credit and usefulness, and became the most base and despicable people under the sun, trodden under foot of the Gentiles. Daniel, and other pious Jews, were of great use in their generation; but the idolatrous Jews then, and the unbelieving Jews now since the preaching of the gospel, have been, and are, of no common service, not fit for any work. 2. Being so, it is given to the fire for fuel, Eze 15:6. Note, Those who are not fruitful to the glory of God's grace will be fuel to the fire of his wrath; and thus, if they give not honour to him, he will get himself honour upon them, honour that will shine brightly in that flaming fire by which impenitent sinners will be for ever consumed. He will not be a loser at last by any of his creatures. The Lord has made all things for himself, yea, even the wicked, that would not otherwise be for him, for the day of evil (Pro 16:4); and in those who would not glorify him as the God to whom duty belongs he will be glorified as the God to whom vengeance belongs. The fire of God's wrath had before devoured both the ends of the Jewish nation (Eze 15:4), Samaria and the cities of Judah; and now Jerusalem, that was the midst of it, was thrown into the fire, to be burnt too, for it is meet for no work; it will not be wrought upon, by any of the methods God has taken, to be serviceable to him. The inhabitants of Jerusalem were like a vine-branch, rotten and awkward; and therefore (Eze 15:7), "I will set my face against them, to thwart all their counsels," as they set their faces against God, to contradict his word and defeat all his designs. It is decreed; the consumption is determined: I will make the land quite desolate, and therefore, when they go out from one fire, another fire shall devour them (Eze 15:7); the end of one judgment shall be the beginning of another, and their escape from one only a reprieve till another comes; they shall go from misery in their own country to misery in Babylon. Those who kept out of the way of the sword perished by famine or pestilence. When one descent of the Chaldean forces upon them was over, and they thought, Surely the bitterness of death is past, yet soon after they returned again with double violence, till they had made a full end. Thus they shall know that I am the Lord, a God of almighty power, when I set my face against them. Note, God shows himself to be the Lord, by perfecting the destruction of his implacable enemies as well as the deliverances of his obedient people. Those whom God sets his face, though they may come out of one trouble little hurt, will fall into another; though they come out of the pit, they will be taken in the snare (Isa 24:18); though they escape the sword of Hazael, they will fall by that of Jehu (Kg1 19:17); for evil pursues sinners. Nay, though they go out from the fire of temporal judgments, and seem to die in peace, yet there is an everlasting fire that will devour them; for, when God judges, first or last he will overcome, and he will be known by the judgments which he executes. See Mat 3:10; Joh 15:6.

Ezekiel Chapter 16

Still God is justifying himself in the desolations he is about to bring upon Jerusalem; and very largely, in this chapter, he shows the prophet, and orders him to show the people, that he did but punish them as their sins deserved. In the foregoing chapter he had compared Jerusalem to an unfruitful vine, that was fit for nothing but the fire; in this chapter he compares it to an adulteress, that, in justice, ought to be abandoned and exposed, and he must therefore show the people their abominations, that they might see how little reason they had to complain of the judgments they were under. In this long discourse are set forth, I. The despicable and deplorable beginnings of that church and nation (Eze 16:3-5). II. The many honours and favours God had bestowed upon them (Eze 16:6-14). III. Their treacherous and ungrateful departures from him to the services and worship of idols, here represented by the most impudent whoredom (v. 15-34). IV. A threatening of terrible destroying judgments, which God would bring upon them for this sin (Eze 16:35-43). V. An aggravation both of their sin and of their punishment, by comparison with Sodom and Samaria (v. 44-59). VI. A promise of mercy in the close, which God would show to a penitent remnant (Eze 16:60-63). And this is designed for admonition to us.

Ezekiel 16:1

Ezekiel is now among the captives in Babylon; but, as Jeremiah at Jerusalem wrote for the use of the captives though they had Ezekiel upon the spot with them (ch. 29), so Ezekiel wrote for the use of Jerusalem, though Jeremiah himself was resident there; and yet they were far from looking upon it as an affront to one another's help both by preaching and writing. Jeremiah wrote to the captives for their consolation, which was the thing they needed; Ezekiel here is directed to write to the inhabitants of Jerusalem for their conviction and humiliation, which was the thing they needed.

I. This is his commission (Eze 16:2): "Cause Jerusalem to know her abominations (that is, her sins); set them in order before her." Note, 1. Sins are not only provocations which God is angry at, but abominations which he hates, as contrary to his nature, and which we ought to hate, Jer 44:4. 2. The sins of Jerusalem are in a special manner so. The practice of profaneness appears most odious in those that make a profession of religion. 3. Though Jerusalem is a place of great knowledge, yet she is loth to know her abominations; so partial are men in their own favour that they are hardly made to see and own their own badness, but deny it, palliate or extenuate it. 4. It is requisite that we should know our sins, that we may confess them, and may justify God in what he brings upon us for them. 5. It is the work of ministers to cause sinners, sinners in Jerusalem, to know their abominations, to set before them the glass of the law, that in it they may see their own deformities and defilements, to tell them plainly of their faults. Thou art the man.

II. That Jerusalem may be made to know her abominations, and particularly the abominable ingratitude she had been guilty of, it was requisite that she should be put in mind of the great things God had done for her, as the aggravations of her bad conduct towards him; and, to magnify those favours, she is in these verses made to know the meanness and baseness of her original, from what poor beginnings God raised her, and how unworthy she was of his favour and of the honour he had put upon her. Jerusalem is here put for the Jewish church and nation, which is here compared to an outcast child, base-born and abandoned, which the mother herself has no affection nor concern for. 1. The extraction of the Jewish nation was mean: "Thy birth is of the land of Canaan (Eze 16:3); thou hadst from the very first the spirit and disposition of a Canaanite." The patriarchs dwelt in Canaan, and they were there but strangers and sojourners, had no possession, no power, not one foot of ground of their own but a burying-place. Abraham and Sarah were indeed their father and mother, but they were only inmates with the Amorites and Hittites, who, having the dominion, seemed to be as parents to the seed of Abraham, witness the court Abraham made to the children of Seth (Gen 23:4, Gen 23:8), the dependence they had upon their neighbours the Canaanites, and the fear they were in of them, Gen 13:7; Gen 34:30. If the patriarchs, at their first coming to Canaan, had conquered it, and made themselves masters of it, this would have put an honour upon their family and would have looked great in history; but, instead of that, they went from one nation to another (Psa 105:13), as tenants from one farm to another, almost as beggars from one door to another, when they were but few in number, yea, very few. And yet this was not the worst; their fathers had served other gods in Ur of the Chaldees (Jos 24:2); even in Jacob's family there were strange gods, Gen 35:2. Thus early had they a genius leading them to idolatry; and upon this account their ancestors were Amorites and Hittites. 2. When they first began to multiply their condition was really very deplorable, like that of a new-born child, which must of necessity die from the womb if the knees prevent it not, Job 3:11, Job 3:12. The children of Israel, when they began to increase into a people and became considerable, were thrown out from the country that was intended for them; a famine drove them thence. Egypt was the open field into which they were cast; there they had no protection or countenance from the government they were under, but, on the contrary, were ruled with rigour, and their lives embittered; they had no encouragement given them to build up their families, no help to build up their estates, no friends or allies to strengthen their interests. Joseph, who had been the shepherd and stone of Israel, was dead; the king of Egypt, who should have been kind to them for Joseph's sake, set himself to destroy this man-child as soon as it was born (Rev 12:4), ordered all the males to be slain, which, it is likely, occasioned the exposing of many as well as Moses, to which perhaps the similitude here has reference. The founders of nations and cities had occasion for all the arts and arms they were masters of, set their heads on work, by policies and stratagems, to preserve and nurse up their infant states. Tantae molis erat Romanam condere gentem-So vast were the efforts requisite to the establishment of the Roman name. Virgil. But the nation of Israel had no such care taken of it, no such pains taken with it, as Athens, Sparta, Rome, and other commonwealths had when they were first founded, but, on the contrary, was doomed to destruction, like an infant new-born, exposed to wind and weather, the navel-string not cut, the poor babe not washed, not clothed, no swaddled, because not pitied, Eze 16:4, Eze 16:5. Note, We owe the preservation of our infant lives to the natural pity and compassion which the God of nature has put into the hearts of parents and nurses towards new-born children. This infant is said to be cast out, to the loathing of her person; it was a sign that she was loathed by those that bore her, and she appeared loathsome to all that looked upon her. The Israelites were an abomination to the Egyptians, as we find Gen 43:32; Gen 46:34. Some think that this refers to the corrupt and vicious disposition of that people from their beginning: they were not only the weakest and fewest of all people (Deu 7:7), but the worst and most ill-humoured of all people. God giveth thee this good land, not for thy righteousness, for thou art a stiff-necked people, Deu 9:6. And Moses tells them there (Eze 16:24), You have been rebellious against the Lord from the day that I knew you. They were not suppled, nor washed, nor swaddled; they were not at all tractable or manageable, nor cast into any good shape. God took them to be his people, not because he saw any thing in them inviting or promising, but so it seemed good in his sight. And it is a very apt illustration of the miserable condition of all the children of men by nature. As for our nativity, in the day that we were born we were shapen in iniquity and conceived in sin, our understandings darkened, our minds alienated from the life of God, polluted with sin, which rendered us loathsome in the eyes of God. Marvel not then that we are told, You must be born again.

Ezekiel 16:6

In there verses we have an account of the great things which God did for the Jewish nation in raising them up by degrees to be very considerable. 1. God saved them from the ruin they were upon the brink of in Egypt (Eze 16:6): "When I passed by thee, and saw thee polluted in thy own blood, loathed and abandoned, and appointed to die, as sheep for the slaughter, then I said unto thee, Live. I designed thee for life when thou wast doomed to destruction, and resolved to save thee from death." Those shall live to whom God commands life. God looked upon the world of mankind as thus cast off, thus cast out, thus polluted, thus weltering in blood, and his thoughts towards it were thoughts of good, designing it life, and that more abundantly. By converting grace, he says to the soul, Live. 2. He looked upon them with kindness and a tender affection, not only pitied them, but set his love upon them, which was unaccountable, for there was nothing lovely in them; but I looked upon thee, and, behold, thy time was the time of love, Eze 16:8. It was the kindness and love of God our Saviour that sent Christ to redeem us, that sends the Spirit to sanctify us, that brought us out of a state of nature into a state of grace. That was a time of love indeed, distinguishing love, when God manifested his love to us, and courted our love to him. Then was I in his eyes as one that found favour, Sol 8:10. 3. He took them under his protection: "I spread my skirt over thee, to shelter thee from wind and weather, and to cover thy nakedness, that the shame of it might not appear." Boaz spread his skirt over Ruth, in token of the special favour he designed her, Rut 3:9. God took them into his care, as an eagle bears her young ones upon her wings, Deu 32:11, Deu 32:12. When God owned them for his people, and sent Moses to Egypt to deliver them, which was an expression of the good-will of him that dwelt in the bush, then he spread his skirt over them. 4. He cleared them from the reproachful character which their bondage in Egypt laid them under (Eze 16:9): "Then washed I thee with water, to make thee clean, and anointed thee with oil, to make thee sweet and supple thee." All the disgrace of their slavery was rolled away when they were brought, with a high hand and a stretched-out arm, into the glorious liberty of the children of God. When God said, Israel is my son, my first-born-Let my people go, that they may serve me, that word, backed as it was with so many works of wonder, thoroughly washed away their blood; and when God led them under the convoy of the pillar of cloud and fire he spread his skirt over them. 5. He multiplied them and built them up into a people. This is here mentioned (Eze 16:7) before his spreading his skirt over them, because their numbers increased exceedingly while they were yet bond-slaves in Egypt. They multiplied as the bud of the field in spring time; they waxed great, exceedingly mighty, Exo 1:7. 20. Their breasts were fashioned when they were formed into distinct tribes and had officers of their own (Exo 5:19); their hair grew when they grew numerous, whereas they had been naked and bare, very few and therefore contemptible. 6. He admitted them into covenant with himself. See what glorious nuptials this poor forlorn infant is preferred to at last. How she is dignified who at first had scarcely her life given her for a prey: I swore unto thee and entered into covenant with thee. This was done at Mount Sinai: "when the covenant between God and Israel was sealed and ratified then thou becamest mine." God called them his people, and himself the God of Israel. Note, Those to whom God gives spiritual life he takes into covenant with himself; by that covenant they become his subjects and servants, which intimates their duty-his portion, his treasure, which intimates their privilege; and it is confirmed with an oath, that we might have strong consolation. 7. He beautified and adorned them. This maid cannot forget her ornaments, and she is gratified with abundance of them, Eze 16:10-13. We need not be particular in the application of these. Her wardrobe was well furnished with rich apparel; they had embroidered work to wear, shoes of fine badgers' skins, linen girdles, and silk veils, bracelets and necklaces, jewels and ear-rings, and even a beautiful crown, or coronet. Perhaps this may refer to the jewels and other rich goods which they took from the Egyptians, which might well be spoken of thus long after as a merciful circumstance of their deliverance, when it was spoken of long before, Gen 15:14. They shall come out with great substance. Or it may be taken figuratively for all those blessings of heaven which adorned both their church and state. In a little time they came to excellent ornaments, Eze 16:7. The laws and ordinances which God gave them were to them as ornaments of grace to the head and chains about the neck, Pro 1:9. God's sanctuary, which he set up among them, was a beautiful crown upon their head; it was the beauty of holiness. 8. He fed them with abundance, with plenty, with dainty: Thou didst eat fine flour, and honey, and oil-manna, angels' food-honey out of the rock, oil out of the flinty rock. In Canaan they did eat bread to the full, the finest of the wheat, Deu 32:13, Deu 32:14. Those whom God takes into covenant with himself are fed with the bread of life, clothed with the robe of righteousness, adorned with the graces and comforts of the spirit. The hidden man of the heart is that which is incorruptible. 9. He gave them great reputation among their neighbours, and made them considerable, acceptable to their friends and allies and formidable to their adversaries: Thou didst prosper into a kingdom (Eze 16:13), which speaks both dignity and dominion; and, They renown went forth among the heathen for thy beauty, Eze 16:14. The nations about had their eye upon them, and admired them for the excellent laws by which they were governed, the privilege they had of access to God, Deu 4:7, Deu 4:8. Solomon's wisdom, and Solomon's temple, were very much the renown of that nation; and, if we put all the privileges of the Jewish church and kingdom together, we must own that it was the most accomplished beauty of all the nations of the earth. The beauty of it was perfect; you could not name the thing that would be the honour of a people but it was to be found in Israel, in David's and Solomon's time, when that kingdom was in its zenith-piety, learning, wisdom, justice, victory, peace, wealth, and all sure to continue if they had kept close to God. It was perfect, saith God, through my comeliness which I had put upon thee, through the beauty of their holiness, as they were a people set apart for God, and devoted to him, to be to him for a name, and for a praise, and for a glory. It was this that put a lustre upon all their other honours and was indeed the perfection of their beauty. We may apply this spiritually. Sanctified souls are truly beautiful; they are so in God's sight, and they themselves may take the comfort of it. But God must have all the glory, for they were by nature deformed and polluted, and, whatever comeliness they have, it is that which God has put upon them and beautified them with, and he will be well pleased with the work of his own hands.

Ezekiel 16:15

In these verses we have an account of the great wickedness of the people of Israel, especially in worshipping idols, notwithstanding the great favours that God had conferred upon them, by which, one would think, they should have been for ever engaged to him. This wickedness of theirs is here represented by the lewd and scandalous conversation of that beautiful maid which was rescued from ruin, brought up and well provided for by a kind friend and benefactor, that had been in all respects as a father and a husband to her. Their idolatry was the great provoking sin that they were guilty of; it began in the latter end of Solomon's time (for from Samuel's till then I do not remember that we read any thing of it), and thenceforward continued more or less the crying sin of that nation till the captivity; and, though it now and then met with some check from the reforming kings, yet it was never totally suppressed, and for the most part appeared to a high degree impudent and barefaced. They not only worshipped the true God by images, as the ten tribes by the calves at Dan and Bethel, but they worshipped false gods, Baal and Moloch, and all the senseless rabble of the pagan deities.

This is that which is here all along represented (as often elsewhere) under the similitude of whoredom and adultery, 1. Because it is the violation of a marriage-covenant with God, forsaking him and embracing the bosom of a stranger; it is giving that affection and that service to his rivals which are due to him alone. 2. Because it is the corrupting and defiling of the mind, and the enslaving of the spiritual part of the man, and subjecting it to the power and dominion of sense, as whoredom is. 3. Because it debauches the conscience, sears and hardens it; and those who by their idolatries dishonour the divine nature, and change the truth of God into a lie and his glory into shame, God justly punishes by giving them over to a reprobate mind, to dishonour the human nature with vile affections, Rom 1:23, etc. It is a besotting bewitching sin; and, when men are given up to it, they seldom recover themselves out of the snare. 4. Because it is a shameful scandalous sin for those that have joined themselves to the Lord to join themselves to an idol. Now observe here,

I. What were the causes of this sin. How came the people of God to be drawn away to the service of idols? How came a virgin so well taught, so well educated, to be debauched? Who would have thought it? But, 1. They grew proud (Eze 16:15): "Thou trustedst to thy beauty, and didst expect that that should make thee an interest, and didst play the harlot because of thy renown." They thought, because they were so complimented and admired by their neighbours, that, further to ingratiate themselves with them and return their compliments, they must join with them in their worship and conform to their usages. Solomon admitted idolatry, to gratify his wives and their relations. Note, Abundance of young people are ruined by pride and particularly pride in their beauty. Rara est concordia formae atque pudicitiae-Beauty and chastity are seldom associated 2. They forgot their beginning (Eze 16:22) "Thou hast not remembered the days of thy youth, how poor, and mean, and despicable thou wast, and what great things God did for thee and what lasting obligations he laid upon thee thereby." Note, It should be an effectual check to our pride and sensuality to consider what we are and how much we are beholden to the free grace of God. 3. They were weak in understanding and in resolution (Eze 16:30): How weak is thy heart, seeing thou dost all these things. Note, The strength of men's lusts is an evidence of the weakness of their hearts; they have no acquaintance with themselves, nor government of themselves. She is weak, and yet an imperious whorish woman. Note, Those that are most foolish are commonly most imperious, and think themselves fit to manage others when they are far from being able to manage themselves.

II. What were the particulars of it. 1. They worshipped all the idols that came in their way, all that they were ever courted to the worship of; they were at the beck of all their neighbours (Eze 16:15): Thou pouredst out thy fornications on every one that passed by; his it was. They were ready to close with every temptation of this kind, though ever so absurd. No foreign idol could be imported, no new god invented, but they were ready to catch at it, as a common trumpet that prostitutes herself to all comers and multiplies her whoredoms, Eze 16:25. Thus some common drunkards will be company for every one that puts up the finger to them; how weak are the hearts of such! 2. They adorned their idol-temples, and groves, and high places, with the fine rich clothing that God had given them (Eze 16:16, Eze 16:18): Thou deckedst thy high places with divers colours, with the coats of divers colours, like Joseph's, which God had given them as particular marks of his favour, and hast played the harlot (that is, worshipped idols) thereupon. Of this he saith, "The like things shall not come, neither shall it be so; that is, this is a thing by no means to be suffered; I will never endure such practices as these without showing my resentments." 3. They made images for worship of the jewels which God had given them (Eze

16:17): The jewels of my gold and my silver which I had given thee. Note, It is God that gives us our gold and silver; the products of trade, of art and industry, are the gifts of God's providence to us, as well as the fruits of the earth. And what God gives us the use of he still retains a property in. "It is my silver and my gold, though I have given it to thee." It is his still, so that we ought to serve and honour him with it, and are accountable to him for the disposal of it. Every penny has God's image upon it as well as Caesar's. Should we make our silver and gold, our plate, money, and jewels, the matter of our pride and contention, our covetousness and prodigality, if we duly considered that they were God's silver and his gold? The Israelites began betimes to turn their jewels into idols, when Aaron made the golden calf of their earrings. 4. They served their idols with the good things which God gave them for their own use and to serve him with (Eze 16:18): "Thou hast set my oil and my incense before the, upon their altars, as perfumes to these dunghill-deities; my meat, and fine flour, and oil, and that honey which Canaan flowed with, and wherewith I fed thee, thou hast regaled them and their hungry priests with, hast made an offering of it to them for a sweet savour, to purify them, and procure acceptance with them: and thus it was, saith the Lord God; it is too plain to be denied, too bad to be excused. These things thou hast done. He that knows all things knows it." See how fond they were of their idols, that they would part with that which was given them for the necessary subsistence of themselves and their families to honour them with, which may shame our niggardliness and strait-handedness in the service of the true and living God. 5. They had sacrificed their children to their idols. This is insisted upon here, and often elsewhere, as one of the worst instances of their idolatry, as indeed there was none in which the devil triumphed so much over the children of men, both their natural reason and their natural affection, as in this (see Jer 7:31; Jer 19:5; Jer 32:35): Thou hast taken thy sons and thy daughters, and not only made them to pass through the fire, or between two fires, in token of their being dedicated to Moloch, but thou hast sacrificed them to be devoured, Eze 16:20. Never was there such an instance of the degenerating of the paternal authority into the most barbarous tyranny as this was. Yet that was not the worst of it: it was an irreparable wrong to God himself, who challenged a special property in their children more than in their gold and silver and their meat: They are my children (Eze 16:21), the sons and daughters which thou hast borne unto me, Eze 16:20. He is the Father of spirits, and rational souls are in a particular manner his; and therefore the taking away of life, human life, unjustly, is a high affront to the God of life. But the children of Israelites were his by a further right; they were the children of the covenant, born in God's house. He had said to Abraham, I will be a God to thee and to thy seed; they had the seal of the covenant in their flesh from eight days old; they were to bear God's name, and keep up his church; to murder them was in the highest degree inhuman, but to murder them in honour of an idol was in the highest degree impious. One cannot think of it without the utmost indignation: to see the pitiless hands of the parents shedding the guiltless blood of their own children, and by offering those pieces of themselves to the devil for buying sacrifices openly avowing the offering up of themselves to him for living sacrifices! How absurd was this, that the children which were born to God should be sacrificed to devils! Note, The children of parents that are members of the visible church are to be looked upon as born unto God, and his children,;

as such, and under that character, we are to love them, and pray for them, bring them up for him, and, if he calls for them, cheerfully part with them to him; for may he not do what he will with his own? Upon this instance of their idolatry, which indeed ought not to pass without a particular brand, this remark is made (Eze 16:20), Is this of thy whoredoms a small matter? which intimates that there were those who made a small matter of it, and turned it into a jest. Note, There is no sin so heinous, so apparently heinous, which men of profligate consciences will not make a mock at. But is whoredom, is spiritual whoredom, a small matter? Is it a small matter for men to make their children brutes and the devil their god? It will be a great matter shortly. 6. They built temples in honour of their idols, that others might be invited to resort thither and join with them in the worship of their idols: "After all thy wickedness of this kind committed in private, for which, woe, woe, unto thee" (that comes in in a sad parenthesis, denoting those to be in a woeful condition who are going on in sin, and giving them warning in time, if they would but take it), "thou hast at length arrived at such a pitch of impudence as to proclaim it; thou hast long had a whore's heart, but now thou hast come to have a whore's forehead, and canst not blush," Eze 16:23-35. Thou hast built there an eminent place, a brothel-house (so the margin reads it), and such their idol temples were. Thou hast made for thyself a high place, for one idol or other, in every street, and at every head of the way; and again Eze 16:31. They did all they could to seduce and debauch others, and to spread the contagion, by making the temptations to idolatry as strong as possibly they could; and hereby the ringleaders in idolatry did but make themselves vile, and even those that had courted them to it, finding themselves outdone by them, began to be surfeited with the abundance and violence of their idolatries: Thou hast made thy beauty to be abhorred, even by those that had admired it. The Jewish nation, by leaving their own God, and doting on the gods of the nations round about them, had made themselves mean and despicable in the eyes even of their heathen neighbours; much more was their beauty abhorred by all that were wise and good, and had any concern for the honour of God and religion. Note, Those shame themselves that bring a reproach on their profession. And justly will that beauty, that excellency, at length be made the object of the loathing of others which men have made the matter of their own pride.

III. What were the aggravations of this sin.

1. They were fond of the idols of those nations which had been their oppressors and persecutors. As, (1.) The Egyptians. They were a people notorious for idolatry, and for the most sottish senseless idolatries; they had of old abused Israel by their barbarous dealings, and of late by their treacherous dealings-were always either cruel or false to them; and yet so infatuated were they that they committed fornication with the Egyptians their neighbours, not only by joining with them in their idolatries, but by entering into leagues and alliances with them, and depending upon them for help in their straits, which was an adulterous departure from God. (2.) The Assyrians. They had also been vexatious to Israel: "And yet thou hast played the whore with them (Eze 16:28); though they lived at a greater distance, yet thou hast entertained their idols and their superstitious usages, and so hast multiplied thy fornications unto Chaldea, hast borrowed

images of gods, patterns of altars, rites of sacrificing, and one foolery or other of that kind, from that remote country, that enemy's country, and hast imported them into the land of Canaan, enfranchised and established them there." Thus Mr. George Herbert long since foretold, or feared at least,

That Seine shall swallow Tiber, and the Thames

By letting in them both pollute her streams.

2. They had been under the rebukes of Providence for their sins, and yet they persisted in them (Eze 16:27): I have stretched out my hand over thee, to threaten and frighten thee. So God did before he laid his hand upon them to ruin and destroy them; and that is his usual method, to try to bring men to repentance first by less judgments. He did so here. Before he brought such a famine upon them as broke the staff of bread he diminished their ordinary food, but them short before he cut them off. When the overplus is abused, it is just with God to diminish that which is for necessity. Before he delivered them to the Chaldeans to be destroyed he delivered them to the daughters of the Philistines to be ridiculed for their idolatries; for they hated them, and, though they were idolaters themselves, yet were ashamed of the lewd way of the Israelites, who had grown more profane in their idolatries than any of their neighbours, who changed their gods, whereas other nations did not change theirs, Jer 2:10, Jer 2:11. For this they were justly chastised by the Philistines. Or it may refer to the inroads which the Philistines made upon the south of Judah in the reign of Ahaz, by which it was weakened and impoverished, and which was the beginning of sorrows to them (Ch2 28:18); but they did not take warning by those judgments, and therefore were justly abandoned to ruin at last. Note, In the account which impenitent sinners shall be called to they will be told not only of the mercies for which they have been ungrateful, but of the afflictions under which they have been incorrigible, Amo 4:11.

3. They were insatiable in their spiritual whoredom: Thou couldst not be satisfied, Eze 16:28 and again Eze 16:29. When they had multiplied their idols and superstitious usages beyond measure, yet still they were enquiring after new gods and new fashions in worship. Those that in sincerity join themselves to the true God find enough in him for their satisfaction; and, though they still desire more of God, yet they never desire more than God. But those that forsake this living fountain for broken cisterns will find themselves soon surfeited, but never satisfied; they have soon enough of the gods they have, and are still enquiring after more.

4. They were at great expense with their idolatry, and laid out a great deal of wealth in purchasing patterns of images and altars, and hiring priests to attend upon them from other countries. Harlots generally had their hire; but this impudent adulteress, instead of being hired to serve idols, hired idols to protect her and accept her homage. This is much insisted on, Eze 16:31-34. "In this respect the contrary is in thee from other women in thy whoredoms: others are courted, but thou makest court to those that do not follow thee, art fond of making leagues and

alliances with those heathen nations that despise thee; others have gifts given them, but thou givest thy gifts, the gifts which God had graciously given thee, to thy idols; herein thou art like a wife that commits adultery, not for gain, as harlots do, but entirely for the sin's sake." Note, Spiritual lusts, those of the mind, such as theirs after idols were, are often as strong and impetuous as any carnal lusts are. And it is a great aggravation of sin when men are their own tempters, and, instead of proposing to themselves any worldly advantage by their sin, are at great expense with it; such are transgressors without cause (Psa 25:3), wicked transgressors indeed.

And now is not Jerusalem in all this made to know her abominations? For what greater abominations could she be guilty of than these? Here we may see with wonder and horror what the corrupt nature of men is when God leaves them to themselves, yea, though they have the greatest advantages to be better and do better. And the way of sin is down-hill. Nitimur in vetitum-We incline to what is forbidden.

Ezekiel 16:35

Adultery was by the law of Moses made a capital crime. This notorious adulteress, the criminal at the bar, being in the foregoing verses found guilty, here has sentence passed upon her. It is ushered in with solemnity, Eze 16:35. The prophet, as the judge, in God's name calls to her, O harlot! hear the word of the Lord. Our Saviour preached to harlots, for their conversion, to bring them into the kingdom of God, not as the prophet here, to expel them out of it. Note, An apostate church is a harlot. Jerusalem is so if she become idolatrous. How has the faithful city become a harlot! Rome is so represented in the Revelation, when it is marked for ruin, as Jerusalem here. Rev 17:1, Come, and I will show thee the judgments of the great whore. Those who will not hear the commanding word of the Lord and obey it shall be made to hear the condemning word of the Lord and shall tremble at it. Let us attend while judgment is given.

I. The crime is stated and the articles of the charge are summed up (Eze 16:36) and (as is usual) with the attendant aggravations (Eze 16:43); for when God speaks in wrath he will be justified, and clear when he judges, clear when he is judged; and sinners, when they are condemned, shall have their sins so set in order before them that their mouth shall be stopped and they shall not have a word to object against the equity of the sentence. The crimes which this harlot stands convicted of, and is now to be condemned for, are, 1. The violation of the first two commandments of the first table by idolatry, which is here called her whoredoms with her lovers (so she called them, Hos 2:12, because she loved them as if they had been indeed her benefactors), that is, with all the idols of her abominations, the abominable idols which she served and worshipped. This was the sin which provoked God to jealousy. 2. The violation of the first two commandments of the second table by the murder of their own innocent infants: The blood of thy children which thou didst give unto them. It is not strange if those that have cast off God and his fear break through the strongest and most sacred bonds of natural affection. Their sins are aggravated from the consideration, (1.) Of the dishonour they had thereby done to

cxl

themselves: "Hereby thy filthiness was poured out; the uncleanness that was in thy heart was hereby discovered and brought to light, and thy nakedness was exposed to view, and thou wast thereby exposed to contempt." God is displeased with his professing people for shaming themselves by their sins. (2.) Their base ingratitude is another aggravation of their sins: "Thou hast not remembered the days of thy youth, and the kindness that was done thee then, when otherwise thou wouldst have perished," Eze 16:43. And, (3.) The vexation which their sins gave to God, whom they ought to have pleased: "Thou hast fretted me in all these things, not only angered me, but grieved me." It is a strange expression, and, one would think, enough to melt a heart of stone, that the great God, who cannot admit any uneasiness, is pleased to speak of the sins and follies of his professing people as fretting to him. Forty years long was I grieved with this generation.

II. The sentence is passed in general: I will judge thee as women that break wedlock and shed blood are judged (Eze 16:38), and those two crimes were punished with death, with an ignominious death. "Thou hast shed blood, and therefore I will give thee blood; thou hast broken wedlock, and therefore I will give it thee, not only in justice, but in jealousy, not only as a righteous Judge, but as an injured and incensed husband, who will not spare in the day of vengeance," Pro 6:34, Pro 6:35. He will recompense their way upon their head, Eze 16:43. In all the judgments God executes upon sinners we must see their own way recompensed upon their head; they are dealt with not only as they deserved, but as they procured. It is the end which their sin, as a way, had a direct tendency to. More particularly, 1. This criminal must be (as is usually done with criminals) exposed to public shame, Eze 16:37. Malefactors are not executed privately, but are made a spectacle to the world. Care is here taken to bring spectators together: "All those whom thou hast loved, with whom thou hast taken pleasure, shall come to be witnesses of the execution, that they may take warning and prevent their own like ruin; and those also whom thou hast hated, who will insult over thee and triumph in thy fall." Both ways the calamities of Jerusalem will be aggravated, that they will be the grief of her friends and the joy of her foes. These shall not only be gathered around her, but gathered against her; even those with whom she took unlawful pleasure, with whom she contracted unlawful leagues, the Egyptians and Assyrians, shall now contribute to her ruin. As, when a man's ways please the Lord, he makes even his enemies to be at peace with him, so when a man's ways displease the Lord he makes even his friends to be at war with him; and justly makes those a scourge and a plague to sinners, and instruments of their destruction, who were their tempters, and with whom they were partakers in wickedness. Those whom they have suffered to strip them of their virtue shall see them stripped, and perhaps help to strip them, of all their other ornaments; to see the nakedness of the land will they come. It is added, to the same purport (Eze 16:41), I will execute judgments upon thee in the sight of many women; thou shalt be made an example of in terrorem- that others may see and fear and do no more presumptuously. 2. The criminal is condemned to die, for her sins are such as death is the wages of (Eze 16:40): They shall bring up a company (that is, a company shall be brought up) against thee, and they shall stone thee with stones, and thrust thee through with their swords; so great a death, so many deaths in one, is this adulteress adjudged to. When the walls of Jerusalem were battered down with stones shot against them, and the inhabitants of Jerusalem were put to the sword, then this sentence was executed in the letter of it. 3. The estate of the criminal is confiscated, and all that belonged to her destroyed with her (Eze 16:39): They shall throw down thy eminent place, and (Eze 16:41) they shall burn thy houses, as the habitations of bad women are destroyed, in detestation of their lewdness. Their high places, erected in honour of their idols, by which they thought to ingratiate themselves with their neighbours, shall be an offence to them, and even they shall break them down. It was long the complaint, even in some of the best reigns of the kings of Judah, that the high places were not taken away; but now the army of the Chaldeans, when they lay all waste, shall break them down. If iniquity be not taken away by the justice of the nation, it shall be taken away by the judgments of God upon the nation. 4. Thus both the sin and the sinners shall be abolished together, and an end put to both: Thou shalt cease from playing the harlot; there shall be no remainders of idolatry in the land, because the inhabitants shall be wholly extirpated, and they shall give no more hire because they shall have no more to give. Some that will not leave their sins live till their sins leave them. When all that with which they honoured their idols is taken from them they shall not give hire any more (Eze 16:41): "Then thou shalt not commit this lewdness of sacrificing thy children, which was a crime provoking above all thy abominations, for thy children shall all be cut off by the sword or carried into captivity, so that thou shalt have none to sacrifice," Eze 16:43. Or it may be meant of the reformation of those of them that escape and survive the punishment; they shall take warning, and shall do no more presumptuously. The captivity in Babylon made the people of Israel to cease for ever from playing the harlot; it effectually cured them of their inclination to idolatry. And then all shall be well, when this is the fruit, even the taking away of sin; then (Eze 16:42) my jealousy shall depart. I will be quiet, and no more angry. When we begin to be at war with sin God will be at peace with us; for he continues the affliction no longer than till it has done its work. When sin departs God's jealousy will soon depart, for he is never jealous but when we give him just cause to be so. Yet some understand this as a threatening of utter ruin, that God will make a full end and the fire of his anger shall burn as long as there is any fuel for it. His fury shall rest upon them, and not remove. Compare this with that doom of unbelievers, Joh 3:36. The wrath of God abideth on them. They shall drink the dregs of the cup, and then God will be no more angry, for he is eased of his adversaries (Isa 1:24), is satisfied in the abandoning of them, and therefore will be no more angry, because there are no more for his anger to fasten upon. They had fretted him, when judgment and mercy were contesting; but now he is quiet, as he will be in the eternal damnation of sinners, wherein he will be glorified, and therefore he will be satisfied.

Ezekiel 16:44

The prophet here further shows Jerusalem her abominations, by comparing her with those places that had gone before her, and showing that she was worse than any of them, and therefore should, like them, be utterly and irreparably ruined. We are all apt to judge of ourselves by comparison, and to imagine that we are sufficiently good if we are but as good as such and such, who are thought passable; or that we are not dangerously bad if we are no worse than such and such, who, though bad, are not of the worst. Now God by the prophet shows Jerusalem,

I. That she was as bad as her mother, that is, as the accursed devoted Canaanites that were the possessors of this land before her. Those that use proverbs, as most people do, shall apply that proverb to Jerusalem, As is the mother, so is her daughter, Eze 16:44. She is her mother's own child. The Jews are as like the Canaanites in temper and inclination as if they had been their own children. The character of the mother was that she loathed her husband and her children, she had all the marks of an adulteress; and that is the character of the daughter: she forsakes the guide of her youth, and is barbarous to the children of her own bowels. When God brought Israel into Canaan he particularly warned them not to do according to the abominations of the men of that land, who went before them (for which it had spued them out, Lev 18:27, Lev 18:28), the monuments of whose idolatry, with the remains of the idolaters themselves, would be a continual temptation to them; but they learned their way, and trod in their steps, and were as well affected to the idols of Canaan as ever they were (Psa 106:38), and thus, in respect of imitation, it might truly be said that their mother was a Hittite and their father an Amorite (Eze 16:45), for they resembled them more than Abraham and Sarah.

II. That she was worse than her sisters Sodom and Samaria, that were adulteresses too, that loathed their husbands and their children, that were weary of the gods of their fathers, and were for introducing new gods, a-la-mode-quite in style, that came newly up, and new fashions in religion, and were given to change. On this comparison between Jerusalem and her sisters the prophet here enlarges, that he might either shame them into repentance or justify God in their ruin. Observe,

1. Who Jerusalem's sisters were, Eze 16:45. Samaria and Sodom. Samaria is called the elder sister, or rather the greater, because it was a much larger city and kingdom, richer and more considerable, and more nearly allied to Israel. If Jerusalem look northward, this is partly on her left hand. This city of Samaria, and the towns and villages, that were as daughters to that mother-city, these had been lately destroyed for their spiritual whoredom. Sodom, and the adjacent towns and villages that were her daughters, dwelt at Jerusalem's right hand, and was her less sister, less than Jerusalem, less than Samaria, and these were of old destroyed for their corporeal whoredom, Jde 1:7.

2. Wherein Jerusalem's sins resembled her sisters', particularly Sodom's (v. 49): This was the iniquity of Sodom (it is implied, and this is thy iniquity too), pride, fulness of bread, and abundance of idleness. Their going after strange flesh, which was Sodom's most flagrant wickedness, is not mentioned, because notoriously known, but those sins which did not look so black, but opened the door and led the way to these more enormous crimes, and began to fill that measure of her sins, which was filled up at length by their unnatural filthiness. Now these initiating sins were, (1.) Pride, in which the heart lifts up itself above and against both God and

cxliii

man. Pride was the first sin that turned angels into devils, and the garden of the Lord into a hell upon earth. It was the pride of the Sodomites that they despised righteous Lot, and would not bear to be reproved by him; and this ripened them for ruin. (2.) Gluttony, here called fulness of bread. It was God's great mercy that they had plenty, but their great sin that they abused it, glutted themselves with it, ate to excess and drank to excess, and made that the gratification of their lusts which was given them to be the support of their lives. (3.) Idleness, abundance of idleness, a dread of labour and a love of ease. Their country was fruitful, and the abundance they had they came easily by, which was a temptation to them to indulge themselves in sloth, which disposed them to all that abominable filthiness which kindled their flames. Note, Idleness is an inlet to much sin. The men of Sodom, who were idle, were wicked, and sinners before the Lord exceedingly, Gen 13:13. The standing waters gather filth and the sitting bird is the fowler's mark. When David arose from off his bed at evening he saw Bathsheba. Quaeritur, Aegisthus quare sit factus adulter? In promptu causa est; desidiosus erat-What made Aegisthus an adulterer? Indolence. (4.) Oppression: Neither did she strengthen the hands of the poor and needy; probably it is implied that she weakened their hands and broke their arms; however, it was bad enough that, when she had so much wealth, and consequently power and interest and leisure, she did nothing for the relief of the poor, in providing for whose wants those that themselves are full of bread may employ their time well; they need not be so abundantly idle as too often they are. These were the sins of the Sodomites, and these were Jerusalem's sins. Their pride, the cause of their sins, is mentioned again (Eze 16:50): They were haughty, with the horrid effects of their sins, their abominations which they committed before God. Men arrive gradually at the height of impiety and wickedness. Nemo repente fit turpissimus-No man reaches the height of vice at once. But, where pride has got the ascendant in a man, he is in the high road to all abominations.

3. How much the sins of Jerusalem exceeded those of Sodom and Samaria; they were more heinous in the sight of God, either in themselves or by reason of several aggravations: "Thou hast not only walked after their ways, and trod in their steps, but hast quite outdone them in wickedness, Eze 16:47. Thou thoughtest it a very little thing to do as they did; didst laugh at them as sneaking sinners and silly ones; thou wouldst be more cunning, more daring, in wickedness, wouldst triumph more boldly over thy convictions, and bid more open defiance to God and religion: 'if a man will break, let him break for something.' Thus thou wast corrupted more than they in all thy ways." Jerusalem was more polite, and therefore sinned with more wit, more art and ingenuity, than Sodom and Samaria could. Jerusalem had more wealth and power, and its government was more absolute and arbitrary, and therefore had the more opportunity of oppressing the poor, and shedding malignant influences around her, than Sodom and Samaria had. Jerusalem had the temple, and the ark, and the priesthood, and kings of the house of David; and therefore the wickedness of that holy city, that was so dignified, so near, so dear to God, was more provoking to him than the wickedness of Sodom and Samaria, that had not Jerusalem's privileges and means of grace. Sodom has not done as thou hast done, Eze 16:48. This agrees with what Christ says. Mat 11:24, It shall be more tolerable for the land of Sodom in the day of judgment than for thee. The kingdom of the ten tribes had been very wicked; and yet Samaria has

not committed half thy sins (Eze 16:51), has not worshipped half so many idols, nor slain half so many prophets. It was bad enough that those of Jerusalem were guilty of Sodom's sins, Sodomy itself not excepted, Kg1 14:24; Kg2 23:7. And though the Dead Sea, the standing monument of Sodom's sin and ruin, bordered upon their country (Num 34:12), and that sulphureous lake was always under their nose (God having taken away Sodom and her daughters in such way and manner as he saw good, as he says here, Eze 16:50, so as that one thing should effectually make their overthrow an example to those that afterwards should live ungodly, Pe2 2:6), yet they did not take warning, but multiplied their abominations more than they; and, (1.) By this they justified Sodom and Samaria, Eze 16:51. They pretended, in their haughtiness and superciliousness, to judge them, and in the days of old, when they retained their integrity, they did judge them, Eze 16:52. But now they justify them comparatively: Sodom and Samaria are more righteous than thou, that is, less wicked. It will look like some extenuation of their sins that, bad as they were, Jerusalem was worse, though it was God's own city. Not that it will serve for a plea to justify Sodom, but it condemns Jerusalem, against which Sodom and Samaria will rise up in judgment. (2.) For this they ought themselves to be greatly ashamed: "Thou who hast judged thy sisters, and cried out shame on them, now bear thy own shame, for thy sins which thou hast committed, which, though of the same kind with theirs, yet, being committed by thee, are more abominable than theirs," Eze 16:52. This may be taken either as foretelling their ruin (Thou shalt bear thy shame) or as inviting them to repentance: "Be thou confounded and bear thy shame; take the shame to thyself that is due to thee." It may be hoped that sinners will forsake their sins when they begin to be heartily ashamed of them. And therefore they shall go into captivity, and there they shall lie, that they may be confounded in all that they have done, because they had been a comfort and encouragement to Sodom and Samaria, Eze 16:54. Note, There is nothing in sin which we have more reason to be ashamed of than this, that by our sin we have encouraged others in sin, and comforted them in that for which they must be grieved or they are undone. Another reason why they must now be ashamed is because in the day of their prosperity they had looked with so much disdain upon their neighbours: Thy sister Sodom was not mentioned by thee in the day of they pride, Eze 16:56. They thought Sodom not worthy to be named the same day with Jerusalem, little dreaming that Jerusalem would at length lie under a worse and more scandalous character than Sodom herself. Those that are high may perhaps come to stand upon a level with those they contemn. Or "Sodom was not mentioned, that is, the warning designed to be given to thee by Sodom's ruin was not regarded." If the Jews had but talked more frequently and seriously to one another, and to their children, concerning the wrath of God revealed from heaven against Sodom's ungodliness and unrighteousness, it might have kept them in awe, and prevented their treading in their steps; but they kept the thought of it at a distance, would not bear the mention of it, and (as the ancients say) put Isaiah to death for putting them in mind of it, when he called them rulers of Sodom and people of Gomorrah, Isa 1:10. Note, Those are but preparing judgments for themselves that will not take notice of God's judgments upon others.

4. What desolations God had brought and was bringing upon Jerusalem for these wickednesses,

wherein they had exceeded Sodom and Samaria. (1.) She has already long ago been disgraced, and has fallen into contempt, among her neighbours (Eze 16:57): Before her wickedness was discovered, before she came to be so grossly and openly flagitious, she bore the just punishment of her secret and more concealed lewdness, when she fell under the reproach of the daughters of Syria, of the Philistines, who were said to despise her and be ashamed of her (Eze 16:27), and under the reproach of all that were round about her, which seems to refer to the descent made upon Judah by the Syrians in the days of Ahaz, and soon after another by the Philistines, Ch2 28:5, Ch2 28:18. Note, Those that disgrace themselves by yielding to their lusts will justly be brought into disgrace by being made to yield to their enemies; and it is observable that before God brought potent enemies upon them, for their destruction, he brought enemies upon them that were less formidable, for their reproach. If less judgments would do the work, God would not send greater. In this thou hast borne thy lewdness, Eze 16:58. Those that will not cast off their sins by repentance and reformation shall be made to bear their sins to their confusion. (2.) She is now in captivity, or hastening into captivity, and therein is reckoned with, not only for her lewdness (Eze 16:58), but for her perfidiousness and covenant-breaking (Eze 16:59): "I will deal with thee as thou hast done; I will forsake thee as thou hast forsaken me, and cast thee off as thou hast cast me off, for thou hast despised the oath, in breaking the covenant." This seems to be meant of the covenant God made with their fathers at Mount Sinai, whereby he took them and theirs to be a peculiar people to himself. They flattered themselves with a conceit that because God had hitherto continued his favour to them, notwithstanding their provocations, he would do so still. "No," says God, "you have broken covenant with me, have despised both the promises of the covenant and the obligations of it, and therefore I will deal with thee as thou hast done." Note, Those that will not adhere to God as their God have no reason to expect that he should continue to own them as his people. (3.) The captivity of the wicked Jews, and their ruin, shall be as irrevocable as that of Sodom and Samaria. In this sense, as a threatening, most interpreters take Eze 16:53, Eze 16:55. "When I shall bring again the captivity of Sodom and Samaria, and when they shall return to their former estate, then I will bring again the captivity of thy captives in the midst of them, and as it were for their sakes, and under their shadow and protection, because they are more righteous than thou, and then thou shalt return to thy former estate." But Sodom and Samaria were never brought back, nor ever returned to their former estate, and therefore let not Jerusalem expect it, that is, those who now remained there, whom God would deliver to be removed into all the kingdoms of the earth for their hurt, Jer 24:9, Jer 24:10. Sooner shall the Sodomites arise out of the salt sea, and the Samaritans return out of the land of Assyria, than they enjoy their peace and prosperity again; for, to their shame be it spoken, it is a comfort to those of the ten tribes, who are dispersed and in captivity, to see those of the two tribes who had been as bad as they, or worse, in like manner dispersed and in captivity; and therefore they shall live and die, shall stand and fall, together. The bad ones of both shall perish together; the good ones of both shall return together. Note, Those who do as the worst of sinners do must expect to fare as they fare. Let my enemy be as the wicked.

Ezekiel 16:60

Here, in the close of the chapter, after a most shameful conviction of sin and a most dreadful denunciation of judgments, mercy is remembered, mercy is reserved, for those who shall come after. As was when God swore in his wrath concerning those who came out of Egypt that they should not enter Canaan, "Yet" (says God) "your little ones shall;" so here. And some think that what is said of the return of Sodom and Samaria (Eze 16:53, Eze 16:55), and of Jerusalem with them, is a promise; it may be understood so, if by Sodom we understand (as Grotius and some of the Jewish writers do) the Moabites and Ammonites, the posterity of Lot, who once dwelt in Sodom; their captivity was returned (Jer 48:47; Jer 49:6), as was that of many of the ten tribes, and Judah's with them. But these closing verses are, without doubt, a previous promise, which was in part fulfilled at the return of the penitent and reformed Jews out of Babylon, but was to have its full accomplishment in gospel-times, and in that repentance and that remission of sins which should then be preached with success to all nations, beginning at Jerusalem. Now observe here,

I. Whence this mercy should take rise-from God himself, and his remembering his covenant with them (Eze 16:60): Nevertheless, though they had been so provoking, and God had been provoked to such a degree that one would think they could never be reconciled again, yet "I will remember my covenant with thee, that covenant which I made with thee in the days of thy youth, and will revive it again. Though thou hast broken the covenant (Eze 16:59), I will remember it, and it shall flourish again." See how much it is our comfort and advantage that God is pleased to deal with us in a covenant-way, for thus the mercies of it come to be sure mercies and everlasting (Isa 55:3); and, while this root stands firmly in the ground, there is hope of the tree, though it be cut down, that through the scent of water it will bud again. We do not find that they put him in mind of the covenant, but ex mero motu-from his own mere good pleasure, he remembers it as he had promised. Lev 26:42, Then will I remember my covenant, and will remember the land. He that bids us to be ever mindful of the covenant no doubt will himself be ever mindful of it, the word which he commanded (and what he commands stands fast for ever) to a thousand generations.

II. How they should be prepared and qualified for this mercy (Eze 16:61): "Thou shalt remember thy ways, thy evil ways; God will put thee in mind of them, will set them in order before thee, that thou mayest be ashamed of them." Note, God's good work in us commences and keeps pace with his good-will towards us. When he remembers his covenant for us, that he may not remember our sins against us, he puts us upon remembering our sins against ourselves. And if we will but be brought to remember our ways, how crooked and perverse they have been and how we have walked contrary to God in them, we cannot but be ashamed; and, when we are so, we are best prepared to receive the honour and comfort of a sealed pardon and a settled peace.

III. What the mercy is that God has in reserve for them. 1. He will take them into covenant with himself (Eze 16:60): I will establish unto thee an everlasting covenant; and again (Eze 16:62), I will establish, re-establish, and establish more firmly than ever, my covenant with thee.

Note, It is an unspeakable comfort to all true penitents that the covenant of grace is so well ordered in all things that every transgression in the covenant does not throw us out of the covenant, for that is inviolable. 2. He will bring the Gentiles into church-communion with them (Eze 16:61): "Thou shalt receive thy sisters, the Gentile nations that are found about thee, thy elder and thy younger, greater than thou art and less, ancient nations and modern, and I will give them unto thee for daughters; they shall be founded, nursed, taught, and educated, by that gospel, that word of the Lord, which shall go forth from Zion and from Jerusalem; so that all the neighbours shall call Jerusalem mother, while the church continues there, and shall acknowledge the Jerusalem which is from above, and which is free, to be the mother of us all, Gal 4:26. They shall be thy daughters, but not by thy covenant, not by the covenant of peculiarity, not as being proselytes to the Jewish religion and subject to the yoke of the ceremonial law, but as being converts with thee to the Christian religion." Or not by thy covenant may mean, "not upon such terms as thou shalt think fit to impose upon them as conquered nations, as captives and homagers to whom thou mayest give law at pleasure" (such a dominion as that the carnal Jews hope to have over the nations); "no, they shall be thy daughters by my covenant, the covenant of grace made with thee and them in concert, as in indenture tripartite. I will be a Father, a common Father, both to Jews and Gentiles, and so they shall become sisters to one another. And, when thou shalt receive them, thou shalt be ashamed of thy own evil ways wherein thou wast conformed to them. Thou shalt blush to look a Gentile in the face, remembering how much worse than the Gentiles thou wast in the day of thy apostasy."

IV. What the fruit and effect of this will be. 1. God will hereby be glorified (Eze 16:62): "Thou shalt know that I am the Lord. It shall hereby be known that the God of Israel is Jehovah, a God of power, and faithful to his covenant; and thou shalt know it who hast hitherto lived as if thou didst not know or believe it." It had often been said in wrath, You shall know that I am the Lord, shall know it to your cost; here it is said in mercy, You shall know it to your comfort; and it is one of the most precious promises of the new covenant which God has made with us that all shall know him from the least to the greatest. 2. They shall hereby be more humbled and abased for sin (Eze 16:63): "That thou mayest be the more confounded at the remembrance of all that thou hast done amiss, mayest reproach thyself for it and call thyself a thousand times unwise, undutiful, ungrateful, and unlike what thou wast, and mayest never open thy mouth any more in contradiction to God, reflection on him, or complaints of him, but mayest be for ever silent and submissive because of thy shame." Note, Those that rightly remember their sins will be truly ashamed of them; and those that are truly ashamed of their sins will see great reason to be patient under their afflictions, to be dumb, and not open their mouths against what God does. But that which is most observable is, that all this shall be when I am pacified towards thee, saith the Lord God. Note, It is the gracious ingenuousness of true penitents that the clearer evidences and the fuller instances they have of God's being reconciled to them the more grieved and ashamed they are that ever they have offended God. God is in Jesus Christ pacified towards us; he is our peace, and it is by his cross that we are reconciled, and in his gospel that God is reconciling the world to himself. Now the consideration of this should be powerful to melt our hearts into a godly sorrow for sin. This is repenting because the kingdom of heaven is at hand. The prodigal, after he had received the kiss which assured him that his father was pacified towards him, was ashamed and confounded, and said, Father, I have sinned against heaven and before thee. And the more our shame for sin is increased by the sense of pardoning mercy the more will our comfort in God be increased.

Ezekiel Chapter 17

God was, in the foregoing chapter, reckoning with the people of Judah, and bringing ruin upon them for their treachery in breaking covenant with him; in this chapter he is reckoning with the king of Judah for his treachery in breaking covenant with the king of Babylon; for when God came to contend with them he found many grounds of his controversy. The thing was now in doing: Zedekiah was practising with the king of Egypt underhand for assistance in a treacherous project he had formed to shake off the yoke of the king of Babylon, and violate the homage and fealty he had sworn to him. For this God by the prophet here, I. Threatens the ruin of him and his kingdom, by a parable of two eagles and a vine (Eze 17:1-10), and the explanation of that parable (Eze 17:11-21). But, in the close, II. He promises hereafter to raise the royal family of Judah again, the house of David, in the Messiah and his kingdom (Eze 17:22-24).

We must take all these verses together, that we may have the parable and the explanation of it at one view before us, because they will illustrate one another. 1. The prophet is appointed to put forth a riddle to the house of Israel (Eze 17:2), not to puzzle them, as Samson's riddle was put forth to the Philistines, not to hide the mind of God from them in obscurity, or to leave them in uncertainty about it, one advancing one conjecture and another another, as is usual in expounding riddles; no, he is immediately to tell them the meaning of it. Let him that speaks in an unknown tongue pray that he may interpret, Col 14:13. But he must deliver this message in a riddle or parable that they might take the more notice of it, might be the more affected with it themselves, and might the better remember it and tell it to others. For these reasons God often used similitudes by his servants the prophets, and Christ himself opened his mouth in parables. Riddles and parables are used for an amusement to ourselves and an entertainment to our friends. The prophet must make use of these to see if in this dress the things of God might find acceptance, and insinuate themselves into the minds of a careless people. Note, Ministers should study to find out acceptable words, and try various methods to do good; and, as far as they have reason to think will be for edification, should both bring that which is familiar into their preaching and their preaching too into their familiar discourse, that there may not be so vast a dissimilitude as with some there is between what they say in the pulpit and what they say out. 2. He is appointed to expound this riddle to the rebellious house, Eze 17:12. Though being rebellious they might justly have been left in ignorance, to see and hear and not perceive, yet the thing shall be explained to them: Know you not what these things mean? Those that knew the story, and what was now in agitation, might make a shrewd guess at the meaning of this riddle, but, that they might be left without excuse, he is to give it to them in plain terms, stripped of the metaphor. But the enigma was first propounded for them to study on awhile, and to send to their friends at Jerusalem, that they might enquire after and expect the solution of it some time after.

Let us now see what the matter of this message is.

I. Nebuchadnezzar had some time ago carried off Jehoiachin, the same that was called Jeconiah, when he was but eighteen years of age and had reigned in Jerusalem but three months, him and his princes and great men, and had brought them captives to Babylon, Kg2 24:12. This in the parable is represented by an eagle's cropping the top and tender branch of a cedar, and carrying it into a land of traffic, a city of merchants (Eze 17:3, Eze 17:4), which is explained Eze 17:12. The king of Babylon took the king of Jerusalem, who was no more able to resist him than a young twig of a tree is to contend with the strongest bird of prey, that easily crops it off, perhaps towards the making of her nest. Nebuchadnezzar, in Daniel's vision, is a lion, the king of beasts (Dan 7:4); there he has eagle's wings, so swift were his motions, so speedy were his conquests. Here, in this parable, he is an eagle, the king of birds, a great eagle, that lives upon spoil and rapine, whose young ones suck up blood, Job 39:30. His dominion extends itself far and wide, like the great and long wings of an eagle; the people are numerous, for it is full of feathers; the court is splendid, for it has divers colours, which look like embroidering, as the word is. Jerusalem is Lebanon, a forest of houses, and very pleasant. The royal family is the cedar; Jehoiachin is the top branch, the top of the young twigs, which he crops off. Babylon is the land of traffic and city of merchants where it is set. And the king of Judah, being of the house of David, will think himself much degraded and disgraced to be lodged among tradesmen; but he must make the best of it.

II. When he carried him to Babylon he made his uncle Zedekiah king in his room, Eze 17:5, Eze 17:6. His name was Mattaniah-the gift of the Lord, which Nebuchadnezzar changed into Zedekiah-the justice of the Lord, to remind him to be just like the God he called his, for fear of his justice. This was one of the seed of the land, a native, not a foreigner, not one of his Babylonian princes; he was planted in a fruitful field, for so Jerusalem as yet was; he placed it by great waters, where it would be likely to grow, like a willow-tree, which grows quickly, and grows best in moist ground, but is never designed nor expected to be a stately tree. He set it with care and circumspection (so some read it); he wisely provided that it might grow, but that it might not grow too big. He took of the king's seed (so it is explained, Eze 17:13) and made a covenant with him that he should have the kingdom, and enjoy the regal power and dignity, provided he held it as his vassal, dependent on him and accountable to him. He took an oath of him, made him swear allegiance to him, swear by his own God, the God of Israel, that he would be a faithful tributary to him, Ch2 36:13. He also took away the mighty of the land, the chief of the men of war, partly as hostages for the performance of the covenant, and partly that, the land being thereby weakened, the king might be the less able, and therefore the less in temptation, to break his league. What he designed we are told (Eze 17:14): That the kingdom might be base, in respect both of honour and strength, might neither be a rival with its powerful neighbours, nor a terror to its feeble ones, as it had been, that it might not left up itself to vie with the kingdom of Babylon, or to bear down any of the petty states that were in subjection to it. But yet he designed that by the keeping of this covenant it might stand, and continue a kingdom. Hereby the pride and ambition of that haughty potentate would be gratified, who aimed to be like the Most High (Isa 14:14), to have all about him subject to him. Now see here, 1. How sad a change sin made with the royal family of Judah. Time was when all the nations about were tributaries to that; now that has not only lost its dominion over other nations, but has itself become a tributary. How has the gold become dim! Nations by sin sell their liberty, and princes their dignity, and profane their crowns by casting them to the ground. 2. How wisely Zedekiah did for himself in accepting these terms, though they were dishonourable, when necessity brought him to it. A man may live very comfortably and contentedly, though he cannot bear a part, and make a figure, as formerly. A kingdom may stand firmly and safely, though it do not stand so high as it has sometimes done; and so may a family.

III. Zedekiah, while he continued faithful to the king of Babylon, did very well, and, if he would but have reformed his kingdom, and returned to God and his duty, he would have done better, and by that means might soon have recovered his former dignity, Eze 17:6. This plant grew, and though it was set as a willow-tree, and little account was made of it, yet it became a spreading vine of low stature, a great blessing to his own country, and his fruits made glad their hearts; and it is better to be a spreading vine of low stature than a lofty cedar of no use. Nebuchadnezzar was pleased, for the branches turned towards him, and rested on him as the vine on the wall, and he had his share of the fruits of this vine; the roots thereof too were under him, and at his disposal. The Jews had reason to be pleased, for they sat under their own vine, which brought forth branches, and shot forth sprigs, and looked pleasant and promising. See how gradually the judgments of God came upon this provoking people, how God gave them respite and so gave them space to repent. He made their kingdom base, to try if that would humble them, before he made it no kingdom; yet left it easy for them, to try if that would win upon them to return to him, that the troubles threatened might be prevented.

IV. Zedekiah knew not when he was well off, but grew impatient of the disgrace of being a tributary to the king of Babylon, and, to get clear of it, entered into a private league with the king of Egypt. He had no reason to complain that the king of Babylon put any new hardships upon him or improved his advantages against him, that he oppressed or impoverished his country, for, as the prophet had said before (Eze 17:6) to aggravate his treachery, he shows again (Eze 17:8) what a fair way he was in to be considerable: He was planted in a good soil by great waters; his family was likely enough to be built up, and his exchequer to be filled, in a little time, so that, if he had dealt faithfully, he might have been a goodly vine. But there was another great eagle that he had an affection for, and put a confidence in, and that was the king of Egypt, Eze 17:7. Those two great potentates, the kings of Babylon and Egypt, were but two great eagles, birds of prey. This great eagle of Egypt is said to have great wings, but not to be long-winged as the king of Babylon, because, though the kingdom of Egypt was strong, yet it was not of such a vast extent as that of Babylon was. The great eagle is said to have many feathers, much wealth and many soldiers, which he depended upon as a substantial defence, but which really were no more than so may feathers. Zedekiah, promising himself liberty, made himself a vassal to the king of Egypt, foolishly expecting ease by changing his master. Now this vine did secretly and under-hand bend her roots towards the king of Egypt, that great eagle, and after awhile did openly shoot forth her branches towards him, give him an intimation how much she coveted an alliance with him, that he might water it by the furrows of her plantation, whereas it was planted by great waters, and did not need any assistance from him. This is expounded, Eze 17:15. Zedekiah rebelled against the king of Babylon in sending his ambassadors into Egypt, that they might give him horses and much people, to enable him to contend with the king of Babylon. See what a change sin had made with the people of God! God promised that they should be a numerous people, as the sand of the sea; yet now, if their king had occasion for much people, he must send to Egypt for them, they being for sin diminished and brought low, Psa 107:39. See also the folly of fretful discontented spirits, that ruin themselves by striving to better themselves, whereas they might be easy and happy enough if they would but make the best of that which is.

V. God here threatens Zedekiah with the utter destruction of him and his kingdom, and, in displeasure against him, passes that doom upon him for his treacherous revolt from the king of Babylon. This is represented in the parable (Eze 17:9, Eze 17:19) by the plucking up of this vine by the roots, the cutting off of the fruit, and the withering of the leaves, the leaves of her spring, when they are in their greenness (Job 8:12), before they begin in autumn to wither of themselves. The project shall be blasted; it shall utterly wither. The affairs of this perfidious prince shall be ruined past retrieve; as a vine when the east wind blasts it, so that it shall be fit for nothing but the fire (as we had it in that parable, Eze 15:4), it shall wither even in the furrows where it grew, though they were ever so well watered. It shall be destroyed without great power or many people to pluck it up; for what need is there of raising the militia to pluck up a vine? Note, God can bring great things to pass without much ado. He needs not great power and many people to effect his purposes; a handful will serve if he pleases. He can without any difficulty ruin a sinful king and kingdom, and make no more of it than we do of rooting up a tree that cumbers the ground. In the explanation of the parable the sentence is very largely recorded: Shall be prosper? Eze 17:15. Can he expect to do ill and fare well? Nay, shall he that does such wicked things escape? Shall he break the covenant, and be delivered from that vengeance which is the just punishment of his treachery? No; can he expect to do ill and not suffer ill? Let him hear his doom.

1. It is ratified by the oath of God (Eze 17:16): As I live, saith the Lord God, he shall die for it. This intimates how highly God resented the crime, and how sure and severe the punishment of it would be. God swears in his wrath, as he did Psa 95:11. Note, As God's promises are confirmed with an oath, for comfort to the saints, so are his threatenings, for terror to the wicked. As sure as God lives and is happy (I may add, and as long), so sure, so long, shall impenitent sinners die and be miserable.

2. It is justified by the heinousness of the crime he had been guilty of. (1.) He had been very ungrateful to his benefactor, who had made him king, and undertook to protect him, had made him a prince when he might as easily have made him a prisoner. Note, It is a sin against God to be unkind to our friends and to lift up the heel against those that have helped to raise us. (2.) He had been very false to him whom he had covenanted with. This is mostly insisted on: He despised the oath. When his conscience or friends reminded him of it he made a jest of it, put on a daring resolution, and broke it, Eze 17:15, Eze 17:16, Eze 17:18, Eze 17:19. He broke through it, and took a pride in making nothing of it, as a great tyrant in our own day, whose maxim (they say) it is, That princes ought not to be slaves to their word any further than it is for their interest. That which aggravated Zedekiah's perfidiousness was that the oath by which he had bound himself to the king of Babylon was, [1.] A solemn oath. An emphasis is laid upon this (Eze 17:18): When, lo, he had given his hand, as a confederate with the king of Babylon, not only as his subject, but as his friend, the joining of hands being a token of the joining of hearts. [2.] As sacred oath. God says (Eze 17:19): It is my oath that he has despised and my covenant that he has broken. In every solemn oath God is appealed to as a witness of the sincerity of him that swears, and invocated as a judge and revenger of his treachery if he now swear falsely or at any time hereafter break his oath. But the oath of allegiance to a prince is particularly called the oath of God (Ecc 8:2), as if that had something in it more sacred than another oath; for princes are ministers of God to us for good, Rom 13:4. Now Zedekiah's breaking this oath and covenant is the sin which God will recompense upon his own head (Eze 17:19), the trespass which he has trespassed against God, for which God will plead with him, Eze 17:20. Note, Perjury is a heinous sin and highly provoking to the God of heaven. It would not serve for an excuse, First, That he who took this oath was a king, a king of the house of David, whose liberty and dignity might surely set him above the obligation of oaths. No; though kings are gods to us, they are men to God, and not exempt from his law and judgment. The prince is doubtless as firmly bound before God to the people by his coronation-oath as the people are to the princes by the oath of allegiance. Secondly, Nor that this oath was sworn to the king of Babylon, a heathen prince, worse than a heretic, with whom the church of Rome says, No faith is to be kept. No; though Nebuchadnezzar was a worshipper of false gods, yet the true God will avenge this quarrel when one of his worshippers breaks his league with him; for truth is a debt due to all men; and, if the professors of the true religion deal perfidiously with those of a false religion, their profession will be so far from excusing, much less justifying them, that it aggravates their sin, and God will the more surely and severely punish it, because by it they give occasion to the enemies of the Lord to blaspheme; as that Mahometan prince, who, when the Christians broke their league with him, cried out, O Jesus! are these thy Christians? Thirdly, Nor would it justify him that the oath was extorted from him by a conqueror, for the covenant was made upon a valuable consideration. He held his life and crown upon this condition, that he should be faithful and bear true allegiance to the king of Babylon; and, if he enjoy the benefit of his bargain, it is very unjust if he do not observe the terms. Let him know then that, having despised the oath, and broken the covenant, he shall not escape. And if the contempt and violation of such an oath, such a covenant

as this, would be so punished, of how much sorer punishment shall those be thought worthy who break covenant with God (when, lo, they had given their hand upon it that they would be faithful), who tread under foot the blood of that covenant as an unholy thing? Between the covenants there is no comparison.

3. It is particularized in divers instances, wherein the punishment is made to answer the sin. (1.) He had rebelled against the king of Babylon, and the king of Babylon should be his effectual conqueror. In the place where that king dwells whose covenant he broke, even with him in the midst of Babylon he shall die,Eze 17:16. He thinks to get out of his hands, but he shall fall, more than before, into his hands. God himself will now take part with the king of Babylon against him: I will spread my net upon him, Eze 17:20. God has a net for those who deal perfidiously and think to escape his righteous judgments, in which those shall be taken and held who would not be held by the bond of an oath and covenant. Zedekiah dreaded Babylon: "Thither I will bring him," says God, "and plead with him there." Men will justly be forced upon that calamity which they endeavour by sin to flee from. (2.) He had relied upon the king of Egypt, and the king of Egypt should be his ineffectual helper: Pharaoh with his mighty army shall not make for him in the war (Eze 17:17), shall to him no service, nor give any check to the progress of the Chaldean forces; he shall not assist him in the siege by casting up mounts and building forts, nor in battle by cutting off many person. Note, Every creature is that to us which God makes it to be; and he commonly weakens and withers that arm of flesh which we trust in and stay ourselves upon. Now was again fulfilled what was spoken on a former similar occasion (Isa 30:7), The Egyptians shall help in vain. They did so; for though, upon the approach of the Egyptian army, the Chaldeans withdrew from the siege of Jerusalem, upon their retreat they returned to it again and took it. It should seem, the Egyptians were not hearty, had strength enough, but no good-will, to help Zedekiah. Note, Those who deal treacherously with those who put a confidence in them will justly be dealt treacherously with by those they put a confidence in. Yet the Egyptians were not the only states Zedekiah stayed himself upon; he had bands of his own to stand by him, but those bands, though we may suppose they were veteran troops and the best soldiers his kingdom afforded, shall become fugitives, shall quit their posts, and make the best of their way, and shall fall by the sword of the enemy, and the remains of them shall be scattered, Eze 17:21. This was fulfilled when the city was broken up and all the men of war fled, Jer 52:7. This you shall now that I the Lord have spoken it. Note, Sooner or later God's word will prove itself; and those who will not believe shall find by experience the reality and weight of it.

Ezekiel 17:22

When the royal family of Judah was brought to desolation by the captivity of Jehoiachin and Zedekiah it might be asked, "What has now become of the covenant of royalty made with David, that his children should sit upon his throne for evermore? Do the sure mercies of David prove thus unsure?" To this it is sufficient for the silencing of the objectors to answer that the promise was conditional. If they will keep my covenant, then they shall continue, Psa 132:12. But David's posterity broke the condition, and so forfeited the promise. But the unbelief of man shall not invalidate the promise of God. He will find out another seed of David in which it shall be accomplished; and that is promised in these verses.

I. The house of David shall again be magnified, and out of its ashes another phoenix shall arise. The metaphor of a tree, which was made us of in the threatening, is here presented in the promise, Eze 17:22, Eze 17:23. This promise had its accomplishment in part when Zerubbabel, a branch of the house of David, was raised up to head the Jews in their return out of captivity, and to rebuild the city and temple and re-establish their church and state; but it was to have its full accomplishment in the kingdom of the Messiah, who was a root out of a dry ground, and to whom God, according to promise, gave the throne of his father David, Luk 1:32. 1. God himself undertakes the reviving and restoring of the house of David. Nebuchadnezzar was the great eagle that had attempted the re-establishing of the house of David in a dependence upon him, Eze 17:5. But the attempt miscarried; his plantation withered and was plucked up. "Well," says God, "the next shall be of my planting: I will also take of the highest branch of the high cedar and I will set it." Note, As men have their designs, God also has his designs; but his will prosper when theirs are blasted. Nebuchadnezzar prided himself in setting up kingdoms at his pleasure, Dan 5:19. But those kingdoms soon had an end, whereas the God of heaven sets up a kingdom that shall never be destroyed, Dan 2:44. 2. The house of David is revived in a tender one cropped from the top of his young twigs. Zerubbabel was so; that which was hopeful in him was but the day of small things (Zac 4:10), yet before him great mountains were made plain. Our Lord Jesus was the highest branch of the high cedar, the furthest of all from the root (for soon after he appeared the house of David was all cut off and extinguished), but the nearest of all to heaven, for his kingdom was not of this world. He was taken from the top of the young twigs, for he is the man, the branch, a tender plant, and a root out of a dry ground (Isa 53:2), but a branch of righteousness, the planting of the Lord, that he may be glorified. 3. This branch is planted in a high mountain (Eze 17:22), in the mountain of the height of Israel, Eze 17:23. Thither he brought Zerubbabel in triumph; there he raised up his son Jesus, sent him to gather the lost sheep of the house of Israel that were scattered upon the mountains, set him his king upon his holy hill of Zion, sent forth the gospel from Mount Zion, the word of the Lord from Jerusalem; there, in the height of Israel, a nation which all its neighbours had an eye upon as conspicuous and illustrious, was the Christian church first planted. The churches of Judea were the most primitive churches. The unbelieving Jews did what they could to prevent its being planted there; but who can pluck up what God will plant? 4. Thence it spreads far and wide. The Jewish state, though it began very low in Zerubbabel's time, was set as a tender branch, which might easily be plucked up, yet took root, spread strangely, and after some time became very considerable; those of other nations, fowl of every wing, put themselves under the protection of it. The Christian church was at first like a grain of mustard-seed, but became, like this tender branch, a great tree, its beginning small, but its latter end increasing to admiration. When the Gentiles flocked into the church then did the fowl of every wing (even the birds of prey, which those preyed upon, as the wolf and the lamb feeding together, Isa 11:6) come and dwell under the shadow of this goodly cedar. See Dan 4:21.

II. God himself will herein be glorified, Eze 17:24. The setting up of the Messiah's kingdom in the world shall discover more clearly than ever to the children of men that God is the King of all the earth, Psa 47:7. Never was there a more full conviction given of this truth, that all things are governed by an infinitely wise and mighty Providence, than that which was given by the exaltation of Christ and the establishment of his kingdom among men; for by that it appeared that God has all hearts in his hand, and the sovereign disposal of all affairs. All the trees of the field shall know, 1. That the tree which God will have to be brought down, and dried up, shall be so, though it be ever so high and stately, ever so green and flourishing. Neither honour nor wealth, neither external advancements nor internal endowments, will secure men from humbling withering providence. 2. That the tree which God will have to be exalted, and to flourish, shall so be, shall so do, though ever so low, and ever so dry. The house of Nebuchadnezzar, that now makes so great a figure, shall be extirpated, and the house of David, that now makes so mean a figure, shall become famous again; and the Jewish nation, that is now despicable, shall be considerable. The kingdom of Satan, that has borne so long, so large, a sway, shall be broken, and the kingdom of Christ, that was looked upon with contempt. shall be established. The Jews, who, in respect of church-privileges, had been high and green, shall be thrown out, and the Gentiles, who had been low and dry trees, shall be taken in their room, Isa 54:1. All the enemies of Christ shall be abased and made his footstool, and his interests shall be confirmed and advanced: I the Lord have spoken (it is the decree, the declared decree, that Christ must be exalted, must be the headstone of the corner), and I have done it, that is, I will do it in due time, but it is as sure to be done as if it were done already. With men saying and doing are two things, but they are not so with God. What he has spoken we may be sure that he will do, nor shall one iota or tittle of his word fall to the ground, for he is not a man, that he should lie, or the son of man, that he should repent either of his threatenings or of his promises.

Ezekiel Chapter 18

Perhaps, in reading some of the foregoing chapters, we may have been tempted to think ourselves not much concerned in them (though they also were written for our learning); but this chapter, at first view, appears highly and nearly to concern us all, very highly, very nearly; for, without particular reference to Judah and Jerusalem, it lays down the rule of judgment according to which God will deal with the children of men in determining them to their everlasting state, and it agrees with that very ancient rule laid down, Gen 4:7, "If though doest well, shalt thou not be accepted?" But, "if not, sin," the punishment of sin,"lies at the door." Here is, I. The corrupt proverb used by the profane Jews, which gave occasion to the message here sent them, and made it necessary for the justifying of God in his dealings with them (Eze 18:1-3). II. The reply given to this proverb, in which God asserts in general his own sovereignty and justice (Eze 18:4). Woe to the wicked; it shall be ill with them (Eze 18:4, Eze 18:20). But say to the righteous, It shall be ill with them (Eze 18:4, Eze 18:20). But say to the righteous, It shall be well with them (Eze 18:5-9). In particular, as to the case complained of, he assures us, 1. That it shall be ill with a wicked man, though he had a good father (Eze 18:10-13). 2. That it shall be well with a good man, though he had a wicked father (Eze 18:14-18). And therefore in this God is righteous (Eze 18:19, Eze 18:20). 3. That it shall be well with penitents, though they began ever so ill (Eze 18:21-23 and Eze 18:27, Eze 18:28). 4. That it shall be ill with apostates, though they began ever so well (Eze 18:24, Eze 18:26). And the use of all this is, (1.) To justify God and clear the equity of all his proceedings (Eze 18:25, Eze 18:29). (2.) To engage and encourage us to repent of our sins and turn to God (Eze 18:30-32). And these are things which belong to our everlasting peace. O that we may understand and regard them before they be hidden from our eyes!

Ezekiel 18:1

Evil manners, we say, beget good laws; and in like manner sometimes unjust reflections occasion just vindications; evil proverbs beget good prophecies. Here is,

I. An evil proverb commonly used by the Jews in their captivity. We had one before (Eze 12:22) and a reply to it; here we have another. That sets God's justice at defiance: "The days are prolonged and every vision fails; the threatenings are a jest." This charges him with injustice, as if the judgments executed were a wrong: "You use this proverb concerning the land of Israel, now that it is laid waste by the judgments of God, saying, The fathers have eaten sour grapes and the children's teeth are set on edge; we are punished for the sins of our ancestors, which is as great an absurdity in the divine regimen as if the children should have their teeth set on edge, or stupefied, by the fathers' eating sour grapes, whereas, in the order of natural causes, if men eat or drink any thing amiss, they only themselves shall suffer by it." Now, 1. It must be owned that there was some occasion given for this proverb. God had often said that he would visit the iniquity of the fathers upon the children, especially the sin of idolatry, intending thereby to express the evil of sin, of that sin, his detestation of it, and just indignation against it, and the heavy punishments he would bring upon idolaters, that parents might be restrained from sin by their affection to their children and that children might not be drawn to sin by their reverence for their parents. He had likewise often declared by his prophets that in bringing the present ruin upon Judah and Jerusalem he had an eye to the sins of Manasseh and other preceding kings; for, looking upon the nation as a body politic, and punishing them with national judgments for national sins, and admitting the maxim in our law that a corporation never dies, reckoning with them now for the iniquities of former ages was but like making a man, when he is old, to possess the iniquities of his youth, Job 13:26. And there is no unrighteousness with God in doing so. But, 2. They intended it as a reflection upon God, and an impeachment of his equity in his proceedings against them. Thus far that is right which is implied in this proverbial saying, That those who are guilty of wilful sin eat sour grapes; they do that which they will feel from, sooner or later. The grapes may look well enough in the temptation, but they will be bitter as bitterness itself in the reflection. They will set the sinner's teeth on edge. When conscience is awake, and sets the sin in order before them, it will spoil the relish of their comforts as when the teeth are set on edge. But they suggest it as unreasonable that the children should smart for the fathers' folly and feel the pain of that which they never tasted the pleasure of, and that God was unrighteous in thus taking vengeance and could not justify it. See how wicked the reflection is, how daring the impudence; yet see how witty it is, and how sly the comparison. Many that are impious in their jeers are ingenious in their jests; and thus the malice of hell against God and religion is insinuated and propagated. It is here put into a proverb, and that proverb used, commonly used; they had it up ever and anon. And, though it had plainly a blasphemous meaning, yet they sheltered themselves under the similitude from the imputation of downright blasphemy. Now by this it appears that they were unhumbled under the rod, for, instead of condemning themselves and justifying God, they condemned him and justified themselves; but woe to him that thus strives with his Maker.

II. A just reproof of, and reply to, this proverb: What mean you by using it? That is the reproof. "Do you intend hereby to try it out with God? Or can you think any other than that you will hereby provoke him to be angry with you will he has consumed you? Is this the way to reconcile yourselves to him and make your peace with him?" The reply follows, in which God tells them,

1. That the use of the proverb should be taken away. This is said, it is sworn (Eze 18:3): You shall not have occasion any more to use this proverb; or (as it may be read), You shall not have the use of this parable. The taking away of this parable is made the matter of a promise, Jer 31:29. Here it is made the matter of a threatening. There it intimates that God will return to them in ways of mercy; here it intimates that God would proceed against them in ways of judgment. He will so punish them for this impudent saying that they shall not dare to use it any more; as in

another case, Jer 23:34, Jer 23:36. God will find out effectual ways to silence those cavillers. Or God will so manifest both to themselves and others that they have wickedness of their own enough to bring all these desolating judgments upon them that they shall no longer for shame lay it upon the sins of their fathers that they were thus dealt with: "Your own consciences shall tell you, and all your neighbours shall confirm it, that you yourselves have eaten the same sour grapes that your fathers ate before you, or else your teeth would not have been set on edge."

2. That really the saying itself was unjust and a causeless reflection upon God's government. For,

(1.) God does not punish the children for the fathers' sins unless they tread in their fathers' steps and fill up the measure of their iniquity (Mat 23:32), and then they have no reason to complain, for, whatever they suffer, it is less than their own sin has deserved. And, when God speaks of visiting the iniquity of the fathers upon the children, that is so far from putting any hardship upon the children, to whom he only renders according to their works, that it accounts for God's patience with the parents, whom he therefore does not punish immediately, because he lays up their iniquity for their children, Job 21:19.

(2.) It is only in temporal calamities that children (and sometimes innocent ones) fare the worse for their parents' wickedness, and God can alter the property of those calamities, and make them work for good to those that are visited with them; but as to spiritual and eternal misery (and that is the death here spoken of) the children shall by no means smart for the parents' sins. This is here shown at large; and it is a wonderful piece of condescension that the great God is pleased to reason the case with such wicked and unreasonable men, that he did not immediately strike them dumb or dead, but vouchsafed to state the matter before them, that he may be clear when he is judged. Now, in his reply,

[1.] He asserts and maintains his own absolute and incontestable sovereignty: Behold, all souls are mine, Eze 18:4. God here claims a property in all the souls of the children of men, one as well as another. First, Souls are his. He that is the Maker of all things is in a particular manner the Father of spirits, for his image is stamped on the souls of men; it was so in their creation; it is so in their renovation. He forms the spirit of man within him, and is therefore called the God of the spirits of all flesh, of embodied spirits. Secondly, All souls are his, all created by him and for him, and accountable to him. As the soul of the father, so the soul of the son, is mine. Our earthly parents are only the fathers of our flesh; our souls are not theirs; God challenges them. Now hence it follows, for the clearing of this matter, 1. That God may certainly do what he pleases both with fathers and children, and none may say unto him, What doest thou? He that gave us our being does us no wrong if he takes it away again, much less when he only takes away some of the supports and comforts of it; it is as absurd to quarrel with him as for the thing formed to say to him that formed it, Why hast thou made me thus? 2. That God as certainly bears a good-will both to father and son, and will put no hardship upon either. We are sure that God hates nothing that he has made, and therefore (speaking of the adult, who are capable of acting for themselves) he has such a kindness for all souls that none die but through their own default. All souls are his, and therefore he is not partial in his judgment of them. Let us subscribe to his interest in us and dominion over us. He says, All souls are mine; let us answer, "Lord, my soul is thine; I devote it to thee to be employed for thee and made happy in thee." It is with good reason that God says, "My son, give me thy heart, for it is my own," to which we must yield, "Father, take my heart, it is thy own."

[2.] Though God might justify himself by insisting upon his sovereignty, yet he waives that, and lays down the equitable and unexceptionable rule of judgment by which he will proceed as to particular persons; and it is this:-First, The sinner that persists in sin shall certainly die, his iniquity shall be his ruin: The soul that sins shall die, shall die as a soul can die, shall be excluded from the favour of God, which is the life and bliss of the soul, and shall lie for ever under his wrath, which is its death and misery. Sin is the act of the soul, the body being only the instrument of unrighteousness; it is called the sin of the soul, Mic 6:7. And therefore the punishment of sin is the tribulation and the anguish of the soul, Rom 2:9. Secondly, The righteous man that perseveres in his righteousness shall certainly live. If a man be just, have a good principle, a good spirit and disposition, and, as an evidence of that, do judgment and justice (Eze 18:5), he shall surely live, saith the Lord God, Eze 18:9. He that makes conscience of conforming in every thing to the will of God, that makes it his business to serve God and his aim to glorify God, shall without fail be happy here and for ever in the love and favour of God; and, wherein he comes short of his duty, it shall be forgiven him, through a Mediator. Now here is part of the character of this just man. 1. He is careful to keep himself clean from the pollutions of sin, and at a distance from all the appearances of evil. (1.) From sins against the second commandment. In the matters of God's worship he is jealous, for he knows God is so. He has not only not sacrificed in the high places to the images there set up, but he has not so much as eaten upon the mountains, that is, not had any communion with idolaters by eating things sacrificed to idols, Col 10:20. He would not only not kneel with them at their altars, but not sit with them at their tables in their high places. He detests not only the idols of the heathen but the idols of the house of Israel, which were not only allowed of, but generally applauded and adored, by those that were accounted the professing people of God. He has not only not worshipped those idols, but he has not so much as lifted up his eyes to them; he has not given them a favourable look, has had no regard at all to them, neither desired their favour nor dreaded their frowns. He has observed so many bewitched by them that he has not dared so much as to look at them, lest he should be taken in the snare. The eyes of idolaters are said to go a whoring, Eze 6:9. See Deu 4:19. (2.) From sins against the seventh commandment. He is careful to possess his vessel in sanctification and honour, and not in the lusts of uncleanness; and therefore he has not dared to defile his neighbour's wife, nor said or done any thing which had the least tendency to corrupt or debauch her, no, nor will he make any undue approaches to his own wife when she is put apart for her uncleanness, for it was forbidden by the law,Lev 18:19; Lev 20:18. Note, It is an essential branch of wisdom and justice to keep the appetites of the body always in subjection to reason and virtue.

(3.) From sins against the eighth commandment. He is a just man, who has not, by fraud and under colour of law and right, oppressed any, and who has not with force and arms spoiled any by violence, not spoiled them of their goods or estates, much less of their liberties and lives, Eze 18:7. Oppression and violence were the sins of the old world, that brought the deluge, and are sins of which still God is and will be the avenger. Nay, he is one that has not lent his money upon usury, nor taken increase (Eze 18:8), though, being done by contract, it may seem free from injustice (Volenti non fit injuria-What is done to a person with his own consent is no injury to him), yet, as far as it is forbidden by the law, he dares not do it. A moderate usury they were allowed to receive from strangers, but not from their brethren. A just man will not take advantage of his neighbour's necessity to make a prey of him, nor indulge himself in ease and idleness to live upon the sweat and toil of others, and therefore will not take increase from those who cannot make increase of what he lends them, nor be rigorous in exacting what was agreed for from those who by the act of God are disabled to pay it; but he is willing to share in loss as well as profit. Qui sentit commodum, sentire debet et onus-He who enjoys the benefit should bear the burden. 2. He makes conscience of doing the duties of his place. He has restored the pledge to the poor debtor, according to the law. Exo 22:26. "If thou take thy neighbour's raiment for a pledge, the raiment that is for necessary use, thou shalt deliver it to him again, that he may sleep in his own bedclothes." Nay, he has not only restored to the poor that which was their own, but has given his bread to the hungry. Observe, It is called his bread, because it is honestly come by; that which is given to some is not unjustly taken from others; for God has said, I hate robbery for burnt-offerings. Worldly men insist upon it that their bread is their own, as Nabal, who therefore would not give of it to David (Sal 25:11); yet let them know that it is not so their own but that they are bound to do good to others with it. Clothes are necessary as well as food, and therefore this just man is so charitable as to cover the naked also with a garment, Eze 18:7. The coats which Dorcas had made for the poor were produced as witnesses of her charity, Act 9:39. This just man has withdrawn his hands from iniquity, Eze 18:8. If at any time he has been drawn in through inadvertency to that which afterwards has appeared to him to be a wrong thing, he does not persist in it because he has begun it, but withdraws his hand from that which he now perceives to be iniquity; for he executes true judgment between man and man, according as his opportunity is of doing it (as a judge, as a witness, as a juryman, as a referee), and in all commerce is concerned that justice be done, that no man be wronged, that he who is wronged be righted, and that every man have his own, and is ready to interpose himself, and do any good office, in order hereunto. This is his character towards his neighbours; yet it will not suffice that he be just and true to his brother, to complete his character he must be so to his God likewise (Eze 18:9): He has walked in my statutes, those which relate to the duties of his immediate worship; he has kept those and all his other judgments, has had respect to them all, has made it his constant care and endeavour to conform and come up to them all, to deal truly, that so he may approve himself faithful to his covenant with God, and, having joined himself to God, he does not treacherously depart from him, nor dissemble with him. This is a just man, and living he shall live; he shall certainly live, shall have life and shall have it more abundantly, shall live truly, live comfortably, live eternally. Keep the commandments, and thou shalt enter into life, Mat 19:17.

Ezekiel 18:10

God, by the prophet, having laid down the general rule of judgment, that he will render eternal life to those that patiently continue in well-doing, but indignation and wrath to those that do not obey the truth, but obey unrighteousness (Rom 2:7, Rom 2:8), comes, in these verses, to show that men's parentage and relation shall not alter the case either one way or other.

I. He applied it largely and particularly both ways. As it was in the royal line of the kings of Judah, so it often happens in private families, that godly parents have wicked children and wicked parents have godly children. Now here he shows,

1. That a wicked man shall certainly perish in his iniquity, though he be the son of a pious father. If that righteous man before described beget a son whose character is the reverse of his father's, his condition will certainly be so too. (1.) It is supposed as no uncommon case, but a very melancholy one, that the child of a very godly father, notwithstanding all the instructions given him, the good education he has had and the needful rebukes that have been given him, and the restraints he has been laid under, after all the pains taken with him and prayers put up for him, may yet prove notoriously wicked and vile, the grief of his father, the shame of his family, and the curse and plague of his generation. He is here supposed to allow himself in all those enormities which his good father dreaded and carefully avoided, and to shake off all those good duties which his father made conscience of and took satisfaction in; he undoes all that his father did, and goes counter to his example in every thing. He is here described to be a highwayman-a robber and a shedder of blood. He is an idolater: He has eaten upon the mountains (Eze 18:11) and has lifted up his eyes to the idols, which his good father never did, and has come at length not only to feast with the idolaters, but to sacrifice with them, which is here called committing abomination, for the way of sin is down-hill. He is an adulterer, has defiled his neighbour's wife. He is an oppressor even of the poor and needy; he robs the spital, and squeezes those who, he knows, cannot defend themselves, and takes a pride and pleasure in trampling upon the weak and impoverishing those that are poor already. He takes away from those to whom he should give. He has spoiled by violence and open force; he has given forth upon usury, and so spoiled by contract; and he has not restored the pledge, but unjustly detained it even when the debt was paid. Let those good parents that have wicked children not look upon their case as singular; it is a case put here; and by it we see that grace does not run in the blood, nor always attend the means of grace. The race is not always to the swift, nor the battle to the strong, for then the children that are well taught would do well, but God will let us know that his grace is his own and his Spirit a free-agent, and that though we are tied to give our children a good education he is not tied to bless it. In this, as much as any thing, appears the power of original sin and the necessity of special grace. (2.) We are here assured that this wicked man shall perish for ever in his iniquity, notwithstanding his being the son of a good father. He may perhaps prosper awhile in the world,

for the sake of the piety of his ancestors, but, having committed all these abominations, and never repented of them, he shall not live, he shall not be happy in the favour of God; though he may escape the sword of men, he shall not escape the curse of God. He shall surely die; he shall be for ever miserable; his blood shall be upon him. He may thank himself; he is his own destroyed. And his relation to a good father will be so far from standing him in stead that it will aggravate his sin and his condemnation. It made his sin the more heinous, nay, it made him really the more vile and profligate, and, consequently, will make his misery hereafter the more intolerable.

2. That a righteous man shall be certainly happy, though he be the son of a wicked father. Though the father did eat the sour grapes, if the children do not meddle with them, they shall fare never the worse for that. Here, (1.) It is supposed (and, blessed be God, it is sometimes a case in fact) that the son of an ungodly father may be godly, that, observing how fatal his father's errors were, he may be so wise as to take warning, and not tread in his father's tests, Eze 18:14. Ordinarily, children partake of the parents' temper and are drawn in to imitate their example; but here the son, instead of seeing his father's sins, and, as is usual, doing the like, sees them and dreads doing the like. Men indeed do not gather grapes of thorns, but God sometimes does, takes a branch from a wild olive and grafts it into a good one. Wicked Ahaz begets a good Hezekiah, who sees all his father's sins which he has done, and though he will not, like Ham, proclaim his father's shame, or make the worst of it, yet he loathes it, and blushes at it, and thinks the worse of sin because it was the reproach and ruin of his own father. He considers and does not such like; he considers how ill it became his father to do such things, what an offence it was to God and all good men, what a wound and dishonour he got by it, and what calamities he brought into his family, and therefore he does not such like. Note, If we did but duly consider the ways of wicked men, we should all dread being associates with them and followers of them. The particulars are here again enumerated almost in the same words with that character given of the just man (Eze 18:6, etc.), to show how good men walk in the same spirit and in the same steps. This just man here, when he took care to avoid his father's sins, took care to imitate his grandfather's virtues; and, if we look back, we shall find some examples for our imitation, as well as others for our admonition. This just man can not only say, as the Pharisee, I am no adulterer, no extortioner, no oppressor, no usurer, no idolater; but he has given his bread to the hungry and covered the naked. He has taken off his hand from the poor; where he found his father had put hardships upon poor servants, tenants, neighbours, he eased their burden. He did not say, "What my father has done I will abide by, and if it was a fault it was his and not mine;" as Rehoboam, who contemned the taxes his father had imposed. No; he takes his hand off from the poor, and restores them to their rights and liberties again, Eze 18:15-17. Thus he has executed God's judgments and walked in his statutes, not only done his duty for once, but one on in a course and way of obedience. (2.) We are assured that the graceless father alone shall die in his iniquity, but his gracious son shall fare never the worse for it. As for his father (Eze 18:18), because he was a cruel oppressor, and did hurt, nay, because, though he had wealth and power, he did not with them do good among his people, lo, even he, great as he is, shall die in his iniquity, and be undone for ever; but he that

clxiv

kept his integrity shall surely live, shall be easy and happy, and he shall not die for the iniquity of his father. Perhaps his father's wickedness has lessened his estate and weakened his interest, but it shall be no prejudice at all to his acceptance with God and his eternal welfare.

II. He appeals to themselves then whether they did not wrong God with their proverb. "Thus plain the case is, and yet you say, Does not the son bear the iniquity of the father? No, he does not; he shall not if he will himself do that which is lawful and right," Eze 18:19. But this people that bore the iniquity of their fathers had not done that which is lawful and right, and therefore justly suffered for their own sin and had no reason to complain of God's proceedings against them as at all unjust, though they had reason to complain of the bad example their fathers had left them as very unkind. Our fathers have sinned and are not, and we have borne their iniquity, Lam 5:7. It is true that there is a curse entailed upon wicked families, but it is as true that the entail may be cut off by repentance and reformation; let the impenitent and unreformed therefore thank themselves if they fall under it. The settled rule of judgment is therefore repeated (Eze 18:20): The soul that sins shall die, and not another for it. What direction God has given to earthly judges (Deu 24:16) he will himself pursue: The son shall not die, not die eternally, for the iniquity of the father, if he do not tread in the steps of it, nor the father for the iniquity of the son, if he endeavour to do his duty for the preventing of it. In the day of the revelation of the righteous judgment of God, which is now clouded and eclipsed, the righteousness of the righteous shall appear before all the world to be upon him, to his everlasting comfort and honour, upon him as a robe, upon his as a crown; and the wickedness of the wicked shall be upon him, to his everlasting confusion, upon him as a chain, upon him as a load, as a mountain of lead to sink him to the bottomless pit.

Ezekiel 18:21

We have here another rule of judgment which God will go by in dealing with us, by which is further demonstrated the equity of his government. The former showed that God will reward or punish according to the change made in the family or succession, for the better or for the worse; here he shows that he will reward or punish according to the change made in the person himself, whether for the better or the worse. While we are in this world we are in a state of probation; the time of trial lasts as long as the time of life, and according as we are found at last it will be with us to eternity. Now see here,

I. The case fairly stated, much as it had been before (Eze 3:18, etc.), and here it is laid down once (Eze 18:21-24) and again (Eze 18:26-28), because it is a matter of vast importance, a matter of life and death, of life and death eternal. Here we have,

1. A fair invitation given to wicked people, to turn from their wickedness. Assurance is here given us that, if the wicked will turn, he shall surely live, Eze 18:21, Eze 18:27. Observe,

(1.) What is required to denominate a man a true convert, how he must be qualified that he may be entitled to this act of indemnity. [1.] The first step towards conversion is consideration (Eze 18:28): Because he considers and turns. The reason why sinners go on in their evil ways is because they do not consider what will be in the end thereof; but if the prodigal once come to himself, if he sit down and consider a little how bad his state is and how easily it may be bettered, he will soon return to his father (Luk 15:17), and the adulteress to her first husband when she considers that then it was better with her than now, Hos 2:7. [2.] This consideration must produce an aversion to sin. When he considers he must turn away from his wickedness, which denotes a change in the disposition of the heart; he must turn from his sins and his transgression, which denotes a change in the life; he must break off from all his evil courses, and, wherein he has done iniquity, must resolve to do so no more, and this from a principle of hatred to sin. What have I to do any more with idols? [3.] This aversion to sin must be universal; he must turn from all his sins and all his transgressions, without a reserve for any Delilah, any house of Rimmon. We do not rightly turn from sin unless we truly hate it, and we do not truly hate sin, as sin, if we do not hate all sin. [4.] This must be accompanied with a conversion to God and duty; he must keep all God's statutes (for the obedience, if it be sincere, will be universal) and must do that which is lawful and right, that which agrees with the word and will of God, which he must take for his rule, and not the will of the flesh and the way of the world.

(2.) What is promised to those that do thus turn from sin to God. [1.] They shall save their souls alive, Eze 18:27. They shall surely live, they shall not die, Eze 18:21. and again Eze 18:28. Whereas it was said, The soul that sins it shall die, yet let not those that have sinned despair but that the threatened death may be prevented if they will but turn and repent in time. When David penitently acknowledges, I have sinned, he is immediately assured of his pardon: "The Lord has taken away thy sin, thou shalt not die (Sa2 12:13), thou shalt not die eternally." He shall surely live; he shall be restored to the favour of God, which is the life of the soul, and shall not lie under his wrath, which is as messengers of death to the soul. [2.] The sins they have repented of and forsaken shall not rise up in judgment against them, nor shall they be so much as upbraided with them: All his transgressions that he has committed, though numerous, though heinous, though very provoking to God, and redounding very much to his dishonour, yet they shall not be mentioned unto him (Eze 18:22), not mentioned against them; not only they shall not be imputed to him to ruin him, but in the great day they shall not be remembered against him to grieve or shame him; they shall be covered, shall be sought for and not found. This intimates the fulness of pardoning mercy; when sin is forgiven it is blotted out, it is remembered no more. [3.] In their righteousness they shall live; not for their righteousness, as if that were the purchase of their pardon and bliss and an atonement for their sins, but in their righteousness, which qualifies them for all the blessings purchased by the Mediator, and is itself one of those blessings.

(3.) What encouragement a repenting returning sinner has to hope for pardon and life according to this promise. He is conscious to himself that his obedience for the future can never be a valuable compensation for his former disobedience; but he has this to support himself with, that

God's nature, property, and delight, is to have mercy and to forgive, for he has said (Eze 18:23): "Have I any pleasure at all that the wicked should die? No, by no means; you never had any cause given you to think so." It is true God has determined to punish sinners; his justice calls for their punishment, and, pursuant to that, impenitent sinners will lie for ever under his wrath and curse; that is the will of his decree, his consequent will, but it is not his antecedent will, the will of his delight. Though the righteousness of his government requires that sinners die, yet the goodness of his nature objects against it. How shall I give thee up, Ephraim? It is spoken here comparatively; he has not pleasure in the ruin of sinners, for he would rather they should turn from their ways and live; he is better pleased when his mercy is glorified in their salvation than when his justice is glorified in their damnation.

2. A fair warning given to righteous people not to turn from their righteousness,Eze 18:24-26. Here is, (1.) The character of an apostate, that turns away from his righteousness. He never was in sincerity a righteous man (as appears by that of the apostle, Jo1 2:19, If they had been of us, they would, no doubt, have continued with us), but he passed for a righteous man. He had the denomination and all the external marks of a righteous man; he thought himself one, and others thought him one. But he throws of his profession, leaves his first love, disowns and forsakes the truth and ways of God, and so turns away from his righteousness as one sick of it, and now shows, what he always had, a secret aversion to it; and, having turned away from his righteousness, he commits iniquity, grows loose, and profane, and sensual, intemperate, unjust, and, in short, does according to all the abominations that the wicked man does; for, when the unclean spirit recovers his possession of the heart, he brings with him seven other spirits more wicked than himself and they enter in and dwell there,Luk 11:26. (2.) The doom of an apostate: Shall he live because he was once a righteous man? No; factum non dicitur quod non perseverat- that which does not abide is not said to be done. In his trespass (Eze 18:24) and for his iniquity (that is the meritorious cause of his ruin), for the iniquity that he has done, he shall die, shall die eternally, Eze 18:26. The backslider in heart shall be filled with his own ways. But will not his former professions and performances stand him in some stead-will they not avail at least to mitigate his punishment? No: All his righteousness that he has done, though ever so much applauded by men, shall not be mentioned so as to be either a credit or a comfort to him; the righteousness of an apostate is forgotten, as the wickedness of a penitent is. Under the law, if a Nazarite was polluted he lost all the foregoing days of his separation (Num 6:12), so those that have begun in the spirit and end in the flesh may reckon all their past services and sufferings in vain (Gal 3:3, Gal 3:4); unless we persevere we lose what we have gained, Jo2 1:8.

II. An appeal to the consciences even of the house of Israel, though very corrupt, concerning God's equity in all these proceedings; for he will be justified, as well as sinners judged, out of their own mouths. 1. The charge they drew up against God is blasphemous, Eze 18:25, Eze 18:29. The house of Israel has the impudence to say, The way of the Lord is not equal, than which nothing could be more absurd as well as impious. He that formed the eye, shall he not see? Can his ways be unequal whose will is the eternal rule of good and evil, right and wrong? Shall not the Judge of all the earth do right? No doubt he shall; he cannot do otherwise. 2. God's reasonings with them are very gracious and condescending, for even these blasphemers God would rather have convinced and saved than condemned. One would have expected that God would immediately vindicate the honour of his justice by making those that impeached it eternal monuments of it. Must those be suffered to draw another breath that have once breathed out such wickedness as this? Shall that tongue ever speak again any where but in hell that has once said, The ways of the Lord are not equal? Yes, because this is the day of God's patience, he vouchsafes to argue with them; and he requires them to own, for it is so plain that they cannot deny, (1.) The equity of his ways: Are not my ways equal? No doubt they are. He never lays upon man more than is right. In the present punishments of sinners and the afflictions of his own people, yea, and in the eternal damnation of the impenitent, the ways of the Lord are equal. (2.) The iniquity of their ways: "Are not your ways unequal? It is plain that they are, and the troubles you are in you have brought upon your own heads. God does you no wrong, but you have wronged yourselves." The foolishness of man perverts his way, makes that unequal, and then his heart frets against the Lord, as if his ways were unequal,Pro 19:3. In all our disputes with God, and in all his controversies with us, it will be found that his ways are equal, but ours are unequal, that he is in the right and we are in the wrong.

Ezekiel 18:30

We have here the conclusion and application of this whole matter. After a fair trial at the bar of right reason the verdict is brought in on God's side; it appears that his ways are equal. Judgment therefore is next to be given; and one would think it should be a judgment of condemnation, nothing short of Go, you cursed, into everlasting fire. But, behold, a miracle of mercy; the day of grace and divine patience is yet lengthened out; and therefore, though God will at last judge every one according to his ways, yet he waits to be gracious, and closes all with a call to repentance and a promise of pardon upon repentance.

I. Here are four necessary duties that we are called to, all amounting to the same:-1. We must repent; we must change our mind and change our ways; we must be sorry for what we have done amiss and ashamed of it, and go as far as we can towards the undoing of it again. 2. We must turn ourselves from all our transgressions, Eze 18:30 and again Eze 18:32. Turn yourselves, face about; turn from sin, nay, turn against it as the enemy you loathe, turn to God as the friend you love. 3. We must cast away from us all our transgressions; we must abandon and forsake them with a resolution never to return to them again, give sin a bill of divorce, break all the leagues we have made with it, throw it overboard, as the mariners did Jonah (for it has raised the storm), cast it out of the soul, and crucify it as a malefactor. 4. We must make us a new heart and a new spirit. This was the matter of a promise, Eze 11:19. Here it is the matter of a precept. We must do our endeavour, and then God will not be wanting to us to give us his grace. St. Austin well explains this precept. Deus non jubet impossibilia, sed jubendo monet et facere quod possis et petere quod non possis-God does not enjoin impossibilities, but by his commands admonishes us to do what is in our power and to pray for what is not.

II. Here are four good arguments used to enforce these calls to repentance:-1. It is the only way, and it is a sure way, to prevent the ruin which our sins have a direct tendency to: So iniquity shall not be your ruin, which implies that, if we do not repent, iniquity will be our ruin, here and for ever, but that, if we do, we are safe, we are snatched as brands out of the burning. 2. If we repent not, we certainly perish, and our blood will be upon our own heads. Why will you die, O house of Israel? What an absurd thing it is for you to choose death and damnation rather than life and salvation. Note, The reason why sinners die is because they will die; they will go down the way that leads to death, and not come up to the terms on which life is offered. Herein sinners, especially sinners of the house of Israel, are most unreasonable and act most unaccountably. 3. The God of heaven has no delight in our ruin, but desires our welfare (Eze 18:32): I have no pleasure in the death of him that dies, which implies that he has pleasure in the recovery of those that repent; and this is both an engagement and an encouragement to us to repent. 4. We are made for ever if we repent: Turn yourselves, and live. He that says to us, Repent, thereby says to us, Live, yea, he says to us, Live; so that life and death are here set before us.

Ezekiel Chapter 19

Ezekiel

The scope of this chapter is much the same with that of the 17th, to foretel and lament the ruin of the house of David, the royal family of Judah, in the calamitous exit of the four sons and grandsons of Josiah-Jehoahaz, Jehoiakim, Jeconiah, and Zedekiah, in whom that illustrious line of kings was cut off, which the prophet is here ordered to lament (Eze 19:1). And he does it by similitudes. I. The kingdom of Judah and house of David are here compared to a lioness, and those princes to lions, that were fierce and ravenous, but were hunted down and taken in nets (Eze 19:2-9). II. That kingdom and that house are here compared to a vine, and these princes to branches, which had been strong and flourishing, but were now broken off and burnt (Eze 19:10-14). This ruin of that monarchy was now in the doing, and this lamentation of it was intended to affect the people with it, that they might not flatter themselves with vain hopes of the lengthening out of their tranquility.

Ezekiel 19:1

Here are, I. Orders given to the prophet to bewail the fall of the royal family, which had long made so great a figure by virtue of a covenant of royalty made with David and his seed, so that the eclipsing and extinguishing of it are justly lamented by all who know what value to put upon the covenant of our God, as we find, after a very large account of that covenant with David (Psa 89:3, Psa 89:20, etc.), a sad lamentation for the decays and desolations of his family (v. 38, 39): But thou hast cast off and abhorred, hast made void the covenant of thy servant and profaned his crown, etc. The kings of Judah are here called princes of Israel; for their glory was diminished and they had become but as princes, and their purity was lost; they had become corrupt and idolatrous as the kings of Israel, whose ways they had learned. The prophet must take up a lamentation for them; that is, he must describe their lamentable fall as one that did himself lay it to heart, and desired that those he preached and wrote to might do so to. And how can we expect that others should be affected with that which we ourselves are not affected with? Ministers, when they boldly foretel, must yet bitterly lament the destruction of sinners, as those that have not desired the woeful day. He is not directed to give advice to the princes of Israel (that had been long and often done in vain), but, the decree having gone forth, he must take up a lamentation for them.

II. Instructions given him what to say. 1. He must compare the kingdom of Judah to a lioness, so wretchedly degenerated was it from what it had been formerly, when it sat as a queen among the nations, Eze 19:2. What is thy mother? thine, O king? (we read of Solomon's crown wherewith his mother crowned him, that is, his people, Sol 3:11), thine, O Judah? The royal family is as a mother to the kingdom, a nursing mother. She is a lioness, fierce, and cruel, and ravenous. When they had left their divinity they soon lost their humanity too; and, when they feared not God, neither did they regard man. She lay down among lions. God had said, The people shall dwell alone, but they mingled with the nations and learned their works. She nourished her whelps among young lions, taught the young princes the way of tyrants, which was then used by the arbitrary kings of the east, filled their heads betimes with notions of their absolute despotic power, and possessed them with a belief that they had a right to enslave their subjects, that their liberty and property lay at their mercy: thus she nourished her whelps among young lions. 2. He must compare the kings of Judah to lions' whelps, Eze 19:3. Jacob had compared Judah, and especially the house of David, to a lion's whelp, for its being strong and formidable to its enemies abroad (Gen 49:9, He is an old lion; who shall stir him up?) and, if they had adhered to the divine law and promise, God would have preserved to them the might, and majesty, and dominion of a lion, and does it in Christ, the Lion of the tribe of Judah. But these lions' whelps were so to their own subjects, were cruel and oppressive to them, preyed upon their estates and liberties; and, when they thus by their tyranny made themselves a terror to those whom they ought to have protected, it was just with God to make those a terror to them whom otherwise they might have subdued. Here is lamented, (1.) The sin and fall of Jehoahaz, one of the whelps of this lioness. He became a young lion (Eze 19:3); he was made king, and thought he was made so that he might do what he pleased, and gratify his own ambition, covetousness, and revenge, as he had a mind; and so he was soon master of all the arts of tyranny; he learned to catch the prey and devoured men. When he got power into his hand, all that had before in any thing disobliged him were made to feel his resentments and become a sacrifice to his rage. But what came of it? He did not prosper long in his tyranny: The nations heard of him (Eze 19:4), heard how furiously he drove at his first coming to the crown, how he trampled upon all that is just and sacred, and violated all his engagements, so that they looked upon him as a dangerous neighbour, and prosecuted him accordingly, as a multitude of shepherds is called forth against a lion roaring on his prey, Isa 31:4. And he was taken, as a beast of prey, in their pit. His own subjects durst not stand up in defence of their liberties, but God raised up a foreign power that soon put an end to his tyranny, and brought him in chains to the land of Egypt. Thither Jehoahaz was carried captive, and never heard of more. (2.) The like sin and fall of his successor Jehoiakim. The kingdom of Judah for some time expected the return of Jehoahaz out of Egypt, but at length despaired of it, and then took another of the lion's whelps, and made him a young lion, Eze 19:5. And he, instead of taking warning by his brother's fate to use his power with equity and moderation, and to seek the good of his people, trod in his brother's steps: He went up and down among the lions, Eze 19:6. He consulted and conversed with those that were fierce and furious like himself, and took his measures from them, as Rehoboam took the advice of the rash and hot-headed young men. And he soon learned to catch the prey, and he devoured men (Eze 19:6); he seized his subjects' estates, fined and imprisoned them, filled his treasury by rapine and injustice, sequestrations and confiscations, fines and forfeitures, and swallowed up all that stood in his way. He had got the art of discovering what effects men had that lay concealed, and where the treasures were which they had hoarded up; he knew their desolate places (Eze 19:7), where they his their money and sometimes hid themselves; he knew where to find both out; and by his oppression he laid waste their cities, depopulated them by forcing the inhabitants to remove their families to some place of safety. The land was desolate, and the country villages were deserted; and though there was great plenty, and a fulness of all good things, yet people quitted it all for fear of the noise of his roaring. He took a pride in making all his subjects afraid of him, as the lion makes all the beasts of the forest to tremble (Amo 3:8), and by his terrible roaring so astonished them that they fell down for fear, and, having not spirit to make their escape, became an easy prey to him, as they say the lions do. He hectored, and threatened, and talked big, and bullied people out of what they had. Thus he thought to establish his own power, but it had a contrary effect, it did but hasten his own ruin (Eze 19:8): The nations set against him on every side, to restrain and reduce his exorbitant power, which they joined in confederacy to do for their common safety; and they spread their net over him, formed designs against him. God brought against Jehoiakim bands of the Syrians, Moabites, and Ammonites, with the Chaldees (Kg2 24:2), and he was taken in their pit. Nebuchadnezzar bound him in fetters to carry him to Babylon, Ch2 36:6. They put this lion within grates, bound him in chains, and brought him to the king of Babylon, Ch2 36:9. What became of him we know not; but his voice was nowhere heard roaring upon the mountains of Israel. There was an end of his tyranny: he was buried with the burial of an ass (Jer 22:19), though he had been as a lion, the terror of the mighty in the land of the living. Note, The righteousness of God is to be acknowledged when those who have terrified and enslaved others are themselves terrified and enslaved, when those who by the abuse of their power to destruction which was given them for edification make themselves as wild beasts, as roaring lions and ranging bears (for such, Solomon says, wicked rulers are over the poor people, Pro 28:15), are treated as such-when those who, like Ishmael, have their hand against every man, come at last to have every man's hand against them. It was long since observed that bloody tyrants seldom die in peace, but have blood given them to drink, for they are worthy.

Ad generum Cereris sine caede et sanguine pauci

Descendunt reges et sicca morte tyranni-

How few of all the boastful men that reign

Descend in peace to Pluto's dark domain!

-Juvenal

Ezekiel 19:10

Jerusalem, the mother-city, is here represented by another similitude; she is a vine, and the princes are her branches. This comparison we had before, Eze 15:1. Jerusalem is as a vine; the Jewish nation is so: Like a vine in they blood (Eze 19:10), the blood-royal, like a vine set in blood and watered with blood, which contributes very much to the flourishing and fruitfulness of vines, as if the blood which had been shed had been designed for the fattening and improving of the soil, in such plenty was it shed; and for a time it seemed to have that effect, for she was fruitful and full of branches by reason of the waters, the many waters near which she was planted. Places of great wickedness may prosper for a while; and a vine set in blood may be full of branches. Jerusalem was full of able magistrates, men of sense, men of learning and experience, that were strong rods, branches of this vine of uncommon bulk and strength, or poles for the support of this vine, for such magistrates are. The boughs of this vine had grown to such maturity that they were fit to make white staves of for the sceptres of those that bore rule, Eze 19:11. And those are strong rods that are fit for sceptres, men of strong judgments and strong resolutions that are fit for magistrates. When the royal family of Judah was numerous, and the courts of justice were filled with men of sense and probity, then Jerusalem's stature was exalted among thick branches; when the government is in good able hands a nation is thereby made considerable Then she was not taken for a weak and lowly vine, but she appeared in her height, a distinguished city, with the multitude of her branches. Tanquam lenta solent inter viburna cupressi-Midst humble withies thus the cypress soars. "In thy quietness" (so some read that, Eze 19:10, which we translate in thy blood) "thou wast such a vine as this." When Zedekiah was quiet and easy under the king of Babylon's yoke his kingdom flourished thus. See how slow God is to anger, how he defers his judgments, and waits to be gracious. 2. This vine is now quite destroyed. Nebuchadnezzar, being highly provoked by Zedekiah's treachery, plucked it up in fury (Eze 19:12), ruined the city and kingdom, and cut off all the branches of the royal family that fell in his way. The vine was cut off close to the ground, though not plucked up by the roots. The east wind dried up the fruit that was blasted. The young people fell by the sword, or were carried into captivity. The aspect of it had nothing that was pleasing, the prospect nothing that was promising. Her strong rods were broken and withered; her great men were cut off, judges and magistrates deposed. The vine itself is planted in the wilderness, Eze 19:13. Babylon was as a wilderness to those of the people that were carried captives thither; the land of Judah was as a wilderness to Jerusalem, now that the whole country was ravaged and laid waste by the Chaldean army-a fruitful land turned into barrenness. "It is burnt with fire (Psa 80:16) and that fire has gone out of a rod of her branches (Eze 19:14); the king himself, by rebelling against the king of Babylon, has given occasion to all this mischief. She may thank herself for the fire that consumes her; she has by her wickedness made herself like tinder to the sparks of God's wrath, so that her own branches serve as fuel for her own consumption; in them the fire is kindled which devoured the fruit, the sins of the elder being the judgments which destroy the younger; her fruit is burned with her own branches, so that she has no strong rod to be a sceptre to rule, none to be found now that are fit for the government or dare take this ruin under their hand, as the complaint is (Isa 3:6, Isa 3:7), none of the house of David left that have a right to rule, no wise men, or men of sense, that are able to rule." It goes ill with any state, and is likely to go worse, when it is thus deprived of the blessings of government and has no strong rods for sceptres. Woe unto thee, O land! when thy king is a child, for it is as well to have no rod as not a strong rod. Those strong rods, we have reason to fear, had been instruments of oppression, assistant to the king in catching the prey and devouring men, and now they are destroyed with him. Tyranny is the inlet to anarchy; and, when the rod of government is turned into the serpent of oppression, it is just with God to say, "There shall be no strong rod to be a sceptre to rule; but let men be as are the fishes of the sea, where the greater devour the less." Note, This is a lamentation and shall be for a lamentation. The prophet was bidden (Eze 19:1) to take up a lamentation; and, having done so, he leaves it to be made use of by others. "It is a lamentation to us of this age, and, the desolations continuing long, it shall be for a lamentation to those that shall come after us; the child unborn will rue the destruction made of Judah and Jerusalem by the present judgments. They were a great while in coming; the bow was long in the drawing; but now that they have come they will continue, and the sad effects of them will be entailed upon posterity." Note, Those who fill up the measure of their fathers' sins are laying up in store for their children's sorrows and furnishing them with matter for lamentation; and nothing is more so than the overthrow of government.

Ezekiel Chapter 20

In this chapter, I. The prophet is consulted by some of the elders of Israel (Eze 20:1). II. He is instructed by his God what answer to give them. He must, 1. Signify God's displeasure against them (Eze 20:2, Eze 20:3). And, 2. He must show them what just cause he had for that displeasure, by giving them a history of God's grateful dealings with their fathers and their treacherous dealings with God. (1.) In Egypt (Eze 20:5-9). (2.) In the wilderness (v. 10-26). (3.) In Canaan (Eze 20:27-32). 3. He must denounce the judgments of God against them (Eze 20:33-36). 4. He must tell them likewise what mercy God had in store for them, when he would bring a remnant of them to repentance, re-establish them in their own land, and set up his sanctuary among them again (Eze 20:37-44). 5. Here is another word dropped towards Jerusalem, which is explained and enlarged upon in the next chapter (Eze 20:45-49).

Ezekiel 20:1

Here is, 1. The occasion of the message which we have in this chapter. That sermon which we had ch. 18 was occasioned by their presumptuous reflections upon God; this was occasioned by their hypocritical enquiries after him. Each shall have his own. This prophecy is exactly dated, in the seventh year of the captivity, about two years after Ezekiel began to prophesy. God would have them to keep account how long their captivity lasted, that they might see how the years went on towards their deliverance, though very slowly. Certain of the elders of Israel came to enquire of the Lord, not statedly (as those Eze 8:1), but, as it should seem, occasionally, and upon a particular emergency. Whether they were of those that were now in captivity, or elders lately come from Jerusalem upon business to Babylon, is not certain; but, by what the prophet says to them (Eze 20:32), it should seem, their enquiry was whether now that they were captives in Babylon, at a distance from their own country, where they had not only no temple, but no synagogue, for the worship of God, it was not lawful for them, that they might ingratiate themselves with their lords and masters, to join with them in their worship and do as the families of these countries do, that serve wood and stone. This matter was palliated as well as it would bear, like Naaman's pleading with Elisha for leave to bow in the house of Rimmon, in compliment to the king; but we have reason to suspect that their enquiry drove at this. Note, Those hearts are wretchedly hardened which ask God leave to go on in sin, and that when they are suffering for it. They came and sat very demurely and with a show of devotion before the prophet, Eze 33:31. 2. The purport of this message. (1.) They must be made to know that God is angry with them; he takes it as an affront that they come to enquire of him when they are resolved to go on still in their trespasses: As I live, saith the Lord God, I will not be enquired of by you, Eze 20:3. Their shows of devotion shall be neither acceptable to God nor advantageous to themselves. God will not take notice of their enquiries, nor give them any satisfactory answers. Note, A hypocritical attendance on God and his ordinances is so far from being pleasing to him that it is provoking. (2.) They must be made to know that God is justly angry with them (Eze 20:4): "Wilt thou judge them, son of man, wilt thou judge them? Thou art a prophet, surely thou wilt not plead for them, as an intercessor with God; but surely thou wilt pass sentence on them as a judge for God. See, I have set thee over the nation; wilt thou not declare to them the judgments of the Lord? Cause them therefore to know the abominations of their fathers." So the orders run now, as before (Eze 16:2) he must cause them to know their own abominations. Though their own abominations were sufficient to justify God in the severest of his proceedings against them, yet it would be of use for them to know the abominations of their fathers, that they might see what a righteous thing it was with God now at last to cut them off from being a people, who from the first were such a provoking people.

Ezekiel 20:5

The history of the ingratitude and rebellion of the people of Israel here begins as early as their beginning; so does the history of man's apostasy from his Maker. No sooner have we read the story of our first parents' creation than we immediately meet with that of their rebellion; so we see here it was with Israel, a people designed to represent the body of mankind both in their dealings with God and in his with them. Here is,

I. The gracious purposes of God's law concerning Israel in Egypt, where they were bond-slaves to Pharaoh. Be it spoken, be it written, to the immortal honour of free grace, that then and there, 1. He chose Israel to be a peculiar people to himself, though their condition was bad and their character worse, that he might have the honour of mending both. He therefore chose them, because they were the seed of the house of Jacob, the posterity of that prince with God, that he might keep the oath which he had sworn unto their fathers, Deu 7:7, Deu 7:8. 2. He made himself known to them by his name Jehovah (a new name, Exo 6:3), when by reason of their servitude they had almost lost the knowledge of that name by which he was known to their fathers, God Almighty. Note, As the foundation of our blessedness is laid in God's choosing us, so the first step towards it is God's making himself known to us. And whatever distance we are at, whatever distress we are in, he that made himself known to Israel even in the land of Egypt can find us out, and follow us with the gracious discoveries and manifestations of his favour. 3. He made over himself to them as their God in covenant: I lifted up my hand unto them, saying it, and confirming it with an oath. "I am the Lord your God, to whom you are to pay your homage, and from whom and in whom you are to expect your bliss." 4. He promised to bring them out of Egypt; and made good what he promised. He lifted up his hand, that is, he swore unto them, that he would deliver them; and, they being very unworthy, and their deliverance very unlikely, it was requisite that the promise of it should be confirmed by an oath. Or, He lifted up his hand, that is, he put forth his almighty power to do it; he did it with an outstretched arm, Psa 136:12. 5. He assured them that he would put them in possession of the land of Canaan. He therefore brought them out of Egypt, that he might bring them into a land that he had spied out for them, a second garden of Eden, which was the glory of all lands. So he found it, the climate being temperate, the soil fruitful, the situation pleasant, and every thing agreeable (Deu 8:7; Deu 11:12); or, however this might be, so he made it, by setting up his sanctuary in it.

II. The reasonable commands he gave them, and the easy conditions of his covenant with them at that time. Having told them what they might expect from him, he next tells them what was all he expected from them; it was no more than this (Eze 20:7): "Cast you away every man his images that he uses for worship, that are the adorations, but should be the abominations, of his eyes. Let him abominate them, and put them out of his sight, and defile not yourselves with the idols of Egypt." Of these, it seems, many of them were fond; the golden calf was one of them. It was just, and what might reasonably be expected, that, being delivered from the Egyptian slavery, they should quit the Egyptian idolatry, especially when God, at bringing them out, executed judgment upon the gods of Egypt (Num 33:4) and thereby showed himself above them. And, whatever other idols they might have an inclination to, one would think they should have had a rooted aversion to the gods of Egypt for Egypt's sake, which had been to them a house of bondage. Yet, it seems, they needed this caution, and it is backed with a good reason: I am the Lord your God, who neither need an assistant nor will admit a rival.

III. Their unreasonable disobedience to these commands, for which God might justly have cut them off as soon as ever they were formed into a people (Eze 20:8): They rebelled against God, not only refused to comply with his particular precepts, but shook off their allegiance, and in effect told him that they should be at liberty to worship what God they pleased. And even then when God came down to deliver them, and sent Moses for that purpose, yet they would not forsake the idols of Egypt, which perhaps made them speak so affectionately of the onions of Egypt (Num 11:5), for among other things the Egyptians worshipped an onion. It was strange that all the plagues of Egypt would not prevail to cure them of their affection to the idols of Egypt. For this God said he would pour out his fury upon them, even while they were yet in the midst of the land of Egypt. Justly might he have said, "Let them die with the Egyptians." This magnifies the riches of God's goodness, that he was pleased to work so great a salvation for them even when he saw them ripe for ruin. Well might Moses tell them, It is not for your righteousness, Duet. Eze 9:4, Eze 9:5.

IV. The wonderful deliverance which God wrought for them, notwithstanding. Though they forfeited the favour while it was in the bestowing, and when God would have healed them then their iniquity was discovered (Hos 7:1), yet mercy rejoiced against judgment, and God did what he designed purely for his own name's sake, Eze 20:9. When nothing in us will furnish him with a reason for his favours he furnishes himself with one. God made himself known to them in the sight of the heathen when he ordered Moses publicly to say to Pharaoh, Israel is my son, my first-born, let them go, that they may serve me. Now, if he had left them to perish for their wickedness as they deserved, the Egyptians would have reflected upon him for it, and his name would have been polluted, which ought to be sanctified and shall be so. Note, The church is secured, even when it is corrupt, because God will secure his own honour.

Ezekiel 20:10

The history of the struggle between the sins of Israel, by which they endeavoured to ruin themselves, and the mercies of God, by which he endeavoured to save them and make them happy, is here continued: and the instances of that struggle in these verses have reference to what passed between God and them in the wilderness, in which God honoured himself and they shamed themselves. The story of Israel in the wilderness is referred to in the New Testament (1 Co. 10 and Heb. 3), as well as often in the Old, for warning to us Christians; and therefore we are particularly concerned in these verses. Observe,

1. The great things God did for them, which he puts them in mind of, not as grudging them his favours, but to show how ungrateful they had been. And we say, If you call a man ungrateful, you can call him no worse. It was a great favour, 1. That God brought them forth out of Egypt (Eze 20:10), though, as it follows, he brought them into the wilderness and not into Canaan immediately. It is better to be at liberty in a wilderness than bond-slaves in a land of plenty, to enjoy God and ourselves in solitude than to lose both in a crowd; yet there were many of them who had such base servile spirits as not to understand this, but, when they met with the difficulties of a desert, wished themselves in Egypt again. 2. That he gave them the law upon Mount Sinai (Eze 20:11), not only instructed them concerning good and evil, but by his authority bound them from the evil and to the good. He gave them his statutes, and a valuable gift it was. Moses commanded them a law that was the inheritance of the congregation of Israel, Deu 33:4. God made them to know his judgments, not only enacted laws for them, but showed them the reasonableness and equity of those laws, with what judgment they were formed. The laws he gave them they were encouraged to observe and obey; for, if a man do them, he shall even live in them; in keeping God's commandments there is abundance of comfort and a great reward. Christ says, If thou wilt into enter life, and enjoy it, keep the commandments. Though those who are the most strict in their obedience are thus far unprofitable servants that they do no more than is their duty to do, yet it is thus richly recompensed: This do, and thou shalt live. The Chaldee says, He shall live an eternal life in them. St. Paul quotes this (Gal 3:12) to show that the law is not of faith, but proposes life upon condition of perfect obedience, which we are not capable of rendering, and therefore must have recourse to the grace of the gospel, without which we are all undone. 3. That he revived the ancient institution of the sabbath day, which was lost and forgotten while they were bond-slaves in Egypt; for their task-masters there would by no means allow them to rest one day in seven. In the wilderness indeed every day was a day of rest; for what need had those to labour who lived upon manna, and whose raiment waxed not old? But one day in seven must be a holy rest (Eze 20:12): I gave them my sabbaths to be a sign between me and them (the institution of the sabbath was a sign of God's good-will to them, and their observance of it a sign of their regard to him), that they might know that I am the Lord that

clxxviii

sanctify them. By this God made it to appear that he had distinguished them from the rest of the world, and designed to model them for a peculiar people to himself; and by their attendance on God in solemn assemblies on sabbath days they were made to increase in the knowledge of God, in an experimental knowledge of the powers and pleasures of his sanctifying grace. Note, (1.) Sabbaths are privileges, and are so to be accounted; the church acknowledges as a great favour, in that chapter which is parallel to this and seems to have a reference to this (Neh 9:14), Thou madest known unto them thy holy sabbaths. (2.) Sabbaths are signs; it is a sign that men have a sense of religion, and that there is some good correspondence between them and God, when they make conscience of keeping holy and sabbath day. (3.) Sabbaths, if duly sanctified, are the means of our sanctification; if we do the duty of the day, we shall find, to our comfort, it is the Lord that sanctifies us, makes us holy (that is, truly happy) here, and prepares us to be happy (that is, perfectly holy) hereafter.

II. Their disobedient undutiful conduct towards God, for which he might justly have thrown them out of covenant as soon as he had taken them into covenant (Eze 20:13): They rebelled in the wilderness. There where they received so much mercy from God, and had such a dependence upon him, and were in their way to Canaan, yet there they broke out in many open rebellions against the God that led them and fed them. They did not only not walk in God's statutes, but they despised his judgments as not worth observing; instead of sanctifying the sabbaths, they polluted them, greatly polluted them; one gathered sticks, many went out to gather manna on this day. Hereupon God was ready sometimes to cut them off; he said, more than once, that he would consume them in the wilderness. But Moses interceded, so did God's own mercy more powerfully, and most of all a concern for his own glory, that his name might not be polluted and profaned among the heathen (Eze 20:14), that the Egyptians might not say that for mischief he brought them thus far, or that he was not able to bring them any further, or that he had no such good land as was talked of to bring them to, Exo 32:12; Num 14:13, etc. Note, God's strongest reasons for his sparing mercy are those which are fetched from his own glory.

III. God's determination to cut off that generation of them in the wilderness. He who lifted up his hand for them (Eze 20:6) now lifted up his hand against them; he who by an oath confirmed his promise to bring them out of Egypt now by an oath confirmed his threatenings that he would not bring them into Canaan (Eze 20:15, Eze 20:16): I lifted up my hand unto them, saying, As truly as I live, these men who have tempted me these ten times shall never see the land which I swore unto their fathers, Num 14:22, Num 14:23; Psa 95:11. By their contempt of God's laws, and particularly of his sabbaths, they put a bar in their own door; and that which was at the bottom of their disobedience to God, and their neglect of his institutions, was a secret affection to the gods of Egypt: Their heart went after their idols. Note, The bias of the mind towards the world and the flesh, the money and the belly (those two great objects of spiritual idolatry), is the root of bitterness from which springs all disobedience to the divine law. The heart that goes after those idols despises God's judgments.

IV. The reservation of a seed that should be admitted upon a new trial, and the instructions given to that seed, Eze 20:17. Though they thus deserved ruin, and were doomed to it, yet my eye spared them. When he looked upon them he had compassion on them, and did not make an end of them, but reprieved them till a new generation was reared. Note, It is owing purely to the mercy of God that he has not long ago made an end of us. This new generation is well educated. Moses in Deuteronomy reported and enforce the laws which had been given to those that came out of Egypt, that their children might have them as it were sounding in their ears afresh when they entered Canaan (Eze 20:18): "I said unto their children in the wilderness, in the plains of Moab, Walk in the statutes of your God and walk not in the statutes of your fathers; do not imitate their superstitious usages nor retain their foolish wicked customs; away with their vain conversation, which has nothing else to say for itself but that it was received by the tradition of your fathers, Pe1 1:18. Defile not yourselves with their idols, for you see how odious they rendered themselves to God by them. But keep my judgments and hallow my sabbaths," Eze 20:19, Eze 20:20. Note, If parents be careless, and do not give their children good instructions as they ought, the children ought to make up the want by studying the word of God so much the more carefully and diligently themselves when they grow up; and the bad examples of parents must be made use of by their children for admonition, and not for imitation.

V. The revolt of the next generation from God, by which they also made themselves obnoxious to the wrath of God (Eze 20:21): The children rebelled against me too. And the same that was said of the fathers' rebellion is here said of the children's, for they were a seed of evil-doers. Moses told them that he knew their rebellion and their stiff neck, Deu 31:27. And Deu 9:24, You have been rebellious against the Lord from the day that I knew you. They walked not in my statutes (Eze 20:21); nay, they despised my statutes, Eze 20:24. Those who disobey God's statutes despise them, they show that they have a mean opinion of them and of him whose statutes they are. They polluted God's sabbaths, as their fathers. Note, The profanation of the sabbath day is an inlet to all impiety; those who pollute holy time will keep nothing pure. It was said of the fathers (Eze 20:16) that their heart went after their idols; they worshipped idols because they had an affection for them. It is said of the children (Eze 20:24) that their eyes went after their fathers' idols; they had grown atheistical, and had no affection for any gods at all, but they worshipped their fathers' idols because they were their fathers' and they had them before their eyes. They were used to them; and, if they must have gods, they would have such as they could see, such as they could manage. And that which aggravated their disobedience to God's statutes was that, if they had done them, they might have lived in them (Eze 20:21), might have been a happy thriving people. Note, Those that go contrary to their duty go contrary to their interest; they will not obey, will not come to Christ, that they may have life, Joh 5:40. And it is therefore just that those who will not live and flourish as they might in their obedience should die and perish in their disobedience. Now the great instance of that generation's rebellion and inclination to idolatry was the iniquity of Peor, as that of their fathers was the golden calf. Then the anger of the Lord was kindled against Israel, Num 25:3. Then there was a plague in the congregation of the Lord, which, if it had not been seasonably stayed by Phinehas's zeal, had cut them all off; and yet they owned, in Joshua's time, We ware not cleansed from that iniquity unto this day, Jos 22:17; Psa 106:29. Then it was that God said he would pour out his fury upon them (Eze 20:21), that he lifted up his hand unto them in the wilderness, when they were a second time just ready to enter Canaan, that he would scatter them among the heathen. This very thing he said to them by Moses in his parting song, Deu 32:20. Because they provoked him to jealousy with strange gods, he said, I will hide my face form them; and (Eze 20:26, Eze 20:27) he said, I would scatter them into corners, were it not that I feared the wrath of the enemy, which explains this (Eze 20:21, Eze 20:22), I said I would pour out my fury upon them, but I withdrew my hand for my name's sake. Note, When the corruptions of the visible church are such, and so provoking, that we have reason to fear its total extirpation, yet then we may be confident of this, to our comfort, that God will secure his own honour, by making good his purpose, that while the world stands he will have a church in it.

VI. The judgments of God upon them for their rebellion. They would not regard the statutes and judgments by which God prescribed them their duty, but despised them, and therefore God gave them statutes and judgments which were not good, and by which they should not live, Eze 20:25. By this we may understand the several ways by which God punished them while they were in the wilderness-the plague that broke in upon them, the fiery serpent, and the like-which, in allusion to the law they had broken, are called judgments, because inflicted by the justice of God, and statutes, because he gave orders concerning them and commanded desolations as sometimes he had commanded deliverances, and appointed Israel's plagues as he had done the plagues of Egypt. When God said, I will consume them in a moment (Num 16:21), when he said, Take the heads of the people and hang them up (Num 25:4), when he threatened them with the curse and obliged them to say Amen to every curse (Deu 27:26), then he gave them judgments by which they should not live. More is implied than is expressed; they are judgments by which they should die. Those that will not be bound by the precepts of the law shall be bound by the sentence of it; for one way or other the word of God will take hold of men, Zac 1:6. Spiritual judgments are the most dreadful; and these God punished them with. The statutes and judgments which the heathen observed in the worship of their idols were not good, and in practising them they could not live; and God gave them up to those. He made their sin to be their punishment, gave them up to a reprobate mind, as he did the Gentile idolaters (Rom 1:24, Rom 1:26), gave them up to their own heart's lusts (Psa 81:12), punished them for those superstitious customs which were against the written law by giving them up to those which were against the very light and law of nature; he left them to themselves to be guilty of the most impure idolatries, as in the worship of Baal-peor (he polluted them, that is, her permitted them to pollute themselves, in their own gifts, Eze 20:26), and of the most barbarous idolatries, as in the worship of Moloch, when they caused their children, especially their first-born, which God challenged a particular property in (the first-born of thy sons shalt thou give unto me), to pass through the fire, to be sacrificed to their idols; that thus he might make them desolate, not only that he might justly do it, but that he might do it by their own hands; for this must needs be a great weakening to their families and a diminution of the honour and strength of their country. Note, God sometimes makes sin to be its own punishment, and yet is not the author of sin; and there needs no more to make men miserable than to give them up to their own vile appetites and passions. Let them be put into the hand of their own counsels, and they will ruin themselves and make themselves desolate. And thus God makes them know that he is the Lord, and that he is a righteous God, which they themselves will be compelled to own when they see how much their wilful transgressions contribute to their own desolations. Note, Those who will not acknowledge God as the Lord their ruler shall be made to acknowledge him as the Lord their judge when it is too late.

Ezekiel 20:27

Here the prophet goes on with the story of their rebellions, for their further humiliation, and shows,

I. That they had persisted in them after they were settled in the land of Canaan. Though God had so many times testified his displeasure against their wicked courses, "yet in this (that is, in the very same thing) your fathers have blasphemed me, continued to affront me, that they also have trespassed a trespass against me," Eze 20:27. Note, It is a great aggravation of sin when men will not take warning by the mischievous consequences of sin in those that have gone before them: this is blaspheming God; it is speaking reproachfully of his judgments, as if they were of no significancy and were not worth regarding. 1. God had made good his promise: I brought them into the land that I had sworn to give them. Though their unbelief and disobedience had made the performance slow, and much retarded it, yet it did not make the promise of no effect. They were often very near being cut off in the wilderness, but a step between them and ruin, and yet they came to Canaan at last. Note, Even God's Israel get to heaven by hell-gates; so many are their transgressions, and so strong their corruptions, that it is a miracle of mercy they are happy at last; as hypocrites go to hell by heaven-gates. The righteous scarcely are saved. Per tot discrimina rerum tendimus ad coelum-Ten thousand dangers fill the road to heaven. 2. They had broken his precept by their abominable idolatries. God had appointed them to destroy all the monuments of idolatry, that they might not be tempted to desert his sanctuary; but, instead of defacing them, they fell in love with them, and when they saw every high hill whence they had the most delightful prospects, and all the thick trees where they had the most delightful shades (the former to show forth their pompous idolatries, the latter to conceal their shameful ones), there they offered their sacrifices and made their sweet savour, which should have been presented upon God's altar only. There they presented the provocation of their offering (Eze 20:28), that is, their offerings, which, instead of pacifying God, or pleasing him, were highly provoking-sacrifices which, though costly, yet being misplaced, were an abomination to the Lord. 3. They obstinately persisted herein notwithstanding all the admonitions that were given them (Eze 20:29): "Then I told them, by my servants the prophets, told them where the high place was, to which they went; nay, I put them upon considering it, and asking their own consciences concerning it, by putting this question to them, Which is the high place whereunto you go? What do you find there so inviting that you will leave God's altars, where he requires your attendance, to frequent such places as he has forbidden you to worship in? Do you not know that those high places are of a heathenish extraction, and that the things which the Gentiles sacrificed they sacrificed to devils and not to God? Did not Moses tell you so? Deu 32:17. And will you have fellowship with devils? What is that high place to which you go when you turn your back on God's altars? O foolish Israelites, who or what has bewitched you, that you will forsake the fountain of life for broken cisterns, that worship which God appoints, and will accept, for that which he forbids, which he abhors, and which he will punish?" And yet the name is called Bamah unto this day; they will have their way, let God and his prophets say what they please to the contrary. They are wedded to their high places; even in the best reigns those were not taken away; you could not prevail to take away the name of Bamah-the high place, out of their mouths, but still they would have that in the place of their worship. The sin and the sinner are with difficulty parted.

II. That this generation, after they were unsettled, continued under the dominion of the same corrupt inclinations to idolatry, Eze 20:30. He must say to the present house of Israel, some of whose elders were now sitting before him, "Are you polluted after the manner of your fathers? After all that God has said against you by a succession of prophets, and done against you by a series of judgments, yet will you take no warning? Will you still be as bad as your fathers were, and commit the same abominations that they committed? I see you will; you are bent upon returning to the old abominations; you offer your gifts in the high places, and you make your sons to pass through the fire; either you actually do it or you do it in purpose and imagination, and so you continue idolaters to this day." These elders seem now to have been projecting a coalition with the heathen; their hearts they will reserve for the God of Israel, but their knees they will be at liberty to bow to the gods of the nations among whom they live, that they may have the more respect and the fairer quarter among them. Now the prophet is here ordered to tell those who were forming this scheme, and were for compounding the matter between God and Baal, that they should have no comfort or benefit from either. 1. They should have no benefit by their consulting in private with the prophets of the Lord; for, because they were hearkening after idols, God would have nothing to do with them (Eze 20:31): As I live, saith the Lord God, I will not be enquired of by you. What he had said before (Eze 20:3), having largely shown how just it was, he here repeats, as that which he would abide by. Let them not think that they honoured him by their enquiries, nor expect an answer of peace from him, as long as they continued in love and league with their idols. Note, Those reap no benefit by their religion that are not entire and sincere in it; nor can we have any comfortable communion with God in ordinances of worship unless we be inward and upright with him therein. We make nothing of our profession if it be but a profession. Nay, 2. They should have no benefit from their conforming in public to the practice of their neighbours (Eze 20:32): "That which comes into your mind as a piece of refined politics in the present difficult juncture, and which you would be advised to for your own preservation, and that you may not by being singular expose yourselves to abuses, it shall not be at all, it shall turn to no account to you. You say, 'We will be as the heathen, we will join with them in worshipping their gods, though at the same time we do not believe them to be gods, but wood and stone, and then we should be taken as the families of the countries; they will not know, or in a little while will have forgotten, that we are Jews, and will allow us the same privileges with their own countrymen.' Tell them," says God, "that this project shall never prosper. Either their neighbours will not admit them to join with them in their worship, or, if they do, will think never the better, but the worse, of them for it, and will look upon them as dissemblers, and not fit to be trusted, who are thus false to their God, and put a cheat upon their neighbours." Note, There is nothing got by sinful compliances; and the carnal projects of hypocrites will stand them in no stead. It is only integrity and uprightness that will preserve men, and recommend them to God and man.

<h2 style="text-align:center">Ezekiel 20:33</h2>

The design which was now on foot among the elders of Israel was that the people of Israel, being scattered among the nations, should lay aside all their peculiarities and conform to those among whom they lived; but God had told them that the design should not take effect, Eze 20:32. Now, in these verses, he shows particularly how it should be frustrated. They aimed at the mingling of the families of Israel with the families of the countries; but it will prove in the issue that the wicked Israelites, notwithstanding their compliances, shall not mingle with them in their prosperity, but shall be distinguished from them for destruction; for idolatrous Israelites, that are apostates from God, shall be sooner and more sorely punished than idolatrous Babylonians that never knew the way of righteousness. Read and tremble at the doom here passed upon them; it is backed with an oath not to be reversed: As I live, saith the Lord God, thus and thus will I deal with you. They think to make both Jerusalem and Babylon their friends by halting between two; but God threatens that neither of them shall serve for a rest or refuge for them.

I. Babylon shall not protect them, nor any of the countries of the heathen; for God will cast them out of his protection and then what prince, what people, what place, can serve to be a sanctuary to them? God was Israel's King of old, and had they continued his loyal subjects he would have ruled over them with care and tenderness for their good, but now with a stretched-out arm, and with fury poured out, will I rule over them, Eze 20:33. That power which should have been exerted fore their protection shall be exerted for their destruction. Note, There is no shaking off God's dominion; rule he will, either with the golden sceptre or with the iron rod; and those that will not yield to the power of his grace shall be made to sink under the power of his wrath. Now when God is angry with them, though they may think that they shall be lost in the crowd of the heathen among whom they are scattered, they will be disappointed; for (Eze 20:34) I will gather you out of the countries wherein you are scattered, as, when the rebels are dispersed in battle, those that have escaped the sword of war are pursued and brought together out of all the places whither they were scattered, to be punished by the sword of justice. They shall be brought into the wilderness of the people (Eze 20:35), either into Babylon, which is called a wilderness (Eze 19:13), and the desert of the sea (Isa 21:1), or into some place which, though full of people, shall be to them as the wilderness was to Israel after they came out of Egypt, a place where God will plead with them face to face, as he pleaded with their fathers in the wilderness of Egypt (Eze 20:36),-where their carcases shall fall and where he will swear concerning them that they shall never return to Canaan, as he did swear concerning their fathers that they should never come into Canaan,-where he will avenge the breach of his law with as much terror as that with which he gave it in the wilderness of Sinai. Note, God has a good action against apostates, and will find not only time, but a proper place, to plead with them in upon that action, a wilderness even in the midst of the people for that purpose.

II. Israel shall be no more able to protect them than Babylon could; nor shall their relation to God's people stand them in any more stead for the other world than their compliance with idolaters shall for this world; nor shall they stand in the congregation of the righteous any more than in the congregation of evil-doers; for there will come a distinguishing day, when God will separate between the precious and the vile; he will cause them, as the shepherd causes his sheep, to pass under the rod, when he tithes them (Lev 27:32), that he may mark which is for God. God will take particular notice of each of them, one by one, as sheep are counted, and he will bring them into the bond of the covenant (Eze 20:37); he will try them and judge of them according to the tenour of the covenant, and the difference made between some and others by the blessings and curses of the covenant. Or it may refer to those among them that repented and reformed; he will cause them to pass under the rod of affliction, and, having done them good by it, he will bring them again into the bond of the covenant, will be to them a God in covenant, and use them again as heirs of promise.

1. He will separate the wicked from among them (Eze 20:38): "I will purge out from among you the rebels, who have been a grief and scandal to you, and who have by their rebellions brought all these calamities upon you." The judgments of God shall find them out, and their naming the name of Israel shall be no shelter to them. They shall be brought out of the countries where they sojourn, and shall not have that rest in them which they promised themselves. But they shall not enter into the land of Israel, nor enjoy the benefit of that rest which God has promised to his people. Note, Though godly people may share with the wicked in the calamities of the world, yet wicked people shall have no share with the godly in the heavenly Canaan; but it shall be part of the blessedness of that world that they shall be purged out from among them, the tares from the wheat, the chaff from the corn, Eze 13:9. But wherever these idolaters of the house of Israel were contriving to worship both God and their idols, thinking to please both, God here protests against it (Eze 20:39), as Elijah had done in his name: "If the Lord be God, then follow him, but, if Baal, then follow him; if you will serve your idols, do, and take what comes of it; but then do not pretend relation to God and a religious regard to him, nor pollute his holy name with your gifts at his altar." Spiritual judgments are the sorest judgments. Two of that kind of judgments are threatened in this verse against those that were for dividing between the God of Israel and the gods of the nations:-(1.) That they should be given up to the service of their idols. To them he said ironically, "Since you will not hearken unto me, go you, serve every one his idols, now that you think it will be for your interest, and hereafter also. You shall go on in it.

Ephraim is joined to idols, let him alone; let him take his course, and see what he will get by it at last." Note, Those who think to serve themselves by sin will find in the end that they have but enslaved themselves to sin. (2.) That they should be cut off from the service of God and communion with God: "You shall not pollute my holy name with your vain oblations, Isa 1:11. You bring your gifts in your hands, wherewith you pretend to honour me, but at the same time you bring your idols in your hearts, and therefore you do but pollute me, which I will not suffer any more," Amo 5:21, Amo 5:22. Note, Those are justly forbidden God's house that profane his house.

2. He will separate them to himself again. (1.) He will gather them in mercy out of the countries whither they were scattered, to be monuments of mercy, as the incorrigible were gathered to be vessels of wrath, Eze 20:41. Not one of God's jewels shall be lost in the lumber of this world. (2.) He will bring them to the land of Israel, which he had promised to give to their fathers; and the discontinuance of their possession shall be no defeasance of their right; it is the land of Israel still, and thither God will bring them safely again, Eze 20:42. (3.) He will re-establish his ordinances among them, will set up his sanctuary in his holy mountain, which is here called the mountain of the height of Israel; for, though the Mount Zion was none of the highest mountains, yet the temple there was one of the highest honours of Israel. It is promised that those who preserved their integrity, and would not serve idols, in other lands, shall return to their prosperity and shall serve the true God in their own land: All of them in the land shall serve me. Note, It is the true happiness of a people, and a sure token for good to them, when there is a prevailing disposition in them to serve God. Whereas God had forbidden the idolaters to bring their gifts to his altar, of these he will require offerings and first-fruits, and will accept them, Eze 20:40. What he does not require he will not accept, but what is done with a regard to his precepts he will be well pleased with. He will accept them with their sweet savour, or savour of rest (Eze 20:41), as being very grateful to him and what he takes a complacency in; whereas, to hypocritical worshippers, he says, I will not smell in your solemn assemblies. (4.) He will give them true repentance for their sins, Eze 20:43. When they find how gracious God is to them they will be overcome with his kindness, and blush to think of their bad behaviour towards so good a God: "There, in my holy mountain, when you come to enjoy the privileges of that again, there shall you remember your doings, wherein you have been defiled." Note, The more conversant we are with God's holiness the more we shall see of the odious nature of sin. There you shall loathe yourselves in your own sight. Note, Ingenuous evangelical repentance makes people loathe themselves for their sins, as Job 42:5, Job 42:6. (5.) He will give them the knowledge of himself: They shall know by experience that he is the Lord, that he is a God of almighty power and inexhaustible goodness, kind to his people and faithful to his covenant with them. Note, All the favours we receive from God should lead us into a more intimate acquaintance with him. (6.) He will do all this for his own name's sake, notwithstanding their undeservings and ill-deservings (Eze 20:44); he has wrought with them, that is, wrought for them, wrought in favour of them, wrought in concurrence with them, they doing their endeavour; he has wrought with them purely for his name's sake. His reasons were all fetched from himself. Had he dealt with them according

to their wicked ways and their corrupt doings, though they were the better and sounder part of the house of Israel, he would have left them to be scattered and lost with the rest; but he recovered and restored them for the sake of his own name, not only that it might not be polluted (Eze 20:14), but that he might be sanctified in them before the heathen (Eze 20:41), that he might sanctify himself (so the word is); for it is God's work to glorify his own name. He will do well for his people that he may have the glory of it, that he may manifest himself to be a God pardoning sin and so keeping promise, that his people may praise him, and that their neighbours may likewise take notice of him, as they did when God burned again their captivity, Psa 126:3. Then said they among the heathen, The Lord has done great things for them.

Ezekiel 20:45

We have here a prophecy of wrath against Judah and Jerusalem, which would more fitly have begun the next chapter than conclude this; for it has no dependence on what goes before, but that which follows in the beginning of the next chapter is the explication of it, when the people complained that this was a parable which they understood not. In this parable, 1. It is a forest that is prophesied against, the forest of the south field, Judah and Jerusalem. These lay south from Babylon, where Ezekiel now was, and therefore he is directed to set his face towards the south (Eze 20:46), to intimate to them that God had set his face against them, was displeased with them, and determined to destroy them. But, though it be a message of wrath which he has to deliver, he must deliver it with mildness and tenderness; he must drop his word towards the south; his doctrine must distil as the rain (Deu 32:2), that people's hearts might be softened by it, as the earth by the river of God, which drops upon the pastures of the wilderness (Psa 65:12) and which a south land more especially calls for, Jos 15:19. Judah and Jerusalem are called forests, not only because they had been full of people, as a wood of trees, but because they had been empty of fruit, for fruit-trees grow not in a forest; and a forest is put in opposition to a fruitful field,Isa 32:15. Those that should have been as the garden of the Lord, and his vineyard, had become like a forest, all overgrown with briers and thorns; and those that are so, that bring not forth the fruits of righteousness, God's word prophesies against. 2. It is a fire kindled in his forest that is prophesied of, Eze 20:47. All those judgments which wasted and consumed both the city and the country-sword, famine, pestilence, and captivity, are signified by this fire. (1.) It is a fire of God's own kindling: I will kindle a fire in thee; the breath of the Lord is not as a drop, but as a stream, of brimstone to set it on fire, Isa 30:33. He that had been himself a protecting fire about Jerusalem is now a consuming fire in it. All flesh shall see by the fury of this fire, and the desolations it shall make, especially when they compare it with the sins which had made them fuel for this fire, that it is the Lord that has kindled it (Eze 20:48), as a just avenger of his own injured honour. (2.) This conflagration shall be general: all orders and degrees of men shall be devoured by it-young and old, rich and poor, high and low. Even green trees, which the fire does not easily fasten upon, shall be devoured by this fire; even good people shall some of them be involved in these calamities; and if this be done in the green trees, what shall be done in the dry? The dry trees shall be as tinder and touch-wood to this fire. All faces (that is, all that covers the face of the earth) from the south of Canaan to the north, from Beer-sheba to Dan, shall be burnt therein. (3.) The fire shall not be quenched; no attempts to give check to the dissolution shall prevail. When God will ruin a nation, who or what can save it?

Now observe, 1. The people's reflection upon the prophet on occasion of this discourse. They said, Does he not speak parables? This was the language either of their ignorance or infidelity (the plainest truths were as parables to them), or of their malice and ill-will to the prophet. Note. It is common for those who will not be wrought upon by the word to pick quarrels with it; it is either too plain or too obscure, too fine or too homely, too common or too singular; something or other is amiss in it. 2. The prophet's complaint to God: Ah, Lord God! they say so and so of me. Note, It is a comfort to us, when people speak ill of us unjustly, that we have a God to complain to.

Ezekiel Chapter 21

Ezekiel

In this chapter we have, I. An explication of the prophecy in the close of the foregoing chapter concerning the fire in the forest, which the people complained they could not understand (Eze 21:1-5), with directions to the prophet to show himself deeply affected with it (Eze 21:6, Eze 21:7). II. A further prediction of the sword that was coming upon the land, by which all should be laid waste; and this expressed very emphatically (Eze 21:8-17). III. A prospect given of the king of Babylon's approach to Jerusalem, to which he was determined by divination (Eze 21:18-24). IV. Sentence passed upon Zedekiah king of Judah (Eze 21:25-27). V. The destruction of the Ammonites by the sword foretold (Eze 21:28-32). Thus is this chapter all threatenings.

Ezekiel 21:1

The prophet had faithfully delivered the message he was entrusted with, in the close of the foregoing chapter, in the terms wherein he received it, not daring to add his own comment upon it; but, when he complained that the people found fault with him for speaking parables, the word of the Lord came to him again, and gave him a key to that figurative discourse, that with it he might let the people into the meaning of it and so silence that objection. For all men shall be rendered inexcusable at God's bar and every mouth shall be stopped. Note, He that speaks with tongues should pray that he may interpret, Col 14:13. When we speak to people about their souls we should study plainness, and express ourselves as we may be the best understood. Christ expounded his parables to his disciples, Mar 4:34. 1. The prophet is here more plainly directed against whom to level the arrow of this prophecy. He must drop his word towards the holy places (Eze 21:2), towards Canaan the holy land, Jerusalem the holy city, the temple the holy house. These were highly dignified above other places; but, when they polluted them, that word which used to drop in the holy places shall now drop against them: Prophesy against the land of Israel. It was the honour of Israel that it had prophets and prophecy; but these, being despised by them, are turned against them. And justly is Zion battered with her own artillery, which used to be employed against her adversaries, seeing she knew not how to value it. 2. He is instructed, and is to instruct the people, in the meaning of the fire that was threatened to consume the forest of the south: it signified a sword drawn, the sword of war which should make the land desolate (Eze 21:3): Behold, I am against thee, O land of Israel! There needs no more to make a people miserable than to have God against them; for as, if he be for us, we need not fear, whoever are against us, so, if he be against us, we cannot hope, whoever are for us. And God's professing people, when they revolt from him, set him against them, who used to be for them. Was the fire there of God's kindling? The sword here is his sword, which he has prepared, and which he will give commission to; it is he that will draw it out of its sheath, where it had laid quiet and threatened no harm. Note, When the sword is unsheathed among the nations God's hand must be eyed and owned in it. Did the fire devour every green tree and every dry tree? The sword in like manner shall cut off the righteous and the wicked. Good and bad were involved in the common calamities of the nation; the righteous were cut off from the land of Israel when they were sent captives in Babylon, though perhaps few or none of them were cut off from the land of the living; and it was a threatening omen to the land of Israel that in the beginning of its troubles such excellent men as Daniel and his fellows, and Ezekiel, were cut off from it and conveyed to Babylon. But though the sword cut off the righteous and the wicked (for it devours one as well as another, Sa2 11:25), yet far be it from us to think that the righteous are as the wicked, Gen 18:25. No; God's graces and comforts make a great difference when his providence seems to make none. The good figs are sent into Babylon for their good, Jer 24:5, Jer 24:6. It is only in outward appearance that there is one event to the righteous and to the wicked, Ecc 9:2. But it speaks the greatness of God's displeasure against the land of Israel. Well might it be said, His eye shall not spare, when it shall not spare, no, not the righteous in it. Since there are not righteous men sufficient to save the land, to make the justice of God the more illustrious the few that there are shall suffer with it, and God's mercy shall make it up to them some other way. Did the fire burn up all faces from the south to the north? The sword shall go forth against all flesh from the south to the north, shall go forth, as God's sword, with a commission that cannot be contested, with a force that cannot be resisted. Were all flesh made to know that God kindled the fire? They shall be made to know that he has drawn forth the sword, Eze 21:5. And, lastly, Shall the fire that is kindled never be quenched? So when this sword of the Lord is drawn against Judah and Jerusalem the scabbard is thrown away, and it shall never be sheathed: It shall not return any more, till it has made a full end. 3. The prophet is ordered, by expressions of his own grief and concern for these calamities that were coming on, to try to make impressions of the like upon the people. When he has delivered his message he must sigh (Eze 21:6), must fetch many deep sighs, with the breaking of his loins; he must sign as if his heart would burst, sigh with bitterness, with other expressions of bitter sorrow, and this publicly, in the sight of those to whom he delivered the foregoing message, that this might be a sermon to their eyes as that was to their ears; and it was well if both would work upon them. The prophet must sign, though it was painful to himself and made his breast sore, and though it is probable that the profane among the people would ridicule him for it and call him a whining canting preacher. But, if we be beside ourselves it is to God; and, if this be to be vile, we will be yet more so. Note, Ministers, if they would affect others with the things they speak of, must show that they are themselves in the greatest sincerity affected with them, and must submit to that which may create uneasiness to themselves, so that it will promote the ends of their ministry. The people, observing the prophet to sigh so much and seeing no visible occasion for it, would ask, "Wherefore sighest thou? These sighs have some mystical meaning; let us know what it is." And he must answer them (Eze 21:7): "It is for the tidings, the heavy tidings, that we shall hear shortly; the tidings come (the judgments come which we hear the tidings of), they come apace, and then you will all sigh; nay, that will not serve. every heart shall melt and every spirit fail; your courage will all be gone and you will have no animating considerations to support yourselves with. And, when heart and spirit fail, it will follow of course that all hands will be feeble and unable to fight, and all knees will be weak as water and unable to flee or to stand their ground." Those who have God for them when flesh and heart fail have him to be the strength of their heart; but those who have God against them have no cordial for a fainting spirit, but are as Belshazzar when his thoughts troubled him, Dan 5:6. But some people are worse frightened than hurt; may not the case be so here and the event prove better than likely? No: Behold it cometh, and shall be brought to pass. It is not a bugbear that they are frightened with, but according to the fear so is the wrath, and more grievous than is feared.

Ezekiel 21:8

Here is another prophecy of the sword, which is delivered in a very affecting manner; the expressions here used are somewhat intricate, and perplex interpreters. The sword was unsheathed in the foregoing verses; here it is fitted up to do execution, which the prophet is commanded to lament. Observe,

I. How the sword is here described. 1. It is sharpened, that it may cut and wound, and make a sore slaughter. The wrath of God will put an edge upon it; and, whatever instruments God shall please to make use of in executing his judgments, he will fill them with strength, courage, and fury, according to the service they are employed in. Out of the mouth of Christ goes a sharp sword,Rev 19:15. 2. It is furbished, that it may glitter, to the terror of those against whom it is drawn. It shall be a kind of flaming sword. If it have rusted in the scabbard for want of use, it shall be rubbed and brightened; for though the glory of God's justice may seem to have been eclipsed for a while, during the day of his patience and the delay of his judgments, yet it will shine out again and be made to glitter. 3. It is a victorious sword, nothing shall stand before it (Eze 21:10): It contemneth the rod of my son as every tree. Israel, said God once, is my son, my first-born. The government of that people was called a rod, a strong rod; we read (Eze 19:11) of the strong rods they had for sceptres. But when the sword of God's justice is drawn it contemns this rod, makes nothing of it; though it be a strong rod, and the rod of his son, it is no more than any other tree. When God's professing people have revolted from him, and are in rebellion against him, his sword despises them. What are they to him more than another people? The marginal reading gives another notion of this sword: It is the rod of my son; and we know of whom God has said (Psa 2:7), Thou art my Son, this day have I begotten thee, and (Eze 21:9) Thou shalt break them with a rod of iron. This sword is that rod of iron which contemns every tree and will bear it down. Or, This sword is the rod of my son, a correcting rod, for the chastening of the transgression of God's people (Sa2 7:14), not to cut them off from being a people. It is a sword to others, a rod to my son.

II. How the sword is here put into the hand of the executioners: "It is the rod of my Son, and he has given it that it may be handled (Eze 21:11), that it may be made use of for the end for which it was drawn. It is given into the hand, not of the fencer to be played with, but of the slayer to do execution with. The sword of war my Son makes use of as a sword of justice, and to him all judgment is committed. It is made bright (Eze 21:15), it is wrapped up, that it may be kept safe, and clean, and sharp for the slaughter, not as Goliath's sword was wrapped up in a cloth only for a memorial," Sa1 21:9.

III. How the sword is directed, and against whom it is sent (Eze 21:12): It shall be upon my people; they shall fall by this sword. It is repeated again, as that which is scarcely credible, that the sword of the heathen shall be upon God's own people; nay, it shall be upon all the princes of Israel; their dignity and power as princes shall be no more their security than their profession of religion as princes of Israel. But, if the sword be at any time upon God's people, have they not comfort within sufficient to arm them against every thing in it that is frightful? Yes, they have, while they conduct themselves as becomes his people; but these had not done so, and therefore terrors, by reason of the sword, shall be upon those that call themselves my people. Note, While good men are quiet, not only from evil, but from the fear of it, wicked men are disturbed not only with the sword, but with the terrors of it, arising from a consciousness of their own guilt. This sword is directed particularly against the great men, for they had been the greatest sinners among them; they had altogether broken the yoke and burst the bonds (Jer 5:5), and therefore with them in a special manner God's controversy is, who had been the ringleaders in sin. The sword of the slain is the sword of the great men that are slain, Eze 21:14. Though they have furnished themselves with places of retirement, places of concealment, where they flatter themselves with hopes that they shall be safe, they will find that the sword will enter into their privy chambers, and find them out there, as the frogs, when they were one of Egypt's plagues, found admission into the chambers of their kings. The sword, the point of this sword, is directed against their gates, against all their gates (Eze 21:15), against all those things with which they thought to keep it out and fortify themselves against it. Note, The strongest gates, though they be gates of brass, ever so well barred, ever so well guarded, are no fence against the point of the sword of God's judgments. But when that is pointed against sinners, 1. They are ready to fear the worst; their hearts faint, so that they are not able to make any resistance. 2. The worst comes; whatever resistance they make, it is to no purpose, but they are ruined, and their ruins are multiplied. But what need have we to observe the particular directions of this sword when it has a general commission, is sent with a running warrant? (Eze 21:16): "Go thee, one way or other, which way thou wilt, turn to the right hand or to the left, thou wilt find those that are obnoxious, for there are none free from guilt; and thou hast authority against them, for there are none exempt from punishment; and therefore, whithersoever thy face is set, that way do thou proceed, and, like Jonathan's sword, from the blood of the slain, from the fat of the mighty, thou shalt never return empty," Sa2 1:22. Note, So full is the world of wicked people that, which way soever God's judgments go forth, they will find work, will find matter to work upon. That fire will never go out on this earth for want of fuel. And such various methods God has of meeting with sinners that the sword of his justice is still as it was at first when it flamed in the hand of the cherubim: it turns every way, Gen 3:24.

IV. What is the nature of this sword, and what are the intentions and limitations of it as to the people of God, Eze 21:13. It is a correction; it is designed to be so; the sword to others is a rod to them. This is a comfortable word which comes in in the midst of these terrible ones, though it be expressed somewhat obscurely. 1. The people of God begin to be afraid that the sword will contemn even the rod, that the sword will go on with such fury that it will despise its commission to be a rod only, will forget its bounds and become a sword indeed, even to God's own people. They fear lest the Chaldeans' sword, which is the rod of God's anger, contemn its being called a rod, and become as the axe that boasts itself against him that heweth therewith or the staff that lifts up itself as if it were no wood, Isa 10:15. Or, "What if the sword contemn even the rod? that is, what if this sword make the former rods, as that or Sennacherib, to be contemned as nothing to this? What if this should prove not a correcting rod, but a destroying sword, to make a full end of our church and nation?" This is that which the thinking, but timorous, few are apprehensive of. Note, When threatening judgments are abroad it is good to suppose the worst that may be the consequences of them, that we may provide accordingly. What if the sword contemn the tribe or sceptre? namely, that of Judah and the house of David (so some think Shebet here signifies); what if it should aim at the ruin of our government? If it do, the Lord is righteous and will be gracious notwithstanding. But, 2. These fears are silenced with an assurance that it is not so; the sword shall not forget itself, nor the errand on which it is sent: It is a trial, and it is no more than a trial. He that sends it makes what use of it, and sets what bounds to it, he pleases. Here shall its proud waves be stayed. Note, It is matter of comfort to the people of God, when his judgments are abroad, and they are ready to tremble for fear of them, that, whatever they are to others, to them they are but trials; and, when they are tried, they shall come forth as gold, and the proving of their faith shall be the improving of it.

V. Here the prophet and the people must show themselves affected with these judgments threatened. 1. The prophet must be very serious in denouncing these judgments. He must say, A sword! a sword! Eze 21:9. Let him not study for fine words, and a variety of quaint expressions; when the town is on fire people do not so give notice of it, but cry, with a frightful doleful voice, Fire! fire! So must the prophet cry, A sword! a sword! and (Eze 21:14), Let the sword be doubled the third time in thy preaching. God speaks once, yea, twice, yea, thrice; it were well if men, after all, would perceive and regard it. It shall be doubled the third time in God's providence; for it was Nebuchadnezzar's third descent upon Jerusalem that made a full end of it. Ruin comes gradually, but at last comes effectually, upon a provoking people. Yet this is not all: the prophet is not only as a herald at arms to proclaim war, and to cry, A sword! a sword! once and again, and a third time, but, as a person nearly concerned, he must cry and howl (Eze 21:12), must sadly lament the desolations that the sword would make, as one that did himself not only sympathize with the sufferers, but feel from the sufferings. Again (Eze 21:14), Prophesy, and smite thy hands together, wring thy hands, as lamenting the desolation, or clap thy hands, as by thy prophecy instigating and encouraging those that were to be the instruments of it, or as one standing amazed at the suddenness and severity of the judgment. The prophet must smite his hands together; for (says God) I will also smite my hands together, Eze 21:17. God is in earnest in pronouncing this sentence upon them, and therefore the prophet must show himself in earnest in publishing it. God's smiting his hands together, as well as the prophet's smiting, is in token of a holy indignation at their wickedness, which was really very astonishing. When Balak's anger was kindled against Balaam he smote his hands together, Num 24:10. Note, God and his ministers are justly angry at those who might be saved and yet will be ruined. Some make it an expression of triumph and exultation, agreeing with that (Isa 1:24), Ah! I will ease me of my adversaries; and that (Pro 1:26), I also will laugh at their calamity. And so it follows here, I will cause my fury to rest, not only it shall be perfected, but it shall be pleased. And observe with what solemnity, with what authority, this sentence is ratified: "I the Lord have said it, who can and will make good what I have said. I have said it, and will never unsay it. I have said it, and who can gainsay it?" 2. The people must be very serious in the prospect of these judgments. An intimation of this comes in in a parenthesis (Eze 21:10): Should we then make mirth? Seeing God has drawn the sword, and the prophet sighs and cries, Should we then make mirth? The prophet seems to give this as a reason why he sighs; as Neh 2:3, Why should not my countenance be sad, when Jerusalem lies waste? Note, Before we allow ourselves to be merry, we ought to consider whether we should be merry or no. Should we make mirth, we who are sentenced to the sword, who lie under the wrath and curse of God? Shall we make mirth as other people, who have gone a whoring from our God? Hos 9:1. Should we now make mirth, when the hand of God has gone out against us, when God's judgments are abroad in the land and he by them calls to weeping and mourning? Isa 22:11, Isa 22:13. Shall we now make mirth as the king and Haman, when the church is in perplexity (Est 3:15), when we should be grieving for the affliction of Joseph? Amo 6:6.

Ezekiel 21:18

The prophet, in the verses before, had shown them the sword coming; he here shows them that sword coming against them, that they might not flatter themselves that by some means or other it should be diverted a contrary way.

I. He must see and show the Chaldean army coming against Jerusalem and determined by a supreme power so to do. The prophet must appoint him two ways, that is, he must upon a paper draw out two roads (Eze 21:19), as sometimes is done in maps; and he must bring the king of Babylon's army to the place where the roads part, for there they will make a stand. They both come out of the same land; but when they come to the place where one road leads to Rabbath, the head city of the Ammonites, and the other to Jerusalem, he makes a pause; for, though he is resolved to be the ruin of both, yet he is not determined which to attack first; here his politics and his politicians leave him at a loss. The sword must go either to Rabbath or to Judah in Jerusalem. Many of the inhabitants of Judah had now taken shelter in Jerusalem, and all the interests of the country were bound up in the safety of the city, and therefore it is called Judah in Jerusalem the defenced; so strongly fortified was it, both by nature and art, that it was thought impregnable, Lam 4:12. The prophet must describe this dilemma that the king of Babylon is at (Eze 21:21); for the king of Babylon stood (that is, he shall stand considering what course to take) at the head of the two ways. Though he was a prince of great foresight and great resolution, yet, it seems, he knew neither his own interest nor his own mind. Let not the wise man then glory in his wisdom nor the mighty man in his arbitrary power, for even those that may do what they will seldom know what to do for the best. Now observe, 1. The method he took to come to a resolution; he used divination, applied to a higher and invisible power, perhaps to the determination of Providence by a lot, in order to which he made his arrows bright, that were to be drawn for the lots, in honour of the solemnity. Perhaps Jerusalem was written on one arrow and Rabbath on the other, and that which was first drawn out of the quiver he determined to attack first. Or he applied to the direction of some pretended oracle: he consulted with images or teraphim, expecting to receive audible answers from them. Or to the observations which the augurs made upon the entrails of the sacrifices: he looked in the liver, whether the position of that portended good or ill luck. Note, It is a mortification to the pride of the wise men of the earth that in difficult cases they have been glad to make their court to heaven for direction; as it is an instance of their folly that they have taken such ridiculous ways of doing it, when in cases proper for an appeal to Providence it is sufficient that the lot be cast into the lap, with that prayer, Give a perfect lot, and a firm belief that the disposal thereof is not fortuitous, but of the Lord, Pro 16:33. 2. The resolution he was hereby brought to. Even by these sinful practices God served his own purposes and directed him to go to Jerusalem, Eze 21:22. The divination for Jerusalem happened to be at his right hand, which, according to the rules of divination, determined him that way. Note, What services God designs men for he will be sure in his providence to lead them to, though perhaps they themselves are not aware what guidance they are under. Well, Jerusalem being the mark set up, the campaign is presently opened with the siege of that important place. Captains are appointed for the command of the forces to be employed in the siege, who must open the mouth in the slaughter, must give directions to the soldiers what to do and make speeches to animate them. Orders are given to provide every thing necessary for carrying on the siege with vigour; battering rams must be prepared and forts built. O what pains, what cost, are men at to destroy one another!

II. He must show both the people and the prince that they bring this destruction upon themselves by their own sin.

1. The people do so, Eze 21:23, Eze 21:24. They slight the notices that are given them of the judgment coming. Ezekiel's prophecy is to them a false divination; they are not moved or awakened to repentance by it. When they hear that Nebuchadnezzar by his divination is directed to Jerusalem, and assured of success in that enterprise, they laugh at it and continue secure, calling it a false divination; because they have sworn oaths, that is, they have joined in a solemn league with the Egyptians, and they depend upon the promise they have made them to raise the siege, or upon the assurances which the false prophets have given them that it shall be raised. Or it may refer to the oaths of allegiance they had sworn to the king of Babylon, but had violated, for which treachery of theirs God had given them up to a judicial blindness, so that the fairest

warnings given them were slighted by them as false divinations. Note, It is not strange if those who make a jest of the most sacred oaths can make a jest likewise of the most sacred oracles; for where will a profane mind stop? But shall their unbelief invalidate the counsel of God? Are they safe because they are secure? By no means; nay, the contempt they put upon divine warnings is a sin that brings to remembrance their other sins, and they may thank themselves if they be now remembered against them. (1.) Their present wickedness is discovered. Now that God is contending with them so perverse and obstinate are they that whatever they offer in their own defence does but add to their offence; they never conducted themselves so ill as they did now that they had the loudest call given them to repent and reform: "So that in all your doings your sins do appear. Turn yourselves which way you will, you show a black side." This is too true of every one of us; for not only there is none that lives and sins not, but there is not a must man upon earth that does good and sins not. Our best services have such allays of weakness, and folly, and imperfection, and so much evil is present with us even when we would do good, that we may say, with sorrow and shame, In all our doings, and in all our sayings too, our sins do appear, and witness against us, so that if we were under the law we were undone. (2.) This brings to mind their former wickedness: "You have made your iniquity to be remembered, not by yourselves that it might be repented of, but by the justice of God that it might be reckoned for. Your own sins make the sins of your fathers to be remembered against you, which otherwise you should never have smarted for." Note, God remembers former iniquities against those only who by the present discoveries of their wickedness show that they do not repent of them. (3.) That they may suffer for all together, they are turned over to the destroyed, that they may be taken (v. 23): "You shall be taken with the hand that God had appointed to seize you and to hold you and out of which you cannot escape." Men are said to be God's hand when they are made use of as the ministers of his justice, Psa 17:14. Note, Those who will not be taken with the word of God's grace shall at last be taken by the hand of his wrath.

2. The prince likewise brings his ruin upon himself. Zedekiah is the prince of Israel, to whom the prophet here, in God's name, addresses himself; and, if he had not spoken in God's name, he would not have spoken so boldly, so bluntly; for is it fit to say to a king, Thou art wicked? (1.) He gives him his character,Eze 21:25. Thou profane and wicked prince of Israel! He was not so bad as some of his predecessors, and yet bad enough to merit his character. He was himself profane, lost to every thing that is virtuous and sacred. And he was wicked, as he promoted sin among his people; he sinned, and made Israel to sin. Note, Profaneness and wickedness are bad in any, but worst of all in a prince, a prince of Israel, who as an Israelite should know better himself, and as a prince should set a better example and have a better influence on those about him. (2.) He reads him his doom. His iniquity has an end; the measure of it is full, and therefore his day has come, the day of his punishment, the day of divine vengeance. Note, Though those who are wicked and profane may flourish awhile, yet their day will come to fall. The sentence here passed is, [1.] That Zedekiah shall be deposed. He has forfeited his crown, and he shall no longer wear it; he has by his profaneness profaned his crown, and it shall be cast to the ground (Eze 21:26): Remove the diadem. Crowns and diadems are losable things; it is only in the other

world that there is a crown of glory that fades not away, a kingdom that cannot be moved. The Chaldee paraphrase expounds it thus: Take away the diadem from Seraiah the chief priest, and I will take away the crown from Zedekiah the king; neither this nor that shall abide in his place, but shall be removed. This shall not be the same, not the same that he has been; this not this (so the word is); profane and wicked perhaps he is as he has been. Note, Men lose their dignity by their iniquity. Their profaneness and wickedness remove their diadem, and take off their crown, and make them the reverse of what they were. [2.] That great confusion and disorder in the state shall follow hereupon. Every thing shall be turned upside down. The conqueror shall take a pride in exalting him that is low and abasing him that is high, preferring some and degrading others, at his pleasure, without any regard either to right or merit. [3.] Attempts to re-establish the government shall be blasted and come to nothing, Gedaliah's particularly, and Ishmael's who was of the seed-royal (to which the Chaldee paraphrase refers this); neither of them shall be able to make any thing of it. I will overturn, overturn, overturn, first one project and then another; for who can build up what God will throw down? [4.] This monarchy shall never be restored till it is fixed for perpetuity in the hands of the Messiah. There shall be no more kings of the house of David after Zedekiah, till Christ comes, whose right the kingdom is, who is that seed of David in whom the promise was to have its full accomplishment, and I will give it to him. He shall have the throne of his father David, Luk 1:32. Immediately before the coming of Christ there was a long eclipse of the royal dignity, as there was also a failing of the spirit of prophecy, that his shining forth in the fulness of time both as king and prophet might appear the more illustrious. Note, Christ has an incontestable title to the dominion and sovereignty both in the church and in the world; the kingdom is his right. And, having the right, he shall in due time have the possession: I will give it to him; and there shall be a general overturning of all rather than he shall come short of his right, and a certain overturning of all the opposition that stands in his way to make room for him, Dan 2:45; Col 15:25. This is mentioned here for the comfort of those who feared that the promise made in David would fail for evermore. "No," says God, "that promise is sure, for the Messiah's kingdom shall last for ever."

Ezekiel 21:28

The prediction of the destruction of the Ammonites, which was effected by Nebuchadnezzar about five years after the destruction of Jerusalem, seems to come in here upon occasion of the king of Babylon's diverting his design against Rabbath, when he turned it upon Jerusalem. Upon this the Ammonites grew very insolent, and triumphed over Jerusalem; but the prophet must let them know that forbearance is no acquittance; the reprieve is not a pardon; their day also is at hand; their turn comes next, and it will be but a poor satisfaction to them that they are to be devoured last, to be last executed.

I. The sin of the Ammonites is here intimated; it is their reproach, Eze 21:28. 1. The reproach they put upon themselves when they hearkened to their false prophets (for such it seems there were among them as well as among the Jews), who pretended to foretel their perpetual safety in the midst of the desolations that were made of the countries round about them: "They see vanity unto thee and divine a lie, Eze 21:29. They flatter thee with promises of peace, and thou art such a fool as to suffer thyself to be imposed upon by them and to encourage them therein by giving credit to them." Note, Those that feed themselves with a self-conceit in the day of their prosperity prepare matter for a self-reproach in the day of their calamity. 2. The reproach they put upon the Israel of God, when they triumphed in their afflictions, and thereby added affliction to them, which was very barbarous and inhuman. Their divines, by puffing them up with a conceit that they were a better people than Israel, being spared when they were cut off, and with a confidence that their prosperity should always continue, made them so very haughty and insolent that they did even tread on the necks of the Israelites that were slain, slain by the wicked Chaldeans, who had commission to execute God's judgments upon them when their iniquity had an end, that is, when the measure of it was full. We shall meet with this again, Eze 25:3, etc. Note, Those are ripening apace for misery who trample upon the people of God in their distress, whereas they ought to tremble when judgment begins at the house of God.

II. The utter destruction of the Ammonites is threatened. For the reproach cast on the church by her neighbours will be returned into their own bosom, Psa 79:12. Let us see how terrible the threatening is and the destruction will be. 1. It shall come from the wrath of God, who resents the indignities and injuries done to his people as done to himself (Eze 21:31): I will pour out my indignation as a shower of fire and brimstone upon thee. The least drop of divine indignation and wrath will create tribulation and anguish enough to the soul of man that does evil; what then would a full stream of that indignation and wrath do? "I will blow against thee in the fire of my wrath; that is, I will blow up the fire of my wrath against thee; it shall burn with the utmost vehemence." Thou shalt be for fuel to this fire, Eze 21:32. Note, Wicked men make themselves fuel to the fire of God's wrath; they are consumed by it, and it is inflamed by them. 2. It shall be effected by the sword of war; to them he must cry, as before to Israel, because they had triumphed in Israel's overthrow: The sword, the sword is drawn (Eze 21:28, compare Eze 21:9, Eze 21:10); it is drawn to consume because of the glittering, because it is brandished and glitters, and is fit to be made use of. God's executions will answer his preparations. This sword, when it is drawn, shall not return into its sheath (Eze 21:30) till it has done the work for which it was drawn. When the sword is drawn it does not return till God causes it to return, and he is in one mind and who can turn him? Who can change his purpose? 3. The persons employed in it are brutish men, and skilful to destroy. Men of such a bad character as this, who have the wit of men to do the work of wild beasts-human reason, which makes them skilful, but no human compassion, which makes them skilful only to destroy-though they are the scandal of mankind, yet sometimes are made use of to serve God's purposes. God delivers the Ammonites into the hands of such, and justly, for they themselves were brutish, and delighted in the destruction of God's Israel. We have reason to pray, as Paul desired to be prayed for, that we may be delivered from wicked and unreasonable men (Th2 3:2), men that seem made for doing mischief. 4. The place where they should thus be reckoned with: "I will judge thee where thou wast created, where thou wast first formed into a people, and where thou hast been settled ever since, and therefore where thou seemest to have taken root; the land of thy nativity shall be the land of thy destruction." Note, God can bring ruin upon us even where we are most secure, and turn us out of that land which we thought we had a title to not to be disputed and a possession of not to be disturbed. Thy blood shall be shed not only in thy borders, but in the midst of thy land. Lastly, I shall be an irreparable ruin: "Though thou mayest think to recover thyself, it is in vain to think of it; thou shalt be no more remembered with any respect," Psa 9:6. Justly is their name blotted out who would have Israel's name for ever lost.

Ezekiel Chapter 22

Ezekiel

Here are three separate messages which God entrusts the prophet to deliver concerning Judah and Jerusalem, and all to the same purport, to show them their sins and the judgments that were coming upon them for those sins. I. Here is a catalogue of their sins, by which they had exposed themselves to shame and for which God would bring them to ruin (v. 1-16). II. They are here compared to dross, and are condemned as dross to the fire (Eze 22:17-22). III. All orders and degrees of men among them are here found guilty of the neglect of the duty of their place and of having contributed to the national guilt, which therefore, since none appeared as intercessors, they must all expect to share in the punishment of (Eze 22:23-31).

Ezekiel 22:1

In these verses the prophet by a commission from Heaven sits as a judge upon the bench, and Jerusalem is made to hold up her hand as a prisoner at the bar; and, if prophets were set over other nations, much more over God's nation, Jer 1:10. This prophet is authorized to judge the bloody city, the city of bloods. Jerusalem is so called, not only because she had been guilty of the particular sin of blood-shed, but because her crimes in general were bloody crimes (Eze 7:23), such as polluted her in her blood, and for which she deserved to have blood given her to drink. Now the business of a judge with a malefactor is to convict him of his crimes, and then to pass sentence upon him for them. These two things Ezekiel is to do here.

I. He is to find Jerusalem guilty of many heinous crimes here enumerated in a long bill of indictment, and it is billa vera-a true bill; so he writes upon it whose judgment we are sure is according to truth. He must show her all her abominations (Eze 22:2), that God may be justified in all the desolations brought upon her. Let us take a view of all the particular sins which Jerusalem here stands charged with; and they are all exceedingly sinful.

1. Murder: The city sheds blood, not only in the suburbs, where the strangers dwell, but in the midst of it, where, one would think, the magistrates would, if any where, be vigilant. Even there people were murdered either in duels or by secret assassinations and poisonings, or in the courts of justice under colour of law, and there was no care taken to discover and punish the murderers according to the law (Gen 9:6), no, nor so much as the ceremony used to expiate an uncertain murder (Deu 21:1), and so the guilt and pollution remains upon the city. Thus thou hast become guilty in thy blood that thou hast shed, Eze 22:4. This crime is insisted most upon, for it was Jerusalem's measure-filling sin more than any; it is said to be that which the Lord would not pardon, Kg2 24:4. (1.) The princes of Israel, who should have been the protectors of injured

cc

innocence, every one were to their power to shed blood, Eze 22:6. They thirsted for it, and delighted in it, and whoever came within their power were sure to feel it; whoever lay at their mercy were sure to find none. (2.) There were those who carried tales to shed blood, Eze 22:9. They told lies of men to the princes, to whom they knew it would be pleasing, to incense them against them; or they betrayed what passed in private conversation, to make mischief among neighbours, and set them together by the ears, to bite, and devour, and worry one another, even to death. Note, Those who, by giving invidious characters and telling ill-natured stories of their neighbours, sow discord among brethren, will be accountable for all the mischief that follows upon it; as he that kindles a fire will be accountable for all the hurt it does. (3.) There were those who took gifts to shed blood (Eze 22:12), who would be hired with money to swear a man out of his life, or, if they were upon a jury, would be bribed to find an innocent man guilty. When so much barbarous bloody work of this kind was done in Jerusalem we may well conclude, [1.] That men's consciences had become wretchedly profligate and seared and their hearts hardened; for those would stick at no wickedness who would not stick at this. [2.] That abundance of quiet, harmless, good people were made away with, whereby, as the guilt of the city was increased, so the number of those that should have stood in the gap to turn away the wrath of God was diminished.

2. Idolatry: She makes idols against herself to destroy herself, Eze 22:3. And again (Eze 22:4), Thou hast defiled thyself in thy idols which thou hast made. Note, Those who make idols for themselves will be found to have made them against themselves, for idolaters put a cheat upon themselves and prepare destruction for themselves; besides that thereby they pollute themselves, they render themselves odious in the eyes of the just and jealous God, and even their mind and conscience are defiled, so that to them nothing is pure. Those who did not make idols themselves were yet found guilty of eating upon the mountains, or high places (Eze 22:9), in honour of the idols and in communion with idolaters.

3. Disobedience to parents (Eze 22:7): In thee have the children set light by their father and mother, mocked them, cursed them, and despised to obey them, which was a sign of a more than ordinary corruption of nature as well as manners, and a disposition to all manner of disorder, Isa 3:5. Those that set light by their parents are in the highway to all wickedness. God had made many wholesome laws for the support of the paternal authority, but no care was taken to put them in execution; nay, the Pharisees in their day taught children, under pretence of respect to the Corban, to set light by their parents and refuse to maintain them, Mat 15:5.

4. Oppression and extortion. To enrich themselves they wronged the poor (Eze 22:7): They dealt by oppression and deceit with the stranger, taking advantage of his necessities, and his ignorance of the laws and customs of the country. In Jerusalem, that should have been a sanctuary to the oppressed, they vexed the fatherless and widows by unreasonable demands and inquisitions, or troublesome law-suits, in which might prevails against right. "Thou hast taken usury and increase (Eze 22:12); not only there are those in thee that do it, but thou hast done it."

It was an act of the city or community; the public money, which should have been employed in public charity, was put out to usury, with extortion. Thou hast greedily gained of thy neighbours by violence and wrong. For neighbours to gain by one another in a way of fair trading is well, but those who are greedy of gain will not be held within the rules of equity.

5. Profanation of the sabbath and other holy things. This commonly goes along with the other sins for which they here stand indicted (Eze 22:8): Thou hast despised my holy things, holy oracles, holy ordinances. The rites which God appointed were thought too plain, too ordinary; they despised them, and therefore were fond of the customs of the heathen. Note, Immorality and dishonesty are commonly attended with a contempt of religion and the worship of God. Thou hast profaned my sabbaths. There was not in Jerusalem that face of sabbath-sanctification that one would have expected in the holy city. Sabbath-breaking is an iniquity that is an inlet to all iniquity. Many have owned it to contribute as much to their ruin as any thing.

6. Uncleanness and all manner of seventh-commandment sins, fruits of those vile affections to which God in a way of righteous judgment gives men up, to punish them for their idolatry and profanation of holy things. Jerusalem had been famous for its purity, but now in the midst of thee they commit lewdness (Eze 22:9); lewdness goes bare-faced, though in the most scandalous instances, as that of a man's having his father's wife, which is the discovery of the father's nakedness (Eze 22:10) and is a sin not to be named among Christians without the utmost detestation (Col 5:1), and was made a capital crime by the law of Moses, Lev 20:11. The time to refrain from embracing has not been observed (Ecc 3:6), for they have humbled her that was set apart for her pollution. They made nothing of committing lewdness with a neighbour's wife, with a daughter-in-law, or a sister, Eze 22:11. And shall not God visit for these things?

7. Unmindfulness of God was at the bottom of all this wickedness (Eze 22:12): "Thou hast forgotten me, else thou wouldst not have done thus." Note, Sinners do that which provokes God because they forget him; they forget their descent from him, dependence on him, and obligations to him; they forget how valuable his favour is, which they make themselves unfit for, and how formidable his wrath, which they make themselves obnoxious to. Those that pervert their ways forget the Lord their God, Jer 3:21.

II. He is to pass sentence upon Jerusalem for these crimes.

1. Let her know that she has filled up the measure of her iniquity, and that her sins are such as forbid delays and call for speedy vengeance. She has made her time to come (Eze 22:3), her days to draw near; and she has come to her years of maturity for punishment (Eze 22:4), as an heir that has come to age and is ready for his inheritance. God would have borne longer with them, but they had arrived at such a pitch of impudence in sin that God could not in honour give them a further day. Note, Abused patience will at last be weary of forbearing. And, when sinners (as Solomon speaks) grow overmuch wicked, they die before their time (Ecc 7:17) and shorten their

reprieves.

2. Let her know that she has exposed herself, and therefore God has justly exposed her, to the contempt and scorn of all her neighbours (Eze 22:4): I have made thee a reproach to the heathen, both those who are near, who are eye-witnesses of Jerusalem's apostasy and degeneracy, and those afar off, who, though at a distance, will think it worth taking notice of (Eze 22:5); they shall all mock thee. While they were reproached by their neighbours for their adherence to God it was their honour, and they might be sure that God would roll away their reproach. But, now that they are laughed at for their revolt from God, they must lie down in their shame, and must say, The Lord is righteous. They make a mock at Jerusalem, both because her sins had been very scandalous (she is infamous, polluted in name, and has quite lost her credit), and because her punishment is very grievous-she is much vexed and frets without measure at her troubles. Note, Those who fret most at their troubles have commonly those about them who will be so much the more apt to make a jest of them.

3. Let her know that God is displeased, highly displeased, at her wickedness, and does and will witness against it (Eze 22:13): I have smitten my hand at thy dishonest gain. God, both by his prophets and by his providence, revealed his wrath from heaven against their ungodliness and unrighteousness, the oppressions they were guilty of, though they got by them, and their murders (the blood which has been in the midst of thee), and all their other sins. Note, God has sufficiently discovered how angry he is at the wicked courses of his people; and, that they may not say that they have not had fair warning, he smites his hand against the sin before he lays his hand upon the sinner. And this is a good reason why we should despise dishonest gain, even the gain of oppressions, and shake our hands from holding bribes, because these are sins against which God shakes his hands, Isa 33:15.

4. Let her know that, proud and secure as she is, she is no match for God's judgments, Eze 22:14. (1.) She is assured that the destruction she has deserved will come: I the Lord have spoken it, and will do it. He that is true to his promises will be true to his threatenings too, for he is not a man that he should repent. (2.) It is supposed that she thinks herself able to contend with God, and so stand a siege against his judgments. She bade defiance to the day of the Lord,Isa 5:19. But, (3.) She is convinced of her utter inability to make her part good with him: "Can thy heart endure, or can thy hand be strong, in the days that I shall deal with thee? Thou thinkest thou hast to do only with men like thyself, but shalt be made to know that thou fallest into the hands of a living God." Observe here, [1.] There is a day coming when God will deal with sinners, a day of visitation. He deals with some to bring them to repentance, and there is no resisting the force of convictions when he sets them on; he deals with others to bring them to ruin. He deals with sinners in this life, when he brings upon them his sore judgments; but the days of eternity are especially the days in which God will deal with them, when the full vials of God's wrath will be poured out without mixture. [2.] The wrath of God against sinners, when he comes to deal with them, will be found both intolerable and irresistible. There is no heart stout enough to endure it;

it is none of the infirmities which the spirit of a man will sustain. Damned sinners can neither forget nor despise their torments, nor have they any thing wherewith to support themselves under their torments. There are no hands strong enough either to ward off the strokes of God's wrath or to break the chains with which sinners are bound over to the day of wrath. Who knows the power of God's anger?

5. Let her know that, since she has walked in the way of the heathen, and learned their works, she shall have enough of them (Eze 22:15): "I will not only send thee among the heathen, out of thy own land, but I will scatter thee among them and disperse thee in the countries, to be abused and insulted over by strangers." And since her filthiness and filthy ones continued in her, notwithstanding all the methods God had taken to refine her (she would not be made clean, Jer 13:27), he will be his judgments consume her filthiness out of her; he will destroy those that are incurably bad and reform those that are inclined to be good.

6. Let her know that God has disowned her and cast her off. He had been her heritage and portion; but now (Eze 22:16), "Thou shalt take thy inheritance in thyself, shift for thyself, make the best hand thou canst for thyself, for God will no longer undertake for thee." Note, Those that give up themselves to be ruled by their lusts will justly be given up to be portioned by them. Those that resolve to be their own masters, let them expect no other comfort and happiness than what their own hands can furnish them with, and a miserable portion it will prove. Verily, I say unto you, They have their reward. Thou in thy life-time receivedst thy good things. These are the same with this, "Thou shalt take thy inheritance in thyself, and then, when it is too late, shalt own in the sight of the heathen that I am the Lord, who alone am a portion sufficient for my people." Note, Those that have lost their interest in God will know how to value it.

Ezekiel 22:17

The same melancholy string is still harped upon, and various turns are given it, to make it affecting, that it may be influencing. The prophet must here show, or at least it is here shown him, that the whole house of Israel has become as dross and that as dross they shall be consumed. What David has said concerning the wicked ones of the world is here said concerning the wicked ones of the church, now that it is corrupt and degenerate (Psa 119:119): Thou puttest away all the wicked of the earth like dross.

I. See here how the wretched degeneracy of the house of Israel is described. That state, in David's and Solomon's time, had been a head of gold; when the kingdoms were divided it was as the arms of silver. But now, 1. It has degenerated into baser metal, of no value in comparison with what it formerly was: They are all brass, and tin, and iron, and lead, which some make to signify divers sorts of sinners among them. Their being brass denotes the impudence of some in their wickedness; they are brazen-faced, and cannot blush; their shoes had been iron and brass (Deu 33:25), but now their brow is so, Isa 48:4. Their being tin denotes the hypocritical profession of piety with which many of them cover their iniquity; they have a specious show, but no intrinsic worth. Their being iron denotes the cruel disposition of some, and their delight in war, according to the character of the iron age. Their being lead denotes their dulness, sottishness, and stupidity: though soft and pliable to evil, yet heavy and not movable to good. How has the gold become dross! How has the most fine gold changed! So is Jerusalem's degeneracy bewailed, Lam 4:1. Yet this is not the worst; these metals, though of less value, are yet of good use. But, 2. The house of Israel has become dross to me. So she is in God's account, whatever she is in her own and her neighbours' account. They were silver, but now they are even the dross of silver; the word signifies all the dirt, and rubbish, and worthless stuff, that are separated from the silver in the washing, melting, and refining of it. Note, Sinners, and especially degenerate professors, are in God's account as dross, vile, and contemptible, and of no account, as the evil figs which could not be eaten, they were so evil. They are useless and fit for nothing; of no consistency with themselves and no service to man.

II. How the woeful destruction of this degenerate house of Israel is foretold. They are all gathered together in Jerusalem; thither people fled from all parts of the country as to a city of refuge, not only because it was a strong city, but because it was the holy city. Now God tells them that their flocking into Jerusalem, which they intended for their security, should be as the gathering of various sorts of metal into the furnace or crucible, to be melted down, and to have the dross separated from them. They are in the midst of Jerusalem, surrounded by the forces of the enemy; and, being thus enclosed, 1. The fire of God's wrath shall be kindled upon this furnace, and it shall be blown, to make it burn fiercely and strongly, Eze 22:20, Eze 22:21. God will gather them in his anger and fury. The blowing of the fire makes a great noise, so will the judgments of God upon Jerusalem. When God stirs up himself to execute judgments upon a provoking people, from the consideration of his own glory and the necessity of making some examples, then he may be said to blow the fire of his wrath against sin and sinners, to heat the furnace seven times hotter. 2. The several sorts of metal gathered in it shall be melted; by a complication of judgments, as by a raging fire, their constitution shall be dissolved, they shall lose all their former shape and strength, and shall be utterly unable to stand before the wrath of God. The various sorts of sinners shall be melted down together, and united in a common overthrow, as brass and lead in the same furnace, as trees are bound in bundles for the fire. They came together into Jerusalem as a place of defence, but God brought them together there as unto a place of execution. 3. God will leave them in the furnace (Eze 22:20): I will gather you into the furnace and will leave you there. When God brings his own people into the furnace he sits by them, as the refiner by his gold, to see that they be not continued there any longer than is fitting and needful; but he will bring these people into the furnace, as men throw dross into it, which they design shall be consumed, and therefore are in no care about it, but leave it there. Compare with this Hos 5:14, I will tear and go away. 4. Hereby the dross shall be wholly separated and the good metal purified, the impenitent shall be destroyed and the penitent reformed and fitted for deliverance. Take away the dross from the silver, and there shall come forth a vessel for the finer, Pro 25:4. This judgment shall do that in the house of Israel for the doing of which other methods had been tried in vain, and reprobate silver shall they no more be called, Jer 6:30.

Ezekiel 22:23

Here is, I. A general idea given of the land of Israel, how well it deserved the judgments coming to destroy it and how much it needed these judgments to refine it. Let the prophet tell her plainly, "Thou art the land that is not cleansed, not refined as metal is, and therefore needest to be again put into the furnace. Means and methods of reformation have been ineffectual; thou art not rained upon in the day of indignation." This was one of the judgments which God brought upon them in the day of his wrath, he withheld the rain from them, Jer 14:4. Or, "When thou art under the tokens of God's displeasure, even in the day of indignation thou art not rained upon; thou hast not received instruction by the prophets, whose doctrine is said to descend as the rain." Or, "When thou art corrected thou art not cleansed; thy filth is not carried away as that in the streets is by a sweeping rain. Nay, though it be a day of indignation with thee, yet thy filthiness, which should be done away, has become more offensive, as that of a city is in dry weather, when it is not rained upon." Or, "Thou hast nothing to refresh and comfort thyself with in the day of indignation; thou art not rained upon by divine consolations." So the rich man in torment had not a drop of water, or rain, to cool his tongue.

II. A particular charge drawn up against the several orders and degrees of men among them, which shows that they had all helped to fill the measure of the nation's guilt, but none had done any thing towards the emptying of it; they are therefore all alike.

1. They have every one corrupted his way, and those who should have been the brightest examples of virtue were ringleaders in iniquity and patterns of vice.

(1.) The prophets, who pretended to make known the mind of God to them, were not only deceivers, but devourers (Eze 22:25), and hardened them in their wickedness both by their preaching, wherein they promised them impunity and prosperity, and by their conversation, in which they were as profligate as any. There is a conspiracy of her prophets against God and religion, against the true prophets and all good men; they conspired together to be all in one song, as Ahab's prophets were, to assure them of peace in their sinful ways. Note, The unity which is found among pretenders to infallibility, and which they so much boast of, is only the result of a secret conspiracy against the truth. Satan is not divided against himself. The prophets are in conspiracy with the murderers and oppressors, to patronise and protect them in their wickedness, and justify what they did with their false prophecies, provided they may come in sharers with them in the profits of it. They are like a roaring lion ravening the prey; they thunder out threats against those whose ruin is aimed at, terrify them, or make them odious to the people, and so make themselves masters, [1.] Of their lives: They have devoured souls, have been accessory to the shedding of the blood of many an innocent person, and so have made many to become sorrowful widows who were comfortable wives. They have persecuted those to death who witnessed against their pretensions to prophecy and would not be imposed upon by their counterfeit commission. Or, They devoured souls by flattering sinners into a false peace and a vain hope, and seducing them into the paths of sin, which would be their eternal ruin. Note, Those who draw men to wickedness, and encourage them in it, are the devourers and murderers of their souls. [2.] Of their estates. When Naboth is slain they take possession of his vineyard; They have seized the treasure and precious things, as forfeited; some way or other they had of devouring the widows' houses, as the Pharisees, Mat 23:14. Or, They got this treasure, and all these precious things, as fees for false and flattering prophecies; for he that puts not into their mouths, they even prepare war against him, Mic 3:5. It was said with Jerusalem when such men as these passed for prophets.

(2.) The priests, who were teachers by office, and had the custody of the sacred things, and should have called the false prophets to account, were as bad as they,Eze 22:26. [1.] They violated the law of God, which they should have observed and taught others to observe. They made no conscience of the law of the priesthood, but openly broke it, and with contempt, as Hophni and Phinehas. They did what they had a mind, with an express non obstante-notwithstanding to the word of God. And how should those teach the people their duty who lived in contradiction to their own? [2.] They profaned God's holy things, about which they were to minister, and which they ought to have restrained others from the profanation of. They suffered those to eat of the holy things who were unqualified by the law. The table of the Lord was contemptible with them. By dealing in holy things with such unhallowed hands they did themselves profane them. [3.] They did not themselves put a difference, nor did they show the people how to put a difference, between the holy and profane, the clean and the unclean, according to the directions and distinctions of the law. They did not exclude those from God's courts who were excluded by the law, nor teach the people to observe the difference the law had made between food clean and unclean, between times and places holy and common; but they lived at large themselves and encouraged the people to do so too. [4.] They hid their eyes from God's sabbaths; they took no care about them; it was all one to them whether God's sabbaths were kept holy or no; they neither gave countenance to those who observed them nor check to those who profaned them, nor did they themselves show any regard to them or veneration for them. They winked at those who did servile works on that day, and looked another way when they should have inspected the behaviour of the people on sabbath days. God's sabbaths have such a beauty and glory put upon them by the divine institution as may command respect; but they hid their eyes from them and would not see that excellency in them. [5.] By all this God himself was profaned among them; his authority was slighted, his goodness made light of, and the highest affront and contempt imaginable were put upon his holiness. Note, The profanation of the honour of the scriptures, of sabbaths and sacred things, is a profanation of the honour of God himself, who is interested in them.

(3.) The princes, who should have interposed with their authority to redress these grievances, were as daring transgressors of the law as any (Eze 22:27): They are like wolves ravening the prey; for such is power without justice and goodness to direct it. All their business was to gratify, [1.] Their own pride and ambition, by making themselves arbitrary and formidable. [2.] Their own malice and revenge, by shedding blood and destroying souls, sacrificing to their cruelty all those that stood in their way or had in any thing disobliged them. [3.] Their own avarice; all they aim at is to get dishonest gain, by crushing and oppressing their subject. Lucri bonus est odor ex re qualibet. Rem, rem, quocunque modo rem-Sweet is the odour of gain, from whatever substance it ascends. Money, money, by fairness or by fraud, get money. But, though they had power sufficient to carry them on in their oppressive courses, yet how could they answer it both to their credit and to their consciences? We are told how (Eze 22:28): The prophets daubed them with untempered mortar, told them in God's name (horrid wickedness!) that there was no harm in what they did, that they might dispose of the lives and estates of their subjects as they pleased, and could do no wrong, nay, that in prosecuting such and such whom they had marked out they did God service; and thus they stopped the mouth of their consciences. They also justified what they did, to the people, nay, and magnified it as if it were all for the public good, and so saved their reputation, and kept their oppressed subjects from murmuring. Note, Daubing prophets are the great supporters of ravening princes, but will prove at last their great deceivers, for they daub with untempered mortar which will not hold, nor will the wall stand long that is built up with it. They pretend to be seers, but they see vanity; they pretend to be diviners, but they divine lies; they pretend a warrant from Heaven for what they say, and that it is all as true as gospel; they say, Thus saith the Lord God, but it is all a sham, for the Lord has not spoken any such thing.

(4.) The people that had any power in their hands learned of their princes to abuse it, Eze 22:29. Those that should have complained of the oppression of the subject, and have put in a claim of rights on behalf of the injured, that should have stood up for liberty and property, were themselves invaders of them: The people of the land have used oppression and exercised robbery. The rich oppress the poor, masters their servants, landlords their tenants, and even parents their own children; nay, the buyers and sellers will find some way to oppress one another. This is such a sin as, when it is national, is indeed a national judgment, and is threatened as such. Isa 3:5, The people shall be oppressed every one by his neighbour. It is an aggravation of the sin that they have vexed the poor and needy, whom they should have relieved, and have oppressed the stranger and deprived him of his right, to whom they ought to have been not only just, but kind. Thus was the apostasy universal and the disease epidemical.

2. There is none that appears as an intercessor for them (v. 30): I sought for a man among them that should stand in the gap, but I found none. Note, (1.) Sin makes a gap in the hedge of protection that is about a people at which good things run out from them and evil things pour in upon them, a gap by which God enters to destroy them. (2.) There is a way of standing in the gap, and making up the breach against the judgments of God, by repentance, and prayer, and reformation. Moses stood in the gap when he made intercession for Israel to turn away the wrath of God, Psa 106:23. (3.) When God is coming forth against a sinful people to destroy them he expects some to intercede for them, and enquires if there be but one that does; so much is it his

desire and delight to show mercy. If there be but a man that stands in the gap, as Abraham for Sodom, he will discover him and be well pleased with him. (4.) It bodes ill to a people when judgments are breaking in upon them, and the spirit of prayer is restrained, so that not one is found that will either give them a good word or speak a good word for them. (5.) When it is so, what can be expected but utter ruin? Therefore have I poured out my indignation upon them (Eze 22:31), have given it full scope, that it may come upon them in a full stream; yet, whatever God's wrath inflicts upon a people, it is their own way that is therein recompensed upon their heads, and God deals with them no worse, but even much better, than their iniquity deserves.

Ezekiel Chapter 23

Ezekiel

This long chapter (as before ch. 16 and 20) is a history of the apostasies of God's people from him and the aggravations of those apostasies under the similitude of corporal whoredom and adultery. Here the kingdoms of Israel and Judah, the ten tribes and the two, with their capital cities, Samaria and Jerusalem, are considered distinctly. Here is, I. The apostasy of Israel and Samaria from God (Eze 23:1-8) and their ruin for it (Eze 23:9, Eze 23:10). II. The apostasy of Judah and Jerusalem from God (Eze 23:11-21) and sentence passed upon them, that they shall in like manner be destroyed for it (Eze 23:22-35). III. The joint wickedness of them both together (Eze 23:36-44) and the joint ruin of them both (Eze 23:45-49). And all that is written for warning against the sins of idolatry, and confidence in an arm of flesh, and sinful leagues and confederacies with wicked people (which are the sins here meant by committing whoredom), is that others may hear and fear, and not sin after the similitude of the transgressions of Israel and Judah.

Ezekiel 23:1

God had often spoken to Ezekiel, and by him to the people, to this effect, but now his word comes again; for God speaks the same thing once, yea, twice, yea, many a time, and all little enough, and too little, for man perceives it not. Note, To convince sinners of the evil of sin, and of their misery and danger by reason of it, there is need of line upon line, so loth we are to know the worst of ourselves. The sinners that are here to be exposed are two women, two kingdoms, sister-kingdoms, Israel and Judah, daughters of one mother, having been for a long time but one people. Solomon's kingdom was so large, so populous, that immediately after his death it divided into two. Observe, 1. Their character when they were one (Eze 23:3): They committed whoredoms in Egypt, for there they were guilty of idolatry, as we read before, Eze 20:8. The representing of those sins which are most provoking to God and most ruining to a people by the sin of whoredom plainly intimates what an exceedingly sinful sin uncleanness is, how offensive, how destructive. Doubtless it is itself one of the worst of sins, for the worst of other sins are compared to it here and often elsewhere, which should increase our detestation and dread of all manner of fleshly lusts, all appearances of them and approaches to them, as warring against the soul, infatuating sinners, bewitching them, alienating their minds from God and all that is good, debauching conscience, rendering them odious in the eyes of the pure and holy God, and drowning them at last in destruction and perdition. 2. Their names when they became two, Eze 23:4. The kingdom of Israel is called the elder sister, because that first made the breach, and separated from the family both of kings and priests that God had appointed-the greater sister (so the word is), for ten tribes belonged to that kingdom and only two to the other. God says of them both, They were mine, for they were the seed of Abraham his friend and of Jacob his chosen; they were in covenant with God, and carried about with them the sign of their circumcision, the seal of the covenant. They were mine; and therefore their apostasy was the highest injustice. It was alienating God's property, it was the basest ingratitude to the best of benefactors, and a perfidious treacherous violation of the most sacred engagements. Note, Those who have been in profession the people of God, but have revolted from him, have a great deal to answer for more than those who never made any such profession. "They were mine; they were espoused to me, and to me they bore sons and daughters;" there were many among them that were devoted to God's honour, and employed in his service, and were the strength and beauty of these kingdoms, as children are of the families they are born in. In this parable Samaria and the kingdom of Israel shall bear the name of Aholah-her own tabernacle, because the places of worship which that kingdom had were of their own devising, their own choosing, and the worship itself was their own invention; God never owned it. Her tabernacle to herself (so some render it); "let her take it to herself, and make her best of it." Jerusalem and the kingdom of Judah bear the name of Aholibah-my tabernacle is in her, because their temple was the place which God himself had chosen to put his name there. He acknowledged it to be his, and honoured them with the tokens of his presence in it. Note, Of those that stand in relation to God, and make profession of his name, some have greater privileges and advantages than others; and, as those who have greater are thereby rendered the more inexcusable if they revolt from God, so those who have less will not thereby be rendered inexcusable. 3. The treacherous departure of the kingdom of Israel from God (Eze 23:5): Aholah played the harlot when she was mine. Though the ten tribes had deserted the house of David, yet God owned them for his still; though Jeroboam, in setting up the golden calves, sinned, and made Israel to sin, yet, as long as they worshipped the God of Israel only, though by images, he did not quite cast them off. But they way of sin is down-hill. Aholah played the harlot, brought in the worship of Baal (Kg1 16:31), set up that other god, that dunghill-god, in competition with Jehovah (Kg1 18:21), as a vile adulteress dotes on her lovers, because they are well dressed and make a figure, because they are young and handsome (Eze 23:6), clothed with blue, captains and rulers, desirable young men, genteel, and that pass for men of honour, so she doted upon her neighbours, particularly the Assyrians, who had extended their conquests near them; she admired their idols and worshipped them, admired the pomp of their courts and their military strength and courted alliances with them upon any terms, as if her own God were not sufficient to be depended upon. We find one of the kings of Israel giving a thousand talents to the king of Assyria, to engage him in his interests, Kg2 15:19. She doted on the chosen men of Assyria, as worthy to be trusted and employed in the service of the state (Eze 23:7), and on all their idols with which she defiled herself. Note, Whatever creature we dote upon, pay homage to, and put a confidence in, we make an idol of that creature; and whatever we make an idol of we defile ourselves with. And now again the conviction looks back as far as the original of their nation: Neither left she her whoredoms which she brought from Egypt, Eze 23:8. Their being idolaters in Egypt was a thing never to be forgotten-that they should be in love with Egypt's idols even when they were continually in fear of Egypt's tyrants and task-masters! But (as some have observed) therefore, at that time, when Satan boasted of his having walked through the earth as all his own, to disprove his pretensions God did not say, Hast thou considered my people Israel in Egypt? (for they had become idolaters, and were not to be boasted of), but, Hast thou considered my servant Job in the land of Uz? And this corrupt disposition in them, when they were first formed into a people, is an emblem of that original corruption which is born with us and is woven into our constitution, a strong bias towards the world and the flesh, like that in the Israelites towards idolatry; it was bred in the bone with them, and was charged upon them long after, that they left not their whoredoms brought from Egypt. It would never out of the flesh, though Egypt had been a house of bondage to them. Thus the corrupt affections and inclinations which we brought into the world with us we have not lost, nor got clear of, but still retain them, though the iniquity we were born in was the source of all the calamities which human life is liable to. 4. The destruction of the kingdom of Israel for their apostasy from God (Eze 23:9, Eze 23:10): I have delivered her into the hand of her lovers. God first justly gave her up to her lust (Ephraim is joined to idols, let him alone), and then gave her up to her lovers. The neighbouring nations, whose idolatries she had conformed to and whose friendship she had confided in, and in both had affronted God, are now made use of as the instruments of her destruction. The Assyrians, on whom she doted, soon spied out the nakedness of the land, discovered her blind side, on which to attack her, stripped her of all her ornaments and all her defences, and so uncovered her, and made her naked and bare, carried her sons and daughters into captivity, slew her with the sword, and quite destroyed that kingdom and put an end to it. We have the story at large Kg2 17:6, etc., where the cause of the ruin of that once flourishing kingdom by the Assyrians is shown to be their forsaking the God of Israel, fearing other gods, and walking in the statutes of the heathen; it was for this that God was very angry with them and removed them out of his sight, Eze 23:18. And that the Assyrians, whom they had been so fond of, should be employed in executing judgments upon them was very remarkable, and shows how God, in a way of righteous judgment, often makes that a scourge to sinners which they have inordinately set their hearts upon. The devil will for ever be a tormentor to those impenitent sinners who now hearken to him and comply with him as a tempter. Thus Samaria became famous among women, or infamous rather; she became a name (so the word is); not only she came to be the subject of discourse, and much talked of, as the desolations of cities and kingdoms fill the newspapers, but she was thus ruined for her idolatries in terrorem-for warning to all people to take heed of doing likewise; as the public execution of notorious malefactors makes them such a name, such an ill name, as may serve to frighten others from those wicked courses which have brought them to a miserable and shameful end. Deu 21:21, All Israel shall hear and fear.

Ezekiel 23:11

The prophet Hosea, in his time, observed that the two tribes retained their integrity, in a great measure, when the ten tribes had apostatized (Hos 11:12, Ephraim indeed compasses me about with lies, but Judah yet rules with God and is faithful with the saints; and this was justly expected from them: Hos 4:15, Though thou Israel play the harlot, yet let not Judah offend); but this lasted not long. By some unhappy matches made between the house of David and the house of Ahab the worship of Baal had been brought into the kingdom of Judah, but had been by the reforming kings worked out again; and at the time of the captivity of the ten tribes, which was in the reign of Hezekiah, things were in a good posture: but it lasted not long. In the reign of Manasseh, soon after the kingdom of Judah had seen the destruction of the kingdom of Israel, they became more corrupt than Israel had been in their inordinate love of idols, Eze 23:11. Instead of being made better by the warning which that destruction gave them, they were made worse by it, as if they were displeased because the Lord had made that breach upon Israel, and for that reason became disaffected to him and to his service. Instead of being made to stand in awe of him as a jealous God, they therefore grew strange to him, and liked those gods better that would admit of partners with them. Note, Those may justly expect God's judgments upon themselves who do not take warning by his judgments upon others, who see in others what is the end of sin and yet continue to make a light matter of it. But it is bad indeed with those who are made worse by that which should make them better, and have their lusts irritated and exasperated by that which was designed to suppress and subdue them. Jerusalem grew worse in her whoredoms than her sister Samaria had been in her whoredoms. This was observed before (Eze 16:51), Neither has Samaria committed half of thy sins.

I. Jerusalem, that had been a faithful city, became a harlot, Isa 1:21. She also doted upon the Assyrians (Eze 23:12), joined in league with them, joined in worship with them, grew to be in love with their captains and rulers, and cried them up as finer and more accomplished gentlemen than any that ever the land of Israel produced. "See how richly, how neatly, they are dressed, clothed most gorgeously; how well they sit a horse; they are horsemen riding on horses; how charmingly they look, all of them desirable young men." And thus they grew to affect every thing that was foreign and to despise their own nation; and even the religion of it was mean and homely, and not to be compared with the curiosity and gaiety of the heathen temples. Thus she increased her whoredoms; she fell in love, fell in league, with the Chaldeans. Hezekiah himself was faulty this way when he was proud of the court which the king of Babylon made to him and complimented his ambassadors with the sight of all his treasures, Isa 39:2. And the humour increased (Eze 23:14); she doted upon the pictures of the Babylonian captains (Eze 23:15, Eze 23:16), joined in alliance with that kingdom, invited them to come and settle in Jerusalem, that they might refine the genius of the Jewish nation and make it more polite; nay, they sent for patterns of their images, altars, and temples, and made use of them in their worship. Thus was she polluted with her whoredoms (Eze 23:17), and thereby she discovered her own whoredom (Eze 23:18), her own strong inclination to idolatry. And when she had had enough of the Chaldeans, and grew tired of them and disposed to break her league with them, as Jehoiakim and Zedekiah did, her mind being alienated from them, she courted the Egyptians, doted upon their paramours (Eze 23:20), would come into an alliance with them, and, to strengthen the alliance, would join with them in their idolatries and then depend upon them to be their protectors from all other nations; for so wise, so rich, so strong, was the Egyptian nation, and came to such perfection in idolatry, that there was no nation now which they could take such satisfaction in as in Egypt. Thus they called to remembrance the days of their youth (Eze 23:19), the lewdness of their youth, Eze 23:21. 1. They pleased themselves with the remembrance of it. When they began to set their affections upon Egypt, they encouraged themselves to put a confidence in that kingdom, because of the old acquaintance they had with it, as if they still retained the gust and relish of the leeks and onions they ate there, or rather of the idolatrous worship they learned there, and brought up with them thence. When they began an acquaintance with Egypt they remembered how merrily their fathers worshipped the golden calf, what music and dancing they had at that sport, which they learned in Egypt; and they hoped they should now have a fair pretence to come to that again. Thus she multiplied her whoredoms, repeated her former whoredoms, and encouraged herself to close with present temptations, by calling to remembrance the days of her youth. Note, Those who, instead of reflecting upon their former sins with sorrow and shame, reflect upon them with pleasure and pride, contract new guilt thereby, strengthen their own corruptions, and in effect bid defiance to repentance. This is returning with the dog to his vomit. 2. They called it God's remembrance, and provoked him to remember it against them. God had said indeed that he would reckon with them for the golden calf, that idol of Egypt (Exo 32:34); but such was his patience that he seemed to have forgotten it till they, by their league now with the Egyptians against the Chaldeans, did, as it were, put him in mind of it; and in the day when he visits he will now, as he has said, visit for that. It is very observable how this adulteress changes her lovers: she dotes first on the Assyrians; then she thought the Chaldeans finer and courted them; after a while her mind was alienated from them, and she thought the Egyptians more powerful (Eze 23:20) and she must contract an intimacy with them. This shows the folly, (1.) Of fleshly lusts; when they are indulged they grow humoursome and fickle, are soon surfeited but never satisfied; they must have variety, and what is loved one day is loathed the next. Unius adulterium matrimonium vocant-One adultery is called marriage, as Seneca observes. (2.) Of idolatry. Those who think one God too little will not think a hundred sufficient, but will still be for trying more, as finding all insufficient. (3.) Of seeking to creatures for help; we go from one to another, but are disappointed in them all, and can never rest till we have made the God of Israel our help.

II. The faithful God justly gives a bill of divorce to this now faithless city, that has become a harlot. His jealousy soon discovered her lewdness (Eze 23:13): I saw that she was defiled, that she was debauched, and saw which way her inclination was, that the two sisters both took one way, and that Jerusalem grew worse than Samaria. For, if we stretch out our hand to a strange god, will not God search this out? No doubt he will; and when he has found it can he be pleased with it? No (Eze 23:18): Then my mind was alienated from her, as it was from her sister. How could the pure and holy God any longer take delight in such a lewd generation? Note, Sin alienates God's mind from the sinner, and justly, for it is the alienation of the sinner's mind from God; but woe, and a thousand woes, to those from whom God's mind is alienated; for whom he turns from he will turn against.

Ezekiel 23:22

Jerusalem stands indicted by the name of Aholibah, for that she, as a false traitor to her sovereign Lord the God of heaven, not having his fear before her eyes, but moved by the instigation of the devil, had revolted from her allegiance to him, had compassed and imagined to shake off his government, had kept up a correspondence had joined in confederacy with his enemies, and the pretenders to a deity, in contempt of his crown and dignity. To this indictment she has pleaded, Not guilty: I am not polluted; I have not gone after Baalim. But it is found against her by the notorious evidence of the fact, and she stands convicted of it, nor has any thing material to offer why judgment should not be given and execution awarded according to law. In these verses, therefore, we have the sentence.

I. Her old confederates must be her executioners; and those whom she had courted to be her leaders in sin are now to be employed as instruments of her punishment (Eze 23:22): "I will raise up thy lovers against thee, the Chaldeans, whom formerly thou didst so much admire and covet an acquaintance with, but from whom thy mind is since alienated and with whom thou hast perfidiously broken covenant." They are called thy lovers (Eze 23:22) and yet (Eze 23:28) those whom thou hatest. Note, It is common for sinful love soon to turn into hatred; as Amnon's to Tamar. Those of headstrong and unreasonable passions are often very hot against those persons and things that a little before they were as hot for. Fools run into extremes; nay, and wise men may see cause to change their sentiments. And therefore, as we should rejoice and weep as if we rejoiced not and wept not, so we should love and hate as if we loved not and hated not. Ita ama tanquam osurus-Love as one who may have cause to feel aversion.

II. The execution to be done upon her is very terrible.

1. Her enemies shall come against her on every side (Eze 23:22), those of the several nations that constituted the Chaldean army (Eze 23:23), all of them great lords and renowned, whose pomp, and grandeur, and splendid appearance made them look the more amiable when they came as friends to protect and patronise Jerusalem, but the more formidable when they came to chastise its treachery and aimed at no less than its ruin. (1.) They shall come with a great deal of military force (Eze 23:24), with chariots and wagons furnished with all necessary provisions for a camp, with arms and ammunition, bag and baggage, with a vast army, and well armed. (2.) They shall have justice on their side: "I will set judgment before them" (they shall have right with them as well as might; for the king of Babylon had just cause to make war upon the king of Judah, because he had broken his league with him), "and therefore they shall judge thee, not only according to God's judgments, as the instruments of his justice, to punish thee for the indignities done to him, but according to their judgments, according to the law of nations, to punish thee for thy perfidious dealings with them." (3.) They shall prosecute the war with a great deal of fury and resentment. It being a war of revenge, they shall deal with thee hatefully, Eze 23:29. This will make the execution the more severe that their swords will be dipped in poison. Thou hatest

them, and they shall deal hatefully with thee; those that hate will be hated and will be hatefully dealt with. (4.) God himself will lead them on, and his anger shall be mingled with theirs (Eze 23:25): I will set my jealousy against thee; that shall kindle this fire, and then they shall deal furiously with thee. If men deal ever so hatefully, ever so furiously, with us, yet, if we have God on our side, we need not fear them; they can do us no real hurt. But if men deal furiously with us, and God set his jealousy against us too, what will become of us?

2. The particulars of the sentence here passed upon this notorious adulteress are, (1.) That all she has shall be seized on. The clothes and the fair jewels, with which she had endeavoured to recommend herself to her lovers, these she shall be stripped of, Eze 23:26. All those things that were the ornaments of their state shall be taken away: "They shall take away all thy labour, all that thou hast gotten by thy labour, and shall leave thee naked and bare," Eze 23:29. Both city and country shall be impoverished and all the wealth of both swept away. (2.) That her children shall go into captivity. "They shall take thy sons and thy daughters, and make slaves of them (Eze 23:25); for they are children of whoredoms, unworthy the dignities and privileges of Israelites," Hos 2:4. (3.) That she shall be stigmatized and deformed: "They shall take away thy nose and thy ears, shall mark thee for a harlot, and render thee for ever odious," Eze 23:25. This intimates the many cruelties of the Chaldean soldiers towards the Jews that fell into their hands, whom, it is probable, they used barbarously. Some will have this to be understood figuratively; and by the nose they think is meant the kingly dignity, and by the ears that of the priesthood. (4.) That she shall be exposed to shame: Thy lewdness and thy whoredoms shall be discovered (Eze 23:29), as, when a malefactor is punished, all his crimes are ripped up, and repeated to his disgrace; what was secret then comes to light, and what was done long since is then called to mind. (5.) That she shall be quite cut off and ruined: "The remnant of thy people that have escaped the famine and pestilence shall fall by the sword; and the residue of thy houses that have not been battered down about thy ears shall be devoured by the fire," Eze 23:25. And this shall be the end of Jerusalem.

III. Because she has trod in the steps of Samaria's sins, she must expect no other than Samaria's fate. It is common, in giving judgment, to have an eye to precedents; so has God in passing this sentence on Jerusalem (Eze 23:31, etc.): "Thou hast walked in the way of thy sister, notwithstanding the warning thou hast had given thee, by the fatal consequences of her wickedness; and therefore I will give her cup, her portion of miseries, into thy hand, the cup of the Lord's fury, which will be to thee a cup of trembling." Now, 1. This cup is said to be deep and large, and to contain much (Eze 23:32), abundance of God's wrath and abundance of miseries, the fruits of that wrath. It is such a cup as that which we read of, Jer 25:15, Jer 25:16. The cup of divine vengeance holds a great deal, and so those will find into whose hand it shall be put. 2. They shall be made to drink the very dregs of this cup, as the wicked are said to do (Psa 75:8): "Thou shalt drink it and suck it out, not because it is pleasant, but because it is forced upon thee (Eze 23:34); thou shalt break the shreds thereof, and pluck off thy own breasts, for indignation at the extreme bitterness of this cup, being full of the fury of the Lord (Isa 51:20), as men in great anguish tear their hair, and throw every thing from them. Finding there is no remedy, but it must be drank (for I have spoken it, saith the Lord God), thou shalt have no manner of patience in the drinking of it." 3. They shall be intoxicated by it, made sick, and be at their wits' end, as men in drink are, staggering, and stumbling, and ready to fall (Eze 23:33): Thou shalt be filled with drunkenness and sorrow. Note, Drunkenness has sorrow attending it, to such a degree that the utmost confusion and astonishment are here represented by it. Who would think that that which is such a force upon nature, such a scandal to it, which deprives men of their reason, disorders them to the last degree, and is therefore expressive of the greatest misery, should yet be with many a beloved sin, that they should damn their own souls to distemper their own bodies? Who has woe and sorrow like them? Pro 23:29. 4. Being so intoxicated, they shall become, as drunkards deserve to be, a laughing-stock to all about them (Eze 23:32): Thou shalt be laughed to scorn and had in derision, as acting ridiculously in every thing thou goest about. When God is about to ruin a people he makes their judges fools and pours contempt on their princes, Job 12:17, Job 12:21.

IV. In all this God will be justified, and by all this they will be reformed; and so the issue even of this will be God's glory and their good. 1. They have been bad, very bad, and that justifies God in all that is brought upon them (Eze 23:30): I will do these things unto thee because thou hast gone a whoring after the heathen, and (Eze 23:35) because thou hast forgotten me and cast me behind thy back. Note, Forgetfulness of God, and a contempt of him, of his eye upon us and authority over us, are at the bottom of all our treacherous adulterous departures from him. Therefore men wander after idols, because they forget God, and their obligations to him; nor could they look with so much desire and delight upon the baits of sin if they did not first cast God behind their back, as not worthy to be regarded. And those who put such an affront upon God, how can they think but that it should turn upon themselves at last? Therefore bear thou also thy lewdness and thy whoredoms; that is, thou shalt suffer the punishment of them, and thou alone must bear the blame. Men need no more to sink them than the weight of their own sins; and those who will not part with their lewdness and their whoredoms must bear them. 2. They shall be better, much better, and this fire, though consuming to many, shall be refining to a remnant (Eze 23:27): Thus will I make thy lewdness to cease from thee. The judgments which were brought upon them by their sins parted between them and their sins, and taught them at length to say, What have we to do any more with idols? Observe, (1.) How inveterate the disease was: Thy whoredoms were brought from the land of Egypt. Their disposition to idolatry was early and innate, their practice of it was ancient, and had gained a sort of prescription by long usage. (2.) How complete the cure was notwithstanding: "Though it has taken root, yet it shall be made to cease, so that thou shalt not so much as lift up thy eyes to the idols again, nor remember Egypt with pleasure any more." They shall avoid the occasions of this sin, for they shall not so much as look upon an idol, lest their hearts should unawares walk after their eyes. And they shall abandon all inclinations to it: "They shall not remember Egypt; they shall not retain any of that affection for idols which they had from the very infancy of their nation." They got it, through the corruption of nature, in their bondage in Egypt, and lost it, through the grace of God, in their captivity in Babylon, which this was the blessed fruit of, even the taking away of sin, of that sin; so that whereas, before the captivity, no nation (all things considered) was more impetuously bent upon idols and idolatry than they were, after that captivity no nation was more vehemently set against idols and idolatry than they were, insomuch that at this day the image-worship which is practised in the church of Rome confirms the Jews as much as any thing in their prejudices against the Christian religion.

Ezekiel 23:36

After the ten tribes were carried into captivity, and that kingdom was made quite desolate, the remains of it by degrees incorporated with the kingdom of Judah, and gained a settlement (many of them) in Jerusalem; so that the two sisters had in effect become one again; and therefore, in these verses, the prophet takes those to task jointly who were thus conjoined: "Wilt thou judge Aholah and Aholibah together? Eze 23:36. Wilt thou go about to frame an excuse for them? Thou seest the matter is so bad as not to bear an excuse." Or, rather, "Thou shalt now be employed, in God's name, to judge them, Eze 20:4. The matter is rather worse than better since the union."

I. Let them be made to see the sins they are guilty of: Declare unto them openly and boldly their abominations. 1. They have been guilty of gross idolatry, here called adultery. With their idols they have committed adultery (Eze 23:37), have broken their marriage-covenant with God, have lusted after the gratifications of a carnal sensual mind in the worship of God. This is the first and worst of the abominations he is to charge them with. 2. They have committed the most barbarous murders, in sacrificing their children to Moloch, a sin so unnatural that they deserve to hear of it upon all occasions: Blood is in their hands, innocent blood, the blood of their own children, which they have caused to pass through the fire (Eze 23:37), not that they might be dedicated to the idols, but that they might be devoured, a sign that they loved their idols better than that which was dearest to them in the world. 3. They have profaned the sacred things with which God had dignified and distinguished them: This they have done unto me, this indignity, this injury, Eze 23:38. Every contempt put upon that which is holy reflects upon him who is the fountain of holiness, and from a relation to whom whatever is called holy has its denomination. God had set up his sanctuary among them, but they defiled it, by making it a house of merchandise, a den of thieves; nay, and much worse; there they set up their idols and worshipped them, and there they shed the blood of God's prophets. God had revealed to them his holy sabbaths, but they profaned them, by doing all manner of servile work therein, or perhaps by sports and recreations on that day, not only practised, but allowed and encouraged by authority. They defiled the sanctuary on the same day that they profaned the sabbath. To defile the sanctuary was bad enough on any day, but to do it on the sabbath day was an aggravation. We commonly say, The better day the better deed; but here, the better day the worse deed. God takes notice of the circumstances of sin which add to the guilt. He shows (Eze 23:39) what was their profanation both of the sanctuary and of the sabbath. They slew their children, and sacrificed them to their idols, to the great dishonour both of God and of human nature; and then came, on the same day, their hands imbrued with the blood of their children and their clothes stained with it, to attend in God's sanctuary, not to ask pardon for what they had done, but to present themselves before him, as other Israelites did, expecting acceptance with him, notwithstanding these villanies which they were guilty of; as if God either did not know their wickedness or did not hate it. Thus they profaned the sanctuary, as if that were a protection to the worst of malefactors; for thus they did in the midst of his house. Note, It is a profanation of God's solemn ordinances when those that are grossly and openly profane and vicious impudently and impenitently so intrude upon the services and privileges of them. Give not that which is holy unto dogs. Friend, how camest thou in hither? 4. They have courted foreign alliances, been proud of them, and reposed a confidence in them. This also is represented by the sin of adultery, for it was a departure from God, not only to whom alone they ought to pay their homage and not to idols, but in whom alone they ought to put their trust, and not in creatures. Israel was a peculiar people, must dwell alone and not be reckoned among the nations; and they profane their crown, and lay their honour in the dust, when they covet to be like them or in league with them. But this they have now done; they have entered into strict alliances with the Assyrians, Chaldeans, and Egyptians, the most renowned and potent kingdoms at that time; but they scorned alliances with the petty kingdoms and states that lay near them, which yet might have been of more real service to them. Note, Affecting an acquaintance and correspondence with great people has often been a snare to good people. Let us see how Jerusalem courts her high allies, thinking thereby to make herself considerable. (1.) She privately requested that a public embassy might be sent to her (Eze 23:40): You sent a messenger for men to come from far. It seems, then, that the neighbours had no desire to come into a confederacy with Jerusalem, but she thrust herself upon them, and sent under-hand to desire them to court her: and, lo, they came. The wisest and best may be drawn unavoidably into company and conversation with profane and wicked people: but it is no sign either of wisdom or goodness to covet an intimacy with such and to court it. (2.) Great preparation was made for the reception of these foreign ministers, for their public entry and public audience, which is compared to the pains that an adulteress takes to make herself look handsome. Jezebel-like, thou paintedst thy face and deckedst thyself with ornaments, Eze 23:40. The king and princes made themselves new clothes, fitted up the rooms of state, beautified the furniture, and made it look fresh. Thou sattest upon a stately bed (Eze 23:41), a stately throne; a table was prepared, whereon thou has set my oil and my incense. This was either, [1.] A feast for the ambassadors, a noble treat, agreeable to the other preparations. There was incense to perfume the room and oil to anoint their heads. Or, [2.] An altar already furnished for the ambassadors' use in the worship of their idols, to let them know that the Israelites were not so strait-laced but that they could allow foreigners the free exercise of their religion among them, and furnish them with chapels, yea, and complimented them so far as to join with them in their devotions; though the law of their God was against it, yet they could easily dispense with themselves to oblige a friend. The oil and incense God calls his, not only because they were the gift of his providence, but because they should have been offered at his altar, which was an aggravation of their sin in serving idols and idolaters with them. See Hos 2:8. (3.) There was great joy at their coming, as if it were such a blessing as never happened to Jerusalem before (Eze 23:42): A voice of a multitude being at east was with her. The people were very easy, for they thought themselves very safe and happy now that they had such powerful allies; and therefore attended the ambassadors with loud huzzas and acclamations of joy. A great confluence of people there was to the court upon this occasion. The men of the common sort were there to grace the solemnity, and to increase the crowd; and with them were brought Sabeans from the wilderness. The margin reads it drunkards from the wilderness, that would drink healths to the prosperity of this grand alliance, and force them upon others, and be most noisy in shouting upon this occasion. Whoever they were, in honour of the ambassadors they put bracelets upon their hands and beautiful crowns upon their heads, which made the cavalcade appear very splendid. (4.) God by his prophets warned them against making these dangerous leagues with foreigners (Eze 23:43): "Then said I unto her that was old in adulteries, that from the first was fond of leagues with the heathen, of matching with their families (Jdg 3:6), and afterwards of making alliances with their kingdoms, and, though often disappointed therein, would never be dissuaded from it (this was the adultery she was old in), I said, Will they now commit whoredoms with her and she with them? Surely experience and observation will by this time have convinced both them and her that an alliance between the nation of the Jews and a heathen nation can never be for the advantage of either." They are iron and clay, that will not mix, nor will God bless such an alliance, or smile upon it. But, it seems, her being old in these adulteries, instead of weaning her from them, as one would expect, does but make her the more impudent and insatiable in them; for, though she was thus admonished of the folly of it, yet they went in unto her, Eze 23:44. A bargain was soon clapped up, and a league made, first with this, and then with the other, foreign state. Samaria did so, Jerusalem did so, like lewd women. They could not rest satisfied in the embraces of God's laws and care, and the assurances of protection he gave them; they could not think his covenant with them security enough. But they must by treaties and leagues, politic ones (they thought) and well-concerted, throw themselves into the arms of foreign princes, and put their interests under their protection. Note, Those hearts go a whoring from God that take a complacency in the pomp of the world and put a confidence in its wealth, and in an arm of flesh, Jer 17:5.

II. Let them be made to foresee the judgments that are coming upon them for these sins (Eze 23:45): The righteous men, they shall judge them. Some make the instruments of their destruction to be the righteous men that shall judge them. The Assyrians that destroyed Samaria, the Chaldeans that destroyed Jerusalem, those were comparatively righteous, had a sense of justice between man and man and justly resented the treachery of the Jewish nation; however, they executed God's judgments, which, we are sure, are all righteous. Others understand it of the prophets, whose office it was, in God's name, to judge them and pass sentence upon them. Or we may take it as an appeal to all righteous men, to all that have a sense of equity; they shall all judge concerning these cities, and agree in their verdict, that forasmuch as they have been notoriously guilty of adultery and murder, and the guilt is national, therefore they ought to suffer the pains and penalties which by law are inflicted upon women in their personal capacity that shed blood and are adulteresses. Righteous men will say, "Why should bloody filthy cities escape any better than bloody filthy persons? Judge, I pray thee," Isa 5:3. This judgment being given by the righteous men, the righteous God will award execution. See here, 1. What the execution will be,Eze 23:46, Eze 23:47. The same as before, Eze 23:23, etc. God will bring a company of enemies upon them, who shall be made to serve his holy purposes even when they are serving their own sinful appetites and passions. These enemies shall easily prevail, for God will give them into their hands to be removed and spoiled; this company shall stone them with stones as malefactors, shall single them out and dispatch them with their swords; and, as was sometimes done in severe executions (witness that of Achan), they shall slay their children and burn their houses. 2. What will be the effects of it. (1.) Thus they shall suffer for their sins: Their lewdness shall be recompensed upon them (Eze 23:49); and they shall bear the sins of their idols, Eze 23:35, Eze 23:49. Thus God will assert the honour of his broken law and injured government, and let the world know what a just and jealous God he is. (2.) Thus they shall be broken off from their sins: I will cause lewdness to cease out of the land, Eze 23:27, Eze 23:48. The destruction of God's city, like the death of God's saints, shall do that for them which ordinances and providences before could not do; it shall quite take away their sin, so that Jerusalem shall rise out of its ashes a new lump, as gold comes out of the furnace purified from its dross. (3.) Thus other cities and nations will have fair warning given them to keep themselves from idols. That all women may be taught not to do after your lewdness. This is the end of the punishment of malefactors, that they may be made examples to others, who will see and fear. Smite the scorner and the simple will beware. The judgments of God upon some are designed to teach others, and happy are those who receive instruction from them not to tread in the steps of sinners, lest they be taken in their snares; those who would be taught this must know God is the Lord (Eze 23:49), that he is the governor of the world, a God that judges in the earth, and with whom there is no respect of persons.

Ezekiel Chapter 24

Here are two sermons in this chapter, preached on a particular occasion, and they are both from Mount Sinai, the mount of terror, both from Mount Ebal, the mount of curses; both speak the approaching fate of Jerusalem. The occasion of them was the king of Babylon's laying siege to Jerusalem, and the design of them is to show that in the issue of that siege he should be not only master of the place, but destroyer of it. I. By the sign of flesh boiling in a pot over the fire are shown the miseries that Jerusalem should suffer during the siege, and justly, for her filthiness (Eze 24:1-14). II. By the sign of Ezekiel's not mourning for the death of his wife is shown that the calamities coming upon Jerusalem were too great to be lamented, so great that they should sink down under them into a silent despair (Eze 24:15-27).

Ezekiel 24:1

We have here,

I. The notice God gives to Ezekiel in Babylon of Nebuchadnezzar's laying siege to Jerusalem, just at the time when he was doing it (Eze 24:2): "Son of man, take notice, the king of Babylon, who is now abroad with his army, thou knowest not where, set himself against Jerusalem this same day." It was many miles, it was many days' journey, from Jerusalem to Babylon. Perhaps the last intelligence they had from the army was that the design was upon Rabbath of the children of Ammon and that the campaign was to be opened with the siege of that city. But God knew, and could tell the prophet, "This day, at this time, Jerusalem is invested, and the Chaldean army has sat down before it." Note, As all times, so all places, even the most remote, are present with God and under his view. He tells the prophet, that the prophet might tell the people, that so when it proved to be punctually true, as they would find by the public intelligence in a little time, it might be a confirmation of the prophet's mission, and they might infer that, since he was right in his news, he was so in his predictions, for he owed both to the same correspondence he had with Heaven.

II. The notice which he orders him to take of it. He must enter it in his book, memorandum, that in the ninth year of Jehoiachin's captivity (for thence Ezekiel dated, Eze 1:2, which was also the ninth year of Zedekiah's reign, for he began to reign when Jehoiachin was carried off), in the tenth month, on the tenth day of the month, the king of Babylon laid siege to Jerusalem; and the date here agrees exactly with the date in the history, Kg2 25:1. See how God reveals things to his servants the prophets, especially those things which serve to confirm their word, and so to confirm their own faith. Note, It is good to keep an exact account of the date of remarkable occurrences, which may sometimes contribute to the manifesting of God's glory so much the more in them, and the explaining and confirming of scripture prophecies. Known unto God are all his works.

III. The notice which he orders him to give to the people thereupon, the purport of which is that this siege of Jerusalem, now begun, will infallibly end in the ruin of it. This he must say to the rebellious house, to those of them that were in Babylon, to be by them communicated to those that were yet in their own land. A rebellious house will soon be a ruinous house.

1. He must show them this by a sign; for that stupid people needed to be taught as children are. The comparison made use of is that of a boiling pot. This agrees with Jeremiah's vision many years before, when he first began to be a prophet, and probably was designed to put them in mind of that (Jer 1:13, I see a seething pot, with the face towards the north; and the explanation of it, Eze 24:15, makes it to signify the besieging of Jerusalem by the northern nations); and, as this comparison is intended to confirm Jeremiah's vision, so also to confront the vain confidence of the princes of Jerusalem, who had said (Jer 11:3), This city is the caldron and we are the flesh, meaning, "We are as safe here as if we were surrounded with walls of brass." "Well," says God, "it shall be so; you shall be boiled in Jerusalem, as the flesh in the caldron, boiled to pieces; let the pot be set on with water in it (Eze 24:4); let it be filled with the flesh of the choice of the flock (Eze 24:5), with the choice pieces (Eze 24:4), and the marrow-bones, and let the other bones serve for fuel, that, one way or other, either in the pot or under it, the whole beast may be made use of." A fire of bones, though it be a slow fire (for the siege was to be long), is yet a sure and lasting fire; such was God's wrath against them, and not like the crackling of thorns under a pot, which has noise and blaze, but no intense heat. Those that from all parts of the country fled into Jerusalem for safety would be sadly disappointed when the siege laid to it would soon make the place too hot for them; and yet there was not getting out of it, but they must be forced to abide by it, as the flesh in a boiling pot.

2. He must give them a comment upon this sign. It is to be construed as a woe to the bloody city, Eze 24:6. And again (Eze 24:9), being bloody, let it go to pot, to be boiled; that is the fittest place for it. Let us here see,

(1.) What is the course God takes with it. Jerusalem, during the siege, is like a pot boiling over the fire, all in a heat, all in a hurry. [1.] Care is taken to keep a good fire under the pot, which signifies the closeness of the siege, and the many vigorous attacks made upon the city by the besiegers, and especially the continued wrath of God burning against them (Eze 24:9): I will make the pile for fire great. Commission is given to the Chaldeans (Eze 24:10) to heap on wood, and kindle the fire, to make Jerusalem more and more hot to the inhabitants. Note, The fire which God kindles for the consuming of impenitent sinners shall never abate, much less go out, for want of fuel. Tophet has fire and much wood,Isa 30:33. [2.] The meat, as it is boiled, is taken out, and given to the Chaldeans for them to feast upon. "Consume the flesh; let it be thoroughly boiled, boiled to rags. Spice it well, and make it savoury, for those that will fees sweetly upon it. Let the bones be burnt." either the bones under the pot ("let them be consumed with the other fuel") or, as some think, the bones in the pot-"let it boil so furiously that not only the flesh may be sodden, but even the bones softened; let all the inhabitants of Jerusalem be by sickness, sword, and famine, reduced to the extremity of misery." And then (Eze 24:6), "Bring it out piece by piece; let every man be delivered into the enemy's hand, to be either put to the sword or made a prisoner. Let them be an easy prey to them, and let the Chaldeans fall upon them as eagerly as a hungry man does upon a good dish of meat when it is set before him. Let no lot fall upon it; every piece in the pot shall be fetched out and devoured, first or last, and therefore it is no matter for casting lots which shall be fetched out first." It was a very severe military execution when David measured Joab with two lines to put to death and one full line to keep alive, Sa2 8:2. But here is no line, no lot of mercy, made use of; all goes one way, and that is to destruction. [3.] When all the broth is boiled away the pot is set empty upon the coals, that it may burn too, which signifies the setting of the city on fire, Eze 24:11. The scum of the meat, or (as some translate it) the rust of the meat, has so got into the pot that there is no making it clean by washing or scouring it, and therefore it must be done by fire; so let the filthiness be burnt out of it, or, rather, melted in it and burnt with it. Let the vipers and their nest be consumed together.

(2.) What is the quarrel God has with it. He would not take these severe methods with Jerusalem but that he is provoked to it; she deserves to be thus dealt with, for, [1.] It is a bloody city (Eze 24:7, Eze 24:8): Her blood is in the midst of her. Many a barbarous murder has been committed in the very heart of the city; nay, and they have a disposition to cruelty in their hearts; they inwardly delight in blood-shed, and so it is in the midst of them. Nay, they commit their murders in the face of the sun, and openly and impudently avow them, in defiance of the justice both of God and man. She did not pour out the blood she shed upon the ground, to cover it with dust, as being ashamed of the sin or afraid of the punishment. She did not look upon it as a filthy thing, proper to be concealed (Deu 23:13), much less dangerous. Nay, she poured out the innocent blood she shed upon a rock, where it would not soak in, upon the top of a rock, in despite of divine views and vengeance. They shed innocent blood under colour of justice; so that they gloried in it, as if they had done God and the country good service, so put it, as it were, on the top of a rock. Or it may refer to the sacrificing of their children on their high places, perhaps on the top of rocks. Now thus they caused fury to come up and take vengeance, Eze 24:8. It could not be avoided but that God must in anger visit for these things; his soul must be avenged on such a nation as this. It is absolutely necessary that such a bloody city as this should have blood given her to drink, for she is worthy, for the vindicating of the honour of divine justice. And, the crime having been public and notorious, it is fit that the punishment should be so too: I have set her blood on the top of a rock. Jerusalem was to be made an example, and therefore was made a spectacle, to the world; God dealt with her according to the law of retaliation. It is fit that those who sin before all should be rebuked before all; and that the reputation of those should not be consulted by the concealment of their punishment who were so impudent as not to desire the concealment of their sin. [2.] It is a filthy city. Great notice is taken, in this explanation of the comparison, of the scum of this pot, which signifies the sin of Jerusalem, working up and appearing when the judgments of God were upon her. It is the pot whose scum is therein and has not gone out of it, Eze 24:6. The great scum that went not forth out of her (Eze 24:12), that stuck to the pot when all was boiled away, and was molten in it (Eze 24:11), some of this runs over into the fire (Eze 24:12), inflames that, and makes it burn the more furiously, but it shall all be consumed at last, Eze 24:11. When the hand of God had gone out against them, instead of humbling themselves under it, repenting and reforming, and accepting the punishment of their iniquity, they grew more impudent and outrageous in sin, quarrelled with God, persecuted his prophets, were fierce to one another, enraged to the last degree against the Chaldeans, snarled at the stone, gnawed their chain, and were like a wild bull in a net. This as their scum; in their distress they trespassed yet more against the Lord, like that king Ahaz,Ch2 28:22. There is little hope of those who are made worse by that which should make them better, whose corruptions are excited an exasperated by those rebukes both of the word and of the providence of God which were designed for the suppressing and subduing of them, or of those whose scum boiled up once in convictions, and confessions of sin, as if it would be taken off by reformation, but afterwards returned again, in a revolt from their good overtures; and the heart that seemed softened is hardened again. This was Jerusalem's case: She has wearied with lies, wearied her God with purposes and promises of amendment, which she never stood to, wearied herself with her carnal confidences, which have all deceived her, Eze 24:12. Note, Those that follow after lying vanities weary themselves with the pursuit. Now see her doom, Eze 24:13, Eze 24:14. Because she is incurably wicked she is abandoned to ruin, without remedy. First, Methods and means of reformation had been tried in vain (Eze 24:13): "In thy filthiness is lewdness; thou hast become obstinate and impudent in it; thou hast got a habit of it, which is confirmed by frequent acts. In thy filthiness thee is a rooted lewdness; as appears by this, I have purged thee and thou wast not purged. I have given thee medicine, but it has done thee no good. I have used the means of cleansing thee, but they have been ineffectual; the intention of them has not been answered." Note, It is sad to think how many there are on whom ordinances and providences are all lost. Secondly, It is therefore resolved that no more such methods shall be sued: Thou shalt not be purged from thy filthiness any more. The fire shall no longer be a refining fire, but a consuming fire, and therefore shall not be mitigated and shortened, as it has been, but shall be continued in extremity, till it has done its destroying work. Note, Those that will not be healed are justly given up and their case adjudged desperate. There is a day coming when it will be said, He that is filthy, let him be filthy still. Thirdly, Nothing remains then but to bring them to utter ruin: I will cause my fury to rest upon thee. This is the same with what is said of the later Jews, that wrath has come upon them to the uttermost, Th1 2:16. They deserve it: According to thy doings they shall judge thee, Eze 24:14. And God will do it. The sentence is bound on with repeated ratifications, that they might be awakened to see how certain their ruin was: "I the Lord have spoken it, who am able to make good what I have spoken; it shall come to pass, nothing shall prevent it, for I will do it myself, I will not go back upon any entreaties; the decree has gone forth, and I will not spare in compassion to them, neither will I repent." He will neither change his mind nor his way. Hereby the prophet was forbidden to interceded for them, and they were forbidden to flatter themselves with hopes of an escape. God hath said it, and he will do it. Note, The declarations of God's wrath against sinners are as inviolable as the assurances he has given of favour to his people; and the case of such is sad indeed, who have brought it to this issue, that either God must be false or they must be damned.

Ezekiel 24:15

These verses conclude what we have been upon all along from the beginning of this book, to wit, Ezekiel's prophecies of the destruction of Jerusalem; for after this, though he prophesied much concerning other nations, he said no more concerning Jerusalem, till he heard of the destruction of it, almost three years after, Eze 33:21. He had assured them, in the former part of this chapter, that there was no hope at all of the preventing of the trouble; here he assures them that they should not have the ease of weeping for it. Observe here,

I. The sign by which this was represented to them, and it was a sign that cost the prophet very dear; the more shame for them that when he, by a divine appointment, was at such an expense to affect them with what he had to deliver, yet they were not affected by it

1. He must lose a good wife, that should suddenly be taken from him by death. God gave him notice of it before, that it might be the less surprise to him (Eze 24:16): Behold, I take away from thee the desire of thy eyes with a stroke. Note, (1.) A married state may very well agree with the prophetical office; it is honourable in all, and therefore not sinful in ministers. (2.) Much of the comfort of human life lies in agreeable relations. No doubt Ezekiel found a prudent tender yoke-fellow, that shared with him in his griefs and cares, to be a happy companion in his captivity. (3.) Those in the conjugal relation must be to each other not only a covering of the eyes (Gen 20:16), to restrain wandering looks after others; but a desire of the eyes, to engage pleasing looks on one another. A beloved wife is the desire of the eyes, which find not any object more grateful. (4.) That is least safe which is most dear; we know not how soon the desire of our eyes may be removed from us and may become the sorrow of our hearts, which is a good reason why those that have wives should be as though they had none, and those who rejoice in them as though they rejoiced not, Col 7:29, Col 7:30. Death is a stroke which the most pious, the most useful, the most amiable, are not exempted from. (5.) When the desire of our eyes is taken away with a stroke we must see and own the hand of God in it: I take away the desire of thy eyes. He takes our creature-comforts from us when and how he pleases; he gave them to us, but reserved to himself a property in them; and may he not do what he will with his own? (6.) Under afflictions of this kind it is good for us to remember that we are sons of men; for so God calls the prophet here. If thou art a son of Adam, thy wife is a daughter of Eve, and therefore a dying creature. It is an affliction which the children of men are liable to; and shall the earth be forsaken for us? According to this prediction, he tells us (Eze 24:18), I spoke unto the people in the morning; for God sent his prophets, rising up early and sending them; then he thought, if ever, they would be

disposed to hearken to him. Observe, [1.] Though God had given Ezekiel a certain prospect of this affliction coming upon him, yet it did not take him off from his work, but he resolved to go on in that. [2.] We may the more easily bear an affliction if it find us in the way of our duty; for nothing can hurt us, nothing come amiss to us, while we keep ourselves in the love of God.

2. He must deny himself the satisfaction of mourning for his wife, which would have been both an honour to her and an ease to the oppression of his own spirit. He must not use the natural expressions of sorrow, Eze 24:16. He must not give vent to his passion by weeping, or letting his tears run down, though tears are a tribute due to the dead, and, when the body is sown, it is fit that it should thus be watered. But Ezekiel is not allowed to do this, though he thought he had as much reason to do it as any man and would perhaps be ill thought of by the people if he did it not. Much less might he use the customary formalities of mourners. He must dress himself in his usual attire, must bind his turban on him, here called the tire of his head, must put on his shoes, and not go barefoot, as was usual in such cases; he must not cover his lips, not throw a veil over his face (as mourners were wont to do, Lev 13:45), must not be of a sorrowful countenance, appearing unto men to fast, Mat 6:18. He must not eat the bread of men, nor expect that his neighbours and friends should send him in provisions, as usually they did in such cases, presuming the mourners had no heart to provide meat for themselves; but, if it were sent, he must not eat of it, but go on in his business as at other times. It could not but be greatly against the grain to flesh and blood not to lament the death of one he loved so dearly, but so God commands; and I did in the morning as I was commanded. He appeared in public, in his usual habit, and looked as he used to do, without any signs of mourning. (1.) Here there was something peculiar, and Ezekiel, to make himself a sign to the people, must put a force upon himself and exercise an extraordinary piece of self-denial. Note, Our dispositions must always submit to God's directions, and his command must be obeyed even in that which is most difficult and displeasing to us. (2.) Though mourning for the dead be a duty, yet it must always be kept under the government of religion and right reason, and we must not sorrow as those that have no hope, nor lament the loss of any creature, even the most valuable, and that which we could worst spare, as if we had lost our God, or as if all our happiness were gone with it; and, of this moderation in mourning, ministers, when it is their case, ought to be examples. We must at such a time study to improve the affliction, to accommodate ourselves to it, and to get our acquaintance with the other world increased, by the removal of our dear relations, and learn with holy Job to bless the name of the Lord even when he takes as well as when he gives.

II. The explication and application of this sign. The people enquired the meaning of it (Eze 24:19): Wilt thou not tell us what these things are to us that thou doest so? They knew that Ezekiel was an affectionate husband, that the death of his wife was a great affliction to him, and that he would not appear so unconcerned at it but for some good reason and for instruction to them; and perhaps they were in hopes that it had a favourable signification, and gave them an intimation that God would now comfort them again according to the time he had afflicted them, and make them look pleasant again. Note, When we are enquiring concerning the things of God our enquiry must be, "What are those thing to us? What are we concerned in them? What conviction, what counsel, what comfort, do they speak to us? Wherein do they reach our case?" Ezekiel gives them an answer verbatim-word for word as he had received it from the Lord, who had told him what he must speak to the house of Israel.

1. Let them know that as Ezekiel's wife was taken from him by a stroke so would God take from them all that which was dearest to them, v. 21. If this was done to the green tree, what shall be done to the dry? If a faithful servant of God was thus afflicted only for his trial, shall such a generation of rebels against God go unpunished? By this awakening providence God showed that he was in earnest in his threatenings, and inexorable. We may suppose that Ezekiel prayed that, if it were the will of God, his wife might be spared to him, but God would not hear him; and should he be heard then in his intercessions for this provoking people? No, it is determined: God will take away the desire of your eyes. Note, The removal of the comforts of others should awaken us to think of parting with ours too; for are we better than they? We know not how soon the same cup, or a more bitter one, may be put into our hands, and should therefore weep with those that weep, as being ourselves also in the body. God will take away that which their soul pities, that is, of which they say, What a pity is it that it should be cut off and destroyed! That for which your souls are afraid (so some read it); you shall lose that which you most dread the loss of. And what is that? (1.) That which was their public pride, the temple: "I will profane my sanctuary, by giving that into the enemy's hand, to be plundered and burnt." This was signified by the death of a wife, a dear wife, to teach us that God's sanctuary should be dearer to us, and more the desire of our eyes, than any creature-comfort whatsoever. Christ's church, that is his spouse, should be ours too. Though this people were very corrupt, and had themselves profaned the sanctuary, yet it is called the desire of their eyes. Note, Many that are destitute of the power of godliness are yet very fond of the form of it; and it is just with God to punish them for their hypocrisy by depriving them of that too. The sanctuary is here called the excellency of their strength; they had many strong-holds and places of defence, but the temple excelled them all. It was the pride of their strength; they prided in it as their strength that they were the temple of the Lord, Jer 7:4. Note, The church-privileges that men are proud of are profaned by their sins, and it is just with God to profane them by his judgments. And with these God will take away, (2.) That which was their family-pleasure, which they looked upon with delight: "Your sons and your daughters (which are the dearer to you because they are but few left of many, the rest having perished by famine and pestilence) shall fall by the sword of the Chaldeans." What a dreadful spectacle would it be to see their own children, pieces, pictures, of themselves, whom they had taken such care and pains to bring up, and whom they loved as their own souls, sacrificed to the rage of the merciless conquerors! This, this, was the punishment of sin.

2. Let them know that as Ezekiel wept not for his affliction so neither should they weep for theirs. He must say, You shall do as I have done, Eze 24:22. You shall not mourn nor weep, Eze 24:23. Jeremiah had told them the same, that men shall not lament for the dead nor cut themselves (Jer 16:6); not that there shall be any such merciful circumstance without, or any

such degrees of wisdom and grace within, as shall mitigate and moderate the sorrow; but they shall not mourn, for, (1.) Their grief shall be so great that they shall be quite overwhelmed with it; their passions shall stifle them, and they shall have no power to ease themselves by giving vent to it. (2.) Their calamities shall come so fast upon them, one upon the neck of another, that by long custom they shall be hardened in their sorrows (Job 6:10) and perfectly stupefied, and moped (as we say), with them. (3.) They shall not dare to express their grief, for fear of being deemed disaffected to the conquerors, who would take their lamentations as an affront and disturbance to their triumphs. (4.) They shall not have hearts, nor time, nor money, wherewith to put themselves in mourning, and accommodate themselves with the ceremonies of grief: "You will be so entirely taken up with solid substantial grief that you will have no room for the shadow of it." (5.) Particular mourners shall not need to distinguish themselves by covering their lips, and laying aside their ornaments, and going barefoot; for it is well known that every body is a mourner. (6.) There shall be none of that sense of their affliction and sorrow for it which would help to bring them to repentance, but that only which shall drive them to despair; so it follows: "You shall pine away for your iniquities, with seared consciences and reprobate minds, and you shall mourn, not to God in prayer and confession of sin, but one towards another," murmuring, and fretting, and complaining of God, thus making their burden heavier and their wound more grievous, as impatient people do under their afflictions by mingling their own passions with them.

III. An appeal to the event, for the confirmation of all this (Eze 24:24): "When this comes, as it is foretold, when Jerusalem, which is this day besieged, is quite destroyed and laid waste, which now you cannot believe will ever be, then you shall know that I am the Lord God, who have given you this fair warning of it. Then you will remember that Ezekiel was to you a sign." Note, Those who regard not the threatenings of the word when they are preached will be made to remember them when they are executed. Observe,

1. The great desolation which the siege of Jerusalem should end in (Eze 24:25): In that day, that terrible day, when the city shall be broken up, I will take from them, (1.) That which they depended on-their strength, their walls, their treasures, their fortifications, their men of war; none shall stand them in stead. (2.) That which they boasted of-the joy of their glory, that which they looked upon as most their glory, and which they most rejoiced in, the temple of their God and the palaces of their princes. (3.) That which they delighted in, which was the desire of their eyes, and on which they set their minds. Note, Carnal people set their minds upon that on which they can set their eyes; they look at, and dote upon, the things that are seen; and it is their folly to set their minds upon that which they have no assurance of and which may be taken from them in a moment, Pro 23:5. Their sons and their daughters were all this-their strength, and joy, and glory; and these shall go into captivity.

2. The notice that should be brought to the prophet, not be revelation, as the notice of the siege was brought to him (Eze 24:2), but in an ordinary way (Eze 24:26): "He that escapes in that day

shall, by a special direction of Providence, come to thee, to bring thee intelligence of it," which we find was done, Eze 33:21. The ill-news came slowly, and yet to Ezekiel and his fellow-captives it came too soon.

3. The divine impression which he should be under upon receiving that notice,Eze 24:27. Whereas, from this time to that, Ezekiel was thus far dumb that he prophesied no more against the land of Israel, but against the neighbouring nations, as we shall find in the following chapters, then he shall have orders given him to speak again to the children of his people (Eze 33:2, Eze 33:22); then his mouth shall be opened. He was suspended from prophesying against them in the mean time, because, Jerusalem being besieged, his prophecies could not be sent into the city,-because, when God was speaking so loudly by the rod, there was the less need of speaking by the word,-and because then the accomplishment of his prophecies would be the full confirmation of his mission, and would the more effectually clear the way for him to begin again. It being referred to that issue, that issue must be waited for. Thus Christ forbade his disciples to preach openly that he was Christ till after his resurrection, because that was to be the full proof of it. "But then thou shalt speak with the greater assurance, and the more effectually, either to their conviction or to their confusion." Note, God's prophets are never silenced but for wise and holy ends. And when God gives them the opening of the mouth again (as he will in due time, for even the witnesses that are slain shall arise) it shall appear to have been for his glory that they were for a while silent, that people may the more certainly and fully know that God is the Lord.

Ezekiel Chapter 25

Ezekiel

Judgment began at the house of God, and therefore with them the prophets began, who were the judges; but it must not end there, and therefore they must not. Ezekiel had finished his testimony which related to the destruction of Jerusalem. As to that he was ordered to say no more, but stand upon his watch-tower and wait the issue; and yet he must not be silent; there are divers nations bordering upon the land of Israel, which he must prophesy against, as Isaiah and Jeremiah had done before; and must proclaim God's controversy with them, chiefly for the injuries and indignities which they had done to the people of God in the day of their calamity. In this chapter we have his prophecy, I. Against the Ammonites (Eze 25:1-7). II. Against the Moabites (Eze 25:8-11). III. Against the Edomites (Eze 25:11-14). IV. Against the Philistines (Eze 25:15-17). That which is laid to the charge of each of them is their barbarous and insolent conduct towards God's Israel, for which God threatens to put the same cup of trembling into their hand. God's resenting it thus would be an encouragement to Israel to believe that though he had dealt thus severely with them yet he had not cast them off, but would still own them and plead their cause.

Ezekiel 25:1

Here, I. The prophet is ordered to address himself to the Ammonites, in the name of the Lord Jehovah the God of Israel, who is also the God of the whole earth. But what can Chemosh, the god of the children of Ammon, say, in answer to it? He is bidden to set his face against the Ammonites, for he is God's representative as a prophet, and thus he must signify that God set his face against them, for the face of the Lord is against those that do evil, Psa 34:16. He must speak with boldness and assurance, as one that knew whose errand he went upon, and that he should be borne out in delivering it. He must therefore set his face as a flint, Isa 1:7. He must show his displeasure against these proud enemies of Israel, and face them down, though they were very impudent, and thus must show that, though he had prophesied so much and so long against Israel, yet still he was for Israel, and, while he witnessed against their corruptions, he adhered to and gloried in God's covenant with them. Note, Those are miserable that have the preaching and praying of God's prophets against them, against whom their faces are set.

II. He is directed what to say to them. Ezekiel is now a captive in Babylon, and has been so many years, and knows little of the state of his own nation, much less of the nations that were about it; but God tells him both what they were doing and what he was about to do with them. And thus by the spirit of prophecy he is enabled to speak as pertinently to their case as if he had been among them.

1. He must upbraid the Ammonites with their insolent and barbarous triumphs over the people of Israel in their calamities, Eze 25:3. The Ammonites said, when all went against the Jews, Aha! so would we have it. They were glad to see, (1.) The temple burned, the sanctuary profaned by the victorious Chaldeans. This is put first, to intimate what was the cause of the controversy; they had an enmity to the Jews for the sake of their religion, though it was only some poor remains of the profession of it that were to be found among them. (2.) The nation ruined. They rejoiced when the land of Israel was made desolate, the cities burnt, the country wasted, and both depopulated, and when the house of Judah went into captivity. When they had not power to oppress God's Israel themselves they were pleased to see the Chaldeans oppress them, partly because they envied their wealth and the good land they enjoyed, partly because they feared their growing power, and partly because they hated their religion and the divine oracles they were favoured with. It is repeated again (Eze 25:6): They clapped with their hands, to irritate the rage of the Chaldeans, and to set them on as dogs upon the game; or they clapped their hands in triumph, attended this tragedy with their Plaudite-Give us your applause, thinking it well acted; never was there any thing more diverting or entertaining to them. They stamped with their feet, ready to leap and dance for joy upon this occasion; they not only rejoiced in heart, but they could not forbear showing it, though every one that had any sense of honour and humanity would cry shame upon them for it, especially considering that they rejoiced thus, not for any thing they got by Israel's fall (if so, they would have been the more excusable: most people are for themselves); but this as purely from a principle of malice and enmity: Thou hast rejoiced in heart with all thy despite (which signifies both scorn and hatred) against the land of Israel. Note, The people of God have always had a great deal of ill-will borne them by this wicked world; and their calamities have been their neighbours' entertainments. See to what unnatural instances of malice the enmity that is in the seed of the serpent against the seed of the woman will carry them. The Ammonites, of all people, should not have rejoiced in Jerusalem's ruin, but should rather have trembled, because they themselves had such a narrow escape at the same time; it was but "cross or pile" [the toss of a halfpenny] which should be besieged first, Rabbath or Jerusalem, Eze 21:20. And they had reason to think that the king of Babylon would set upon them next. But thus were their hearts hardened to their ruin, and their insolence against Jerusalem was to them an evident token of perdition, Phi 1:28. It is a very wicked thing to be glad at the calamities of any, especially of God's people, and a sin that God will surely reckon for; such delight has God in showing mercy, and so backward is he to punish, that nothing is more pleasing to him than to be stopped in the ways of his judgments by intercessions, not any thing more provoking than to help forward the affliction when he is but a little displeased, Zac 1:15.

2. He must threaten the Ammonites with utter ruin for this insolence which they were guilty of. God turns away his wrath from Israel against them, as is said, Pro 24:17, Pro 24:18. God is jealous for his people's honour, because his own is so nearly interested in it. And therefore those that touch that shall be made to know that they touch the apple of his eye. He had before predicted the destruction of the Ammonites, Eze 21:28. Had they repented, that would have been revoked; but now it is ratified. (1.) A destroying enemy is brought against them: I will deliver

thee to the men of the east, first to the Chaldeans, who came from the north-east, and whose army, under the command of Nebuchadnezzar, destroyed the country of the Ammonites, about five years after the destruction of Jerusalem (as Josephus relates, Antiq. 10.181), and then to the Arabians, who were properly the children of the east, who, when the Chaldeans had made the country desolate, and quitted it, came and took possession of it for themselves, probably with the consent of the conquerors. Shepherds' tents were their palaces; these they set up in the country of the Ammonites; there they made their dwellings, Eze 25:4. They enjoyed the products of the country: They shall eat thy fruit and drink thy milk; and the milk from the cattle is the fruit of the ground at second-hand. They made use even of the royal city for their cattle (Eze 25:5): I will make Rabbath, that was a nice and splendid city, to be a stable for camels; for its new masters, whose wealth lies all in cattle, will not think they can put the palaces of Rabbath to a better use. Rabbath had been a habitation of brutish men; justly therefore is it now made a stable for camels and the country a couching-lace for flocks, more innocent beasts than those with which it had been before replenished. (2.) God himself acts as an enemy to them (Eze 25:7): I will stretch out my hand upon thee, a hand that will reach far and strike home, which there is no resisting the blow of, for it is a mighty hand, nor bearing the weight of, for it is a heavy hand. God's hand stretched out against the Ammonites will not only deliver them for a spoil to the heathen, so that all their neighbours shall prey upon them, but will cut them off from the people and made them perish out of the countries, so that there shall be no remains of them in that place. Compare with this, Jer 49:1, etc. What can sound more terrible than that resolution (Eze 25:7), I will destroy thee? For the almighty God is able both to save and to destroy, and it is a fearful thing to fall into his hands. Both the threatenings here (Eze 25:5 and Eze 25:7) conclude with this, You shall know that I am the Lord. For, [1.] Thus God will maintain his own honour, and will make it appear that he is the God of Israel, though he suffers them for a time to be captives in Babylon. [2.] Thus he will bring those that were strangers to him into an acquaintance with him, and it will be a blessed effect of their calamities. Better know God and be poor than be rich and ignorant of him.

Ezekiel 25:8

Three more of Israel's ill-natured neighbours are here arraigned, convicted, and condemned to destruction, for contributing to and triumphing in Jerusalem's fall.

I. The Moabites. Seir, which was the seat of the Edomites, is joined with them (Eze 25:8), because they said the same as the Moabites; but they were afterwards reckoned with by themselves, Eze 25:12. Now observe,

1. What was the sin of the Moabites; they said, Behold, the house of Judah is like unto all the heathen. They triumphed, (1.) In the apostasies of Israel, were please to see them forsake their God and worship idols, and hoped that in a while their religion would be quite lost and forgotten and the house of Judah would be like all the heathen, perfect idolaters. When those that profess

religion walk unworthy of their profession they encourage the enemies of religion to hope that it will in time sink, and be run down, and quite abandoned; but let the Moabites know that, though there are those of the house of Judah who have made themselves like the heathen, yet there is a remnant that retain their integrity, the religion of the house of Judah shall recover itself, its peculiarities shall be preserved, it shall not lose itself among the heathen, but distinguish itself from them, till it deliver itself honourably into a better institution. (2.) In the calamities of Israel. They said, "The house of Judah is like all the heathen, in as bad a state as they; their God is no more able to deliver them from this overflowing scourge of these parts of the world than the gods of the heathen are to deliver them. Where are the promises they gloried in and all the wonders which they and their fathers told us of? What the better are they for the covenant of peculiarity, upon which they so much valued themselves? Those that looked with so much scorn upon all the heathen are now set upon a level with them, or rather sunk below them." Note, Those who judge only by outward appearance are ready to conclude that the people of God have lost all their privileges when they have lost their worldly prosperity, which does not follow, for good men, even in affliction, in captivity among the heathen, have graces and comforts within sufficient to distinguish them from all the heathen. Though the event seem one to the righteous and wicked, yet indeed it is vastly different.

2. What should be the punishment of Moab for this sin; because they triumphed in the overthrow of Judah, their country shall be in like manner overthrown with that of the Ammonites, who were guilty of the same sin (Eze 25:9, Eze 25:10): "I will open the side of Moab, will uncover its shoulder, will take away all its defences, that it may become an easy prey to any that will make a prey of it." (1.) See here how it shall be exposed; the frontier-towns, that were its strength and guard, shall be demolished by the Chaldean forces, and laid open. Some of the cities are here named, which are said to be the glory of the country, which they trusted in, and boasted of as impregnable; these shall decay, be deserted, or betrayed, or fall into the enemies' hands, so that Moab shall lie exposed, and whoever will may penetrate into the heart of the country. Note, Those who glory in any other defence and protection than that of the divine power, providence, and promise, will sooner or later see cause to be ashamed of their glorying. (2.) See here to whom it shall be exposed: The men of the east, when they come to take possession of the country of the Ammonites, shall seize that of the Moabites too. God, the Lord of all lands, will give them that land; for the kingdoms of men he gives to whomsoever he will. The Arabians, who are shepherds, and live quietly, plain men dwelling in tents, shall by an overruling Providence be put in possession of the land of the Moabites, who are soldiers, men of war, and cunning hunters, that live turbulently. The Chaldeans shall get it by war, and the Arabians shall enjoy it in peace. Concerning the Ammonites it is said, They shall no more be remembered among the nations (Eze 25:10), for they had been accessory to the murder of Gedaliah, Jer 40:14. But of the Moabites it is said, I will execute judgments upon Moab; they shall feel the weight of God's displeasure, but perhaps not to that degree that the Ammonites shall; however, so far as that they shall know that I am the Lord, that the God of Israel is a God of power, and that his covenant with his people is not broken.

II. The Edomites, the posterity of Esau, between whom and Jacob there had been an old enmity. And here is,

1. The sin of the Edomites, Eze 25:12. They not only triumphed in the ruin of Judah and Jerusalem, as the Moabites and Ammonites had done, but they took advantage from the present distressed state to which the Jews were reduced to do them some real mischiefs, probably made inroads upon their frontiers and plundered their country: Edom has dealt against the house of Judah by taking vengeance. The Edomites had of old been tributaries to the Jews, according to the sentence that the elder should serve the younger. In Jehoram's time they revolted. Amaziah severely chastised them (Kg2 14:7), and for this they took vengeance. Now they would pay off all the old scores, and not only incensed the Babylonians against Jerusalem, crying, Rase it, rase it (Psa 137:7), but cut off those that escaped, as we find in the prophecy of Obadiah, which is wholly directed against Edom, Eze 25:11, Eze 25:12, etc. It is called here revenging a revenge, which intimates that they were not only eager upon it, but very cruel in it, and recompensed to the Jews more than double. "Herein he has greatly offended." Note, It is a great offence to God for us to revenge ourselves upon our brother; for God has said, Vengeance is mine. We are forbidden to revenge or to bear a grudge. Suppose Judah had been hard upon Edom formerly, it was a base thing for the Edomites now, in revenge for it, to smite them secretly. But the Jews had a divine warrant to reign over the Edomites, for that therefore they ought not to have made reprisals; and it was the more disingenuous for them to retain the old enmity when God had particularly commanded his people to forget it. Deu 23:7, Thou shalt not abhor an Edomite.

2. The judgments threatened against them for this sin. God will take them to task for it (Eze 25:13): I will stretch out my hand upon Edom Their country shall be desolate from Teman, which lay in the south part of it; and they shall fall by the sword unto Dedan, which lay north; the desolations of war should go through the nation. (1.) They had taken vengeance, and therefore God will lay his vengeance upon them (Eze 25:14): They shall know my vengeance. Those that will not leave it to God to take vengeance for them may expect that he will take vengeance on them; and those that will not believe and fear his vengeance shall be made to know and feel his vengeance; they shall be dealt with according to God's anger and according to his fury, not according to the weakness of the instruments that are employed in it, but according to the strength of the arm that employs them. (2.) They had taken vengeance on Israel, and God will lay his vengeance on them by the hand of his people Israel. They suffered much by the Chaldeans, which seems to be referred to, Jer 49:8. But besides that there were saviours to come upon Mount Zion, who should judge the mount of Esau (Oba 1:21), and Israel's Redeemer comes with dyed garments from Bozrah (Isa 63:1), this implies a promise that Israel should recover itself again to such a degree as to be in a capacity of curbing the insolence of its neighbours. And we find (1 Macc. 5:3) that Judas Maccabeus fought against the children of Esau in Idumea, gave them a great overthrow, abated their courage, and took their spoil; and Josephus says (Antiq. 13.257), that Hircanus made the Edomites tributaries to Israel. Note, The equity of God's judgments is to be observed when he not only avenges injuries upon those that did them, but by

those against whom they were done.

III. The Philistines. And, 1. Their sin is much the same with that of the Edomites: They have dealt by revenge with the people of Israel, and have taken vengeance with a despiteful heart, not to disturb them only, but to destroy them, for the old hatred (Eze 25:15), the old grudge they bore them, or (as the margin reads it) with perpetual hatred, a hatred that began long since and which they resolved to continue. The anger was implacable: they dealt by revenge, traded in the acts of malice; it was their constant practice, and their heart, their spiteful heart, was upon it. 2. Their punishment likewise is much the same, Eze 25:16. Those that were for destroying God's people shall themselves be cut off and destroyed; and (Eze 25:17) those that were for avenging themselves shall find that God will execute great vengeance upon them. This was fulfilled when that country was wasted by the Chaldean army, not long after the destruction of Jerusalem, which is foretold, Jer 47:1-7. It was strange that these nations, which bordered upon the land of Israel, were not alarmed by the success of the Chaldean army, and made to tremble in the apprehension of their own danger; when their neighbour's house was on fire it was time to look to their own; but their impiety and malice made them forget their politics, till God by his judgments convinced them that the cup was going round, and they were the less safe for being secure.

Ezekiel Chapter 26

The prophet had soon done with those four nations that he set his face against in the foregoing chapters; for they were not at that time very considerable in the world, nor would their fall make any great noise among the nations nor any figure in history. But the city of Tyre is next set to the bar; this, being a place of vast trade, was known all the world over; and therefore here are three whole chapters, this and the two that follow, spent in the prediction of the destruction of Tyre. We have "the burden of Tyre," Isa. 23. It is but just mentioned in Jeremiah, as sharing with the natives in the common calamity, Jer 25:22; Jer 27:3; Jer 47:4. But Ezekiel is ordered to be copious upon that head. In this chapter we have, I. The sin charged upon Tyre, which was triumphing in the destruction of Jerusalem (Eze 26:2). II. The destruction of Tyrus itself foretold. 1. The extremity of this destruction: it shall be utterly ruined (Eze 26:4-6, Eze 26:12-14). 2. The instruments of this destruction, many nations (Eze 26:3), and the king of Babylon by name with his vast victorious army (Eze 26:7-11). 3. The great surprise that this should give to the neighbouring nations, who would all wonder at the fall of so great a city and be alarmed at it (Eze 26:15-21).

Ezekiel 26:1

This prophecy is dated in the eleventh year, which was the year that Jerusalem was taken, and in the first day of the month, but it is not said what month, some think the month in which Jerusalem was taken, which was the fourth month, others the month after; or perhaps it was the first month, and so it was the first day of the year. Observe here,

I. The pleasure with which the Tyrians looked upon the ruins of Jerusalem. Ezekiel was a great way off, in Babylon, but God told him what Tyrus said against Jerusalem (Eze 26:2): "Aha! she is broken, broken to pieces, that was the gates of the people, to whom there was a great resort and where there was a general rendezvous of all nations, some upon one account and some upon another, and I shall get by it; all the wealth, power, and interest, which Jerusalem had, it is hoped, shall be turned to Tyre, and so now that she is laid waste I shall be replenished." We do not find that the Tyrians had such a hatred and enmity to Jerusalem and the sanctuary as the Ammonites and Edomites had, or were so spiteful and mischievous to the Jews. They were men of business, and of large acquaintance and free conversation, and therefore were not so bigoted, and of such a persecuting spirit, as the narrow souls that lived retired and knew not the world. All their care was to get estates, and enlarge their trade, and they looked upon Jerusalem not as an enemy, but as a rival. Hiram, king of Tyre, was a good friend to David and Solomon, and we do not read of any quarrels the Jews had with the Tyrians; but Tyre promised herself that the fall of

Jerusalem would be an advantage to her in respect of trade a commerce, that now she shall have Jerusalem's customers, and the great men from all parts that used to come to Jerusalem for the accomplishing of themselves, and to spend their estates there, will now come to Tyre and spend them there; and whereas many, since the Chaldean army became so formidable in those parts, had retired into Jerusalem, and brought their estates thither for safety, as the Rechabites did, now they will come to Tyre, which, being in a manner surrounded with the sea, will be thought a place of greater strength than Jerusalem, and thus the prosperity of Tyre will rise out of the ruins of Jerusalem. Note, To be secretly pleased with the death or decay of others, when we are likely to get by it, with their fall when we may thrive upon it, is a sin that does most easily beset us, but is not thought to be such a bad thing, and so provoking to God, as really it is. We are apt to say, when those who stand in our light, in our way, are removed, when they break of fall into disgrace, "We shall be replenished now that they are laid waste." But this comes from a selfish covetous principle, and a desire to be placed alone in the midst of the earth, as if we grudged that any should live by us. This comes from a want of that love to our neighbour as to ourselves which the law of God so expressly requires, and from that inordinate love of the world as our happiness which the love of God so expressly forbids. And it is just with God to blast the designs and projects of those who thus contrive to raise themselves upon the ruins of others; and we see they are often disappointed.

II. The displeasure of God against them for it. The providence of God had done well for Tyrus. Tyrus was a pleasant and wealthy city, and might have continued so if she had, as she ought to have done, sympathized with Jerusalem in her calamities and sent her an address of condolence; but when, instead of that, she showed herself pleased with her neighbour's fall, and perhaps sent an address of congratulation to the conquerors, then God says, Behold, I am against thee, O Tyrus! Eze 26:3. And let her not expect to prosper long if God be against her.

1. God will bring formidable enemies upon her: Many nations shall come against thee, an army made up of many nations, or one nation that shall be as strong as many. Those that have God against them may expect all the creatures against them; for what peace can those have with whom God is at war? They shall come pouring in as the waves of the sea, one upon the neck of another, with an irresistible force. The person is named that shall bring this army upon them- Nebuchadnezzar king of Babylon, a king of kings, that had many kings tributaries to him and dependents on him, besides those that were his captives, Song 2:37, 38. He is that head of gold. He shall come with a vast army, horses and chariots, etc., all land-forces. We do not find that he had any naval force, or any thing wherewith he might attack it by sea, which made the attempt the more difficult, as we find Eze 29:18, where it is called a great service which he served against Tyrus. He shall besiege it in form (Eze 26:8), make a fort, and cast a mount, and (Eze 26:9) shall set engines of war against the walls. His troops shall be so numerous as to raise a dust that shall cover the city, Eze 26:10. They shall make a noise that shall even shake the walls; and they shall shout at every attack, as soldiers do when they enter a city that is broken up; the horses shall prance with so much fury and violence that they shall even tread down the streets though so

ever well paved.

2. They shall do terrible execution. (1.) The enemy shall make themselves masters of all their fortifications, shall destroy the walls and break down the towers, Eze 26:4. For what walls are so strongly built as to be a fence against the judgments of God? Her strong garrisons shall go down to the ground, Eze 26:11. And the walls shall be broken down, Eze 26:12. The city held out a long siege, but it was taken at last. (2.) A great deal of blood shall be shed: Her daughters who are in the field, the cities upon the continent, which were subject to Tyre as the mother-city, the inhabitants of them shall be slain by the sword, Eze 26:6. The invaders begin with those that come first in their way. And (Eze 26:11) he shall slay thy people with the sword; not only the soldiers that are found in arms, but the burghers, shall be put to the sword, the king of Babylon being highly incensed against them for holding out so long. (3.) The wealth of the city shall all become a spoil to the conqueror (Eze 26:12): They shall make a prey of the merchandise. It was in hope of the plunder that the city was set upon with so much vigour. See the vanity of riches, that they are kept for the owners to their hurt; they entice and recompense thieves, and not only cease to benefit those who took pains for them and were duly entitled to them, but are made to serve their enemies, who are thereby put into a capacity of doing them so much the more mischief. (4.) The city itself shall be laid in ruins. All the pleasant houses shall be destroyed (Eze 26:12), such as were pleasantly situated, beautified, and furnished, shall become a heap of rubbish. Let none please themselves too much in their pleasant houses, for they know not how soon they may see the desolation of them. Tyre shall be utterly ruined; the enemy shall not only pull down the houses, but shall carry away the stones and the timber, and shall lay them in the midst of the water, not to be recovered, or ever made use of again. Nay (Eze 26:4), I will scrape her dust from her; not only shall the loose dust be blown away, but the very ground it stands upon shall be torn up by the enraged enemy, carried off, and laid in the midst of the water, Eze 26:12. The foundation is in the dust; that dust shall be all taken away, and then the city must fall of course. When Jerusalem was destroyed it was ploughed like a field, Mic 3:12. But the destruction of Tyre is carried further than that; the very soil of it shall be scraped away, and it shall be made like the top of a rock (Eze 26:4, Eze 26:14), pure rock that has no earth to cover it; it shall only be a place for the spreading of nets (Eze 26:5, Eze 26:14); it shall serve fishermen to dry their nets upon and mend them. (5.) There shall be a full period to all its mirth and joy (Eze 26:13): I will cause the noise of thy songs to cease. Tyre had been a joyous city (Isa 23:7).; with her songs she had courted customers to deal with her in a way of trade. But now farewell all her profitable commerce and pleasant conversation; Tyre is no more a place either of business or of sport. Lastly, It shall be built no more (Eze 26:14), not built any more as it had been, with such state and magnificence, nor built any more in the same place, within the sea, nor built any where for a long time; the present inhabitants shall be destroyed or dispersed, so that this Tyre shall be no more. For God has spoken it (Eze 26:5, Eze 26:14); and when what he has said is accomplished they shall know thereby that he is the Lord, and not a man that he should lie nor the son of man that he should repent.

The utter ruin of Tyre is here represented in very strong and lively figures, which are exceedingly affecting.

1. See how high, how great, Tyre had been, how little likely ever to come to this. The remembrance of men's former grandeur and plenty is a great aggravation of their present disgrace and poverty. Tyre was a renowned city (Eze 26:17), famous among the nations, the crowning city (so she is called Isa 23:8), a city that had crowns in her gift, honoured all she smiled upon, crowned herself and all about her. She was inhabited of seas, that is, of those that trade at sea, of those who from all parts came thither by sea, bringing with them the abundance of the seas and the treasures hidden in the sand. She was strong in the sea, easy of access to her friends, but to her enemies inaccessible, fortified by a wall of water, which made her impregnable. So that she with her pomp, and her inhabitants with their pride, caused their terror to be on all that haunted that city, and upon any account frequented it. It was well fortified, and formidable in the eyes of all that acquainted themselves with it. Every body stood in awe of the Tyrians and was afraid of disobliging them. Note, Those who know their strength are too apt to cause terror, to pride themselves in frightening those they are an over-match for.

2. See how low, how little, Tyre is made, Eze 26:19, Eze 26:20. This renowned city is made a desolate city, is no more frequented as it has been; there is no more resort of merchants to it; it is like the cities not inhabited, which are no cities, and having none to keep them in repair, will go to decay of themselves. Tyre shall be like a city overflowed by an inundation of waters, which cover it, and upon which the deep is brought up. As the waves had formerly been its defence, so now they shall be its destruction. She shall be brought down with those that descend into the pit, with the cities of the old world that were under water, and with Sodom and Gomorrah, that lie in the bottom of the Dead Sea. Or, she shall be in the condition of those who have been long buried, of the people of old time, who are old inhabitants of the silent grace, who are quite rotted away under ground and quite forgotten above ground; such shall Tyre be, free among the dead, set in the lower parts of the earth, humbled, mortified, reduced. It shall be like the places desolate of old, as well as like persons dead of old; it shall be like other cities that have formerly been in like manner deserted and destroyed. It shall not be inhabited again; none shall have the courage to attempt the rebuilding of it upon that spot, so that it shall be no more; The Tyrians shall be lost among the nations, so that people will look in vain for Tyre in Tyre: Thou shalt be sought for, and never found again. New persons may build a new city upon a new spot of ground hard by, which they may call Tyre, but Tyre, as it is, shall never be any more. Note, The strongest cities in this world, the best-fortified and best-furnished, are subject to decay, and may in a little time be brought to nothing. In the history of our own island many cities are spoken of as in being when the Romans were here which now our antiquaries scarcely know where to look for, and of which there remains no more evidence than Roman urns and coins digged up there sometimes accidentally. But in the other world we look for a city that shall stand for ever and flourish in

perfection through all the ages of eternity.

3. See what a distress the inhabitants of Tyre are in (Eze 26:15): There is a great slaughter made in the midst of thee, many slain, and great men. It is probable that, when the city was taken, the generality of the inhabitants were put to the sword. Then did the wounded cry, and they cried in vain, to the pitiless conquerors; they cried quarter, but it would not be given them; the wounded are slain without mercy, or, rather, that is the only mercy that is shown them, that the second blow shall rid them out of their pain.

4. See what a consternation all the neighbours are in upon the fall of Tyre. This is elegantly expressed here, to show how astonishing it should be. (1.) the islands shall shake at the sound of thy fall (Eze 26:15), as, when a great merchant breaks, all that he deals with are shocked by it, and begin to look about them; perhaps they had effects in his hands, which they are afraid they shall lose. Or, when they see one fail and become bankrupt of a sudden, in debt a great deal more than he is worth, it makes them afraid for themselves, lest they should do so too. Thus the isles, which thought themselves safe in the embraces of the sea, when they see Tyrus fall, shall tremble and be troubled, saying, "What will become of us?" And it is well if they make this good use of it, to take warning by it not to be secure, but to stand in awe of God and his judgments. The sudden fall of a great tower shakes the ground round about it; thus all the islands in the Mediterranean Sea shall feel themselves sensibly touched by the destruction of Tyre, it being a place they had so much knowledge of, such interests in, and such a constant correspondence with. (2.) The princes of the sea shall be affected with it, who ruled in those islands. Or the rich merchants, who live like princes (Isa 23:8), and the masters of ships, who command like princes, these shall condole the fall of Tyre in a most compassionate and pathetic manner (Eze 26:16): They shall come down from their thrones, as neglecting the business of their thrones and despising the pomp of them. They shall lay away their robes of state, their broidered garments, and shall clothe themselves all over with tremblings, with sackcloth that will make them shiver. Or they shall by their own act and deed make themselves to tremble upon this occasion; they shall sit upon the ground in shame and sorrow; they shall tremble every moment at the thought of what has happened to Tyre, and for fear of what may happen to themselves; for what island is safe if Tyre be not? They shall take up a lamentation for thee, shall have elegies and mournful poems penned upon the fall of Tyre, Eze 26:17. How art thou destroyed! [1.] It shall be a great surprise to them, and they shall be affected with wonder, that a place so well fortified by nature and art, so famed for politics and so full of money, which is the sinews of war, that held out so long and with so much bravery, should be taken at last (Eze 26:21): I make thee a terror. Note, It is just with God to make those a terror to their neighbours, by the suddenness and strangeness of their punishment, who make themselves a terror to their neighbours by the abuse of their power. Tyre had caused her terror (Eze 26:17) and now is made a terrible example. [2.] It shall be a great affliction to them, and they shall be affected with sorrow (Eze 26:17); they shall take up a lamentation for Tyre, as thinking it a thousand pities that such a rich and splendid city should be thus laid in ruins. When Jerusalem, the holy city, was destroyed, there were no such lamentations

for it; it was nothing to those that passed by (Lam 1:12); but when Tyre, the trading city, fell, it was universally bemoaned. Note, Those who have the world in their hearts lament the loss of great men more than the loss of good men. [3.] It shall be a loud alarm to them: They shall tremble in the day of thy fall, because they shall have reason to think that their own turn will be next. If Tyre fall, who can stand? Howl, fir-trees, if such a cedar be shaken. Note, The fall of others should awaken us out of our security. The death or decay of others in the world is a check to us, when we dream that our mountain stands strongly and shall not be moved.

5. See how the irreparable ruin of Tyre is aggravated by the prospect of the restoration of Israel. Thus shall Tyre sink when I shall set glory in the land of the living, Eze 26:20. Note, (1.) The holy land is the land of the living; for none but holy souls are properly living souls. Where living sacrifices are offered to the living God, and where the lively oracles are, there the land of the living is; there David hoped to see the goodness of the Lord, Psa 27:13. That was a type of heaven, which is indeed the land of the living. (2.) Though this land of the living may for a time lie under disgrace, yet God will again set glory in it; the glory that had departed shall return, and the restoration of what they had been deprived of shall be so much more their glory. God will himself be the glory of the lands that are the lands of the living. (3.) It will aggravate the misery of those that have their portion in the land of the dying, of those that are for ever dying, to behold the happiness of those, at the same time, that shall have their everlasting portion in the land of the living. When the rich man was himself in torment he saw Lazarus in the bosom of Abraham, and glory set for him in the land of the living.

Ezekiel Chapter 27

Still we are attending the funeral of Tyre and the lamentations made for the fall of that renowned city. In this chapter we have, I. A large account of the dignity, wealth, and splendour of Tyre, while it was in its strength, the vast trade it drove, and the interest it had among the nations (v. 1-25), which is designed to make its ruin the more lamentable. II. A prediction of its fall and ruin, and the confusion and consternation which all its neighbours shall thereby be put into (Eze 27:26-36). And this is intended to stain the pride of all worldly glory, and, by setting the one over-against the other, to let us see the vanity and uncertainty of the riches, honours, and pleasures of the world, and what little reason we have to place our happiness in them or to be confident of the continuance of them; so that all this is written for our learning.

Ezekiel 27:1

Here, I. The prophet is ordered to take up a lamentation for Tyrus, Eze 27:2. It was yet in the height of its prosperity, and there appeared not the least symptom of its decay; yet the prophet must lament it, because its prosperity is its snare, is the cause of its pride and security, which will make its fall the more grievous. Even those that live at ease are to be lamented if they be not preparing for trouble. He must lament it because its ruin is hastening on apace; it is sure, it is near; and though the prophet foretel it, and justify God in it, yet he must lament it. Note, We ought to mourn for the miseries of other nations, as well as for our own, out of an affection for mankind in general; it is a part of the honour we owe to all men to bewail their calamities, even those which they have brought upon themselves by their own folly.

II. He is directed what to say, and to say it in the name of the Lord Jehovah, a name not unknown in Tyre, and which shall be better known, Eze 26:6.

1. He must upbraid Tyre with her pride: O Tyrus! thou hast said, I am of perfect beauty (Eze 27:3), of universal beauty (so the word is), every way accomplished, and therefore every where admired. Zion, that had the beauty of holiness, is called indeed the perfection of beauty (Psa 50:2); that is the beauty of the Lord. But Tyre, because well-built and well-filled with money and trade, will set up for a perfect beauty. Note, It is the folly of the children of this world to value themselves on the pomp and pleasure they live in, to call themselves beauties for the sake of them, and, if in these they excel others, to think themselves perfect. But God takes notice of the vain conceits men have of themselves in their prosperity when the mind is lifted up with the condition, and often, for the humbling of the spirit, finds a way to bring down the estate. Let none reckon themselves beautified any further than they are sanctified, nor say that they are of

perfect beauty till they come to heaven.

2. He must upbraid Tyre with her prosperity, which was the matter of her pride. In elegies it is usual to insert encomiums of those whose fall we lament; the prophet, accordingly, praises Tyre for all that she had that was praiseworthy. He has nothing to say of her religion, her piety, her charity, her being a refuge to the distressed or using her interest to do good offices among her neighbours; but she lived great, and had a great trade, and all the trading part of mankind made court to her. The prophet must describe her height and magnificence, that God may be the more glorified in her fall, as the God who looks upon every one that is proud and abases him, hides the proud in the dust together, and binds their faces in secret, Job 40:12.

(1.) The city of Tyre was advantageously situated, at the entry of the sea (Eze 27:3), having many commodious harbours each way, not as cities seated on rivers, which the shipping can come but one way to. It stood at the east end of the Mediterranean, very convenient for trade by land into all the Levant parts; so that she became a merchant of the people for many isles. Lying between Greece and Asia, it became the great emporium, or mart-town, the rendezvous of merchants from all parts: They borders are in the heart of the seas, Eze 27:4. It was surrounded with water, which was a great advantage to its trade; it was the darling of the sea, laid in its bosom, in its heart. Note, It is a great convenience, upon many accounts, to live in an island: seas are the most ancient land-mark, not which our fathers have set, but the God of our fathers, and which cannot be removed as other land-marks may, nor so easily got over. The people so situated may the more easily dwell alone, if they please, as not reckoned among the nations, and yet, if they please, may the more easily traffic abroad and keep a correspondence with the nations. We therefore of this island must own that he who determines the bounds of men's habitations has determined well for us.

(2.) It was curiously built, according as the fashion then was; and, being a city on a hill, it made a glorious show and tempted the ships that sailed by into her ports (Eze 27:4): They builders have perfected thy beauty; they have so improved in architecture that nothing appears in the buildings of Tyre that can be found fault with; and yet it wants that perfection of beauty into which the Lord does and will build up his Jerusalem.

(3.) It had its haven replenished with abundance of gallant ships, Isa 33:21. The ship-carpenters did their part, as well as the house-carpenters theirs. The Tyrians are thought to be the first that invented the art of navigation; at least they improved it, and brought it to as great a perfection perhaps as it could be without the loadstone. [1.] They made the boards, or planks, for the hulk of the ship, of fir-trees fetched from Senir, a mount in the land of Israel, joined with Hermon,Sol 4:8. Planks of fir were smooth and light, but not so lasting as our English oak. [2.] They had cedars from Lebanon, another mountain of Israel, for their masts, Eze 27:5. [3.] They had oaks from Bashan (Isa 2:13), to make oars of; for it is probable that their ships were mostly galleys, that go with oars. The people of Israel built few ships for themselves, but they furnished the

Tyrians with timber for shipping. Thus one country uses what another produced, and so they are serviceable one to another, and cannot say to each other, I have no need of thee. [4.] Such magnificence did they affect in building their ships that they made the very benches of ivory, which they fetched from the isles of Chittim, from Italy or Greece, and had workmen from the Ashurites or Assyrians to make them, so rich would they have their state-rooms in their ships to be. [5.] So very prodigal were they that they made their sails of fine linen fetched from Egypt, and that embroidered too, Eze 27:7. Or it may be meant of their flags (which they hoisted to notify what city they belonged to), which were very costly. The word signifies a banner as well as a sail. [6.] They hung those rooms on ship-board with blue and purple, the richest cloths and richest colours they could get from the isles they traded with. For though Tyre was itself famous for purple, which is therefore called the Tyrian dye, yet they must have that which was far-fetched.

(4.) These gallant ships were well-manned, by men of great ingenuity and industry. The pilots and masters of the ships, that had command in their fleets, were of their own city, such as they could put a confidence in (Eze 27:8): Thy wise men, O Tyrus! that were in thee, were thy pilots. But, for common sailors, they had men from other countries; The inhabitants of Arvad and Zidon were thy mariners. These came from cities hear them; Zidon was sister to Tyre, not two leagues off, to the northward; there they bred able seamen, which it is the interest of the maritime powers to support and give all the countenance they can to. They sent to Gebal in Syria for calkers, or strengtheners of the clefts or chinks, to stop them when the ships come home, after long voyages, to be repaired. To do this they had the ancients and wise men (Eze 27:9); for there is more need of wisdom and prudence to repair what has gone to decay than to build anew. In public matters there is occasion for the ancients and wise men to be the repairers of the breaches and the restorers of paths to dwell in. Nay, all the countries they traded with were at their service, and were willing to send men into their pay, to put their youths apprentice in Tyre, or to put them on board their fleets; so that all the ships in the sea with their mariners were ready to occupy thy merchandise. Those that give good wages shall have hands at command.

(5.) Their city was guarded by a military force that was very considerable, Eze 27:10, Eze 27:11. The Tyrians were themselves wholly given to trade; but it was necessary that they should have a good army on foot, and therefore they took those of other states into their pay, such as were fittest for service, though they had them from afar (which perhaps was their policy), from Persia, Lud, and Phut. These bore their arms when there was occasion, and in time of peace hung up the shield and buckler in the armoury, as it were to proclaim peace, and let the world know that they had at present no need of them, but they were ready to be taken down whenever there was occasion for them. Their walls were guarded by the man of Arvad; their towers were garrisoned by the Gammadim, robust men, that had a great deal of strength in their arms; yet the vulgar Latin renders it pygmies, men no longer than one's arm. They hung their shields upon the walls in their magazines or places of arms; or hung them out upon the walls of the city, that none might dare to approach them, seeing how well provided they were with all things necessary for their own defence. "Thus they set forth thy comeliness (Eze 27:10), and made they beauty perfect," Eze 27:11. It contributed as much as any thing to the glory of Tyre that it had those of all the surrounding nations in its service, except the land of Israel (though it lay next them), which furnished them with timber, but we do not find that it furnished them with men; that would have trenched upon the liberty and dignity of the Jewish nation, Ch2 2:17, Ch2 2:18. It was also the glory of Tyre that it had such a militia, so fit for service, and in constant pay, and such an armoury, like that in the tower of David, where hung the shields of mighty men, Sol 4:4. It is observable that there and here the armouries are said to be furnished with shields and helmets, defensive arms, not with swords and spears, offensive, though it is probable that there were such, to intimate that the military force of a people must be intended only for their own protection and not to invade and annoy their neighbours, to secure their own right, not to encroach upon the rights of others.

(6.) They had a vast trade and a correspondence with all parts of the known world. Some nations they dealt with in one commodity and some in another, according as either its products or its manufactures were, and the fruits of nature or art were, with which it was blessed. This is very much enlarged upon here, as that which was the principal glory of Tyre, and which supported all the rest. We do not find any where in scripture so many nations named together as are here; so that this chapter, some think, gives much light to the first account we have of the settlement of the nations after the flood, Gen. 10. The critics have abundance of work here to find out the several places and nations spoken of. Concerning many of them their conjectures are different and they leave us in the dark and at much uncertainty; it is well that it is not material. Modern surveys come short of explaining the ancient geography. And therefore we will not amuse ourselves here with a particular enquiry either concerning the traders or the goods they traded in. We leave it to the critical expositors, and observe that only which is improvable. [1.] We have reason to think that Ezekiel knew little, of his own knowledge, concerning the trade of Tyre. He was a priest, carried away captive far enough from the neighbourhood of Tyre, we may suppose when he was young, and there he had been eleven years. And yet he speaks of the particular merchandises of Tyre as nicely as if he had been comptroller of the custom-house there, by which it appears that he was divinely inspired in what he spoke and wrote. It is God that saith this, Eze 27:3. [2.] This account of the trade of Tyre intimates to us that God's eye is upon men, and that he takes cognizance of what they do when they are employed in their worldly business, not only when they are at church, praying and hearing, but when they are in their markets and fairs, and upon the exchange, buying and selling, which is a good reason why we should in all our dealings keep a conscience void of offence, and have our eye always upon him whose eye is always upon us. [3.] We may here observe the wisdom of God, and his goodness, as the common Father of mankind, in making one country to abound in one commodity and another in another, and all more or less serviceable either to the necessity or to the comfort or ornament of human life. Non omis fert omnia tellus-One land does not supply all the varieties of produce. Providence dispenses its gifts variously, some to each, and all to none, that there may be a mutual commerce among those whom God has made of one blood, though they are made to dwell on all the face of the earth,Act 17:26. Let every nations therefore thank God for the productions of its country; though they be not so rich as those of others, yet there is use for them in the public service of the world. [4.] See what a blessing trade and merchandise are to mankind, especially when followed in the fear of God, and with a regard not only to private advantage, but to a common benefit. The earth is full of God's riches, Psa 104:24. There is a multitude of all kinds of riches in it (as it is here, Eze 27:12), gathered off its surface and dug out of its bowels. The earth is also full of the fruits of men's ingenuity and industry, according as their genius leads them. Now by exchange and barter these are made more extensively useful; thus what can be spared is helped off, and what is wanted is fetched in, in lieu of it, from the most distant countries. Those that are not tradesmen themselves have reason to thank God for tradesmen and merchants, by whom the productions of other countries are brought to our hands, as those of our own are by our husbandmen. [5.] Besides the necessaries that are here traded in, see what abundance of things are here mentioned that only serve to please fancy, and are made valuable only by men's humour and custom; and yet God allows us to use them, and trade in them, and part with those things for them which we can spare that are of an intrinsic worth much beyond them. Here are horns of ivory and ebony (Eze 27:15), that are brought for a present, exposed to sale, and offered in exchange, or (as some think) presented to the city, or the great men of it, to obtain their favour. Here are emeralds, coral, and agate (Eze 27:16), all precious stones, and gold (Eze 27:22), which the world could better be without than iron and common stones. Here are, to please the taste and smell, the chief of all spices (Eze 27:22), cassia and calamus (Eze 27:19), and, for ornament, purple, broidered work, and fine linen (Eze 27:16), precious clothes for chariots (Eze 27:20), blue clothes (which Tyre was famous for), broidered work, and chests of rich apparel, bound with rich cords, and made of cedar, a sweet wood to perfume the garments kept in them, Eze 27:24. Upon the review of this invoice, or bill of parcels, we may justly say, What a great many things are here that we have no need of, and can live very comfortably without! [6.] It is observable that Judah and the land of Israel were merchants in Tyre too; in a way of trade they were allowed to converse with the heathen. But they traded mostly in wheat, a substantial commodity, and necessary, wheat of Minnith and Pannag, two countries in Canaan famous for the best wheat, as some think. The whole land indeed was a land of wheat (Deu 8:8); it had the fat of kidneys of wheat, Deu 32:14. Tyre was maintained by corn fetched from the land of Israel. They traded likewise in honey, and oil, and balm, or rosin; all useful things, and not serving to pride or luxury. And the land which these were the staple commodities of was that which was the glory of all lands, which God reserved for his peculiar people, not those that traded in spices and precious stones; and the Israel of God must reckon themselves well provided for if they have food convenient; for those that are acquainted with the delights of the children of God will not set their hearts on the delights of the sons and daughters of men, or the treasures of kings and provinces. We find indeed that the New Testament Babylon trades in such things as Tyre traded in, Rev 18:12, Rev 18:13. For, notwithstanding its pretensions to sanctity, it is a mere worldly interest. [7.] Though Tyre was a city of great merchandise, and they got abundance by buying and selling, importing commodities from one place and exporting them to another, yet manufacture-trades were not neglected. The wares of their own making, and a multitude of such wares, are here spoken of, Eze 27:16, Eze 27:18. It is the wisdom of a nation to encourage art and industry, and not to bear hard upon the handicraft-tradesmen; for it contributes much to the wealth and honour of a nation to send abroad wares of their own making, which may bring them in the multitude of all riches. [8.] All this made Tyrus very great and very proud: The ships of Tarshish did sing of thee in they market (Eze 27:25); thou wast admired and cried up by all the nations that had dealings with thee; for thou wast replenished in wealth and number of people, wast beautified, and made very glorious, in the midst of the seas. Those that grow very rich are cried up as very glorious; for riches are glorious things in the eyes of carnal people, Gen 31:1.

Ezekiel 27:26

We have seen Tyre flourishing; here we have Tyre falling, and great is the fall of it, so much the greater for its having made such a figure in the world. Note, The most mighty and magnificent kingdoms and states, sooner or later, have their day to come down. They have their period; and, when they are in their zenith, they will begin to decline. But the destruction of Tyre was sudden. Her sun went down at noon. And all her wealth and grandeur, pomp and power, did but aggravate her ruin, and make it the more grievous to herself and astonishing to all about her. Now observe here, 1. How the ruin of Tyrus will be brought about,Eze 27:26. She is as a great ship richly laden, that is split or sunk by the indiscretion of her steersmen: Thy rowers have themselves brought thee into great and dangerous waters; the governors of the city, and those that had the management of their public affairs, by some mismanagement or other involved them in that war with the Chaldeans which was the ruin of their state. By their insolence, by some affront given to the Chaldeans or some attempt made upon them, in confidence of their own ability to contend with them, they provoked Nebuchadnezzar to make a descent upon them, and, by their obstinacy in standing it out to the last, enraged him to such a degree that he determined on the ruin of their state, and, like an east wind, broke them in the midst of the seas. Note, It is ill with a people when those that sit at the stern, instead of putting them into the harbour, run them aground. 2. How great and general the ruin will be. All her wealth shall be buried with her, her riches, her fairs, and her merchandise (Eze 27:27); all that had any dependence upon her, and dealings with her, in trade, in war, in conversation, shall ball with her into the midst of the seas, in the day of her ruin. Note, Those who make creatures their confidence, place their happiness in their interest in them and rest their hopes upon them, will of course fall with them; happy therefore are those that have the God of Jacob for their help, and whose hope is in the Lord their God, who lives for ever. 3. What sad lamentation would be made for the destruction of Tyre. The pilots, her princes and governors, when they see how wretchedly they have mismanaged and how much they have contributed to their own ruin, shall cry out so loud as to make even the suburbs shake (Eze 27:28), such a vexation shall it be to them to reflect upon their own bad conduct. The inferior officers, that were as the mariners of the state, shall be forced to come down from their respective posts (Eze 27:29), and they shall cry out against thee, as having deceived them, in not proving so well able to hold out as they thought thou hadst been; they shall cry bitterly for the common ruin, and their own share in it. They shall use all the most solemn expressions of grief; they shall cast dust on their heads, in indignation against themselves, shall wallow themselves in ashes, as having bid a final farewell to all ease and pleasure; they shall make themselves bald (Eze 27:31), with tearing their hair; and, according to the custom of great mourners, those shall gird themselves with sackcloth who used to wear fine linen, and, instead of merry songs, they shall weep with bitterness of heart. Note, Losses and crosses are very grievous, and hard to be borne, to those that have long been wallowing in pleasure and sleeping in carnal security. 4. How Tyre should be upbraided with her former honour and prosperity (Eze 27:32, Eze 27:33); she that was Tyrus the renowned shall now be called Tyrus the destroyed in the midst of the sea. "What city is like Tyre? Did ever any city come down from such a height of prosperity to such a depth of adversity? Time was when thy wares, those of thy own making and those that passed through thy hands, went forth out of the seas, and were exported to all parts of the world; then thou filledst many people, and didst enrich the kings of the earth and their kingdoms." The Tyrians, though they bore such a sway in trade, were yet, it seems, fair merchants, and let their neighbours not only live, but thrive by them. All that dealt with them were gainers; they did not cheat or oppress the people, but did enrich them with the multitude of their merchandise. "But now those that used to be enriched by thee shall be ruined with thee" (as is usual in trade); "when thou shalt be broken, and all thou hast is seized on, all thy company shall fall too," Eze 27:34. There is an end of Tyre, that made such a noise and bustle in the world. This great blaze goes out in a snuff. 5. How the fall of Tyre should be matter of terror to some and laughter to others, according as they were differently interested and affected. Some shall be sorely afraid, and shall be troubled (Eze 27:35), concluding it will be their own turn to fall next. Others shall hiss at her (Eze 27:36), shall ridicule her pride, and vanity, and bad management, and think her ruin just. She triumphed in Jerusalem's fall, and there are those that will triumph in hers. When God casts his judgments on the sinner men also shall clap their hands at him and shall hiss him out of his place, Job 27:22, Job 27:23. Is this the city which men called the perfection of beauty?

Ezekiel Chapter 28

In this chapter we have, I. A prediction of the fall and ruin of the king of Tyre, who, in the destruction of that city, is particularly set up as a mark for God's arrows (Eze 28:1-10). II. A lamentation for the king of Tyre, when he has thus fallen, though he falls by his own iniquity (Eze 28:11-19). III. A prophecy of the destruction of Zidon, which as in the neighbourhood of Tyre and had a dependence upon it (Eze 28:20-23). IV. A promise of the restoration of the Israel of God, though in the day of their calamity they were insulted over by their neighbours (Eze 28:24-26).

Ezekiel 28:1

We had done with Tyrus in the foregoing chapter, but now the prince of Tyrus is to be singled out from the rest. Here is something to be said to him by himself, a message to him from God, which the prophet must send him, whether he will hear or whether he will forbear.

I. He must tell him of his pride. His people are proud (Eze 27:3) and so is he; and they shall both be made to know that God resists the proud. Let us see, 1. What were the expressions of his pride: His heart was lifted up, Eze 28:2. He had a great conceit of himself, was puffed up with an opinion of his own sufficiency, and looked with disdain upon all about him. Out of the abundance of the pride of his heart he said, I am a god; he did not only say it in his heart, but had the impudence to speak it out. God has said of princes, They are gods (Psa 82:6); but it does not become them to say so of themselves; it is a high affront to him who is God alone, and will not give his glory to another. He thought that the city of Tyre had as necessary a dependence upon him as the world has upon the God that made it, and that he was himself independent as God and unaccountable to any. He thought himself to have as much wisdom and strength as God himself, and as incontestable an authority, and that his prerogatives were as absolute and his word as much a law as the word of God. He challenged divine honours, and expected to be praised and admired as a god, and doubted not to be deified, among other heroes, after his death as a great benefactor to the world. Thus the king of Babylon said, I will be like the Most High (Isa 14:14), not like the Most Holy. "I am the strong God, and therefore will not be contradicted, because I cannot be controlled. I sit in the seat of God; I sit as high as God, my throne equal with his. Divisum imperium cum Jove Caesar habet-Caesar divides dominion with Jove. I sit as safely as God, as safely in the heart of the seas, and as far out of the reach of danger, as he in the height of heaven." He thinks his guards of men of war about his throne as pompous and potent as the hosts of angels that are about the throne of God. He is put in mind of his meanness and mortality, and, since he needs to be told, he shall be told, that self-evident truth, Thou art a man, and not God, a depending creature; thou art flesh, and not spirit, Isa 31:3. Note, Men must be made to know that they are but men, Psa 9:20. The greatest wits, the greatest potentates, the greatest saints, are men, and not gods. Jesus Christ was both God and man. The king of Tyre, though he has such a mighty influence upon all about him, and with the help of his riches bears a mighty sway, though he has tribute and presents brought to his court with as much devotion as if they were sacrifices to his altar, though he is flattered by his courtiers and made a god of by his poets, yet, after all, he is but a man; he knows it; he fears it. But he sets his heart as the heart of God; "Thou hast conceited thyself to be a god, hast compared thyself with God, thinking thyself as wise and strong, and as fit to govern the world, as he." It was the ruin of our first parents, and ours in them, that they would be as gods, Gen 3:5. And still that corrupt nature which inclines men to set up themselves as their own masters, to do what they will, and their own carvers, to have what they will, their own end, to live to themselves, and their own felicity, to enjoy themselves, sets their hearts as the heart of God, invades his prerogatives, and catches at the flowers of his crown- a presumption that cannot go unpunished.

2. We are here told what it was that he was proud of. (1.) His wisdom. It is probable that this prince of Tyre was a man of very good natural parts, a philosopher, and well read in all the parts of learning that were then in vogue, at least a politician, and one that had great dexterity in managing the affairs of state. And then he thought himself wiser than Daniel, Eze 28:3. We found, before, that Daniel, though now but a young man, was celebrated for his prevalency in prayer, Eze 14:14. Here we find he was famous for his prudence in the management of the affairs of this world, a great scholar and statesman, and withal a great saint, and yet not a prince, but a poor captive. It was strange that under such external disadvantages his lustre should shine forth, so that he had become wise to a proverb. When the king of Tyre dreams himself to be a god he says, I am wiser than Daniel. There is no secret that they can hide from thee. Probably he challenged all about him to prove him with questions, as Solomon was proved, and he had unriddled all their enigmas, had solved all their problems, and none of them all could puzzle him. He had perhaps been successful in discovering plots, and diving into the counsels of the neighbouring princes, and therefore thought himself omniscient, and that no thought could be withholden from him; therefore he said, I am a god. Note, Knowledge puffeth up; it is hard to know much and not to know it too well and to be elevated with it. He that was wiser than Daniel was prouder than Lucifer. Those therefore that are knowing must study to be humble and to evidence that they are so. (2.) His wealth. That way his wisdom led him; it is not said that by his wisdom he searched into the arcana either of nature or government, modelled the state better than it was, or made better laws, or advanced the interests of the commonwealth of learning; but his wisdom and understanding were of use to him in traffic. As some of the kings of Judah loved husbandry (Ch2 26:10), so the king of Tyre loved merchandise, and by it he got riches, increased his riches, and filled his treasures with gold and silver, Eze 28:4, Eze 28:5. See what the wisdom of this world is; those are cried up as the wisest men that know how to get money and by right or wrong to raise estates; and yet really this their way is their folly, Psa 49:13. It was the folly of the king of Tyre, [1.] That he attributed the increase of his wealth to himself and not to the

providence of God, forgetting him who gave him power to get wealth, Deu 8:17, Deu 8:18. [2.] That he thought himself a wise man because he was a rich man; whereas a fool may have an estate (Ecc 2:19), yea, and a fool may get an estate, for the world has been often observed to favour such, when bread is not to the wise, Ecc 9:11. [3.] That his heart was lifted up because of his riches, because of the increase of his wealth, which made him so haughty and secure, so insolent and imperious, and which set his heart as the heart of God. The man of sin, when he had a great deal of worldly pomp and power, showed himself as a god, Th2 2:4. Those who are rich in this world have therefore need to charge that upon themselves which the word of God charges upon them, that they be not high-minded, Ti1 6:17.

II. Since pride goes before destruction, and a haughty spirit before a fall, he must bell him of that destruction, of that fall, which was now hastening on as the just punishment of his presumption in setting up himself a rival with God. "Because thou hast pretended to be a god (Eze 28:6), therefore thou shalt not be long a man," Eze 28:7. Observe here,

1. The instruments of his destruction: I will bring strangers upon thee-the Chaldeans, whom we do not find mentioned among the many nations and countries that traded with Tyre, ch. 27. If any of those nations had been brought against it, they would have had some compassion upon it, for old acquaintance-sake; but these strangers will have none. They are people of a strange language, which the king of Tyre himself, wise as he is, perhaps understands not. They are the terrible of the nations; it was an army made up of many nations, and it was at this time the most formidable both for strength and fury. These God has at command, and these he will bring upon the king of Tyre.

2. The extremity of the destruction: They shall draw their swords against the beauty of thy wisdom (Eze 28:7), against all those things which thou gloriest in as thy beauty and the production of thy wisdom. Note, It is just with God that our enemies should make that their prey which we have made our pride. The king of Tyre's palace, his treasury, his city, his navy, his army, these he glories in as his brightness, these, he thinks, made him illustrious and glorious as a god on earth. But all these the victorious enemy shall defile, shall deface, shall deform. He thought them sacred, things that none durst touch; but the conquerors shall seize them as common things, and spoil the brightness of them. But, whatever becomes of what he has, surely his person is sacred. No (Eze 28:8): They shall bring thee down to the pit, to the grave; thou shalt die the death. And, (1.) It shall not be an honourable death, but an ignominious one. He shall be so vilified in his death that he may despair of being deified after his death. He shall die the deaths of those that are slain in the midst of the seas, that have no honour done them at their death, but their dead bodies are immediately thrown overboard, without any ceremony or mark of distinction, to be a feast for the fish. Tyre is likely to be destroyed in the midst of the sea (Eze 27:32) and the prince of Tyre shall fare no better than the people. (2.) It shall not be a happy death, but a miserable one. He shall die the deaths of the uncircumcised (Eze 28:10), of those that are strangers to God and not in covenant with him, and therefore die under his wrath and

curse. It is deaths, a double death, temporal and eternal, the death both of body and soul. He shall die the second death; that is dying miserably indeed. The sentence of death here passed upon the king of Tyre is ratified by a divine authority: I have spoken it, saith the Lord God. And what he has said he will do. None can gainsay it, nor will he unsay it.

3. The effectual disproof that this will be of all his pretensions to deity (Eze 28:9): "When the conqueror sets his sword to thy breast, and thou seest no way of escape, wilt thou then say, I am God? Wilt thou then have such a conceit of thyself as thou now hast? No; thy being overpowered by death, and by the fear of it, will force thee to own that thou art not a god, but a weak, timorous, trembling, dying man. In the hand of him that slays thee (in the hand of God, and of the instruments that he employed) thou shalt be a man, and not God, utterly unable to resist, and help thyself." I have said, You are gods; but you shall die like men, Psa 82:6, Psa 82:7. Note, Those who pretend to be rivals with God shall be forced one way or other to let fall their claims. Death at furthest, when we come into his hand, will make us know that we are men.

Ezekiel 28:11

As after the prediction of the ruin of Tyre (ch. 26) followed a pathetic lamentation for it (ch. 27), so after the ruin of the king of Tyre is foretold it is bewailed.

I. This is commonly understood of the prince who then reigned over Tyre, spoken to, Eze 28:2. His name was Ethbaal, or Ithobalus, as Diodorus Siculus calls him that was king of Tyre when Nebuchadnezzar destroyed it. He was, it seems, upon all external accounts an accomplished man, very great and famous; but his iniquity was his ruin. Many expositors have suggested that besides the literal sense of this lamentation there is an allegory in it, and that it is an allusion to the fall of the angels that sinned, who undid themselves by their pride. And (as is usual in texts that have a mystical meaning) some passages here refer primarily to the king of Tyre, as that of his merchandises, others to the angels, as that of being in the holy mountain of God. But, if there be any thing mystical in it (as perhaps there may), I shall rather refer it to the fall of Adam, which seems to be glanced at, Eze 28:13. Thou hast been in Eden the garden of God, and that in the day thou wast created.

II. Some think that by the king of Tyre is meant the whole royal family, this including also the foregoing kings, and looking as far back as Hiram, king of Tyre. The then governor is called prince (Eze 28:2); but he that is here lamented is called king. The court of Tyre with its kings had for many ages been famous; but sin ruins it. Now we may observe two things here:-

1. What was the renown of the king of Tyre. He is here spoken of as having lived in great splendour, Eze 28:12-15. He as a man, but it is here owned that he was a very considerable man and one that made a mighty figure in his day. (1.) He far exceeded other men. Hiram and other kings of Tyre had done so in their time; and the reigning king perhaps had not come short of any

ccliii

of them: Thou sealest up the sum full of wisdom and perfect in beauty. But the powers of human nature and the prosperity of human life seemed in him to be at the highest pitch. He was looked upon to be as wise as the reason of men could make him, and as happy as the wealth of this world and the enjoyment of it could make him; in him you might see the utmost that both could do; and therefore seal up the sum, for nothing can be added; he is a complete man, perfect in suo genere-in his kind. (2.) He seemed to be as wise and happy as Adam in innocency (Eze 28:13): "Thou hast been in Eden, even in the garden of God; thou hast lived as it were in paradise all thy days, hast had a full enjoyment of every thing that is good for food or pleasant to the eyes, and an uncontroverted dominion over all about thee, as Adam had." One instance of the magnificence of the king of Tyre is, that he outdid all others princes in jewels, which those have the greatest plenty of that trade most abroad, as he did: Every precious stone was his covering. There is a great variety of precious stones; but he had of every sort and in such plenty that besides what were treasured up in his cabinet, and were the ornaments of his crown, he had his clothes trimmed with them; they were his covering. Nay (Eze 28:14), he walked up and down in the midst of the stones of fire, that is, these precious stones, which glittered and sparkled like fire. His rooms were in a manner set round with jewels, so that he walked in the midst of them, and then fancied himself as glorious as if, like God, he had been surrounded by so many angels, who are compared to a flame of fire. And, if he be such an admirer of precious stones as to think them as bright as angels, no wonder that he is such an admirer of himself as to think himself as great as God. Nine several sorts of previous stones are here named, which were all in the high priest's ephod. Perhaps they are particularly named because he, in his pride, used to speak particularly of them, and tell those about him, with a great deal of foolish pleasure, "This is such a precious stone, of such a value, and so and so are its virtues." Thus is he upbraided with his vanity. Gold is mentioned last, as far inferior in value to those precious stones; and he used to speak of it accordingly. Another thing that made him think his palace a paradise was the curious music he had, the tabrets and pipes, hand-instruments and wind-instruments. The workmanship of these was extraordinary, and they were prepared for him on purpose; prepared in thee, the pronoun is feminine-in thee, O Tyre! or it denotes that the king was effeminate in doting on such things. They were prepared in the day he was created, that is, either born, or created king; they were made on purpose to celebrate the joys either of his birthday or of his coronation-day. These he prided himself much in, and would have all that came to see his palace take notice of them. (3.) He looked like an incarnate angel (Eze 28:14): Thou art the anointed cherub that covers or protects; that is, he looked upon himself as a guardian angel to his people, so bright, so strong, so faithful, appointed to this office and qualified for it. Anointed kings should be to their subjects as anointed cherubim, that cover them with the wings of their power; and, when they are such, God will own them. Their advancement was from him: I have set thee so. Some think, because mention was made of Eden, that it refers to the cherub set on the east of Eden to cover it, Gen 3:24. He thought himself as able to guard his city from all invaders as that angel was for his charge. Or it may refer to the cherubim in the most holy place, whose wings covered the ark; he thought himself as bright as one of them. (4.) He appeared in as much splendour as the high priest when he was clothed with his garments for glory and beauty: "Thou wast upon the holy mountain of God, as president of the temple built on that holy mountain; thou didst look as great, and with as much majesty and authority, as ever the high priest did when he walked in the temple, which was garnished with precious stones (Ch2 3:6), and had his habit on, which had precious stones both in the breast and on the shoulders; in that he seemed to walk in the midst of the stones of fire." Thus glorious is the king of Tyre; at least he thinks himself so.

2. Let us now see what was the ruin of the king of Tyre, what it was that stained his glory and laid all this honour in the dust (Eze 28:15): "Thou wast perfect in thy ways; thou didst prosper in all thy affairs and every thing went well with thee; thou hadst not only a clear, but a bright reputation, from the day thou wast created, the day of thy accession to the throne, till iniquity was found in thee; and that spoiled all." This may perhaps allude to the deplorable case of the angels that fell, and of our first parents, both of whom were perfect in their ways till iniquity was found in them. And when iniquity was once found in him it increased; he grew worse and worse, as appears (Eze 28:18): "Thou hast defiled thy sanctuaries; thou hast lost the benefit of all that which thou thoughtest sacred, and in which, as in a sanctuary, thou thoughtest to take refuge; these thou hast defiled, and so exposed thyself by the multitude of thy iniquities." Now observe,

(1.) What the iniquity was that was the ruin of the king of Tyre. [1.] The iniquity of his traffic (so it is called, Eze 28:18), both his and his people's, for their sin is charged upon him, because he connived at it and set them a bad example (Eze 28:16):By the multitude of thy merchandise they have filled the midst of thee with violence, and thus thou hast sinned. The king had so much to do with his merchandise, and was so wholly intent upon the gains of that, that he took no care to do justice, to give redress to those that suffered wrong and to protect them from violence; nay, in the multiplicity of business, wrong was done to many by oversight; and in his dealings he made use of his power to invade the rights of those he dealt with. Note, Those that have much to do in the world are in great danger of doing much amiss; and it is hard to deal with many without violence to some. Trades are called mysteries; but too many make them mysteries of iniquity. [2.] His pride and vain-glory (Eze 28:17): "Thy heart was lifted up because of thy beauty; thou wast in love with thyself, and thy own shadow. And thus thou hast corrupted thy wisdom by reason of the brightness, the pomp and splendour, wherein thou livedst." He gazed so much upon this that it dazzled his eyes and prevented him from seeing his way. He appeared so puffed up with his greatness that it bereaved him both of his wisdom and of the reputation of it. He really became a fool in glorying. Those make a bad bargain for themselves that part with their wisdom for the gratifying of their gaiety, and, to please a vain humour, lose a real excellency.

(2.) What the ruin was that this iniquity brought him to. [1.] He was thrown out of his dignity and dislodged from his palace, which he took to be his paradise and temple (Eze 28:16): I will cast thee as profane out of the mountain of God. His kingly power was high as a mountain, setting him above others; it was a mountain of God, for the powers that be are ordained of God, and have something in them that is sacred; but, having abused his power, he is reckoned profane, and is therefore deposed and expelled. He disgraces the crown he wears, and so has forfeited it, and shall be destroyed from the midst of the stones of fire, the precious stones with which his palace was garnished, as the temple was; and they shall be no protection to him. [2.] He was exposed to contempt and disgrace, and trampled upon by his neighbours: "I will cast thee to the ground (Eze 28:17), will cast thee among the pavement-stones, from the midst of the precious stones, and will lay thee a rueful spectacle before kings, that they may behold thee and take warning by thee not to be proud and oppressive." [3.] He was quite consumed, his city and he in it: I will bring forth a fire from the midst of thee. The conquerors, when they have plundered the city, will kindle a fire in the heart of it, which shall lay it, and the palace particularly, in ashes. Or it may be taken more generally for the fire of God's judgments, which shall devour both prince and people, and bring all the glory of both to ashes upon the earth; and this fire shall be brought forth from the midst of thee. All God's judgments upon sinners take rise from themselves; they are devoured by a fire of their own kindling. [4.] He was hereby made a terrible example of divine vengeance. Thus he is reduced in the sight of all those that behold him (Eze 28:18): Those that know him shall be astonished at him, and shall wonder how one that stood so high could be brought so low. The king of Tyre's palace, like the temple at Jerusalem, when it is destroyed shall be an astonishment and a hissing, Ch2 7:20, Ch2 7:21. So fell the king of Tyre.

Ezekiel 28:20

God's glory is his great end, both in all the good and in all the evil which proceed out of the mouth of the Most High; so we find in these verses. 1. God will be glorified in the destruction of Zidon, a city that lay near to Tyre, was more ancient, but not so considerable, had a dependence upon it and stood and fell with it. God says here, I am against thee, O Zidon! and I will be glorified in the midst of thee, Eze 28:22. And again, "Those that would not know be gentler methods shall be made to know that I am the Lord, and I alone, and that I am a just and jealous God, when I shall have executed judgments in her, destroying judgments, when I shall have done execution according to justice and according to the sentence passed, and so shall be sanctified in her." The Zidonians, it should seem, were more addicted to idolatry than the Tyrians were, who, being men of business and large conversation, were less under the power of bigotry and superstition. The Zidonians were noted for the worship of Ashtaroth; Solomon introduced it, Kg1 11:5. Jezebel was daughter to the king of Zidon, who brought the worship of Baal into Israel (Kg1 16:31); so that God had been much dishonoured by the Zidonians. Now, says he, I will be glorified, I will be sanctified. The Zidonians were borderers upon the land of Israel, where God was known, and where they might have got the knowledge of him and have learned to glorify him; but, instead of that, they seduced Israel to the worship of their idols. Note, When God is sanctified he is glorified, for his holiness is his glory; and those whom he is not sanctified and glorified by he will be sanctified and glorified upon, by executing judgments upon them, which declare him a just avenger of his own and his people's injured honour. The judgments that shall be executed upon Zidon are war and pestilence, two wasting depopulating judgments, Eze 28:23. They are God's messengers, which he sends on his errands, and they shall accomplish that for which he sends them. Pestilence and blood shall be sent into her streets; there the dead bodies of those shall lie who perished, some by the plague, occasioned perhaps through ill diet when the city was besieged, and some by the sword of the enemy, most likely the Chaldean armies, when the city was taken, and all were put to the sword. Thus the wounded shall be judged; when they are dying of their wounds they shall judge themselves, and others shall say, They justly fall. Or, as some read it, They shall be punished by the sword, that sword which has commission to destroy on every side. It is God that judges, and he will overcome. Nor is it Tyre and Zidon only on which God would execute judgments, but on all those that despised his people Israel, and triumphed in their calamities; for this was now God's controversy with the nations that were round about them, Eze 28:26. Note, When God's people are under his correcting hand for their faults he takes care, as he did concerning malefactors that were scourged, that they shall not seem vile to those that are about them, and therefore takes it ill of those who despise them and so help forward the affliction when he is but a little displeased, Zac 1:15. God regards them even in their low estate; and therefore let not men despise them. 2. God will be glorified in the restoration of his people to their former safety and prosperity. God had been dishonoured by the sins of his people, and their sufferings too had given occasion to the enemy to blaspheme (Isa 52:5); but God will now both cure them of their sins and ease them of their troubles, and so will be sanctified in them in the sight of the heathen, will recover the honour of his holiness, to the satisfaction of all the world, Eze 28:25. For, (1.) They shall return to the possession of their own land again: I will gather the house of Israel out of their dispersions, in answer to that prayer (Psa 106:27), Save us, O Lord our God! and gather us from among the heathen; and in pursuance of that promise (Deu 30:4), Thence will the Lord thy God gather thee. Being gathered, they shall be brought in a body, to dwell in the land that I have given to my servant Jacob. God had an eye to the ancient grant, in bringing them back, for that remained in force, and the discontinuance of the possession was not a defeasance of the right. He that gave it will again give it. (2.) They shall enjoy great tranquillity there. When those that have been vexatious to them are taken off they shall live in quietness; there shall be no more a pricking brier nor a grieving thorn, Eze 28:24. They shall have a happy settlement, for they shall build houses, and plant vineyards; and they shall enjoy a happy security and serenity there; they shall dwell safely, shall dwell with confidence, and there shall be none to disquiet them or make them afraid, Eze 28:26. This never had full accomplishment in the body of that people, for after their return out of captivity they were ever and anon molested by some bad neighbour or other. Nor has the gospel-church been ever quite free from pricking briers and grieving thorns; yet sometimes the church has rest, and believers always dwell safely under the divine protection and may be quiet from the fear of evil. But the full accomplishment of this promise is reserved for the heavenly Canaan, when all the saints shall be gathered together, and every thing that offends shall be removed, and all griefs and fears for ever banished.

Ezekiel Chapter 29

Three chapters we had concerning Tyre and its king; next follow four chapters concerning Egypt and its king. This is the first of them. Egypt had formerly been a house of bondage to God's people; of late they had had but too friendly a correspondence with it, and had depended too much upon it; and therefore, whether the prediction reached Egypt or no, it would be of use to Israel, to take them off from their confidence in their alliance with it. The prophecies against Egypt, which are all laid together in these four chapters, were of five several dates; the first in the 10th year of the captivity (Eze 29:1), the second in the 27th (Eze 29:17), the third in the 11th year and the first month (Eze 30:20), the fourth in the 11th year and the third month (Eze 31:1), the fifth in the 12th year (Eze 32:1), and another in the same year (Eze 29:17). In this chapter we have, I. The destruction of Pharaoh foretold, for his dealing deceitfully with Israel (Eze 29:1-7). II. The desolation of the land of Egypt foretold (Eze 29:8-12). III. A promise of the restoration thereof, in part, after forty years (Eze 29:13-16). IV. The possession that should be given to Nebuchadnezzar of the land of Egypt (Eze 29:17-20). V. A promise of mercy to Israel (Eze 29:21).

Ezekiel 29:1

Here is, I. The date of this prophecy against Egypt. It was in the tenth year of the captivity, and yet it is placed after the prophecy against Tyre, which was delivered in the eleventh year, because, in the accomplishment of the prophecies, the destruction of Tyre happened before the destruction of Egypt, and Nebuchadnezzar's gaining Egypt was the reward of his service against Tyre; and therefore the prophecy against Tyre is put first, that we may the better observe that. But particular notice must be taken of this, that the first prophecy against Egypt was just at the time when the king of Egypt was coming to relieve Jerusalem and raise the siege (Jer 37:5), but did not answer the expectations of the Jews from them. Note, It is good to foresee the failing of all our creature-confidences, then when we are most in temptation to depend upon them, that we may cease from man.

II. The scope of this prophecy. It is directed against Pharaoh king of Egypt, and against all Egypt, Eze 29:2. The prophecy against Tyre began with the people, and then proceeded against the prince. But this begins with the prince, because it began to have its accomplishment in the insurrections and rebellions of the people against the prince, not long after this.

III. The prophecy itself. Pharaoh Hophrah (for so was the reigning Pharaoh surnamed) is here represented by a great dragon, or crocodile, that lies in the midst of his rivers, as Leviathan in the waters, to play therein, Eze 29:3. Nilus, the river of Egypt, was famed for crocodiles. And what is the king of Egypt, in God's account, but a great dragon, venomous and mischievous? Therefore says God, I am against thee. I am above thee; so it may be read. How high soever the princes and potentates of the earth are, there is a higher than they (Ecc 5:8), a God above them, that can control them, and, if they be tyrannical and oppressive, a God against them, that will be free to reckon with them. Observe here,

1. The pride and security of Pharaoh. He lies in the midst of his rivers, rolls himself with a great deal of satisfaction in his wealth and pleasures; and he says, My river is my own. He boasts that he is an absolute prince (his subjects are his vassals; Joseph bought them long ago, Gen 47:23),-that he is a sole prince, and has neither partner in the government nor competitor for it,-that he is out of debt (what he has is his own, and none of his neighbours have any demands upon him),-that he is independent, neither tributary nor accountable to any. Note, Worldly carnal minds please themselves with, and pride themselves in, their property, forgetting that whatever we have we have only the use of it, the property is in God. We ourselves are not our own, but his. Our tongues are not our own, Psa 12:4. Our river is not our own, for its springs are in God. The most potent prince cannot call what he has his own, for, though it be so against all the world, it is not so against God. But Pharaoh's reason for his pretensions is yet more absurd: My river is my own, for I have made it for myself. Here he usurps two of the divine prerogatives, to be the author and the end of his own being and felicity. He only that is the great Creator can say of this world, and of every thing in it, I have made it for myself. He calls his river his own because he looks not unto the Maker thereof, nor has respect unto him that fashioned it long ago, Isa 22:11. What we have we have received from God and must use for God, so that we cannot say, We made it, much less, We made it for ourselves; and why then do we boast? Note, Self is the great idol that all the world worships, in contempt of God and his sovereignty.

2. The course God will take with this proud man, to humble him. He is a great dragon in the waters, and God will accordingly deal with him, Eze 29:4, Eze 29:5. (1.) He will draw him out of his rivers, for he has a hook and a cord for this leviathan, with which he can manage him, though none on earth can (Job 41:1): "I will bring thee up out of the midst of thy rivers, will cast thee out of thy palace, out of thy kingdom, out of all those things in which thou takest such a complacency and placest such a confidence." Herodotus related of this Pharaoh, who was now king of Egypt, that he had reigned in great prosperity for twenty-five years, and was so elevated with his successes that he said that God himself would not cast him out of his kingdom; but he shall soon be convinced of his mistake, and what he depended on shall be no defence. God can force men out of that in which they are most secure and easy. (2.) All his fish shall be drawn out with him, his servants, his soldiers, and all that had a dependence on him, as he thought, but really such as he had dependence upon. These shall stick to his scales, adhere to their king, resolving to live and die with him. But, (3.) The king and his army, the dragon and all the fish that stick to his scales, shall perish together, as fish cast upon dry ground, and shall be meat to the beasts and fowls, Eze 29:5. Now this is supposed to have had its accomplishment soon after,

when this Pharaoh, in defence of Aricius king of Libya, who had been expelled his kingdom by the Cyrenians, levied a great army, and went out against the Cyrenians, to re-establish his friend, but was defeated in battle, and all his forces were put to flight, which gave such disgust to his kingdom that they rose in rebellion against him. Thus was he left thrown into the wilderness, he and all the fish of the river with him. Thus issue men's pride, and presumption, and carnal security. Thus men justly lose what they might call their own, under God, when they call it their own against him.

3. The ground of the controversy God has with the Egyptians; it is because they have cheated his people. They encouraged them to expect relief and assistance from them when they were in distress, but failed them (Eze 29:6, Eze 29:7): Because they have been a staff of reed to the house of Israel. They pretended to be a staff for them to lean upon, but, when any stress was laid upon them, they were either weak and could not or treacherous and would not do that for them which was expected. They broke under them, to their great disappointment and amazement, so that they rent their shoulder and made all their loins to be at a stand. The king of Egypt, it is probable, had encouraged Zedekiah to break his league with the king of Babylon, with a promise that he would stand by him, which, when he failed to do, to any purpose, it could not but put them into a great consternation. God had told them, long since, that the Egyptians were broken reeds, Isa 30:6, Isa 30:7. Rabshakeh had told them so, Isa 36:6. And now they found it so. It was indeed the folly of Israel to trust them, and they were well enough served when they were deceived in them. God was righteous in suffering them to be so. But that is no excuse at all for the Egyptians' falsehood and treachery, nor shall it secure them from the judgments of that God who is and will be the avenger of all such wrongs. It is a great sin, and very provoking to God, as well as unjust, ungrateful, and very dishonourable and unkind, to put a cheat upon those that put a confidence in us.

Ezekiel 29:8

This explains the foregoing prediction, which was figurative, and looks something further. Here is a prophecy,

I. Of the ruin of Egypt. The threatening of this is very full and particular; and the sin for which this ruin shall be brought upon them is their pride, Eze 29:9. They said, The river is mine and I have made it; therefore their land shall spue them out. 1. God is against them, both against the king and against the people, against thee and against thy rivers. Waters signify people and multitudes, Rev 17:15. 2. Multitudes of them shall be cut off by the sword of war, a sword which God will bring upon them to destroy both man and beast, the sword of civil war. 3. The country shall be depopulated. The land of Egypt shall be desolate and waste (Eze 29:9), the country not cultivated, the cities not inhabited. The wealth of both was their pride, and that God will take away. It shall be utterly waste (wastes of waste, so the margin reads it), and desolate (Eze 29:10); neither men nor beasts shall pass through it, nor shall it be inhabited (Eze 29:11); it shall be desolate in the midst of the countries that are so, Eze 29:12. This was the effect not so much of those wars spoken of before, which were made by them, but of the war which the king of Babylon made upon them. It shall be desolate from one end of the land to the other, from the tower of Syene even unto the border of Ethiopia. The sin of pride is enough to ruin a whole nation. 4. The people shall be dispersed and scattered among the nations (Eze 29:12), so that those who thought the balance of power was in their hand should now become a contemptible people. Such a fall does a haughty spirit go before.

II. Of the restoration of Egypt after awhile, Eze 29:13. Egypt shall lie desolate forty years (Eze 29:12) and then I will bring again the captivity of Egypt, Eze 29:14. Some date the forty years from Nebuchadnezzar's destroying Egypt, others from the desolation of Egypt some time before; however, they end about the first year of Cyrus, when the seventy years' captivity of Judah ended, or soon after. Then this prediction was accomplished, 1. That God will gather the Egyptians out of all the countries into which they were dispersed, and make them to return to the land of their habitation, and give them a settlement there again, Eze 29:14. Note, Though God will find out a way to humble the proud, yet he will not contend for ever, no, not with them in this world. 2. That yet they shall not make a figure again as they have done. Egypt shall be a kingdom again, but it shall be the basest of the kingdoms (Eze 29:15); it shall have but little wealth and power, and shall not extend its conquests as formerly; it shall be the tail of the nations, and not the head. It is a mercy that it shall become a kingdom again, but, to humble it, it shall be a despicable kingdom; it shall be a long time before it recover any thing like its ancient lustre. For two reasons it shall be thus mortified:-(1.) That it may not domineer over its neighbours, that it may not exalt itself above the nations, nor rule over the nations, as it has done, but that it may know what it is to be low and despised. Note, Those who abuse their power will justly be stripped of it; and God, as King of nations, will find out a way to maintain the injured rights and liberties, not only of his own, but of other nations. (2.) That it may not deceive the people of God (Eze 29:16): It shall no more be the confidence of the house of Israel; they shall no more be in temptation to trust in it as they have done, which is a sin that brings their iniquity to remembrance, that is, provokes God to punish them not for that only, but for all their other sins. Or it puts them in mind of their idolatries to return to them, when they look to the idolaters, to repose a confidence in them. Note, The creatures we confide in are often therefore ruined, because there is no other way effectually to cure us of our confidence in them. Rather than Israel shall be ensnared again, the whole land of Egypt shall be laid waste. He that once gave Egypt for their ransom (Isa 43:3) will now give Egypt for their cure; and it shall be destroyed rather than Israel shall not in this particular be reformed. God, not only in justice, but in wisdom and goodness to us, breaks those creature-stays which we lean too much upon, and makes them to be no more, that they may be no more our confidence.

Ezekiel 29:17

The date of this prophecy is observable; it was in the twenty-seventh year of Ezekiel's captivity, sixteen years after the prophecy in the former part of the chapter, and almost as long after those which follow in the next chapters; but it comes in here for the explication of all that was said against Egypt. After the destruction of Jerusalem Nebuchadnezzar spent two or three campaigns in the conquest of the Ammonites and Moabites and making himself master of their countries. Then he spent thirteen years in the siege of Tyre. During all that time the Egyptians were embroiled in war with the Cyrenians and one with another, by which they were very much weakened and impoverished; and just at the end of the siege of Tyre God delivers this prophecy to Ezekiel, to signify to him that that utter destruction of Egypt which he had foretold fifteen or sixteen years before, which had been but in part accomplished hitherto, should now be completed by Nebuchadnezzar. The prophecy which begins here, it should seem, is continued to the twentieth verse of the next chapter. And Dr. Lightfoot observes that it is the last prophecy we have of this prophet, and should have been last in the book, but is laid here, that all the prophecies against Egypt might come together. The particular destruction of Pharaoh-Hophrah, foretold in the former part of this chapter, was likewise foretold Jer 44:30. This general devastation of Egypt by Nebuchadnezzar was foretold Jer 43:10. Observe,

I. What success God would give to Nebuchadnezzar and his forces against Egypt. God gave him that land, that he might take the spoil and prey of it, Eze 29:19, Eze 29:20. It was a cheap and easy prey. He subdued it with very little difficulty; the blood and treasure expended upon the conquest of it were inconsiderable. But it was a rich prey, and he carried off a great deal from it that was of value. Their having been divided among themselves, no doubt, gave a common enemy great advantage against them, who, when they had been so long preying upon one another, soon made a prey of them all. En! quo discordia cives perduxit miseros-What wretchedness does civil discord bring! Jeremiah foretold that Nebuchadnezzar should array himself with the land of Egypt as a shepherd puts on his coat, which intimates what a rich and cheap prey it should be.

II. Upon what considerations God would give Nebuchadnezzar this success against Egypt; it was to be a recompence to him for the hard service with which he had caused his army to serve against Tyre, Eze 29:18, Eze 29:20. 1. The taking of Tyre was a tedious piece of work; it cost Nebuchadnezzar abundance of blood and treasure. It held out thirteen years; all that time the Chaldean army was hard at it, to make themselves masters of it. A large current of the sea, between Tyre and the continent, was filled up with earth, and many other difficulties which were thought insuperable they had to struggle with; but so great a prince, having begun such an undertaking, thought himself bound in honour to push it on, whatever it cost him. How many thousand lives have been sacrificed to such points of honour as this as! In prosecuting this siege every head was made bald, and every shoulder peeled, with carrying burdens and labouring in the water when they had a strong tide and a strong town to contend with. Egypt, a large kingdom, being divided within itself, is easily conquered; Tyre, a single city, being unanimous, is with difficulty subdued. Those that have much to do in the world find some affairs go on a great deal more readily and easily than others. But, 2. In this service God own that they wrought for him,Eze 29:20. He set them at work, for the humbling of a proud city and its king, though they meant not so, neither did their heart think so, who were employed in it. Note, Even great men and bad men are tools that God makes use of, and are working for him even when they are pursuing their own covetous and ambitious designs; so wonderfully does God overrule all to his own glory. Yet, 3. For this service he had no wages nor his army. He was at a vast expense to take Tyre; and when he had it, though it was a very rich city, and he promised himself good plunder for his army from it, he was disappointed; the Tyrians sent away by ship their best effects, and threw the rest into the sea, so that they had nothing but bare walls. Thus are the children of this world ordinarily frustrated in their highest expectations from it. Therefore, 4. He shall have the spoil of Egypt to recompense him for his service against Tyre. Note, God will be behind-hand with none for any service they do for him, but, one way or other, will recompense them for it; none shall kindle a fire on his altar for nought. The service done for him by worldly men, with worldly designs, shall be recompensed with a mere worldly reward, which his faithful servants, that have a sincere regard to his will and glory, would not be put off with. This accounts for the prosperity of wicked men in this world; God is in it paying them for some service or other, in which he has made use of them. Verily they have their reward. Let none envy it them. The conquest of Egypt is spoken of as Nebuchadnezzar's full reward, for that completed his dominion over the then known world in a manner; that was the last of the kingdoms he subdued; when he was master of that he became the head of gold.

III. The mercy God had in store for the house of Israel soon after. When the tide is at the highest it will turn, and so it will when it is at the lowest. Nebuchadnezzar was in the zenith of his glory when he had conquered Egypt, but within a year after he ran mad (Song 4), was so seven years, and within a year or two after he had recovered his senses he resigned his life. When he was at the highest Israel was at the lowest; then were they in the depth of their captivity, their bones dead and dry; but in that day the horn of the house of Israel shall bud forth, Eze 29:21. The day of their deliverance shall begin to dawn, and they shall have some little reviving in their bondage, in the honour that shall be done, 1. To their princes; they are the horns of the house of Israel, the seat of their glory and power. These began to bud forth when Daniel and his fellows were highly preferred in Babylon; Daniel sat in the gate of the city; Shadrach, Meshach, and Abednego, were set over the affairs of the province (Dan 2:49); these were all of the king's seed, and of the princes, Dan 1:3. And it was within a year after the conquest of Egypt that they were thus preferred; and, soon after, three of them were made famous by the honour God put upon them in bringing them alive out of the burning fiery furnace. This might very well be called the budding forth of the horn of the house of Israel. And, some years after, this promise had a further accomplishment in the enlargement and elevation of Jehoiachin king of Judah, Jer 52:31, Jer 52:32. They were both tokens of God's favour to Israel, and happy omens. 2. To their prophets. And I will give thee the opening of the mouth. Though none of Ezekiel's prophecies, after this, are recorded, yet we have reason to think he went on prophesying, and with more liberty and boldness, when Daniel and his fellows were in power, and would be ready to protect him not only from the Babylonians, but from the wicked ones of his own people. Note, It bodes well to a people when God enlarges the liberties of his ministers and they are countenanced and encouraged in their work.

Ezekiel Chapter 30

Ezekiel

In this chapter we have, I. A continuation of the prophecy against Egypt, which we had in the latter part of the foregoing chapter, just before the desolation of that once flourishing kingdom was completed by Nebuchadnezzar, in which is foretold the destruction of all her allies and confederates, all her interests and concerns, and the several steps which the king of Babylon should take in pushing on this destruction (v. 1-19). II. A repetition of a former prophecy against Egypt, just before the desolation of it begun by their own bad conduct, which gradually weakened them and prepared the way for the king of Babylon (Eze 30:20-26). It is all much to the same purport with what we had before.

Ezekiel 30:1

The prophecy of the destruction of Egypt is here very full and particular, as well as, in the general, very frightful. What can protect a provoking people when the righteous God comes forth to contend with them?

I. It shall be a very lamentable destruction, and such as shall occasion great sorrow (Eze 30:2, Eze 30:3): "Howl you; you may justly shriek now that it is coming, for you will be made to shriek and make hideous outcries when it comes. Cry out, Woe worth the day! or, Ah the day! alas because of the day! the terrible day! Woe and alas! For the day is near; the day we have so long dreaded, so long deserved. It is the day of the Lord, the day in which he will manifest himself as a God of vengeance. You have your day now, when you carry all before you, and trample on all about you, but God will have his day shortly, the day of the revelation of his righteous judgment," Psa 37:13. It will be a cloudy day, that is, dark and dismal, without the shining forth of any comfort; and it shall threaten a storm-fire, and brimstone, and a horrible tempest. It shall be the time of the heathen, of reckoning with the heathen for all their heathenish practices, that time which David spoke of when God would pour out his fury upon the heathen (Psa 79:6), when they should sink, Psa 9:15.

II. It shall be the destruction of Egypt, and of all the states and countries in confederacy with her and in her neighbourhood. 1. Egypt herself shall fall (Eze 30:4): The sword shall come upon Egypt, the sword of the Chaldeans, and it shall be a victorious sword, for the slain shall fall in Egypt, fall by it, fall before it. Is the country populous? They shall take away her multitude. Is it strong, and well-fixed? Her foundations shall be broken down, and then the fabric, though built ever so fine, ever so high, will fall of course. 2. Her neighbours and inmates shall fall with her. When the slain fall so thickly in Egypt great pain shall be in Ethiopia, both that in Africa, which is in the neighbourhood of Egypt on one side, and that in Asia, which is near to it on the other side. When their neighbour's house was on fire they could not but apprehend their own in danger; nor were their fears groundless, for they shall all fall with them by the sword,Eze 30:5. Ethiopia and Libya (Cush and Phut, so the Hebrew names are, two of the sons of Ham who are mentioned, and Mizraim, that is, Egypt, between them,Gen 10:6), and the Lydians (who were famous archers, and are spoken of as confederates with Egypt, Jer 46:9), these shall fall with Egypt and Chub (the Chaldeans, the inhabitants of the inner Libya); these and others were the mingled people; there were those of all these and other countries who upon some account or other resided in Egypt, as did also the men of the land that is in league, some of the remains of the people of Israel and Judah, the children of the covenant, or league, as they are called (Act 3:25), the children of the promise,Gal 4:28. These sojourned in Egypt contrary to God's command, and these shall fall with them. Note, Those that will take their lot with God's enemies shall have their lot with them, yea, though they be in profession the men of the land that is in league with God.

III. All that pretend to support the sinking interests of Egypt shall come down under her, shall come down with her (Eze 30:6): Those that uphold Egypt shall fall, and then Egypt must fall of course. See the justice of God; Egypt pretended to uphold Jerusalem when that was tottering, but proved a deceitful reed; and now those that pretended to uphold Egypt shall prove no better. Those that deceive others are commonly paid in their own coin; they are themselves deceived. 1. Does Egypt think herself upheld by the absolute authority and dominion of her king? The pride of her power shall come down, Eze 30:6. The power of the king of Egypt was his pride; but that shall be broken, and humbled. 2. Is the multitude of her people her support? These shall fall by the sword, even from the tower of Syene, which is in the utmost corner of the land, from that side of it by which the enemy shall enter. Both the countries and the cities, the husbandmen and the merchants, shall be desolate, Eze 30:7, as before, Eze 29:12. Even the multitude of Egypt shall be made to cease, Eze 30:10. That populous country shall be depopulated. The land shall be even filled with the slain, Eze 30:11. 3. Is the river Nile her support, and are the several channels of it a defence to her? "I will make the rivers dry (Eze 30:12), so that those natural fortifications which were thought impregnable, because impassable, shall stand them in no stead." 4. Are her idols a support to her? They shall be destroyed; those imaginary upholders shall appear more than ever to be imaginary, for so images are when they pretend to be deliverers and strongholds (Eze 30:13): I will cause their images to cease out of Noph. 5. Is her royal family her support? There shall be no more a prince in the land of Egypt; the royal family shall be extirpated and extinguished, which had continued so long. 6. Is her courage her support, and does she think to uphold herself by the bravery of her men of war, who have now of late been inured to service? That shall fail: I will put a fear in the land of Egypt. 7. Is the rising generation her support? is she upheld by her children, and does she think herself happy because she has her quiver full of them? Alas! the young men shall fall by the sword (Eze 30:17) and the daughters shall go into captivity (Eze 30:18), and so she shall be robbed of all her hopes.

IV. God shall inflict these desolating judgments on Egypt (Eze 30:8): They shall know that I am the Lord, and greater than all gods, than all their gods, when I have set a fire in Egypt. The fire that consumes nations is of God's kindling; and, when he sets fire to a people, all their helpers shall be destroyed. Those that go about to quench the fire shall themselves be devoured by it; for who can stand before him when he is angry? When he pours out his fury upon a place, when he sets fire to it (Eze 30:15, Eze 30:16), neither its strength nor its multitude can stand it in any stead.

V. The king of Babylon and his army shall be employed as instruments of this destruction: The multitude of Egypt shall be made to cease and be quite cut off by the hand of the king of Babylon, Eze 30:10. Those that undertook to protect Israel from the king of Babylon shall not be able to protect themselves. It is said of the Chaldeans, who should destroy Egypt, 1. That they are strangers (Eze 30:12), who therefore shall show no compassion for old acquaintance-sake, but shall behave strangely towards them. 2. That they are the terrible of the nations (Eze 30:11), both in respect of force and in respect of fierceness; and, being terrible, they shall make terrible work. (3.) That they are the wicked, who will not be restrained by reason and conscience, the laws of nature or the laws of nations, for they are without law: I will sell the land into the hand of the wicked. They do violence unjustly, as they are wicked; yet, so far as they are instruments in God's hand of executing his judgments, it is on his part justly done. Note, God often makes one wicked man a scourge to another; and even wicked men acquire a title to prey, jure belli-by the laws of war, for God sells it into their hands.

VI. No place in the land of Egypt shall be exempted from the fury of the Chaldean army, not the strongest, not the remotest: The sword shall go through the land. Various places are here named: Pathros, Zoan, and No (Eze 30:14), Sin and Noph (Eze 30:15, Eze 30:16), Aven and Pi-beseth (Eze 30:17), and Tehaphnehes, Eze 30:18. These shall be made desolate, shall be fired, and God's judgments shall be executed upon them, and his fury poured out upon them. Their strength and multitude shall be cut off; they shall have great pain, shall be rent asunder with fear, and shall have distresses daily. Their day shall be darkened; their honours, comforts, and hopes, shall be extinguished. Their yokes shall be broken, so that they shall no more oppress and tyrannize as they have done. The pomp of their strength shall cease, and a cloud shall cover them, a cloud so thick that through it they shall not see any hopes, nor shall their glory be seen, or shine further. And, lastly, the Ethiopians, who are at a distance from them, as well as those who are mingled with them, shall share in their pain and terror. God will by his providence spread the rumour, and the careless Ethiopians shall be made afraid, Eze 30:9. Note, God can strike a terror upon those that are most secure; fearfulness shall, when he pleases, surprise the most presumptuous hypocrites.

The close of this prediction leaves, 1. The land of Egypt mortified: Thus will I execute judgments on Egypt, Eze 30:19. The destruction of Egypt is the executing of judgments, which intimates not only that it is done justly, for its sins, but that it is done regularly and legally, by a judicial sentence. All the executions God does are according to his judgments. 2. The God of Israel herein glorified: They shall know that I am the Lord. The Egyptians shall be made to know it and the people of God shall be made to know it better. The Lord is known by the judgments which he executes.

Ezekiel 30:20

This short prophecy of the weakening of the power of Egypt was delivered about the time that the army of the Egyptians, which attempted to raise the siege of Jerusalem, was frustrated in its enterprises, and returned re infect-without accomplishing their purpose; whereupon the king of Babylon renewed the siege and carried his point. The kingdom of Egypt was very ancient, and had been for many ages considerable. That of Babylon had but lately arrived at its great pomp and power, being built upon the ruins of the kingdom of Assyria. Now it is with them as it is with families and states, some are growing up, others are declining and going back; one must increase and the others must of course decrease.

I. It is here foretold that the king of Egypt shall grow weaker and weaker. The extent of his territories shall be abridged, his wealth and power shall be diminished, and he shall become less able than ever to help either himself or his friend. 1. This was in part done already (Eze 30:21): I have broken the arm of Pharaoh, some time ago. One arm of that kingdom might well be reckoned broken when the king of Babylon routed the forces of Pharaoh-Necho at Carchemish (Jer 46:2), and made himself master of all that pertained to Egypt from the river of Egypt to Euphrates, Kg2 24:7. Egypt had been long in gathering strength and extending its dominions, and therefore, that there may be a proportion observed in providence, it loses its strength slowly and by degrees. It was soon after the king of Egypt slew good king Josiah, and in the same reign, that its arm was thus broken, and it received that fatal blow which it never recovered. Before Egypt's heart and neck were broken its arm was. God's judgments come upon a people by steps, that they may meet him repenting. When the arm of Egypt is broken it shall not be bound up to be healed, for none can heal the wounds that God gives but he himself. Those whom he disarms, whom he disables, cannot again hold the sword. 2. This was to be done again. One arm was broken before, and something was done towards the setting of it, towards the healing of the deadly wound that was given to the beast. But now (Eze 30:22), I am against Pharaoh, and will break both his arms, both the strong and that which was broken and set again. Note, If less judgments do not prevail to humble and reform sinners, God will send greater. Now God will cause the sword to fall out of his hand, which he caught hold of as thinking himself strong enough to hold it. It is repeated (Eze 30:24), I will break Pharaoh's arms. He had been a cruel oppressor to the people of God formerly, and of late the staff of a broken rod to them; and now God by breaking his arms reckons with him for both. God justly breaks that power which is abused either to put wrongs upon people or to put cheats upon them. But this is not all; (1.) The king of Egypt shall be dispirited when he finds himself in danger of the king of Babylon's forces: he shall groan before him with the groaning of a deadly wounded man. Note, It is common for those that are most elated in their prosperity to be most dejected and disheartened in their adversity. Pharaoh, even before the sword touches him, shall groan as if he had received his death's wound. (2.) The people of Egypt shall be dispersed (Eze 30:23 and again Eze 30:26): I will scatter them among the nations. Other nations had mingled with them (Eze 30:5); now they shall be mingled with other nations, and seek shelter in them, and so be made to know that the Lord is righteous.

II. It is here foretold that the king of Babylon shall grow stronger and stronger,Eze 30:24, Eze 30:25. Put strength into the king of Babylon's arms, that he may be able to go through the service he is designed for. 2. That he will put a sword, his sword, into the king of Babylon's hand, which signified his giving him a commission and furnishing him with arms for carrying on a war, particularly against Egypt. Note, As judges on the bench, like Pilate (Joh 19:11), so generals in the field, like Nebuchadnezzar, have no power but what is given them from above.

Ezekiel Chapter 31

The prophecy of this chapter, as the two chapters before, is against Egypt, and designed for the humbling and mortifying of Pharaoh. In passing sentence upon great criminals it is usual to consult precedents, and to see what has been done to others in the like case, which serves both to direct and to justify the proceedings. Pharaoh stands indicted at the bar of divine justice for his pride and haughtiness, and the injuries he had done to God's people; but he thinks himself so high, so great, as not to be accountable to any authority, so strong, and so well guarded, as not to be conquerable by any force. The prophet is therefore directed to make a report to him of the case of the king of Assyria, whose head city was Nineveh. I. He must show him how great a monarch the king of Assyria had been, what a vast empire he had, what a mighty sway he bore; the king of Egypt, great as he was could not go beyond him (Eze 31:3-9). II. He must then show him how like he was to the king of Assyria in pride and carnal security (Eze 31:10). III. He must next read him the history of the fall and ruin of the king of Assyria, what a noise it made among the nations and what a warning it gave to all potent princes to take heed of pride (Eze 31:11-17). IV. He must leave the king of Egypt to apply all this to himself, to see his own face in the looking-glass of the king of Assyria's sin, and to foresee his own fall through the perspective glass of his ruin (Eze 31:18).

Ezekiel 31:1

This prophecy bears date the month before Jerusalem was taken, as that in the close of the foregoing chapter about four months before. When God's people were in the depth of their distress, it would be some comfort to them, as it would serve likewise for a check to the pride and malice of their neighbours, that insulted over them, to be told from heaven that the cup was going round, even the cup of trembling, that it would shortly be taken out of the hands of God's people and put into the hands of those that hated them, Isa 51:22, Isa 51:23. In this prophecy,

I. The prophet is directed to put Pharaoh upon searching the records for a case parallel to his own (Eze 31:2): Speak to Pharaoh and to his multitude, to the multitude of his attendants, that contributed so much to his magnificence, and the multitude of his armies, that contributed so much to his strength. These he was proud of, these he put a confidence in; and they were as proud of him and trusted as much in him. Now ask him, Whom art thou like in thy greatness? We are apt to judge of ourselves by comparison. Those that think highly of themselves fancy themselves as great and as good as such and such, that have been mightily celebrated. The flatterers of princes tell them whom they equal in pomp and grandeur. "Well," says God, "let him pitch upon the most famous potentate that ever was, and it shall be allowed that he is like him in greatness and no way inferior to him; but, let him pitch upon whom he will, he will find that his day came to fall; he will see there was an end of all his perfection, and must therefore expect the end of his own in like manner." Note, The falls of others, both into sin and ruin, are intended as admonitions to us not to be secure or high-minded, nor to think we stand out of danger.

II. He is directed to show him an instance of one whom he resembles in greatness, and that was the Assyrian (Eze 31:3), whose monarchy had continued from Nimrod. Sennacherib was one of the mighty princes of that monarchy; but it sunk down soon after him, and the monarchy of Nebuchadnezzar was built upon its ruins, or rather grafted upon its stock. Let us now see what a flourishing prince the king of Assyria was. He is here compared to a stately cedar, Eze 31:3. The glory of the house of David is illustrated by the same similitude, Eze 17:3. The olive-tree, the fig-tree, and the vine, which were all fruit-trees, had refused to be promoted over the trees because they would not leave their fruitfulness (Jdg 9:8, etc.), and therefore the choice falls upon the cedar, that is stately and strong, and casts a great shadow, but bears no fruit. 1. The Assyrian monarch was a tall cedar, such as the cedars in Lebanon generally were, of a high stature, and his top among the thick boughs; he was attended by other princes that were tributaries to him, and was surrounded by a life-guard of brave men. He surpassed all the princes in his neighbourhood; they were all shrubs to him (Eze 31:5): His height was exalted above all the trees of the field; they were many of them very high, but he overtopped them all, Eze 31:8. The cedars, even those in the garden of Eden, which we may suppose were the best of the kind, would not hide him, but his top branches outshot theirs. 2. He was a spreading cedar; his branches did not only run up in height, but run out in breadth, denoting that this mighty prince was not only exalted to great dignity and honour, and had a name above the names of the great men of the earth, but that he obtained great dominion and power; his territories were large, and he extended his conquests far and his influences much further. This cedar, like a vine, sent forth his branches to the sea, to the river, Psa 80:11. His boughs were multiplied; his branches became long (Eze 31:5); so that he had a shadowing shroud, Eze 31:3. This contributed very much to his beauty, that he grew proportionably large as well as high. He was fair in his greatness, in the length of his branches (Eze 31:7), very comely as well as very stately, fair by the multitude of his branches,Eze 31:9. His large dominions were well managed, like a spreading tree that is kept in shape and good order by the skill of the gardener, so as to be very beautiful to the eye. His government was as amiable in the eyes of wise men as it was admirable in the eyes of all men. The fir-trees were not like his boughs, so straight, so green, so regular; nor were the branches of the chestnut-trees like his branches, so thick, so spreading. In short, no tree in the garden of God, in Eden, in Babylon (for that stood where paradise was planted), where there was every tree that was pleasant to the sight (Gen 2:9), was like to this cedar in beauty; that is, in all the surrounding nations there was no prince so much admired, so much courted, and whom every body was so much in love with, as the king of Assyria. Many of them did virtuously, but he excelled them all, outshone them all. All the trees of Eden envied him, Eze 31:9. When they found they could not compare with him they were angry and grieved that he so far outdid them, and secretly grudged him the praise due to him. Note, It is the unhappiness of those who in any thing excel others that thereby they make themselves the objects of envy; and who can stand before envy? 3. He was serviceable, as far as a standing growing cedar could be, and that was only by his shadow (Eze 31:6): All the fowls of heaven, some of all sorts, made their nests in his boughs, where they were sheltered from the injuries of the weather. The beasts of the field put themselves under the protection of his branches. There they were levant-rising up, and couchant-lying down; there they brought forth their young; for they had there a natural covert from the heat and from the storm. The meaning of all is, Under his shadow dwelt all great nations; they all fled to him for safety, and were willing to swear allegiance to him if he would undertake to protect them, as travellers in a shower come under thick trees for shelter. Note, Those who have power ought to use it for the protection and comfort of those whom they have power over; for to that end they are entrusted with power. Even the bramble, if he be anointed king, invites the trees to come and trust in his shadow, Jdg 9:15. But the utmost security that any creature, even the king of Assyria himself, can give, is but like the shadow of a tree, which is but a scanty and slender protection, and leaves a man many ways exposed. Let us therefore flee to God for protection, and he will take us under the shadow of his wings, where we shall be warmer and safer than under the shadow of the strongest and stateliest cedar, Psa 17:8; Psa 91:4. 4. He seemed to be settled and established in his greatness and power. For, (1.) It was God that made him fair, Eze 31:9. For by him kings reign. He was comely with the comeliness that God put upon him. Note, God's hand must be eyed and owned in the advancement of the great men of the earth, and therefore we must not envy them; yet that will not secure the continuance of their prosperity, for he that gave them their beauty, if they be deprived of it, knows how to turn it into deformity. (2.) He seemed to have a good bottom. This cedar was not like the heath in the desert, made to inhabit the parched places (Jer 17:6); it was not a root in a dry ground, Isa 53:2. No; he had abundance of wealth to support his power and grandeur (Eze 31:4): The waters made him great; he had vast treasures, large stores and magazines, which were as the deep that set him up on high, constant revenues coming in by taxes, customs, and crown-rents, which were as rivers running round about his plants; these enabled him to strengthen and secure his interests every where, for he sent out his little rivers, or conduits, to all the trees of the field, to water them; and when they had maintenance from the king's palace (Ezr 4:14), and their country was nourished by the king's country (Act 12:20), they would be serviceable and faithful to him. Those that have wealth flowing upon them in great rivers find themselves obliged to send it out again in little rivers; for, as goods are increased, those are increased that eat them, and the more men have the more occasion they have for it; yea, and still the more they have occasion for. The branches of this cedar became long, because of the multitude of waters which fed them (Eze 31:5 and Eze 31:7); his root was by great waters, which seemed to secure it that its leaf should never wither (Psa 1:3), that it should not see when heat came, Jer 17:8. Note, Worldly people may seem to have an established prosperity, yet it only seems so, Job 5:3; Psa 37:35.

Ezekiel 31:10

We have seen the king of Egypt resembling the king of Assyria in pomp, and power, and prosperity, how like he was to him in his greatness; now here we see,

I. How he does likewise resemble him in his pride, Eze 31:10. For, as face answers to face in a glass, so does one corrupt carnal heart to another; and the same temptations of a prosperous state by which some are overcome are fatal to many others too. "Thou, O king of Egypt! hast lifted up thyself in height, hast been proud of thy wealth and power, Eze 29:3. And just so he (that is, the king of Assyria); when he had shot up his top among the thick boughs his heart was immediately lifted up in his height, and he grew insolent and imperious, set God himself at defiance, and trampled upon his people;" witness the messages and letter which the great king, the king of Assyria, sent to Hezekiah, Isa 36:4. How haughtily does he speak of himself and his own achievements! how scornfully of that great and good man! There were other sins in which the Egyptians and the Assyrians did concur, particularly that of oppressing God's people, which is charged upon them both together (Isa 52:4); but here that sin is traced up to its cause, and that was pride; for it is the contempt of the proud that they are filled with. Note, When men's outward condition rises their minds commonly rise with it; and it is very rare to find a humble spirit in the midst of great advancements.

II. How he shall therefore resemble him in his fall; and for the opening of this part of the comparison,

1. Here is a history of the fall of the king of Assyria. For his part, says God (Eze 31:11), I have therefore, because he was thus lifted up, delivered him into the hand of the mighty one of the heathen. Cyaxares, king of the Medes, in the twenty-sixth year of his reign, in conjunction with Nebuchadnezzar king of Babylon in the first year of his reign, destroyed Nineveh, and with it the Assyrian empire. Nebuchadnezzar, though he was not then, yet afterwards became, very emphatically, the mighty one of the heathen, most mighty among them and most mighty over them, to prevail against them.

(1.) Respecting the fall of the Assyrian three things are affirmed:-[1.] It is God himself that orders his ruin: I have delivered him into the hand of the executioner; I have driven him out. Note, God is the Judge, who puts down one and sets up another (Psa 75:7); and when he pleases he can extirpate and expel those who think themselves, and seem to others, to have taken deepest root. And the mightiest ones of the heathens could not gain their point against those they contended with if the Almighty did not himself deliver them into their hands. [2.] It is his own sin that procures his ruin: I have driven him out for his wickedness. None are driven out from their honour, power, and possessions, but it is for their wickedness. None of our comforts are ever lost but what have been a thousand times forfeited. If the wicked are driven away, it is in their wickedness. [3.] It is a mighty one of the heathen that shall be the instrument of his ruin; for God often employs one wicked man in punishing another. He shall surely deal with him, shall know how to manage him, great as he is. Note, Proud imperious men will, sooner or later, meet with their match.

(2.) In this history of the fall of the Assyrian observe, [1.] A continuation of the similitude of the cedar. He grew very high, and extended his boughs very far; but his day comes to fall. First, This stately cedar was cropped: The terrible of the nations cut him off. Soldiers, who being both armed and commissioned to kill, and slay, and destroy, may well be reckoned among the terrible of the nations. They have lopped off his branches first, have seized upon some parts of his dominion and forced them out of his hands; so that in all mountains and valleys of the nations about, in the high-lands and low-lands, and by all the rivers, there were cities or countries that were broken off from the Assyrian monarchy, that had been subject to it, but had either revolted or were recovered from it. Its feathers were borrowed; and, when every bird had fetched back its own, it was naked like the stump of a tree. Secondly, It was deserted: All the people of the earth, that had fled to him for shelter, have gone down from his shadow and have left him. When he was disabled to give them protection they thought they no longer owed him allegiance. Let not great men be proud of the number of those that attend them and have a dependence upon them; it is only for what they can get. When Providence frowns upon them their retinue is soon dispersed and scattered from them. Thirdly, It was insulted over, and its fall triumphed in (Eze 31:13): Upon his ruin shall all the fowls of the heaven remain, to tread upon the broken branches of this cedar. Its fall is triumphed in by the other trees, who were angry to see themselves overtopped so much: All the trees of Eden, that were cut down and had fallen before him, all that drank water of the rain of heaven, as the stump of the tree that is left in the south is said to be wet with the dew of heaven (Dan 4:23) and to bud through the scent of water (Job 14:9), shall be comforted in the nether parts of the earth when they see this proud cedar brought as low as themselves. Solamen miseris socios habuisse doloris-To have companions in woe is a solace to those who suffer. But, on the contrary, the trees of Lebanon, that are yet standing in their height and strength, mourned for him, and the trees of the field fainted for him, because they could not but read their own destiny in his fall. Howl, fir-trees, if the cedar be shaken, for they cannot expect to stand long, Zac 11:2. [2.] An explanation of the similitude of the cedar. By the cutting down of this cedar is signified the slaughter of this mighty monarch and all his adherents and supporters; they are all delivered to death, to fall by the sword, as the cedar by the axe. He and his princes, who, he said, were altogether kings, go down to the grace, to the nether parts of the earth, in the midst of the children of men, as common persons of no quality or distinction. They died like men (Psa 82:7); they were carried away with those that go down to the pit, and their pomp did neither protect them nor descend after them. Again (Eze 31:16), He was cast down to hell with those that descend into the pit; he went into the state of the dead, and was buried as others are, in obscurity and oblivion. Again (Eze 31:17), They all that were his arm, on whom he stayed, by whom he acted and exerted his power, all that dwelt under his shadow, his subjects and allies, and all that had any dependence on him, they all went down into ruin, down into the grace with him, unto those that were slain with the sword, to those that were cut off by untimely deaths before them, under the load of guilt and shame. When great men fall a great many fall with them, as a great many in like manner have fallen before them. [3.] What God designed, and aimed at, in bringing down this mighty monarch and his monarchy. He designed thereby, First, To give an alarm to the nations about, to put them all to a stand, to put them all to a gaze (Eze 31:16): I made the nations to shake at the sound of his fall. They were all struck with astonishment to see so mighty a prince brought down thus. It give a shock to all their confidences, every one thinking his turn would be next. When he went down to the grace (Eze 31:15) I caused a mourning, a general lamentation, as the whole kingdom goes into mourning at the death of the king. In token of this general grief, I covered the deep for him, put that into black, gave a stop to business, in complaisance to this universal mourning. I restrained the floods, and the great waters were stayed, that they might run into another channel, that of lamentation. Lebanon particularly, the kingdom of Syria, that was sometimes in confederacy with the Assyrian, mourned for him; as the allies of Babylon, Rev 18:9. Secondly, To give an admonition to the nations about, and to their kings (Eze 31:14): To the end that none of all the trees by the waters, though ever so advantageously situated, may exalt themselves for their height, may be proud and conceited of themselves and shoot up their top among the thick boughs, looking disdainfully upon others, nor stand upon themselves for their height, confiding in their own politics and powers, as if they could never be brought down. Let them all take warning by the Assyrian, for he once held up his head as high, and thought he kept his footing as firm, as any of them; but his pride went before his destruction, and his confidence failed him. Note, The fall of proud presumptuous men is intended for warning to others to keep humble. It would have been well for Nebuchadnezzar, who was himself active in bringing down the Assyrian, if he had taken the admonition.

2. Here is a prophecy of the fall of the king of Egypt in like manner, Eze 31:18. He thought himself like the Assyrian in glory and greatness, over-topping all the trees of Eden, as the cypress does the shrubs. "But thou also shalt be brought down, with the other trees that are pleasant to the sight, as those in Eden. Thou shalt be brought to the grave, to the nether or lower parts of the earth; thou shalt lie in the midst of the uncircumcised, that die in their uncleanness, die ingloriously, die under a curse and at a distance from God; then shall those whom thou hast trampled upon triumph over thee, saying, This is Pharaoh and all his multitude. See how mean he looks, how low he lies; see what all his pomp and pride have come to; here is all that is left of him." Note, Great men and great multitudes, with the great figure and great noise they make in the world, when God comes to contend with them, will soon become little, less than nothing, such as Pharaoh and all his multitude.

Ezekiel Chapter 32

Still we are upon the destruction of Pharaoh and Egypt, which is wonderfully enlarged upon, and with a great deal of emphasis. When we read so very much of Egypt's ruin, no less than six several prophecies at divers times delivered concerning it, we are ready to think, Surely there is some special reason for it. And, I. Perhaps it may look as far back as the book of Genesis, where we find (Gen 15:14) that God determined to judge Egypt for oppressing his people; and, though that was in part fulfilled in the plagues of Egypt and the drowning of Pharaoh, yet, in this destruction, here foretold, those old scores were reckoned for, and that was to have its full accomplishment. II. Perhaps it may look as far forward as the book of the Revelation, where we find that the great enemy of the gospel-church, that makes war with the Lamb, is spiritually called Egypt, Rev 11:8. And, if so, the destruction of Egypt and its Pharaoh was a type of the destruction of that proud enemy; and between this prophecy of the ruin of Egypt and the prophecy of the destruction of the antichristian generation there is some analogy. We have two distinct prophecies in this chapter relating to Egypt, both in the same month, one on the 1st day, the other that day fortnight, probably both on the sabbath day. They are both lamentations, not only to signify how lamentable the fall of Egypt should be, but to intimate how much the prophet himself should lament it, from a generous principle of love to mankind. The destruction of Egypt is here represented under two similitudes:-1. The killing of a lion, or a whale, or some such devouring creature (v. 1-16). 2. The funeral of a great commander or captain-general (v. 17-32). The two prophecies of this chapter are much of the same length.

Ezekiel 32:1

Here, I. The prophet is ordered to take up a lamentation for Pharaoh king of Egypt, Eze 32:2. It concerns ministers to be much of a serious spirit, and, in order thereunto, to be frequent in taking up lamentations for the fall and ruin of sinners, as those that have not desired, but dreaded, the woeful day. Note, Ministers that would affect others with the things of God must make it appear that they are themselves affected with the miseries which sinners bring upon themselves by their sins. It becomes us to weep and tremble for those that will not weep and tremble for themselves, to try if thereby we may set them a weeping, set them a trembling.

II. He is ordered to show cause for that lamentation.

1. Pharaoh has been a troubler of the nations, even of his own nation, which he should have procured the repose of: He is like a young lion of the nations (Eze 32:2), loud and noisy, hectoring and threatening as a lion when he roars. Great potentates, if they by tyrannical and

oppressive, are in God's account no better than beasts of prey. He is like a whale, or dragon, like a crocodile (so some) in the seas, very turbulent and vexatious, as the leviathan that makes the deep to boil like a pot, Job 41:31. When Pharaoh engaged in an unnecessary war with the Cyrenians he came forth with his rivers, with his armies, troubled the waters, disturbed his own kingdom and the neighbouring nations, fouled the rivers, and made them muddy. Note, A great deal of disquiet is often given to the world by the restless ambition and implacable resentments of proud princes. Ahab is he that troubles Israel, and not Elijah.

2. He that has troubled others must expect to be himself troubled; for the Lord is righteous, Jos 7:25.

(1.) This is set forth here by a comparison. Is Pharaoh like a great whale, which, when it comes up the river, gives great disturbance, a leviathan which Job cannot draw out with a hook? (Job 41:1), yet God has a net for him which is large enough to enclose him and strong enough to secure him (Eze 32:3): I will spread my net over thee, even the army of the Chaldeans, a company of many people; they shall force him out of his fastnesses, dislodge him out of his possessions, throw him like a great fish upon dry ground, upon the open field (Eze 32:4), where being out of his element, he must die of course, and be a prey to the birds and beasts, as was foretold, Eze 29:5. What can the strongest fish do to help itself when it is out of the water and lies gasping? The flesh of this great whale shall be laid upon the mountains (Eze 32:5) and the valleys shall be filled with his height. Such numbers of Pharaoh's soldiers shall be slain that the dead bodies shall be scattered upon the hills and there shall be heaps of them piled up in the valleys. Blood shall be shed in such abundance as to swell the rivers in the valleys. Or, Such shall be the bulk, such the height, of this leviathan, that, when he is laid upon the ground, he shall fill a valley. Such vast quantities of blood shall issue from this leviathan as shall water the land of Egypt, the land wherein now he swims, now he sports himself, Eze 32:6. It shall reach to the mountains, and the waters of Egypt shall again be turned into blood by this means: The rivers shall be full of thee. The judgments executed upon Pharaoh of old are expressed by the breaking of the heads of leviathan in the waters, Psa 74:13, Psa 74:14. But now they go further; this old serpent not only has now his head bruised, but is all crushed to pieces.

(2.) It is set forth by a prophecy of the deep impression which the destruction of Egypt should make upon the neighbouring nations; it would put them all into a consternation, as the fall of the Assyrian monarchy did, Eze 31:15, Eze 31:16. When Pharaoh, who had been like a blazing burning torch, is put out and extinguished it shall make all about him look black, Eze 32:7. The heavens shall be hung with black, the stars darkened, the sun eclipsed, and the moon be deprived of her borrowed light. It is from the upper world that this lower receives its light; and therefore (Eze 32:8), when the bright lights of heaven are made dark above, darkness by consequence is set upon the land, upon the earth; so it shall be on the land of Egypt. Here the plague of darkness, which was upon Egypt of old for three days, seems to be alluded to, as, before, the turning of the waters into blood. For, when former judgments are forgotten, it is just that they should be repeated. When their privy-counsellors, and statesmen, and those that have the direction of the public affairs, are deprived of wisdom and made fools, and the things that belong to their peace are hidden from their eyes, then their lights are darkened and the land is in a mist. This is foretold, Isa 19:13. The princes of Zoan have become fools. Now upon the spreading of the report of the fall of Egypt, and the bringing of the news to remote countries, countries which they had not known (Eze 32:9), people shall be much affected, and shall feel themselves sensibly touched by it. [1.] It shall fill them with vexation to see such an ancient, wealthy, potent kingdom thus humbled and brought down, and the pride of worldly glory, which they have such a value for, stained. The hearts of many people will be vexed to see the word of the God of Israel fulfilled in the destruction of Egypt, and that all the gods of Egypt were not able to relieve it. Note, The destruction of some wicked people is a vexation to others. [2.] It shall fill them with admiration (Eze 32:10): They shall be amazed at thee, shall wonder to see such great riches and power come to nothing, Rev 18:17. Note, Those that admire with complacency the pomp of this world will admire with consternation the ruin of that pomp, which to those that know the vanity of all things here below is no surprise at all. [3.] It shall fill them with fear: even their kings (that think it their prerogative to be secure) shall be horribly afraid for thee, concluding their own house to be in danger when their neighbour's is on fire. When I shall brandish my sword before them they shall tremble every man for his own life. Note, When the sword of God's justice is drawn against some, to cut them off, it is thereby brandished before others, to give them warning. And those that will not be admonished by it, and made to reform, shall yet be frightened by it, and made to tremble. They shall tremble at every moment, because of thy fall. When others are ruined by sin we have reason to quake for fear, as knowing ourselves guilty and obnoxious. Who is able to stand before this holy Lord God?

(3.) It is set forth by a plain and express prediction of the desolation itself that should come upon Egypt. [1.] The instruments of the desolation appear here very formidable. It is the sword of the king of Babylon, that warlike, that victorious prince, that shall come upon thee (Eze 32:11), the swords of the mighty, even the terrible of the nations, all of them (Eze 32:12), an army that there is no standing before. Note, Those that delight in war, and are upon all occasions entering into contention, may expect, some time or other, to be engaged with those that will prove too hard for them. Pharaoh had been forward to quarrel with his neighbour and to come forth with his rivers, with his armies,Eze 32:2. But God will now give him enough of it. [2.] The instances of the desolation appear here very frightful, much the same with what we had before,Eze 29:10-12; Eze 30:7. First, The multitude of Egypt shall be destroyed, not decimated, some picked out to be made examples, but all cut off. Note, The numbers of sinners, though they be a multitude, will neither secure them against God's power nor entitle them to his pity. Secondly, The pomp of Egypt shall be spoiled, the pomp of their court, what they have been proud of. Note, in renouncing the pomps of this world we did ourselves a great kindness, for they are things that are soon spoiled and that cheat their admirers. Thirdly, The cattle of Egypt, that used to feed by the rivers, shall be destroyed (Eze 32:13), either cut off by the sword or carried off for a prey. Egypt was famous for horses, which would be an acceptable booty to the

Chaldeans. The rivers shall be no more frequented as they have been by man and beast, that came thither to drink. Fourthly, The waters of Egypt, that used to flow briskly, shall now grow deep, and slow, and heavy, and shall run like oil (Eze 32:14), a figurative expression signifying that there should be such universal sadness and heaviness upon the whole nation that even the rivers should go softly and silently like mourners, and quite forget their rapid motion. Fifthly, The whole country of Egypt shall be stripped of its wealth; it shall be destitute of what whereof it was full (Eze 32:15), corn, and cattle, and all the pleasant fruits of the earth; when those are smitten that dwell therein the ground is untilled, and that which is gathered becomes an easy prey to the invader. Note, God can soon empty those of this world's goods that have the greatest fulness of those things and are full of them, that enjoy most and have their hearts set upon those enjoyments. The Egyptians were full of their pleasant and plentiful country, and its rich productions. Every one that talked with them might perceive how much it filled them. But God can soon make their country destitute of that whereof it is full; it is therefore our wisdom to be full of treasures in heaven. When the country is made destitute, 1. It shall be an instruction to them: Then shall they know that I am the Lord. A sensible conviction of the vanity of the world, and the fading perishing nature of all things in it, will contribute much to our right knowledge of God as our portion and happiness. 2. It shall be a lamentation to all about them: The daughters of the nations shall lament her (Eze 32:16), either because, being in alliance with her, they share in her grievances and suffer with her, or, being admirers of her, they at least share in her grief and sympathize with her. They shall lament for Egypt and all her multitude; it shall excite their pity to see so great a devastation made. By enlarging the matters of our joy we increase the occasions of our sorrow.

Ezekiel 32:17

This prophecy concludes and completes the burden of Egypt, and leaves it and all its multitude in the pit of destruction.

I. We are here invited to attend the funeral of that once flourishing kingdom, to lament its fall, and to take a view of those who attend it to the grave and accompany it in the grave.

1. This dead corpse of a kingdom is here brought to the grave. The prophet is ordered to cast them down to the pit (Eze 32:18), to foretel their destruction as one that had authority, as Jeremiah was set over the kingdoms, Jer 1:10. He must speak in God's name, and as from him who will cast them down. Yet he must foretel it as one that had an affectionate concern for them; he must wail for the multitude of Egypt, even when he casts them down. When Egypt is slain, let her have an honourable funeral, befitting her quality; let her be buried with the daughters of the famous nations, in their burying-places and with the same ceremony. It is but a poor allay to the reproach and terror of death to be buried with those that were famous; yet this is all that is allowed to Egypt. Shall Egypt think to exempt herself from the common fate of proud and imperious nations? No; she must take her lot with them (Eze 32:19): "Whom dost thou surpass in

beauty? Art thou so much fairer than any other nation that thou shouldst expect therefore to be excused? No; others as fair as thou have sunk into the pit; go down therefore, and be thou laid with the uncircumcised. Thou art like them and art likely to lie among them. The multitude of Egypt shall all fall in the midst of those that are slain with the sword, now that there is a general slaughter made among the nations." Egypt with the rest must drink of the bloody cup, and therefore she is delivered to the sword, to the sword of war (but, in God's hand, the sword of justice), is delivered to be publicly executed. Draw her and all her multitude; draw them either as the dead bodies of great men are drawn in honour to the grave, in a hearse, or as malefactors are drawn in disgrace to the place of execution, on a sledge; draw them to the pit, and let them be made a spectacle to the world.

2. This corpse of a kingdom is bid welcome to the grave, and Pharaoh is made free of the congregation of the dead, and admitted into their regions, not without some pomp and ceremony. As the surprising fall of the king of Babylon is thus illustrated, Hell from beneath is moved for thee to meet thee at thy coming, and to introduce thee into those mansions of darkness (Isa 14:9, etc.), so here (Eze 32:21), They shall speak to him out of the midst of hell, as it were congratulating his arrival and calling him to join with them in acknowledging that which neither he nor they would be brought to own when they were in their pomp and pride, that it is in vain to think of contesting with God, and none ever hardened their hearts against him and prospered. They shall say to him, and to those that pretended to help him, Where are you now? What have you brought your attempts to at last? Divers nations are here mentioned as gone down to the grave before Egypt that are ready to give her a scornful reception and upbraid her with coming to them at last. These nations here spoken of were probably such as had been of late years ruined and wasted by the king of Babylon, and their princes cut off; let Egypt know that she has neighbour's fare. When she goes to the grave she does but migrare ad plures-migrate to the majority; there are innumerable before her. But it is observable that though Judah and Jerusalem were just about this time, or a little before, utterly ruined and laid waste, yet they are not mentioned here among the nations that welcome Egypt to the pit; for though they suffered the same things that these nations suffered, and by the same hand, yet the kind intentions of their affliction, and its happy issue at last, and the mercy God had yet in reserve for them, altered the property of it; it was not to them a going down to the pit, as it was to the heathen; they were not smitten as others were, nor slain according to the slaughter of other nations, Isa 27:7. But let us see who those are that have gone to the grave before Egypt, that lie uncircumcised, slain by the sword, with whom she must now take up her lodging. (1.) There lie the Assyrian empire, and all the princes and mighty men of that monarchy (Eze 32:22): Asshur is there and all her company, all the countries that were tributaries to and had dependence upon that crown. That mighty potentate who used to lie in state, with his guards and grandees about him, now lies in obscurity, with his graves about him and his soldiers in them, unable any longer to do him service or honour; they are all of them slain, fallen by the sword. The number of their months was cut off in the midst, and, being bloody and deceitful men, they were not suffered to live out half their days. Their braves were set in the sides of the pit, all in a row, like beds in a common chamber, Eze

32:23. All their company is such as were slain, fallen by the sword; a vast congregation there is of such, who had caused terror in the land of the living. But as the death of those to whom they were a terror put an end to their fears (in the grave the prisoners rest together and hear not the voice of the oppressor, Job 3:18), so the death of these mighty men puts an end to their terrors. Who is afraid of a dead lion? Note, Death will be a king of terrors to those who, instead of making themselves blessings, make themselves terrors, in their generation. (2.) There lies the kingdom of Persia, which perhaps within the memory of man at that time had been wasted and brought down: There is Elam and all her multitude, the king of Elam and his numerous armies, Eze 32:24, Eze 32:25. They also had caused their terror in the land of the living, had made a fearful noise and bluster among the nations in their day. But Elam has now a grave by herself, and the graves of the common people round about her, fallen by the sword; she has her bed in the midst of the slain that went down uncircumcised, unsanctified, unholy, and not in covenant with God. They have borne their shame with those that go down to the pit; they have fallen under the common disgrace and mortification of mankind, that they die and are buried; nay, they die under particular marks of ignominy, which God and man put upon them. Note, Those who cause their terror shall, sooner or later, bear their shame, and be made a terror to themselves. The king of Elam is put in the midst of those that are slain. All the honour he can now pretend to is to be buried in the chief sepulchre. (3.) There lies the Scythian power, which, about this time, was busy in the world. Meshech and Tubal, those barbarous northern nations, had lately made a descent upon the Medes, and caused their terror among them, lived among them upon free quarter for some years, making every thing their own that they could lay their hands on; but at length Cyaxares, king of the Medes, drew them by a wile into his power, but off abundance of them, and obliged them to quit his country, Eze 32:26. There lie Meshech and Tubal, and all their multitude; there is a burying place for them, with their chief commander in the midst of them, all of them uncircumcised, slain by the sword. These Scythians, dying ingloriously as they lived, are not laid, as the other nations spoken of before, in the bed of honour (Eze 32:27): They shall not lie with the mighty, shall not be buried in state, as those are, even by consent of the enemy, that are slain in the field of battle, that go down to their graves with their weapons of war carried before the hearse, or trailed after it, that have particularly their swords laid under their heads, as if they could sleep the sweeter in the grave when they laid their heads on such a pillow. These Scythians are not buried with these marks of honour, but their iniquities shall be upon their sons; they shall, for their iniquity, be left unburied, though they were the terror even of the mighty in the land of the living. (4.) There lies the kingdom of Edom, which had flourished long, but about this time, at least before the destruction of Egypt, was made quite desolate, as was foretold, Eze 25:13. Among the sepulchres of the nations there is Edom, Eze 32:29. There lie, not dignified with monuments or inscriptions, but mingled with common dust, her kings and all her princes, her wise statesmen (which Edom was famous for), and her brave soldiers. These with their might are laid by those that were slain by the sword; their might could not prevent it, nay, their might helped to procure it, for that both encouraged them to engage in war and incensed their neighbours against them, who thought it necessary to curb their growing greatness. A great deal of pains they took to ruin themselves, as many do, who with their might, with all their might, are laid by those that were slain with the sword. The Edomites retained circumcision, being of the seed of Abraham. But that shall stand them in no stead; they shall lie with the uncircumcised. (5.) There lie the princes of the north, and all the Zidonians. These were as well acquainted with maritime affairs as the Egyptians were, who relied much upon that part of their strength, but they have gone down with the slain (Eze 32:30), down to the pit. Now they are ashamed of their might, ashamed to think how much they boasted of it and trusted to it; and, as the Edomites with their might, so these with their terror, are laid with those that are slain by the sword and are forced to take their lot with them. They bear their shame with those that go down to the pit, die in as much disgrace as those that are cut off by the hand of public justice. (6.) All this is applied to Pharaoh and the Egyptians, who have no reason to flatter themselves with hopes of tranquillity when they see how the wisest, and wealthiest, and strongest, of their neighbours have been laid waste (Eze 32:28): "Yea, thou shalt be broken in the midst of the uncircumcised; when God is pulling down the unhumbled and unreformed nations thou must expect to come down with them." [1.] It will be some extenuation of the miseries of Egypt to observe that it has been the case of so many great and mighty nations before (Eze 32:31): Pharaoh shall see them and be comforted; it will be some ease to his mind that he is not the first king that has been slain in battle-his not the first army that has been routed, his not the first kingdom that has been made desolate. Mr. Greenhill observes here, "The comfort which wicked ones have after death is poor comfort, not real, but imaginary." They will find little satisfaction in having so many fellow-sufferers; the rich man in hell dreaded it. It is only in point of honour that Pharaoh can see and be comforted. [2.] But nothing will be an exemption from these miseries; for (Eze 32:32) I have caused my terror in the land of the living. Great men have caused their terror, have studied how to make every body fear them. Oderint dum metuant-Let them hate, so that they do but fear. But now the great God has caused his terror in the land of the living; and therefore he laughs at theirs, because he sees that his day is coming, Psa 37:13. In this day of terror Pharaoh and all his multitude shall be laid with those that are slain by the sword.

II. The view which this prophecy gives us of ruined states may show us something, 1. Of this present world, and the empire of death in it. Come, and see the calamitous state of human life; see what a dying world this is. The strong die, the mighty die, Pharaoh and all his multitude. See what a killing world this is. They are all slain with the sword. As if men did not die fast enough of themselves, men are ingenious at finding out ways to destroy one another. It is not only a great pit, but a great cock-pit. 2. Of the other world. Though it is the destruction of nations as such that perhaps is principally intended here, yet here is a plain allusion to the final and everlasting ruin of impenitent sinners, of those that are uncircumcised in heart; they are slain by the sword of divine justice; their iniquity is upon them, and with it they bear their shame. Those, Christ's enemies, that would not have him to reign over them, shall be brought forth and slain before him, though they be as pompous, though they be as numerous, as Pharaoh and all his multitude.

Ezekiel Chapter 33

The prophet has now come off his circuit, which he went as judge, in God's name, to try and pass sentence upon the neighbouring nations, and, having finished with them, and read them all their doom, in the eight chapters foregoing, he now returns to the children of his people, and receives further instructions what to say to them. I. He must let them know what office he was in among them as a prophet, that he was a watchman, and had received a charge concerning them, for which he was accountable (Eze 33:1-9). The substance of this we had before, Eze 3:17, etc. II. He must let them know upon what terms they stand with God, that they are upon their trial, upon their good behaviour, that if a wicked man repent he shall not perish, but that if a righteous man apostatize he shall perish (Eze 33:10-20). III. Here is a particular message sent to those who yet remained in the land of Israel, and (which is very strange) grew secure there, and confident that they should take root there again, to tell them that their hopes would fail them because they persisted in their sins (Eze 33:21-29). IV. Here is a rebuke to those who personally attended Ezekiel's ministry, but were not sincere in their professions of devotion (Eze 33:30-33).

Ezekiel 33:1

The prophet had been, by express order from God, taken off from prophesying to the Jews, just then when the news came that Jerusalem was invested, and close siege laid to it, Eze 24:27. But now that Jerusalem is taken, two years after, he is appointed again to direct his speech to them; and there his commission is renewed. If God had abandoned them quite, he would not have sent prophets to them; nor, if he had not had mercy in store for them, would he have shown them such things as these. In these verses we have,

I. The office of a watchman laid down, the trust reposed in him, the charge given him, and the conditions adjusted between him and those that employ him, Eze 33:2, Eze 33:6. 1. It is supposed to be a public danger that gives occasion for the appointing of a watchman-when God brings the sword upon a land, Eze 33:2. The sword of war, whenever it comes upon a land, is of God's bringing; it is the sword of the Lord, of his justice, how unjustly soever men draw it. At such a time, when a country is in fear of a foreign invasion, that they may be informed of all the motions of the enemy, may not be surprised with an attack, but may have early notice of it, in order to their being at their arms and in readiness to give the invader a warm reception, they set a man of their coast, some likely person, that lives upon the borders of their country, where the threatened danger is expected, and is therefore well acquainted with all the avenues of it, and make him their watchman. Thus wise are the children of this world in their generation. Note, One man may be of public service to a whole country. Princes and statesmen are the watchmen of a kingdom; they are continually to employ themselves, and, if occasion be, as watchmen, to expose themselves for the public safety. 2. It is supposed to be a public trust that is lodged in the watchman and that he is accountable to the public for the discharge of it. His business is, (1.) To discover the approaches and advances of the enemy; and therefore he must not be blind nor asleep, for then he cannot see the sword coming. (2.) To give notice of them immediately by sound of trumpet, or, as sentinels among us, by the discharge of a gun, as a signal of danger. A special trust and confidence is reposed in him by those that set him to be their watchman that he will faithfully do these two things; and they venture their lives upon his fidelity. Now, [1.] If he do his part, if he be betimes aware of all the dangers that fall within his cognizance, and give warning of them, he has discharged his trust, and has not only delivered his soul, but earned his wages. If the people do not take warning, if they either will not believe the notice he gives them, will not believe the danger to be so great or so near as really it is, or will not regard it, and so are surprised by the enemy in their security, it is their own fault; the blame is not to be laid upon the watchman, but their blood is upon their own head. If any person goes presumptuously into the mouth of danger, though he heard the sound of the trumpet, and was told by it where the danger was, and so the sword comes and takes him away in his folly, he is felo de se-a suicide; foolish man, he has destroyed himself. But, [2.] If the watchman do not do his duty, if he might have seen the danger, and did not, but was asleep, or heedless, or looking another way, or if he did see the danger (for so the case is put here) and shifted only for his own safety, and blew not the trumpet to warn the people, so that some are surprised and cut off in their iniquity (Eze 33:6), cut off suddenly, without having time to cry, Lord, have mercy upon me, time to repent and make their peace with God (which makes the matter much the worse, that the poor creature is taken away in his iniquity), his blood shall be required at the watchman's hand; he shall be found guilty of his death, because he did not give him warning of his danger. But if the watchman do his part, and the people do theirs, all is well; both he that gives warning and he that takes warning have delivered their souls.

II. The application of this to the prophet, Eze 33:7, Eze 33:9.

1. He is a watchman to the house of Israel. He had occasionally given warning to the nations about, but to the house of Israel he was a watchman by office, for they were the children of the prophets and the covenant They did not set him for a watchman, as the people of the land, Eze 33:2 (for they were not so wise for their souls as to secure the welfare of them, as they would have been for the protection of their temporal interests); but God did it for them; he appointed them a watchman.

2. His business as a watchman is to give warning to sinners of their misery and danger by reason of sin. This is the word he must hear from God's mouth and speak to them. (1.) God has said, The wicked man shall surely die; he shall be miserable. Unless he repent, he shall be cut off from God and all comfort and hope in him, shall be cut off from all good. He shall fall and lie for ever under the wrath of God, which is the death of the soul, as his favour is its life. The righteous

God has said it, and will never unsay it, nor can all the world gainsay it, that the wages of sin is death. Sin, when it is finished, brings froth death. The wrath of God is revealed from heaven, not only against wicked nations, speaking ruin to them as nations, but against wicked persons, speaking ruin to them in their personal capacity, their personal interests, which pass into the other world and last to eternity, as national interests do not. (2.) It is the will of God that the wicked man should be warned of this: Warn them from me. This intimates that there is a possibility of preventing it, else it were a jest to give warning of it; nay, and that God is desirous it should be prevented. Sinners are therefore warned of the wrath to come, that they may flee from it, Mat 3:7. (3.) It is the work of ministers to give him warning, to say to the wicked, It shall be ill with thee, Isa 3:11. God ways in general, The soul that sinneth it shall die. The minister's business is to apply this to particular persons, and to say, "O wicked man! thou shalt surely die, whoever thou art; if thou go on still in thy trespasses, they will inevitably be thy ruin. O adulterer! O robber! O drunkard! O swearer! O sabbath-breaker! thou shalt surely die." And he must say this, not in passion, to provoke the sinner, but in compassion, to warn the wicked from hi way, warn him to turn from it, that he may live. This is to be done by the faithful preaching of the word in public, and by personal application to those whose sins are open.

3. If souls perish through his neglect of his duty, he brings guilt upon himself. "If the prophet do not warn the wicked of the ruin that is at the end of his wicked way, that wicked man shall die in his iniquity; for, though the watchman did not do his part, yet the sinner might have taken warning from the written word, from his own conscience, and from God's judgments upon others, by which his mouth shall be stopped, and God will be justified in his destruction." Note, It will not serve impenitent sinners to plead in the great day that their watchmen did not give them warning, that they were careless and unfaithful; for, though they were so, it will be made to appear that God left not himself without witness. "But he shall not perish alone in his iniquity; the watchman also shall be called to an account: His blood will I require at thy hand. The blind leader shall fall with the blind follower into the ditch." See what a desire God has of the salvation of sinners, in that he resents it so ill if those concerned do not what they can to prevent their destruction. And see what a great deal those ministers have to answer for another day who palliate sin, and flatter sinners in their evil way, and by their wicked lives countenance and harden them in their wickedness, and encourage them to believe that they shall have peace though they go on.

4. If he do his duty, he may take the comfort of it, though he do not see the success of it (Eze 33:9): "If thou warn the wicked of his way, if thou tell him faithfully what will be the end thereof, and call him earnestly to turn from it, and he do not turn, but persist in it, he shall die in his iniquity, and the fair warning given him will be an aggravation of his sin and ruin; but thou hast delivered thy soul." Note, It is a comfort to ministers that they may through grace save themselves, though they cannot be instrumental to save so many as they wish of those that hear them.

Ezekiel 33:10

These verses are the substance of what we had before (Eze 18:20, etc.) and they are so full and express a declaration of the terms on which people stand with God (as the former were of the terms on which ministers stand) that it is no wonder that they are here repeated, as those were, though we had the substance of them before. Observe here,

I. The cavils of the people against God's proceedings with them. God was now in his providence contending with them, but their uncircumcised hearts were not as yet humbled, for they were industrious to justify themselves, though thereby they reflected on God. Two things they insisted upon, in their reproaches of God, and in both they added iniquity to their sin and misery to their punishment:-1. They quarrelled with his promises and favours, as having no kindness nor sincerity in them, Eze 33:10. God had set life before them, but they plead that he had set it out of their reach, and therefore did but mock them with the mention of it. The prophet had said, some time ago (Eze 24:23), You shall pine away for your iniquities; with that word he had concluded his threatenings against Judah and Jerusalem; and this they now upbraided him with, as if it had been spoken absolutely, to drive them to despair; whereas it was spoken conditionally, to bring them to repentance. Thus are the sayings of God's ministers perverted by men of corrupt minds, who are inclined to pick quarrels. He puts them in hopes of life and happiness; and herein they would make him contradict himself; "for" (say they) "if our transgressions and our sins be upon us, as thou hast often told us they are, and if we must, as thou sayest, pine away in them, and wear out a miserable captivity in a fruitless repentance, how shall we then live? If this be our doom, there is no remedy. We die, we perish, we all perish." Note, It is very common for those that have been hardened with presumption when they were warned against sin to sink into despair when they are called to repent, and to conclude there is no hope of life for them. 2. They quarrelled with his threatenings and judgments, as having no justice or equity in them. They said, The way of the Lord is not equal (Eze 17:20), suggesting that God was partial in his proceedings, that with him there was respect of persons and that he was more severe against sin and sinners than there was cause.

II. Here is a satisfactory answer given to both these cavils.

1. Those that despaired of finding mercy with God are here answered with a solemn declaration of God's readiness to show mercy, Eze 33:11. When they spoke of pining away in their iniquity God sent the prophet to them, with all speed, to tell them that though their case was sad it was not desperate, but there was yet hope in Israel. (1.) It is certain that God has no delight in the ruin of sinners, nor does he desire it. If they will destroy themselves, he will glorify himself in it, but he has no pleasure in it, but would rather they should turn and live, for his goodness is that attribute of his which is most his glory, which is most his delight. He would rather sinners should turn and live than go on and die. He has said it, he has sworn it, that by these two immutable things, in both which it is impossible for God to lie, we might have strong

consolation. We have his word and his oath; and, since he could swear by no greater, he swears by himself: As I live. They questioned whether they should live, though they did repent and reform; yea, says God, as sure as I live, true penitents shall live also; for their life is hid with Christ in God. (2.) It is certain that God is sincere and in earnest in the calls he gives sinners to repent: Turn you, turn you, from your evil way. To repent is to turn from our evil way; this God requires sinners to do; this he urges them to do by repeated pressing instances: Turn you, turn you. O that they would be prevailed with to turn, to turn quickly, without delay! This he will enable them to do if they will but frame their doings to turn to the Lord, Hos 5:4. For he has said, I will pour out my Spirit unto you, Pro 1:23. And in this he will accept of them; for it is not only what he commands, but what he courts them to. (3.) It is certain that, if sinners perish in their impenitency, it is owing to themselves; they die because they will die; and herein they act most absurdly and unreasonably: Why will you die, O house of Israel? God would have heard them, and they would not be heard.

2. Those that despaired of finding justice with God are here answered with a solemn declaration of the rule of judgment which God would go by in dealing with the children of men, which carries along with it the evidence of its own equity; he that runs may read the justice of it. The Jewish nation, as a nation, was now dead; it was ruined to all intents and purposes. The prophet must therefore deal with particular persons, and the rule of judgment concerning them is much like that concerning a nation, Jer 18:8-10. If God speak concerning it to build and to plant, and it do wickedly, he will recall his favours and leave it to ruin. But if he speak concerning it to pluck up and destroy, and it repent, he will revoke the sentence and deliver it. So it is here. In short, The most plausible professors, if they apostatize, shall certainly perish for ever in their apostasy from God; and the most notorious sinners, if they repent, shall certainly be happy for ever in their return to God. This is here repeated again and again, because it ought to be again and again considered, and preached over to our own hearts. This was necessary to be inculcated upon this stupid senseless people, that said, The way of the Lord is not equal; for these rules of judgment are so plainly just that they need no other confirmation of them than the repetition of them.

(1.) If those that have made a great profession of religion throw off their profession, quit the good ways of God and grow loose and carnal, sensual and worldly, the profession they made and all the religious performances with which they had for a great while kept up the credit of their profession shall stand them in no stead, but they shall certainly perish in their iniquity, Eze 33:12, Eze 33:13, Eze 33:18. [1.] God says to the righteous man that he shall surely live, Eze 33:13. He says it by his word, by his ministers. He that lives regularly, his own heart tells him, his neighbours tell him, He shall live. Surely such a man as this cannot but be happy. And it is certain, if he proceed and persevere in his righteousness, and if, in order to that, he be upright and sincere in it, if he be really as good as he seems to be, he shall live; he shall continue in the love of God and be for ever happy in that love. [2.] Righteous men, who have very good hopes of themselves and whom others have a very good opinion of, are yet in danger of turning to iniquity by trusting to their righteousness. So the case is put here: If he trust to his own righteousness, and commit iniquity, and come to make a trade of sin-if he not only take a false step, but turn aside into a false way and persist in it. This may possibly be the case of a righteous man, and it is the effect of his trusting to his own righteousness. Note, Many eminent professors have been ruined by a proud conceitedness of themselves and confidence in themselves. He trust to the merit of his own righteousness, and thinks he has already made God so much his debtor that now he may venture to commit iniquity, for he has righteousness enough in stock to make amends for it; he fancies that whatever evil deeds he may do hereafter he can be in no danger from them, having so many good deeds beforehand to counterbalance them. Or, He trust to the strength of his own righteousness, thinks himself now so well established in a course of virtue that he may thrust himself into any temptation and it cannot overcome him, and so by presuming on his own sufficiency he is brought to commit iniquity. By making bold on the confines of sin he is drawn at length into the depths of hell. This ruined the Pharisees; they trusted to themselves that they were righteous, and that their long prayers, and fasting twice in the week, would atone for their devouring widows' houses. [3.] If righteous men turn to iniquity, and return not to their righteousness, they shall certainly perish in their iniquity, and all the righteousness they have formerly done, all their prayers, and all their alms, shall be forgotten. No mention shall be made, no remembrance had, of their good deeds; they shall be overlooked, as if they had never been. The righteousness of the righteous shall not deliver him from the wrath of God, and the curse of the law, in the day of his transgression. When he becomes a traitor and a rebel, and takes up arms against his rightful Sovereign, it will not serve for him to plead in his own defence that formerly he was a loyal subject, and did many good services to the government. No; he shall not be able to live. The remembrance of his former righteousness shall be no satisfaction either to God's justice or his own conscience in the day that he sins, but rather shall, in the estimate of both, highly aggravate the sin and folly of his apostasy. And therefore for his iniquity that he committed he shall die, Eze 33:13. And again (Eze 33:18), He shall even die thereby; and it is owing to himself.

(2.) If those that have lived a wicked life repent and reform, forsake their wicked ways and become religious, their sins shall be pardoned, and they shall be justified and saved, if they persevere in their reformation. [1.] God says to the wicked, "Thou shalt surely die. The way that thou art in leads to destruction. The wages of thy sin is death, and thy iniquity will shortly be thy ruin." It was said to the righteous man, Thou shalt surely live, for his encouragement to proceed and persevere in the way of righteousness; but he made an ill use of it, and was emboldened by it to commit iniquity. It was said to the wicked man, Thou shalt surely die, for warning to him not to persist in his wicked ways; and he makes a good use of it, and is quickened thereby to return to God and duty. Thus even the threatenings of the word are to some, by the grace of God, a savour of life unto life, while even the promises of the word become to others, by their own corruption, a savour of death unto death. When God says to the wicked man, Thou shalt surely die, die eternally, it is to frighten him, not out of his wits, but out of his sins. [2.] There is many a wicked man who was hastening apace to his own destruction who yet is wrought upon by the grace of God to return and repent, and live a holy life. He turns from his sin (Eze 33:14), and is resolved that he will have no more to do with it; and, as an evidence of his repentance for wrong done, he restores the pledge (Eze 33:15) which he had taken uncharitably from the poor, he gives again that which he had robbed and taken unjustly from the rich. Nor does he only cease to do evil, but he learns to do well; he does that which is lawful and right, and makes conscience of his duty both to God and man-a great change, since, awhile ago, he neither feared God nor regarded man. But many such amazing changes, and blessed ones, have been wrought by the power of divine grace. He that was going on in the paths of death and the destroyer now walks in the statues of life, in the way of God's commandments, which has both life in it (Pro 12:28) and life at the end of it, Mat 19:17. And in this good way he perseveres without committing iniquity, though not free from remaining infirmity, yet under the dominion of no iniquity. He repents not of his repentance, nor returns to the commission of those gross sins which he before allowed himself in. [3.] He that does thus repent and return shall escape the ruin he was running into, and his former sins shall be no prejudice to his acceptance with God. Let him not pine away in his iniquity, for, if he confess and forsake it, he shall find mercy. He shall surely live; he shall not die, Eze 33:15. Again (Eze 33:16), He shall surely live. Again (Eze 33:19), He has done that which is lawful and right, and he shall live thereby. But will not his wickednesses be remembered against him? No; he shall not be punished for them (Eze 33:12): As for the wickedness of the wicked, though it was very heinous, yet he shall not fall thereby in the day that he turns from his wickedness. Now that it has become his grief it shall not be his ruin. Now that there is a settled separation between him and sin there shall be no longer a separation between him and God. Nay, he shall not be so much as upbraided with them (Eze 33:16): None of his sins that he has committed shall be mentioned unto him, either as a clog to his pardon or an allay to the comfort of it, or as any blemish and diminution to the glory that is prepared for him.

Now lay all this together, and then judge whether the way of the Lord be not equal, whether this will not justify God in the destruction of sinners and glorify him in the salvation of penitents. The conclusion of the whole matter is (Eze 33:20): "O you house of Israel, though you are all involved now in the common calamity, yet there shall be a distinction of persons made in the spiritual and eternal state, and I will judge you every one after his ways." Though they were sent into captivity by the lump, good fish and bad enclosed in the same net, yet there he will separate between the precious and the vile and will render to every man according to his works. Therefore God's way is equal and unexceptionable; but, as for the children of thy people, God turns them over to the prophet, as he did to Moses (Exo 32:7): "They are thy people; I can scarcely own them for mine." As for them, their way is unequal; this way which they have got of quarrelling with God and his prophets is absurd and unreasonable. In all disputes between God and his creatures it will certainly be found that he is in the right and they are in the wrong.

Ezekiel 33:21

Here we have,

cclxxxix

I. The tidings brought to Ezekiel of the burning of Jerusalem by the Chaldeans. The city was burnt in the eleventh year of the captivity and the fifth month, Jer 52:12, Jer 52:13. Tidings hereof were brought to the prophet by one that was an eye-witness of the destruction, in the twelfth year, and the tenth month (Eze 33:21), which was a year and almost five months after the thing was done; we may well suppose that, there being a constant correspondence at this time more than ever kept up between Jerusalem and Babylon, he had heard the news long before. But this was the first time he had an account of it from a refugee, from one who escaped, who could be particular, and would be pathetic, in the narrative of it. And the sign given him was the coming of such a one to him as had himself narrowly escaped the flames (Eze 24:26): He that escapes in that day shall come unto thee, to cause thee to hear it with thy ears, to hear it more distinctly than ever, from one that could say, Quaeque ipse miserrima vidi-These miserable scenes I saw.

II. The divine impressions and influences he was under, to prepare him for those heavy tidings (Eze 33:22): The hand of the Lord was upon me before he came, and had opened my mouth to speak to the house of Israel what we had in the former part of this chapter. And now he was no more dumb; he prophesied now with more freedom and boldness, being by the event proved a true prophet, to the confusion of those that contradicted him. All the prophecies from ch. 24 to this chapter have relation purely to the nations about, it is probable that the prophet, when he received them from the Lord, did not deliver them by word of mouth, but in writing; for he could not Say to the Ammonites, Say unto Tyrus, Say unto Pharaoh, etc., so and so, but by letters directed to the persons concerned, as Zacharias, when he could not speak, wrote; and herein he was as truly executing his prophetic office as ever. Note, Even silenced ministers may be doing a great deal of good by writing letters and making visits. But now the prophet's mouth is opened, that he may speak to the children of his people. It is probable that he had, during these three years, been continually speaking to them as a friend, putting them in mind of what he had formerly delivered to them, but that he never spoke to them as a prophet, by inspiration, till now, when the hand of the Lord came upon him, renewed his commission, gave him fresh instructions, and opened his mouth, furnished him with power to speak to the people as he ought to speak.

III. The particular message he was entrusted with, relating to these Jews that yet remained in the land of Israel, and inhabited the wastes of that land, Eze 33:24. See what work sin had made. The cities of Israel had now become the wastes of Israel, for they lay all in ruins; some few that had escaped the sword and captivity still continued there and began to think of re-settling. This was so long after the destruction of Jerusalem that it was some time before this that Gedaliah (a modest humble man) and his friends were slain; but probably at this time Johanan, and the proud men that joined with him, were at the height (Jer 43:2); and before they came to a resolution to go into Egypt, wherein Jeremiah opposed them, it is probable that the project was to establish themselves in the wastes of the land of Israel, in which Ezekiel here opposed them, and probably despatched the message away by the person that brought him the news of Jerusalem's destruction. Or, perhaps, those here prophesied against might be some other party of Jews, that remained in the land, hoping to take root there and to be sole masters of it, after Johanan and his forces had gone into Egypt. Now here we have,

1. An account of the pride of these remaining Jews, who dwelt in the wastes of the land of Israel. Though the providence of God concerning them had been very humbling, and still was very threatening, yet they were intolerably haughty and secure, and promised themselves peace. He that brought the news to the prophet that Jerusalem was smitten could not tell him (it is likely) what these people said, but God tells him, They say, "The land is given us for inheritance, Eze 33:24. Our partners being gone, it is now all our own by survivorship, or, for want of heirs, it comes to us as occupants; we shall now be placed alone in the midst of the earth and have it all to ourselves." This argues great stupidity under the weighty hand of God, and a reigning selfishness and narrow-spiritedness; they pleased themselves in the ruin of their country as long as they hoped to find their own account in it, cared not though it were all waste, so that they might have the sole property-a poor inheritance to be proud of! They have the impudence to compare their case with Abraham's, glorying in this, We have Abraham to our father. "Abraham," say they, "was one, one family, and he inherited the land, and lived many years in the peaceable enjoyment of it; but we are many, many families, more numerous than he; the land is given us for inheritance." (1.) They think they can make out as good a title from God to this land as Abraham could: "If God gave this land to him, who was but one worshipper of him, as a reward of his service, much more will he give it to us, who are many worshippers of him, as the reward of our service." This shows the great conceit they had of the own merits, as if they were greater than those of Abraham their father, who yet was not justified by works. (2.) They think they can make good the possession of this land against the Chaldeans and all others invaders, as well as Abraham could against those that were competitors with him for it: "If he, who was but one, could hold it, much more shall we, who are many, and have many more at command than his 300 trained servants." This shows the confidence they had in their own might; they had got possession, and were resolved to keep it.

2. A check to this pride. Since God's providences did neither humble them nor terrify them, he sends them a message sufficient to do both.

(1.) To humble them, he tells them of the wickedness they still persisted in, which rendered them utterly unworthy to possess this land, so that they could not expect God should give it to them. They had been followed with one judgment after another, but they had not profited by those means of grace as might be expected; they were still unreformed, and how could they expect that they should possess the land? "Shall you possess the land? What! such wicked people as you are? How shall I put thee among the children, and give thee a pleasant land? Jer 3:19. Surely you never reflect upon yourselves, else you would rather wonder that you are in the land of the living than expect to possess this land. For do you now know how bad you are?" [1.] "You make no conscience of forbidden fruit, forbidden food: You eat with the blood," directly contrary to one of the precepts given to Noah and his sons when God gave them possession of the earth,

Gen 9:4. [2.] "Idolatry, that covenant-breaking sin, that sin which the jealous God has been in a particular manner provoked by to lay your country waste, is still the sin that most easily besets you and which you have a strong inclination to: You lift up your eyes towards your idols, which is a sign that though perhaps you do not bow your knee to them so much as you have done, yet you set your hearts upon them and hanker after them." [3.] "You are as fierce, and cruel, and barbarous as ever: You shed blood, innocent blood." [4.] "You confide in your own strength, your own arm, your own bow, and have no dependence on, or regard to, God and his providence: You stand upon your sword (Eze 33:26); you think to carry all before you, and make all your own, by force of arms." How can those expect the inheritance of Isaac (as these did) who are of Ishmael's disposition, that had his hand against every man (Gen 16:12), and Esau's resolution to live by his sword? Gen 27:40. We met with those (Gen 32:27) who, when they died, thought they could not lie easy underground unless they had their swords under their heads. Here we meet with those who, while they live, think they cannot stand firmly above ground unless they have their swords under their feet, as if swords were both the softest pillows and the strongest pillars; though it was sin, it was sin, that first drew the sword. But, blessed be God, there are those who know better, who stand upon the support of the divine power and promise and lay their heads in the bosom of divine love, not trusting in their own sword, Psa 44:3. [5.] "You are guilty of all manner of abominations, and, particularly, you defile every one his neighbour's wife, which is an abomination of the first magnitude, and shall you possess the land? What! such vile miscreants as you?" Note, Those cannot expect to possess the land, nor to enjoy any true comfort or happiness here or hereafter, who live in rebellion against the Lord.

(2.) To terrify them, he tells them of the further judgments God had in store for them, which should make them utterly unable to possess this land, so that they could not stand it out against the enemy. Do they say that they shall possess the land? God has said they shall not, he has sworn it, As I live, saith the Lord. Though he has sworn that he delights not in the death of sinners, yet he has sworn also that those who persist in impenitency and unbelief shall not enter into his rest. [1.] Those that are in the cities, here called the wastes, shall fall by the sword, either by the sword of the Chaldeans, who come to avenge the murder of Gedaliah, or by one another's swords, in their intestine broils. [2.] Those that are in the open field shall be devoured by wild beasts, which swarmed, of course, in the country when it was dispeopled, and there were none to master them and keep them under, Exo 23:29. When the army of the enemy had quitted the country still there was no safety in it. Noisome beasts constituted one of the four sore judgments, Eze 14:15. [3.] Those that are in the forts and in the caves, that think themselves safe in artificial or natural fastnesses, because men's eyes cannot discover them nor men's darts reach them, there the arrows of the Almighty shall find them out; they shall die of the pestilence. [4.] The whole land, even the land of Israel, that had been the glory of all lands, shall be most desolate, Eze 33:28. It shall be desolation, desolation, all over as desolate as desolation itself can make it. The mountain of Israel, the fruitful mountains, Zion itself the holy mountain not excepted, shall be desolate, the roads unfrequented, the houses uninhabited, that none shall pass through; as it was threatened (Deu 28:62), You shall be left few in number. [5.] The pomp of her strength, whatever she glories in as her pomp and trusts to as her strength, shall be made to cease. [6.] The cause of all this was very bad; it is for all their abominations which they have committed. It is sin that does all this mischief, that makes nations desolate; and therefore we ought to call it an abomination. [7.] Yet the effect of all this will be very good: Then shall they know that I am the Lord, am their Lord, and shall return to their allegiance, when I have made the land most desolate. Those are untractable unteachable indeed that are not made to know their dependence upon God when all their creature-comforts fail them and are made desolate.

Ezekiel 33:30

The foregoing verses spoke conviction to the Jews who remained in the land of Israel, who were monuments of sparing mercy and yet returned not to the Lord; in these verses those are reproved who were now in captivity in Babylon, under divine rebukes, and yet were not reformed by them. They are not indeed charged with the same gross enormities that the others are charged with. They made some show of religion and devotion; but their hearts were not right with God. The thing they are here accused of is mocking the messengers of the lord, one of their measure-filling sins, which brought this ruin upon them, and yet they were not cured of it. Two ways they mocked the prophet Ezekiel:-

I. By invidious ill natured reflections upon him, privately among themselves, endeavouring by all means possible to render him despicable. The prophet did not know it, but charitably thought that those who spoke so well to him to his face, with so much seeming respect and deference, would surely not speak ill of him behind his back. But God comes and tells him, The children of thy people are still talking against thee (Eze 33:30), or talking of thee, no good, I doubt. Note, Public persons are a common theme or subject of discourse; every one takes a liberty to censure them at pleasure. Faithful ministers know not how much ill is said of them every day; it is well that they do not; for, if they did, it might prove a discouragement to them in their work not to be easily got over. God takes notice of all that is said against his ministers, not only what is decreed against them, or sworn against them, not only what is written against them, or spoken with solemnity and deliberation, but of what is said against them in common talk, among neighbours when they meet in an evening, by the walls and in the doors of their houses, where whatever freedom of speech they use, if they reproach and slander any of God's ministers, God will reckon with them for it; his prophets shall not be made the song of the drunkards always. They had no crime to lay to the prophet's charge, but they loved to talk of him in a careless, scornful, bantering way; they said, jokingly, "Come, and let us hear what is the word that comes forth from the Lord; perhaps it will be something new, and will entertain us, and furnish us with matter for discourse." Note, Those have arrived as a great pitch of profaneness who can make so great a privilege, and so great a duty, as the preaching and hearing of the word of God, a matter of sport and ridicule, yea though it be not done publicly, but in private conversation among themselves. Serious things should be spoken of seriously.

II. By dissembling with him in their attendance upon his ministry. Hypocrites mock God and mock his prophets. But their hypocrisy is open before God, and the day is coming when, as here, it will be laid open. Observe here,

1. The plausible profession which these people made and the speciousness of their pretensions. They are like those (Mat 15:8) who draw nigh to God with their mouths and honour him with their lips, but their hearts are far from him. (1.) They were diligent and constant in their attendance upon the means of grace: They come unto thee as the people come. In Babylon they had no temple or synagogue, but they went to the prophet's house (Eze 8:1), and there, it is probable, they spent their new moons and their sabbaths in religious exercises,Kg2 4:23. When the prophet was bound the word of the Lord was not bound; and the people, when they had not the help for their souls that they wished for, were thankful for what they had; it was a reviving in their bondage. Now these hypocrites came, according to the coming of the people, as duly and as early as any of the prophet's hearers. Their being said to come as the people came seems to intimate that the reason why they came was because other people came; they did not come out of conscience towards God, but only for company, for fashion-sake, and because it was now the custom of their countrymen. Note, Those that have no inward principle of love to God's ordinances may yet be found much in the external observance of them. Cain brought his sacrifice as well as Abel; and the Pharisee went up to the temple to pray as well as the publican. (2.) They behaved themselves very decently and reverently in the public assembly; there were none of them whispering, or laughing, or gazing about them, or sleeping. But they sit before thee as my people, with all the shows of gravity, and sereneness, and composure of mind. They sit out the time, without weariness, or wishing the sermon done. (3.) They were very attentive to the word preached: "They are not thinking of something else, but they hear thy words, and take notice of what thou sayest." (4.) They pretended to have a great kindness and respect for the prophet. Though, behind his back, they could not give him a good word, yet, to his face, they showed much love to him and his doctrine; they pretended to have a great concern lest he should spend himself too much in preaching or expose himself to the Chaldeans, for they would be thought to be some of his best friends and well-wishers. (5.) They took a great deal of pleasure in the word; they delighted to know God's word, Isa 58:2. Herod heard John Baptist gladly, Mar 6:20. Thou art unto them as a very lovely song. Ezekiel's matter was surprising, his language fine, his expressions elegant, his similitudes apt, his voice melodious, and his delivery graceful; so that they could sit with as much pleasure to hear him preach as (if I may speak in the language of our times) to see a play or an opera, or to hear a concert of music. Ezekiel was to them as one that had a pleasant voice and could sing well, or play well on an instrument. Note, Men may have their fancies pleased by the word, and yet not have their consciences touched nor their hearts changed, the itching ear gratified and yet not the corrupt nature sanctified.

2. The hypocrisy of these professions and pretensions; it is all a sham, it is all a jest. (1.) They have no cordial affection for the word of God. While they show much love it is only with the mouth, from the teeth outward, but their heart goes after their covetousness; they are as much set

upon the world as ever, as much in love and league with it as ever. Hearing the word is only their diversion and recreation, a pretty amusement now and then for an hour or two. But still their main business is with their farm and merchandise; the bent and bias of their souls are towards them, and their inward thoughts are employed in projects about them. Note, Covetousness is the ruining sin of multitudes that make a great profession of religion; it is the love of the world that secretly eats the love of God out of their hearts. The cares of this world and the deceitfulness of riches are the thorns that choke the seed, and choke the soul too. And those neither please God nor profit themselves who, when they are hearing the word of God, are musing upon their worldly affairs. God has his eye on the hearts that do so. (2.) They yield no subjection to it. They hear thy words, but it is only a hearing that they give thee, for they will not do them, Eze 33:31. And again (Eze 33:32), they do them not. They will not be persuaded by all the prophet can say, either by authority or argument, to cross themselves in any instance, to part with any one beloved sin, or apply themselves to any one duty that is against the grain to flesh and blood. Note, There are many who take pleasure in hearing the word, but make no conscience of doing it; and so they build upon the sand, and deceive themselves.

3. Let us see what will be in the end hereof: Shall their unbelief and carelessness make the word of God of no effect? By no means. (1.) God will confirm the prophet's word, though they contemn it, and make light of it, Eze 33:33. What he says will come to pass, and not one jot or one tittle shall fall to the ground. Note, The curses of the law, though they may be bantered by profane wits, cannot be baffled. (2.) They themselves shall rue their folly when it is too late. When it comes to pass they shall know, shall know to their cost, know to their confusion, that a prophet has been among them, though they made no more of him than as one that had a pleasant voice. Note, Those who will not consider that a prophet is among them, and who improve not the day of their visitation while it is continued, will be made to remember that a prophet has been among them when the things that belong to their peace are hidden from their eyes. The day is coming when vain and worldly men will have other thoughts of things than now they have, and will feel a weight in that which they made light of. They shall know that a prophet has been among them when they see the event exactly answer the prediction, and the prophet himself shall be a witness against them that they had fair warning given them, but would not take it. When Ezekiel is gone, whom now they speak against, and there is no more any prophet, nor any to show them how long, then they will remember that once they had a prophet, but knew not how to use him well. Note, Those who will not know the worth of mercies by the improvement of them will justly be made to know the worth of them by the want of them, as those who should desire to see one of the days of the Son of man, which now they slighted, and might not see it.

Ezekiel Chapter 34

The iniquities and calamities of God's Israel had been largely and pathetically lamented before, in this book. Now in this chapter the shepherds of Israel, their rulers both in church and state, are called to an account, as having been very much accessory to the sin and ruin of Israel, by their neglecting to do the duty of their place. Here is, I. A high charge exhibited against them for their negligence, their unskillfulness, and unfaithfulness in the management of public affairs (Eze 34:1-6 and Eze 34:8). II. Their discharge from their trust, for their insufficiency and treachery (Eze 34:7-10). III. A gracious promise that God would take care of his flock, though they did not, and that it should not always suffer as it had done by their mal-administrations (Eze 34:11-16). IV. Another charge exhibited against those of the flock that were fat and strong, for the injuries they did to those that were weak and feeble (Eze 34:17-22). V. Another promise that God would in the fulness of time send the Messiah, to be the great and good Shepherd of the sheep, who should redress all grievances and set every thing to rights with the flock (Eze 34:23-31).

Ezekiel 34:1

The prophecy of this chapter is not dated, nor any of those that follow it, till ch. 40. It is most probable that it was delivered after the completing of Jerusalem's destruction, when it would be very seasonable to enquire into the causes of it.

I. The prophet is ordered to prophesy against the shepherds of Israel-the princes and magistrates, the priests and Levites, the great Sanhedrim or council of state, or whoever they were that had the direction of public affairs in a higher or lower sphere, the kings especially, for there were two of them now captives in Babylon, who, as well as the people, must have their transgressions shown them, that they might repent, as Manasseh in his captivity. God has something to say to the shepherds, for they are but under-shepherds, accountable to him who is the great Shepherd of Israel, Psa 80:1. And that which he says is, Woe to the shepherds of Israel! Though they are shepherds, and shepherds of Israel, yet he must not spare them, must not flatter them. Note, If men's dignity and power do not, as they ought, keep them from sin, they will not serve to exempt them from reproof, to excuse their repentance, or to secure them from the judgments of God if they do not repent. We had a woe to the pastors, Jer 23:1. God will in a particular manner reckon with them if they be false to their trust.

II. He is here directed what to charge the shepherds with, in God's name, as the ground of God's controversy with them; for it is not a causeless quarrel. Two things they are charged with:-

1. That all their care was to advance and enrich themselves and to make themselves great. Their business was to take care of those that were committed to their charge: Should not the shepherds feed the flocks? No doubt they should; they betray their trust if they do not. Not that they are to put the meat into their mouths, but to provide it for them and bring them to it. But these shepherds made this the least of their care; they fed themselves, contrived every thing to gratify and indulge their own appetite, and to make themselves rich and great, fat and easy. They made sure of the profits of their places; they did eat the fat, the cream (so some), for he that feeds a flock eats of the milk of it (Col 9:7), and they made sure of the best of the milk. They made sure of the fleece, and clothed themselves with the wool, getting into their hands as much as they could of the estates of their subjects, yea, and killed those that were well fed, that what they had might be fed upon, as Naboth was put to death for his vineyard. Note, There is a woe to those who are in public trusts, but consult only their own private interest, and are more inquisitive about the benefice than about the office, what money is to be got than what good to be done. It is an old complaint, All seek their own, and too many more than their own. 2. That they took no care for the benefit and welfare of those that were committed to their charge: You feed not the flock. They neither knew how to do it, so ignorant were they, nor would they take any pains to do it, so lazy and slothful were they; nay, they never desired nor designed it, so treacherous and unfaithful were they. (1.) They did not do their duty to those of the flock that were distempered, did not strengthen them, nor heal them, nor bind them up, Eze 34:4. When any of the flock were sick or hurt, worried or wounded, it was all one to them whether they lived or died; they never looked after them. The princes and judges took no care to right those that suffered wrong or to shelter injured innocency. They took no care of the poor to see them provided for; they might starve, for them. The priests took no care to instruct the ignorant, to rectify the mistakes of those that were in error, to warn the unruly, or to comfort the feeble-minded. The ministers of state took no care to check the growing distempers of the kingdom, which threatened the vitals of it. Things were amiss, and out of course, every where, and nothing was done to rectify them. (2.) They did not do their duty to those of the flock that were dispersed, that were driven away by the enemies that invaded the country, and were forced to seek for shelter where they could find a place, or that wandered of choice upon the mountains and hills (Eze 34:6), where they were exposed to the beasts of prey and became meat to them, Eze 34:5. Every one is ready to seize a waif and stray. Some went abroad and begged, some went abroad and traded, and thus the country became thin of inhabitants, and was weakened and impoverished, and wanted hands both in the fields of corn and in the fields of battle, both in harvest and in war: My flock was scattered upon all the face of the earth, Eze 34:6. And they were never enquired after, were never encouraged to return to their own country: None did search or seek after them. Nay, with force and cruelty they ruled them, which drove more away, and discouraged those that were driven away from all thoughts of returning. Their case is bad who have reason to expect better treatment among strangers than in their own country. It may be meant of those of the flock that went astray from God and their duty; and the priests, that should have taught the good knowledge of the Lord, used no means to convince and reclaim them, so that they became an easy prey to

seducers. Thus were they scattered because there was no shepherd, Eze 34:5. There were those that called themselves shepherds, but really they were not. Note, Those that do not do the work of shepherds are unworthy of the name. And if those that undertake to be shepherds are foolish shepherds (Zac 11:15), if they are proud and above their business, idle and do not love their business, or faithless and unconcerned about it, the case of the flock is as bad as if it were without a shepherd. Better no shepherd than such shepherds. Christ complains that his flock were as sheep having no shepherd, when yet the scribes and Pharisees sat in Moses' seat, Mat 9:36. It is ill with the patient when his physician is his worst disease, ill with the flock when the shepherds drive them away and disperse them, by ruling them with force.

Ezekiel 34:7

Upon reading the foregoing articles of impeachment drawn up, in God's name, against the shepherds of Israel, we cannot but look upon the shepherds with a just indignation, and upon the flock with a tender compassion. God, by the prophet, here expresses both in a high degree; and the shepherds are called upon (Eze 34:7, Eze 34:9) to hear the word of the Lord, to hear this word. Let them hear how little he regards them, who made much of themselves, and how much he regards the flock, which they made nothing of; both will be humbling to them. Those that will not hear the word of the Lord giving them their direction shall be made to hear the word of the Lord reading them their doom. Now see here,

I. How much displeased God is at the shepherds. Their crimes are repeated, Eze 34:8. God's flock became a prey to the deceivers first that drew them to idolatry, and then to the destroyers that carried them into captivity; and these shepherds took no care to prevent either the one or the other, but were as if there had been no shepherds; and therefore God says (Eze 34:10), and confirms it with an oath (Eze 34:8), I am against the shepherds. They had a commission from God to feed the flock, and made use of this name in what they did, expecting he would stand by them. "No," says God, "so far from that, I am against them." Note, It is not our having the name and authority of shepherds that will engage God for us, if we do not the work enjoined us, and be not faithful to the trust reposed in us. God is against them, and they shall know it; for, 1. They shall be made to account for the manner in which they have discharged their trust: "I will require my flock at their hands, and charge it upon them that so many of them are missing." Note, Those will have a great deal to answer for in the judgment-day who take upon them the care of souls and yet take no care of them. Ministers must watch and work as those that must give account, Heb 13:17. 2. They shall be deprived officio et beneficio-both of the work and of the wages. They shall cease from feeding the flock, that is, from pretending to feed it. Note, It is just with God to take out of men's hands that power which they have abused and that trust which they have betrayed. But, if this were all their punishment, they could bear it well enough; therefore it is added, "Neither shall the shepherds feed themselves any more, for I will deliver my flock from their mouth, which, instead of protecting, they had made a prey of." Note, Those that are enriching themselves with the spoils of the public cannot expect that they shall always be

ccxcviii

suffered to do so. Nor will God always permit his people to be trampled upon by those that should support them, but will find a time to deliver them from the shepherds their false friends, as well as from the lions their open enemies.

II. How much concerned God is for the flock; he speaks as if he were the more concerned for them because he saw them thus neglected, for with him the fatherless finds mercy. Precious promises are made here upon the occasion, which were to have their accomplishment in the return of the Jews out of their captivity and their re-establishment in their own land. Let the shepherds hear this word of the Lord, and know that they have no part nor lot in the matter. But let the poor sheep hear it and take the comfort of it. Note, Though magistrates and ministers fail in doing their part, for the good of the church, yet God will not fail in doing his; he will take the flock into his own hand rather than the church shall come short of any kindness he has designed for it. The under-shepherds may prove careless, but the chief Shepherd neither slumbers nor sleeps. They may be false, but God abides faithful.

1. God will gather his sheep together that were scattered, and bring those back to the fold that had wandered from it: "I, even I, who alone can do it, will do it, and will have all the glory of it. I will both search my sheep and find them out (Eze 34:11) as a shepherd does (Eze 34:12), and bring them back as he does the stray-sheep, upon his shoulders, from all the places where they have been scattered in the cloudy and dark day." There are cloudy and dark days, windy and stormy ones, which scatter God's sheep, which send them hither and thither, to divers and distant places, in quest of secrecy and safety. But, (1.) Wherever they are the eye of God will find them out; for his eyes run to and fro through the earth, in favour of them. I will seek out my sheep; and not one that belongs to the fold, though driven ever so far off, shall be lost. The Lord knows those that are his; he knows their work and where they dwell (Rev 2:13), and where they are hidden. (2.) When his time shall come his arms will fetch them home (Eze 34:13): I will bring them out from the people. God will both incline their hearts to come by his grace and will by his providence open a door for them and remove every difficulty that lies in the way. They shall not return one by one, clandestinely stealing away, but they shall return in a body: "I will gather them from the countries into which they are dispersed, not only the most considerable families of them, but every particular person. I will seek that which was lost and bring again that which was driven away," Eze 34:16. This was done when so many thousand Jews returned triumphantly out of Babylon, under the conduct of Zerubbabel, Ezra, and others. When those that have gone astray from God into the paths of sin are brought back by repentance, when those that erred come to the acknowledgment of the truth, when God's outcasts are gathered and restored, and religious assemblies, that were dispersed, rally again, upon the ceasing of persecution, and when the churches have rest and liberty, then this promise has a further accomplishment.

2. God will feed his people as the sheep of his pasture, that had been famished. God will bring the returning captives safely to their own land (Eze 34:13), will feed them upon the mountains of Israel, and that is a good pasture, and a fat pasture (Eze 34:14); there shall their feeding be, and

there shall be their fold; and it is a good fold. There God will not only feed them, but cause them to lie down (Eze 34:15), which denotes a comfortable rest after they had tired themselves with their wanderings, and a constant continuing residence; they shall not be driven out again from these green pastures, as they have been, nor shall they be disturbed, but shall lie down in a sweet repose and there shall be none to make them afraid. Psa 23:2, He makes me to lie down in green pastures. Compare this with the like promise (Jer 23:3, Jer 23:4), when God restored them not only to the milk and honey of their own land, to the enjoyment of its fruits, but to the privileges of his sanctuary on Mount Zion, the chief of the mountains of Israel. When they had an altar and a temple again, and the benefit of a settled priesthood, then they were fed in a good pasture.

3. He will succour those that are hurt, will bind up that which was broken and strengthen that which was sick, will comfort those that mourn in Zion and with Zion. If ministers, who should speak peace to those who are of a sorrowful spirit, neglect their duty, yet the Holy Ghost the Comforter will be faithful to his office. But, as it follows, the fat and the strong shall be destroyed. He that has rest for disquieted saints has terror to speak to presumptuous sinners. As every valley shall be filled, so every mountain and hill shall be brought low, Luk 3:5.

Ezekiel 34:17

The prophet has no more to say to the shepherds, but he has now a message to deliver to the flock. God had ordered him to speak tenderly to them, and to assure them of the mercy he had in store for them. But here he is ordered to make a difference between some and others of them, to separate between the precious and the vile and then to give them a promise of the Messiah, by whom this distinction should be effectually made, partly at his first coming (for for judgment he came into this world, Joh 9:39, to fill the hungry with good things and to send the rich empty away, Luk 1:53), but completely at his second coming, when he shall, as it is here said, judge between cattle and cattle, as a shepherd divides between the sheep and the goats, and shall set the sheep on his right hand and the goats on his left (Mat 25:32, Mat 25:33), which seems to have reference to this. We have here,

I. Conviction spoken to those of the flock that were fat and strong, the rams and the he-goats (Eze 34:17), those that, though they had not power, as shepherds and rulers, to oppress with, yet, being rich and wealthy, made use of the opportunity which this gave them to bear hard upon their poor neighbours. Those that have much would have more, and, if they set to it, will have more, so many ways have they of encroaching upon their poor neighbours, and forcing from them the one ewe-lamb, Sa2 12:4. Do not the rich oppress the poor merely with the help of their riches, and draw them before the judgment-seats? Jam 2:6. Poor servants and tenants are hardly used by their rich lords and masters. The rams and the he-goats not only kept all the good pasture to themselves, ate the fat and drank the sweet, but they would not let the poor of the flock have any comfortable enjoyment of the little that was left them; they trod down the residue of the pastures and fouled the residue of the waters, so that the flock was obliged to eat that which they had trodden into the dirt, and drink that which they had muddied, Eze 34:18, Eze 34:19. This intimates that the great men not only by extortion and oppression made and kept their neighbours poor, and scarcely left them enough to subsist on, but were so vexatious to them that what little coarse fare they had was embittered to them. And this seemed a small thing to them; they thought there was no harm in it, as if it were the privilege of their quality to be injurious to all their neighbours. Note, Many that live in pomp and at ease themselves care not what straits those about them are reduced to, so they may but have every thing to their mind. Those that are at ease, and the proud, grudge that any body should live by them with any comfort. But this as not all; they not only robbed the poor, to make them poorer, but were troublesome to the sick and weak of the flock (Eze 34:21): They thrust with side and shoulder those that were feeble (for the weakest goes to the wall) and pushed the diseased with their horns, because they knew they could be too hard for them, when they durst not meddle with their match. It has been observed concerning sheep that if one of the flock be sick and faint the rest will secure it as well as they can, and shelter it from the scorching heat of the sun; but these, on the contrary, were most injurious to the diseased. Those that they could not serve themselves of they did what they could to rid the country of, and so scattered them abroad, as if the poor, whom, Christ says, we must have always with us, were public nuisances, not to be relieved, but sent far away from us. Note, It is a barbarous thing to add affliction to the afflicted. Perhaps these rams and he-goats are designed to represent the scribes and Pharisees, for they are such troublers of the church as Christ himself must come to deliver it from, Eze 34:23. They devoured widows' houses, took away the key of knowledge, corrupted the pure water of divine truths, and oppressed the consciences of men with the traditions of the elders, besides that they were continually vexatious and injurious to the poor of the flock that waited on the Lord, Zac 11:11. Note, It is no new thing for the flock of God to receive a great deal of damage and mischief from those that are themselves of the flock, and in eminent stations in it, Act 20:30.

II. Comfort spoken to those of the flock that are poor and feeble, and that wait for the consolation of Israel (Eze 34:22): "I will save my flock, and they shall no more be spoiled as they have been by the beasts of prey, by their own shepherds or by the rams and he-goats among themselves." Upon this occasion, as is usual in the prophets, comes in a prediction of the coming of the Messiah, and the setting up of his kingdom, and the exceedingly great and precious benefits which the church should enjoy under the protection and influence of that kingdom. Observe what is here foretold,

1. Concerning the Messiah himself. (1.) He shall have his commission from God himself: I will set him up (Eze 34:23); I will raise him up, Eze 34:29. He sanctified and sealed him, appointed and anointed him. (2.) He shall be the great Shepherd of the sheep, who shall do that for his flock which no one else could do. He is the one Shepherd, under whom Jews and Gentiles should be one fold. (3.) He is God's servant, employed by him and for him, and doing all in obedience to his will, with an eye to his glory-his servant, to re-establish his kingdom among men and advance the interests of that kingdom. (4.) He is David, one after God's own heart, set as his

King upon the holy hill of Zion, made the head of the corner, with whom the covenant of royalty is made, and to whom God would give the throne of his father David. He is both the root and offspring of David. (5.) He is the plant of renown, because a righteous branch (Jer 23:5), a branch of the Lord, that is beautiful and glorious, Isa 4:2. He has a name above every name, a throne above every throne, and may therefore well be called a branch of renown. Some understand it of the church, the planting of the Lord, Isa 61:3. Its name shall be remembered (Psa 45:17) and Christ's in it.

2. Concerning the great charter by which the kingdom of the Messiah should be incorporated, and upon which it should be founded (Eze 34:25): I will make with them a covenant of peace. The covenant of grace is a covenant of peace. In it God is at peace with us, speaks peace to us, and assures us of peace, of all good, all the good we need to make us happy. The tenour of this covenant is: "I the Lord will be their God, a God all-sufficient to them (Eze 34:24), will own them and will be owned by them; in order to this my servant David shall be a prince among them, to reduce them to their allegiance, to receive their homage, and to reign over them, in them, and for them." Note, Those, and those only, that have the Lord Jesus for their prince have the Lord Jehovah for their God. And then they, even the house of Israel, shall be my people. If we take God to be our God, he will take us to be his people. From this covenant between God and Israel there results communion: "I the Lord their God am with them, to converse with them; and they shall know it, and have the comfort of it."

3. Concerning the privileges of those that are the faithful subjects of this kingdom of the Messiah and interested in the covenant of peace. These are here set forth figuratively, as the blessings of the flock. But we have a key to it, Eze 34:31. Those that belong to this flock, though they are spoken of as sheep, are really men, men that have the Lord for their God, and are in covenant with him. Now to them it is promised,

(1.) That they shall enjoy a holy security under the divine protection. Christ, our good Shepherd, has caused the evil beasts to cease out of the land (Eze 34:25), having vanquished all our spiritual enemies, broken their power, and triumphed over them; the roaring lion is not a roaring devouring lion to them; they shall no more be a prey to the heathen nor the heathen a terror to them, neither shall the beasts of the land devour them. Sin and Satan, death and hell, are conquered. And then they shall dwell safely, not only in the folds, but in the fields, in the wilderness, in the woods, where the beasts of prey are; they shall not only dwell there, but they shall sleep there, which denotes not only that the beasts being made to cease there shall be no danger, but, their consciences being purified and pacified, they shall be in no apprehension of danger; not only safe from evil, but quiet from the fear of evil. Note, Those may lay down and sleep securely, sleep at ease, that have Christ for their prince; for he will be their protector, and make them to dwell in safety. None shall hurt them, nay, none shall make them afraid. If God be for us, who can be against us? Therefore will not we fear, though the earth be removed. Through Christ, God delivers his people not only from the things they have reason to fear, but from their fear even of death itself, from all that fear that has torment. This safety from evil is promised (Eze 34:27): They shall be safe in their land, in no danger of being invaded and enslaved, though their great plenty be a temptation to their neighbours to desire their land; and that which shall make them think themselves safe is their confidence in the wisdom, power, and goodness of God: They shall know that I am the Lord. All our disquieting fears arise from our ignorance of God and mistakes concerning him. Their experience of his particular care concerning them encourages their confidence in him: "I have broken the bands of their yoke, with which they have been brought and held down under oppression, and have delivered them out of the hand of those that served themselves of them, whence they shall argue, He that has delivered does and will, therefore will we dwell safely." This is explained, and applied to our gospel-state, Luk 1:74. That we, being delivered out of the hand of our enemies, might serve him without fear, as those may do that serve him in faith.

(2.) That they shall enjoy a spiritual plenty of all good things, the best things, for their comfort and happiness: They shall no more be consumed with hunger in the land, Eze 34:29. Famine and scarcity, when Israel was punished with that judgment, turned as much to their reproach among the heathen as any other, because the fruitfulness of Canaan was so much talked of. But now they shall not bear that shame of the heathen any more For the showers shall come down in their season, even showers of blessing, Eze 34:26. Christ is a Shepherd that will feed his people; and they shall go in and out, and find pasture. [1.] They shall not be consumed with hunger; for they shall not be put off with the world for a portion, which is not bread, which satisfies not, and which leaves those that are put off with it to be consumed with hunger. The ordinances of the ceremonial law are called beggarly elements, for there was little in them, compared with the Christian institutes, wherewith the mower fills his hand and he that binds sheaves his bosom. Those that hunger and thirst after righteousness shall not be consumed with that hunger, for they shall be filled. And he that drinks of the water that Christ gives him, the still waters by which he leads his sheep, shall never thirst. [2.] Showers of blessings shall come upon them, Eze 34:26, Eze 34:27. The heavens shall yield their dews; the trees of the field also shall yield their fruit. The seat of this plenty is God's hill, his holy hill of Zion, for on that mountain, in the gospel church, it is, that God has made to all nations a feast; to that those must join themselves who would partake of gospel benefits. The cause of this plenty is the showers that come down in their season, that descend upon the mountains of Zion, the graces of Christ, his doctrine that drops as the dew, the graces of Christ, and the fruits and comforts of his Spirit, by which we are made fruitful in the fruits of righteousness. The instances of this plenty are the blessings of heaven poured down upon us and the productions of grace brought forth by us, our comfort in God's favour and God's glory in our fruit-bearing. The extent of this plenty is very large, to all the places round about my hill; for out of Zion shall go forth the law, shall go forth light to a dark world, and the river that shall water a dry and desert world; all that are in the neighbourhood of Zion shall fare the better for it; and the nearer the church the nearer its God. And, lastly, The effect of this plenty is, I will make them a blessing, eminently and exemplarily blessed, patterns of happiness, Isa 19:24. Or, They shall be blessings to all about them, diffusively useful. Note,

Those that are the blessed of the Lord must study to make themselves blessings to the world. He that is good, let him do good; he that has received the gift, the grace, let him minister the same.

Now this promise of the Messiah and his kingdom spoke much comfort to those to whom it was then made, for they might be sure that God would not utterly destroy their nation, how low soever it might be brought, as long as that blessing was in the womb of it, Isa 65:8. But it speaks much more comfort to us, to whom it is fulfilled, who are the sheep of this good Shepherd, are fed in his pastures, and blessed with all spiritual blessings in heavenly things by him.

Ezekiel Chapter 35

It was promised, in the foregoing chapter, that when the time to favour Zion, yea, the set time, should come, especially the time for sending the Messiah and setting up his kingdom in the world, God would cause the enemies of his church to cease and the blessings and comforts of the church to abound. This chapter enlarges upon the former promise, concerning the destruction of the enemies of the church; the next chapter upon the latter promise, the replenishing of the church with blessings. Mount Seir (that is, Edom) is the enemy prophesied against in this chapter, but fitly put here, as in the prophecy of Obadiah, for all the enemies of the church; for, as those all walked in the way of Cain that hated Abel, so those all walked in the way of Esau who hated Jacob, but over whom Jacob, by virtue of a particular blessing, was to have dominion. Now here we have, I. The sin charged upon the Edomites, and that was their spite and malice to Israel (Eze 35:5, Eze 35:10-13). II. The ruin threatened, that should come upon them for this sin. God will be against them (Eze 35:3) and then their country shall be laid waste (Eze 35:4), depopulated, and made quite desolate (Eze 35:6-9), and left so when other nations that had been wasted should recover themselves (Eze 35:14, Eze 35:15).

Ezekiel 35:1

Mount Seir was mentioned as partner with Moab in one of the threatenings we had before (Eze 25:8); but here it is convicted and condemned by itself, and has woes of its own. The prophet must boldly set his face against Edom, and prophesy particularly against it; for the God of Israel has said, O Mount Seir! I am against thee. Note, Those that have God against them have the word of God against them, and the face of his ministers, nor dare they prophesy any good to them, but evil. The prophet must tell the Edomites that God has a controversy with them, and let them know,

I. What is the cause and ground of that controversy, Eze 35:5. God espouses his people's cause, and will plead it, takes what is done against them as done against himself, and will reckon for it; and it is upon their account that God now contends with the Edomites. 1. Because of the enmity they had against the people of God, that was rooted in the heart. "Thou hast had a perpetual hatred to them, to the very name of an Israelite." The Edomites kept up an hereditary malice against Israel, the same that Esau bore to Jacob, because he got the birth-right and the blessing. Esau had been reconciled to Jacob, had embraced and kissed him (Gen. 33), and we do not find that ever he quarrelled with him again. But the posterity of Esau would never be reconciled to the seed of Jacob, but hated them with a perpetual hatred. Note, Children will be more apt to imitate the vices than the virtues of their parents, and to tread in the steps of their sin than in the steps of their repentance. Parents should therefore be careful not to set their children any bad example, for though, through the grace of God, they may return, and prevent the mischief of what they have done amiss to themselves, they may not be able to obviate the bad influence of it upon their children. It is strange how deeply rooted national antipathies sometimes are, and how long they last; but it is not to be wondered at that profane Edomites hate pious Israelites, since the old enmity that was put between the seed of the woman and the seed of the serpent (Gen 3:15) will continue to the end. Marvel not if the world hate you. 2. Because of the injuries they had done to the people of God. They shed their blood by the force of the sword, in the time of their calamity; they did not attack them as fair and open enemies, but laid wait for them, to cut off those of them that had escaped (Oba 1:14), or they drove them back upon the sword of the pursuers, by which they fell. It was cowardly, as well as barbarous, to take advantage of their distress; and for neighbours, with whom they had lived peaceably, to smite them secretly when strangers openly invaded them. It was in the time that their iniquity had an end, when the measure of it was full and destruction came. Note, Even those that suffer justly, and for their sins, are yet to be pitied and not trampled upon. If the father corrects one child, he expects the rest should tremble at it, not triumph in it.

II. What should be the effect and issue of that controversy. If God stretch out his hand against the country of Edom, he will make it most desolate, Eze 35:3. Desolation and desolation. 1. The inhabitants shall be slain with the sword (Eze 35:6): I will prepare thee unto blood. Edom shall be gradually weakened, and so be the more easily conquered, and the enemy shall gather strength the more effectually to subdue it. Thus preparation is in the making a great while before for this destruction. Thou hast not hated blood; it implies, "Thou hast delighted in it and thirsted after it." Those that do not keep up a rooted hatred of sin, when a temptation to it is very strong, will be in danger of yielding to it. Some read it, "Unless thou hatest blood" (that is, "unless thou dost repent, and put off this bloody disposition) blood shall pursue thee." And then it is an intimation that the judgment may yet be prevented by a thorough reformation. If he turn not, he will whet his sword, Psa 7:12. But, if he turn, he will lay it by. Blood shall pursue thee, the guilt of the blood which thou hast shed or the judgment of blood; thy blood-thirsty enemies shall pursue thee, which way soever thou seekest to make thy escape. A great and general slaughter shall be made of the Idumeans, such as had been foretold (Isa 34:6): The mountains and hills, the valleys and rivers, shall be filled with the slain, Eze 35:8. The pursuers shall overtake those that flee and shall give no quarter, but put them all to the sword. Note, When God comes to make inquisition for blood those that have shed the blood of his Israel shall have blood given them to drink, for they are worthy. Satia te sanguine quem sitisti-Glut thyself with blood, after which thou hast thirsted. 2. The country shall be laid waste. The cities shall be destroyed (Eze 35:4), the country made most desolate (Eze 35:7); for God will cut off from both him that passes out and him that returns; and when the inhabitants are cut off that should keep the cities in repair they will decay and go into ruins, and when those are cut off that should till the land that will soon be over-run with briers and thorns and become a wilderness. Note, Those that help forward the desolations of Israel may expect to be themselves made desolate. And that which completes the judgment is that Edom shall be made perpetual desolations (Eze 35:9) and the cities shall never return to their former state, nor the inhabitants of them come back from their captivity and dispersion. Note, Those that have a perpetual enmity to God and his people, as the carnal mind has, can expect no other than to be made a perpetual desolation. Implacable malice will justly be punished with irreparable ruin.

Ezekiel 35:10

Here is, I. A further account of the sin of the Edomites, and their bad conduct towards the people of God. We find the church complaining of them for setting on the Babylonians, and irritating them against Jerusalem, saying, Rase it, rase it, down with it, down with it (Psa 137:7), inflaming a rage that needed no spur; here it is further charged upon them that they triumphed in Jerusalem's ruin and in the desolations of the country. Many blasphemies they spoke against the mountains of Israel, saying, with pride and pleasure, They are laid desolate, Eze 35:12. Note, The troubles of God's church, as they give proofs of the constancy and fidelity of its friends, so they discover and draw out the corruptions of its enemies, in whom there then appears more brutish malice than one would have thought of. Now their triumphing in Jerusalem's ruin is here said to proceed, 1. From a sinful passion against the people of Israel; from anger and envy, and hatred against them (Eze 35:11), that perpetual hatred spoken of Eze 35:5. Though they were not a match for them, and therefore could not do them a mischief themselves, yet they were glad when the Chaldeans did them a mischief. 2. From a sinful appetite to the land of Israel. They pleased themselves with hopes that when the people of Israel were destroyed they should be let into the possession of their country, which they had so often grudged and envied them. They thought they could make out something of a title to it, ob defectum sanguinis-for want of other heirs. If Jacob's issue fail, they think that they are next in the entail, and that the remainder will be to his brother's issue: "These two nations of Judah and Israel shall be mine. Now is the time for me to put in for them." At least they hope to come in as first occupants, being near neighbours: We will possess it when it is deserted. Ceditur occupanti-Let us get possession and that will be title enough. Note, Those have the spirit of Edomites who desire the death of others because they hope to get by it, or are pleased with their failing because they expect to come into their business. When we see the vanity of the world in the disappointments, losses, and crosses, that others meet with in it, instead of showing ourselves, upon such an occasion, greedy of it, we should rather be made thereby to sit more loose to it, and both take our affections off it and lower our expectations from it. But in this case of the Edomites' coveting the land of Israel, and gaping for it, there was a particular affront to God, when they said, "These lands are given us to devour, and we shall have our bellies full of their riches." God says, You have boasted against me and have multiplied your words against me; for they expected possession upon a vacancy, because Israel was driven out, whereas the Lord was still there,Eze 35:10. His temple indeed was burnt, and the other tokens of his presence were gone; but his promise to give that land to the seed of Jacob for an inheritance was not made void, but remained in full force and virtue; and by that promise he did in effect still keep possession for Israel, till they should in due time be restored to it. That was Immanuel's land (Isa 8:8); in that land he was to be born, and therefore that people shall continue in it of whom he is to be born, till he has passed his time in it, and then let who will take it. The Lord is there, the Lord Jesus is to be there; and therefore Israel's discontinuance of possession is no defeasance of their right, but it shall be kept for them, and they shall have, hold, and enjoy it by virtue of the divine grant, till the promise of this Canaan shall by the Messiah be changed into the promise of a far better. Note, It is a piece of presumption highly offensive to God for Edomites to lay claim to those privileges and comforts that are peculiar to God's chosen Israel and are reserved for them. It is blasphemy against the mountains of Israel, the holy mountains, to say, because they are for the present made a prey of and trodden under foot of the Gentiles (Rev 11:2), even the holy city itself, that therefore the Lord has forsaken them, their God has forgotten them. The apostle will by no means admit such a thought as this, that God hath cast away his people, Rom 11:1. No; though they are cast down for a time, they are not cast off for ever. Those reproach the Lord who say they are.

II. The notice God took of the barbarous insolence of the Edomites, and the doom passed upon them for it: I have heard all thy blasphemies, Eze 35:12. And again (Eze 35:13), You have multiplied your words against me, and I have heard them, I have observed them, I have kept an account of them. Note, In the multitude of words, not one escapes God's cognizance; let men speak ever so much, ever so fast, though they multiply words, which they themselves regard not, but forget immediately, yet none of them are lost in the crowd, not the most idle words; but God hears them, and will be able to charge the sinner with them. All the haughty and hard speeches, particularly, which are spoken against the Israel of God, the words which are magnified (as it is in the margin, Eze 35:13) as well as the words which are multiplied, God takes notice of. For, as the most trifling words are not below his cognizance, so the most daring are not above his rebuke. I have heard all thy blasphemies. This is a good reason why we should bear reproach as if we heard it not, because God will hear, Psa 38:13, Psa 38:15. God has heard the Edomites' blasphemy; let them therefore hear their doom, Eze 35:14, Eze 35:15. It was a national sin (the blasphemies charged upon them were the sense and language of all the Edomites), and therefore shall be punished with a national desolation. And, 1. It shall be a distinguishing punishment. As God has peculiar favours for Israelites, so he has peculiar plagues for Edomites: so that "When the whole earth rejoices I will make thee desolate; when other nations have their desolations repaired, to their joy, thine shall be perpetual," Eze 35:9. 2. The punishment shall answer to the sin: "As thou didst rejoice in the desolation of the house of Israel, God will give thee enough of desolation; since thou art so fond of it, thou shalt be desolate; I will make thee so." Note, Those who, instead of weeping with the mourners, make a jest of their grievances, may justly be made to weep like the mourners, and themselves to feel the weight, to feel the smart, of those grievances which they set so light by. Some read Eze 35:14 so as to complete the resemblance between the sin and the punishment: The whole earth shall rejoice when I make thee desolate, as thou didst rejoice when Israel was made desolate. Those that are glad at the death and fall of others may expect that others will be glad of their death, of their fall. 3. In the destruction of the enemies of the church God designs his own glory, and we may be sure that he will not come short of his design. (1.) That which he intends is to manifest himself, as a just and jealous God, firm to his covenant and faithful to his people and their injured cause (Eze 35:11): I will make myself known among them when I have judged thee. The Lord is and will be known by the judgments which he executes. (2.) His intention shall be fully answered; not only his own people shall be made to know it to their comfort, but even the Edomites themselves, and all the other enemies of his name and people, shall know that he is the Lord, Eze 35:4, Eze 35:9, Eze 35:15. As the works of creation and common providence demonstrate that there is a God, so the care taken of Israel shows that Jehovah, the God of Israel, is that God alone, the true and living God.

Ezekiel Chapter 36

Ezekiel

We have done with Mount Seir, and left it desolate, and likely to continue so, and must now turn ourselves, with the prophet, to the mountains of Israel, which we find desolate too, but hope before we have done with the chapter to leave in better plight. Here are two distinct prophecies in this chapter:-I. Here is one that seems chiefly to relate to the temporal estate of the Jews, wherein their present deplorable condition is described and the triumphs of their neighbours in it; but it is promised that their grievances shall be all redressed and that in due time they shall be settled again in their own land, in the midst of peace and plenty (Eze 36:1-15). II. Here is another that seems chiefly to concern their spiritual estate, wherein they are reminded of their former sins and God's judgments upon them, to humble them for their sins and under God's mighty hand (Eze 36:16-20). But it is promised, 1. That God would glorify himself in showing mercy to them (Eze 36:21-24). 2. That he would sanctify them, by giving them his grace and fitting them for his service; and this for his own name's sake and in answer to their prayers (Eze 36:25-38).

Ezekiel 36:1

The prophet had been ordered to set his face towards the mountains of Israel and prophesy against them, Eze 6:2. Then God was coming forth to contend with his people; but now that God is returning in mercy to them he must speak good words and comfortable words to these mountains, Eze 36:1 and again Eze 36:4. You mountains of Israel, hear the word of the Lord; and what he says to them he says to the hills, to the rivers, to the valleys, to the desolate wastes in the country, and to the cities that are forsaken, Eze 36:4. and again Eze 36:6. The people were gone, some one way and some another; nothing remained there to be spoken to but the places, the mountains and valleys; these the Chaldeans could not carry away with them. The earth abides for ever. Now, to show the mercy God had in reserve for the people, he is to speak of him as having a dormant kindness for the place, which, if the Lord had been pleased for ever to abandon, he would not have called upon to hear the word of the Lord, nor would he as at this time have shown it such things as these. Here is,

I. The compassionate notice God takes of the present deplorable condition of the land of Israel. It has become both a prey and a derision to the heathen that are round about, Eze 36:4. 1. It has become a prey to them; and they are all enriched with the plunder of it. When the Chaldeans had conquered them all their neighbours flew to the spoil as to a shipwreck, every one thinking all his own that he could lay his hands on (Eze 36:3): They have made you desolate, and swallowed you up on every side, that you might be a possession to the heathen, to the residue of them, even such as had themselves narrowly escaped the like desolation. No one thought it any crime to strip an

Israelite. Turba Romae sequitur fortunam ut semper-The mob of Rome still praise the elevated and despise the fallen. It is the common dry, when a man is down, Down with him. 2. It has become a derision to them. They took all they had and laughed at them when they had done. The enemy said, "Aha! even the ancient high places are ours in possession, Eze 36:2. Neither the antiquity, nor the dignity, neither the sanctity nor the fortifications, of the land of Israel, are its security, but we have become masters of it all." The more honours that land had been adorned with, and the greater figure it had made among the nations, the more pride and pleasure did they take in making a spoil of it, which is an instance of a base and sordid spirit; for the more glorious and prosperity was the more piteous is the adversity. God takes notice of it here as an aggravation of the present calamity of Israel: You are taken up in the lips of talkers and are an infamy of the people,Eze 36:3. All the talk of the country about was concerning the overthrow of the Jewish nation; and every one that spoke of it had some peevish ill-natured reflection or other upon them. They were the scorning of those that were at ease and the contempt of the proud, Psa 123:4. There are some that are noted for talkers, that have something to say of every body, but cannot find in their hearts to speak well of any body; God's people, among such people, were sure to be a reproach when the crown had fallen from their head. Thus it was the lot of Christianity, in its suffering days, to be every where spoken against.

II. The expressions of God's just displeasure against those who triumphed in the desolations of the land of Israel, as many of its neighbours did, even the residue of the brethren, and Idumea particularly. Let us see, 1. How they dealt with the Israel of God. They carved out large possessions to themselves out of their land, out of God's land; for so indeed it was: "They have appointed my land into their possession (Eze 36:5), and so not only invaded their neighbour's property, but intrenched upon God's prerogative." It was the holy land which they laid their sacrilegious hands upon. They did not own any dependence upon God, as the God of that land, nor acknowledge any remaining interest that Israel had in it, but cast it out for a prey, as if they had won it in a lawful war. And this they did without any dread of God and his judgments and without any compassion for Israel and their calamities, but with the joy of all their hearts, because they got by it, and with despiteful minds to Israel that lost by it. Increasing wealth, by right or wrong, is all the joy of a worldly heart; and the calamities of God's people are all the joy of a despiteful mind. And those that had not an opportunity of making a prey of God's people made a reproach of them; so that they were the shame of the heathen, Eze 36:6. Every body ridiculed them and made a jest of them; and the truth is they had by their own sin made themselves vile; so that God was righteous herein, but men were unrighteous and very barbarous. 2. How God would deal with those who were thus in word and deed abusive to his people. He has spoken against the heathen; he has passed sentence upon them; he has determined to reckon with them for it, and this in the fire of his jealousy, both for his own honour and for the honour of his people, Eze 36:5. Having a love for both as strong as death, he has a jealousy for both as cruel as the grave. They spoke in their malice against God's people, and he will speak in his jealousy against them; and it is easy to say which will speak most powerfully. God will speak in his jealousy and in his fury, Eze 36:6. Fury is not in God; but he will exert his power against them and handle them as severely as men do when they are in a fury. He will so speak to them in his wrath as to vex them in his sore displeasure. What he says he will stand to, for it is backed with an oath. He has lifted up his hand and sworn by himself, has sworn and will not repent. And what is it that is said with so much heat, and yet with so much deliberation? It is this (Eze 36:7), Surely the heathen that are about you, they shall bear their shame. Note, The righteous God, to whom vengeance belongs, will render shame for shame. Those that put contempt and reproach upon God's people will, sooner or later, have it burned upon themselves, perhaps in this world (either their follies or their calamities, their miscarriages or their mischances, shall be their reproach), at furthest in that day when all the impenitent shall rise to shame and everlasting contempt.

III. The promises of God's favour to his Israel and assurances given of great mercy God had in store for them. God takes occasion from the outrage and insolence of their enemies to show himself so much the more concerned for them and ready to do them good, as David hoped that God would recompense him good for Shimei's cursing him. Let them curse, but bless thou. In this way, as well as others, the enemies of God's people do them real service, even by the injuries they do them, against their will and beyond their intention. We shall have no reason to complain if, the more unkind men are, the more kind God is-if, the more kindly he speaks to us by his word and Spirit, the more kindly he acts for us in his providence. The prophet must say so to the mountains of Israel, which were now desolate and despised, that God is for them and will burn to them, Eze 36:9. As the curse of God reaches the ground for man's sake, so does the blessing. Now that which is promised is, 1. That their rightful owners should return to the possession of them: My people Israel are at hand to come, Eze 36:8. Though they are at a great distance from their own country, though they are dispersed in many countries, and though they are detained by the power of their enemies, yet they shall come again to their own border, Jer 31:17. The time is at hand for their return. Though there were above forty years of the seventy (perhaps fifty) yet remaining, it is spoken of as near, because it is sure, and there were some among them that should live to see it. A thousand years are with God but as one day. The mountains of Israel are now desolate; but God will cause men to walk upon them again, even his people Israel, not as travellers passing over them, but as inhabitants-not tenants, but freeholders: They shall possess thee, not for term of life, but for themselves and their heirs; thou shalt be their inheritance. It was a type of the heavenly Canaan, to which all God's children are heirs, every Israelite indeed, and into which they shall shortly be all brought together, out of the countries where they are now scattered. 2. That they should afford a plentiful comfortable maintenance for their owners at their return. When the land had enjoyed her sabbaths for so many years, it should be so much the more fruitful afterwards, as we should be after rest, especially a sabbath rest: You shall be tilled and sown (Eze 36:9) and shall yield your fruit to my people Israel, Eze 36:8. Note, It is a blessing to the earth to be made serviceable to men, especially to good men, that will serve God with cheerfulness in the use of those good things which the earth serves up to them. 3. That the people of Israel should have not only a comfortable sustenance, but a comfortable settlement, in their own land: The cities shall be inhabited; the wastes shall be builded, Eze 36:10 And I will settle you after your old estates, Eze 36:11. Their own sin had unsettled them, but now God's favour shall resettle them. When the prodigal son has become a penitent he is settled again in his father's house, according to his former estate. Bring hither the first robe, and put it on him. Nay, I will do better unto you now than at your beginnings. There is more joy for the sheep that is brought back than there would have been if it had never gone astray. And God sometimes multiplies his people's comforts in proportion to the time that he has afflicted them. Thus God blessed the latter end of Job more than his beginning, and doubled to him all he had. 4. That the people, after their return, should be fruitful, and multiply, and replenish the land, so that it should not only be inhabited again, but as thickly inhabited, and as well peopled, as ever. God will bring back to it all the house of Israel, even all of it (observe what an emphasis is laid upon that, Eze 36:10), all whose spirits God stirred up to return; and those only were reckoned of the house of Israel, the rest had cut themselves off from it; or, though but few, in comparison, returned at first, yet afterwards, at divers times, they all returned; and then (says God) I will multiply these men (Eze 36:10), multiply man and beast; and they shall increase, Eze 36:11. Note, God's kingdom in the world is a growing kingdom; and his church, though for a time it may be diminished, shall recover itself and be again replenished. 5. That the reproach long since cast upon the land of Israel by the evil spies, and of late revived, that it was a land that ate up the inhabitants of it by famine, sickness, and the sword, should be quite rolled away, and there should never be any more occasion for it. Canaan had got into a bad name. It had of old spued out the inhabitants (Lev 18:28), the natives, the aborigines, which was turned to its reproach by those that should have put another construction upon it, Num 13:32. It had of late devoured the Israelites, and spued them out too; so that it was commonly said of it, It is a land which, instead of supporting its nations or tribes that inhabit it, bereaves them, overthrows them, and causes them to fall; it is a tenement which breaks all the tenants that come upon it. This character it had got among the neighbours; but God now promises that it shall be so no more: Thou shalt no more bereave them of men (Eze 36:12), shalt devour men no more, Eze 36:14. But the inhabitants shall live to a good old age, and not have the number of their months cut off in the midst. Compare this with that promise,Zac 8:4. Note, God will take away the reproach of his people by taking away that which was the occasion of it. When the nation is made to flourish in peace, plenty, and power, then they hear no more the shame of the heathen (Eze 36:15), especially when it is reformed; when sin, which is the reproach of any people, particularly of God's professing people, is taken away, then they hear no more the reproach of the people. Note, When God returns in mercy to a people that return to him in duty, all their grievances will be soon redressed and their honour retrieved.

Ezekiel 36:16

When God promised the poor captives a glorious return, in due time, to their own land, it was a great discouragement to their hopes that they were unworthy, utterly unworthy, of such a favour; therefore, to remove that discouragement, God here shows them that he would do it for them purely for his own name's sake, that he might be glorified in them and by them, that he might manifest and magnify his mercy and goodness, that attribute which of all others is most his glory. And, the restoration of that people being typical of our redemption by Christ, this is intended further to show that the ultimate end aimed at in our salvation, to which all the steps of it were made subservient, was the glory of God. To this end Christ directed all he did in that short prayer, Father, glorify thy name; and God declared it was his end in all he did in the immediate answer given to that prayer, by a voice from heaven: I have glorified it, and I will glorify it yet again, Joh 12:28. Now observe here,

I. How God's name had suffered both by the sins and by the miseries of Israel; and this was more to be regretted than all their sorrow, which they had brought upon themselves; for the honour of God lies nearer the hearts of good men than any interests of their own. 1. God's glory had been injured by the sin of Israel when they were in their own land, Eze 36:17. It was a good land, a holy land, a land that had the eye of God upon it. But they defiled it by their own way, their wicked way; that is our own way, the way of our own choice; and we ourselves must bear the blame and shame of it. The sin of a people defiles their land, renders it abominable to God and uncomfortable to themselves; so that they cannot have any holy communion with him nor with one another. What was unclean might not be made use of. By the abuse of the gifts of God's bounty to us we forfeit the use of them; and, the mind and conscience being defiled with guilt, no comfort is allowed us, nothing is pure to us. Their way in the eye of God was like the pollution of a woman during the days of her separation, which shut her out from the sanctuary and made very things she touched ceremonially unclean, Lev 15:19. Sin is that abominable thing which the Lord hates, and which he cannot endure to look upon. They shed blood and worshipped idols (Eze 36:18) and with those sins defiled the land. For this God poured out his fury upon them, scattered them among the heathen. Their own land was sick of them, and they were sent into other lands. Herein God was righteous, and was justified in what he did; none could say that he did them any wrong, nay, he did justice to his own honour, for he judged them according to their way and according to their doings, Eze 36:19. And yet, the matter being not rightly understood, he was not glorified in it; for the enemies did say, as Moses pleaded the Egyptians would say if he had destroyed them in the wilderness, that for mischief he brought them forth. Their neighbours considered them rather as a holy people than as a sinful people, and therefore took occasion from the calamities they were in, instead of glorifying God, as they might justly have done, to reproach him and put contempt upon him; and God's name was continually every day blasphemed by their oppressors, Isa 52:5. 2. When they entered into the land of the heathen God had no glory by them there; but, on the contrary, his holy name was profaned, Eze 36:20. (1.) It was profaned by the sins of Israel; they were no credit to their profession wherever they went, but, on the contrary, a reproach to it. The name of God and his holy religion was blasphemed through them, Rom 2:24. When those that pretended to be in relation to God, in covenant and communion with him, were found corrupt in their morals, slaves to their appetites and passions, dishonest in their dealings, and false to their words and the trust reposed in them, the enemies of the Lord had thereby great occasion given them to blaspheme, especially when they quarrelled with their God for correcting them, than which nothing could be more scandalous. (2.) It was profaned by the sufferings of Israel; for from them the enemies of God took occasion to reproach God, as unable to protect his own worshippers and to make good his own grants. They said, in scorn, "These are the people of the land, these wicked people (you see he could not keep them in their obedience to his precepts), these miserable people-you see he could not keep them in the enjoyment of his favours. These are the people that came out of Jehovah's land, they are the very scum of the nations. Are these those that had statues so righteous whose lives are so unrighteous? Is this the nation that is so much celebrated for a wise and understanding people, and that is said to have God so nigh unto them? Do these belong to that brave, that holy nation, who appear here so vile, so abject?" Thus God sold his people and did not increase his wealth by their price, Psa 44:12. The reproach they were under reflected upon him.

II. Let us now see how God would retrieve his honour, secure it, and advance it, by working a great reformation upon them and then working a great salvation for them. He would have scattered them among the heathen, were it not that he feared the wrath of the enemy, Deu 32:26, Deu 32:27. But, though they were unworthy of his compassion, yet he had pity for his own holy name, and a thousand pities it was that that should be trampled upon and abused. He looked with compassion on his own honour, which lay bleeding among the heathen, on that jewel which was trodden into the dirt, which the house of Israel, even in the land of their captivity, had profaned, Eze 36:21. In pity to that God brought them out from the heathen, because their sins were more scandalous there than they had been in their own land. "Therefore I will gather you out of all countries and bring you into your own land, Eze 36:24. Not for your sake, because you are worthy of such a favour, for you are most unworthy, but for my holy name's sake (Eze 36:22), that I may sanctify my great name," Eze 36:23. Observe, by the way, God's holy name is his great name. His holiness is his greatness; so he reckons it himself. Nor does any thing make a man truly great but being truly good, and partaking of God's holiness. God will magnify his name as a holy name, for he will sanctify it: I will sanctify my name which you have profaned. When God performs that which he has sworn by his holiness, then he sanctifies his name. The effect of this shall be very happy: The heathen shall know that I am the Lord when I shall be sanctified in you before their eyes and yours. When God proves his own holy name, and his saints praise it, then he is sanctified in them, and this contributes to the propagating of the knowledge of him. Observe, 1. God's reasons of mercy are all fetched from within himself; he will bring his people out of Babylon, not for their sakes, but for his own name's sake, because he will be glorified. 2. God's goodness takes occasion from man's badness to appear so much the more illustrious; therefore he will sanctify his name by the pardon of sin, because it has been profaned by the commission of sin.

Ezekiel 36:25

The people of God might be discouraged in their hopes of a restoration by the sense not only of their unworthiness of such a favour (which was answered, in the foregoing verses, with this, that God, in doing it, would have an eye to his own glory, not to their worthiness), but of their unfitness for such a favour, being still corrupt and sinful; and that is answered in these verses, with a promise that God would by his grace prepare and qualify them for the mercy and then bestow it on them. And this was in part fulfilled in that wonderful effect which the captivity in Babylon had upon the Jews there, that it effectually cured them of their inclination to idolatry. But it is further intended as a draught of the covenant of grace, and a specimen of those spiritual blessings with which we are blessed in heavenly things by that covenant. As (ch. 34) after a promise of their return the prophecy insensibly slid into a promise of the coming of Christ, the great Shepherd, so here it insensibly slides into a promise of the Spirit, and his gracious influences and operations, which we have as much need of for our sanctification as we have of Christ's merit for our justification.

I. God here promises that he will work a good work in them, to qualify them for the good work he intended to bring about for them, Eze 36:25-27. We had promises to the same purport, Eze 11:18-20. 1. That God would cleanse them from the pollutions of sin (Eze 36:25): I will sprinkle clean water upon you, which signifies both the book of Christ sprinkled upon the conscience to purify that and to take away the sense of guilt (as those that were sprinkled with the water of purification were thereby discharged from their ceremonial uncleanness) and the grace of the Spirit sprinkled on the whole soul to purify it from all corrupt inclinations and dispositions, as Naaman was cleansed from his leprosy by dipping in Jordan. Christ was himself clean, else his blood could not have been cleansing to us; and it is a Holy Spirit that makes us holy: From all your filthiness and from all your idols will I cleanse you. And (Eze 36:29) I will save you from all your uncleannesses. Sin is defiling, idolatry particularly is so; it renders sinners odious to God and burdensome to themselves. When guilt is pardoned, and the corrupt nature sanctified, then we are cleansed from our filthiness, and there is no other way of being saved from it. This God promises his people here, in order to his being sanctified in them, Eze 36:23. We cannot sanctify God's name unless he sanctify our hearts, nor live to his glory, but by his grace. 2. That God would give them a new heart, a disposition of mind excellent in itself and vastly different from what it was before. God will work an inward change in order to a universal change. Note, All that have an interest in the new covenant, and a title to the new Jerusalem, have a new heart and a new spirit, and these are necessary in order to their walking in newness of life. This is that divine nature which believers are by the promises made partakers of. 3. That, instead of a heart of stone, insensible and inflexible, unapt to receive any divine impressions and to return any devout affections, God would give a heart of flesh, a soft and tender heart, that has spiritual senses exercised, conscious to itself of spiritual pains and pleasures, and complying in every thing with the will of God. Note, Renewing grace works as great a change in the soul as the turning of a dead stone into living flesh. 4. That since, besides our inclination to sin, we complain of an inability to do our duty, God will cause them to walk in his statutes, will not only show them the way of his statutes before them, but incline them to walk in it, and thoroughly furnish them with wisdom and will, and active powers, for every good work. In order to this he will put his Spirit within them, as a teacher, guide, and sanctifier. Note, God does not force men to walk in his statutes by external violence, but causes them to walk in his statutes by an internal principle. And observe what use we ought to make of this gracious power and principle promised us, and put within us: You shall keep my judgments. If God will do his part according to the promise, we must do ours according to the precept. Note, The promise of God's grace to enable us for our duty should engage and quicken our constant care and endeavour to do our duty. God's promises must drive us to his precepts as our rule, and then his precepts must send us back to his promises for strength, for without his grace we can do nothing.

II. God here promises that he will take them into covenant with himself. The sum of the covenant of grace we have, Eze 36:28. You shall be my people, and I will be your God. It is not, "If you will be my people, I will be your God" (though it is very true that we cannot expect to have God to be to us a God unless we be to him a people), but he has chosen us, and loved us, first, not we him; therefore the condition is of grace, is by promise, as well as the reward; not of merit, not of works: "You shall be my people; I will make you so; I will give you the nature and spirit of my people, and then I will be your God." And this is the foundation and top-stone of a believer's happiness; it is heaven itself, Rev 21:3, Rev 21:7.

III. He promises that he will bring about all that good for them which the exigence of their case calls for. When they are thus prepared for mercy, 1. Then they shall return to their possessions and be settled again in them (Eze 36:28): You shall dwell in the land that I gave to your fathers. God will, in bringing them back to it, have an eye not to any merit of theirs, but to the promise made to the fathers; for therefore he gave it to them at first, Deu 7:7, Deu 7:8. Therefore he is gracious, because he has said that he will be so. This shall follow upon the blessed reformation God would work among them (Eze 36:33): "In the day that I shall have cleansed you from all your iniquities, and so shall have made you meet for the inheritance, I will cause you to dwell in the cities, and so put you in possession of the inheritance." This is God's method of mercy indeed, first to part men from their sins, and then to restore them to their comforts. 2. Then they shall enjoy a plenty of all good things. When they are saved from their uncleanness, from their sins which kept good things from them, then I will call for the corn and will increase it, Eze 36:29. Plenty comes at God's call, and the plenty he calls for shall be still growing; and when he speaks the word the fruit both of the tree and of the field shall multiply. As the inhabitants multiply the productions shall multiply for their maintenance; for he that sends mouths will send meat. Famine was one of the judgments which they had laboured under, and it had been as much as any a reproach to them, that they should be starved in a land so famed for fruitfulness. But now I will lay no famine upon you; and none are under that rod without having it laid on by him. Then they shall receive no more reproach of famine, shall never be again upbraided with that, nor shall it ever be said that God is a Master that keeps his servants to short allowance. Nay, they shall not only be cleared from the reproach of famine, but they shall have the credit of abundance. The land that had long lain desolate in the sight of all that passed by, that looked upon it, some with contempt and some with compassion, shall again be tilled (Eze 36:34), and, having long lain fallow, it will now be the more fruitful. Observe, God will call for the corn and yet they must till the ground for it. Note, Even promised mercies must be laboured for; for the promise is not to supersede, but to quicken and encourage our industry and endeavour. And such a blessing will God command on the hand of the diligent that all who pass by shall take notice of it, with wonder, Eze 36:35. They shall say, "See what a blessed change here is, how this land that was desolate has become like the garden of Eden, the desert turned again into a paradise," Note, God has honours in reserve for his people to be crowned with sufficient to counterbalance the contempt they are now loaded with, and in them he will be honoured. This wonderful increase both of the people of the land and of its products is compared (Eze 36:38) to the large flocks of cattle that are brought to Jerusalem, to be sacrificed at one of the solemn feasts. Even the cities that now lie waste shall be filled with flocks of men, not like the flocks with which the pastures are covered over (Psa 65:13), but like the holy flock which is brought to the courts of the Lord's house. Note, Then the increase of the numbers of a people is honourable and comfortable indeed when they are all dedicated to God as a holy flock, to be presented to him for living sacrifices. Crowds are a lovely sight in God's temple.

IV. He shows what shall be the happy effects of this blessed change. 1. It shall have a happy effect upon the people of God themselves, for it shall bring them to an ingenuous repentance for their sins (Eze 36:31): Then shall you remember your own evil ways and shall loathe yourselves. See here what sin is; it is an abomination, a loathsome thing, that abominable thing which the Lord hates. See what is the first step towards repentance; it is remembering our own evil ways, reflecting seriously upon the sins we have committed and being particular in recapitulating them. We must remember against ourselves not only our gross enormities, our own evil ways, but our defects and infirmities, our doings that were not good, not so good as they should have been; not only our direct violations of the law, but our coming short of it. See what is evermore a companion of true repentance, and that is self-loathing, a holy shame and confusion of face: "You shall loathe yourselves in your own sight, seeing how loathsome you have made yourselves in the sight of God." Self-love is at the bottom of sin, which we cannot but blush to see the absurdity of; but our quarrelling with ourselves is in order to our being, upon good grounds, reconciled to ourselves. And, lastly, see what is the most powerful inducement to an evangelical repentance, and that is a sense of the mercy of God; when God settles them in the midst of plenty, then they shall loathe themselves for their iniquities. Note, The goodness of God should overcome our badness and lead us to repentance. The more we see of God's readiness to receive us into favour upon our repentance the more reason we shall see to be ashamed of ourselves that we could ever sin against so much love. That heart is hard indeed that will not be thus melted. 2. It shall have a happy effect upon their neighbours, for it shall bring them to a more clear knowledge of God (Eze 36:36): "Then the heathen that are left round about you, that spoke ignorantly of God (for so all those do that speak ill of him) when they saw the land of Israel desolate, shall begin to know better, and to speak more intelligently of God, being convinced that he is able to rebuild the most desolate cities and to replant the most desolate countries, and that, though the course of his favours to his people may be obstructed for a time, they shall not be cut off for ever." They shall be made to know the truth of divine revelation by the exact agreement which they shall discern between God's word which he has spoken to Israel and his works which he has done for them: I the Lord have spoken it, and I will do it. With us saying and doing are two things, but they are not so with God.

V. He proposes these things to them, not as the recompence of their merits, but as the return of their prayers.

1. Let them not think that they have deserved it: Not for your sakes do I this, be it known to you (Eze 36:22, Eze 36:32); no, be you ashamed and confounded for your own ways. God is doing this, all this which he has promised; it is as sure to be done as if it were done already, and present events have a tendency towards it. But then, (1.) They must renounce the merit of their own good works, and be brought to acknowledge that it is not for their sakes that it is done; so, when God brought Israel into Canaan the first time, an express caveat was entered against this thought. Deu 9:4-6, It is not for thy righteousness. It is not for the sake of any of their good qualities or good deeds, not because God had any need of them, or expected any benefit by them. No, in showing mercy he acts by prerogative, not for our deserts, but for his own honour. See how emphatically this is expressed: Be it known to you, it is not for your sakes, which intimates that we are apt to entertain a high conceit of our own merits and are with difficulty persuaded to disclaim a confidence in them. But, one way or other, God will make all his favourites to know and own that it is his grace, and not their goodness, his mercy, and not their merit, that made them so; and that therefore not unto them, not unto them, but unto him, is all the glory due. (2.) They must repent of the sin of their own evil ways. They must own that the mercies they receive from God are not only not merited, but that they are a thousand times forfeited; and therefore they must be so far from boasting of their good works that they must be ashamed and confounded for their evil ways, and then they are best prepared for mercy.

2. Yet let them know that they must desire and expect it (Eze 36:37): I will yet for this be enquired of by the house of Israel. God has spoken, and he will do it, and he will be sought unto for it. He requires that his people should seek unto him, and he will incline their hearts to do it, when he is coming towards them in ways of mercy. (1.) They must pray for it, for by prayer God is sought unto, and enquired after. What is the matter of God's promises must be the matter of our prayers. By asking for the mercy promised we must give glory to the donor, express a value for the gift, own our dependence, and put honour upon prayer which God has put honour upon. Christ himself must ask, and then God will give him the heathen for his inheritance, must pray the Father, and then he will send the Comforter; much more must we ask that we may receive. (2.) They must consult the oracles of God, and thus also God is sought unto and enquired after. The mercy must be, not an act of providence only, but a child of promise; and therefore the promise must be looked at, and prayer made for it with an eye of faith fastened upon the promise, which must be both the guide and the ground of our expectations. Both these ways we find God enquired of by Daniel, in the name of the house of Israel, when he was about to do those great things for them; he consulted the oracles of God, for he understood by books, the book of the prophet Jeremiah, both what was to be expected and when; and then he set his face to seek God

by prayer, Dan 9:2, Dan 9:3. Note, Our communion with God must be kept up by the word and prayer in all the operations of his providence concerning us and in both he must be enquired of.

Ezekiel Chapter 37

The threatenings of the destruction of Judah and Jerusalem for their sins, which we had in the former part of this book, were not so terrible, but the promises of their restoration and deliverance for the glory of God, which we have here in the latter part of the book, are as comfortable; and as those were illustrated with many visions and similitudes, for the awakening of a holy fear, so are these, for the encouraging of a humble faith. God had assured them, in the foregoing chapter, that he would gather the house of Israel, even all of it, and would bring them out of their captivity, and return them to their own land; but there were two things that rendered this very unlikely:-I. That they were so dispersed among their enemies, so destitute of all helps and advantages which might favour or further their return, and so dispirited likewise in their own minds; upon all these accounts they are here, in vision, compared to a valley full of the dry bones of dead men, which should be brought together and raised to life. The vision of this we have (Eze 37:1-10) and the explication of it, with its application to the present case (Eze 37:11-14). II. That they were so divided among themselves, too much of the old enmity between Judah and Ephriam remaining even in their captivity. But, as to this, by a sign of two sticks made one in the hand of the prophet is foreshown the happy coalition that should be, at their return, between the two nations of Israel and Judah (Eze 37:15-22). In this there was a type of the uniting of Jews and Gentiles, Jews and Samaritans, in Christ and his church. And so the prophet slides into a prediction of the kingdom of Christ, which should be set up in the world with God's tabernacle in it, and of the glories and graces of that kingdom (Eze 37:23-28).

Ezekiel 37:1

Here is, I. The vision of a resurrection from death to life, and it is a glorious resurrection. This is a thing so utterly unknown to nature, and so contrary to its principles (a privatione ad habitum non datur regressus-from privation to possession there is no return), that we could have no thought of it but by the word of the Lord; and that it is certain by that word that there shall be a general resurrection of the dead some have urged from this vision, "For" (say they) "otherwise it would not properly be made a sign for the confirming of their faith in the promise of their deliverance out of Babylon, as the coming of the Messiah is mentioned for the confirming of their faith touching a former deliverance," Isa 7:14. But,

1. Whether it be a confirmation or no, it is without doubt a most lively representation of a threefold resurrection, besides that which it is primarily intended to be the sign of. (1.) The resurrection of souls from the death of sin to the life or righteousness, to a holy, heavenly, spiritual, and divine life, by the power of divine grace going along with the word of Christ, Joh

5:24, Joh 5:25. (2.) The resurrection of the gospel church, or any part of it, from an afflicted persecuted state, especially under the yoke of the New Testament Babylon, to liberty and peace. (3.) The resurrection of the body at the great day, especially the bodies of believers that shall rise to life eternal.

2. Let us observe the particulars of this vision.

(1.) The deplorable condition of these dead bones. The prophet was made, [1.] to take an exact view of them. By a prophetic impulse and a divine power he was, in vision, carried out and set in the midst of a valley, probably that plain spoken of Eze 3:22, where God then talked with him; and it was full of bones, of dead men's bones, not piled up on a heap, as in a charnel-house, but scattered upon the face of the ground, as if some bloody battle had been fought here, and the slain left unburied till all the flesh was devoured or putrefied, and nothing left but the bones, and those disjointed from one another and dispersed. He passed by them round about, and he observed not only that they were very many (for there are multitudes gone to the congregation of the dead), but that, lo, they were very dry, having been long exposed to the sun and wind. The bones that have been moistened with marrow (Job 21:24), when they have been any while dead, lose all their moisture, and are dry as dust. The body is now fenced with bones (Job 10:11), but then they will themselves be defenceless. The Jews in Babylon were like those dead and dry bones, unlikely ever to come together, to be so much as a skeleton, less likely to be formed into a body, and least of all to be a living body. However, they lay unburied in the open valley, which encouraged the hopes of their resurrection, as of the two witnesses, Rev 11:8, Rev 11:9. The bones of Gog and Magog shall be buried (Eze 39:12, Eze 39:15), for their destruction is final; but the bones of Israel are in the open valley, under the eye of Heaven, for there is hope in their end. [2.] He was made to own their case deplorable, and not to be helped by any power less than that of God himself (Eze 37:3): "Son of man, can these bones live? Is it a thing likely? Cast thou devise how it should be done? Can thy philosophy reach to put life into dry bones, or thy politics to restore a captive nation?" "No," says the prophet, "I know not how it should be done, but thou knowest." He does not say, "They cannot live," lest he should seem to limit the Holy One of Israel; but, "Lord, thou knowest whether they can and whether they shall; if thou dost not put life into them, it is certain that they cannot life." Note, God is perfectly acquainted with his own power and his own purposes, and will have us to refer all to them, and to see and own that his wondrous works are such as could not be effected by any counsel or power but his own.

(2.) The means used for the bringing of these dispersed bones together and these dead and dry bones to life. It must be done by prophecy. Ezekiel is ordered to prophesy upon these bones (Eze 37:4 and again Eze 37:9), to prophesy to the wind. So he prophesied as he was commanded, Eze 37:7, Eze 37:10. [1.] He must preach, and he did so; and the dead bones lived by a power that went along with the word of God which he preached. [2.] He must pray, and he did so; and the dead bones were made to live in answer to prayer; for a spirit of life entered into them. See the efficacy of the word and prayer, and the necessity of both, for the raising of dead souls. God bids his ministers prophesy upon the dry bones. Say unto them, Live; yea, say unto them, Live; and they do as they are commanded, calling to them again and again, O you dry bones! hear the word of the Lord. But we call in vain, still they are dead, still they are very dry; we must therefore be earnest with God in prayer for the working of the Spirit with the word: Come, O breath! and breathe upon them. God's grace can save souls without our preaching, but our preaching cannot save them without God's grace, and that grace must be sought by prayer. Note, Ministers must faithfully and diligently use the means of grace, even with those that there seems little probability of gaining upon. To prophesy upon dry bones seems as great a penance as to water a dry stick; and yet, whether they will hear or forbear, we must discharge our trust, must prophesy as we are commanded, in the name of him who raises the dead and is the fountain of life.

(3.) The wonderful effect of these means. Those that do as they are commanded, as they are commissioned, in the face of the greatest discouragements, need not doubt of success, for God will own and enrich his own appointments. [1.] Ezekiel looked down and prophesied upon the bones in the valley, and they became human bodies. First, That which he had to say to them was that God would infallibly raise them to life: Thus saith the Lord God unto these bones, You shall live, Eze 37:5 and again Eze 37:6. And he that speaks the word will thereby do the work; he that says, They shall live, will make them alive: He will clothe them with skin and flesh (Eze 37:6), as he did at first, Job 10:11. He that made us so fearfully and wonderfully, and curiously wrought us, can in like manner new-make us, for his arm is not shortened. Secondly, That which was immediately done for them was that they were moulded anew into shape. We may well suppose it was with great liveliness and vigour that the prophet prophesied, especially when he found what he said begin to take effect. Note, The opening, sealing, and applying of the promises, are the ordinary means of our participation of a new and divine nature. As Ezekiel prophesied in this vision there was a noise, a word of command, from heaven, seconding what he said; or it signified the motion of the angels that were to be employed as the ministers of the divine Providence in the deliverance of the Jews, and we read of the noise of their wings (Eze 1:24) and the sound of their going, Sa2 5:24. And, behold, a shaking, or commotion, among the bones. Even dead and dry bones begin to move when they are called to hear the word of the Lord. This was fulfilled when, upon Cyrus's proclamation of liberty, those whose spirits God had stirred up began to think of making use of that liberty, and getting ready to be gone. When there was a noise, behold, a shaking; when David heard the sound of the going on the tops of the mulberry-trees then he bestirred himself; then there was a shaking. When Paul heard the voice saying, Why persecutest thou me? behold, a shaking of the dry bones; he trembled and was astonished. But this was not all: The bones came together bone to his bone, under a divine direction; and, though there is in man a multitude of bones, yet of all the bones of those numerous slain not one was missing, not one missed its way, not one missed its place, but, as it were by instinct, each knew and found its fellow. The dispersed bones came together and the displaced bones were knit together, the divine power supplying that to these dry bones which in a living body every joint supplies. Thus shall it be in the resurrection of the dead; the scattered atoms shall be ranged and marshalled in their proper place and order, and every bone come to his bone, by the same wisdom and power by which the bones were first formed in the womb of her that is with child. Thus it was in the return of the Jews; those that were scattered in several parts of the province of Babylon came to their respective families, and all as it were by consent to the general rendezvous, in order to their return. By degrees sinews and flesh came upon these bones, and the skin covered them, Eze 37:8. This was fulfilled when the captives got their effects about them, and the men of their place helped them with silver, and gold, and whatever they needed for their remove, Ezr 1:4. But still there was no breath in them; they wanted spirit and courage for such a difficult and hazardous enterprise as this was of returning to their own land. [2.] Ezekiel then looked up and prophesied to the wind, or breath, or spirit, and said, Come, O breath! and breathe upon these slain. As good have been still dry bones as dead bodies: but as for God his work is perfect; he is not the God of the dead, but of the living; therefore breathe upon them that they may live. In answer to this request, the breath immediately came into them, Eze 37:10. Note, the spirit of life is from God; he at first in the creation breathed into man the breath of life, and so he will at last in the resurrection. The dispirited despairing captives were wonderfully animated with resolution to break through all the discouragements that lay in the way of their return and applied themselves to it with all imaginable vigour. And then they stood upon their feet, an exceedingly great army; not only living men, but effective men, fit for service in the wars and formidable to all that gave them any opposition. Note, With God nothing is impossible. He can out of stones raise up children unto Abraham and out of dead and dry bones levy an exceedingly great army to fight his battles and plead his cause.

II. The application of this vision to the present calamitous condition of the Jews in captivity: These bones are the whole house of Israel, both the ten tribes and the two. See in this what they are and what they shall be.

1. The depth of despair to which they are now reduced, Eze 37:11. They all give up themselves for lost and gone; they say, "Our bones are dried, our strength is exhausted, our spirits are gone, our hope is all lost; every thing we looked for succour and relief from fails us, and we are cut off for our parts. Let who will cherish some hope, we see no ground for any." Note, When troubles continue long, hopes have been often frustrated, and all creature-confidences fail, it is not strange if the spirits sink; and nothing but an active faith in the power, promise, and providence of God will keep them from quite dying away. 2. The height of prosperity to which, notwithstanding this, they shall be advanced: "therefore, because things have come thus to the last extremity, prophesy to them, and tell them, now is God's time to appear for them. Jehovah-jireh-in the mount of the Lord it shall be seen, Eze 37:12-14. Tell them," (1.) "That they shall be brought out of the land of their enemies, where they are as it were buried alive: I will open your graves." Those shall be restored, not only whose bones are scattered at the grave's mouth (Psa 141:7), but who are buried in the grave; though the power of the enemy is like the bars of the pit, which one would think it impossible to break through, strong as death and cruel as the grave, yet it shall be conquered. God can bring his people up from the depths of the earth, Psa 71:20. (2.) "That they shall be brought into their own land, where they shall live in prosperity: I will bring you into the

land of Israel (Eze 37:12) and place you there (Eze 37:14), and will put my spirit in you and then you shall live." Note, Then God puts spirit in us to good purpose, and so that we shall indeed live, when he puts his Spirit in us. And (lastly) in all this God will be glorified: You shall know that I am the Lord (Eze 37:13), and that I have spoken it and performed it, Eze 37:14. Note, God's quickening the dead redounds more than any thing to his honour, and to the honour of his word, which he has magnified above all his name, and will magnify more and more by the punctual accomplishment of every tittle of it.

Ezekiel 37:15

Here are more exceedingly great and precious promises made of the happy state of the Jews after their return to their own land; but they have a further reference to the kingdom of the Messiah and the glories of gospel-times.

I. It is here promised that Ephraim and Judah shall be happily united in brotherly love and mutual serviceableness; so that whereas, ever since the desertion of the ten tribes from the house of David under Jeroboam, there had been continual feuds and animosities between the two kingdoms of Israel and Judah, and it is to be feared there had been some clashings between them even in the land of their captivity (Ephraim upon all occasions envying Judah and Judah vexing Ephraim), now it should be no longer, but there should be a coalition between them, and, notwithstanding the old differences that had been between them, they should agree to love one another and to do one another all good offices. This is here illustrated by a sign. The prophet was to take two sticks, and write upon one, For Judah (including Benjamin, those of the children of Israel that were his companions), upon the other, For Joseph, including the rest of the tribes, Eze 37:16. These two sticks must be so framed as to fall into one in his hand, Eze 37:17. The people took notice of this, and desired him to tell them the meaning of it, for they knew he did not play with sticks for his diversion, as children do. Those that would know the meaning should ask the meaning of the word of God which they read and hear, and of the instituted signs by which spiritual and divine things are represented to us; the ministers' lips should keep the knowledge thereof and the people should ask it at their mouth, Mal 2:7. It is a necessary question for grown people, as well as children, to ask, What mean you by this service, by this sign? Exo 12:26. The meaning was that Judah and Israel should become one in the hand of God, Eze 37:19. 1. They shall be one, one nation, Eze 37:22. They shall have no separate interests, and, consequently, no divided affections. There shall be no mutual jealousies and animosities, no remembrance, no remains, of their former discord. But there shall be a perfect harmony between them, a good understanding one of another, a good disposition one to another, and a readiness to all good offices and services for one another's credit and comfort. They had been two sticks crossing and thwarting one another, nay, beating and bruising one another; but now they shall become one, supporting and strengthening one another. Vix unita fortior-Force added to force is proportionally more efficient. Behold, how good and how pleasant a thing it is to see Judah and Israel, that had long been at variance, now dwelling together in unity. Then they shall become acceptable to their God, amiable to their friends, and formidable to their enemies, Isa 11:13, Isa 11:14. 2. They shall be one in God's hand; by his power they shall be united, and, being by his hand brought together, his hand shall keep them together, so that they shall not fly off, to be separated again. They shall be one in his hand, for his glory shall be the centre of their unity and his grace the cement of it. In him, in a regard to him and in his service and worship, they shall unite, and so shall become one. Both sides shall agree to put themselves into his hand, and so they shall be one. Qui conveniunt in aliquo tertio inter se conveniunt-Those who agree in a third agree with each other. Note, Those are best united that are one in God's hand, whose union with each other results from their union with Christ and their communion with God through him, Eph 1:10. One in us, Joh 17:21. 3. They shall be one in their return out of captivity (Eze 37:21): I will take them from among the heathen, and gather them on every side, and bring them together incorporated into one body to their own land. They shall be one in their separation from the heathen with whom they had mingled themselves: they shall both agree to part from them, and take their affections off from them, and no longer to comply with their usages, and then they will soon agree to join together in walking according to the rule of God's word. Their having been joint-sufferers will contribute to this blessed comprehension, when they begin to come to themselves and to consider things. Put many pieces of metal together into the furnace, and, when they are melted, they will run all together. It was time for them to strengthen one another when their oppressors were so busy to weaken and ruin them all. Likewise their being joint-sharers in the favour of God, and the great and common deliverance wrought out for them all, should help to unite them. God's loving them all was a good reason why they should love one another. Times of common joy, as well as times of common suffering, should be healing loving times. 4. They shall all be the subjects of one king, and so they shall become one. The Jews, after their return, were under one government, and not divided as formerly. But this certainly looks further, to the kingdom of Christ; he is that one King in allegiance to whom all God's spiritual Israel shall cheerfully unite, and under whose protection they shall all be gathered. All believers unite in one Lord, one faith, and one baptism. And the uniting of Jews and Gentiles in the gospel church, their becoming one fold under Christ the one great Shepherd, is doubtless the union that is chiefly looked at in this prophecy. By Christ and partition-wall between them was taken down, and the enmity slain, and of them twain was made one new man, Eph 2:14, Eph 2:15.

II. It is here promised that the Jews shall by their captivity be cured of their inclination to idolatry; this shall be the happy fruit of that affliction, even the taking away of their sin (Eze 37:23): Neither shall they defile themselves any more with their idols, those detestable defiling things, no, nor with any of their former transgressions. Note, When one sin is sincerely parted with all sin is abandoned too, for he that hates sin, as sin, will hate all sin. And those that are cured of their spiritual idolatry, their inordinate affection to the world and the flesh, that no longer make a god of their money or their belly, have a happy blow given to the root of all their transgressions. Two ways God will take to cure them of their idolatry:-1. By bringing them out of the way of temptation to it: "I will save them out of all their dwelling-places wherein they have sinned, because there they met with the occasion of sin and allurements to it." Note, It is our wisdom to avoid the places where we have been overcome by temptations to sin, not to remain in them, or return to them, but to save ourselves out of them, as we would out of infected places; see Zac 2:7; Rev 18:4. And it is a great mercy when God, in his providence, saves us out of the dwelling-places where we have sinned, and keeps us from harm by keeping us out of harm's way, in answer to our prayer, Lead us not into temptation, but deliver us from evil. 2. By changing the disposition of their mind: "I will cleanse them (Eze 37:28); that is, I will sanctify them, will work in them an aversion to the pollutions of sin and a complacency in the pleasures of holiness, and then you may be sure they will not defile themselves any more with their idols." Those whom God has cleansed he will keep clean.

III. It is here promised that they shall be the people of God, as their God, and the subjects and sheep of Christ their King and Shepherd. These promises we had before, and they are here repeated (Eze 37:23, Eze 37:24) for the encouragement of the faith of Israel: They shall be my people, to serve me, and I will be their God, to save them and to make them happy. David, my servant, shall be king over them, to fight their battles, to protect them from injury, and to rule them, and overrule all things that concern them for their good. He shall be their shepherd, to guide them and provide for them. Christ is this David, Israel's King of old; and those whom he subdues to himself, and makes willing in the day of his power, he makes to walk in his judgments and to keep his statutes.

IV. It is here promised that they shall dwell comfortably, Eze 37:25, Eze 37:26. They shall dwell in the land of Israel; for where else should Israelites dwell? And many things will concur to make their dwelling agreeable. 1. They shall have it by covenant; they shall come in again upon their old title, by virtue of the grant made unto Jacob, God's servant. As Christ was David, God's servant, so the church is Jacob, his servant too; and the members of the church shall come in for a share, as born in God's house. He will make a covenant of peace with them (Eze 37:26), and in pursuance of that covenant he will place them, and multiply them. Note, Temporal mercies are doubly sweet when they come from the promise of the covenant, and not merely from common providence. 2. They shall come to it by prescription: "It is the land wherein your fathers have dwelt, and for that reason you cannot but have a special kindness for it, which God will graciously gratify." It was the inheritance of their ancestors, and therefore shall be theirs. They are beloved for their fathers' sakes. 3. They shall have it entailed upon them and the heirs of their body, and shall have their families built up, so that it shall not be lost for want of heirs. They shall dwell therein all their time, and never be turned out of possession, and they shall leave it for an inheritance to their children and their children's children for ever, who shall enjoy it when they are gone, the prospect of which will be a satisfaction to them. 4. They shall live under a good government, which will contribute very much to the comfort of their lives: My servant David shall be their prince for ever. This can be no other than Christ, of whom it was said, when he was brought into the world, He shall reign over the house of Jacob for ever, Luk 1:33. Note, It is the unspeakable comfort of all Christ's faithful subjects that, as his kingdom is everlasting, so he is an everlasting King, he lives to reign for ever; and, as sure and as long as he lives and reigns, they shall live and reign also. 5. The charter by which they hold all their privileges is indefeasible. God's covenant with them shall be an everlasting covenant; so the covenant of grace is, for it secures to us an everlasting happiness.

V. It is here promised that God will dwell among them; and this will make them dwell comfortably indeed: I will set my sanctuary in the midst of them for evermore; my tabernacle also shall be with them, Eze 37:26, Eze 37:27. 1. They shall have the tokens of God's special presence with them and his gracious residence among them. God will in very deed dwell with them upon the earth, for where his sanctuary is he is; when they profaned his sanctuary he took it from them (Isa 64:11), but now that they are purified God will dwell with them again. 2. They shall have opportunity of conversing with God, of hearing from him, speaking to him, and so keeping up communion with him, which will be the comfort of their lives. 3. They shall have the means of grace. By the oracles of God in his tabernacle they shall be made wiser and better, and all their children shall be taught of the Lord. 4. Thus their covenant relation to God shall be improved and the bond of it strengthened: "I will be their God and they shall be my people, and they shall know it by having my sanctuary among them, and shall have the comfort of it."

VI. Both God and Israel shall have the honour of this among the heathen, Eze 37:26. "Now the heathen observe how Israel have profaned their own crown by their sins, and God has profaned it by his judgments; but then, when Israel is reformed and God has returned in mercy to them, the very heathen shall be made to know that the Lord sanctifies Israel, has a title to them and an interest in them more than other people, because his sanctuary is, and shall be, in the midst of them." Note, God designs the sanctification of those among whom he sets up his sanctuary. And blessed and holy are those who, enjoying the privileges of the sanctuary, give such proofs and evidences of their sanctification that the heathen may know it is no less than the almighty grace of God that sanctifies them. Such have God's sanctuary in the midst of them, the kingdom of God within them, in the principles of the spiritual life, and shall have it so for evermore in the enjoyments of an eternal life.

Ezekiel Chapter 38

This chapter, and that which follows it, are concerning Gog and Magog, a powerful enemy to the people of Israel, that should make a formidable descent upon them, and put them into a consternation, but their army should be routed and their design defeated; and this prophecy, it is most probable, had its accomplishment some time after the return of the people of Israel out of their captivity, whether in the struggles they had with the kings of Syria, especially Antiochus Epiphanes, or perhaps in some other way not recorded, we cannot tell. If the sacred history of the Old Testament had reached as far as the prophecy, we should have been better able to understand these chapters, but, for want of that key, we are locked out of the meaning of them. God had by the prophet assured his people of happy times after their return to their own land; but lest they should mistake the promises which related to the kingdom of the Messiah and the spiritual privileges of that the kingdom of the Messiah and the spiritual privileges of that kingdom, as if from them they might promise themselves an uninterrupted temporal prosperity, he here tells them, as Christ told his disciples to prevent the like mistake, that in the world they shall have tribulation, but they may be of good cheer, for they shall be victorious at last. This prophecy here of Gog and Magog is without doubt alluded to in that prophecy which relates to the latter days, and which seems to be yet unfulfilled (Rev 20:8), that Gog and Magog shall be gathered to battle against the camp of the saints, as the Old Testament prophecies of the destruction of Babylon are alluded to, Rev. 18. But, in both, the Old Testament prophecies had their accomplishment in the Jewish church as the New Testament prophecies shall have when the time comes in the Christian church. In this chapter we have intermixed, I. The attempt that Gog and Magog should make upon the land of Israel, the vast army they should bring into the field, and their vast preparations (Eze 38:4-7), their project and design in it (Eze 38:8-13), God's hand in it (Eze 38:4). II. The great terror that this should strike upon the land of Israel (Eze 38:15, Eze 38:16, Eze 38:18-20). III. The divine restraint that these enemies should be under, and the divine protection that Israel should be under (Eze 38:2-4 and Eze 38:14). IV. The defeat that should be given to those enemies by the immediate hand of God (Eze 38:21-23), which we shall hear more of in the next chapter.

Ezekiel 38:1

The critical expositors have enough to do here to enquire out Gog and Magog. We cannot pretend either to add to their observations or to determine their controversies. Gog seems to be the king and Magog the kingdom; so that Gog and Magog are like Pharaoh and the Egyptians. Some think they find them afar off, in Scythia, Tartary, and Russia. Others think they find them nearer the land of Israel, in Syria, and Asia the Less. Ezekiel is appointed to prophesy against

Gog, and to tell him that God is against him, Eze 38:2, Eze 38:3. Note, God does not only see those that are now the enemies of his church and set himself against them, but he foresees those that will be so and lets them know by his word that he is against them too, and yet is pleased to make use of them to serve his own purposes, for the glory of his own name; surely their wrath shall praise him, and the remainder thereof he will restrain, Psa 76:10. Let us observe here,

I. The confusion which God designed to put this enemy to. It is remarkable that this is put first in the prophecy; before it is foretold that God will bring him forth against Israel it is foretold that God will put hooks into his jaws and turn him back (Eze 38:4), that they might have assurance of their deliverance before they had the prospect given them of their danger. Thus tender is God of the comfort of his people, thus careful that they may not be frightened; even before the trouble begins he tells them it will end well.

II. The undertaking which he designed to engage him in, in order to this defeat and disappointment. 1. The nations that shall be confederate in this enterprise against Israel are many, and great, and mighty (Eze 38:5, Eze 38:6), Persia, Ethiopia, etc. Antiochus had an army made up of all the nations here named, and many others. These people had been at variance with one another, and yet in combination against Israel. How are those increased that trouble God's people! 2. They are well furnished with arms and ammunition, and bring a good train of artillery into the field-horses and horsemen (Eze 38:4) bravely equipped with all sorts of armour, bucklers and shields for defence, and all handling swords for offence. Orders are given to make all imaginable preparation for this expedition (Eze 38:7): "Be thou prepared, and do thou prepare. See what warlike preparations thou hast already in store, and, lest that should not suffice, make further preparation, thou and all thy company," Let Gog himself be a guard to the rest of the confederates. As commander-in-chief, let him engage to take care of them and their safety; let him pass his word for their security, and take them under his particular protection. The leaders of an army, instead of exposing their soldiers needlessly and presumptuously, and throwing away their lives upon desperate undertakings, should study to be a guard to them, and, whenever they send them forth in danger, should contrive to support and cover them. This call to prepare seems to be ironical-Do thy worst, but I will turn thee back; like thatIsa 8:9. Gird yourselves, and you shall be broken in pieces. 3. Their design is against the mountains of Israel (Eze 38:8), against the land that is brought back from the sword. It is not long since it was harassed with the sword of war, and it has been always wasted, more or less, with one judgment or other; it is but newly gathered out of many people, and brought forth out of the nations; it has enjoyed comparatively but a short breathing-time, has scarcely recovered any strength since it was brought down by war and captivity; and therefore its neighbours need not fear its being too great, nay, and therefore it is very barbarous to pick a quarrel with it so soon. It is a people that dwell safely, all of them, in unwalled villages, very secure, and having neither bars nor gates, Eze 38:11. It is a certain sign that they intend no mischief to their neighbours, for they fear no mischief from them. It cannot be thought that those will offend others who do not take care to defend themselves; and this aggravates the sin of these invaders. It is base and barbarous to devise evil against thy neighbour while he dwells securely by thee, and has no distrust of thee, Pro 3:29. But see here how the clouds return after the rain in this world, and what little reason we have ever to be secure till we come to heaven. It is not long since Israel was brought back from the sword of one enemy, and behold the sword of another is drawn against it. Former troubles will not excuse us from further troubles; but when we think we have put off the harness, at least for some time, by a fresh and sudden alarm we may be called to gird it on again; and therefore we must never boast nor be off our guard. 4. That which the enemy has in view, in forming this project, is to enrich himself and to make himself master, not of the country, but of the wealth of it, to spoil and plunder it, and make a prey of it: At the same time that God intends to bring this matter about things shall come into the mind of this enemy, and he shall think an evil thought, Eze 38:10. Note, All the mischief men do, and particularly the mischief they do to the church of God, arises from evil thoughts that come into their mind, ambitious thoughts, covetous thoughts, spiteful thoughts against those that are good, for the sake of their goodness. It came into Antiochus's mind what a singular people these religious Jews were, and how their worship witnessed against and condemned the idolatries of their neighbours, and therefore, in enmity to their religion, he would plague them. It came into his mind what a wealthy people they were, that they had gotten cattle and goods in the midst of the land (Eze 38:12), and withal how weak they were, how unable to make any resistance, how easy it would be to carry off what they had, and how much glory this rapine would add to his victorious sword; these things coming into his mind, and one evil thought drawing on another, he came at last to this resolve (Eze 38:11, Eze 38:12): "I will go up to the land of unwalled villages; yea, that I will; it will cost me nothing to make them all my own. I will go and disturb those that are at rest, without giving them any notice, not to crush their growing greatness, or chastise their insolence, or make reprisals upon them for any wrong they have done us (they had none of these pretences to make war upon them), but purely to take a spoil and to take a prey" (Eze 38:12), in open defiance to all the laws of justice and equity, as much as the highwayman's killing the traveller that he may take his money. These were the thoughts that came into the mind of this wicked prince, and God knew them; nay, he knew them before they came into his mind, for he understands our thoughts afar off, Psa 139:2. 5. According to the project thus formed he pours in all his forces upon the land of Israel, and finds those that are ready to come in to his assistance with the same prospects (Eze 38:9): "Thou shalt ascent and come like a storm, with all the force, and fury, and fierceness imaginable, and thou shalt be like a cloud to cover the land, to darken it, and to threaten it, thou and not only all thy bands, all the force thou canst bring into the field, but many people with thee" (such as are spoken of Eze 38:13), "Sheba and Dedan, the Arabians and the Edomites, and the merchants of Tarshish, of Tyre and Sidon and other maritime cities, they and their young lions that are greedy of spoil and live upon it, shall say, Hast thou come to take the spoil of this land?" Yes he has; and therefore they wish him success. Or perhaps they envy him, or grudge it to him. "Hast thou come for riches who art thyself so rich already?" Or, knowing that God was on Israel's side, they thus ridicule his attempts, foreseeing that they would be baffled and that he would be disappointed of the prey he promised himself. Or, if he come to take the prey, they will come and join with him, and add to his forces. When Lysias, who was general of Antiochus's army, came against the Jews, the neighbouring nations joined with him (1 Macc. 3:41), to share in the guilt, in hopes to share in the prey. When thou sawest a thief then thou consentedst with him.

Ezekiel 38:14

This latter part of the chapter is a repetition of the former; the dream is doubled, for the thing is certain and to be very carefully regarded.

I. It is here again foretold that this spiteful enemy should make a formidable descent upon the land of Israel (Eze 38:15): "Thou shalt come out of the north parts (Syria lay on the north of Canaan) with a mighty army, shalt come like a cloud, and cover the land of my people Israel," Eze 38:16. These words (Eze 38:14), When my people Israel dwell safely, shalt thou not know it? may be taken two ways:-1. As intimating his inducements to this attempt. "Thou shalt have intelligence brought thee how securely, and therefore how carelessly, the people of Israel dwell, which shall give rise to thy project against them; for when thou knowest not only what a rich, but what an easy prey they are likely to be, thou wilt soon determine to fall upon them" Note, God's providence is to be acknowledged in the occasion, the small occasion perhaps, that is given, and that not designedly neither, to those first thoughts from which great enterprises take their original. God, to bring about his own purposes, lets men know that which yet he knows they will make a bad use of, as here. Or, 2. As intimating his disappointment in this attempt, which here, as before, the prophecy begins with: "When my people Israel dwell safely, not in their own apprehension only, but in reality, forasmuch as they dwell safely under the divine protection, shalt not thou be made to know it by the fruitlessness of thy endeavours to destroy them?" Thou shalt soon find that there is no enchantment against Jacob, that no weapon formed against them shall prosper; thou shalt know to thy cost, shalt know to thy shame, that though they have no walls, nor bars, nor gates, they have God himself, a wall of fire, round about them, and that he who touches them touches the apple of his eye; whosoever meddles with them meddles to his own hurt. And it is for the demonstrating of this to all the world that God will bring this mighty enemy against his people. Those that gathered themselves against Israel said, Let us take the spoil and take they prey, but they knew not the thoughts of the Lord, Mic 4:11, Mic 4:12. I will bring thee against my land. This is strange news, that God will not only permit his enemies to come against his own children, but will himself bring them; but, if we understand what he aims at, we shall be well reconciled even to this: it is "that the heathen may know me to be the only living and true God when I shall be sanctified in thee, O Gog! that is, in thy defeat and destruction before their eyes, that all the nations may see, and say, There is none like unto the God of Jeshurun, that rides on the heavens for the help of his people." Note, God brings his people into danger and distress that he may have the honour of bringing about their deliverance, and suffers the enemies of his church to prevail awhile, though they profane his name by their sin, that he may have the honour of prevailing at last and sanctifying his own name in their ruin. Now it is said, This shall be in the latter days, namely, in the latter days of the Old Testament church; so the mischief that Antiochus did to Israel was; but in the latter days of the New Testament church another like enemy should arise, that should in like manner be defeated. Note, Effectual securities are treasured up in the word of God against the troubles and dangers the church may be brought into a great while hence, even in the latter days.

II. Reference is herein had to the predictions of the former prophets (Eze 38:17): Art thou he of whom I have spoken in old time, of whom Moses spoke in his prophecy of the latter days (Deu 32:43, He will render vengeance to his adversaries), and David, Psa 9:15 (The heathen are sunk down into the pit that they made) and often elsewhere in the Psalms? This is the leviathan of whom Isaiah spoke (Isa 27:1), that congress of the nations of which Joel spoke, Joe 3:1. Many of the prophets had perhaps spoken particularly of this event, though it be not written, as they all had spoken and written too that which is applicable to it. Note, There is an amiable admirable harmony and agreement between the Lord's prophets, though they lived in several ages, for they were all guided by one and the same Spirit.

III. It is here foretold that this furious formidable enemy should be utterly cut off in this attempt upon Israel, and that it should issue in his own ruin. This is supposed by many to have its accomplishment in the many defeats given by the Maccabees to the forces of Antiochus and the remarkable judgments of God executed upon his own person, for he died of sore diseases. But these things are here foretold, as usual, in figurative expressions, which we are not to look for the literal accomplishment of, and yet they might be fulfilled nearer the letter than we know of. 1. God will be highly displeased with this bold invader: When he comes up in pride and anger against the land of Israel, and thinks to carry all before him with a high hand, then God's fury shall come up in his face, which is an allusion to the manner of men, whose colour rises in their faces when some high affront is offered them and they are resolved to show their resentment of it,Eze 38:18. God will speak against them in his jealousy for his people and in the fire of his wrath against his and their enemies, Eze 38:19. See how God's permitting sin, his laying occasions of sin before men, and his making use of it to serve his own purposes, consist with his hatred of sin and his displeasure against it. God brings this enemy against his land, letting him know what an easy prey it might be and determining thereby to glorify himself; and yet, when he comes against the land, God's fury comes up, and he speaks to him in the fire of his wrath. If any ask, Why does he thus find fault? for who has resisted his will? It is easy to answer, Nay, but, O man! who art thou that repliest against God? 2. His forces shall be put into the greatest confusion and consternation imaginable (Eze 38:19): There shall be a great shaking of them in the land of Israel, a universal concussion (Eze 38:20), such as shall affect the fishes and fowls, the beasts and creeping things, and much more the men that are upon the face of the earth, who sooner receive impressions of fear. There shall be such an earthquake as shall throw down the mountains, those natural heights, and the steep places, towers and walls, those artificial heights; they shall all fall to the ground. Some understand this of the fright which the land of Israel should be put into by the fury of the enemy. But it is rather to be understood of the fright which the enemy should be put into by the wrath of God; all those things which they both raise themselves and stay themselves upon shall be shaken down, and their hearts shall fail them. 3. He shall be routed and utterly ruined; both earth and heaven shall be armed against him (1.) The earth shall muster up its forces to destroy him. If the people of Israel have not strength and courage to resist him, God will call for a sword against him, Eze 38:21. And he has swords always at command, that are bathed in heaven, Isa 35:5. Throughout all the mountains of Israel, where he hoped to meet with spoil to enrich him, he shall meet with swords to destroy him, and, rather than fail, every man's sword shall be against his brother, as in the day of Midian, Psa 83:9. The great men of Syria shall undermine and overthrow one another, shall accuse one another, shall fight duels with one another. Note, God can, and often does, make the destroyers of his people to be their own destroyers and the destroyers of one another. However, he will himself be their destroyer, will take the work into his own hand, that it may be done thoroughly (Eze 38:22): I will plead against him with pestilence and blood. Note, Whom God acts against he pleads against; he shows them the ground of his controversy with them, that their mouths may be stopped, and he may be clear when he judges. (2.) The artillery of heaven shall also be drawn out against them: I will rain upon him an overflowing rain, Eze 38:22. He comes like a storm upon Israel, Eze 38:9. But God will come like a storm upon him, will rain upon him great hailstones as upon the Canaanites (Jos 10:11), fire and brimstone as upon Sodom, and a horrible tempest, Psa 11:6. Thus the Gog and Magog in the New Testament shall be devoured with fire from heaven, and cast into the lake of brimstone, Rev 20:9, Rev 20:10. That will be the everlasting portion of all the impenitent implacable enemies of God's church and people. 4. God, in all this, will be glorified. The end he aimed at (Eze 38:16) shall be accomplished (Eze 38:23): Thus will I magnify myself and sanctify myself. Note, In the destruction of sinners God makes it to appear that he is a great and holy God, and he will do so to eternity. And, if men do not magnify and sanctify him as they ought, he will magnify himself, and sanctify himself; and this we should desire and pray for daily, Father, glorify thy own name.

Ezekiel Chapter 39

This chapter continues and concludes the prophecy against Gog and Magog, in whose destruction God crowns his favour to his people Israel, which shines very brightly after the scattering of that black cloud in the close of this chapter. Here is, I. An express prediction of the utter destruction of Gog and Magog, agreeing with what we had before (Eze 39:1-7). II. An illustration of the vastness of that destruction, in three consequences of it: the burning of their weapons (Eze 39:8-10), the burning of their slain (Eze 39:11-16), and the feasting of the fowls with the dead bodies of those that were unburied (Eze 39:17-22). III. A declaration of God's gracious purposes concerning his people Israel, in this and his other providences concerning them, and a promise of further mercy that he had yet in store for them (Eze 39:23-29).

Ezekiel 39:1

This prophecy begins as that before (Eze 38:3, Eze 38:4, I am against thee, and I will turn thee back); for there is need of line upon line, both for the conviction of Israel's enemies and the comfort of Israel's friends. Here, as there, it is foretold that God will bring this enemy from the north parts, as formerly the Chaldeans were fetched from the north, Jer 1:14 (Omne malum ab aquilone-Every evil comes from the north), and, long after, the Roman empire was overrun by the northern nations, that he will bring him upon the mountains of Israel (Eze 39:2), first as a place of temptation, where the measures of his iniquity shall be filled up, and then as a place of execution, where his ruin shall be completed. And that is it which is here enlarged upon. 1. His soldiers shall be disarmed and so disabled to carry on their enterprise. Though the men of might may find their hands, yet to what purpose, when they find it is put out of their power to do mischief, when God shall smite their bow out of their left hand and their arrow out of their right? Eze 39:3. Note, The weapons formed against Zion shall not prosper. 2. He and the greatest part of his army shall be slain in the field of battle (Eze 39:4): Thou shalt fall upon the mountains of Israel; there they sinned, and there they shall perish, even upon the holy mountains of Israel, for there broke he the arrows of the bow, Psa 76:3. The mountains of Israel shall be moistened, and fattened, and made fruitful, with the blood of the enemies. "Thou shalt fall upon the open field (Eze 39:5) and shalt not be able even there to make thy escape." Even upon the mountains he shall not find a pass that he shall be able to maintain, and upon the open field he shall not find a road that he shall be able to make his escape by. He and his bands; his regular troops, and the people that are with him that follow the camp to share in the plunder, shall all fall with him. Note, Those that cast in their lot among wicked people (Pro 1:14), that they may have one purse with them, must expect to take their lot with them, and fare as they fare, taking the worse with the better. There shall be such a general slaughter made that but a sixth part shall be left (Eze

39:2), the other five shall all be cut off. Never was army so totally routed as this. And, for its greater infamy and reproach, their bodies shall be a feast to the birds of prey, Eze 39:4. Compare Eze 39:17, Thou shalt fall, for I have spoken it. Note, Rather shall the most illustrious princes (Antiochus was called Epiphanes-the illustrious) and the most numerous armies fall to the ground than any word of God; for he that has spoken will make it good. 3. His country also shall be made desolate: I will send a fire on Magog (Eze 39:6) and among those that dwell carelessly, or confidently, in the isles, that is, the nations of the Gentiles. He designed to destroy the land of Israel, but shall not only be defeated in that design, but shall have his own destroyed by some fire, some consuming judgment or other. Note, Those who invade other people's rights justly lose their own. 4. God will by all this advance the honour of his own name, (1.) Among his people Israel; they shall hereby know more of God's name, of his power and goodness, his care of them, his faithfulness to them. His providence concerning them shall lead them into a better acquaintance with him; every providence should do so, as well as every ordinance: I will make my holy name known in the midst of my people. In Judah is God known; but those that know much of God should know more of him; we should especially increase in the knowledge of his name as a holy name. They shall know him as a God of perfect purity and rectitude and that hates all sin, and then it follows, I will not let them pollute my holy name any more. Note, Those that rightly know God's holy name will not dare to profane it; for it is through ignorance of it that men make light of it and make bold with it. And this is God's method of dealing with men, first to enlighten their understandings, and by that means to influence the whole man; he first makes us to know his holy name, and so keeps us from polluting it and engages us to honour it. And this is here the blessed effect of God's glorious appearances on the behalf of his people. Thus he completes his favours, thus he sanctifies them, thus he makes them blessings indeed; by them he instructs his people and reforms them. When the Almighty scattered kings for her she was white as snow in Salmon, Psa 68:14. (2.) Among the heathen; those that never knew it, or would not own it, shall know that I am the Lord, the Holy One in Israel. They shall be made to know by dear bought experience that he is a God of power, and his people's God and Saviour; and it is in vain for the greatest potentates to contend with him; none ever hardened their heart against him and prospered.

Ezekiel 39:8

Though this prophecy was to have its accomplishment in the latter days, yet it is here spoken of as if it were already accomplished, because it is certain (Eze 39:8): "Behold it has come, and it is done; it is as sure to be done when the time shall come as if it were done already; this is the day whereof I have long and often spoken, and, though it has been long in coming, yet at length it has come." Thus it was said unto John (Rev 21:6), It is done. To represent the routing of the army of Gog as very great, here are three things specified as the consequences of it. It was God himself that gave the defeat; we do not find that the people of Israel drew a sword or struck a stroke: but,

I. They shall burn their weapons, their bows and arrows, which fell out of their hands (Eze

39:3), their shields and bucklers, their javelins, spears, leading staves, truncheons, and half-pikes, every thing that is combustible. They shall not lay them up in their armouries, nor reserve them for their own use, lest they should be tempted to put a confidence in them, but they shall burn them; not all at once, for a bonfire (to what purpose would be that waste?) but as they had occasion to use them for fuel in their houses, instead of other fire-wood, so that they should have no occasion to take wood out of the field or forests for seven years together (Eze 39:10), such vast quantities of weapons shall there be left upon the open field where the enemy fell, and in the roads which they passed in their flight. The weapons were dry and fitter for fuel than green wood; and, by saving the wood in their coppices and forests, they gave it time to grow. Though the mountains of Israel produce plenty of all good things, yet it becomes the people of Israel to be good husbands of their plenty and to save what they can for the benefit of those that come after them, as Providence shall give them opportunity to do so. We may suppose that when those who dwelt in the cities of Israel came forth to spoil those who spoiled them, and make reprisals upon them, they found upon them silver, and gold, and ornaments; yet no mention is made of any thing particularly that they converted to their own use but the wood of the weapons for fuel, which is one of the necessaries of human life, to teach us to think it enough if we be well supplied with those, though we have but little of the delights and gaieties of it and of those things which we may very well live without. And every time they put fuel to the fire, and warmed themselves at it, they would be put in mind of the number and strength of their enemies, and the imminent peril they were in of falling into their hands, which would help to enlarge their hearts in thankfulness to that God who had so wonderfully, so seasonably, delivered them. As they sat by the fire with their children about them (their fire-side), they might from it take occasion to tell them what great things God had done for them.

II. They shall bury their dead. Usually, after a battle, when many are slain, the enemy desire time to bury their own dead. But here the slaughter shall be so general that there shall not be a sufficient number of the enemies left alive to bury the dead. And, besides, the slain lie so dispersed on the mountains of Israel that it would be a work of time to find them out; and therefore it is left to the house of Israel to bury them as a piece of triumph in their overthrow. 1. A place shall be appointed on purpose for the burying of them, the valley of the passengers, on the east of the sea, either the salt sea or the sea of Tiberias, a valley through which there was great passing and repassing of travellers between Egypt and Chaldea. There shall be such a multitude of dead bodies, putrefying above ground, with such a loathsome stench, that the travellers who go that way shall be forced to stop their noses. See what vile bodies ours are; when the soul has been a little while from them the smell of them becomes offensive, no smell more nauseous or more noxious. There therefore where the greatest number lay slain shall the burying-place be appointed. In the place where the tree falls there let it lie. And it shall be called, The valley of Hamon-gog, that is, of the multitude of Gog; for that was the thing which was in a particular manner to be had in remembrance. How numerous the forces of the enemy were which God defeated and destroyed for the defence of his people Israel! 2. A considerable time shall be spent in burying them, no less than seven months (Eze 39:12), which is a further intimation that the slain of the Lord in this action should be many and that great care should be taken by the house of Israel to leave none unburied, that so they might cleanse the land from the ceremonial pollution it contracted by the lying of so many dead corpses unburied in it, for the prevention of which it was appointed that those who were hanged on a tree should be speedily taken down and buried, Deut, Eze 21:23. This is an intimation that times of eminent deliverances should be times of reformation. The more God has done for the saving of a land from ruin the more the inhabitants should do for the cleansing of the land from sin. 3. Great numbers shall be employed in this work: All the people of the land shall be ready to lend a helping hand to it, Eze 39:13. Note, Every one should contribute the utmost he can in his place towards the cleansing of the land from the pollutions of it, and from every thing that is a reproach to it. Sin is a common enemy, which every man should take up arms against. In publico discrimine unusquisque homo miles est-In the season of public danger every man becomes a soldier. And whoever shall assist in this work it shall be to them a renown; though the office of grave-makers, or common scavengers of the country, seem but mean, yet, when it is for the cleansing and purifying of the land from dead works, it shall be mentioned to their honour. Note, Acts of humanity add much to the renown of God's Israel; it is a credit to religion when those that profess it are ready to every good work; and a good work it is to bury the dead, yea, though they be strangers and enemies to the commonwealth of Israel, for even they shall rise again. It shall be a renown to them in the day when God will be glorified. Note, It is for the glory of God when his Israel do that which adorns their profession; others will see their good works and glorify their Father, Mat 5:16. And when God is honoured he will put honour upon his people. His glory is their renown. 4. Some particular persons shall make it their business to search out the dead bodies, or any part of them that should remain unburied. The people of the land will soon grow weary of burying the pollutions of the country, and therefore they shall appoint men of continual employment, that shall apply themselves to it and do nothing else till the land be thoroughly cleansed; for, otherwise, that which is every one's work would soon become nobody's work. Note, Those that are engaged in public work, especially for the cleansing and reforming of a land, ought to be men of continual employments, men that will stick to what they undertake and go through with it, men that will apply themselves to it; and those that will do good according to their opportunities will find themselves continually employed. 5. Even the passengers shall be ready to give information to those whose business it is to cleanse the land of what public nuisances they meet with, which call for their assistance. Those that pass through the land, though they will not stay to bury the dead themselves, lest they should contract a ceremonial pollution, will yet give notice of those that they find unburied. If they but discover a bone, they will set up a sign, that the buriers may come and bury it, and that, till it is buried, others may take need of touching it, for which reason their sepulchres among the Jews were whitened, that people might keep at a distance from them. Note, When good work is to be done every one should lend a hand to further it, even the passengers themselves, who must not think themselves unconcerned, in a common calamity, or a common iniquity, to put a stop to it. Those whose work it is to cleanse the land must not countenance any thing in it that is defiling; though it were not the body, but only the bone, of a man, that was found unburied, they must encourage those who will give information of it (private information, by a sign, concealing the informer), that they may take it away, and bury it out of sight. Nay, after the end of seven months, which was allowed them for this work, when all is taken away that appeared at first view, they shall search for more, that what is hidden may be brought to light; they shall search out iniquity till they find none. In memory of this they shall give a new name to their city. It shall be called Hamonah-The multitude. O what a multitude of our enemies have we of this city buried! Thus shall they cleanse the land, with all this care, with all this pains, Eze 39:16. Note, After conquering there must be cleansing. Moses appointed those Israelites that had been employed in the war with the Midianites to purify themselves, Num 31:24. Having received special favours from God, let us cleanse ourselves from all filthiness.

III. The birds and beasts of prey shall rest upon the carcases of the slain while they remain unburied and it shall be impossible to prevent them, Eze 39:17, etc. We find a great slaughter represented by this figure, Rev 19:17, etc., which is borrowed from this.

1. There is a general invitation given, Eze 39:17. It is to the fowl of every wing and to every beast of the field, from the greatest to the least, that preys upon carcases, from the eagle to the raven, from the lion to the dog; let them all gather themselves on every side; here is meat enough for them, and they are all welcome. Let them come to God's sacrifice, to his feast; so the margin reads it. Note, The judgments of God, executed upon sin and sinners, are both a sacrifice and a feast, a sacrifice to the justice of God and a feast to the faith and hope of God's people. When God broke the head of leviathan, he gave him to be meat to Israel, Psa 74:14. The righteous shall rejoice as at a feast when he sees the vengeance, and shall wash his foot, as at a feast, in the blood of the wicked. This sacrifice is upon the mountains of Israel; these are the high places, the altars, where God has been dishonoured by the idolatries of the people, but where he will now glorify himself in the destruction of his enemies.

2. There is great preparation made: They shall eat the flesh of the mighty and drink the blood of the princes of the earth, Eze 39:18, Eze 39:19. (1.) It is the flesh and blood of men that they shall be treated with. This has sometimes been an instance of the rebellion of the inferior creatures against man their master, which is an effect of his rebellion against God his Maker. (2.) It is the flesh and blood of great men, here called rams, and bullocks, and great goats, all of them fatlings of Bashan. It is the blood of the princes of the earth that they shall regale themselves with. What a mortification is this to the princes of the blood, as they call themselves, that God can make that blood, that royal blood, which swells their veins, a feast for the birds and beasts of prey! (3.) It is the flesh and blood of wicked men, the enemies of God's church and people, that they are invited to. They had accounted the Israel of God as sheep for the slaughter, and now they shall themselves be so accounted; they had thus used the dead bodies of Gods' servants (Psa 79:2), or would have done, and now it shall come upon themselves.

3. They shall all be fed, they shall all be feasted to the full (Eze 39:19, Eze 39:20): "You shall eat fat, and drink blood, which are satiating surfeiting things. The sacrifice is great and the feast upon the sacrifice is accordingly: You shall be filled at my table." Note, God keeps a table for the inferior creatures; he provides food for all flesh. The eyes of all wait upon him, and he satisfies their desires, for he keeps a plentiful table. And if the birds and beasts shall be filled at God's table, which he has prepared for them, much more shall his children be abundantly satisfied with the goodness of his house, even of his holy temple. They shall be filled with horses and chariots; that is, those who ride in the chariots, mighty men and men of war, who triumphed over nations, are now themselves triumphed over by the ravens of the valley and the young eagles, Pro 30:17. They thought to make an easy prey of God's Israel, and now they are themselves an easy prey to the birds and beasts. See how evil pursues sinners even after death. This exposing of their bodies to be a prey is but a type and sign of those terrors which, after death, shall prey upon their consciences (which the poetical fictions represented by a vulture continually pecking at the heart), and this shame is but an earnest of the everlasting shame and contempt they shall rise to.

IV. This shall redound very much both to the glory of God and to the comfort and satisfaction of his people. 1. It shall be much for the honour of God, for the heathen shall hereby be made to know that he is the Lord (Eze 39:21): All the heathen shall see and observe my judgments that I have executed, and thereby my glory shall be set among them. This principle shall be admitted and established among them more than ever, that the God of Israel is a great and glorious God. He is known to be so even among the heathen, that have not, or read not, his written word, by the judgments which he executes. 2. It shall be much for the satisfaction of his people; for they shall hereby be made to know that he is their God (Eze 39:22): The house of Israel shall know, abundantly to their comfort, that I am the Lord their God from that day and forward. (1.) He will be so from that day and forward. God's present mercies are pledges and assurances of further mercies. If God evidence to us that he is our God he assures us that he will never leave us. This God is our God for ever and ever. (2.) They shall know it with more satisfaction from that day and forward. They had sometimes been ready to question whether the Lord was with them or no; but the events of this day shall silence their doubts, and, the matter being thus settled and made clear, it shall not be doubted of for the future. As boasting in themselves is hereby for ever excluded, so boasting in God is hereby for ever secured.

Ezekiel 39:23

This is the conclusion of the whole matter going before, and has reference not only to the predictions concerning Gog and Magog, but to all the prophecies of this book concerning the captivity of the house of Israel, and then concerning their restoration and return out of their captivity.

I. God will let the heathen know the meaning of his people's troubles, and rectify the mistake of those concerning them who took occasion from the troubles of Israel to reproach the God of Israel, as unable to protect them and untrue to his covenant with them. When God, upon their reformation and return to him, turned again their captivity, and brought them back to their own land, and, upon their perseverance in their reformation, wrought such great salvations for them as that from the attempts of Gog upon them, then it would be made to appear, even to the heathen that would but consider and compare things, that there was no ground at all for their reflection, that Israel went into captivity, not because God could not protect them, but because they had by sin forfeited his favour and thrown themselves out of his protection (Eze 39:23, Eze 39:24): The heathen shall know that the house of Israel went into captivity for their iniquity, that iniquity which they learned from the heathen their neighbours, because they trespassed against God. That was the true reason why God hid his face from them and gave them into the hand of their enemies. It was according to their uncleanness and according to their transgressions. Now the evincing of this will not only silence their reflections on God, but will redound greatly to his honour; when the troubles of God's people are over, and we see the end of them, we shall better understand them than we did at first. And it will appear much for the glory of God when the world is made to know, 1. That God punishes sin even in his own people, because he hates it most in those that are nearest and dearest to him,Amo 3:2. It is the praise of justice to be impartial. 2. That, when God gives up his people for a prey, it is to correct them and reform them, not to gratify their enemies, Isa 10:7; Isa 42:24. Let not them therefore exalt themselves. 3. That no sooner do God's people humble themselves under the rod than he returns in mercy to them.

II. God will give his own people to know what great favour he has in store for them notwithstanding the troubles he had brought them into (Eze 39:25, Eze 39:26): Now will I bring again the captivity of Jacob.

1. Why now? Now God will have mercy upon the whole house of Israel, (1.) Because it is time for him to stand up for his own glory, which suffers in their sufferings: Now will I be jealous for my holy name, that that may no longer be reproached. (2.) Because now they repent of their sins: They have borne their shame, and all their trespasses. When sinners repent, and take shame to themselves, God will be reconciled and put honour upon them. It is particularly pleasing to God that these penitents look a great way back in their penitential reflections, and are ashamed of all their trespasses which they were guilty of when they dwelt safely in their land and none made them afraid. The remembrance of the mercies they enjoyed in their own land, and the divine protection they were under there, shall be improved as an aggravation of the sins they committed in that land; they dwelt safely, and might have continued to dwell so, and none should have given them any disquiet or disturbance if they had continued in the way of their duty. Nay, therefore they trespassed because they dwelt safely. Outward safety is often a cause of inward security, and that is an inlet to all sin, Ps. 73. Now this they are willing to bear the shame of, and acknowledge that God has justly brought them into a land of trouble, where every one makes them afraid, because they had trespassed against him in a land of peace, where none made them

afraid. And, when they thus humble themselves under humbling providences, God will bring again their captivity: and,

2. What then? When God has gathered them out of their enemies' hands, and brought them home again, (1.) Then God will have the praise of it: I will be sanctified in them in the sight of many nations, Eze 39:27. As God was reproached in the reproach they were under during their captivity, so he will be sanctified in their reformation and the making of them a holy people again, and will be glorified in their restoration and the making of them a happy glorious people again. (2.) Then they shall have the benefit of it (Eze 39:28): They shall know that I am the Lord their God. Note, The providences of God concerning his people, that are designed for their good, have the grace of God going along with them to teach them to eye God as the Lord, and their God, in all; and then they do them good. They shall eye him as the Lord and their God, [1.] In their calamities, that it was he who caused them to be led into captivity; and therefore they must not only submit to his will, but endeavour to answer his end in it. [2.] In their comfort, that it is he who has gathered them to their own land, and left none of them among the heathen. Note, By the variety of events that befal us, if we look up to God in all, we may come to acquaint ourselves better with his various attributes and designs. (3.) Then God and they will never part, Eze 39:29. [1.] God will pour out his Spirit upon them, to prevent their departures from him and returns to folly again, and to keep them close to their duty. And then, [2.] He will never hide his face any more from them, will never suspend his favour as he had done; he will never turn from doing them good, and, in order to that, he will effectually provide that they shall never turn from doing him service. Note, The indwelling of the Spirit is an infallible pledge of the continuance of God's favour. He will hide his face no more from those on whom he has poured out his Spirit. When therefore we pray that God would never cast us away from his presence we must as earnestly pray that, in order to that, he would never take his Holy Spirit away from us, Psa 51:11.

Ezekiel Chapter 40

Ezekiel

The waters of the sanctuary which this prophet saw in vision (Eze 47:1) are a proper representation of this prophecy. Hitherto the waters have been sometimes but to the ankles, in other places to the knees, or to the loins, but now the waters have risen, and have become "a river which cannot be passed over." Here is one continued vision, beginning at this chapter, to the end of the book, which is justly looked upon to be one of the most difficult portions of scripture in all the book of God. The Jews will not allow any to read it till they are thirty years old, and tell those who do read it that, though they cannot understand every thing in it, "when Elias comes he will explain it." Many commentators, both ancient and modern, have owned themselves at a loss what to make of it and what use to make of it. But because it is hard to be understood we must not therefore throw it by, but humbly search concerning it, get as far as we can into it and as much as we can out of it, and, when we despair of satisfaction in every difficulty we meet with, bless God that our salvation does not depend upon it, but that things necessary are plain enough, and wait till God shall reveal even this unto us. These chapters are the more to be regarded because the last two chapters of the Revelation seem to have a plain allusion to them, as Rev 20:1-15 has to the foregoing prophecy of Gog and Magog. Here is the vision of a glorious temple (in this chapter and ch. 41 and 42), of God's taking possession of it (ch. 43), orders concerning the priests that are to minister in this temple (ch. 44), the division of the land, what portion should be allotted for the sanctuary, what for the city, and what for the prince, both in his government of the people and his worship of God (ch. 45), and further instructions for him and the people, ch. 46. After the vision of the holy waters we have the borders of the holy land, and the portions assigned to the tribes, and the dimensions and gates of the holy city, ch. 47, 48. Some make this to represent what had been during the flourishing state of the Jewish church, how glorious Solomon's temple was in its best days, that the captives might see what they had lost by sin and might be the more humbled. But that seems not probable. The general scope of it I take to be, 1. To assure the captives that they should not only return to their own land, and be settled there, which had been often promised in the foregoing chapters, but that they should have, and therefore should be encouraged to build, another temple, which God would own, and where he would meet them and bless them, that the ordinances of worship should be revived, and the sacred priesthood should there attend; and, though they should not have a king to live in such splendour as formerly, yet they should have a prince or ruler (who is often spoken of in this vision), who should countenance the worship of God among them and should himself be an example of diligent attendance upon it, and that prince, priests, and people, should have a very comfortable settlement and subsistence in their own land. 2. To direct them to look further than all this, and to expect the coming of the Messiah, who had before been prophesied of under the name of David because he was the man that projected the building of the temple and that should set up a spiritual temple, even the gospel-church, the glory of which should far exceed that of Solomon's temple, and which should continue to the end of time. The dimensions of these visionary buildings being so large (the new temple more spacious than all the old Jerusalem and the new Jerusalem of greater extent than all the land of Canaan) plainly intimates, as Dr. Lightfoot observes, that these things cannot be literally, but must spiritually, understood. At the gospel-temple, erected by Christ and his apostles, was so closely connected with the second material temple, was erected so carefully just at the time when that fell into decay, that it might be ready to receive its glories when it resigned them, that it was proper enough that they should both be referred to in one and the same vision. Under the type and figure of a temple and altar, priests and sacrifices, is foreshown the spiritual worship that should be performed in gospel times, more agreeable to the nature both of God and man, and that perfected at last in the kingdom of glory, in which perhaps these visions will have their full accomplishment, and some think in some happy and glorious state of the gospel-church on this side heaven, in the latter days.

In this chapter we have, I. A general account of this vision of the temple and city (Eze 40:1-4). II. A particular account of it entered upon; and a description given, 1. Of the outside wall (Eze 40:5). 2. Of the east gate (Eze 40:6-19). 3. Of the north gate (Eze 40:20-23). 4. Of the south gate (Eze 40:24-31) and the chambers and other appurtenances belonging to these gates. 5. Of the inner court, both towards the east and towards the south (Eze 40:32-38). 6. Of the tables (Eze 40:39-43). 7. Of the lodgings for the singers and the priests (Eze 40:44-47). 8. Of the porch of the house (Eze 40:48, Eze 40:49).

Ezekiel 40:1

Here is, 1. The date of this vision. It was in the twenty-fifth year of Ezekiel's captivity (Eze 40:1), which some compute to be the thirty-third year of the first captivity, and is here said to be the fourteenth year after the city was smitten. See how seasonably the clearest and fullest prospects of their deliverance were given, when they were in the depth of their distress, and an assurance of the return of the morning when they were in the midnight of their captivity: "Then the hand of the Lord was upon me and brought me thither to Jerusalem, now that it was in ruins, desolate and deserted"-a pitiable sight to the prophet. 2. The scene where it was laid. The prophet was brought, in the visions of God, to the land of Israel, Eze 40:2. And it was not the first time that he had been brought thither in vision. We had him carried to Jerusalem to see it in its iniquity and shame (Eze 8:3); here he is carried thither to have a pleasing prospect of it in its glory, though its present aspect, now that it was quite depopulated, was dismal. He was set upon a very high mountain, as Moses upon the top of Pisgah, to view this land, which was now a second time a land of promise, not yet in possession. From the top of this mountain he saw as the frame of a city, the plan and model of it; but this city was a temple as large as a city. The New Jerusalem (Rev 21:22) had no temple therein; this which we have here is all temple, which comes much to one. It is a city for men to dwell in; it is a temple for God to dwell in; for in the church on earth God dwells with men, in that in heaven men dwell with God. Both these are framed in the counsel of God, framed by infinite wisdom, and all very good. 3. The particular discoveries of this city (which he had at first a general view of) were made to him by a man whose appearance was like the appearance of brass (Eze 40:3), not a created angel, but Jesus Christ, who should be found in fashion as a man, that he might both discover and build the gospel-temple. He brought him to this city, for it is through Christ that we have both acquaintance with and access to the benefits and privileges of God's house. He it is that shall build the temple of the Lord, Zac 6:13. His appearing like brass intimates both his brightness and his strength. John, in vision, saw his feet like unto fine brass, Rev 1:15. 4. The dimensions of this city or temple, and the several parts of it, were taken with a line of flax and a measuring reed, or rod (Eze 40:3), as carpenters have both their line and a wooden measure. The temple of God is built by line and rule; and those that would let others into the knowledge of it must do it by that line and rule. The church is formed according to the scripture, the pattern in the mount. That is the line and the measuring reed that is in the hand of Christ. With that doctrine and laws ought to be measured, and examined by that; for then peace is upon the Israel of God when they walk according to that rule. 5. Directions are here given to the prophet to receive this revelation from the Lord and transmit it pure and entire to the church, Eze 40:4. (1.) He must carefully observe every thing that was said and done in this vision. His attention is raised and engaged (Eze 40:4): "Behold with thy eyes all that is shown thee (do not only see it, but look intently upon it), and hear with thy ears all that is said to thee; diligently hearken to it, and be sure to set thy heart upon it; attend with a fixedness of thought and a close application of mind." What we see of the works of God, and what we hear of the word of God, will do us no good unless we set out hearts upon it, as those that reckon ourselves nearly concerned in it, and expect advantage to our souls by it. (2.) He must faithfully declare it to the house of Israel, that they may have the comfort of it. Therefore he receives, that he may give. Thus the Revelation of Jesus Christ was lodged in the hands of John, that he might signify it to the churches, Rev 1:1. And, because he is to declare it as a message from God, he must therefore be fully apprised of it himself and much affected with it. Note, Those who are to preach God's word to others ought to study it well themselves and set their hearts upon it. Now the reason given why he must both observe it himself and declare it to the house of Israel is because to this intent he is brought hither, and has it shown to him. Note, When the things of God are shown to us it concerns us to consider to what intent they are shown to us, and, when we are sitting under the ministry of the word, to consider to what intent we are brought thither, that we may answer the end of our coming, and may not receive the grace of God, in showing us such things, in vain.

Ezekiel 40:5

The measuring-reed which was in the hand of the surveyor-general was mentioned before, Eze 40:3. Here we are told (Eze 40:5) what was the exact length of it, which must be observed, because the house was measured by it. It was six cubits long, reckoning, not by the common cubit, but the cubit of the sanctuary, the sacred cubit, by which it was fit that this holy house should be measured, and that was a hand-breadth (that it, four inches) longer than the common cubit: the common cubit was eighteen inches, this twenty-two, see Eze 43:13. Yet some of the critics contend that this measuring-reed was but six common cubits in length, and one handbreadth added to the whole. The former seems more probable. Here is an account,

I. Of the outer wall of the house, which encompassed it round, which was three yards thick and three yards high, which denotes the separation between the church and the world on every side and the divine protection which the church is under. If a wall of this vast thickness will not secure it, God himself will be a wall of fire round about it; whoever attack it will do so at their peril.

II. Of the several gates with the chambers adjoining to them. Here is no mention of the outer court of all, which was called the court of the Gentiles, some think because in gospel-times there should be such a vast confluence of Gentiles to the church that their court should be left unmeasured, to signify that the worshippers in that court should be unnumbered, Rev 7:9, Rev 7:11, Rev 7:12.

1. He begins with the east gate, because that was the usual way of entering into the lower end of the temple, the holy of holies being at the west end, in opposition to the idolatrous heathen that worshipped towards the east. Now, in the account of this gate, observe, (1.) That he went up to it by stairs (Eze 40:6), for the gospel-church was exalted above that of the Old Testament, and when we go to worship God we must ascend; so is the call, Rev 4:1. Come up hither. Sursum corda-Up with your hearts. (2.) That the chambers adjoining to the gates were but little chambers, about ten feet square, Eze 40:7. These were for those to lodge in who attended the service of the house. And it becomes such as are made spiritual priests to God to content themselves with little chambers and not to seek great things to themselves; so that we may but have a place within the verge of God's court we have reason to be thankful though it be in a little chamber, a mean apartment, though we be but door-keepers there. (3.) The chambers, as they were each of them four-square, denoting their stability and due proportion and their exact agreement with the rule (for they were each of them one reed long and one reed broad), so they were all of one measure, that there might be an equality among the attendants on the service of the house. (4.) The chambers were very many; for in our Father's house there are many mansions (Joh 14:2), in his house above, and in that here on earth. In the secret of his tabernacle shall those be hid, and in a safe pavilion, whose desire is to dwell in the house of the Lord all the days of their life, Psa 27:4, Psa 27:5. Some make these chambers to represent the particular congregations of believers, which are parts of the great temple, the universal church, which are, and must be, framed by the scripture-line and rule, and which Jesus Christ takes the measure of, that is, takes cognizance of, for he walks in the midst of the seven golden candle-sticks. (5.) It is said (Eze 40:14), He made also the posts. He that now measured them was the same that made them; for Christ is the builder of his church and therefore is best able to give us the knowledge of it. And his reducing them to the rule and standard is called his making them, for no account is

made of them further than they agree with that. To the law and to the testimony. (6.) Here are posts of sixty cubits, which, some think, was literally fulfilled when Cyrus, in his edict for rebuilding the temple at Jerusalem, ordered that the height thereof should be sixty cubits, that is, thirty yards and more, Ezr 6:3. (7.) Here were windows to the little chambers, and windows to the posts and arches (that is, to the cloisters below), and windows round about (Eze 40:16), to signify the light from heaven with which the church is illuminated; divine revelation is let into it for instruction, direction, and comfort, to those that dwell in God's house, light to work by, light to walk by, light to see themselves and one another by. There were lights to the little chambers; even the least, and least considerable, parts and members of the church, shall have light afforded them. All thy children shall be taught of the Lord. But they are narrow windows, as those in the temple, Kg1 6:4. The discoveries made to the church on earth are but narrow and scanty compared with what shall be in the future state, when we shall no longer see through a glass darkly. (8.) Divers courts are here spoken of, an outermost of all, then an outer court, then an inner, and then the innermost of all, into which the priests only entered, which (some think) may put us in mind "of the diversities of gifts, and graces, and offices, in the several members of Christ's mystical body here, as also of the several degrees of glory in the courts and mansions of heaven, as there are stars in several spheres and stars of several magnitudes in the fixed firmament." English Annotations. Some draw nearer to God than others and have a more intimate acquaintance with divine things; but to a child of God a day in any of his courts is better than a thousand elsewhere. These courts had porches, or piazzas, round them, for the shelter of those that attended in them from wind and weather; for when we are in the way of our duty to God we may believe ourselves to be under his special protection, that he will graciously provide for us, nay, that he will himself be to us a covert from the storm and tempest, Isa 4:5, Isa 4:6. (9.) On the posts were palm-trees engraven (Eze 40:16), to signify that the righteous shall flourish like the palm-tree in the courts of God's house, Psa 92:12. The more they are depressed with the burden of affliction the more strongly do they grow, as they say of the palm-trees. It likewise intimates the saints' victory and triumph over their spiritual enemies; they have palms in their hands (Rev 7:9); but lest they should drop these, or have them snatched out of their hands, they are here engraven upon the posts of the temple as perpetual monuments of their honour. Thanks be to God, who always causes us to triumph. Nay, believers shall themselves be made pillars in the temple of our God, and shall go no more out, and shall have his name engraven on them, which will be their brightest ornament and honour, Rev 3:12. (10.) Notice is here taken of the pavement of the court, Eze 40:17, Eze 40:18. The word intimates that the pavement was made of porphyry-stone, which was of the colour of burning coals; for the brightest and most sparkling glories of this world should be put and kept under our feet when we draw near to God and are attending upon him. The stars are, as it were, the burning coals, or stones of a fiery colour, with which the pavement of God's celestial temple is laid; and, if the pavement of the court be so bright and glittering, how glorious must we conclude the mansions of that house to be!

2. The gates that looked towards the north (Eze 40:20) and towards the south (Eze 40:24), with their appurtenances, are much the same with that towards the east, after the measure of the first

gate, Eze 40:21. But the description is repeated very particularly. And thus largely was the structure of the tabernacle related in Exodus, and of the temple in the books of Kings and Chronicles, to signify the special notice God does take, and his ministers should take, of all that belong to his church. His delight is in them; his eye is upon them. He knows all that are his, all his living temples and all that belongs to them. Observe, (1.) This temple had not only a gate towards the east, to let into it the children of the east, that were famous for their wealth and wisdom, but it had a gate to the north, and another to the south, for the admission of the poorer and less civilized nations. The new Jerusalem has twelve gates, three towards each quarter of the world (Rev 21:13); for many shall come from all parts to sit down there, Mat 8:11. (2.) To those gates they went up by steps, seven steps (Eze 40:22-26), which, as some observe, may remind us of the necessity of advancing in grace and holiness, adding one grace to another, going from step to step, from strength to strength, still pressing forward towards perfection-upward, upward, towards heaven, the temple above.

Ezekiel 40:27

In these verses we have a delineation of the inner court. The survey of the outer court ended with the south side of it. This of the inner court begins with the south side (Eze 40:27), proceeds to the east (Eze 40:32), and so to the north (Eze 40:35); for here is no gate either of the outer or inner court towards the west. It should seem that in Solomon's temple there were gates westward, for we find porters towards the west, Ch1 9:24; Ch1 26:8. But Josephus says that in the second temple there was no gate on the west side. Observe, 1. These gates into the inner court were exactly uniform with those into the outer court, the dimensions the same, the chambers adjoining the same, the galleries or rows round the court the same, and the very engravings on the posts the same. The work of grace, and its workings, are the same, for substance, in grown Christians that they are in young beginners, only that the former have got so much nearer their perfection. The faith of all the saints is alike precious, though it be not alike strong. There is a great resemblance between one child of God and another; for all they are brethren and bear the same image. 2. The ascent into the outer court at each gate was by seven steps, but the ascent into the inner court at each gate was by eight steps. This is expressly taken notice of (Eze 40:31, Eze 40:34, Eze 40:37), to signify that the nearer we approach to God the more we should rise above this world and the things of it. The people, who worshipped in the outer court, must rise seven steps above other people, but the priests, who attended in the inner court, must rise eight steps above them, must exceed them at least one step more than they exceed other people.

Ezekiel 40:39

In these verses we have an account,

I. Of the tables that were in the porch of the gates of the inner court. We find no description of the altars of burnt-offerings in the midst of that court till Eze 43:13. But, because the one altar under the law was to be exchanged for a multitude of tables under the gospel, here is early notice taken of the tables, at our entrance into the inner court; for till we come to partake of the table of the Lord we are but professors at large; our admission to that is our entrance into the inner court. But in this gospel-temple we meet with no altar till after the glory of the Lord has taken possession of it, for Christ is our altar, that sanctifies every gift. Here were eight tables provided, whereon to slay the sacrifices, Eze 40:41. We read not of any tables for this purpose either in the tabernacle or in Solomon's temple. But here they are provided, to intimate the multitude of spiritual sacrifices that should be brought to God's house in gospel-times, and the multitude of hands that should be employed in offering up those sacrifices. Here were the shambles for the altar; here were the dressers on which they laid the flesh of the sacrifice, the knives with which they cut it up, and the hooks on which they hung it up, that it might be ready to be offered on the altar (Eze 40:43), and there also they washed the burnt-offerings (Eze 40:38), to intimate that before we draw near to God's altar we must have every thing in readiness, must wash our hands, our hearts, those spiritual sacrifices, and so compass God's altar.

II. The use that some of the chambers mentioned before were put to. 1. Some were for the singers, Eze 40:44. It should seem they were first provided for before any other that attended this temple-service, to intimate, not only that the singing of psalms should still continue a gospel-ordinance, but that the gospel should furnish all that embrace it with abundant matter for joy and praise, and give them occasion to break forth into singing, which is often foretold concerning gospel times, Psa 96:1; Psa 98:1. Christians should be singers. Blessed are those that dwell in God's house, they will still praising him. 2. Others of them were for the priests, both those that kept the charge of the house, to cleanse it, and to see that none came into it to pollute it, and to keep it in good repair (Eze 40:45), and those that kept the charge of the altar (Eze 40:46), that came near to the Lord to minister to him. God will find convenient lodging for all his servants. Those that do the work of his house shall enjoy the comforts of it.

III. Of the inner court, the court of the priests, which was fifty yards square, Eze 40:47. The altar that was before the house was placed in the midst of this court, over-against the three gates, and, standing in a direct line with the three gates of the outer court, when the gates were set open all the people in the outer court might through them be spectators of the service done at the altar. Christ is both our altar and our sacrifice, to whom we must look with an eye of faith in all our approaches to God, and he is salvation in the midst of the earth (Psa 74:12), to be looked unto from all quarters.

IV. Of the porch of the house. The temple is called the house, emphatically, as if no other house were worthy to be called so. Before this house there was a porch, to teach us not to rush hastily and inconsiderately into the presence of God, but gradually, that is, gravely, and with solemnity, passing first through the outer court, then the inner, then the porch, ere we enter into the house. Between this porch and the altar was a place where the priests used to pray, Joe 2:17. In the porch, besides the posts on which the doors were hung, there were pillars, probably for state and ornament, like Jachin and Boaz-He will establish; in him is strength, Eze 40:49. In the gospel church every thing is strong and firm, and every thing ought to be kept in its place and to be done decently and in order.

Ezekiel 40:1

We have here a very short and ready way taken for the dividing of the land among the twelve tribes, not so tedious and so far about as the way that was taken in Joshua's time; for in the distribution of spiritual and heavenly blessings there is not that danger of murmuring and quarrelling that there is in the participation of the temporal blessings. When God gave to the labourers every one his penny those that were uneasy at it were soon put to silence with, May I not do what I will with my own? And such is the equal distribution here among the tribes. In this distribution of the land we may observe, 1. That it differs very much from the division of it in Joshua's time, and agrees not with the order of their birth, nor with that of their blessing by Jacob or Moses. Simeon here is not divided in Jacob, nor is Zebulun a haven of ships, a plain intimation that it is not so much to be understood literally as spiritually, though the mystery of it is very much hidden from us. In gospel times old things have passed away; behold, all things have become new. The Israel of God is cast into a new method. 2. That the tribe of Dan, which was last provided for in the first division of Canaan (Jos 19:40), is first provided for here, Eze 48:1. Thus in the gospel the last shall be first, Mat 19:30. God, in the dispensation of his grace, does not follow the same method that he does in the disposals of his providence. But Dan had now his portion thereabouts where he had only one city before, northward, on the border of Damascus, and furthest of all from the sanctuary, because that tribe had revolted to idolatry. 3. That all the ten tribes that were carried away by the king of Assyria, as well as the two tribes that were long afterwards carried to Babylon, have their allotment in this visionary land, which some think had its accomplishment in the particular persons and families of those tribes who returned with Judah and Benjamin, of which we find many instances in Ezra and Nehemiah; and it is probable that there were returns of many more afterwards at several times, which are not recorded; and the Jews having Galilee, and other parts, that had been the possessions of the ten tribes, put into their hands, in common with them, they enjoyed them. Grotius says, If the ten tribes had repented and returned to God, as the chief fathers of Judah and Benjamin did, and the priests and Levites (Ezr 1:5), they would have fared as those two tribes did, but they forfeited the benefit of this glorious prophecy by sin. However, we believe it has its designed accomplishment in the establishment and enlargement of the gospel church, and the happy settlement of all those who are Israelites indeed in the sure and sweet enjoyment of the privileges of the new covenant, in which there is enough for all and enough for each. 4. That every tribe in this visionary distribution had its particular lot assigned it by a divine appointment; for it was never the intention of the gospel to pluck up the hedge of property and lay all in common; it was in a way of charity, not of legal right, that the first Christians had all things common (Act 2:44), and many precepts of the gospel suppose that every man should know his own. We must not only acknowledge, but acquiesce in, the hand of God appointing us our lot, and be well pleased with

cccl

it, believing it fittest for us. He shall choose our inheritance for us, Psa 47:4. 5. That the tribes lay contiguous. By the border of one tribe was the portion of another, all in a row, in exact order, so that, like stones in an arch, they fixed, and strengthened, and wedged in one another. Behold how good and how pleasant a thing it is for brethren thus to dwell together! It was a figure of the communion of churches and saints under the gospel-government; thus, though they are many, yet they are one, and should hold together in holy love and mutual assistance. 6. That the lot of Reuben, which before lay at a distance beyond Jordan, now lies next to Judah, and next but one to the sanctuary; for the scandal he lay under, for which he was told he should not excel, began by this time to wear off. What has turned to the reproach of any person or people ought not to be remembered for ever, but should at length be kindly forgotten. 7. That the sanctuary was in the midst of them. There were seven tribes to the north of it and the Levites, the prince's, and the city's portion, with that of five tribes more, to the south of it; so that it was, as it ought to be, in the heart of the kingdom, that it might diffuse its benign influences to the whole, and might be the centre of their unity. The tribes that lay most remote from each other would meet there in a mutual acquaintance and fellowship. Those of the same parish or congregation, though dispersed, and having no occasion otherwise to know each other, yet by meeting statedly to worship God together should have their hearts knit to each other in holy love. 8. That where the sanctuary was the priests were: For them, even for the priests, shall this holy oblation be, Eze 48:10. As, on the one hand, this denotes honour and comfort to ministers, that what is given for their support and maintenance is reckoned a holy oblation to the Lord, so it intimates their duty, which is that, since they are appointed and maintained for the service of the sanctuary, they ought to attend continually to this very thing, to reside on their cures. Those that live upon the altar must serve at the altar, not take the wages to themselves and devolve the work upon others; but how can they serve the altar, his altar they live upon, if they do not live near it? 9. Those priests had the priests' share of these lands that had approved themselves faithful to God in times of trial (Eze 48:11): It shall be for the sons of Zadok, who, it seems, had signalized themselves in some critical juncture, and went not astray when the children of Israel, and the other Levites, went astray. God will put honour upon those who keep their integrity in times of general apostasy, and he has special favours in reserve for them. Those are swimming upwards, and so they will find at last, that are swimming against the stream. 10. The land which was appropriated to the ministers of the sanctuary might by no means be alienated. It was in the nature of the first-fruits of the land, and was therefore holy to the Lord; and, though the priests and Levites had both the use of it and the inheritance of it to them and their heirs, yet they might not sell it nor exchange it, Eze 48:14. It is sacrilege to convert that to other uses which is dedicated to God. 11. The land allotted for the city and its suburbs is called a profane place (Eze 48:15), or common; not but that the city was a holy city above other cities, for the Lord was there, but, in comparison with the sanctuary, it was a profane place. Yet it is too often true in the worst sense that great cities, even those which, like this, have the sanctuary near them, are profane places, and it ought to be deeply lamented. It was the complaint of old, From Jerusalem has profaneness gone forth into all the land, Jer 23:15. 12. The city is made to be exactly square, and the suburbs extending themselves equally on all sides, as the Levites' cities did in the first division of the land (Eze 48:16, Eze 48:17), which, never being literally fulfilled in any city, intimates that it is to be understood spiritually of the beauty and stability of the gospel church, that city of the living God, which is formed according to the wisdom and counsel of God, and is made firm and immovable by his promise. 13. Whereas, before, the inhabitants of Jerusalem were principally of Judah and Benjamin, in whose tribe it lay, now the head city lies not in the particular lot of any of the tribes, but those that serve the city, and bear office in it, shall serve it out of all the tribes of Israel, Eze 48:19. The most eminent men must be picked out of all the tribes of Israel for the service of the city, because many eyes were upon it, and there was great resort to it from all parts of the nation and from other nations. Those that live in the city are said to serve the city, for, wherever we are, we must study to be serviceable to the place, some way or other, according as our capacity is. They must not come out of the tribes of Israel to the city to take their ease, and enjoy their pleasures, but to serve the city, to do all the good they can there, and in so doing they would have a good influence upon the country too. 14. Care was taken that those who applied themselves to public business in the city, as well as in the sanctuary, should have an honourable comfortable maintenance; lands are appointed, the increase whereof shall be food unto those that serve the city, Eze 48:18. Who goes a warfare at his own charges? Magistrates, that attend the service of the state, as well as ministers, that attend the service of the church, should have all due encouragement and support in so doing; and for this cause pay we tribute also. 15. The prince had a lot for himself, suited to the dignity of his high station (Eze 48:21); we took an account of it before, ch. 45. He was seated near the sanctuary, where the testimony of Israel was, and near the city, where the thrones of judgment were, that he might be a protection to both and might see the that duty of both was carefully and faithfully done; and herein he was a minister of God for good to the whole community. Christ is the church's prince, that defends it on every side, and creates a defense; nay, he is himself a defence upon all its glory and encompasses it with his favour. 16. As Judah had his lot next the sanctuary on one side, so Benjamin had, of all the tribes, his lot nearest to it on the other side, which honour was reserved for those who adhered to the house of David and the temple at Jerusalem when the other ten tribes went astray from both. It is enough if treachery and apostasy, upon repentance, he pardoned, but constancy and fidelity shall be rewarded and preferred.

Ezekiel Chapter 41

An account was given of the porch of the house in the close of the foregoing chapter; this brings us to the temple itself, the description of which here given creates much difficulty to the critical expositors and occasions differences among them. Those must consult them who are nice in their enquiries into the meaning of the particulars of this delineation; it shall suffice us to observe, I. The dimensions of the house, the posts of it (Eze 41:1), the door (Eze 41:2), the wall and the side-chambers (Eze 41:5, Eze 41:6), the foundations and wall of the chambers, their doors (Eze 41:8-11), and the house itself (Eze 41:13). II. The dimensions of the oracle, or most holy place (Eze 41:3, Eze 41:4). III. An account of another building over against the separate place (Eze 41:12-15). IV. The manner of the building of the house (Eze 41:7, Eze 41:16, Eze 41:17). V. The ornaments of the house (Eze 41:18-20). VI. The altar of incense and the table (Eze 41:22). VII. The doors between the temple and the oracle (Eze 41:23-26). There is so much difference both in the terms and in the rules of architecture between one age and another, one place and another, that it ought not to be any stumbling-block to us that there is so much in these descriptions dark and hard to be understood, about the meaning of which the learned are not agreed. To one not skilled in mathematics the mathematical description of a modern structure would be scarcely intelligible; and yet to a common carpenter or mason among the Jews at that time we may suppose that all this, in the literal sense of it, was easy enough.

Ezekiel 41:1

We are still attending a prophet that is under the guidance of an angel, and therefore attend with reverence, though we are often at a loss to know both what this is and what it is to us. Observe here, 1. After the prophet had observed the courts he was at length brought to the temple, Eze 41:1. If we diligently attend to the instructions given us in the plainer parts of religion, and profit by them, we shall be led further into an acquaintance with the mysteries of the kingdom of heaven. Those that are willing to dwell in God's courts shall at length be brought into his temple. Ezekiel was himself a priest, but by the iniquity and calamity of the times was cut short of his birthright privilege of ministering in the temple; but God makes up the loss to him by introducing him into this prophetical, evangelical, celestial temple, and employing him to transmit a description of it to the church, in which he was dignified above all the rest of his order. 2. When our Lord Jesus spoke of the destroying of this temple, which his hearers understood of this second temple of Jerusalem, he spoke of the temple of his body (Joh 2:19, Joh 2:21); and with good reason might he speak so ambiguously when Ezekiel's vision had a joint respect to them both together, including also his mystical body the church, which is called the house of God (Ti1 3:15), and all the members of that body, which are living temples, in which the Spirit dwells. 3. The very posts of this temple, the door-posts, were as far one from the other, and consequently the door was as wide, as the whole breadth of the tabernacle of Moses (Eze 41:1), namely, twelve cubits, Exo 26:16, Exo 26:22, Exo 26:25. In comparison with what had been under the law we may say, Wide is the gate which leads into the church, the ceremonial law, that wall of partition which had so much straitened the gate, being taken down. 4. The most holy place was an exact square, twenty cubits each way, Eze 41:4. For the new Jerusalem is exactly square (Rev 21:16), denoting its stability; for we look for a city that cannot be moved. 5. The upper stories were larger than the lower, Eze 41:7. The walls of the temple were six cubits thick at the bottom, five in the middle story, and four in the highest, which gave room to enlarge the chambers the higher they went; but care was taken that the timber might have fast hold (though God builds high, he builds firmly), yet so as not to weaken one part for the strengthening of another; they had hold, but not in the wall of the house. By this spreading gradually, the side-chambers that were on the height of the house (in the uppermost story of all) were six cubits, whereas the lowest were but four; they gained a cubit every story. The higher we build up ourselves in our most holy faith the more should our hearts, those living temples, be enlarged.

Ezekiel 41:12

Here is, 1. An account of a building that was before the separate place (that is, before the temple), at the end towards the west (Eze 41:12), which is here measured, and compared (Eze 41:13) with the measure of the house, and appears to be of equal dimensions with it. This stood in a court by itself, which is measured (Eze 41:15) and its galleries, or chambers belonging to it, its posts and windows, and the ornaments of them, Eze 41:15-17. But what use was to be made of this other building we are not told; perhaps, in this vision, it signified the setting up of a church among the Gentiles not inferior to the Jewish temple, but of quite another nature, and which should soon supersede it. 2. A description of the ornaments of the temple, and the other building. The walls on the inside from top to bottom were adorned with cherubim and palm-trees, placed alternately, as in Solomon's temple, Kg1 6:29. Each cherub is here said to have two faces, the face of a man towards the palm tree on one side and the face of a young lion towards the palm-tree on the other side, Eze 41:19. These seem to represent the angels, who have more than the wisdom of a man and the courage of a lion; and in both they have an eye to the palms of victory and triumph which are set before them, and which they are sure of in all their conflicts with the powers of darkness. And in the assemblies of the saints angels are in a special manner present, Col 11:10. 3. A description of the posts of the doors both of the temple and of the sanctuary; they were squared (Eze 41:21), not round like pillars; and the appearance of the one was as the appearance of the other. In the tabernacle, and in Solomon's temple, the door of the sanctuary, or most holy, was narrower than that of the temple, but here it was fully as broad; for in gospel-times the way into the holiest of all is made more manifest than it was under the Old Testament (Heb 9:8) and therefore the door is wider. These doors are described, Eze 41:23, Eze 41:24. The temple and the sanctuary had each of them its door, and they were two-leaved, folding doors. 4. We have here the description of the altar of incense, here said to be an altar of wood, Eze 41:22. No mention is made of its being over-laid with gold; but surely it was intended to be so, else it would not bear the fire with which the incense was to be burned, unless we will suppose that it served only to put the censers upon. Or else it intimates that the incense to be offered in the gospel-temple shall be purely spiritual, and the fire spiritual, which will not consume an altar of wood. Therefore this altar is called a table. This is the table that is before the Lord. Here, as before, we find the altar turned into a table; for, the great sacrifice being now offered, that which we have to do is to feast upon the sacrifice at the Lord's table. 5. Here is the adorning of the doors and windows with palm-trees, that they might be of a piece with the walls of the house, Eze 41:25, Eze 41:26. Thus the living temples are adorned, not with gold, or silver, or costly array, but with the hidden man of the heart, in that which is not corruptible.

Ezekiel Chapter 42

Ezekiel

This chapter continues and concludes the describing and measuring of this mystical temple, which it is very hard to understand the particular architecture of, and yet more hard to comprehend the mystical meaning of. Here is, I. A description of the chambers that were about the courts, their situation and structure (Eze 42:1-13), and the uses for which they were designed (Eze 42:13,Eze 42:14). II. A survey of the whole compass of ground which was taken up with the house, and the courts belonging to it (Eze 42:15-20).

Ezekiel 42:1

The prophet has taken a very exact view of the temple and the buildings belonging to it, and is now brought again into the outer court, to observe the chambers that were in that square.

I. Here is a description of these chambers, which (as that which went before) seems to us very perplexed and intricate, through our unacquaintedness with the Hebrew language and the rules of architecture at that time. We shall only observe, in general, 1. That about the temple, which was the place of public worship, there were private chambers, to teach us that our attendance upon God in solemn ordinances will not excuse us from the duties of the closet. We must not only worship in the courts of God's house, but must, both before and after our attendance there, enter into our chambers, enter into our closets, and read and meditate, and pray to our Father in secret; and a great deal of comfort the people of God have found in their communion with God in solitude. 2. That these chambers were many; there were three stories of them, and, though the higher stories were not so large as the lower, yet they served as well for retirement, Eze 42:5, Eze 42:6. There were many, that there might be conveniences for all such devout people as Anna the prophetess, who departed not from the temple night or day, Luk 2:37. In my Father's house are many mansions. In his house on earth there are so; multitudes by faith have taken lodgings in his sanctuary, and yet there is room. 3. That these chambers, though they were private, yet were near the temple, within view of it, within reach of it, to teach us to prefer public worship before private (the Lord loves the gates of Zion more than all the dwellings of Jacob, and so must we), and to refer our private worship to the public. Our religious performances in our chambers must be to prepare us for the exercises of devotion in public, and to further us in our improvement of them, as our opportunities are. 4. That before these chambers there were walks of five yards broad (Eze 42:4), in which those that had lodgings in these chambers might meet for conversation, might walk and talk together for their mutual edification, might communicate their knowledge and experiences. For we are not to spend all our time between the church and the chamber, though a great deal of time may be spent to very good purpose in both. But man is made for society, and Christians for the communion of saints; and the duties of that communion we must make conscience of, and the privileges and pleasures of that communion we must take the comfort of. It is promised to Joshua, who was high priest in the second temple, that God will give him places to walk in among those that stand by, Zac 3:7.

II. Here is the use of these chambers appointed, Eze 42:13, Eze 42:14. 1. They were for the priests that approach unto the Lord, that they may be always near their business and may not be non-residents. Therefore they are called holy chambers, because they were for use of those that ministered in holy things during their ministration. Those that have public work to do for God and the souls of men have need to be much in private, to fit themselves for it. Ministers should spend much time in their chambers, in reading, meditation, and prayer, that their profiting may appear; and they ought to be provided with conveniences for this purpose. 2. There the priests were to deposit the most holy things, those parts of the offerings which fell to their share; and there they were to eat them, they and their families, in a religious manner, for the place is holy; and thus they must make a difference between those feasts upon the sacrifice and other meals. 3. There (among other uses) they were to lay their vestments, which God had appointed them to wear when they ministered at the altar, their linen ephods, coats, girdles, and bonnets. We read of the providing of priests garments after their return out of captivity, Neh 7:70, Neh 7:72. When they had ended their service at the altar they must lay by those garments, to signify that the use of them should continue only during that dispensation; but they must put on other garments, such as other people wear, when they approached to those things which were for the people, that is, to do that part of their service which related to the people, to teach them the law and to answer their enquiries. Their holy garments must be laid up, that they may be kept clean and decent for the credit of their service.

Ezekiel 42:15

We have attended the measuring of this mystical temple and are now to see how far the holy ground on which we tread extends; and that also is here measured, and found to take in a great compass. Observe, 1. What the dimensions of it were. It extended each way 500 reeds (Eze 42:16-19), each reed above three yards and a half, so that it reached every way about an English measured mile, which, the ground lying square, was above four miles round. Thus large were the suburbs (as I may call them) of this mystical temple, signifying the great extent of the church in gospel-times, when all nations should be discipled and the kingdoms of the world made Christ's kingdoms. Room should be made in God's courts for the numerous forces of the Gentiles that shall flow into them, as was foretold, Isa 49:18; Isa 60:4. It is in part fulfilled already in the accession of the Gentiles to the church; and we trust it shall have a more full accomplishment when the fulness of the Gentiles shall come in and all Israel shall be saved. 2. Why the dimensions of it were made thus large. It was to make a separation, by putting a very large distance between the sanctuary and the profane place; and therefore there was a wall surrounding it, to keep off those that were unclean and to separate between the previous and the vile. Note, A difference is to be put between common and sacred things, between God's name and other names, between his day and other days, his book and other books, his institutions and other observances; and a distance is to be put between our worldly and religious actions, so as still to go about the worship of God with a solemn pause.

Ezekiel Chapter 43

The prophet, having given us a view of the mystical temple, the gospel-church, as he received it from the Lord, that it might appear not to be erected in vain, comes to describe, in this and the next chapter, the worship that should be performed in it, but under the type of the Old Testament services. In this chapter we have, I. Possession taken of this temple, by the glory of God filling it (Eze 43:1-6). II. A promise given of the continuance of God's presence with his people upon condition of their return to, and continuance in, the instituted way of worship, and their abandoning idols and idolatry (Eze 43:7-12). III. A description of the altar of burnt-offerings (Eze 43:13-17). IV. Directions given for the consecration of that altar (Eze 43:18-27). Ezekiel seems here to stand between God and Israel, as Moses the servant of the Lord did when the sanctuary was first set up.

Ezekiel 43:1

After Ezekiel has patiently surveyed the temple of God, the greatest glory of this earth, he is admitted to a higher form, and honoured with a sight of the glories of the upper world; it is said to him, Come up hither. He has seen the temple, and sees it to be very spacious and splendid; but, till the glory of God comes into it, it is but like the dead bodies he had seen in vision (ch. 37), that had no breath till the Spirit of life entered into them. Here therefore he sees the house filled with God's glory.

I. He has a vision of the glory of God (Eze 43:2), the glory of the God of Israel, that God who is in covenant with Israel, and whom they serve and worship. The idols of the heathen have no glory but what they owe to the goldsmith or the painter; but this is the glory of the God of Israel. This glory came from the way of the east, and therefore he was brought to the gate that leads towards the east, to expect the appearance and approach of it. Christ's star was seen in the east, and he is that other angel that ascends out of the east, Rev 7:2. For he is the morning star, he is the sun of righteousness. Two things he observed in this appearance of the glory of God:-1. The power of his word which he heard: His voice was like a noise of many waters, which is heard very far, and makes impressions; the noise of purling streams is grateful, of a roaring sea dreadful,Rev 1:15; Rev 14:2. Christ's gospel, in the glory of which he shines, was to be proclaimed aloud, the report of it to be heard far; to some it is a savour of life, to others of death, according as they are. 2. The brightness of his appearance which he saw: The earth shone with his glory; for God is light, and none can bear the lustre of his light, none has seen nor can see it. Note, That glory of God which shines in the church shines on the world. When God appeared for David the brightness that was before him dispersed the clouds, Psa 18:12. This appearance of the glory of God to Ezekiel he observed to be the same with the vision he saw when he first received his commission (Eze 1:4), according to that by the river Chebar (Eze 43:3); because God is the same, he was pleased to manifest himself in the same manner, for with him is no variableness. "It was the same" (says he) "as that which I saw when I came to destroy the city, that is, to foretel the city's destruction," which he did with such authority and efficacy, and the event did so certainly answer the prediction, that he might be said to destroy it. As a judge, in God's name, he passed a sentence upon it, which was soon executed. God appeared in the same manner when he sent him to speak words of terror and when he sent him to speak words of comfort; for in both God is and will be glorified. He kills and he makes alive; he wounds and he heals, Deu 32:39. To the same hand that destroyed we must look for deliverance. He has smitten, and he will bind up. Una eademque manus vulnus opemque tulit-The same hand inflicted the wound and healed it.

II. He has a vision of the entrance of this glory into the temple. When he saw this glory he fell upon his face (Eze 43:3), as not able to bear the lustre of God's glory, or rather as one willing to give him the glory of it by a humble and reverent adoration. But the Spirit took him up (Eze 43:5) when the glory of the Lord had come into the house (Eze 43:4), that he might see how the house was filled with it. He saw how the glory of the Lord in this same appearance departed from the temple, because it was profaned, to his great grief; now he shall see it return to the temple to his great satisfaction. See Eze 10:18, Eze 10:19; Eze 11:23. Note, Though God may forsake his people for a small moment, he will return with everlasting loving-kindness. God's glory filled the house as it had filled the tabernacle which Moses set up and the temple of Solomon, Exo 40:34; Kg1 8:10. Now we do not find that ever the Shechinah did in that manner take possession of the second temple, and therefore this was to have its accomplishment in that glory of the divine grace which shines so brightly in the gospel church, and fills it. Here is no mention of a cloud filling the house as formerly, for we now with open face behold the glory of the Lord, in the face of Christ, and not as of old through the cloud of types.

III. He receives instructions more immediately from the glory of the Lord, as Moses did when God had taken possession of the tabernacle (Lev 1:1): I heard him speaking to me out of the house, Eze 43:6. God's glory shining in the church, we must thence expect to receive divine oracles. The man stood by me; we could not bear to hear the voice of God any more than to see the face of God if Jesus Christ did not stand by us as Mediator. Or, if this was a created angel, it is observable that when God began to speak to Ezekiel he stood by and gave way, having no more to say. Nay, he stood by the prophet, as a learner with him; for to the principalities and powers, to the angels themselves, who desire to look into these things, is known by the church the manifold wisdom of God, Eph 3:10. The man stood by him to conduct him thither where he might receive further discoveries, Eze 44:1.

Ezekiel 43:7

God does here, in effect, renew his covenant with his people Israel, upon his retaking possession of the house, and Ezekiel negotiates the matter, as Moses formerly. This would be of great use to the captives at their return both for direction and encouragement; but it looks further, to those that are blessed with the privileges of the gospel-temple, that they may understand how they are before him on their good behaviour.

I. God, by the prophet, puts them in mind of their former provocations, for which they had long lain under the tokens of his displeasure. This conviction is spoken to them to make way for the comforts designed them. Though God gives and upbraids not, it becomes us, when he forgives, to upbraid ourselves with our unworthy conduct towards him. Let them now remember therefore, 1. That they had formerly defiled God's holy name, had profaned and abused all those sacred things by which he had made himself known among them, Eze 43:7. They and their kings had brought contempt on the religion they professed, and their relation to God, by their spiritual whoredom, their idolatry, and by worshipping images, which they called their kings (for so Moloch signifies) or lords (for so Baal signifies), but which were really the carcases of kings, not only lifeless and useless, but loathsome and abominable as dead carcases, in their high places, set up in honour of them. They had defiled God's name by their abominations. And what were they? It was in setting their threshold by my thresholds, and their post by my posts, that is, adding their own inventions to God's institutions, and urging all to a compliance with them, as if they had been of equal authority and efficacy, teaching for doctrines the commandments of men (Isa 29:13); or, rather, setting up altars to their idols even in the courts of the temple, than which a more impudent affront could not be put upon the divine Majesty. Thus they set up a separation wall between him and them, which stopped the current of his favours to them and spoiled the acceptableness of their services to him. See what an indignity sinners do to God, setting up their walls in opposition to his, and thrusting him out from what is his right; and see what injury they do to themselves, for the nearer any come to God with their sins the further they set him at a distance from them. Some give this sense of it: Though their houses joined close to God's house, their posts and thresholds to hi, so that they were in a manner his next neighbours, there was but a wall between me and them (so it is in the margin), so that it might have been expected they would acquaint themselves with him and be in care to please him, yet they were not so much as neighbourly. Note, It often proves too true, The nearer the church the further from God. They were, by profession, in covenant with God, and yet they had defiled the place of his throne and of the soles of his feet, his temple, where he did both reside and reign. Jerusalem is called the city of the great king (Psa 48:2) and his footstool, Psa 99:5; Psa 132:7. Note, When God's ordinances are profaned his holy name is polluted. 2. That for this God had had a controversy with them in their late troubles. They could not condemn him, for he had but brought upon them the desert of their sins: Wherefore I have consumed them in my anger. Note, Those that pollute God's holy name fall under his just displeasure.

II. He calls upon them to repent and reform, and, in order to that, to be ashamed of their iniquities (Eze 43:9): "Now let them put away their whoredom; now that they have smarted so severely for it, and now that God is returning in mercy to them and setting up his sanctuary again in the midst of them, now let them cast away their idols and have no more to do with them, that they may not again forfeit the privileges which they have been taught to know the worth of by the want of them. Let them put away their idols, those loathsome carcases of their kings, far from me, from being a provocation to me." This was seasonable counsel now that the prophet had the model or pattern of the temple to set before them; for, 1. If they see that pattern, they will surely be ashamed of their sins (Eze 43:10): when they see what mercy God has in store for them, notwithstanding their utter unworthiness of it, they will be ashamed to think of their disingenuous conduct towards him. Note, The goodness of God to us should lead us to repentance, especially to a penitential shame. Let them measure the pattern themselves, and see how much it exceeds the former pattern, and guess by that what great things God has in store for them; and surely it will put them out of countenance to think what the desert of their sins was. And then, 2. If they be ashamed of their sins, they shall surely see more of the pattern, Eze 43:11. If they be ashamed of all that they have done, upon a general view of the goodness of God, let them have a more distinct particular account of the temple. Note, Those that improve what they see and know of the goodness of God shall see and know more of it. And then, and not till then, we are qualified for God's favours, when we are truly humbled for our own follies. "Show them the form of the house; let them see what a stately structure it will be; and withal show them the ordinances and laws of it." Note, With the foresights of our comforts it is fit that we should get the knowledge of our duty; with the privileges of God's house we must acquaint ourselves with the rules of it. Show them these ordinances, that they may keep them and do them. Note, Therefore we are made to know our duty, that we may do it, and be blessed in our deed.

III. He promises that they shall be such as they should be, and then he will be to them such as they would have him to be, Eze 43:7. 1. The house of Israel shall no more defile my holy name. This is pure gospel. The precept of the law says, You must not defile my name: the grace of the gospel says, You shall not. Thus what is required in the covenant is promised in the covenant, Jer 32:40. 2. Then I will dwell in the midst of them for ever; and the same again Eze 43:9. God secures to us his good-will be confirming in us his good work. If we do not defile his name, we may be sure that he will not depart from us.

IV. The general law of God's house is laid down (Eze 43:12), That, whereas formerly only the chancel, or sanctuary, was most holy, now the whole mountain of the house shall be so; the whole limit thereof, including all the courts and all the chambers, shall be as the most holy place, signifying that in gospel-times, 1. The whole church shall have the privilege of the holy of holies, that of a near access to God. All believers have now, under the gospel, boldness to enter into the holiest (Heb 10:19), with this advantage, that whereas the high priest entered in the virtue of the blood of bulls and goats, we enter in the virtue of the blood of Jesus, and, wherever we are, we have through him access to the Father. 2. The whole church shall be under a mighty obligation to press towards the perfection of holiness, as he who has called us is holy. All must now be most holy. Holiness becomes God's house for ever, and in gospel-times more than ever. Behold this is the law of the house; let none expect the protection of it that will not submit to this law.

Ezekiel 43:13

This relates to the altar in this mystical temple, and that is mystical too; for Christ is our altar. The Jews, after their return out of captivity, had an altar long before they had a temple, Ezr 3:3. But this was an altar in the temple. Now here we have,

I. The measures of the altar, Eze 43:13. It was six yards square at the top and seven yards square at the bottom; it was four yards and a half high; it had a lower bench or shelf, here called a settle, a yard from the ground, on which some of the priests stood to minister, and another two yards above that, on which others of them stood, and these were each of them half a yard broad, and had ledges on either side, that they might stand firmly upon them. The sacrifices were killed at the table spoken of before, Eze 40:39. What was to be burnt on the altar was given up to those on the lower bench, and handed by them to those on the higher, and they laid it on the altar. Thus in the service of God we must be assistant to one another.

II. The ordinances of the altar. Directions are here given, 1. Concerning the dedication of the altar at first. Seven days were to be spent in the dedication of it, and every day sacrifices were to be offered upon it, and particularly a goat for a sin-offering (Eze 43:25), besides a young bullock for a sin-offering on the first day (Eze 43:19), which teaches us in all our religious services to have an eye to Christ the great sin-offering. Neither our persons nor our performances can be acceptable to God unless sin be taken away, and that cannot be taken away but by the blood of Christ, which both sanctifies the altar (for Christ entered by his own blood, Heb 9:12) and the gift upon the altar. There were also to be a bullock and a ram offered for a burnt-offering (Eze 43:24), which was intended purely for the glory of God, to teach us to have an eye to that in all our services; we present ourselves as living sacrifices, and our devotions as spiritual sacrifices, that we and they may be to him for a name, and for a praise, and for a glory. The dedication of the altar is here called the cleansing and purging of it, Eze 43:20,Eze 43:26. Christ, our altar, though he had no pollution to be cleansed from, yet sanctified himself (Joh 17:19); and when we consecrate the altars of our hearts to God, to have the fire of holy love always burning upon them, we must see that they be purified and cleansed from the love of the world and the lusts of the flesh. It is observable that there are several differences between the rites of dedication here and those which were appointed Ex. 29, to intimate that the ceremonial institutions were mutable things, and the changes in them were earnests of their period in Christ. Only here, according to the general law, that all the sacrifices must be seasoned with salt (Lev 2:13), particular orders are given (Eze 43:24) that the priests shall cast salt upon the sacrifices. Grace is the salt with which all our religious performances must be seasoned, Col 4:6. An everlasting covenant is called a covenant of salt, because it is incorruptible. The glory reserved for us is incorruptible and undefiled; and the grace wrought in us is the hidden man of the heart in that which is not corruptible. 2. Concerning the constant use that should be made of it, when it was dedicated:

ccclxiii

Henceforward the priests shall make their burnt-offerings and peace-offerings upon this altar (Eze 43:27), for therefore it was sanctified, that it might sanctify the gift that was offered upon it. Observe further, (1.) Who were to serve at the altar: The priests of the seed of Zadok, Eze 43:19. That family was substituted in the room of Abiathar by Solomon, and God confirms it. His name signifies righteous, for they are the righteous seed that are priests to God, through Christ the Lord our righteousness. (2.) How they should prepare for this service (Eze 43:26): They shall consecrate themselves, shall fill their hand with the offerings, in token of the giving up of themselves with their offerings to God and to his service. Note, Before we minister to the Lord in holy things we must consecrate ourselves by getting our hands and hearts filled with those things. (3.) How they should speed in it (Eze 43:27): I will accept you. And if God now accept our works, if our services be pleasing to him, it is enough, we need no more. Those that give themselves to God shall be accepted of God, their persons first and then their performances, through the Mediator.

Ezekiel Chapter 44

Ezekiel

In this chapter we have, I. The appropriating of the east gate of the temple to the prince (Eze 44:1-3). II. A reproof sent to the house of Israel for their former profanations of God's sanctuary, with a charge to them to be more strict for the future (Eze 44:4-9). III. The degrading of those Levites that had formerly been guilty of idolatry and the establishing of the priesthood in the family of Zadok, which had kept their integrity (Eze 44:10-16). IV. Divers laws and ordinances concerning the priests (Eze 44:17-31).

Ezekiel 44:1

The prophet is here brought to review what he had before once surveyed; for, though we have often looked into the things of God, they will yet bear to be looked over again, such a copiousness there is in them. The lessons we have learned we should still repeat to ourselves. Every time we review the sacred fabric of holy things, which we have in the scriptures, we shall still find something new which we did not before take notice of. The prophet is brought a third time to the east gate, and finds it shut, which intimates that the rest of the gates were open at all times to the worshippers. But such an account is given of this gate's being shut as puts honour, 1. Upon the God of Israel. It is for the honour of him that the gate of the inner court, at which his glory entered when he took possession of the house, was ever after kept shut, and no man was allowed to enter in by it, Eze 44:2. The difference ever after made between this and the other gates, that this was shut when the others were open, was intended both to perpetuate the remembrance of the solemn entrance of the glory of the Lord into the house (which it would remain a traditional evidence of the truth of) and also to possess the minds of people with a reverence for the Divine Majesty, and with very awful thoughts of his transcendent glory, which was designed in God's charge to Moses at the bush, Put off thy shoe from off thy foot. God will have a way by himself. 2. Upon the prince of Israel, Eze 44:3. It is an honour to him that though he may not enter in by this gate, for no man may, yet, (1.) He shall sit in this gate to eat his share of the peace-offerings, that sacred food, before the Lord. (2.) He shall enter by the way of the porch of that gate, by some little door or wicket, either in the gate or adjoining to it, which is called the say of the porch. This as to signify that God puts some of his glory upon magistrates, upon the princes of his people, for he has said, You are gods. Some by the prince here understand the high priests, or the sagan or second priest; and that he only was allowed to enter by this gate, for he was God's representative. Christ is the high priest of our profession, who entered himself into the holy place, and opened the kingdom of heaven to all believers.

Ezekiel 44:4

This is much to the same purport with what we had in the beginning of ch. 43. As the prophet must look again upon what he had before seen, so he must be told again what he had before heard. Here, as before, he sees the house filled with the glory of the Lord, which strikes an awe upon him, so that he falls prostrate at the sight, the humblest posture of adoration and the expression of a holy awe: I fell upon my face, Eze 44:4. Note, The more we see of the glory of God the more low we shall lie in our own eyes. Now here,

I. God charges the prophet to take a very particular notice of all he saw, and all that was said to him (Eze 44:5): "Behold with thy eyes what is shown thee, particularly the entering in of the house and every going forth of it, all the inlets and all the outlets of the sanctuary;" those he must take special notice of. Note, In acquainting ourselves with divine things we must not aim so much at an abstract speculation of the things themselves as at finding the plain appointed way of converse and communion with those things, that we may go in and out and find pasture. 2. Hear with thy ears all that I say unto thee about the laws and ordinances of the house, which he was to instruct the people in. Note, Those who are appointed to be teachers have need to be very diligent careful learners, that they may neither forget any of the things they are entrusted with nor mistake concerning them.

II. He sends him upon an errand to the people, to the rebellious, even to the house of Israel, Eze 44:6. It is sad to think that the house of Israel should deserve this character from him who perfectly knew them, that a people in covenant with God should be rebellious against him. Who are his subjects if the house of Israel be rebels? But it is an instance of God's rich mercy that, though they had been rebellious, yet, being the house of Israel, he does not cast them off, but sends an ambassador to them, to invite and encourage them to return to their allegiance, which he would not have done if he had been pleased to kill them. The whole race of mankind has fallen under the character here given of the house of Israel; but our Lord Jesus, when he ascended on high, received gifts for men, yea, even for the rebellious also, that, as here, the Lord God might dwell among them, Psa 68:18.

1. He must tell them of their faults, must show them their rebellions, must show the house of Jacob their sins. Note, Those that are sent to comfort God's people must first convince them, and so prepare them for comfort. Let it suffice you of all your abominations, Eze 44:6. Note, It is time for those that have continued long in sin to reckon it long enough, and too long, and to begin to think of taking up in time, and leaving off their evil courses. "Let the time past of your lives suffice, for by this time, surely, you have surfeited upon your abominations and have become sick of them," Pe1 4:3. That which is here charged upon them is, (1.) That they had admitted those to the privileges of the sanctuary that were not entitled to them; whereas God had said, The stranger that comes nigh shall be put to death, they had not only connived at the intrusion of strangers into the sanctuary, but had themselves introduced them (Eze 44:7): You brought in strangers uncircumcised in flesh, and therefore under a legal incapacity to enter into the sanctuary, which was a breaking of the covenant of circumcision, throwing down the hedge

of their peculiarity, and laying themselves in common with the rest of the world. Yet if these strangers had been devout and good, though they were not circumcised, the crime would not have been so great; but they were uncircumcised in heart too, unhumbled, unreformed, and strangers indeed to God and all goodness. When they came to offer sacrifice they brought these with them to feast with them upon the sacrifice, because they were fond of their company, and this was one of their abominations, wherewith they polluted God's sanctuary; it was giving that which was holy unto dogs, Mat 7:6. Note, The admission of those who are openly wicked and profane to special ordinances is a polluting of God's sanctuary and a great provocation to him. (2.) That they had employed those in the service of the sanctuary who were not fit for it. Though none but priests and Levites were to minister in the sanctuary, yet we may suppose that all who were priests and Levites did not immediately attend there, but chosen men of them, who were best qualified, who were most wise, serious, and conscientious, and most likely to keep the charge of the holy things carefully; but, in making this choice, they had not regard to merit and qualification for the work: "You have set keepers of my charge in my sanctuary for yourselves, such as you had some favour or affection for, such as you either had got, or hoped to get, money by, or such as would comply with your humours and would dispense with the laws of the sanctuary to please you; thus you have not kept the charge of my holy things." Note, Those who have the choice of the keepers of the holy things, if, to serve some secular selfish purpose, they choose such as are unfit and unfaithful, will justly have it laid at their door, that they have betrayed the holy things by lodging them in bad hands.

2. He must tell them their duty (Eze 44:9): "No stranger shall enter into my sanctuary till he has first submitted to the laws of it." But, lest any should think that this excluded the penitent believing Gentiles from the church, the stranger here is described to be one that is uncircumcised in heart, not in sincerity consenting to the covenant, nor putting away the filth of the flesh; whereas the believing Gentiles were circumcised with the circumcision made without hands, Col 2:11. This circumcision of the heart, in the spirit, not in the letter, was what the unbelieving Jews were strangers to and unconcerned about, while yet they were zealous to keep out of the sanctuary uncircumcised Gentiles, witness their rage against Paul when they did but suspect him to have brought Greeks into the temple, Act 21:28.

Ezekiel 44:10

The Master of the house, being about to set up house again, takes account of his servants the priests, and sees who are fit to be turned out of their places and who to be kept in, and takes a course with them accordingly.

I. Those who have been treacherous are degraded and put lower those Levites-or priests who were carried down the stream of the apostasy of Israel formerly, who went astray from God after their idols (Eze 44:10), who had complied with the idolatrous kings of Israel or Judah, who ministered to them before their idols (Eze 44:12), bowed with them in the house of Rimmon, or set up altars for them, as Urijah did for Ahaz, and so caused the house of Israel to fall into iniquity, led them to sin and hardened them in sin; for, if the priests go astray, many will follow their pernicious ways. Perhaps in Babylon some of the Jewish priests had complied with the idolaters of the place, to the great scandal of their religion. Now these priests who had thus prevaricated were justly put under the mark of God's displeasure; or, if they were dead (as it is probable that they were, if the crime were committed before the captivity), the iniquity was visited upon their children. Or perhaps it was the whole family of Abiathar that had been guilty of this trespass, which was now called to account for it. And, 1. They are sentenced to be deprived, in part, of their office, and from the dignity of priests are put down into the condition or ordinary Levites. God has lifted up his hand against them, has said it, and sworn it, that they shall bear their iniquity (Eze 44:12); assuredly they shall suffer for it, shall suffer disgrace for it; they shall bear their shame (Eze 44:13), for though they have (we charitably hope) repented of it, yet they shall not come near to do the office of a priest, that is, those parts of the office that were peculiar to them, they shall not come near to any of the holy things within the sanctuary, Eze 44:13. Note, those who have robbed God of his honour will justly be deprived of their honour. And it is really a great punishment to be forbidden to come near to God; and justly might those who have once gone away from him be rejected as unworthy ever to come near to him and put at an everlasting distance. 2. Yet there is a mixture of mercy in this sentence. God deals not in severity, as he might have done, with those who had dealt treacherously with him, but mitigates the sentence, Eze 44:11, Eze 44:14. They are deprived but in part, ab officio-of their office, and, it should seem, not at all beneficio-of their emoluments. They shall help to slay the sacrifice, which the Levites were permitted to do, and which in this temple was done, not at the altar, but at the tables, Eze 40:29. They shall be porters at the gates of the house, and they shall be keepers of the charge of the house, for all the service thereof. Note, Those who may not be fit to be employed in one kind of service may yet be fit to be employed in another; and even those who have offended may yet be made use of, and not quite thrown aside, much less thrown away.

II. Those who have been faithful are honoured and established, Eze 44:15, Eze 44:16. These are remarkably distinguished from the other: "But the sons of Zadok, who kept their integrity in a time of general apostasy, who went not astray when others did, they shall come near to me, shall come near to my table." Note, God will put marks of honour upon those who give proofs of their fidelity and constancy to him in shaking trying times, and will employ those in his service who have kept close to his service when others deserted it and drew back. And it ought to be reckoned a true and great reward of stability in duty to be established in it. If we keep close to God, God will keep us close to him.

Ezekiel 44:17

God's priests must be regulars, not seculars; and therefore here are rules laid down for them to govern themselves by and due encouragement given them to live up to those rules. Directions are here given,

I. Concerning their clothes; they must wear linen garments when they went in to minister or do any service in the inner court, or in the sanctuary, and nothing that was woollen, because it would cause sweat, Eze 44:17, Eze 44:18. They must dress themselves cool, that they might go the more readily about their work; and they had the more need to do so because they were to attend the altars, which had constant fires upon them. And they must dress themselves clean and sweet, and avoid every thing that was sweaty and filthy, to signify the purity of mind with which the service of God is to be attended to. Sweat came in with sin and was part of the curse. In the sweat of thy face shalt thou eat bread. Clothes came in with sin, coats of skins did; and therefore the priests must use as little and as light clothing as possible, and not such as caused sweat. When they had finished their service they must change their clothes again, and lay up their linen garments in the chambers appointed for that purpose, Eze 44:19, as before,Eze 42:14. They must not go among the people with their holy garments on, lest they should imagine themselves sanctified by the touch of them; or, They shall sanctify the people, that is (as it is explained, Eze 42:14), they shall approach to those things which are for the people, in their ordinary garments.

II. Concerning their hair; in that they must avoid extremes on both hands (Eze 44:20): They must not shave their heads, in imitation of the Gentile priests, and as the priests of the Romish church do; nor, on the other hand, must they suffer their locks to grow long, as the beaux, or that they might be thought Nazarites, when really they were not; but they must be grave and modest, must poll their heads and keep their hair short. If a man, especially a minister, wear long hair, it is not becoming (Col 11:14); it is effeminate.

III. Concerning their diet; they must be sure to drink no wine when they went in to minister, lest they should rink to excess, should drink and forget the law, Eze 44:21. It is not for kings to drink wine, more than will do them good, much less for priests. See Lev 10:9; Pro 31:4, Pro 31:5.

IV. Concerning their marriages, Eze 44:22. Here they must consult the credit of their office, and not marry one that had been divorced, that was at least under the suspicion of immodesty, nor a widow, unless she were a priest's widow, that had been accustomed to the usages of the priests' families. Others may do that which ministers may not do, but must deny themselves in, in honour of their character. Their wives as well as themselves must be of good report.

V. Concerning their preaching and church-government. 1. It was part of their business to teach the people; and herein they must approve themselves both skilful and faithful (Eze 44:23): They shall teach my people the difference between the holy and the profane, between good and evil, lawful and unlawful, that they may neither scruple what is lawful nor venture upon what is unlawful, that they may not pollute what is holy nor pollute themselves with what is profane. Ministers must take pains to cause people to discern between the clean and the unclean, that they may not confound the distinctions between right and wrong, nor mistake concerning them, so as to put darkness for light and light for darkness, but may have a good judgment of discretion concerning their own actions. 2. It was part of their business to judge upon appeals made to them (Deu 17:8, Deu 17:9); and in controversy they shall stand in judgment, Eze 44:24. They shall have the honesty to stand up for what is right, and, when they have passed a right judgment, shall have the courage to stand to it and stand by it. They must judge, not according to their own fancies, or inclinations, or secular interests, but according to my judgments; that must be their rule and standard. Note, Ministers must decide controversies according to the word of God, to the law and to the testimony. Sit liber judex-Let the judge be unbiased. Their business is to keep courts in God's name, to preside in the congregations of his people. And herein they must go to the statute-book: They shall keep my statutes in all my assemblies. God calls the assemblies of his people his assemblies, because they are held in his name, to his glory. Ministers are the masters of those assemblies, are to preside in them, and in all their acts must keep close to God's laws. Another part of their work, as church governors, is to hallow God's sabbaths, to do the public work of that day with a becoming care and reverence, as the work of a holy day should be done, and to see that God's people also sanctify that day and do nothing to pollute it.

VI. Concerning their mourning for dead relations; the rule here agrees with the law of Moses, Lev 21:1, Lev 21:11. A priest shall not come near any dead body (for they must be purified from dead works) except of his next relations, Eze 44:25. Decent expressions of a pious sorrow for dear relations, when they are removed by death, are not disagreeable to the character of a minister. Yet by this approach to the dead body of a relation they contracted a ceremonial pollution, from which they must be cleansed by a sin-offering before they went in again to minister, Eze 44:26, Eze 44:27. Note, Though sorrow for the dead is very allowable and commendable, yet there is danger of sinning in it, either by excess or dissimulation; and those tears have too often need to be wept over again.

VII. Concerning their maintenance; they must live upon the altar at which they served, and live comfortably (Eze 44:28): "You shall give them no possession in Israel, no lands or tenements, lest they should be entangled with the affairs of this life;" for God has said, I am their inheritance, and they need no other in reserve; I am their possession, and they need no other in hand. Some land was allowed them (Eze 48:10), but their principal subsistence was by their office. What God appropriated to himself they were the receivers of, for their own proper use and behoof; they lived upon the holy things, and so God himself was the portion both of their inheritance and of their cup. Note, Those who have God for their inheritance and their possession may be content with a little, and ought not to covet a great deal of the possessions and inheritances of this earth. If we have God, we have all; and therefore may well reckon that we have enough. Observe,

1. What the priests were to have from the people, for their maintenance and encouragement. (1.) They must have the flesh of many of the offerings, the sin-offering and trespass-offering, which would supply them and their families with flesh-meat, and the meat-offerings, which would supply them with bread. What we offer to God will redound to our own advantage. (2.)

They must have every dedicated devoted thing in Israel, which was in many cases to be turned into money and given to the priest. This is explained, Eze 44:20. Every oblation or free-will offering (which in times of reformation and devotion would be many and considerable) of all, of every sort of your oblations, shall be the priest's. We have the law concerning them Lev. 27. (3.) They were to have the first of the dough when it was going to the oven, as well as the first of their fruits when they were going to the barn. God, who is the first, must have the first; and, if it belong to him, his priests must have it. We may then comfortably enjoy what we have, when a share of it has been first set apart for works of piety and charity. To this the apostle's rule bears some analogy, to begin the week with laying by for pious uses, Col 16:2. The priests being so well provided for, it would be inexcusable in them if they (contrary to the law which every Israelite is bound by) should eat that which is torn or which died of itself, Eze 44:31. Those that were in want of necessary food might perhaps expect to be dispensed with in such a case. Poverty has its temptations, but the priests were so well provided for that they could have no pretence for it.

2. What the people might expect from the priest for their recompence. Those that are kind to a prophet, to a priest, shall have a prophet's, a priest's reward: That he may cause the blessing to rest in thy house (Eze 44:30), that God may cause it by commanding it, that the priest may cause it by praying for it; and it was part of the priest's work to bless the people in the name of the Lord, not only their congregations, but their families. Note, It is all in all to the comfort of any house to have the blessing of God upon it and to have the blessing to rest in it, to dwell where we dwell and to attend the entail of it upon those that shall come after us. And the way to have the blessing of God abide upon our estates is to honour God with them, and to give him and his ministers, him and his poor, their share out of them. God blesses, he surely blesses, the habitation of those who are thus just, Pro 3:33. And ministers, by instructing and praying for the families that are kind to them, should do their part towards causing the blessing to rest there. Peace be to this house.

Ezekiel Chapter 45

In this chapter is further represented to the prophet, in vision, I. The division of the holy land, so much for the temple, and the priests that attended the service of it (Eze 45:1-4), so much for the Levites (Eze 45:5), so much for the city (Eze 45:6), so much for the prince, and the residue to the people (Eze 45:7, Eze 45:8). II. The ordinances of justice that were given both to prince and people (Eze 45:9-12). III. The oblations they were to offer, and the prince's part in those oblations (Eze 45:13-17). Particularly in the beginning of the year (Eze 45:18-20) and in the passover, and the feast of tabernacles (Eze 45:21-25). And all this seems to point at the new church-state that should be set up under the gospel, which, both for extent and for purity, should far exceed that of the Old Testament.

Ezekiel 45:1

Directions are here given for the dividing of the land after their return to it; and, God having warranted them to do it, would be an act of faith, and not of folly, thus to divide it before they had it. And it would be welcome news to the captives to hear that they should not only return to their own land, but that, whereas they were now but few in number, they should increase and multiply, so as to replenish it. But this never had its accomplishment in the Jewish state after the return out of captivity, but was to be fulfilled in the model of the Christian church, which was perfectly new (as this division of the land was quite different from that in Joshua's time) and much enlarged by the accession of the Gentiles to it; and it will be perfected in the heavenly kingdom, of which the land of Canaan had always been a type. Now, 1. Here is the portion of land assigned to the sanctuary, in the midst of which the temple was to be built, with all its courts and purlieus; the rest round about it was for the priests. This is called (Eze 45:1) an oblation to the Lord; for what is given in works of piety, for the maintenance and support of the worship of God and the advancement of religion, God accepts as given to him, if it be done with a single eye. It is a holy portion of the land, which is to be set out first, as the first-fruits that sanctify the lump. The appropriating of lands for the support of religion and the ministry is an act of piety that bids as fair for perpetuity, and the benefit of posterity, as any. This holy portion of the land was to be measured, and the borders of it fixed, that the sanctuary itself might not have more than its share and in time engross the whole land. So far the lands of the church shall extend and no further; as in our own kingdom donations to the church were of old limited by the statute of mortmain. The lands here allotted to the sanctuary were 25,000 reeds (so our translation makes it, though some make them only cubits) in length, and 10,000 in breadth-about eighty miles one way and thirty miles another way (say some); twenty-five miles one way and ten miles the other way, so others. The priests and Levites that were to come near to minister were to have their dwellings in this portion of the land that was round about the sanctuary, that they might be near their work; whereas by the distribution of land in Joshua's time the cities of the priests and Levites were dispersed all the nation over. This intimates that gospel ministers should reside upon their charge; where their service lies there must they live. 2. Next to the lands of the sanctuary the city-lands are assigned, in which the holy city was to be built, and with the issues and profits of which the citizens were to be maintained (Eze 45:6): It shall be for the whole house of Israel, not appropriated, as before, to one tribe or two, but some of all the tribes shall dwell in the city, as we find they did, Neh 11:1, Neh 11:2. The portion for the city was fully as long, but only half as broad, as that for the sanctuary; for the city was enriched by trade and therefore had the less need of lands. 3. The next allotment after the church-lands and the city-lands is of the crown-lands,Eze 45:7, Eze 45:8. Here is no admeasurement of these, but they are said to lie on the one side and on the other side of the church-lands and city-lands, to intimate that the prince with his wealth and power was to be a protection to both. Some make the prince's share equal to the church's and city's share both together; others make it to be a thirteenth part of the rest of the land, the other twelve parts being for the twelve tribes. The prince that attends continually to the administration of public affairs must have wherewithal to support his dignity, and have abundance, that he may not be in temptation to oppress the people, which yet with many does not prevent that; but the grace of God shall prevent it, for it is promised here, My princes shall no more oppress my people; for God will make the officers peace and the exactors righteousness. Notwithstanding this, we find that after the return of the Jews to their own land the princes were complained of for their exactions. But Nehemiah was one that did not do as the former governors, and yet kept a handsome court, Neh 5:15,Neh 5:18. But so much is said of the prince in this mystical holy state, to intimate that in the gospel-church magistrates should be as nursing fathers to it and Christian princes its patrons and protectors; and the holy religion they profess, as far as they are subject to the power of it, will restrain them from oppressing God's people, because they are more his people than theirs. 4. The rest of the lands were to be distributed to the people according to their tribes, who had reason to think themselves well settled, when they had both the testimony of Israel and the throne of judgment so near them.

Ezekiel 45:9

We have here some general rules of justice laid down both for prince and people, the rules of distributive and commutative justice; for godliness without honesty is but a form of godliness, will neither please God nor avail to the benefit of any people. Be it therefore enacted, by the authority of the church's King and God, 1. That princes do not oppress their subjects, but duly and faithfully administer justice among them (Eze 45:9): "Let it suffice you, O princes of Israel! that you have been oppressive to the people and have enriched yourselves by spoil and violence, that you have so long fleeced the flock instead of feeding them, and henceforward do so no more." Note, Even princes and great men that have long done amiss must at length think it time, high time, to reform and amend; for no prescription will justify a wrong. Instead of saying that they have been long accustomed to oppress, and therefore may persist in it, for the custom will bear them out, they should say that they have been long accustomed to it and therefore, as here, Let the time pass suffice, and let them now remove violence and spoil; let them drop wrongful demands, cancel wrongful usages, and turn out those from employments under them that do violence. Let them take away their exactions, ease their subjects of those taxes which they find lie heavily upon them, and let them execute judgment and justice according to the law, as the duty of their place requires. Note, All princes, but especially the princes of Israel, are concerned to do justice; for of their people God says, They are my people, and they in a special manner rule for God. 2. That one neighbour do not cheat another in commerce (Eze 45:10): You shall have just balances, in which to weigh both money and goods, a just ephah for dry measure of corn and flour, a just bath for the measure of liquids, wine, and oil; and the ephah and bath shall be one measure, the tenth part of a chomer, or cor, Eze 45:11. So that the ephah and bath contained (as the learned Dr. Cumberland has computed) seven wine gallons and four pints, and something more. An omer was but the tenth part of an ephah (Exo 16:36) and the one hundredth part of a chomer, or homer, and contained about six pints. The shekel is here settled (Eze 45:13); it is twenty jerahs, just half a Roman ounce, in our money 2s. 4 1/4d. and almost the eighth part of a farthing, as the aforesaid learned man exactly computes it. By the shekels the maneh, or pound, was reckoned, which, when it was set for a mere weight (says bishop Cumberland), without respect to coinage, contained just 100 shekels, as appears by comparingKg1 10:17, where it is said three manehs, or pounds, of gold, went to one shield, with the parallel place, Ch2 9:16, where it is said 300 shekels of gold went to one shield. But when the maneh is set for a sum of money or coin it contains but sixty shekels, as appears here, where twenty shekels, twenty-five shekels, and fifteen shekels, which in all make sixty, shall be the maneh. But it is thus reckoned because they had one piece of money that weighed twenty shekels, another twenty-five, another fifteen, all of which made up one pound, as a learned writer here observes. Note, It concerns God's Israel to be very honest and just in all their dealings, very punctual and exact in rendering to all their due, and very cautious to do wrong to none, because otherwise they spoil the acceptableness of their profession with God and the reputation of it before men.

Ezekiel 45:13

Having laid down the rules of the righteousness toward men, which is really a branch off true religion, he comes next to give some directions for their religion towards God, which is a branch of universal righteousness.

I. It is required that they offer an oblation to the Lord out of what they have (Eze 45:13): All the people of the land must give an oblation, Eze 45:16. As God's tenants, they must pay a quit-rent to their great landlord. They had offered an oblation out of their real estates (Eze 45:1), a holy portion of their land; now they are directed to offer an oblation out of their personal estates, their goods and chattels, as an acknowledgement of their receivings from him, their dependence on him, and their obligations to him. Note, Whatever our substance is we must honour God with it, by giving him his dues out of it. Not that God has need of or may be benefited by any thing that we can give him, Psa 50:9. No; it is but an oblation; we only offer it to him; the benefit of it returns back to ourselves, to his poor, who, as our neighbours, are ourselves, or to his ministers who serve continually for our good.

II. The proportion of this oblation is here determined, which was not done by the law of Moses. No mention is made of the title, but only of this oblation. And the quantum of this is thus settled:-1. Out of their corn they were to offer a sixtieth part; out of every homer of wheat and barley, which contained ten ephahs, they were to offer the sixth part of one ephah, which was a sixtieth part of the whole,Eze 45:13. 2. Out of their oil (and probably their wine too) they were to offer a hundredth part, for this oblation; out of every cor, or homer, which contained ten baths they were to offer the tenth part of one bath, Eze 45:14. This was given to the altar; for in eery meat-offering there was flour mingled with oil. 3. Out of their flocks they were to give one lamb out of 200; that was the smallest proportion of all, Eze 45:15. But it must be out of the fat pastures of Israel. They must not offer to God that which was taken up from the common, but the fattest and best they had, for burnt-offerings and peace-offerings: the former were offered for the giving of glory to God, the latter for the fetching in of mercy, grace, and peace, from God, and in our spiritual sacrifices these are our two great errands at the throne of grace; but, in order to the acceptance of both, these sacrifices were to make reconciliation for them. Christ is our sacrifice of atonement, by whom reconciliation is made, and to him we must have an eye in our sacrifices of acknowledgment.

III. This oblation must be given for the prince in Israel, Eze 45:16. Some read it to the prince, and understand it of Christ, who is indeed the prince in Israel, to whom we must offer our oblations, and into whose hands we must put them, to be presented to the Father. Or, They shall give it with the prince; every private person shall bring his oblation, to be offered with that of the prince; for it follows (Eze 45:17). It shall be the prince's part to provide all the offerings, to make reconciliation for the house of Israel. The people were to bring their oblations to him according to the foregoing rules, and he was to bring them to the sanctuary, and to make up what fell short out of his own. Note, It is the duty of rulers to take care of religion, and to see that the duties of it be regularly and carefully performed by those under their charge, and that nothing be wanting that is requisite thereto: the magistrate is the keeper of both tables; and it is a happy thing when those that are above others in power and dignity go before them in the service of God.

IV. Some particular solemnities are here appointed.

1. Here is one in the beginning of the year, which seems to be altogether new, and not instituted by the law of Moses; it is the annual solemnity of cleansing the sanctuary. (1.) On the first day of the first month (upon new-year's day) they were to offer a sacrifice for the cleansing of the sanctuary (Eze 45:18), that is, to make atonement for the iniquity of the holy things the year past, that they might bring none of the guilt of them into the services of the new year, and to implore grace for the preventing of that iniquity, and for the better performance of the service of

the sanctuary the ensuing year. And, in token of this, the blood of this sin-offering was to be put upon the posts of the gate of the inner court (Eze 45:19), to signify that by it atonement was intended to be made for the sins of all the servants that attended that house, priests, Levites, and people, even the sins that were found in all their services. Note, Even sanctuaries on earth need cleansing, frequent cleansing; that above needs none. Those what worship God together should often join in renewing their repentance for their manifold defects, and applying the blood of Christ for the pardon of them, and in renewing their covenants to be more careful for the future; and it is very seasonable to begin the year with this work, as Hezekiah did when it had been long neglected, Ch2 29:17. They were here appointed to cleanse the sanctuary upon the first day of the month, because on the fourteenth day of the month they were to eat the passover, an ordinance which, of all Old Testament institutions, had most in it of Christ and gospel grace, and therefore it was very fit that they should begin to prepare for it a fortnight before by cleansing the sanctuary. (2.) This sacrifice was to be repeated on the seventh day of the first month, Eze 45:20. And then it was intended to make atonement for every one that errs, and for him that is simple. Note, He that sins errs and is simple; he mistakes, he goes out of the way, and shows himself to be foolish and unwise. But here it is spoken of those sins which are committed through ignorance, mistake, or inadvertency, whether by any of the priests, or of the Levites, or of the people. Sacrifices were appointed to atone for such sins as men were surprised into, or did before they were aware, which they would not have done if they had known and remembered aright, which they were overtaken in, and for which, afterwards, they condemn themselves. But for presumptuous sins, committed with a high hand, there was no sacrifice appointed, Num 15:30. By these repeated sacrifices you shall reconcile the house, that is, God will be reconciled to it, and continue the tokens of his presence in it, and will let it alone this year also.

2. The passover was to be religiously observed at the time appointed, Eze 45:21. Christ is our passover, that is sacrificed for us. We celebrate the memorial of that sacrifice and feast upon it, triumphing in our deliverance out of the Egyptian slavery of sin and our preservation from the sword of the destroying angel, the sword of divine justice, in the Lord's supper, which is our passover-feast, as the whole Christian life is, and must be, the feast of unleavened bread. It is here appointed that the prince shall prepare a sin-offering, to be offered for himself and the people, a bullock on the first day (Eze 45:22) and a kid of the goats every other day (Eze 45:23), to teach us, in all our attendance upon God for communion with him, to have an eye to the great sin-offering, by which transgression was finished and an everlasting righteousness brought in. On every day of the feast there was to be a burnt-offering, purely for the honour of God, of no less than seven bullocks and seven rams, with their meat-offering, which were wholly consumed upon the altar, and yet no waste, Eze 45:23, Eze 45:24.

3. The feast of tabernacles; that is spoken of next (Eze 45:25), and there is no mention of the feast of pentecost, which came between that of the passover and that of tabernacles. Orders are here given (above what were given by the law of Moses) for the same sacrifices to be offered during the seven days of the passover. See the deficiency of the legal sacrifices for sin; they were

therefore often repeated, not only every year, but every feast, every day of the feast, because they could not make the comers thereunto perfect, Heb 10:1, Heb 10:3. See the necessity of our frequently repeating the same religious exercises. Though the sacrifice of atonement is offered once for all, yet the sacrifices of acknowledgement, that of a broken heart, that of a thankful heart, those spiritual sacrifices which are acceptable to God through Christ Jesus, must be every day offered. We should, as here, fall into a method of holy duties, and keep to it.

Ezekiel Chapter 46

In this chapter we have, I. Some further rules given both to the priests and to the people, relating to their worship (Eze 46:1-15). II. A law concerning the prince's disposal of his inheritance (Eze 46:16-18). III. A description of the places provided for the boiling of the sacrifices and the baking of the meat-offerings (Eze 46:19-24).

Ezekiel 46:1

Whether the rules for public worship here laid down were designed to be observed, even in those things wherein they differed from the law of Moses, and were so observed under the second temple, is not certain; we find not in the history of that latter part of the Jewish church that they governed themselves in their worship by these ordinances, as one would think they should have done, but only by law of Moses, looking upon this then in the next age after as mystical, and not literal. We may observe, in these verses,

I. That the place of worship was fixed, and rules were given concerning that, both to prince and people.

1. The east gate, which was kept shut at other times, was to be opened on the sabbath days, on the moons (Eze 46:1), and whenever the prince offered a voluntary offering, Eze 46:12. Of the keeping of this gate ordinarily shut we read before (Eze 44:2); whereas the other gates of the court were opened every day, this was opened only on high days and on special occasions, when it was opened for the prince, who was to go in by the way of the porch of that gate, Eze 46:2, Eze 46:8. Some think he went in with the priests and Levites into the inner court (for into that court this gate was the entrance), and they observe that magistrates and ministers should join forces, and go the same way, hand in hand, in promoting the service of God. But it should rather seem that he did not go through the gate (as the glory of the Lord had done), though it was open, but he went by the way of the porch of the gate, stood at the post of the gate, and worshipped at the threshold of the gate (Eze 46:2), where he had a full view of the priests' performances at the altar, and signified his concurrence in them, for himself and for the people of the land, that stood behind him at the door of that gate, Eze 46:3. Thus must every prince show himself to be of David's mind, who would very willingly be a door-keeper in the house of his God, and, as the word there is, lie at the threshold, Psa 84:10. Note, The greatest of men are less than the least of the ordinances of God. Even princes themselves, when they draw near to God, must worship with reverence and godly fear, owning that even they are unworthy to approach to him. But Christ is our prince, whom God causes to draw near and approach to him, Jer 30:21.

2. As to the north gate and south gate, by which they entered into the court of the people (not into the inner court), there was this rule given, that whoever came in at the north gate should go out at the south gate, and whoever came in at the south gate should go out at the north gate, Eze 46:9. Some think this was to prevent thrusting and jostling one another; for God is the God of order, and not of confusion. We may suppose that they came in at the gate that was next their own houses, but, when they went away, God would have them go out at that gate which would lead them the furthest way about, that they might have time for meditation; being thereby obliged to go a great way round the sanctuary, they might have an opportunity to consider the palaces of it, and, if they improved their time well in fetching this circuit, they would call it the nearest way home. Some observe that this may remind us, in the service of God, to be still pressing forward (Phi 3:13) and not to look back, and, in our attendance upon ordinances, not to go back as we came, but more holy, and heavenly, and spiritual.

3. It is appointed that the people shall worship at the door of the east gate, where the prince does, he at the head and they attending him, both on the sabbath and on the new moons (Eze 46:3), and that, when they come in and go out, the prince shall be in the midst of them, Eze 46:10. Note, Great men should, by their constant and reverent attendance on God in public worship, give a good example to their inferiors, both engaging them and encouraging them to do likewise. It is a very graceful becoming thing for persons of quality to go to church with their servants, and tenants, and poor neighbours about them, and to behave themselves there with an air of seriousness and devotion; and those who thus honour God with their honour he will delight to honour.

II. That the ordinances of worship were fixed. Though the prince is supposed himself to be a very hearty zealous friend to the sanctuary, yet it is not left to him, no, not in concert with the priests, to appoint what sacrifices shall be offered, but God himself appoints them; for it is his prerogative to institute the rites and ceremonies of religious worship. 1. Every morning, as duly as the morning came, they must offer a lamb for a burnt-offering, Eze 46:13. It is strange that no mention is made of the evening sacrifice; but Christ having come, and having offered himself now in the end of the world (Heb 9:26), we are to look upon him as the evening sacrifice, about the time of the offering up of which he died. 2. On the sabbath days, whereas by the law of Moses four lambs were to be offered (Num 28:9), it is here appointed that (at the prince's charge) there shall be six lambs offered, and a ram besides (Eze 46:4), to intimate how much we should abound in sabbath work, now in gospel-time, and what plenty of the spiritual sacrifices of prayer and praise we should offer up to God on that day; and, if with such sacrifice God is well-pleased, surely we have a great deal of reason to be so. 3. On the new moons, in the beginning of their months, there was over and above the usual sabbath-sacrifices the additional offering of a young bullock, Eze 46:6. Those who do much for God and their souls, stately and constantly, must yet, upon some occasions, do still more. 4. All the sacrifices were to be without blemish; so Christ, the great sacrifice, was (Pe1 1:19), and so Christians, who are to present themselves to God as living sacrifices, should aim and endeavour to be-blameless, and harmless, and without rebuke.

5. All the sacrifices were to have their meat-offerings annexed to them, for so the law of Moses had appointed, to show what a good table God keeps in his house and that we ought to honour him with the fruit of our ground as well as with the fruit of our cattle, because in both he has blessed us, Duet.Eze 28:4. In the beginning, Cain offered the one and Abel the other. Some observe that the meat-offerings here are much larger in proportion than they were by the law of Moses. Then the proportion was three tenth-deals to a bullock, and two to a ram (so many tenth parts of an ephah) and half a hin of oil at the most (Num 15:6-9); but here, for every bullock and every ram, a whole ephah and a whole hin of oil (p. 7), which intimates that under the gospel, the great atoning sacrifice having been offered, these unbloody sacrifices shall be more abounded in; or, in general, it intimates that as now, under the gospel, God abounds in the gifts of his grace to us, more than under the law, so we should abound in the returns of praise and duty to him. But it is observable that in the meat-offering for the lambs the prince is allowed to offer as he shall be able to give (Eze 46:5, Eze 46:7, Eze 46:11), as his hand shall attain unto. Note, Princess themselves must spend as they can afford; and even in that which is laid out in works of piety God expects and requires but that we should do according to our ability, every man as God has prepared him, Col 16:2. God has not made us to serve with an offering (Isa 43:23), but considers our frame and state. Yet this will not countenance those who pretend a disability that is not real, or those who by their extravagances in other things disable themselves to do the good they should. And we find those praised who, in an extraordinary case of charity, went not only to their power, but beyond their power.

Ezekiel 46:16

We have here a law for the limiting of the power of the prince in the disposing of the crown-lands. 1. If he have a son that is a favourite, or has merited well, he may, if he please, as a token of his favour and in recompence for his services, settle some parts of his lands upon him and his heirs for ever (Eze 46:16), provided it do not go out of the family. There may be a cause for parents, when their children have grown up, to be more kind to one than to another, as Jacob gave to Joseph one portion above his brethren, Gen 48:22. 2. Yet, if he have a servant that is a favourite, he may not in like manner settle lands upon him, Eze 46:17. The servant might have the rents, issues, and profits, for such a term, but the inheritance, the jus proprietarium-the right of proprietorship, shall remain in the prince and his heirs. It was fit that a difference should be put between a child and a servant, like that Joh 8:35. The servant abides not in the house for ever, as the son does. 3. What estates he gives his children must be of his own (Eze 46:18): He shall not take of the people's inheritance, under pretence of having many children to provide for; he shall not find ways to make them forfeit their estates, or to force them to sell them and so thrust his subjects out of their possession; but let him and his sons be content with their own. It is far from being a prince's honour to increase the wealth of his family and crown by encroaching upon the rights and properties of his subjects; nor will he himself be a gainer by it at last, for he will be but a poor prince when the people are scattered every man from his possession, when they quit their native country, being forced out of it by oppression, choosing rather to live among strangers that are free people, and where what they have they can call their own, be it ever so little. It is the interest of princes to rule in the hearts of their subjects, and then all they have is, in the best manner, at their service. It is better for themselves to gain their affections by protecting their rights than to gain their estates by invading them.

Ezekiel 46:19

We have here a further discovery of buildings about the temple, which we did not observe before, and those were places to boil the flesh of the offerings in,Eze 46:20. He that kept such a plentiful table at his altar needed large kitchens; and a wise builder will provide conveniences of that kind. Observe, 1. Where those boiling-places were situated. There were some at the entry into the inner court (Eze 46:19) and others under the rows, in the four corners of the outer court, Eze 46:21-23. These were the places where, it is likely, there was most room to spare for this purpose; and this purpose was found for the spare room, that none might be lost. It is a pity that holy ground should be waste ground. 2. What use they were put to. In those places they were to boil the trespass-offering and the sin-offering, those parts of them which were allotted to the priests and which were more sacred than the flesh of the peace-offerings, of which the offerer also had a share. There also they were to bake the meat-offering, their share of it, which they had from the altar for their own tables, Eze 46:20. Care was taken that they should not bear them out into the outer court, to sanctify the people. Let them not pretend to sanctify the people with this holy flesh, and so impose upon them; or let not the people imagine that by touching those sacred things they were sanctified, and made any the better or more acceptable to God. It should seem (from Hag 2:12) that there were those who had such a conceit; and therefore the priests must not carry any of the holy flesh away with them, lest they should encourage that conceit. Ministers must take heed of doing any thing to bolster up ignorant people in their superstitious vanities.

Ezekiel Chapter 47

In this chapter we have, I. The vision of the holy waters, their rise, extent, depth, and healing virtue, the plenty of fish in them, and an account of the trees growing on the banks of them (Eze 47:1-12). II. An appointment of the borders of the land of Canaan, which was to be divided by lot to the tribes of Israel and the strangers that sojourned among them (Eze 47:13-23).

Ezekiel 47:1

This part of Ezekiel's vision must so necessarily have a mystical and spiritual meaning that thence we conclude the other parts of his vision have a mystical and spiritual meaning also; for it cannot be applied to the waters brought by pipes into the temple for the washing of the sacrifices, the keeping of the temple clean, and the carrying off of those waters, for that would be to turn this pleasant river into a sink or common sewer. That prophecy, Zac 14:8, may explain it, of living waters that shall go out from Jerusalem, half of them towards the former sea and half of them towards the hinder sea. And there is plainly a reference to this in St. John's vision of a pure river of water of life, Rev 22:1. That seems to represent the glory and joy which are grace perfected. This seems to represent the grace and joy which are glory begun. Most interpreters agree that these waters signify the gospel of Christ, which went forth from Jerusalem, and spread itself into the countries about, and the gifts and powers of the Holy Ghost which accompanied it, and by virtue of which it spread far and produced strange and blessed effects. Ezekiel had walked round the house again and again, and yet did not till now take notice of those waters; for God makes known his mind and will to his people, not all at once, but by degrees. Now observe,

I. The rise of these waters. He is not put to trace the streams to the fountain, but has the fountain-head first discovered to him (Eze 47:1): Waters issued out from the threshold of the house eastward, and from under the right side of the house, that is, the south side of the alter. And again (Eze 47:2), There ran out waters on the right side, signifying that from Zion should go forth the law and the word of the Lord from Jerusalem, Isa 2:3. There it was that the Spirit was poured out upon the apostles, and endued them with the gift of tongues, that they might carry these waters to all nations. In the temple first they were to stand and preach the words of this life, Act 5:20. They must preach the gospel to all nations, but must begin at Jerusalem, Luk 24:47. But that is not all: Christ is the temple; he is the door; from him those living waters flow, out of his pierced side. It is the water that he gives us that is the well of water which springs up,Joh 4:14. And it is by believing in him that we receive from him rivers of living water; and this spoke he of the Spirit, Joh 7:38, Joh 7:39. The original of these waters was not above-ground, but they sprang up from under the threshold; for the fountain of a believer's life is a mystery; it is hid with

Christ in God, Col 3:3. Some observe that they came forth on the right side of the house to intimate that gospel-blessings are right-hand blessings. It is also an encouragement to those who attend at Wisdom's gates, at the posts of her doors, who are willing to lie at the threshold of God's house, as David was, that they lie at the fountainhead of comfort and grace; the very entrance into God's word gives light and life, Psa 119:130. David speaks it to the praise of Zion, All my springs are in thee, Psa 87:7. They came from the side of the altar, for it is in and by Jesus Christ, the great altar (who sanctifies our gifts to God), that God has blessed us with spiritual blessings in holy heavenly places. From God as the fountain, in him as the channel, flows the river which makes glad the city of our God, the holy place of the tabernacles of the Most High, Psa 46:4. But observe how much the blessedness and joy of glorified saints in heaven exceed those of the best and happiest saints on earth; here the streams of our comfort arise from under the threshold; there they proceed from the throne the throne of God and of the Lamb, Rev 22:1.

II. The progress and increase of these waters: They went forth eastward (Eze 47:3), towards the east country (Eze 47:8), for so they were directed. The prophet and his guide followed the stream as it ran down from the holy mountains, and when they had followed it about a thousand cubits they went over across it, to try the depth of it, and it was to the ankles, Eze 47:3. Then they walked along on the bank of the river on the other side, a thousand cubits more, and then, to try the depth of it, they waded through it the second time, and it was up to their knees, Eze 47:4. They walked along by it a thousand cubits more, and then forded it the third time, and then it was up to their middle-the waters were to the loins. They then walked a thousand cubits further, and attempted to repass it the fourth time, but found it impracticable: The waters had risen, by the addition either of brooks that fell into it above ground or by springs under ground, so that they were waters to swim in, a river that could not be passed over, Eze 47:5. Note, 1. The waters of the sanctuary are running waters, as those of a river, not standing waters, as those of a pond. The gospel, when it was first preached, was still spreading further. Grace in the soul is still pressing forward; it is an active principle, plus ultra-onward still, till it comes to perfection. 2. They are increasing waters. This river, as it runs constantly, so the further it goes the fuller it grows. The gospel-church was very small in its beginnings, like a little purling brook; but by degrees it came to be to the ankles, to the knees: many were added to it daily, and the grain of mustard seed grew up to be a great tree. The gifts of the Spirit increase by being exercised, and grace, where it is true, is growing, like the light of the morning, which shines more and more to the perfect day. 3. It is good for us to follow these waters, and go along with them. Observe the progress of the gospel in the world; observe the process of the work of grace in the heart; attend the motions of the blessed Spirit, and walk after them, under a divine guidance, as Ezekiel here did. 4. It is good to be often searching into the things of God, and trying the depth of them, not only to look on the surface of those waters, but to go to the bottom of them as far as we can, to be often digging, often diving, into the mysteries of the kingdom of heaven, as those who covet to be intimately acquainted with those things. 5. If we search into the things of God, we shall find some things very plain and easy to be understood, as the waters that were but to the ankles, others more difficult, and which require a deeper search, as the water to the knees or the loins, and some quite beyond our reach, which we cannot penetrate into, or account for, but, despairing to find the bottom, must, as St. Paul, sit down at the brink, and adore the depth, Rom 11:33. It has been often said that in the scripture, like these waters of the sanctuary, there are some places so shallow that a lamb may wade through them, and others so deep that an elephant may swim in them. And it is our wisdom, as the prophet here, to begin with that which is most easy, and get our hearts washed with those things before we proceed to that which is dark and hard to be understood; it is good to take our work before us.

III. The extent of this river: It issues towards the east country, but thence it either divide itself into several streams or fetches a compass, so that it goes down into the desert, and so goes into the sea, either into the dead sea, which lay south-east, or the sea of Tiberias, which lay north-east, or the great sea, which lay west, Eze 47:8. This was accomplished when the gospel was preached with success throughout all the regions of Judea and Samaria (Act 8:1), and afterwards the nations about, nay, and those that lay most emote, even in the isles of the sea, were enlightened and leavened by it. The sound of it went forth to the end of the world; and the enemies of it could no more prevail to stop the progress of it than that of a mighty river.

IV. The healing virtue of this river. The waters of the sanctuary, wherever they come and have a free course, will be found a wonderful restorative. Being brought forth into the sea, the sulphureous lake of Sodom, that standing monument of divine vengeance, even those waters shall be healed (Eze 47:8), shall become sweet, and pleasant, and healthful. This intimates the wonderful and blessed change that the gospel would make, wheresoever it came in its power, a a great change, in respect both of character and condition, as the turning of the dead sea into a fountain of gardens. When children of wrath became children of love, and those that were dead in trespasses an sins were made alive, then this was fulfilled. The gospel was as that salt which Elisha cast into the spring of the waters of Jericho, with which he healed them, Kg2 2:20,Kg2 2:21. Christ, coming into the world to be its physician, sent his gospel as the great medicine, the panpharmacon; there is in it a remedy for every malady. Nay, wherever these rivers come, they make things to live (Eze 47:9), both plants and animals; they are the water of life, Rev 22:1, Rev 22:17. Christ came, that we might have life and for that end he sends his gospel. Every thing shall live whither the river comes. The grace of God makes dead sinners alive and living saints lively; everything is made fruitful and flourishing by it. But its effect is according as it is received, and as the mind is prepared and disposed to receive it; for (Eze 47:11) with respect to the marshes and miry places thereof, that are settled in the mire of their own sinfulness, and will not be healed, or settled in the moisture of their own righteousness, and think they need no healing, their doom is, They shall not be healed; the same gospel which to others is a savour of life unto life shall to them be a savour of death unto death; they shall be given to salt, to perpetual barrenness, Deu 29:23. Those that will not be watered with the grace of God, and made fruitful, shall be abandoned to their own hearts' lusts, and left for ever unfruitful. He that is filthy, let him be filthy still. Never fruit grow on thee more for ever. They shall be given to salt, that is, to be monuments of divine justice, as Lot's wife that was turned into a pillar of salt, to season others.

V. The great plenty of fish that should be in this river. Everything living moving thing shall be found here, shall live here (Eze 47:9), shall come on and prosper, shall be the best of the kind, and shall increase greatly; so that there shall be a very great multitude of fish, according to their kinds, as the fish of the great sea, exceedingly many. There shall be as great plenty of the river fish, and as vast shoals of them, as there is of salt-water fish, Eze 47:10. There shall be no great numbers of Christians in the church, and those multiplying like fishes in the rising generations and the dew of their youth. In the creation the waters brought forth the fish abundantly (Gen 1:20, Gen 1:21), and they still live in and by the waters that produced them; so believers are begotten by the word of truth (Jam 1:18), and born by it (Pe1 1:23), that river of God; by it they live, from it they have their maintenance and subsistence; in the waters of the sanctuary they are as in their element, out of them they are as fish upon dry ground; so David was when he thirsted and panted for God, for the living God. Where the fish are known to be in abundance, thither will the fishers flock, and there they will cast their nets; and therefore, to intimate the replenishing of these waters and their being made every way useful, it is here foretold that the fishers shall stand upon the banks of this river, from En-gedi, which lies on the border of the dead sea, to En-eglaim, another city, which joins to that sea, and all along shall spread their nets. The dead sea, which before was shunned as noisome and noxious, shall be frequented. Gospel-grace makes those persons and places which were unprofitable and good for nothing to become serviceable to God and man.

VI. The trees that were on the banks of this river-many trees on the one side and on the other (Eze 47:7), which made the prospect very pleasant and agreeable to the eye; the shelter of these trees also would be a convenience to the fishery. But that is not all (Eze 47:12); they are trees for meat, and the fruit of them shall not be consumed, for it shall produce fresh fruit every month. The leaf shall be for medicine, and it shall not fade. This part of the vision is copied out into St. John's vision very exactly (Rev 22:2), where, on either side of the river, is said to grow the tree of life, which yielded her fruit every month, and the leaves were for the healing of the nations. Christians are supposed to be these trees, ministers especially, trees of righteousness, the planting of the Lord (Isa 61:3), set by the rivers of water, the waters of the sanctuary (Psa 1:3), grafted into Christ the tree of life, and by virtue of their union with him made trees of life too, rooted in him, Col 2:7. There is a great variety of these trees, through the diversity of gifts with which they are endued by that one Spirit who works all in all. They grow on the bank of the river, or they keep close to holy ordinances, and through them derive from Christ sap and virtue. They are fruit-trees, designed, as the fig tree and the olive, with their fruits to honour God and man, Jdg 9:9. The fruit thereof shall be for meat, for the lips of the righteous feed many. The fruits of their righteousness are one way or other beneficial. The very leaves of these trees are for medicine, for bruises and sores, margin. Good Christians with their good discourses, which are as their leaves, as well as with their charitable actions, which are as their fruits, do good to those about them;

they strengthen the weak, and bind up the broken-hearted. Their cheerfulness does good like a medicine, not only to themselves, but to others also. They shall be enabled by the grace of God to persevere in their goodness and usefulness; their leaf shall not fade, or lose its medicinal virtue, having not only life in their root, but sap in all their branches; their profession shall not wither (Psa 1:3), neither shall the fruit thereof be consumed; that is, they shall not lose the principle of their fruitfulness, but shall still bring forth fruit in old age, to show that the Lord is upright (Psa 92:14, Psa 92:15), or the reward of their fruitfulness shall abide for ever; they bring forth fruit that shall abound to their account in the great day, fruit to life eternal; that is indeed fruit which shall not be consumed. They bring new fruit according to their months, some in one month and others in another: so that still there shall be one or other found to serve the glory of God for the purpose he designs. Or each one of them shall bring forth fruit monthly, which denotes an abundant disposition to fruit-bearing (they shall never be weary of well-doing), and a very happy climate, such that there shall be a perpetual spring and summer. And the reason of this extraordinary fruitfulness is because their waters issued out of the sanctuary; it is not to be ascribed to any thing in themselves, but to the continual supplies of divine grace, with which they are watered every moment (Isa 27:3); for, whoever planted them, it was that which gave the increase.

Ezekiel 47:13

We are now to pass from the affairs of the sanctuary to those of the state, from the city to the country. 1. The Land of Canaan is here secured to them for an inheritance (Eze 47:14): I lifted up my hand to give it unto your fathers, that is, promised it upon oath to them and their posterity. Though the possession had been a great while discontinued, yet God had not forgotten his oath which he swore to their fathers. Though God's providences may for a time seem to contradict his promises, yet the promise will certainly take place at last, for God will be ever mindful of his covenant. I lifted up my hand to give it, and therefore it shall without fail fall to you for an inheritance. Thus the heavenly Canaan is sure to all the seed, because it is what God, who cannot lie, has promised. 2. It is here circumscribed, and the bounds and limits of it are fixed, which they must not pass over to encroach upon their neighbours and which their neighbours shall not break through to encroach upon them. We had such a draught of the borders of Canaan when Joshua was to put the people in possession of it, Num 34:1, etc. That begins with the salt sea in the south, goes round and ends there. This begins with Hamath about Damascus in the north, and so goes round and ends there, Eze 47:20. Note, It is God that appoints the bounds of our habitation; and his Israel shall always have cause to say that the lines have fallen to them in pleasant places. The lake of Sodom is here called the east sea, for it, being healed by the waters of the sanctuary, it is no more to be called a salt sea, as it was in Numbers. 3. It is here ordered to be divided among the tribes of Israel, reckoning Joseph for two tribes, to make up the number of twelve, when Levi was taken out to attend the sanctuary, and had his lot adjoining to that (Eze 47:13, Eze 47:21): You shall inherit it, one as well as another, Eze 47:14. The tribes shall have an equal share, one as much as another. As the tribes returned out of Babylon, this seems unequal, because some tribes were much more numerous than the other, and indeed the most were of Judah and Benjamin and very few of the other ten tribes; but as the twelve tribes stand, in type and vision, for the gospel-church, the Israel of God, it was very equal, because we find in another vision an equal number of each of the twelve tribes sealed for the living God, just 12,000 of each, Rev 7:5, etc. And to those sealed ones these allotments did belong. It intimates likewise that all the subjects of Christ's kingdom have obtained like precious faith. Male and female, Jew and Gentile, bond and free, are all alike welcome to Christ and made partakers of him. 4. The strangers who sojourn among them, who shall beget children and be built up into families, and so help to people their country, shall have inheritance among the tribes, as if they had been native Israelites (Eze 47:22, Eze 47:23), which was by no means allowed in Joshua's division of the land. This is an act for a general naturalization, which would teach the Jews who was their neighbour, not those only of their own nation and religion, but those, whoever they were, that they had an opportunity of showing kindness to, because from them they would be willing to receive kindness. It would likewise invite strangers to come and settle among them, and put themselves under the wings of the divine Majesty. But it certainly looks at gospel-times, when the partition-wall between Jew and Gentile was taken down, and both one in Christ, in whom there is no difference, Rom 10:12. This land was a type of the heavenly Canaan, that better country (Heb 11:16), in which believing Gentiles shall have a blessed lot, as well as believing Jews, Isa 56:3.

Ezekiel Chapter 48

In this chapter we have particular directions given for the distribution of the land, of which we had the metes and bounds assigned in the foregoing chapter. I. The portions of the twelve tribes, seven to the north of the sanctuary (Eze 48:1-7) and five to the south (Eze 48:23-29). II. The allotment of land for the sanctuary, and the priests (Eze 48:8-11), for the Levites (Eze 48:12-14), for the city (Eze 48:15-20), and for the prince (Eze 48:21, Eze 48:22). Much of this we had before, ch. 45. III. A plan of the city, its gates, and the new name given to it (v. 30-35), which seals up, and concludes, the vision and prophecy of this book.

Ezekiel 48:31

We have here a further account of the city that should be built for the metropolis of this glorious land, and to be the receptacle of those who would come from all parts to worship in the sanctuary adjoining. It is nowhere called Jerusalem, nor is the land which we have had such a particular account of the dividing of any where called the land of Canaan; for the old names are forgotten, to intimate that the old things are done away, behold all things have become new. Now, concerning this city, observe here, 1. The measures of its out-lets, and the grounds belonging to it, for its several conveniences; each way its appurtenances extended 4500 measures 18,000 in all, Eze 48:35. But what these measures were is uncertain. It is never said, in all this chapter, whether so many reeds (as our translation determines by inserting that word, Eze 48:8, each reed containing six cubits and span, Eze 40:5, and why should the measurer appear with the measuring reed in his hand of that length if he did not measure with that, except where it is expressly said he measured by cubits?) or whether, as others think, it is so many cubits, because those are mentioned Eze 45:2 and Eze 47:3. Yet that makes me incline rather to think that where cubits are not mentioned must be intended so many lengths of the measuring reed. But those who understand it of so many cubits are not agreed whether it be meant of the common cubit, which was half a yard, or the geometrical cubit, which, for better expedition, is supposed to be mostly used in surveying lands, which, some say, contained six cubits, others about three cubits and a half, so making 1000 cubits the same with 1000 paces, that is, an English mile. But our being left at this uncertainty is an intimation that these things are to be understood spiritually, and that what is principally meant is that there is an exact and just proportion observed by Infinite Wisdom in modelling the gospel church, which though now we cannot discern we shall when we come to heaven. 2. The number of its gates. It had twelve gates in all, three on each side, which was very agreeable when it lay four square; and these twelve gates were inscribed to the twelve tribes. Because the city was to be served out of all the tribes of Israel (Eze 48:19) it was fit that each tribe should have its gate; and, Levi being here taken in, to keep to the number twelve Ephraim and Manasseh are made one in Joseph, Eze 48:32. On the north side were the gates of Reuben, Judah, and Levi (Eze 48:31), on the east the gates of Joseph, Benjamin, and Dan (Eze 48:32), on the south the gates of Simeon, Issachar, and Zebulun (Eze 48:33), and on the west the gates of Gad, Asher, and Naphtali, Eze 48:34. Conformable to this, in St. John's vision, the new Jerusalem (for so the holy city is called there, though not here) has twelve gates, three on a side, and on them are written the names of the twelve tribes of the children of Israel, Rev 21:12, Rev 21:13. Note, Into the church of Christ, both militant and triumphant, there is a free access by faith for all that come of every tribe, from every quarter. Christ has opened the kingdom of heaven for all believers. Whoever will may come and take of the water of life, of the tree of life, freely. 3. The name given to this city: From that day, when it shall be newly-erected according to this model, the name of it shall be, not, as before, Jerusalem-The vision of peace, but which is the original of that, and more than equivalent to it, Jehovah Shammah-The Lord is there, Eze 48:35. This intimated, (1.) That the captives, after their return, should have manifest tokens of God's presence with them and his residence among them, both in his ordinances and his providences. They shall have no occasion to ask, as their fathers did, Is the Lord among us, or is he not? for they shall see and say that he is with them of a truth. And then, though their troubles were many and threatening, they were like the bush which burned but was not consumed, because the Lord was there. But when God departed from their temple, when he said, Migremus hinc-Let us go hence, their house was soon left unto them desolate. Being no longer his, it was not much longer theirs. (2.) That the gospel-church should likewise have the presence of God in it, though not in the Shechinah, as of old, yet in a token of it no less sure, that of his Spirit. Where the gospel is faithfully preached, gospel ordinances are duly administered, and God is worshipped in the name of Jesus Christ only, it may truly be said, The Lord is there; for faithful is he that has said, and he will be as good as his word, Lo, I am with you always even unto the end of the world. The Lord is there in his church, to rule and govern it, to protect and defend it, and graciously to accept and own his sincere worshippers, and to be nigh unto them in all that they call upon him for. This should engage us to keep close to the communion of saints, for the Lord is there; and then whither shall we go to better ourselves? Nay, it is true of every good Christian; he dwells in God, and God in him; whatever soul has in it a living principle of grace, it may be truly said, The Lord is There. (3.) That the glory and happiness of heaven should consist chiefly in this, that the Lord is there. St. John's representation of that blessed state does indeed far exceed this in many respects. That is all gold, and pearls, and precious stones; it is much larger than this, and much brighter, for it needs not the light of the sun. But, in making the presence of God the principal matter of its bliss, they both agree. There the happiness of the glorified saints is made to be that God himself shall be with them (Rev 21:3), that he who sits on the throne shall dwell among them, Rev 7:15. And here it is made to crown the bliss of this holy city that the Lord is there. Let us therefore give all diligence to make sure to ourselves a place in that city, that we may be for ever with the Lord.

Made in the USA
Las Vegas, NV
04 October 2021